DAVID FELLMAN

Vilas Professor of Political Science, University of Wisconsin

ADVISORY EDITOR TO DODD, MEAD & COMPANY

CIVIL LIBERTIES
UNDER THE CONSTITUTION

Second Edition

Civil Liberties Under the Constitution

Second Edition

M. GLENN ABERNATHY

University of South Carolina

DODD, MEAD & COMPANY

NEW YORK   TORONTO   1973

To
Glenn, Duncan, and Richard

PREFACE

THE proper study of civil liberties in America involves virtually the whole range of social science techniques and subject matter. It should include constitutional law, political theory, political action, sociology, economics, psychology, history, and the behavioral approaches to decision making, both public and private. Obviously one who attempts to treat civil liberties in a single modest volume is forced to omit most of these approaches and, to that extent, he excludes substantial areas of highly relevant and important material necessary to a solid understanding of civil liberties in America. Choice must be made, however, and for reasons both of personal preference and pedagogical utility, this study concentrates primarily on the constitutional law aspect of civil liberties. Given the importance of the "rule of law" concept in Anglo-American history, it is felt that a firm grasp of the *law* with respect to civil liberties will provide a useful anchor, and a base will be established from which the student can more competently and fruitfully explore other modes of investigating the subject. In short, no limited approach to civil liberties can be more than an introduction to the broad subject, and the student should be warned of this fact at the outset. If this introductory analysis provides a framework for and stimulates interest in further study of so vital a subject, the venture will have been a success.

In this revised edition the primary focus of the original edition has been retained. The revision represents an effort to incorporate the more important court decisions and relevant congressional acts of the past four years. The new cases have been treated largely, though not exclusively, by the addition of a new chapter. Some fifty new cases have been added, with substantial cuttings from thirty-one of the new decisions.

M. GLENN ABERNATHY

Columbia, S. C.
1972

CONTENTS

PREFACE   v

TABLE OF CASES   xiii

CHAPTER 1. The Courts and Civil Rights   1

Limitations on judicial power: failure to litigate; "standing" to sue; nonreviewability of various administrative acts; presumption of validity of official acts; difficulty in extending decisions beyond specific facts and parties involved in litigation; limited remedies for private interference with free choice; political questions.

Remedies available through the Courts: mandamus; injunction; civil damage suit; criminal prosecution; appellate court review; habeas corpus.

CHAPTER 2. Civil Rights in the Federal System   18

     Barron v. *Baltimore* (1833)   20
     Slaughter-House Cases (1873)   26
     Twining v. *New Jersey* (1908)   36

CHAPTER 3. National Protection of Civil Rights   46

National Legislation to Protect Civil Rights   48
     Ex Parte Yarbrough (1884)   50
     United States v. *Classic* (1941)   53
     Civil Rights Cases (1883)   59
     Screws v. *United States* (1945)   66
     United States v. *Price* (1966)   86
Executive Protection of Civil Rights   93

CHAPTER 4. The Rights of the Accused   99

Notice of What Conduct is Made Criminal   100
     The "Void for Vagueness" Rule   100
     Winters v. *New York* (1948)   102
     The Prohibition Against Ex Post Facto Laws   104
     Calder v. *Bull* (1798)   104
     Notice to the Accused of the Offense Charged Against Him   107
     Cole v. *Arkansas* (1948)   107
Unreasonable Searches and Seizures   109
Search With a Valid Warrant   109
     Boyd v. *United States* (1886)   109
     Warden v. *Hayden* (1967)   114
Search and Seizure Without a Warrant   116
     Chimel v. *California* (1969)   118

Brinegar v. United States (1949)   122
Camara v. Municipal Court of San Francisco (1967)   125
Wyman v. James (1971)   128
Admissibility of Evidence Obtained Illegally   131
Mapp v. Ohio (1961)   133
Wiretapping   140
Berger v. New York (1967)   147
Self-Incrimination   150
The Invocation of the Privilege   151
The Scope of the Privilege   155
Ullmann v. United States (1956)   156
The Problem of Immunity and Federalism   160
The Privilege, Registration Laws, and Compulsory Filing   162
Self-Incrimination: Coerced Confessions   163
Brown v. Mississippi (1964)   164
Rochin v. California (1952)   175
Breithaupt v. Abram (1957)   177
The Right to Counsel   181
Johnson v. Zerbst (1938)   182
Powell v. Alabama (1932)   184
Gideon v. Wainwright (1963)   189
Stage at Which the Right to Counsel Accrues   192
Effective Representation by Counsel   193
The Right to Appointed Counsel on Appeal   194
Douglas v. California (1963)   194
The Right to a Fair Hearing   197
In Re Gault (1967)   201
Double Jeopardy   204
Downum v. United States (1963)   205
Double Jeopardy and Criminal Appeals   208
Green v. United States (1957)   208
Benton v. Maryland (1969)   211
Trial for Multiple Related Offenses   212
Ashe v. Swenson (1970)   213
Waller v. Florida (1970)   215
Bartkus v. Illinois (1959)   216
Trial by Jury   220
Patton v. United States (1930)   220
Thiel v. Southern Pacific Company (1946)   225
{ Fay v. New York (1947)   229
{ Bove v. New York (1947)   229
Habeas Corpus   234
Irvin v. Dowd (1961)   237
United States ex rel. Toth v. Quarles (1955)   239
Cruel and Unusual Punishments   243

CHAPTER 5. Religious Freedom   247

Separation of Church and State   249
Aid to Religious Schools   249
Everson v. Board of Education (1947)   249

"Released Time" Programs   254
    Illinois ex rel. *McCollum* v. *Board of Education* (1948)   255
    Zorach v. *Clauson* (1952)   258
The Bible and Prayer in Public Schools   263
    Engel v. *Vitale* (1962)   263
    { *School District of Abington Township* v. *Schempp* (1963)   268
    { *Murray* v. *Curlett* (1963)   268
Sunday Closing Laws and the "Establishment" Clause   278
    McGowan v. *Maryland* (1961)   279
The "Free Exercise" of Religion   284
Permissible Areas of Restraint—Protection of Morals, Health,
    and Safety   285
    Reynolds v. *United States* (1879)   285
    Craig v. *State of Maryland* (1959)   288
Compulsory Patriotic Exercises and Religious Freedom   292
    West Virginia State Board of Education v. *Barnette* (1943)   293
Free Exercise of Religion and the Problems of Sabbatarians   298
    Braunfeld v. *Brown* (1961)   298
Religious Oaths   305
    Torcaso v. *Watkins* (1961)   305
Compulsory Public Education Laws and Religious Freedom   308
    Pierce v. *Society of Sisters* (1925)   309
Prior Restraints on the Free Exercise of Religion   310
    Cantwell v. *Connecticut* (1940)   312
    Kunz v. *New York* (1951)   315
    Cox v. *State of New Hampshire* (1941)   319
The "Free Exercise" Clause and Judicial Settlement of Church Disputes   322
    Watson v. *Jones* (1872)   323
Miscellaneous Establishment and Free Exercise Questions   328

CHAPTER 6. Freedom of Speech, Press, and Assembly   330
The Scope of the Rights   331
Prior Restraints   334
    Near v. *Minnesota* (1931)   336
    Kingsley Books, Inc. v. *Brown* (1957)   341
    Times Film Corporation v. *City of Chicago* (1961)   347
Doctrines Advanced as Tests of Constitutionality of First
    Amendment Restraints   355
    Schenck v. *United States* (1919)   355
Internal Security   373
    Dennis v. *United States* (1951)   374
    Scales v. *United States* (1961)   383
Regulation of Traffic and Maintenance of Public Peace and Order   400
    Edwards v. *South Carolina* (1963)   405
    International Brotherhood of Teamsters v. *Vogt* (1957)   414
Special Aspects of Freedom of Press   418
Free Press *v.* Fair Administration of Justice   418
    Sheppard v. *Maxwell* (1966)   426
Libel   429

Handbill Regulation and "Green River" Ordinances   432
Miscellaneous Regulations Applicable to the Press   435
Obscenity and Pornography   436
  { *Roth* v. *United States* (1957)   438
  { *Alberts* v. *California* (1957)   438

CHAPTER 7. Equal Protection of the Law   453
  Skinner v. *Oklahoma* (1942)   457
  Strauder v. *West Virginia* (1880)   463
  Plessy v. *Ferguson* (1896)   465
  Brown v. *Board of Education of Topeka* (1954)   474
  Brown v. *Board of Education of Topeka* (1955)   479
  Shelley v. *Kraemer* (1948)   482
  Loving v. *Virginia* (1967)   504

CHAPTER 8. Voting and Apportionment   507
Constitutional Limitations on State Voting Regulations   508
  The White Primary Cases   508
  The Grandfather Clauses   512
  Poll Taxes and Literacy Tests   512
Federal Legislation to Protect Voting Rights   517
Apportionment of Legislative Seats and the "Equal Protection" Clause   524
  Baker v. *Carr* (1962)   526
  Lucas v. *Colorado General Assembly* (1964)   537
  Dusch v. *Davis* (1967)   541

CHAPTER 9. Additional Recent Cases   550
Electronic Surveillance   550
  Katz v. *United States* (1967)   550
  United States v. *White* (1971)   552
Interrogation   553
  Orozco v. *Texas* (1969)   553
  Harris v. *New York* (1971)   554
Disruptive Defendants   555
  Illinois v. *Allen* (1970)   555
Trial by Jury   557
  Duncan v. *Louisiana* (1968)   557
  Williams v. *Florida* (1970)   558
Court-Martial Jurisdiction   559
  O'Callahan v. *Parker* (1969)   559
Establishment of Religion   561
  Board of Education v. *Allen* (1968)   561
  Lemon v. *Kurtzman* (1971)   562
  Walz v. *Tax Commission of the City of New York* (1970)   564
  Epperson v. *Arkansas* (1968)   565
Prior Restraints   566
  New York Times Co. v. *United States* (1971)   566
Maintenance of Public Peace and Order   571
  Gregory v. *Chicago* (1969)   571

Brandenburg v. *Ohio* (1969) 573
Note on Libel 574
Obscenity 575
  Stanley v. *Georgia* (1969) 575
  United States v. *Reidel* (1971) 576
Note on War Protestors 577
  Tinker v. *Des Moines School District* (1969) 579
Race Discrimination in the Sale of Property 582
  Jones v. *Alfred Mayer Co.* (1968) 582
Public School Desegregation 583
  Green v. *School Board of New Kent County* (1968) 583
  Swann v. *Charlotte-Mecklenburg Board of Education* (1971) 585
Closing of Public Facilities to Avoid Racial Integration 589
  Palmer v. *Thompson* (1971) 589
Congressional Power over Voting 591
  Oregon v. *Mitchell* (1970) 591
  Perkins v. *Matthews* (1971) 595
Multi-Member Election Districts and the Equal Protection Clause 597
  Whitcomb v. *Chavis* (1971) 597
Constitutionally Permissible Population Variation Among Districts 599
  Abate v. *Mundt* (1971) 599

SELECTED REFERENCES 603

AMENDMENTS TO THE CONSTITUTION OF THE UNITED STATES 615

INDEX 619

TABLE OF CASES

Boldface page numbers indicate that portions of opinions are quoted.

A Book Named "John Cleland's Memoirs of a Woman of Pleasure" v. Attorney General of Massachusetts, 383 U.S. 413 (1966), 445

A Quantity of Copies of Books v. Kansas, 378 U.S. 205 (1964), **446**

Abate v. Mundt, 403 U.S. 182 (1971), 549, **599**

Abbate v. United States, 359 U.S. 187 (1959), 94

Abrams v. United States, 250 U.S. 616 (1919), **357**

Adler v. Board of Education of the City of New York, 342 U.S. 485 (1952), 389

Alberts v. California, 354 U.S. 476 (1957), **438**

Albertson v. Subversive Activities Control Board, 382 U.S. 70 (1965), 163, 397

American Communications Association, CIO v. Douds, 339 U.S. 382 (1950), 369, 388

Anastaplo, In re, 366 U.S. 82 (1961), 392

Anderson v. State, 84 Ga. App. 259, 65 S.E. 2d 848 (1951), 291

Aptheker v. Secretary of State, 378 U.S. 500 (1964), 399

Ashcraft v. Tennessee, 322 U.S. 143 (1944), 167–168

Ashe v. Swenson, 397 U.S. 436 (1970), 213

Associated Press v. N. L. R. B., 301 U.S. 103 (1937), 436

Associated Press v. United States, 326 U.S. 1 (1945), 436

Avery v. Georgia, 345 U.S. 559 (1953), 227

Baer v. City of Bend, 206 Ore. 221, 292 P. 2d 134 (1956), 291

Baker v. Carr, 369 U.S. 186 (1962), 8, **525**

Baldwin v. Franks, 120 U.S. 678 (1887), 58

Ballard v. United States, 329 U.S. 187 (1946), **226**

Bantam Books, Inc. v. Sullivan, 372 U.S. 58 (1963), 449

Barenblatt v. United States, 360 U.S. 109 (1959), 371

Barr v. City of Columbia, 378 U.S. 146 (1964), 489

Barron v. Baltimore, 7 Pet. 243 (1833), 20

Barrows v. Jackson, 346 U.S. 249 (1953), 484

Bartkus v. Illinois, 359 U.S. 121 (1959), 94, **216**

Beck v. Ohio, 379 U.S. 89 (1964), 124

Beilan v. Board of Public Education, 357 U.S. 399 (1958), 390, 392

Bell v. Maryland, 378 U.S. 226 (1964), **489**

Benanti v. United States, 355 U.S. 96 (1957), 144

Bennett v. United States, 145 F.2d 270 (C.A.4th, 1944), 116

Benton v. Maryland, 395 U.S. 784 (1969), 42, 208, **211**

Berger v. New York, 388 U.S. 41 (1967), **146**

Betts v. Brady, 316 U.S. 455 (1942), 187

Blau v. United States, 340 U.S. 159 (1950), 154

Board of Education v. Allen, 392 U.S. 236 (1968), 329, **561**

Bolling v. Sharpe, 347 U.S. 497 (1954), 478

Bouie v. City of Columbia, 378 U.S. 347 (1964), 489

Boyd v. United States, 116 U.S. 616 (1886), 109

Boynton v. Virginia, 364 U.S. 454 (1960), 472

Bove v. New York, 332 U.S. 261 (1947), 229

Brandenburg v. Ohio, 395 U.S. 444 (1969), 388, 573

Breard v. City of Alexandria, 341 U.S. 622 (1951), 433

Breedlove v. Suttles, 302 U.S. 277 (1937), 513

Breithaupt v. Abram, 352 U.S. 432 (1957), 177

Bridges v. California, 314 U.S. 252 (1941), 361, 419, 423

Brinegar v. United States, 338 U.S. 160 (1949), 122

Brock v. North Carolina, 344 U.S. 424 (1953), 205, 210

Brown v. Allen, 344 U.S. 443 (1953), 232, 237, 242

Brown v. Board of Education of Topeka, 347 U.S. 483 (1954), 474

Brown v. Board of Education of Topeka, 349 U.S. 294 (1955), 479

Brown v. Mississippi, 297 U.S. 278 (1936), 164

Buck v. Bell, 274 U.S. 200 (1927), 457

Buchanan v. Warley, 245 U.S. 60 (1917), 468, 481

Burdeau v. McDowell, 256 U.S. 465 (1921), 138

Burroughs v. United States, 290 U.S. 534 (1934), 52

Burstyn v. Wilson, 343 U.S. 495 (1952), 331, 346

Burton v. Wilmington Parking Authority, 365 U.S. 715 (1961), 79, 484

Bute v. Illinois, 333 U.S. 640 (1948), 188

Butler v. Michigan, 352 U.S. 380 (1957), 437

Camara v. Municipal Court of San Francisco, 387 U.S. 523 (1967), 125

Calder v. Bull, 3 Dall. 386 (1798), 104

Callan v. Wilson, 127 U.S. 540 (1888), 191

Cantwell v. Connecticut, 310 U.S. 296 (1940), 42, 312

Carroll v. United States, 267 U.S. 132 (1925), 121

Catlette v. United States, 132 F. 2d 902 (4th Cir. 1943), 75

Chamberlin v. Dade County Board of Public Instruction, 377 U.S. 402 (1964), 278

Chaplinksy v. New Hampshire, 315 U.S. 568 (1942), 404

Cheff v. Schnackenberg, 384 U.S. 373 (1966), 191

Chimel v. California, 395 U.S. 752 (1969), 118

Ciucci v. Illinois, 356 U.S. 571 (1958), 212

Civil Rights Cases, 109 U.S. 3 (1883), 58

Clay (Ali) v. United States, 403 U.S. 698 (1971), 578

Cofer v. United States, 37 F.2d 677 (C.A.5th, 1930), 116

Cole v. Arkansas, 333 U.S. 196 (1948), 107

Colegrove v. Green, 328 U.S. 549 (1946), 8, 524

Colgate v. Harvey, 294 U.S. 404 (1935), 32

Collins v. Hardyman, 341 U.S. 651 (1951), 90

Commercial Pictures v. Regents, 346 U.S. 587 (1954), 347

Communist Party of the United States v. Subversive Activities Control Board, 367 U.S. 1 (1961), 163, 396

Connally v. General Construction Co., 369 U.S. 385 (1926), 101

Corfield v. Coryell, 6 Fed. Cas. No. 3230, 546 (1823), 24

Cox v. Louisiana, 379 U.S. 536 (1965), 409

Cox v. Louisiana, 379 U.S. 559 (1965), 410

Cox v. State of New Hampshire, 312 U.S. 569 (1941), 319, 332, 402

Crescent Oil Co. v. Mississippi, 257 U.S. 129 (1921), 456

Craig v. Harney, 331 U.S. 367 (1947), 421, 423

Craig v. State of Maryland, 220 Md. 590, 155 A.2d 684 (1959), 288

Crawford v. United States, 212 U.S. 183 (1909), 224

Crews v. United States, 160 F.2d 746 (5th Cir. 1947), 75

Crooker v. California, 357 U.S. 433 (1958), 193

Culombe v. Connecticut, 367 U.S. 568 (1961), 169

Curtis Publishing Co. v. Butts, 388 U.S. 130 (1967), 574

Davidson v. New Orleans, 96 U.S. 97 (1878), 33, 99

Davis v. Mann, 377 U.S. 678 (1964), 536

Davis v. Schnell, 81 F. Supp. 872 (D.C., S.D., Ala., 1949), 515

Debs, In re, 158 U.S. 564 (1895), 97

DeJonge v. Oregon, 299 U.S. 353 (1937), 41, 334

Dennis v. United States, 341 U.S. 494 (1951), 369, 372, 374

Dickinson v. United States, 356 U.S. 389 (1953), 307

District of Columbia v. Clawans, 300 U.S. 617 (1937), 191

District of Columbia v. Colts, 282 U.S. 63 (1930), 191, 222

Donahoe v. Richards, 38 Me. 376 (1854), 263

Donaldson v. Read Magazine, 333 U.S. 178 (1948), 353

Dorsey v. Stuyvesant Town Corporation, 299 N.Y. 512, 87 N.E. 2d 541 (1949), 78

Douglas v. Alabama, 380 U.S. 415 (1965), 200

Douglas v. California, 372 U.S. 353 (1963), 194

Downum v. United States, 372 U.S. 734 (1963), 205

Draper v. United States, 358 U.S. 307 (1959), 123

Dugan v. Ohio, 277 U.S. 61 (1928), 198

Duncan v. Louisiana, 391 U.S. 145 (1968), 43, 557

Dusch v. Davis, 387 U.S. 112 (1967), 541

Edwards v. South Carolina, 372 U.S. 229 (1963), 405

Elfbrandt v. Russell, 384 U.S. 11 (1966), 392

Elkins v. United States, 364 U.S. 206 (1960), 138

Engel v. Vitale, 370 U.S. 421 (1962), 263

Epperson v. Arkansas, 393 U.S. 97 (1968), 329, 565

Escobedo v. Illinois, 378 U.S. 478 (1964), 9, 171, 193

Eskridge v. Washington State Board, 357 U.S. 214 (1958), 194

Estes v. Texas, 381 U.S. 532 (1965), 425-426

Everson v. Board of Education, 330 U.S. 1 (1947), 42, 249

Fay v. New York, 332 U.S. 261 (1947), 229

Feiner v. New York, 340 U.S. 315 (1951), 402

Fikes v. Alabama, 352 U.S. 191 (1957), 196

Flast v. Cohen, 392 U.S. 83 (1968), 329

Follett v. Town of McCormick, 321 U.S. 573 (1944), 322

Fortson v. Dorsey, 379 U.S. 433 (1965), 540

Frank v. Maryland, 359 U.S. 360 (1959), 125

Frazier v. United States, 335 U.S. 497 (1948), 224

Freedman v. Maryland, 380 U.S. 51 (1965), 351, 450

Garner v. Board of Public Works, 341 U.S. 716 (1951), 389

Garrison v. Louisiana, 379 U.S. 64 (1964), 431

Gault, In re, 387 U.S. 1 (1967), 192, 201

Gayle v. *Browder,* 352 U.S. 903 (1956), 478

Gideon v. *Wainwright,* 372 U.S. 335 (1963), 18, 43, 171, 189

Gillette v. *United States,* 401 U.S. 437 (1971), 578

Ginzburg v. *United States,* 383 U.S. 463 (1966), 443

Gitlow v. *New York,* 268 U.S. 652 (1925), 41, 333, 359

Goesaert v. *Cleary,* 335 U.S. 464 (1948), 460

Goldman v. *United States,* 316 U.S. 129 (1942), 145

Gray v. *Sanders,* 372 U.S. 368 (1963), 532

Green v. *School Board of New Kent County,* 391 U.S. 430 (1968), 480, 583

Green v. *United States,* 335 U.S. 184 (1957), 208

Greenbelt Cooperative Publishing Ass'n v. *Bresler,* 398 U.S. 6 (1970), 574

Gregory v. *Chicago,* 394 U.S. 111 (1969), 414, 571

Griffin v. *Breckenridge,* 403 U.S. 88 (1971), 90

Griffin v. *California,* 380 U.S. 609 (1965), 42, 152

Griffin v. *Maryland,* 378 U.S. 130 (1964), 489

Griswold v. *Connecticut,* 381 U.S. 479 (1965), 4, 130

Grosjean v. *American Press Co.,* 297 U.S. 233 (1936), 435

Grosso v. *United States,* 390 U.S. 62 (1968), 162

Grovey v. *Townsend,* 294 U.S. 699 (1935), 509, 510

Guinn v. *United States,* 238 U.S. 347 (1915), 512

Guss v. *Utah Labor Relations Boards,* 353 U.S. 1 (1957), 418

Hague v. C.I.O., 307 U.S. 496 (1939), 345

Haley v. *Ohio,* 332 U.S. 596 (1948), 168

Hamilton v. *Alabama,* 368 U.S. 52 (1961), 192

Hannegan v. *Esquire,* 327 U.S. 146 (1946), 14, 352

Harden v. *State of Tennessee,* 188 Tenn. 17, 216 S.W. 2d 708 (1949), 290

Harman v. *Forssenius,* 380 U.S. 528 (1965), 514

Harper v. *Virginia State Board of Elections,* 383 U.S. 663 (1966), 514

Harris v. *New York,* 401 U.S. 222 (1971), 554

Harris v. *South Carolina,* 338 U.S. 68 (1949), 168

Harris v. *United States,* 331 U.S. 145 (1947), 119

Haynes v. *United States,* 390 U.S. 85 (1968), 162

Heart of Atlanta Motel v. *United States,* 379 U.S. 241 (1964), 496

Henderson v. *United States,* 339 U.S. 816 (1950), 472

Henry v. *Rock Hill,* 376 U.S. 776 (1964), 409

Henry v. *United States,* 361 U.S. 98 (1959), 116

Hernandez v. *Texas,* 347 U.S. 475 (1954), 227–28, 465

Hiatt v. *Brown,* 339 U.S. 103 (1950), 239

Hoag v. *New Jersey,* 356 U.S. 464 (1958), 212

Hoffman v. *United States,* 341 U.S. 479 (1951), 153, 154

Holden v. *Hardy,* 169 U.S. 366 (1898), 40

Holmby Productions v. *Vaughn,* 350 U.S. 870 (1955), 347

Holt v. *United States,* 218 U.S. 245 (1910), 174

Home Telephone & Telegraph Co. v. *Los Angeles,* 227 U.S. 278 (1913), 63

Hoyt v. *Florida,* 368 U.S. 57 (1961), 228

Hurtado v. *California,* 110 U.S. 516 (1884), 43, 223

Illinois v. *Allen*, 397 U.S. 337 (1970), 197, **555**

Illinois ex rel. McCollum v. *Board of Education*, 333 U.S. 203 (1948), **255**

International Brotherhood of Teamsters v. *Vogt*, 354 U.S. 284 (1957), **414**

Irvine v. *California*, 374 U.S. 128 (1954), 132

Irvin v. *Dowd*, 366 U.S. 717 (1961), 237, 423

Jackson v. *Denno*, 378 U.S. 368 (1964), 166

Jacobellis v. *Ohio*, 378 U.S. 184 (1964), **441**, 446

Jacobson v. *Massachusetts*, 197 U.S. 11 (1905), 291

James v. *Bowman*, 190 U.S. 127 (1903), 55

Jencks v. *United States*, 353 U.S. 657 (1957), 199

Johnson v. *New Jersey*, 384 U.S. 719 (1966), 174

Johnson v. *United States*, 333 U.S. 10 (1948), 117

Johnson v. *Zerbst*, 304 U.S. 458 (1938), 182, 235

Jones v. *Alfred Mayer Co.*, 392 U.S. 409 (1968), 486, **582**

Jones v. *Cunningham*, 371 U.S. 236 (1963), 236

Jones v. *Georgia*, 57 Ga. App. 344, 195 S.E. 316 (1938), 194

Jones v. *Opelika*, 316 U.S. 584 (1942), 321

Jordan v. *Massachusetts*, 225 U.S. 167 (1912), **223**

Katz v. *United States*, 389 U.S. 347 (1967), 150, **550**

Katzenbach v. *McClung*, 379 U.S. 294 (1964), **497**

Kedroff v. *St. Nicholas Cathedral*, 344 U.S. 94 (1952), **327**

Keokee Consolidated Coke Co. v. *Taylor*, 234 U.S. 224 (1914), 457

Kepner v. *United States*, 195 U.S. 100 (1904), 208

Ker v. *California*, 374 U.S. 23 (1963), 137

Kerr v. *Enoch Pratt Free Library*, 149 F.2d 212 (4th Cir. 1945), 77, 487

Keyishian v. *Board of Regents of New York*, 385 U.S. 589 (1967), 393

Kingsley Books, Inc. v. *Brown*, 354 U.S. 436 (1957), **341**, 450

Klopfer v. *North Carolina*, 386 U.S. 213 (1967), 43

Konigsberg v. *State Bar of California*, 353 U.S. 252 (1957), 391

Konigsberg v. *State Bar of California*, 366 U.S. 36 (1961), 391

Kovacs v. *Cooper*, 336 U.S. 77 (1949), 367, **401**

Kreshik v. *St. Nicholas Cathedral*, 363 U.S. 190 (1960), 328

Krohn v. *Richardson-Merrell, Inc.*, 406 S.W. 2d 166 (Tenn., 1966), 461

Kunz v. *New York*, 340 U.S. 290 (1951), **315**, 345, 432

Lane v. *Wilson*, 307 U.S. 268 (1939), 512

Lanzetta v. *New Jersey*, 306 U.S. 451 (1939), 101

Lassiter v. *Northampton Election Board*, 360 U.S. 45 (1959), **515**

Leary v. *United States*, 395 U.S. 6 (1969), 162

Lee v. *United States*, 343 U.S. 747 (1952), 145, 146

Lem Moon Sing v. *United States*, 158 U.S. 538 (1895), 5

Lemon v. *Kurtzman*, 403 U.S. 602 (1971), 329, **562**

Lerner v. *Casey*, 357 U.S. 468 (1958), 390

Leyra v. *Denno*, 347 U.S. 556 (1954), 168

Linkletter v. *Walker*, 381 U.S. 618 (1965), 139

Lombard v. *Louisiana*, 373 U.S. 267 (1963), 487

Louisiana ex rel. Francis v. *Resweber*, 329 U.S. 459 (1947), 43, 244

Louisiana v. *United States*, 380 U.S. 145 (1965), **516**

Lovell v. *Griffin*, 303 U.S. 444 (1938), 332

Loving v. *Virginia*, 388 U.S. 1 (1967), **504**

Lucas v. *Forty-Fourth General Assembly of Colorado*, 377 U.S. 713 (1964), **536**

Lynch v. *United States*, 189 F.2d 476 (5th Cir. 1951), 80

McCabe v. *Atchison, Topeka & Santa Fe*, 235 U.S. 151 (1914), 470

McCollum v. *Board of Education*, 333 U.S. 203 (1948), 7, **255**

McGowan v. *Maryland*, 366 U.S. 420 (1961), **279**

McKeiver v. *Pennsylvania*, 403 U.S. 528 (1971), 204

McLaughlin v. *Florida*, 379 U.S. 184 (1964), 503

McLaurin v. *Oklahoma State Regents*, 339 U.S. 637 (1950), 472

McNabb v. *United States*, 318 U.S. 332 (1943), 99, 170

Madden v. *Kentucky*, 309 U.S. 83 (1940), 32

Malinski v. *New York*, 324 U.S. 401 (1945), 166, 168

Mallory v. *United States*, 354 U.S. 449 (1957), 170

Malloy v. *Hogan*, 387 U.S. 1 (1964), 42, 152, 160, 161

Mapp v. *Ohio*, 367 U.S. 643 (1961), 42, **133**

Marchetti v. *United States*, 390 U.S. 39 (1968), **162**

Martin v. *Struthers*, 319 U.S. 141 (1943), 433

Maryland Committee for Fair Representation v. *Tawes*, 377 U.S. 656 (1964), 536

Maryland v. *Baltimore Radio Show*, 338 U.S. 912 (1950), 423

Maxwell v. *Dow*, 176 U.S. 581 (1900), 43, 223

Minersville School District v. *Gobitis*, 310 U.S. 586 (1940), **292**

Miranda v. *Arizona*, 384 U.S. 436 (1966), 167, 170, **172**

Missouri ex rel. Gaines v. *Canada*, 305 U.S. 337 (1938), **470**

Mitchell v. *United States*, 313 U.S. 80 (1941), 471

Monitor Patriot Co. v. *Roy*, 401 U.S. 265 (1971), 575

Monroe v. *Pape*, 365 U.S. 167 (1961), 81

Moore v. *Dempsey*, 261 U.S. 86 (1923), 198, 235, 236

Moore v. *Illinois*, 14 How. 13 (1852), 216

Morgan v. *Virginia*, 328 U.S. 373 (1946), 472

Motes v. *United States*, 178 U.S. 458 (1900), 57

Mulloy v. *United States*, 398 U.S. 410 (1970), 578

Murdock v. *Pennsylvania*, 319 U.S. 105 (1943), **321**

Murphy v. *Waterfront Commission of New York Harbor*, 378 U.S. 52 (1964), 160

Murray v. *Curlett*, 374 U.S. 203 (1963), 268

Mutual Film Corporation v. *Industrial Commission*, 236 U.S. 230 (1915), 331

NAACP v. *Alabama*, 357 U.S. 449 (1958), 332, 370, 394

NLRB v. *Consolidated Copper Corp.*, 316 U.S. 105 (1942), **5**

Naim v. *Naim*, 350 U.S. 985 (1956), 503

Nardone v. *United States*, 302 U.S. 379 (1937), 142

Nardone v. *United States*, 308 U.S. 338 (1939), 142

Neagle, In re, 135 U.S. 1 (1890), 97

Near v. *Minnesota*, 283 U.S. 697 (1931), 41, **336**

Nelson v. *County of Los Angeles*, 362 U.S. 1 (1960), 390

New York ex rel. Bryant v. *Zimmerman*, 278 U.S. 63 (1928), 394

New York Times Co. v. *Sullivan*, 376 U.S. 254 (1964), **429**

New York Times v. United States, 403 U.S. 713 (1971), 341, 566

Newberry v. United States, 256 U.S. 232 (1921), 53

Niemotko v. Maryland, 340 U.S. 268 (1951), 345, 455

Nishimura Ekiu v. United States, 142 U.S. 651 (1892), 5

Nixon v. Condon, 286 U.S. 73 (1932), 509

Nixon v. Herndon, 273 U.S. 536 (1927), 508

North Carolina v. Pearce, 395 U.S. 711 (1969), 211

Norton v. Shelby Co., 118 U.S. 425 (1886), 139

O'Callahan v. Parker, 395 U.S. 258 (1969), 241, 559

Oklahoma Press Publishing Co. v. Walling, 327 U.S. 186 (1946), 436

Ogden v. Saunders, 12 Wheat. 213 (1827), 6

Oliver, In re, 333 U.S. 257 (1948), 43, 197

Olmstead v. United States, 277 U.S. 438 (1928), 140

One, Inc. v. Olesen, 355 U.S. 371 (1958), 443

Oregon v. Mitchell, 400 U.S. 112 (1970), 524, 591

Orozco v. Texas, 394 U.S. 324 (1969), 553

Palko v. Connecticut, 302 U.S. 319 (1937), 40, 42, 44, 208, 223

Palmer v. Thompson, 403 U.S. 217 (1971), 506, 589

Parker v. Ellis, 362 U.S. 574 (1960), 236

Parker v. Gladden, 385 U.S. 363 (1966), 223

Patton v. United States, 281 U.S. 276 (1930), 220

Pennekamp v. Florida, 328 U.S. 331 (1946), 361, 421, 423

Pennsylvania v. Nelson, 350 U.S. 497 (1956), 388

Perez v. Lippold [Sharp], 198 P.2d 17 (Calif., 1948), 503

Perkins v. Matthews, 400 U.S. 379 (1971), 524, 595

Peterson v. Greenville, 373 U.S. 244 (1963), 487

Petit v. Minnesota, 177 U.S. 164 (1900), 279

Pierce v. Society of Sisters, 268 U.S. 510 (1925), 309

Plessy v. Ferguson, 163 U.S. 537 (1896), 465

Pointer v. Texas, 380 U.S. 400 (1965), 43, 199

Powell v. Alabama, 287 U.S. 45 (1932), 41, 43, 184

Powell v. Pennsylvania, 127 U.S. 678 (1888), 6

Price v. Johnston, 334 U.S. 266 (1948), 235

Prince v. Massachusetts, 321 U.S. 158 (1944), 289

Quinn v. United States, 349 U.S. 155 (1955), 151

Radice v. New York, 264 U.S. 292 (1924), 460

Raymond v. Chicago Union Traction Co., 207 U.S. 20 (1907), 63

Rea v. United States, 350 U.S. 214 (1956), 138

Regina v. Hicklin (1868), L.R. 3 Q.B. 360, 436

Reitman v. Mulkey, 387 U.S. 369 (1967), 486

Reynolds v. Sims, 377 U.S. 533 (1964), 534

Reynolds v. United States, 98 U.S. 145 (1879), 285

Rice v. Elmore, 165 F.2d 387 (4th Cir., 1947), 511

Rideau v. Louisiana, 373 U.S. 73 (1963), 423

Robinson v. California, 370 U.S. 660 (1962), 43, 245

Robinson v. Florida, 378 U.S. 153 (1964), 489

Rochin v. California, 342 U.S. 165 (1952), 175

Rogers v. Richmond, 365 U.S. 534 (1961), 166

Rogers v. United States, 40 U.S. 367 (1951), 154, 155

Roman v. Sincock, 377 U.S. 695 (1964), 536

Rosenbloom v. Metromedia, 403 U.S. 29 (1971), 574

Roth v. United States, 354 U.S. 476 (1957), 438

Rudolph v. Alabama, 375 U.S. 889 (1963), 245

Saia v. New York, 334 U.S. 558 (1948), 332, 400, 402

Sailors v. Board of Supervisors, 387 U.S. 105 (1967), 541

Sanchez v. Indiana, 199 Ind. 235, 157 N.W. 1 (1927), 194

San Diego Building Trades Council v. Garmon, 359 U.S. 236 (1959), 418

Scales v. United States, 367 U.S. 203 (1961), 383

Schenck v. United States, 249 U.S. 47 (1919), 355

Schmerber v. California, 384 U.S. 757 (1966), 113, 180

Schneiderman v. United States, 320 U.S. 118 (1943), 399

School District of Abington Township v. Schempp, 374 U.S. 203 (1963), 268

Schware v. Board of Bar Examiners, 353 U.S. 232 (1957), 390

Schwartz v. Texas, 344 U.S. 199 (1952), 144

Screws v. United States, 325 U.S. 91 (1945), 65

See v. Seattle, 387 U.S. 541 (1967), 129

Shelley v. Kraemer, 334 U.S. 1 (1948), 482

Shelton v. Tucker, 364 U.S. 479 (1960), 395

Shepherd v. Florida, 341 U.S. 50 (1951), 422

Sheppard v. Maxwell, 384 U.S. 333 (1966), 426

Sherbert v. Verner, 374 U.S. 398 (1963), 303

Sibron v. New York, 392 U.S. 40 (1968), 121

Silverman v. United States, 366 U.S. 505 (1961), 146

Singer v. United States, 380 U.S. 24 (1965), 222

Skinner v. Oklahoma, 316 U.S. 535 (1942), 457

Slaughter-House Cases, 16 Wall. 36 (1873), 26, 32

Slochower v. Board of Higher Education, 350 U.S. 551 (1956), 390

Smith v. Allwright, 321 U.S. 649 (1944), 510

Smith v. California, 361 U.S. 147 (1959), 448

Snowden v. Hughes, 321 U.S. 1 (1944), 32

South v. Peters, 339 U.S. 276 (1950), 525

South Carolina v. Katzenbach, 383 U.S. 30 (1966), 523

Stanley v. Georgia, 394 U.S. 557 (1969), 452, 575

State v. Popolos, 103 A.2d 511 (Me., 1954), 107

State ex rel. Weiss v. District Board of Edgerton, 76 Wis. 177, 44 N.W. 967 (1890), 263

Staub v. City of Baxley, 355 U.S. 313 (1958), 13, 345

Sterling v. Constantin, 287 U.S. 378 (1932), 63

Strauder v. West Virginia, 100 U.S. 303 (1880), 63, 227, 463, 467

Street v. New York, 394 U.S. 576 (1969), 577

Summers, In re, 325 U.S. 561 (1945), 390

Sunshine Book Co. v. Summerfield, 355 U.S. 372 (1958), 443

Superior Films v. Department of Education of Ohio, 346 U.S. 587 (1954), 347

Swann v. Charlotte-Mecklenburg Board of Education, 402 U.S. 1 (1971), 480, 585

Sweatt v. Painter, 339 U.S. 629 (1950), 472

Talley v. California, 362 U.S. 60 (1960), 371, 432

Tancil v. Woolls, 379 U.S. 19 (1964), 506

Terminiello v. Chicago, 337 U.S. 1 (1949), 404

Terry v. Adams, 345 U.S. 461 (1953), 511

Terry v. Ohio, 392 U.S. 1 (1968), 121

Thiel v. Southern Pacific Company, 328 U.S. 217 (1946), 225

Thomas v. Collins, 323 U.S. 516 (1945), 344, 366

Thompson v. Missouri, 171 U.S. 380 (1898), 106

Thompson v. Utah, 170 U.S. 343 (1898), 106

Thornhill v. Alabama, 310 U.S. 88 (1940), 332, 414

Tileston v. Ullman, 318 U.S. 44 (1943), 4

Tilton v. Richardson, 403 U.S. 672 (1971), 564

Times Film Corp. v. City of Chicago, 365 U.S. 43 (1961), 347, 449

Times-Mirror Company v. Superior Court of California, 314 U.S. 252 (1941), 419

Tinker v. Des Moines School District, 393 U.S. 503 (1969), 414, 579

Torcaso v. Watkins, 367 U.S. 488 (1961), 305

Trop v. Dulles, 356 U.S. 86 (1958), 244

Tudor v. Board of Education of Rutherford, 14 N.J. 31 (1953), 276

Tumey v. Ohio, 273 U.S. 510 (1927), 198

Turner v. Louisiana, 379 U.S. 466 (1965), 223, 233

Turner v. Pennsylvania, 338 U.S. 62 (1949), 168

Twining v. New Jersey, 211 U.S. 78 (1908), 35, 100, 152

Ullmann v. United States, 350 U.S. 422 (1956), 155

United States v. Ballard, 322 U.S. 78 (1944), 292

United States v. Brown, 381 U.S. 437 (1965), 398

United States v. Burr [In re Willie], 25 Fed. Cas. 38, No. 14,692 e (C.C.D. Va. 1807), 153

United States v. Carolene Products Company, 304 U.S. 144 (1938), 367

United States v. Classic, 313 U.S. 299 (1941), 53, 64, 509

United States v. Guest, 383 U.S. 745 (1966), 84

United States v. Kahriger, 345 U.S. 22 (1953), 162

United States v. Keen, 26 Fed. Cas. 686 (1839), 208

United States v. Morgan, 346 U.S. 502 (1954), 236

United States v. O'Brien, 391 U.S. 367 (1968), 577

United States v. One Book Called "Ulysses," 5 F. Supp. 182 (1933), 354, 437

United States v. Perez, 9 Wheat. 579 (1824), 205

United States v. Price, 383 U.S. 787 (1966), 84, 86

United States ex rel. Toth v. Quarles, 350 U.S. 11 (1955), 239

United States v. Rabinowitz, 339 U.S. 56 (1950), 118

United States v. Reese, 92 U.S. 214 (1876), 56

United States v. Reidel, 402 U.S. 351 (1971), 452, 576

United States v. Sanges, 144 U.S. 310 (1892), 208

United States v. Seeger, 380 U.S. 163 (1965), 307

United States v. Van Duzee, 140 U.S. 169 (1891), 181

United States v. *Waddell,* 112 U.S. 76 (1884), **57**

United States v. *White,* 322 U.S. 694 (1944), 155

United States v. *White,* 401 U.S. 745 (1971), 150, **552**

United States v. *Williams,* 341 U.S. 70 (1951), 83

United States v. *Wood,* 299 U.S. 123 (1936), 224

Upshaw v. *United States,* 335 U.S. 410 (1948), 170

Valentine v. *Chrestense,* 316 U.S. 52 (1942), 432

Virginia, Ex parte, 100 U.S. 339 (1880), 63, **64**

WMCA, Inc. v. *Lomenzo,* 377 U.S. 633 (1964), 536

Walker v. *Sauvinet,* 92 U.S. 90 (1876), 43

Waller v. *Florida,* 397 U.S. 387 (1970), 215

Walz v. *Tax Commission of the City of New York,* 397 U.S. 664 (1970), 328, **564**

Ward v. *Love County,* 253 U.S. 17 (1920), 63

Warden v. *Hayden,* 387 U.S. 294 (1967), **114**

Washington v. *Texas,* 388 U.S. 14 (1967), 43, **200**

Watts v. *Indiana,* 338 U.S. 49 (1949), 168

Watson v. *Jones,* 13 Wallace 679 (1872), **323**

Weems v. *United States,* 217 U.S. 349 (1910), 244

Weiss v. *United States,* 308 U.S. 321 (1939), 143

Welsh v. *United States,* 398 U.S. 333 (1970), 578

Wesberry v. *Sanders,* 376 U.S. 1 (1964), **533**

West v. *Louisiana,* 194 U.S. 258 (1904), 40

West Virginia Board of Education v. *Barnette,* 319 U.S. 624 (1943), 63, 293

Whitcomb v. *Chavis,* 403 U.S. 124 (1971), 549, **597**

Wieman v. *Updegraff,* 344 U.S. 183 (1952), 389

Wilbur v. *United States,* 281 U.S. 206 (1930), 10

Wilkerson v. *Utah,* 99 U.S. 130 (1879), 244

Williams v. *Florida,* 399 U.S. 78 (1970), 223, **558**

Williams v. *Mississippi,* 170 U.S. 213 (1898), 514

Williams v. *United States,* 341 U.S. 97 (1951), **76**

Williamson v. *Lee Optical Co.,* 348 U.S. 483 (1955), **459**

Winship, In re, 397 U.S. 358 (1970), 204

Winters v. *New York,* 333 U.S. 507 (1948), **102**

Wolf v. *Colorado,* 338 U.S. 25 (1949), 42, **131**

Wood v. *Georgia,* 370 U.S. 375 (1962), 361

Wright v. *Georgia,* 373 U.S. 284 (1963), 104

Wyman v. *James,* 400 U.S. 309 (1971), 128

Yarbrough, Ex parte, 110 U.S. 651 (1884), **50**, 518

Yates v. *United States,* 354 U.S. 298 (1957), 382

Yick Wo v. *Hopkins,* 118 U.S. 356 (1886), **454**

Zorach v. *Clauson,* 343 U.S. 306 (1952), **258**

CHAPTER 1

The Courts and Civil Rights

UNTIL relatively recently, the focal point for official pronouncements concerning the nature and extent of American civil rights has been the judiciary. This is not an unreasonable approach in view of the impact of the institution of judicial review and the habituation of Anglo-Americans to judicial policy-making through centuries of development of the common law. These factors, despite the fact that constitutional conventions or legislative bodies initiated the statements of rights found in the state and federal constitutions, inexorably operate to place the stress on the judiciary as the locus for definitive elaboration of rights. Constitutional challenges to laws or official behavior are expected to reach final resolution only in a court decision, and the higher the court the more nearly final the decision. Despite its oversimplification, there is some element of truth in the statement by presidential candidate Charles Evans Hughes, "We are under the Constitution, but the Constitution is what the judges say it is."

More recently, legislative bodies and administrative agencies have been recognized as important participants in the creation and delineation of rights. Congress, for example, can both create new rights and destroy old ones. In the adoption of the National Labor Relations Act in 1935 a new right of defined categories of workers to organize and bargain collectively was created. And the old right of employers to discharge workers for union activity was demolished. Similarly, in the Civil Rights Act of 1964 a new right of access to places of public accommodation, irrespective of race or religion, was created, while the old right of choice in the operators (absent state laws to the contrary) was removed. In administering the nondiscrimination-in-education provisions of the Civil Rights Act of 1964, the Office of Education has essentially extended the meager phraseology of the Act to embrace additional rights. In great part, however, such participation in the process of rights-definition does not appear to displace the judiciary from its position of primacy in the public mind.

Unfortunately, this attitude sometimes engenders as a corollary the belief that the courts are the omnipresent *guardians* of civil rights. In other words, it is not uncommonly assumed that the courts of the nation stand ever ready to right all wrongs suffered to one's person or liberty or property. In a strictly limited sense this is true. If one has suffered an injury recognized by

1

the law, and if he has the time, money, energy, witnesses, and evidence to prosecute his cause successfully in court, then a remedy is available to him. But this statement camouflages a multitude of barriers to the realization of effective judicial remedies for wronged individuals. Thus while the bulk of this volume places heavy stress on judicial pronouncements defining and analyzing civil rights, it is well to enter a *caveat* initially concerning a number of important factors which serve to limit the effectiveness of courts as *guardians* of civil rights. The purpose of this chapter is to examine these factors, some of which are external to the judicial process and others stemming from the courts' own evaluation of the limits to their appropriate role, and then to define the area in which courts *can* act to protect civil rights.

1. *Failure to Litigate.* At the outset it is clear that the initiative in a civil suit must be taken by the injured party if the courts are to offer any assistance in righting the wrong. Even in criminal actions, a substantial burden rests on the injured party to push forward his cause if he expects satisfaction. If one suffers a criminal wrong, his complaint and testimony (if he is alive to give them) are usually a prerequisite to successful prosecution. And if, instead, he is the victim of an improper prosecution, it is up to him to carry the appeals necessary to try to get a reversal of the conviction. Thus our adversary system demands action, not childlike faith in some future retribution for one's enemies, if the judicial machinery is to be set in motion to safeguard rights. But every day sees abridgments of rights in some form take place with only a very small portion of these leading to actual litigation. Why is this so? Among the more obvious answers are cost, fear of reprisals, delay in reaching final settlement, and perhaps the bad character of the victim. Other factors as well contribute to this reluctance.

Most of us have from time to time suffered an actionable wrong from either private persons or public officials. But we recognize that a certain amount of friction is inevitable in the multitudinous contacts of modern living and prefer to ignore the minor encroachments on our rights. More to the point, one does not lightly undertake a lawsuit if he takes the time to calculate the potential costs in lawyer's fees, witnesses' fees, court costs, and his own time. Particularly is this true when the defendant in such proceedings is "judgment proof"—in other words, out of reach of any judgment against him for lack of money.

Delay in getting a decision more often than not works in favor of the defendant in civil actions. And the courts in many sections of the nation are falling further behind each year in disposing of cases on the dockets. In some of the larger cities, for example, the civil docket for jury trials is three to four years behind. Equity actions, such as a suit for an injunction to prevent impending injury, do not face this problem because they are disposed of without jury determinations. The magistrates' courts and other limited jurisdiction courts are much speedier in their handling of cases, but the quality of their decisions is frequently suspect, and these courts can normally handle only cases at law (no equity jurisdiction) involving relatively small amounts of money. Under such circumstances it is hard to criticize the injured party who throws up his hands in despair and either puts aside any thoughts of bringing suit or, after filing the action, settles out of court for considerably less than the alleged damages. [See Hans Zeisel, Harry Kalven, Jr., and Bernard Buchholz, *Delay in the Court* (Boston: Little, Brown, 1959).]

In the case of various unpopular minority groups or those dependent on the good will of the defendant, there is still additional cause for caution—the fear of reprisals. Economic pressures or even violence may be the reward for attempts to redress grievances through court action. In such event, suffering in silence may well seem to be the wiser course.

In the evolution of the administration of workmen's compensation laws in the various states it was the recognition of just these factors of cost, delay, and fear of reprisals which led legislatures to conclude that the determination of awards to injured employees bringing suit against their employers should be transferred from the courts to administrative agencies. [See Walter F. Dodd, *Administration of Workmen's Compensation* (New York: Oxford University Press, 1936), Chap. IV.]

The heavy hand of officialdom may be visited much more frequently on those who have already had a history of criminal behavior. It is easier for officials to slip beyond the bounds of their authority when dealing with the habitual offender. But this is the class which would be fighting the greatest odds in bringing an action against the offending officials. Thus the questionable character of the would-be plaintiff might lead him to doubt seriously whether he could successfully prosecute a suit to vindicate his rights. Convicts and ex-convicts seldom sue sheriffs and police officers.

To move into slightly more technical aspects than the failure to litigate, there are several factors implicit either in our judicial procedures or statutes which restrict the availability of judicial remedies. Among the more important of these are: the requirement of "standing" to bring suit, the non-reviewability by courts of many administrative acts, the presumption of validity of official acts, the presumption of constitutionality of acts of the legislature, the difficulty of extending decisions beyond the specific facts and parties involved, and, finally, the limited remedies for private interference with free choice.

2. *"Standing" to Sue.* The concept of "standing" to bring suit is a many-faceted problem. Basically, however, it is a requirement that the party bringing suit be able to show an injury recognized by the law, and one for which the law provides a remedy. Thus an individual cannot normally bring suit to redress a wrong suffered by another. (There are, of course, certain necessary exceptions, as in the case of parents, guardians, trustees, and others who may sue in behalf of those under their special care.) In addition, the injury must be real, not fancied, and must be one already suffered or immediately anticipated, not remote and speculative.

A standard illustration of the requirement that one must show injury to have "standing" to sue is the case of *Tileston* v. *Ullman*, 318 U.S. 44 (1943). Dr. Tileston, a Connecticut physician, challenged the constitutionality of a state law prohibiting "the use of drugs or instruments to prevent conception, and the giving of assistance or counsel in their use" on the ground that the law would prevent his giving professional advice to his patients whose lives would be endangered by childbearing. The United States Supreme Court dismissed the action, holding that no question was presented "which appellant has standing to assert." The allegations related to the potential dangers to his patients, not to him, and his patients were not parties to the proceeding. Thus while the law might well present difficult questions of constitutionality, Dr. Tileston was not, in the context of this case, the appropriate person to raise them judicially.

The sequel to the case is *Griswold* v. *Connecticut*, 381 U.S. 479 (1965), in which the same law was again under attack in an appeal to the United States Supreme Court. This time, however, the appellants were appealing from a conviction in a Connecticut court for violation of the law. Since the injury was clear-cut and personal, they had the requisite "standing" to raise the constitutional issue, and the Court responded by rendering a decision on the merits. (A majority of five held the law to be an unconstitutional invasion of the right of privacy of married persons, while two other justices concurred on other grounds.)

Closely akin to this limitation of "standing" is the rule generally followed by judges (unless constitutional provisions require otherwise) that they will not render advisory opinions. One must present a proper case or controversy to a court, in an adversary proceeding, in order to test the validity of a statute or administrative order.

3. *Nonreviewability of Various Administrative Acts.* The ordinary courts are not the only governmental agencies which decide disputes between parties and determine rights of persons. Administrative officials and administrative tribunals serve in a quasijudicial capacity in many very important areas of controversy between private individuals and between individuals and the government. And in many instances the statutes creating such bodies and defining their powers provide that their decisions shall be final and conclusive and not reviewable by the courts. The best illustrations of such powers are found in the authority exercised by immigration officials over aliens desiring entry into the United States. In one such instance, some years past, an alien who was excluded by immigration officials brought a petition for habeas corpus to challenge the order. The statute provided:

All decisions made by the inspection officers or their assistants touching the right of any alien to land, when adverse to such right, shall be final unless appeal be taken to the superintendent of immigration, whose action shall be subject to review by the Secretary of the Treasury.

Except for the statement that the decision "shall be final," the statute was silent concerning review by courts of a determination by the Secretary.

The United States Supreme Court, in *Nishimura Ekiu* v. *United States*, 142 U.S. 651 (1892), held that there was no authority in the courts to review the administrative determination. Justice Gray, speaking for the Court, said that under the act of Congress there could be no doubt that the administrative decision was final and conclusive. The words of the statute were "manifestly intended to prevent the question of an alien immigrant's right to land, when once decided adversely by an inspector, acting within the jurisdiction conferred upon him, from being impeached or reviewed, in the courts or otherwise, save only by appeal to the inspector's official superiors, and in accordance with the provisions of the act."

Shortly thereafter, in *Lem Moon Sing* v. *United States*, 158 U.S. 538 (1895), Justice Harlan spoke for the Court in a similar vein, stating: "The power of Congress ... to prescribe the terms and conditions upon which [aliens] may come to this country, and to have its declared policy in that regard enforced exclusively through executive officers, without judicial intervention, is settled by our previous adjudications."

Even where the courts can review the decisions of administrative officers or tribunals, the law may give only narrow scope to the courts in exercising this power. As an illustration, one can look at the authority of the National Labor Relations Board in determining causes involving alleged unfair labor practices. In one such situation, where the Board ordered reinstatement of employees of a company with back pay, the Court of Appeals refused to enforce the Board's order on the ground that its findings were without *substantial* support in the evidence. In *NLRB* v. *Nevada Consolidated Copper Corp.*, 316 U.S. 105 (1942), the Supreme Court reversed. It found that there was *some* support in the evidence and stated in a *per curiam* opinion:

> We have repeatedly held that Congress, by providing ... that the Board's findings "as to the facts, if supported by evidence, shall be conclusive," precludes the courts from weighing evidence in reviewing the Board's orders, and if the findings of the Board are supported by evidence the courts are not free to set them aside, even though the Board could have drawn different inferences.

Thus it can be seen that even where courts are given some authority to review administrative decisions, they may not be able to disturb reasonable findings of fact. And, after all, the outcome of most administrative determinations of a quasi-judicial nature hinges on the interpretation of the facts in dispute, not on interpretation of laws. [On the scope of review of administrative acts or decisions, see Robert Stern, "Review of Findings of Administrators, Judge, and Juries," 58 *Harv. L. Rev.* 70 (1944).]

4. *Presumption of Validity of Official Acts.* Another feature of judicial operation which limits the chances for successful attack on official restraints lies in the courts' presumption that the acts of public officials are valid. The courts do not automatically presume that all restraints on free choice are improper. The burden is thrown on the person attacking such acts to *prove* that they are improper. This is most readily seen in cases involving the claim

that an act of the legislature is unconstitutional. As Mr. Justice Bushrod Washington wrote, over a century ago, "It is but a decent respect to the wisdom, integrity, and patriotism of the legislative body, by which any law is passed, to presume in favor of its validity, until its violation of the Constitution is proved beyond a reasonable doubt." [*Ogden* v. *Saunders,* 12 Wheat. 213 (1827).]

In the same general direction is the view of judges that acts of administrative officials should be accorded some presumption of validity. Thus a health officer who destroys food alleged by him to be unfit for consumption is presumed to have good reason for his action. The person whose property is so destroyed must bear the burden of proving bad faith on the part of the official, if an action is brought as a consequence.

The point to be made here is that the claimant who protests the operation of a law or the act of a public official must not only show that his view of the matter is a reasonable one, but he must also show that the approach involved in the law or administrative act is clearly an unreasonable one. Thus in *Powell* v. *Pennsylvania,* 127 U.S. 678 (1888), a manufacturer of oleomargarine in Pennsylvania was unable to challenge successfully a state law prohibiting the manufacture of such products in that state. He offered to show by clear and convincing tests that his product was not unhealthful and was clearly safe for human consumption. But since he could not go further and prove that the law was clearly an unreasonable approach to protecting the citizens from unsafe products of other manufacturers, he lost his case. Such a claimant, then, comes into court with the balances tilted against him. He must not merely equalize the weight in the opposite pan; he must add enough extra to tip the balance in his direction.

5. *Difficulty in Extending Decisions Beyond Specific Facts and Parties Involved in Litigation.* Technically, a decision rendered by a court binds only the parties to the suit then under consideration, and binds them only with respect to the controversy in which they are involved. If, however, the decision involves a constitutional question and is determined by the United States Supreme Court, then its effect may be considerably more far-reaching. Under our doctrine of precedent and the application of the national supremacy clause of Article VI of the United States Constitution, all state and federal judges are bound to apply the same constitutional rule if a case arises presenting a similar controversy. The point is, however, that a separate suit may be necessary to get a specific order directing that the Supreme Court's rule be followed. Two things then become apparent. First, a slight alteration of the facts presented may lead to a different decision by the Court in subsequent cases. Second, even if different parties present substantially the same fact situations, one Court decision does not by any means lead to a mass reaction on the part of legislators or administrators throughout the nation to bring their practices in line with the tenor of the Court's requirements.

The result is that inertia or opposition to a holding of a court, even the

United States Supreme Court, could well mean that a prolonged period of litigation would be necessary to lead to even a partial acquiescence in the rule announced. This fact is nowhere better illustrated than in the long history of racial discrimination in according voting rights. The Fifteenth Amendment was proclaimed ratified in the year 1870. Yet even today, a century later, many persons are still denied registration or voting rights solely on the grounds of race.

The words of the Fifteenth Amendment seem clear enough: "The right of citizens of the United States to vote shall not be denied or abridged by the United States or by any State on account of race, color, or previous condition of servitude." But a whole host of devices have been used to defeat the purposes of the Amendment. And in some parts of the South, as each device has been held unconstitutional, a new one has been substituted, which required a new course of litigation. A holding by the Court that denial of membership in the Democratic Party on account of race was unconstitutional did not preclude a state requirement that all applicants for registration give a reasonable interpretation of the United States Constitution. Thus a second case had to be brought and a second decision rendered on the new set of facts.

Even where the facts seem nearly identical, it still may be necessary to get a separate decree from a court in order to secure acquiescence. In 1948 the Supreme Court held unconstitutional as an "establishment of religion" a "released time" program of an Illinois school board under which weekly religious instruction was given to public school students in the school buildings during regular school hours. [*McCollum* v. *Board of Education*, 333 U.S. 203 (1948).] It appears that similar programs are still in operation in various parts of the nation, but unless separate suits are brought to test the validity of such programs under the *McCollum* doctrine, they will continue indefinitely, in the absence of a legislative or administrative policy change. [See Gordon Patric, "The Impact of a Court Decision: Aftermath of the McCollum Case," 6 *J. of Pub. L.* 455 (1957).] This lays open a key difference between the judicial process and the administrative process. The judicial process must await the sufficient irritation of the injured parties to energize its machinery. The administrative process has, by statutory grant, a built-in self-starting mechanism. The National Labor Relations Board, for example, may initiate its own action to halt unfair labor practices. It need not wait for some workman who has a greater than average allotment of courage to step forward and accuse his employer. And, in addition, the administrative tribunal has sufficient personnel to ensure, to a substantial degree at least, that its decisions are followed throughout all industries or areas where they may be applicable.

6. *Limited Remedies for Private Interference with Free Choice.* Another problem in the citizen's search for freedom from restriction lies in the fact that many types of interference stemming from private persons do not constitute actionable wrongs under the law. Private prejudice and private dis-

crimination do not, in the absence of specific statutory provisions, offer grounds for judicial intervention in behalf of the sufferer. If one is denied admission to membership in a social club, for example, solely on the basis of his race or religion or political affiliation, he may understandably smart under the rejection, but the courts cannot help him (again assuming no statutory provision barring such distinctions). This statement is generally true as applied to other more important areas as well: for example, in employment outside the coverage of the Civil Rights Act of 1964, in admission to a purely private school, and in housing if the discrimination is not based on race or religion. To take the latter case, if a man chooses to sell his home to a member of his own economic group only, the courts at present offer no remedy to the would-be purchaser of another class. There are, then, many types of restraints on individual freedom of choice which are beyond the authority of courts to remove or ameliorate.

7. *Political Questions.* Another self-imposed limitation on the courts' area of operation lies in the doctrine of political questions. In brief, this is the view that some problems are pre-eminently political in nature, and solutions should be sought in the political branches rather than in the courts. Even questions which turn on interpretations of the United States Constitution have occasionally been placed in this category, and the courts will refuse a remedy to those who claim injury. An illustration is found in the case of *Colegrove* v. *Green,* 328 U.S. 549 (1946), in which a citizen of Illinois sought a judicial remedy for the glaring inequalities of population in the arrangement of congressional districts in that state. He argued that he and others in the more populous districts were being denied "equal protection of the laws" because of their unequal voting power, in violation of the Fourteenth Amendment. The United States Supreme Court dismissed the case, although only three of the seven justices participating squarely viewed the question as a "political question." While *Baker* v. *Carr,* 369 U.S. 186 (1962), holds that such questions are now justiciable, Justice Frankfurter's statements on political questions in *Colegrove* are still instructive:

> The Constitution has many commands that are not enforceable by courts because they clearly fall outside the conditions and purposes that circumscribe judicial action. Thus, "on demand of the executive authority," Article IV, Section 2, of a State it is the duty of a sister State to deliver up a fugitive from justice. But the fulfillment of this duty cannot be judicially enforced. *Kentucky* v. *Dennison,* 24 How. 66. The duty to see to it that the laws are faithfully executed cannot be brought under legal compulsion. *Mississippi* v. *Johnson,* 4 Wall. 475. Violation of the great guaranty of a republican form of government in States cannot be challenged in the courts. *Pacific Telephone Company* v. *Oregon,* 223 U.S. 118. The Constitution has left the performance of many duties in our governmental scheme to depend on the fidelity of the executive and legislative action and, ultimately, on the vigilance of the people in exercising their political rights.

While there are factors which limit courts in protecting civil liberties, there is, nevertheless, much that they can do in this area. Even in their restricted scope of operation, the courts exercise a vast influence over the activities of both officials and private persons who themselves may never be a party to litigation. Americans have traditionally shown great respect for judicial opinion, despite occasional periods during which the courts have been under heavy fire, and it has sometimes been important in the formation of public opinion.

One of the key powers of the courts is that of judicial review—that is, the authority to review acts of the coordinate branches, in appropriate cases, and to refuse to give effect to such acts on the ground of their unconstitutionality. This power of judicial review is more typically an American judicial power than one belonging to judges in all countries. Many nations today, however, permit the courts at least a limited exercise of this authority. [The standard work on judicial review in America is Charles G. Haines, *The American Doctrine of Judicial Supremacy* (Berkeley: University of California Press, 1932). See also Charles L. Black, Jr., *The People and the Court* (New York: Macmillan, 1960); Edward McWhinney, *Judicial Review in the English-Speaking World* (Toronto: University of Toronto Press, 1956); David Deener, "Judicial Review in Modern Constitutional Systems," 46 *Amer. Pol. Sci. Rev.* 1079 (1952).] Without this vital power, the courts would be obliged to enforce any clear statement of policy by the legislative body, and no independent determination could be made of whether such policy constituted an undue abridgment of individual rights. The United States Supreme Court has almost gone out of the business of declaring acts of Congress unconstitutional, but it still remains rather active in the area of checking excesses of state and local legislative zeal.

Constitutional challenges may be directed to specific administrative practices rather than to a statute, and this, too, is an important aspect of the broad doctrine of judicial review. For example, in *Escobedo* v. *Illinois*, 378 U.S. 478 (1964), the Court considered the constitutionality of a police refusal to allow the accused to consult counsel during interrogation, rather than the constitutionality of a statute. (Under the special circumstances of that case, the Court held the action unconstitutional.) While the bulk of challenged statutes or administrative actions are held valid, the threat of judicial review may serve as an important safeguard against unconstitutional action.

Claims of denials of rights may be based on statutory or common-law grounds as well as on constitutional provisions. Whatever the basis for the alleged right, however, the more important specific *remedies* offered by the judicial process to wronged parties are encompassed in a relatively few procedures. And it is within the framework of these kinds of remedies that the courts serve to protect against injury or to assuage the wounds received.

1. *Mandamus.* Mandamus is an old common-law writ which may be usefully employed against public officials in specified circumstances. Briefly put, it is a writ commanding a public officer to perform some duty which

the laws require him to do but which he refuses or neglects to perform. If he has any discretion in the matter, mandamus cannot be used. But if the law is clear in requiring the performance of some ministerial function, then mandamus may properly be sought to nudge the reluctant or negligent official along in the performance of his duties.

As an illustration, one who is clearly qualified under the law to be registered as a qualified elector may use the remedy of mandamus to force the registrar who arbitrarily denies registration to place his name in the register. Since the writ cannot be employed where the official has discretion, however, it could not issue against the legislature on complaint by teen-age citizens that the voting age should be reduced to eighteen. As the United States Supreme Court stated, in *Wilbur* v. *United States,* 281 U.S. 206, 218 (1930):

Where the duty in a particular situation is so plainly prescribed as to be free from doubt and equivalent to a positive command it is regarded as being so far ministerial that its performance may be compelled by mandamus, unless there be provision or implication to the contrary. But where the duty is not thus plainly prescribed but depends upon a statute the construction or application of which is not free from doubt, it is regarded as involving the character of a judgment or discretion which cannot be controlled by mandamus.

It is important to note as well that the writ does not issue to purely private persons, but can only be directed to public officials or persons performing some quasi-public function. Thus while in its limited area it is useful, the restricted scope of application often makes it necessary for the citizen to seek other remedies.

2. *Injunction.* The injunction is primarily a preventive remedy and issues from a court of equity. It is considerably broader in its applications than mandamus and is far more frequently employed in civil rights questions. It can apply to either ministerial or discretionary functions and to either public officials or private persons. Equity picks up where the law ends and enables a judge to frame an order or decree to fit the necessities of the case under consideration. The injunction is one of the most useful tools of the equity judge. The broad operation of the injunctive remedy is well illustrated by the school segregation cases. The complainants sought injunctions directed to various local school officials ordering them to refrain from enforcing laws requiring racial segregation in the public schools. The 1955 decision of the United States Supreme Court left the lower district court judges free to frame such decrees as appeared advisable to accomplish the ends indicated in the 1954 decision. In some areas of the South, judges issued injunctions to restrain all further attempts to enforce the school segregation laws of the areas involved. In others, special longer range programs of gradual integration were specified in the decrees. In a few instances blanket injunctions were issued to restrain any and all attempts by either officials or private persons to interfere with the integration process.

Thus the injunction is particularly useful where there is a claim that some constitutional right is abridged by the operation of a law or administrative practice and the victim desires the intervention of a court to stop the abridgment. Violation of the terms of either a mandamus or an injunction subjects the violator to the possibility of citation for contempt, with broad leeway given to the judge in determining what punishment to impose.

3. *Civil Damage Suit.* Another important type of legal action to protect rights is the civil damage suit. If a citizen feels that he has been intentionally subjected to a deprivation of a right guaranteed by the law, he can initiate a suit for money damages against the offender. This is possible whether the defendant named is a private person or a public official. A person who without provocation assaults another leaves himself open to a damage suit in which the plaintiff may run up quite a list of items in the bill of damages: hospital or doctor's bills, mental and physical anguish, loss of time from work, and perhaps punitive damages as well. With the increasingly large jury verdicts in tort cases of various sorts, this type of action should pose a substantial deterrent against willful or malicious deprivation of rights. Exceptions are noted, of course, in those cases in which local sentiment runs against the plaintiff because of religion, race, past criminal activity, or some other factor which makes his cause unpopular.

While the civil suit for money damages might be useful in protecting private citizens against other private citizens, a more difficult problem is presented when the defendant is a public official, and the complaint arises from his official performance. If the official acts in good faith but makes an error of judgment, then the decision will normally run against the wronged citizen. The courts recognize that even competent, well-intentioned government personnel are sometimes known to err in the performance of their official duties. It would be a drastic rule indeed which would subject such persons to the expense of paying damages to all citizens who were inconvenienced by these mistakes. Judges and jurors might spend more time as defendants than in the pursuits of their vocations if this were allowed. Thus the plaintiff in such cases has an extra burden of proving willful or malicious deprivation of rights. This is much more difficult, and the difficulty is indicated in the relative rarity with which civil suits are successfully prosecuted against policemen, for example, for damages alleged to have been sustained by private persons in their contacts with these officials.

4. *Criminal Prosecution.* Where the deprivation of one's rights is declared by the law to be a criminal offense, the offender may not only be forced to pay damages, but he also can be put to trial for committing a crime. Suppose one is injured by the unprovoked physical assault of another. Clearly this is a situation which involves the commission of both a private and a public wrong. The victim of such treatment can sue in a civil action for damages, while the government can bring a criminal prosecution. Except in those situations where the victim is locally unpopular for one reason or another, the increasing probability of criminal prosecution has served as

one factor, among others, in lessening the frequency of police brutality in the past two or three decades. [See Caleb Foote, "Tort Remedies for Police Violations of Individual Rights," 39 *Minn. L. Rev.* 493 (1955), and Harry H. Shapiro, "Limitations in Prosecuting Civil Rights Violations," 46 *Cornell L.Q.* 532 (1961).]

5. *Appellate Court Review.* Deprivations of individual rights may take place or may be ignored in the course of judicial proceedings as well as elsewhere in life. Thus there must be some corrective which can operate on even the judicial process. The most important such device is to be found in the review of trial court proceedings by an appellate court. If errors of law are made in the trial court, or if a jury goes beyond its authority in rendering a verdict, then a case would be presented for the appropriate exercise of appellate court review and possible reversal. If a conviction is obtained under circumstances which render the possibility of a fair trial quite remote, such as mob domination or use of perjured testimony or "trial by newspaper," then an appellate court can reverse the conviction and demand a trial under more reasonable and proper conditions.

This power is a very important and highly valuable one. But it must be recognized that there are severe limitations on the effectiveness of this institution as a cure-all for mistakes in trial court proceedings. In the first place, less than five per cent of the decisions of the trial courts in America are appealed. It is probably a fair assumption that in an appreciable number of the mass of unappealed cases reversible error occurred. But appellate review is not automatic, and if the losing party fails to perfect an appeal, the corrective powers of the higher courts cannot be brought to bear. In that event, the trial court decision, right or wrong, stands. In the second place, appellate courts as a general rule examine only the complaint that errors of *law* were made in the trial court, not errors in *fact-finding*. Since the disposition of large numbers of cases turns almost exclusively on the finding of facts, appeals would in most of these be completely futile.

Despite these limitations, the upper courts of both state and federal governments wield substantial powers to correct injustices in the trial courts. And it is argued by many that even where technically they might be powerless to act (e.g., under the rule of not disturbing a lower court finding of fact) there is always some point available on which a decision for reversal and an order for new trial can turn. At times the courts have even reversed on grounds which were not even raised by counsel seeking the review. These are very special cases, however, and the better view is to recognize that the power of review is useful but is by no means a substitute for adequate staffing of the courts of first instance with competent personnel, and a high quality of advocacy on the part of counsel for both sides.

6. *Habeas Corpus.* Another device available to vindicate one's legal rights is the writ of habeas corpus. Important though it is, it should be kept in mind that there are several limitations on its usefulness in the broad area

of protecting personal liberties. Generally speaking, it is a device which can be used to test the legality of a physical restraint or detention. If a person is detained without any formal charge being placed against him, the writ may be used in effect to require that the man be released or a proper charge, supportable by some evidence or reliable information, be placed against him. If a prisoner has been tried and convicted, habeas corpus is still available as a potential remedy, since there is no time limit and no statute of limitations on its use. It cannot, however, be used as a substitute for ordinary appellate review, and the latter is a much broader device for raising issues concerning the interpretations of laws and the conduct of trials. Habeas corpus is referred to as a device for *collateral* attack on detention, since it opens up for investigation only such questions as are considered *jurisdictional* questions. Examples of such questions are whether the trial court which rendered judgment had authority over the person or the offense involved, or whether the prisoner was denied certain constitutional rights such as the right to counsel. On ordinary appellate review a great variety of additional points might be attacked which would be improper under habeas corpus, such as the judge's charge to the jury, the admissibility of evidence, or the competency of certain witnesses to testify. [For an excellent discussion of the history and uses of the writ of habeas corpus, see David Fellman, *The Defendant's Rights* (New York: Rinehart, 1958) Chap. 5.] The writ is of special importance in dealing with detentions by the military, since there is no ordinary review of military court decisions by the civil courts. Thus the only method of bringing issues from the military tribunals to the civil courts is by petition for the writ of habeas corpus. Again it should be noted that in such cases the only ground for relief is that the sentencing court lacked jurisdiction.

Since it is clear that the courts alone cannot adequately safeguard the liberties of the people, the question naturally arises of what additional forces may be deployed to achieve the necessary protection. In approaching the problem it is convenient to look at the various *sources* of interference with our personal freedom. Some may call for a different attack than others.

One important source is the legislative body, and this includes all such bodies from the national Congress down to the municipal council. A rather flagrant example of arbitrary legislative abridgment of rights is that of a municipal ordinance which required labor union organizers to get a permit from the mayor and city council before recruiting new members, and pay a license fee of $2,000, plus $500 for each member obtained! [Held unconstitutional on its face in *Staub* v. *City of Baxley*, 355 U.S. 313 (1958).] The preventive remedies for this source of interference are easily stated, but obviously rather difficult to maintain. First, we must elect a high caliber legislature, and second, we must see that those members of the citizenry who are interested in the protection of civil rights, whether they be a majority or a minority, maintain continual pressure on the legislative body to thwart attempts to adopt such policies as that illustrated above. The ideal may be impossible to attain, but any progress in that direction represents stronger protection of civil liberties.

A second source of abridgments of rights is the administrative process. Modern government by bureaucracy involves a great deal of delegation of decision-making power to what might well be called the fourth branch of the government. Such officials, even when they act in good faith, have the power to impose a tremendous variety of improper limitations on the citizen's exercise of free choices. One example of this sort of restriction was the action of the Postmaster General some years past in withdrawing second-class mail privileges from *Esquire* magazine on the ground that it did not meet the statutory test of being "published for the dissemination of information of a public character, or devoted to literature, the sciences, arts, or some special industry." Actually, he simply disapproved of the contents. Such a withdrawal does not completely bar the designated periodical from the mails, but the first-class rates for mailing are well-nigh prohibitive for commercial publishers in a competitive market. [The Court unanimously held the action to be an unauthorized censorship: *Hannegan* v. *Esquire*, 327 U.S. 146 (1946).]

The nonjudicial remedies against administrative interference are similar to those applicable to the legislature. The prestige of governmental administrative service must be sufficiently enhanced to attract and keep the ablest personnel among the citizenry. Second, the people, both as individuals and as members of organizations, must maintain a continual watch over the actions of administrative officials in those areas where improper interference with private rights is apt to occur. Such abridgments as do occur should be brought promptly to the attention of both administrative supervisors and policy officials who control the agency involved. Similarly, special recognition should be accorded administrative personnel who show particular concern for the rights of the individual. Third, the legislature must be held responsible for exercising care both in its grants of statutory authority to administrators and in its overseeing of their functions.

Making the bureaucracy responsible to the people is one of the most difficult problems in government today. A novel approach to the problem was developed in Sweden in the office of the ombudsman. This official has discretion to investigate any administrative action or governmental agency omission impairing the rights of private persons, either on his own initiative or upon complaint filed with him. Denmark and Norway more recently adopted this institution, and considerable interest is now expressed in the United States. [See Donald C. Rowat, ed., *The Ombudsman: Citizen's Defender* (Toronto: University of Toronto Press, 1965); Walter Gellhorn, *Ombudsmen and Others: Citizens' Protectors in Nine Countries* (Cambridge: Harvard University Press, 1966); Walter Gellhorn, *When Americans Complain: Governmental Grievance Procedures* (Cambridge: Harvard University Press, 1966); Stanley v. Anderson, ed., *Ombudsmen for American Government?* (Englewood Cliffs: Prentice-Hall, 1968).

A third, and more widely publicized, source of violations of civil liberties lies in the personal malice or brutality of officials, particularly police officers. This is illustrated in peculiarly distasteful fashion by the case in which a city police chief and a sheriff's deputy forced a group of Jehovah's Witnesses to drink a half-pint of castor oil, in response to their request for police protection. [Held to come within the scope of acts punishable under the federal civil rights acts: *Catlette* v. *United States*, 132 F.2d 902 (4th C.A., 1943).] Many cases which are far more brutal come to light from time to time. In view of the vast number of daily contacts between police and citizen in the United States, the percentage of brutality cases must be extremely small. At least in this area, however, "small" must not be equated with "negligible." In discussing nonjudicial remedies, there is a strong tendency to propose that this type of evil will be adequately dispelled by the simple expedient of employing only well-educated young men who have passed rigid psychological tests for emotional stability. To some extent, more care in recruitment and training of policemen might well reduce the instances of police lawlessness. Assuredly this is an area in which progress can be made. But the habits and attitudes of the public toward police and law enforcement generally have a direct impact on the practices of the personnel involved. Low budgets and high pressures tend to push enforcement agencies into short-cut procedures. And community demands for unequal treatment of offenders, either on grounds of the character of the offender or of the offense, will usually find their response in the behavior of the enforcement agencies. Only if the community and the police maintain a genuine respect for following lawful procedures can such practices be minimized.

Unequal enforcement that is without brutality presents quite another problem. The average citizen is apt to hold that all criminal laws should be enforced against all offenders. A corollary would be the statement that selective enforcement constitutes a civil rights violation in that it denies equal protection of the laws. This same doctrinaire citizen would probably be enraged, however, if arrested for engaging in a penny-ante poker game on Saturday night with his close friends. As another illustration, laws against adultery are so rarely enforced in this country that one would surely hear indignant cries of "Discrimination!" if a prosecution were actually begun against one of the vast number (according to Professor Kinsey) of ordinary offenders. The suggestion is sometimes made that it would cleanse the consciences of both the police and the public if these rarely enforced criminal laws were repealed altogether. Then the laws remaining could be rewritten to make criminal *only* the specific acts which the community actively wants to see punished, and the police could push forward with full enforcement of *all* the laws. There are several points at which these proposals are open to attack. First, the police, and (if closely questioned) in all probability the public, want to have available a full battery of weapons to use against persons in the community who are patently "undesirable." Then the prosecutor and the police who are forced by public pressures to act against a specific person can roam through the whole long list of criminal acts defined by the statutes or the common law to select the charges which can most easily be substantiated. A notorious but slippery racketeer might then be charged with adultery, when other offenders were overlooked. Admittedly, this is a sort of "The public will have its way" attitude on criminal law enforcement, but conversation with some students of the process would indicate that this conclusion is not too wide of the mark. A second difficulty with the suggested remedies lies in the extreme complexity of the task of statute writing. If the reader will but sit down and try to draft a bill which would punish only the forms of gambling which the average community thinks ought to be subjected to the criminal process, he will see the problem. The attempt to exclude the church bingo game, the matching for coffee, the friendly poker game (do the stakes determine the degree of friendliness?) and the annual bet on the homecoming football game—all of which the average community would probably consider as outside the proper confines of the criminal process— will either leave the statute so ponderous as to be unwieldy (perhaps even unconstitutionally vague) or else will leave loopholes through which the professional gambler can escape. Many enforcement officers much prefer to take a flat prohibition in the law and use the law with discretion. This is another way of saying that what is desired is unequal enforcement, and a serious question may be raised as to whether there is any acceptable realistic alternative. Still a third objection to the remedies proposed lies in the budget process, mentioned above. The law enforcement process is unalterably tied to the appropriation bill. Whatever the criminal code may proscribe, the police can investigate, patrol, and prevent only to the extent that money is appropriated for these purposes. Doubling the appropriation thus could very well have the effect of markedly increasing the statistical crime rate, in the sense that the resulting step-up in police activity would normally lead to the apprehension of more criminals. More financial support should mean a nearer approach to full enforcement of the laws. But in all probability no community gives the enforcement agencies anything approaching the annual sum necessary really to approximate full enforcement of all criminal laws. The police chief simply has to stretch his appropriation to cover as nearly as possible the types of crimes which arouse the greatest public indignation and those which are cheapest to enforce. The twilight zone of unenforced laws is reserved for use against those persons who cannot effectively be reached by the other laws but who have aroused the antagonism of either the public or the officialdom.

The final source of interference with the free choice of individuals is the action of private persons. There are standard judicial remedies for a great many types of private encroachment on private rights, e.g., in the use of the laws of trespass, assault, tort, and others. Nonjudicial remedies which would increase the protection against private interference would basically go in two directions: better enforcement of existing laws and the creation of new rights. Just as government created a new right in the labor field by the laws guaranteeing protection against discrimination for union membership, so governments of the states could create rights in other aspects of man's relations with man. Attempts to go beyond the usual application of standard remedies, however, and reduce further the area of private discrimination touch on the most difficult and sensitive area of all. It is perfectly reasonable to insist that governments act without undue discrimination or favoritism. In the arena of private action, however, the individual should be allowed more room for choice, even though the basic decisions might be considered irrational by others. Governments have stepped in to remove some areas of "free" choice because of inherent inequalities in the bargaining positions of the parties involved and the severe hardships to which large numbers of people might be subjected by others. This has been true, for example, in the matter of minimum wages, maximum hours, and workmen's compensation. In matters generally considered less necessitous than the right to make a living, governments have less frequently interfered with private choices. In the equal accommodations title of the Civil Rights Act of 1964, however, the Congress took action to remove from the area of free choice one of the most exacerbating instances of private discrimination—choice of customers on the basis of race or religion in places of public accommodation.

Freedom to choose associates in either social or vocational activities often leads to exclusivity, and the excluded groups may complain that something must be done by the government to afford them a wider range of choice. The policy which would lead to wider choices for the excluded group must to that extent reduce the freedom of selection of the former. The task of the policy-maker is to weigh the importance of the activity and the number of people involved, and to balance out the conflicting gains and losses in order to make a decision as to whether governmental action will be more or less beneficial than inaction.

In conclusion, one can say that while there is a tremendous area for exploration in the nonjudicial protections which may be offered to civil liberties, the judicial arena is still of vast importance in the field. The Court is, normally, the final judge of what most of the Constitution means; the state and federal courts interpret and apply the laws in appropriate cases; and some of the finest statements in the literature on human rights are to be found in the official opinions of judges on the state and federal bench. Since this is the case, and since this work is predominantly designed to describe the present law in the field of civil rights, the material and comment to follow will center heavily on the questions which have been presented for judicial decision.

CHAPTER 2

Civil Rights in the Federal System

FOR the beginning student in American civil rights, one of the most perplexing features is the complication presented by the federal pattern of government. To such persons it may come as a shock to find that the United States Constitution offers essentially a dual standard for national and state police or courts. The Constitution bars *federal* prosecution for serious crimes without grand jury indictment, but it permits a state to abolish the grand jury altogether. And until 1968 that same Constitution which guarantees the right of trial by jury to all persons charged with *federal* crimes allowed a state, if it chose to do so, to abolish the trial jury in all criminal cases, leaving the verdict to the judge. Further, until the fairly recent decision in *Gideon* v. *Wainwright, 372 U.S. 335 (1963)*, the state could send persons to trial accused of even serious noncapital felonies without benefit of counsel, unless they could afford their own, while the Sixth Amendment demands court-appointed counsel for indigent *federal* defendants in all cases more serious than "petty offenses."

At the core of the matter is the fact that the Bill of Rights to the United States Constitution sets out various limitations on action by the *national* government, but it does not of its own terms in any way limit the *state* governments. Such protection as the Constitution provides against abridgment of civil rights by the state governments is to be found largely in the Civil War Amendments, and even these protections, with the exception of property rights, did not begin to take on substantial importance until the present century was well under way. Of course the most striking single development in the constitutional law of civil rights has been the "nationalization" of rights through the process of gradual "incorporation" of the various protections listed in the Bill of Rights into the "due process" clause of the Fourteenth Amendment. This process has been continuing for nearly half a century, and today most of the safeguards against national action described in the Bill of Rights are similarly operative against state action through the Fourteenth Amendment. Despite this fact, there remain some differences between the two sets of guarantees, and a sophisticated understanding of civil rights in America requires an analysis of the emergence of that law in the framework of the federal system.

To begin with the Philadelphia Convention, the national Constitution was designed to describe the powers and organization of the national government, without attempting to set up simultaneously a general pattern of state government. Certain limitations on state powers are to be found in that document, to be sure, but they are largely due to the desire to protect the integrity of national powers from state interference or to ensure that the states would not thwart the flow of interstate activities by means of burdensome discriminations. It must be recalled that the states existing in 1787 already had their own constitutions and framework of government, and the framers of the national Constitution did not take it upon themselves to tamper with those going concerns except as certain transfers of power from state to nation appeared necessary. In view of the purpose for which the Philadelphia Convention assembled, it would be surprising to find the framers drawing up a detailed list of safeguards to protect the citizen against the *state* government.

From an examination of the general purposes of the framers, it is a relatively easy second step to a realization that the Bill of Rights, added in 1791, protects the citizen only against the actions of the national government. A federal system had been established. Each governmental entity, nation and state, had its own constitution defining governmental organization, powers, and limitations. The state constitutions customarily had bills of rights describing guarantees operating against state officials. The national Bill of Rights operated against the national government. It would have seemed as curious in 1791 to argue that these amendments limited the state governments as it would to have claimed that federal courts were strictly bound by the requirements of state constitutions. The clamor from north to south for the addition of a bill of rights to the proposed Constitution of 1787 stemmed from distrust of national officials, not state officials. And Hamilton's response to such critics is further support for the view that the demands were restricted to protection against national abridgment of rights. In *The Federalist*, No. 84, he stated:

I go further, and affirm that bill of rights, in the sense and to the extent in which they are contended for, are not only unnecessary in the proposed Constitution, but would even be dangerous. They would contain various exceptions to powers not granted; and, on this very account, would afford a colorable pretext to claim more than were granted. For why declare that things shall not be done which there is no power to do? Why, for instance, should it be said that the liberty of the press shall not be restrained, when no power is given by which restrictions may be imposed?

Hamilton was stressing the point that the government was one of delegated powers only, and in the absence of a delegation of authority to restrain the press there was no power to do so. Clearly he was speaking only of the national government, since the states have broad *reserved* powers and are not held to a specific list of enumerated powers as is the national government.

Finally, the group of amendments proposed by the first House of Representatives numbered seventeen, of which only one specifically limited the states. It provided that "no state should infringe the right of trial by jury in criminal cases, nor the rights of conscience, nor the freedom of speech or of the press." It is at least a reasonable conclusion to draw from this fact that the other provisions which omitted any reference to states were not intended to apply to the states. [For possible counter-arguments to this logic, see Herman Pritchett, *The American Constitution* (New York: McGraw-Hill, 1959), p. 371.]

Despite these arguments, a judicial decision was required to dispose of the question finally. The case was *Barron* v. *Baltimore*, decided in 1833. It arose out of alleged damage to a wharf owned by Barron in the course of a paving program carried out by the City of Baltimore. In completing the program, certain streams were diverted from their usual course, and deposits of sand and gravel allegedly were built up at Barron's wharf to such an extent that access of vessels was prevented. A trial court verdict of $4,500 in Barron's favor was reversed by the Maryland Court of Appeals. Claiming that this action was a taking of his property for public use without just compensation, in violation of the Fifth Amendment to the United States Constitution, Barron took the question on writ of error to the United States Supreme Court. His contention was that the Fifth Amendment's broad language ought to be so construed as to restrain not only the power of the United States but also that of the state. The importance of the question from a technical standpoint lay in the fact that unless Barron's contention were upheld, there was no basis for jurisdiction in the Supreme Court, and that Court could go no further into the matter of whether the city had in fact "taken" Barron's property improperly. A holding that the Fifth Amendment did not restrain the state would mean that the state court's decision on the matter was final.

BARRON *v.* BALTIMORE

7 Peters 243 (1833)

Mr. Chief Justice Marshall delivered the opinion of the Court.

The judgment brought up by this writ of error having been rendered by the court of a State, this tribunal can exercise no jurisdiction over it, unless it be shown to come within the provisions of the twenty-fifth section of the Judicial Act.

The plaintiff in error contends that it comes within that clause in the Fifth Amendment to the Constitution, which inhibits the taking of private property for public use, without just compensation. He insists that this amendment, being in favor of the liberty of the citizen, ought to be so construed as to restrain the legislative power of a state, as well as that of the United States. If this proposition be untrue, the Court can take no jurisdiction of the cause.

The question thus presented is, we think, of great importance, but not of much difficulty.

The Constitution was ordained and established by the people of the United States for themselves, for their own government, and not for the government of the individual states. Each state established a constitution for itself, and, in that constitution, provided such limitations and restrictions on the powers of its particular government as its judgment dictated. The people of the United States framed such a government for the United States as they supposed best adapted to their situation, and best calculated to promote their interests. The powers they conferred on this government were to be exercised by itself; and the limitations on power, if expressed in general terms, are naturally, and, we think, necessarily applicable to the government created by the instrument. They are limitations of power granted in the instrument itself; not of distinct governments, framed by different persons and for different purposes.

If these propositions be correct, the Fifth Amendment must be understood as restraining the power of the general government, not as applicable to the states. In their several constitutions they have imposed such restrictions on their respective governments as their own wisdom suggested; such as they deemed most proper for themselves. It is a subject on which they judge exclusively, and with which others interfere no farther than they are supposed to have a common interest.

The counsel for the plaintiff in error insists that the Constitution was intended to secure the people of the several states against the undue exercise of power by their respective state governments; as well as against that which might be attempted by their general government. In support of this argument he relies on the inhibitions contained in the tenth section of the first article.

We think that section affords a strong if not a conclusive argument in support of the opinion already indicated by the Court.

[Here the Chief Justice compares some of the provisions of Article I, Section 9, with similar ones in Article I, Section 10. The former declares that "no bill of attainder or ex post facto law shall be passed." The latter declares that "no State shall pass any bill of attainder or ex post facto law." Marshall points out that despite the general wording of the prohibition in the former section it must be clear that it only applied to the Congress, because otherwise there would be no necessity for adding a separate phrase specifically forbidding the States to do these same things.]

If the original Constitution, in the ninth and tenth sections of the first article, draws this plain and marked line of discrimination between the limitations it imposes on the powers of the general government and on those of the states; if in every inhibition intended to act on state power, words are employed which directly express that intent, some strong reason must be assigned for departing from this safe and judicious course in framing the amendments, before that departure can be assumed.

We search in vain for that reason.

Had the people of the several states, or any of them, required changes in their constitutions; had they required additional safeguards to liberty from the apprehended encroachments of their particular governments, the remedy was in their own hands, and would have been applied by themselves. A convention would have been assembled by the discontented state, and the required improvements would have been made by itself. The unwieldy and cumbrous machinery of procuring a recommendation from two-thirds of Congress, and the assent of three-fourths of their sister states, could never have occurred to any human being as a mode of doing that which might be effected by the state itself. Had the framers of these amendments intended them to be limitations on the powers of the state governments, they would have imitated the framers of the original Constitution, and have expressed that intention. Had Congress engaged in the extraordinary occupation of improving the constitutions of the several states by affording the people additional protection from the exercise of power by their own governments in matters which concerned themselves alone, they would have declared this purpose in plain and intelligible language.

But it is universally understood, it is a part of the history of the day, that the great revolution which established the Constitution of the United States was not effected without immense opposition. Serious fears were extensively entertained that those powers which the patriot statesmen, who then watched over the interests of our country, deemed essential to union, and to the attainment of those invaluable objects for which union was sought, might be exercised in a manner dangerous to liberty. In almost every convention by which the Constitution was adopted, amendments to guard against the abuse of power were recommended. These amendments demanded security against the apprehended encroachments of the general government, not against those of the local governments.

In compliance with a sentiment thus generally expressed, to quiet fears thus extensively entertained, amendments were proposed by the required majority in Congress, and adopted by the states. These amendments contain no expression indicating an intention to apply them to the state governments. This Court cannot so apply them.

We are of opinion that the provision in the Fifth Amendment to the Constitution, declaring that private property shall not be taken for public use without just compensation, is intended solely as a limitation on the exercise of power by the government of the United States, and is not applicable to the legislation of the states. We are therefore of opinion, that there is no repugnancy between the several acts of the general assembly of Maryland, given in evidence by the defendants at the trial of this cause, in the court of that state, and the Constitution of the United States. This Court, therefore, has no jurisdiction of the cause; and it is dismissed.

Despite Marshall's logic and his historical analysis, one might argue that since the First Amendment specifically restricts Congress and the next seven are general in their language, all of these latter amendments were intended to apply fully to all governments within the United States. The answer to this contention is that in reality all of the provisions embodied in the first eight amendments were one lengthy addition to the Constitution, with no necessary logic or subtle unexpressed intent behind the separation into eight articles. Thus the specific application of the opening sentence to Congress should be carried right on through as a limitation on the appropriate arm of the *national* government in each of the provisions of the Bill of Rights.

The citizen of Barron's day might have been impelled by that decision to sit down and browse through the whole Constitution to see just what sort of safeguards that document offered against the improper interference with his rights by the agents of state governments. At that time, 1833, he would have noted the protections in Article I, Section 10, regarding ex post facto laws and bills of attainder, to which Marshall referred in the above case, but virtually nothing else. A keen observer, however, might have spotted a potential weapon in Article IV, which states in Section 2, "The citizens of each State shall be entitled to all privileges and immunities of citizens in the several States." This sentence is not noteworthy for its clarity. The lay reader might readily conjure up an interpretation which would serve as a massive barrier to state deprivations of rights. The judicial interpretations of this clause, however, gave no great encouragement to such a view.

The clause is really a shorthand version of Article 4 of the Articles of Confederation, which in long and somewhat quaint fashion declared:

The better to secure and perpetuate mutual friendship and intercourse among the people of the different states in this Union, the free inhabitants of each of these states—paupers, vagabonds, and fugitives from justice, excepted—shall be entitled to all privileges and immunities of free citizens in the several states; and the people of each state shall have free ingress and regress to and from any other state, and shall enjoy therein all the privileges of trade and commerce, subject to the same duties, impositions, and restrictions, as the inhabitants thereof, respectively....

If one examines the Constitutional provision in the light of its predecessor in the Articles of Confederation, then it immediately becomes apparent that the purpose of the clause was to protect out-of-state residents from burdensome discriminations in favor of local residents. The framers quite reasonably anticipated an ever-increasing flow of interstate travel and interstate commerce and presumably inserted the Article IV provision to safeguard against the erection of improper barriers to that development. [See Roger Howell, "The Privileges and Immunities of State Citizenship," *Johns Hopkins University Studies in History and Political Science*, Vol. XXXVI, No. 3 (1918).] Under such an interpretation, however, it is clear that this clause would afford no solace to the individual who claims that his rights are abridged by his own state. At the outset, then, there is a serious limitation on the usefulness of the clause to protect one's rights broadly against state deprivation.

There is another question to be answered even where the allegation is made that a state has abridged the rights of an out-of-state resident. The question is, just what kinds of rights are protected by the clause? Not until 1825 was there anything approaching an official interpretation of what rights were covered. The controversy leading to this decision arose in New Jersey and concerned rights to gather oysters.

A New Jersey statute prohibited any person not a resident of New Jersey from gathering oysters in the state. One Corfield sailed his boat into the waters of New Jersey and took oysters. His boat was seized, and he sued in trespass. Was New Jersey's reservation of its oysters inconsistent with Article IV, Section 2, of the Constitution? Justice Bushrod Washington, then on circuit, held the question under advisement from October

term, 1824, until April term, 1825, and then gave his famous pronouncement on the meaning of the clause:

We feel no hesitation in confining these expressions to those privileges and immunities which are, in their nature fundamental; which belong, of right, to the citizens
of all free governments; and which have, at all times, been enjoyed by the citizens
of the several states which compose this Union, from the time of their becoming
free, independent, and sovereign. What these fundamental principles are, it would
perhaps be more tedious than difficult to enumerate. [The Justice then proceeds to
risk tedium by recounting quite a list, including protection by the government;
enjoyment of life and liberty; the right to acquire and possess property; the right
of a citizen of one state to pass through, or reside in, other states for purposes of
trade or profession; protection by the writ of habeas corpus; the right to institute
and maintain court actions; exemption from higher taxes than are paid by other
citizens of the state; and the elective franchise, as regulated by the laws of the
particular state in which it is exercised.] These, and many others which might be
mentioned, are, strictly speaking, privileges and immunities. [*Corfield* v. *Coryell*,
6 Fed. Cas. No. 3230, 546, 552 (1823)]

Considering the broad strokes with which Justice Washington outlined
the "privileges and immunities" so protected, one might have expected him
to have held oyster-taking in the protected category. He did not, however,
and made a distinction between the private and personal rights covered and
the common property of the people of a particular state, such as fish. He
further held that the state was under no obligation to share property of
this sort with citizens of other states. The precise holding of the case, with
respect to fisheries, has been followed and even expanded to include game.
But as to the list of general rights mentioned in the opinion, subsequent
construction has in many ways permitted the state to differentiate between
its citizens and nonresidents, or even new residents. Broadly speaking, these
rights are subject to restrictions imposed under the police power of the
state, and the Court has permitted reasonable discriminations by the state
in protecting the health, safety, and welfare of its own citizens. The state
may restrict the right to enter certain professions, such as law, or the right
to sell insurance, to persons who have resided within the state for a prescribed period of time. It may charge nonresidents a higher tuition for its
schools or a higher fee for hunting and fishing. But it may not deny nonresidents access to its courts. [For an analysis of the clause and some of the
major cases concerning it, see E. S. Corwin, ed., *The Constitution of the
United States of America* (U.S. Government Printing Ofc., 1953), pp.
686–693.]

From both standpoints, then—the persons to whom the clause applies
and the rights protected—the conclusion must be that this is a thin reed
on which to rely for remedies against the state. To continue the search,
what remained in the United States Constitution of the pre-Civil War
period which would serve as a safeguard against abridgment of rights by
the state? The answer is clear—nothing at all. The citizen of that period

had to look to his own state laws and state constitution for redress of grievances against the officials of that government.

It should be apparent from this examination that not only did the pre-Civil War Constitution fail to restrain states in their general limitations on personal rights, but it also left the way open for the states to establish substantive and procedural standards in their respective bills of rights which were different from the protections afforded in the Bill of Rights to the United States Constitution. The net result was that the citizen had two separate packets of rights with two separate remedies for abuse, depending on which governmenal entity committed the fault. The fact that many of the guarantees in the state and national constitutions were duplicated should not lead one to the conclusion that his rights against the two governments were identical. As pointed out earlier, even today the state can abolish indictment by grand jury, while the Fifth Amendment makes it mandatory in federal felony cases. This situation, then, is the first complication introduced into the area of civil rights by our federal system of government.

A second complication, and the reason for the chronological references above, was introduced by the addition of the Fourteenth Amendment to the Constitution. The relevant portions of that amendment are found in Section 1:

All persons born or naturalized in the United States, and subject to the jurisdiction thereof, are citizens of the United States and of the State wherein they reside. No State shall make or enforce any law which shall abridge the privileges or immunities of citizens of the United States; nor shall any State deprive any person of life, liberty, or property, without due process of law; nor deny to any person within its jurisdiction the equal protection of the laws.

With the addition of this amendment in 1868 we have the first major *national* restraint upon the governments of the states in the field of civil rights. It is important to note, however, that even this protection does not reach the sort of deprivation caused by private persons. The Fourteenth Amendment is clearly a bar to certain interference occasioned by states, but does not reach the great area of injury inflicted by private action. The problem of defining "state action" will be considered in more detail below.

The immediate question presented by the addition of the Fourteenth Amendment was what kinds of rights and immunities were covered and to what extent they were covered. To be more specific, did this new amendment incorporate the long list of guarantees in the Bill of Rights and require exactly these same standards to be met by all the states? If so, then the troublesome problem of two separate packets of rights would no longer plague us. If not, then at least two alternative interpretations could be made, one of which would make the amendment merely a general statement of principle, and the other build up yet a *third* category of rights and still further complicate the problem. Let us take up the various stages of development to follow the actual line of interpretation.

Over a period of years, class after class of beginning students has been asked to select the phrase from the Fourteenth Amendment which would appear to offer the most substantial protection against encroachment by the state government upon their rights. Almost without fail, the clause selected is, "No State shall make or enforce any law which shall abridge the privileges or immunities of citizens of the United States." And it would seem to be a reasonable choice. The words have the ring of freedom about them. Unfortunately, judicial interpretation has shown this answer to be altogether wrong. The leading decision on what the "privileges and immunities" clause means was rendered in 1873 in the *Slaughter-House Cases*. Professor Charles Fairman has certainly not overstated the point when he says that a full comprehension of this case yields the key to perhaps a good third of the entire constitutional law of the United States.

Despite the fact that the Fourteenth Amendment was primarily enacted to protect the newly freed Negro, it was a group of Southern whites who first invoked the amendment against the carpetbag laws of their own state. In 1869 the Republican legislature of Louisiana passed an act "to protect the health of the city of New Orleans," which incorporated a slaughterhouse company and gave it a twenty-five year monopoly on the slaughtering business in that city. The law required that all other butchers in New Orleans come to that company and pay for the use of its abattoir. The case went up through the state courts with the Republican courts, of course, sustaining the statute. It was argued before the United States Supreme Court that the statute violated four parts of the United States Constitution: the Thirteenth Amendment, and the "privileges and immunities" clause, the "due process" clause, and the "equal protection" clause of the Fourteenth Amendment. Since the main thrust of the opinion was in response to the "privileges and immunities" argument, the other portions of the opinion will be reserved for later discussion.

SLAUGHTER-HOUSE CASES
16 Wallace 36 (1873)

On Writ of Error to the Supreme Court of the State of Louisiana.

Mr. Justice Miller delivered the opinion of the Court.

The plaintiffs in error . . . allege that the Statute is a violation of the Constitution of the United States in these several particulars:

That it creates an involuntary servitude forbidden by the Thirteenth Article of Amendment;

That it abridges the privileges and immunities of citizens of the United States;

That it denies to the plaintiffs the equal protection of the laws; and,

That it deprives them of their property without due process of law; contrary to the provisions of the first section of the Fourteenth Article of Amendment.

This Court is thus called upon for the first time to give construction to these Articles.

We do not conceal from ourselves the great responsibility which this duty devolves upon us. No questions so far-reaching and pervading in their consequences, so profoundly interesting to the people of this country, and so important in their bearing upon the relations of the United States and of the several states to each other, and to the citizens of the states and of the United States have been before this Court during the official life of any of its present members. . . .

[Here the Justice discusses the background of the citizenship clause of Section 1, and the holding in the Dred Scott case, to the effect that a man of African descent, whether a slave or not, was not and could not be a citizen of a state or of the United States.]

To remove this difficulty primarily, and to establish a clear and comprehensive definition of citizenship which should declare what should constitute citizenship of the United States, and also citizenship of a state, the first clause of the first section was framed.

"All persons born or naturalized in the United States, and subject to the jurisdiction thereof, are citizens of the United States and of the State wherein they reside."

The first observation we have to make on this clause is that it puts at rest both the questions which we stated to have been the subject of differences of opinion. It declares that persons may be citizens of the United States without regard to their citizenship of a particular state, and it overturns the Dred Scott decision by making all persons born within the United States and subject to its jurisdiction citizens of the United States. That its main purpose was to establish the citizenship of the Negro can admit of no doubt. The phrase "subject to its jurisdiction" was intended to exclude from its operation children of ministers, consuls, and citizens or subjects of foreign states born within the United States.

The next observation is more important in view of the arguments of counsel in the present case. It is, that the distinction between citizenship of the United States and citizenship of a state is clearly recognized and established. Not only may a man be a citizen of the United States without being a citizen of a state, but an important element is necessary to convert the former into the latter. He must reside within the state to make him a citizen of it, but it is only necessary that he should be born or naturalized in the United States to be a citizen of the Union.

It is quite clear, then, that there is a citizenship of the United States, and a citizenship of a state, which are distinct from each other, and which depend upon different characteristics or circumstances in the individual.

We think this distinction and its explicit recognition in this Amendment of great weight in this argument, because the next paragraph of this same section, which is the one mainly relied on by the plaintiffs in error, speaks only of privileges and immunities of citizens of the United States, and does not speak of those of citizens of the several states. The argument, however, in favor of the plaintiffs rests wholly on the assumption that the citizenship is the same, and the privileges and immunities guaranteed by the clause are the same.

The language is: "No state shall make or enforce any law which shall abridge the privileges or immunities of citizens of the United States." It is a little remarkable, if this clause was intended as a protection to the citizen of a state against the legislative power of his own state, that the words "citizen of the state" should be left out when it is so carefully used, and used in contradistinction to "citizens of the United States" in the very sentence which precedes it. It is too clear for argument that the change in phraseology was adopted understandingly and with a purpose.

Of the privileges and immunities of the citizens of the United States, and of the privileges and immunities of the citizen of the state, and what they respectively are, we will presently consider; but we wish to state here that it is only the former which are placed by this clause under the protection of the Federal Constitution, and that the latter, whatever they may be, are not intended to have any additional protection by this paragraph of the Amendment.

If, then, there is a difference between the privileges and immunities belonging to a citizen of the United States as such, and those belonging to the citizen of the state as such, the latter must rest for their security and protection where they have heretofore rested; for they are not embraced by this paragraph of the Amendment.

The first occurrence of the words "privileges and immunities" in our constitutional history is to be found in the fourth of the Articles of the old Confederation.

[Here the Justice traces the development of the Article IV, Section 2, privileges and immunities clause in the Constitution, and cites Justice Washington's opinion in *Corfield* v. *Coryell*, discussed earlier in this chapter.]

In the case of *Paul* v. *Virginia*, the court, in expounding this clause of the Constitution, says that "the privileges and immunities secured to citizens of each state in the several states, by the provision in question, are those privileges and immunities which are common to the citizens in the latter states under their Constitution and laws by virtue of their being citizens."

The constitutional provision there alluded to did not create those rights, which it called privileges and immunities of citizens of the states. It threw around them in that clause no security for the citizen of the state in which they were claimed or exercised. Nor did it profess to control the power of the state governments over the rights of its own citizens.

Its sole purpose was to declare to the several states, that whatever those rights, as you grant or establish them to your own citizens, or as you limit or qualify, or impose restrictions on their exercise, the same, neither more nor less, shall be the measure of the rights of citizens of other states within your jurisdiction.

It would be the vainest show of learning to attempt to prove by citations of authority, that up to the adoption of the recent Amendments, no claim or pretense was set up that those rights depended on the Federal government for their existence or protection, beyond the very few express limitations which the Federal Constitution imposed upon the states—such, for instance, as the prohibition against ex post facto laws, bills of attainder, and laws impairing the obligation of contracts. But with the exception of these and a few other restrictions, the entire domain of the privileges and immunities of citizens of the states, as above defined, lay within the constitutional and legislative power of the states, and without that of the Federal government. Was it the purpose of the Fourteenth Amendment, by the simple declaration that no state should make or enforce any law which shall abridge the privileges and immunities of citizens of the United States, to transfer the security and protection of all the civil rights which we have mentioned, from the states to the Federal government? And where it is declared that Congress shall have the power to enforce that article, was it intended to bring within the power of Congress the entire domain of civil rights heretofore belonging exclusively to the states?

All this and more must follow, if the proposition of the plaintiffs in error be sound. For not only are these rights subject to the control of Congress whenever in its discretion any of them are supposed to be abridged by state legislation, but that body may also pass laws in advance, limiting and restricting the exercise of legislative power by the states, in their most ordinary and usual functions, as in its judgment it may think proper on all such subjects. And still further, such a construction followed by the reversal of the judgments of the supreme court of Louisiana in these cases would constitute this court a perpetual censor upon all legislation of the states, on the civil rights of their own citizens, with authority to nullify such as it did not approve as consistent with those rights, as they existed at the time of the adoption of this Amendment. The argument, we admit, is not always the most conclusive which is drawn from the consequences urged against the adoption of a particular construction of an instrument. But when, as in the case before us, these consequences are so serious, so far-reaching and pervading, so great a departure from the structure and spirit of our institutions; when the effect is to fetter and degrade the state governments by subjecting them to the control of Congress, in the exercise of powers heretofore universally conceded to them of the most ordinary and fundamental character; when in fact it radically changes the whole theory of the relations of the state and Federal governments to each other and of both these governments to the people; the argument has a force that is irresistible, in the absence of language which expresses such a purpose too clearly to admit of doubt.

We are convinced that no such results were intended by the Congress which proposed these amendments, nor by the legislatures of the states, which ratified them.

Having shown that the privileges and immunities relied on in the argument are those which belong to citizens of the states as such, and that they are left to the state governments for security and protection, and not by this article placed under the special care of the Federal government, we may hold ourselves excused from defining the privileges and immunities of citizens of the United States which no state can abridge, until some case involving those privileges may make it necessary to do so.

But lest it should be said that no such privileges and immunities are to be found if those we have been considering are excluded, we venture to suggest some which owe their existence to the Federal government, its national character, its Constitution, or its laws.

One of these is well described in the case of *Crandall* v. *Nevada*. It is said to be the right of the citizen of this great country, protected by implied guaranties of its Constitution, "to come to the seat of government to assert any claim he may have upon that government, to transact any business he may have with it, to seek its protection, to share its offices, to engage in administering its functions. He has the right of free access to its seaports, through which all operations of foreign commerce are conducted, to the sub-treasuries, land-offices, and courts of justice in the several states." And quoting from the language of Chief Justice Taney in another case, it is said "that, for all the great purposes for which the Federal government was established, we are one people with one common country; we are all citizens of the United States"; and it is as such citizens that their rights are supported in this court in *Crandall* v. *Nevada*.

Another privilege of a citizen of the United States is to demand the care and protection of the Federal government over his life, liberty, and property when on the high seas or within the jurisdiction of a foreign government. Of this there can be no doubt, nor that the right depends upon his character as a citizen of the United States. The right to peaceably assemble and petition for redress of grievances, the privilege of the writ of habeas corpus, are rights of the citizen guarantied by the Federal Constitution. The right to use the navigable waters of the United States, however they may penetrate the territory of the several states, and all rights secured to our citizens by treaties with foreign nations, are dependent upon citizenship of the United States, and not citizenship of a state. One of these privileges is conferred by the very article under consideration. It is that a citizen of the United States can, of his own volition, become a citizen of any state of the Union by a bona fide residence therein, with the same rights as other citizens of that state. To these may be added the rights secured by the thirteenth and fifteenth articles of amendment, and by the other clause of the fourteenth, next to be considered.

But it is useless to pursue this branch of the inquiry, since we are of opinion that the rights claimed by these plaintiffs in error, if they have any existence, are not privileges and immunities of citizens of the United States within the meaning of the clause of the fourteenth amendment under consideration....

Judgment affirmed.

[Justice Field, with Chief Justice Chase and Justices Swayne and Bradley concurring, rendered a dissenting opinion. He stated, in part:]

The amendment does not attempt to confer any new privileges or immunities upon citizens, or to enumerate or define those already existing. It assumes that there are such privileges and immunities which belong of right to citizens as such, and ordains that they shall not be abridged by State legislation. If this inhibition has no reference to privileges and immunities of this character, but only refers, as held by the majority of the court in their opinion, to such privileges and immunities as were before its adoption specially designated in the Constitution or necessarily implied as belonging to citizens of the United States, it was a vain and idle enactment, which accomplished nothing, and most unnecessarily excited Congress and the people on its passage. With privileges and immunities thus designated or implied no State could ever have interfered by its laws, and no new constitutional provision was required to inhibit such interference. The supremacy of the Constitution and the laws of the United States always controlled any State legislation of that character.

Almost without exception, the interpretation given the "privileges and immunities" clause by the Court in the *Slaughter-House Cases* has remained the official view. The result has been that this clause affords no protection to the individual who claims that state officials have deprived him of rights which most of us consider the basic rights: freedom of speech, religious freedom, the right to engage in lawful occupations, freedom from improper police violence, and others of this nature. The initial reaction of many people to a reading of the opinion for the Court is frank surprise. One will frequently hear the remark that such a bad law *must* be unconstitutional, and the Court was derelict in its duty in refusing to hold it so. On the other hand, if Justice Miller's reasoning is carefully examined, it becomes clearer that the overall policy which he set out was beneficial in two important respects.

First, it recognized the existence of the two spheres of authority which the Constitution established in providing for the federal system of government. If we are to have a federal form, the agencies of the national government cannot be permitted to exercise a general supervisory power over every facet of state activity. This would make the states mere administrative subdivisions of the national government. A good case can be made for the unitary form of government, of course, but we have made no constitutional provision for such an arrangement. States are expected to operate more or less autonomously in many areas of policy-making, and it is improper for the arms of the national government to reach down to the purely local level to interfere with this discretionary power. State experiments in unemployment compensation or the use of the merit system of public employment which were dubbed "crackpot" in one period were in a later period adopted by all other states and the national government as well. And policies which are quite congenial to the residents of one state may find stubborn resistance in another. Thus Justice Miller's opinion shows a conscious refusal to stay the power of the state to experiment or to differ with its neighbors in the Union. It can quite properly be characterized as a strong "states-rights" decision.

A second beneficial aspect of the decision lies in the fact that the Court recognized the importance of judicial restraint in matters where the local citizenry should assume responsibility. The federal judges, with life tenure, are largely outside the control of the citizenry. The bench of even the states is not responsive to popular pressures to the degree which the legislative and executive branches are. Thus errors committed by the judges may take longer to correct than would be the case with the other branches. The judge, then, must be constantly mindful of the ballot box as a remedy at least as important and perhaps more appropriate than judicial review for correcting the policy mistakes of governors and legislators.

An important consequence of the decision—whether beneficial or not depends upon the point of view—was its impact upon the possible enforcement legislation which Section 5 of the Fourteenth Amendment empowers Congress to enact. The fact of the matter seems to be that by the narrow coverage allowed to the "privileges and immunities" clause, the Court cut the heart out of one of the most potentially powerful weapons which Congress might have used to legislate in the civil rights area. The only remaining clauses of the amendment of importance for this purpose are the "due process" and the "equal protection" clauses. Looking at these three clauses from the legislator's viewpoint, which would afford the simplest framework for enforcement legislation? It would appear that the "privileges and immunities" clause is tailor-made for such a purpose. All one need do would be to set out a comprehensive list of the vast number of rights which the average person considers to flow from possession of United States citizenship, and then make it a crime for any agent of the state to abridge such rights. The restrictive decision in *Slaughter-House*, however, effectively blocked such an approach. The remaining two clauses are far more elusive as reference points for enforcement legislation. How does one frame a statute to protect a person from state deprivation of his liberty "without due process of law"? Except, perhaps, in the area of racial discrimination, how can a bill-drafter come to grips with the requirement of "equal protection of the laws," which allows so much flexibility in classifying the objects of legislation? Even leaving aside the important political barriers to passing civil rights laws, the technical difficulties in phrasing bills to accomplish the purposes without being unconstitutionally vague are formidable.

The decision in the *Slaughter-House Cases* is thus in the same vein as *Barron* v. *Baltimore*. Federal rights and state rights are two different things, and one must take care to make the proper distinction so that the correct remedy can be selected when abridgment is alleged. To this day, the rule of the *Slaughter-House Cases* with respect to the "privileges and immunities" clause is still good law. The only aberration was in 1935, when the Court held in *Colgate* v. *Harvey*, 296 U.S. 404 (1935), that the right of a citizen of the United States to do business in, or place a loan in, a state other than that of his residence was a privilege of national citizenship. Only five years later, however, the Court expressly overruled that decision in *Madden* v. *Kentucky*, 309 U.S. 83 (1940), and returned to the old interpretation. *Madden* held that for a state to impose on its citizens a higher tax on out-of-state bank deposits than on those deposited within the state was not a violation of the privileges or immunities of national citizenship, since "the right to carry out an incident to a trade, business or calling such as the deposit of money in banks is not a privilege of national citizenship." And in *Snowden* v. *Hughes*, 321 U.S. 1 (1944), the Court held that the right to become a candidate for, and to be elected to, a state office was not among the privileges of United States citizenship but was an attribute of state citizenship. The complainant, then, had to look to his own state constitution and laws for redress of his injury, at least so far as this clause of the Constitution was concerned.

But what of the other two clauses in the Fourteenth Amendment—the "due process" and "equal protection" clauses? Are these no more useful as guarantees against state interference than the "privileges and immunities" clause proved to be? Again, the starting point is the *Slaughter-House* opinion of Justice Miller, but the subsequent developments have been vastly different. The appellants in the case argued most vigorously on the "privileges and immunities" ground, but the latter two clauses were tossed in for good measure. As to these claims, Justice Miller stated:

The argument has not been much pressed in these cases that the defendant's charter deprives the plaintiffs of their property without due process of law, or that it denies to them the equal protection of the law. The first of these paragraphs has been in the Constitution since the adoption of the Fifth Amendment, as a restraint upon the federal power. It is also to be found in some form of expression in the constitutions of nearly all the states, as a restraint upon the power of the states. This law, then, has practically been the same as it now is during the existence of the government, except so far as the present Amendment may place the restraining power over the states in this matter in the hands of the federal government.

We are not without judicial interpretation, therefore, both state and national, of the meaning of this clause. And it is sufficient to say that under no construction of that provision that we have ever seen, or any that we deem admissible, can the restraint imposed by the state of Louisiana upon the exercise of their trade by the butchers of New Orleans be held to be a deprivation of property within the meaning of that provision.

"Nor shall any State deny to any person within its jurisdiction the equal protection of the laws."

In the light of the history of these Amendments, and the pervading purpose of them, which we have already discussed, it is not difficult to give a meaning to this clause. The existence of laws in the states where the newly emancipated Negroes resided, which discriminated with gross injustice and hardship against them as a class, was the evil to be remedied by this clause, and by it such laws are forbidden.

If, however, the states did not conform their laws to its requirements, then by the fifth section of the Article of Amendment Congress was authorized to enforce it by suitable legislation. We doubt very much whether any action of a state not directed by way of discrimination against the Negroes as a class, or on account of their race, will ever be held to come within the purview of this provision. It is so clearly a provision for that race and that emergency, that a strong case would be necessary for its application to any other. But as it is a state that is to be dealt with, and not alone the validity of its laws, we may safely leave that matter until Congress shall have exercised its power, or some case of state oppression, by denial of equal justice in its courts, shall have claimed a decision at our hands. We find no such case in the one before us, and do not deem it necessary to go over the argument again, as it may have relation to this particular clause of the Amendment. . . .

In almost perfunctory fashion, then, Justice Miller denied the contention that the "due process" clause barred the state from enforcing the butcher monopoly law. Except for his statements concerning the recognition of the federal form of government, it is not really clear just why such a law would not constitute a taking of property without due process of law. To fill the gap here, however, one may look to another opinion for the Court filed by Justice Miller a few years later. The case was *Davidson* v. *New Orleans*, 96 U.S. 97 (1878), and dealt with the question of whether a special assessment on certain real estate, for the purpose of draining swamp lands, which allegedly would not benefit the assessed landowner, constituted a taking of property without due process of law. The Louisiana Supreme Court had held against the owner, and the United States Supreme Court reviewed the decision under the question stated. Justice Miller, speaking for the Court, gave a very narrow construction to the clause. In essence, his argument is summarized in the following statements:

It is not possible to hold that a party has, without due process of law, been deprived of his property, when, as regards the issues affecting it, he has, by the laws of the State, a fair trial in a court of justice, according to the modes of proceeding applicable to such a case. . . .

This proposition covers the present case. Before the assessment could be collected, or become effectual, the statute required that the tableau of assessments should be filed in the proper District Court of the State; that personal service of notice, with reasonable time to object, should be served on all owners who were known and within reach of process, and due advertisement made as to those who were unknown, or could not be found. This was complied with; and the party complaining here appeared, and had a full and fair hearing in the court of the first instance, and afterwards in the Supreme Court. If this be not due process of law, then the words can have no definite meaning as used in the Constitution.

[*Judgment affirmed.*]

It is clear from this excerpt of Justice Miller's opinion that to him all that the term "due" process required of the state was "legal" process. If all the forms required by state constitution or statute were met, and if the injured party had his "day in court," then he could not successfully contend that the substance of the law should concern the federal courts under a claim of Fourteenth Amendment violation.

Unlike the "privileges and immunities" clause, however, the "due process" clause underwent a radical change from the interpretation which Justice Miller gave it. The concurring opinion of Justice Bradley in *Davidson* v. *New Orleans* foretold the direction in which later interpretations of the clause would move:

In the conclusion and general tenor of the opinion just read, I concur. But I think it narrows the scope of inquiry as to what is due process of law more than it should do.

It seems to me that private property may be taken by a State without due process of law in other ways than by mere direct enactment, or the want of a judicial proceeding. . . . I think, therefore, we are entitled, under the fourteenth amendment, not only to see that there is some process of law, but "due process of law," provided by the State law when a citizen is deprived of his property; and that, in judging what is "due process of law," respect must be had to the cause and object of the taking, whether under the taxing power, the power of eminent domain, or the power of assessment for local improvements, or none of these; and if found to be suitable or admissible in this special case, it will be adjudged to be "due process of law"; but if found to be arbitrary, oppressive, and unjust, it may be declared to be not "due process of law." Such an examination may be made without interfering with that large discretion which every legislative power has of making wide modifications in the forms of procedure in each case, according as the laws, habits, customs, and preferences of the people of the particular State may require.

The two cases just discussed indicate the strong reluctance of the majority on the United States Supreme Court in the 1870's to allow the Fourteenth Amendment to become a vehicle for wholesale judicial review by that Court of the laws and policies adopted by the states. However, the opinion of

Justice Bradley, just quoted, contained the seeds of development of the "due process" clause into quite a different and stronger weapon of supervision. Beginning in the economic area, with close scrutiny of state laws interfering with the owner's use of property, the Court gradually toward the end of the nineteenth century assumed the power to determine whether such laws were so "arbitrary, oppressive, and unjust" as to amount to a deprivation of property without due process of law. For the purposes of examining non-economic civil rights, such as those generally specified in the national Bill of Rights, the Court was somewhat slower to draw on the "due process" clause as a basis for staying the power of the state. More and more frequently during the latter years of the nineteenth century the Court was criticized for placing the property protection of the Fourteenth Amendment ahead of protection to life and liberty. By the early part of the twentieth century at least some measure of success had been achieved by those who viewed the Fourteenth Amendment as a requirement of some kind of minimal standard in the area of criminal procedure. Efforts were made in arguing some of the cases to prove that in this area the Fourteenth Amendment really represented a shorthand adoption of the procedural guarantees listed in the Bill of Rights, and no state could provide less than this minimum group of safeguards.

One of the most important cases involving this approach was *Twining* v. *New Jersey,* decided in 1908. Counsel for Twining in effect tried to convince the Court that either the "privileges and immunities" clause or the "due process" clause, or both of them, included the whole list of rights which the Bill of Rights protects from national abridgment. The Court's analysis of the issues readily breaks into two parts to answer the contentions made under these two clauses of the Fourteenth Amendment.

Twining and Cornell, directors of a bank in New Jersey, were indicted for having knowingly exhibited a false paper to a state bank examiner with intent to deceive him as to the condition of the bank. At the trial the defendants called no witnesses and did not testify in their own behalf. In his charge to the jury the judge said: "Because a man does not go upon the stand you are not necessarily justified in drawing an inference of guilt. But you have a right to consider the fact that he does not go upon the stand where a direct accusation is made against him."

The defendants were convicted and sentenced to imprisonment for six and four years respectively. This was affirmed by the Court of Errors and Appeals, and the case was then carried to the United States Supreme Court on the claim that the charge to the jury constituted a form of self-incrimination which abridged their privileges and immunities as United States citizens and led to a deprivation of liberty without due process of law. The attempt was to show that the Fifth Amendment's protection against self-incrimination had been included in the Fourteenth Amendment as a protection against the states.

TWINING *v.* NEW JERSEY

211 U.S. 78 (1908)

Justice Moody delivered the opinion of the Court.

[On the "privileges and immunities" issue:]

The defendants contend, in the first place, that the exemption from self-incrimination is one of the privileges and immunities of citizens of the United States which the Fourteenth Amendment forbids the States to abridge. It is not argued that the defendants are protected by that part of the Fifth Amendment which provides that "no person ... shall be compelled in any criminal case to be a witness against himself," for it is recognized by counsel that by a long line of decisions the first ten Amendments are not operative on the States. *Barron* v. *Baltimore,* 7 Pet. 243; ... But it is argued that this privilege is one of the fundamental rights of National citizenship, placed under National protection by the Fourteenth Amendment, and it is specifically argued that the "privileges and immunities of citizens of the United States," protected against State action by that Amendment, include those fundamental personal rights which were protected against National action by the first eight Amendments; that this was the intention of the framers of the Fourteenth Amendment, and that this part of it would otherwise have little or no meaning and effect. These arguments are not new to this court and the answer to them is found in its decisions. The meaning of the phrase "privileges and immunities of citizens of the United States," as used in the Fourteenth Amendment, came under early consideration in the *Slaughter-House Cases,* 16 Wall. 36. . . .

. . . If, then, it be assumed, without deciding the point, that an exemption from compulsory self-incrimination is what is described as a fundamental right belonging to all who live under a free government, and incapable of impairment by legislation or judicial decision, it is, so far as the states are concerned a fundamental right inherent in state citizenship, and is a privilege or immunity of that citizenship only. Privileges and immunities of citizens of the United States, on the other hand, are only such as arise out of the nature and essential character of the national government, or are specifically granted or secured to all citizens or persons by the Constitution of the United States. *Slaughter-House Cases* . . .

Thus, among the rights and privileges of national citizenship recognized by this court are the right to pass freely from state to state (*Crandall* v. *Nevada,* 6 Wall. 35); the right to petition Congress for a redress of grievances (*U.S.* v. *Cruikshank*); the right to vote for national officers (Ex parte *Yarbrough,* 110 U.S. 651); the right to enter the public lands (*U.S.* v. *Waddell,* 112 U.S. 76); the right to be protected against violence while in the lawful custody of a United States marshal (*Logan* v. *U.S.,* 144 U.S. 263); and the right to inform the United States authorities of violation of its laws (*Re Quarles,* 158 U.S. 532) .... But assuming it to be true that the exemption from self-incrimination is not, as a fundamental right of national citizenship, included in the privileges and immunities of citizens of the United States, counsel insist that, as a right specifically granted or secured by the Federal Constitution, it is included in them. This view is based upon the contention which must now be examined, that the safeguards of personal rights which are enumerated in the first eight articles of amendment to the Federal Constitution, sometimes called the Federal Bill of Rights, though they were by those Amendments originally secured only against national action, are among the privileges and immunities of citizens of the United States, which this clause of the Fourteenth

Amendment protects against state action. This view has been, at different times, expressed by justices of this court ... and was undoubtedly that entertained by some of those who framed the Amendment. It is, however, not profitable to examine the weighty arguments in its favor, for the question is no longer open in this court. The right of trial by jury in civil cases, guaranteed by the Seventh Amendment (*Walker* v. *Sauvinet,* 92 U.S. 90), and the right to bear arms, guaranteed by the Second Amendment (*Presser* v. *Illinois,* 116 U.S. 252), have been distinctly held not to be privileges and immunities of citizens of the United States, guaranteed by the Fourteenth Amendment against abridgment by the states, and in effect the same decision was made in respect of the guaranty against prosecution, except by indictment of a grand jury, contained in the Fifth Amendment (*Hurtado* v. *California,* 110 U.S. 516), and in respect of the right to be confronted with witnesses, contained in the Sixth Amendment (*West* v. *Louisiana,* 194 U.S. 258). In *Maxwell* v. *Dow* (176 U.S. 606), where the plaintiff in error had been convicted in a state court of a felony upon an information, and by a jury of eight persons, it was held that the indictment made indispensable by the Fifth Amendment, and the trial by jury, guaranteed by the Sixth Amendment, were not privileges and immunities of citizens of the United States, as those words were used in the Fourteenth Amendment. The discussion in that case ought not to be repeated. All the arguments for the other view were considered and answered, the authorities were examined and analyzed, and the decision rested upon the ground that this clause of the Fourteenth Amendment did not forbid the states to abridge the personal rights enumerated in the first eight Amendments, because those rights were not within the meaning of the clause "privileges and immunities of citizens of the United States.". . . We conclude, therefore, that the exemption from compulsory self-incrimination is not a privilege or immunity of national citizenship guaranteed by this clause of the Fourteenth Amendment against abridgment by the states.

[On the "due process" issue:]

The defendants, however, do not stop here. They appeal to another clause of the Fourteenth Amendment, and insist that the self-incrimination which they allege the instruction to the jury compelled was a denial of due process of law. This contention requires separate consideration, for it is possible that some of the personal rights safeguarded by the first eight Americans against national action may also be safeguarded against state action, because a denial of them would be a denial of due process of law. . . . If this is so, it is not because those rights are enumerated in the first eight Amendments, but because they are of such a nature that they are included in the conception of due process of law. Few phrases of the law are so elusive of exact apprehension as this. Doubtless the difficulties of ascertaining its connotation have been increased in American jurisprudence, where it has been embodied in constitutions and put to new uses as a limit on legislative power. This court has always declined to give a comprehensive definition of it, and has preferred that its full meaning should be gradually ascertained by the process of inclusion and exclusion in the course of the decisions of cases as they arise. There are certain general principles, well settled, however, which narrow the field of discussion, and may serve as helps to correct conclusions. These principles grow out of the proposition universally accepted by American courts on the authority of Coke, that the words "due process of law" are equivalent in meaning to the words "law of the land," contained in that chapter of Magna Charta which provides that "no freeman shall be taken, or imprisoned, or disseised, or outlawed, or exiled, or any wise destroyed; nor shall we go upon him, nor send upon him, but by the lawful judgment of his peers or by the law of the land." . . . From the consideration of the meaning of the words in the light of their historical origin this court has drawn the following conclusions:

First. What is due process of law may be ascertained by an examination of those settled usages and modes of proceedings existing in the common and statute law of England before the emigration of our ancestors, and shown not to have been unsuited to their civil and political condition by having been acted on by them after the settlement of this country. . . . "A process of law," said Mr. Justice Matthews, . . . "which is not otherwise forbidden, must be taken to be due process of law, if it can show the sanction of settled usage both in England and in this country." *Hurtado* v. *California*, 110 U.S. 516, 528.

Second. It does not follow, however, that a procedure settled in English law at the time of the emigration, and brought to this country and practised by our ancestors, is an essential element of due process of law. If that were so, the procedure of the first half of the seventeenth century would be fastened upon the American jurisprudence like a straight-jacket, only to be unloosed by constitutional amendment. That, said Mr. Justice Matthews, in the same case, p. 529, "would be to deny every quality of the law but its age, and to render it incapable of progress or improvement.". . .

Third. But, consistently with the requirements of due process, no change in ancient procedure can be made which disregards those fundamental principles, to be ascertained from time to time by judicial action, which have relation to process of law, and protect the citizen in his private right, and guard him against the arbitrary action of government. This idea has been many times expressed in differing words by this court, and it seems well to cite some expressions of it. . . . "This court has never attempted to define with precision the words 'due process of law.' . . . It is sufficient to say that there are certain immutable principles of justice which inhere in the very idea of free government which no member of the Union may disregard." *Holden* v. *Hardy*, 169 U.S. 366, 389. . . . "The limit of the full control which the state has in the proceedings of its courts, both in civil and criminal cases, is subject only to the qualification that such procedure must not work a denial of fundamental rights or conflict with specific and applicable provisions of the Federal Constitution." *West* v. *Louisiana*, 194 U.S. 258, 263.

The question under consideration may first be tested by the application of these settled doctrines of this court. If the statement of Mr. Justice Curtis, as elucidated in *Hurtado* v. *California*, is to be taken literally, that alone might almost be decisive. For nothing is more certain, in point of historical fact, than that the practice of compulsory self-incrimination in the courts and elsewhere existed for four hundred years after the granting of Magna Charta, continued throughout the reign of Charles I (though then beginning to be seriously questioned), gained at least some foothold among the early colonists of this country, and was not entirely omitted at trials in England until the eighteenth century. . . .

. . . We think it is manifest, from this review of the origin, growth, extent and limits of the exemption from compulsory self-incrimination in the English law, that it is not regarded as a part of the law of the land of Magna Charta or the due process of law, which has been deemed an equivalent expression, but, on the contrary, is regarded as separate from and independent of due process. It came into existence not as an essential part of due process, but as wise and beneficent rule of evidence developed in the course of judicial decision. This is a potent argument when it is remembered that the phrase was borrowed from English law and that to that law we must look at least for its primary meaning.

But ... we prefer to rest our decision on broader grounds, and inquire whether the exemption from self-incrimination is of such a nature that it must be included in the conception of due process. Is it a fundamental principle of liberty and justice which inheres in the very idea of free government and is the inalienable right of a citizen of such a government? ... One aid to the solution of the question is to inquire how the right was rated during the time when the meaning of due process was in a formative state, and before it was incorporated in American constitutional law. Did those who then were formulating and insisting upon the rights of the people entertain the view that the right was so fundamental that there could be no due process without it?

[The Court here reviews the historical background of state law on the subject and especially the attitude of the states at the time of the adoption of the Constitution and the Bill of Rights.] This survey does not tend to show that it was then in this country the universal or even general belief that the privilege ranked among the fundamental and inalienable rights of mankind; and what is more important here, it affirmatively shows that the privilege was not conceived to be inherent in due process of law, but, on the other hand, a right separate, independent, and outside of due process. Congress, in submitting the Amendments to the several states, treated the two rights as exclusive of each other. Such also has been the view of the states in framing their own Constitutions. ... The inference is irresistible that it has been the opinion of constitution makers that the privilege, if fundamental in any sense, is not fundamental in due process of law, nor an essential part of it. ...

... The essential elements of due process of law ... are singularly few, though of wide application and deep significance. ... Due process requires that the court which assumes to determine the rights of parties shall have jurisdiction ... and that there shall be notice and opportunity for hearing given the parties. ... Subject to these two fundamental conditions, which seem to be universally prescribed in all systems of law established by civilized countries, this court has, up to this time, sustained all state laws, statutory or judicially declared, regulating procedure, evidence, and methods of trial, and held them to be consistent with due process of law.

Even if the historical meaning of due process of law and the decisions of this court did not exclude the privilege from it, it would be going far to rate it as an immutable principle of justice which is the inalienable possession of every citizen of a free government. Salutary as the principle may seem to the great majority, it cannot be ranked with the right to hearing before condemnation, the immunity from arbitrary power not acting by general laws, and the inviolability of private property. The wisdom of the exemption has never been universally assented to since the days of Bentham; many doubt it today, and it is best defended not as an unchangeable principle of universal justice but as a law proved by experience to be expedient. ...

Judgment affirmed.

Once again the Court refused to reconsider its narrow construction of the "privileges and immunities" clause laid down in *Slaughter-House Cases.* Further, the opinion clearly states that the Court did not construe the "due process" clause as a total incorporation of all the Bill of Rights guarantees to be applied against the states. But the door was opened to some extent in the area of criminal procedure, and subsequent developments have widened the opening still further.

Justice Moody cautioned that the phrase "due process of law" was "elusive of exact apprehension." But he tried to give a few general guidelines. He pointed out that if a practice is of ancient origin and usage, and if it is not prohibited by law, then it is to be accepted as due process of law. He was unwilling to adopt as a corollary, however, the conclusion that *only* ancient practices could meet the test. Such a view would operate like a straitjacket to stop progress or improvement. Then what is the proper test to apply to newer criminal procedures? Justice Moody quoted two earlier opinions, and then gave his own summary statement: quoting from *Holden* v. *Hardy*, "There are certain immutable principles of justice which inhere in the very idea of free government which no member of the Union may disregard;" and, quoting from *West* v. *Louisiana*, "Such procedure must not work a denial of fundamental rights or conflict with specific and applicable provisions of the Federal Constitution." His own statement was, "Due process requires that the court which assumes to determine the rights of parties shall have jurisdiction . . . and that there shall be notice and opportunity for hearing given the parties."

Justice Cardozo expressed a similar view of the limited scope of the "due process" clause in *Palko* v. *Connecticut*, 302 U.S. 319 (1937), holding that the clause did not bar appeal by the state based on alleged errors of law in criminal cases and subsequent retrial if the state won the appeal. He stated that the only rights covered by the "due process" clause were those which "have been found to be implicit in the concept of ordered liberty, and thus, through the Fourteenth Amendment, become valid as against the States."

To say that the state can run its own affairs as long as it does not violate "immutable principles of justice" or "fundamental rights" is an invitation to every disappointed litigant to claim that in his case the state violated just such principles or rights. The pressures in this direction gradually increased, and in the period since *Twining* hundreds of cases have been reviewed by the Court in which every conceivable facet of the Bill of Rights guarantees has been described by eloquent counsel as an "immutable principle of justice" or a "fundamental right" or as a necessary feature of the requirement of "notice and opportunity for hearing," and therefore forever embedded in the Fourteenth Amendment concept of "due process of law."

Some of these pleas have been sufficiently convincing to lead a majority of the Court to agree with the contentions, and to this extent the procedural guarantees of the Bill of Rights have been incorporated into the Fourteenth Amendment. Thus the cases incorporating guarantees such as the right to counsel and freedom from self-incrimination are the doctrinal offspring of *Twining* v. *New Jersey*. In *Powell* v. *Alabama*, 287 U.S. 45 (1932), for example, holding that due process requires that counsel be afforded by the state to ignorant, illiterate, indigent defendants accused of a capital crime, Justice Sutherland paraphrased the *Twining* opinion in stating:

> It never has been doubted by this court, or any other so far as we know, that notice and hearing are preliminary steps essential to the passing of an enforceable judgment, and that they, together with a legally competent tribunal having jurisdiction of the case, constitute basic elements of the constitutional requirement of due process of law. . . .
>
> What, then, does a hearing include? Historically and in practice, in our own country at least, it has always included the right to the aid of counsel when desired and provided by the party asserting the right. The right to be heard would be, in many cases, of little avail if it did not comprehend the right to be heard by counsel. . . .
>
> . . . All that it is necessary now to decide, as we do decide, is that in a capital case, where the defendant is unable to employ counsel, and is incapable adequately of making his own defense because of ignorance, feeble-mindedness, illiteracy, or the like, it is the duty of the court, whether requested or not, to assign counsel for him as a necessary requisite of due process of law. . . .

The *substantive* rights guaranteed by the Bill of Rights, such as speech, press, and assembly, have also been incorporated into the Fourteenth Amendment, but the vehicle for the expansion here has been the word "liberty" and not the phrase "due process of law." Thus in *Gitlow* v. *New York*, 268 U.S. 652 (1925), the first incorporation case, although the conviction for the crime of criminal anarchy was affirmed, the majority opinion stated that, "For present purposes we may and do assume that freedom of speech and of the press—which are protected by the First Amendment from abridgment by Congress—are among the fundamental personal rights and 'liberties' protected by the due process clause of the Fourteenth Amendment from impairment by the States." For our purposes here, however, it is immaterial which portion of the full "due process" clause has been the vessel to contain the new right. The important point is the extent to which the Fourteenth Amendment now includes Bill of Rights guarantees against state abridgment.

In *Near* v. *Minnesota*, 283 U.S. 697 (1931), the majority opinion stated, "It is no longer open to doubt that the liberty of the press and of speech is within the liberty safeguarded by the due process clause of the Fourteenth Amendment from invasion by state action." By 1937 the Court was willing to add freedom of assembly to the list. In *De Jonge* v. *Oregon*, 299 U.S. 353 (1937), Chief Justice Hughes, speaking for the Court, stated:

> The right of peaceable assembly is a right cognate to those of free speech and free press and is equally fundamental. . . . [T]he right is one that cannot be denied without violating those fundamental principles of liberty and justice which lie at

the base of all civil and political institutions,—principles which the Fourteenth Amendment embodies in the general terms of its due process clause.

Rounding out the incorporation of First Amendment rights into the Fourteenth, the Court in 1940 included religious freedom in the list. The case was *Cantwell* v. *Connecticut*, 310 U.S. 296 (1940), and Justice Roberts, speaking for a unanimous Court, stated:

We hold that the statute, as construed and applied to the appellants, deprives them of their liberty without due process of law in contravention of the Fourteenth Amendment. The fundamental concept of liberty embodied in that Amendment embraces the liberties guaranteed by the First Amendment. The First Amendment declares that Congress shall make no law respecting an establishment of religion or prohibiting the free exercise thereof. The Fourteenth Amendment has rendered the legislatures of the states as incompetent as Congress to enact such laws.

Although Justice Roberts included the prohibition against establishment of religion in his statement, *Cantwell* technically did not present that issue. The issue was squarely presented, however, in *Everson* v. *Board of Education*, 330 U.S. 1 (1947), and the Court held the establishment clause of the First Amendment to be applicable to the states through the Fourteenth Amendment.

The Fourth Amendment's protection against unreasonable searches and seizures was *partially* incorporated into the Fourteenth Amendment by the holding in *Wolf* v. *Colorado*, 338 U.S. 25 (1949), that the security of one's privacy against arbitrary intrusion by the police is "implicit in 'the concept of ordered liberty' and as such enforceable against the States through the Due Process Clause." Not until the decision in *Mapp* v. *Ohio*, 367 U.S. 643 (1961), however, did the Court presumably *fully* incorporate the Fourth Amendment by its holding that not only was an arbitrary search and seizure conducted by state officers unconstitutional, but it was also a violation of the Fourteenth Amendment for them to use evidence so obtained in a criminal prosecution.

In *Malloy* v. *Hogan*, 378 U.S. 1 (1964), the Court held that the Fifth Amendment's exemption from compulsory self-incrimination is also protected by the Fourteenth Amendment against abridgment by the states. And, lest any doubt remained that it was *full* incorporation which was intended, the Court in *Griffin* v. *California*, 380 U.S. 609 (1965), held that adverse comment by the judge on the failure of the accused to take the stand in his defense would violate the Fifth Amendment if occurring in a federal proceeding and, therefore, violated the Fourteenth Amendment in the case under review. The holding of the *Twining* case, then, is no longer ruling law.

In *Benton* v. *Maryland*, 395 U.S. 784 (1969), the Court specifically overruled *Palko* v. *Connecticut* and held that the double jeopardy clause of the Fifth Amendment is applicable to the states through the Fourteenth Amendment.

The Sixth Amendment's guarantee of a jury trial in criminal cases has long been considered inapplicable to state trials, but this right has now been incorporated as a result of the decision in *Duncan* v. *Louisiana,* 391 U.S. 145 (1968). The right to a "public trial" was employed as a Fourteenth Amendment right in *In re Oliver,* 333 U.S. 257 (1948), to reverse a contempt citation imposed during a secret proceeding. The Sixth Amendment also guarantees the accused the right "to be confronted with the witnesses against him," including the right of cross-examination. In *Pointer* v. *Texas,* 380 U.S. 400 (1965), the majority opinion stated:

We hold that petitioner was entitled to be tried in accordance with the protection of the confrontation guarantee of the Sixth Amendment, and that that guarantee, like the right against compelled self-incrimination, is "to be enforced against the States under the Fourteenth Amendment according to the same standards that protect those personal rights against federal encroachment." *Malloy* v *Hogan.* . . .

A further protection of the Sixth Amendment for the criminal defendant is the right "to have compulsory process for obtaining witnesses in his favor." In *Washington* v. *Texas,* 388 U.S. 14 (1967), the Court incorporated this right into the Fourteenth Amendment. It further held that this right was denied by Texas statutes which provided that persons charged or convicted as coparticipants in the same crime could not testify for one another, although there was no bar to their testifying for the state. The final clause of the Sixth Amendment guarantees to defendants in federal prosecutions the right to have "the assistance of counsel" for their defense. As stated earlier, *Powell* v. *Alabama* partially incorporated this right into the Fourteenth Amendment by applying it to certain kinds of capital cases. Shortly thereafter it was extended to all capital cases, and full incorporation was accomplished in *Gideon* v. *Wainwright,* 372 U.S. 335 (1963).

In *Klopfer* v. *North Carolina,* 386 U.S. 213 (1967), the Court incorporated the "speedy trial" provision of the Sixth Amendment, stating: "We hold here that the right to a speedy trial is as fundamental as any of the rights secured by the Sixth Amendment."

Finally, in *Louisiana ex rel. Francis* v. *Resweber,* 329 U.S. 459 (1947), the majority "assumed" that the Eighth Amendment's prohibition against cruel and unusual punishments was binding on the state through the Fourteenth Amendment. This was accepted as a firm holding in *Robinson* v. *California,* 370 U.S. 660 (1962).

The incorporation process has continued since 1925 until at this juncture all of the guarantees of the First, Fourth, and Sixth Amendments, and portions of the Fifth and Eighth, have been incorporated into the Fourteenth Amendment. While it is not anticipated that the entire Bill of Rights will be so incorporated (indictment by grand jury, for example, has gradually been losing favor), some further additions might be made (the Eighth Amendment prohibitions against excessive bail or excessive fines, for example). There still remain, then, some differences between the standards set up by the Bill of Rights for federal proceedings and those which the Fourteenth Amendment has been construed as imposing upon states. If the state wants to abolish grand jury indictment and try criminals upon an information (a sworn written accusation by the prosecutor), the Fourteenth Amendment does not bar it, although the Fifth Amendment would prohibit such a substitution in a federal prosecution for a "capital or otherwise infamous crime." [*Hurtado* v. *California*, 110 U.S. 516 (1884).] If the state wants to expedite decisions by abolishing jury trials altogether in civil cases, it may do so, even though jury trials in suits at common law in federal courts are guaranteed by the Seventh Amendment. [*Walker* v. *Sauvinet*, 92 U.S. 90 (1876).]

The result of the line of decisions amplifying the "due process" clause of the Fourteenth Amendment is that the student of American civil rights must deal with *three separate* packets of rights: (1) the rights and safeguards which the Bill of Rights to the national Constitution guarantees against abridgment by the national government; (2) the rights which make up the minimal requirements for a scheme of "ordered liberty," and which the state cannot abridge without violating the Fourteenth Amendment; and (3) the rights which the state constitution and laws guarantee against abridgment by the state government. [While these categories cover the bulk of the rights protected, there are, of course, a few rights specifically guaranteed in the main body of the Constitution in Article I, Sections 9 and 10 (safeguards against ex post facto laws, bills of attainder, and against suspension of the writ of habeas corpus), and in the Thirteenth, Fifteenth, and Nineteenth Amendments (barring slavery and abridgment of the right to vote based on race or sex).]

Illustrative of the problem, in a general discussion of the right of jury trial in America, it must be pointed out that (1) the Sixth and Seventh Amendments preserve the right to jury trial in the federal courts both in criminal cases and in civil cases at law; (2) the Fourteenth Amendment safeguards the right to jury trial in criminal cases but not in civil cases; and (3) some state constitutions preserve the civil jury in certain cases but abolish it in other types of cases.

It should be kept in mind in comparing the due process requirements of the Fourteenth Amendment with state practices that the state provisions must be of general application. If the state guarantees certain procedures to one religious group, for example, and denies these protections to other sects, then there is a probable violation of the "equal protection" clause, even though the "due process" clause might permit the state to dispense with the procedure altogether. Thus the state can make available or abolish the civil jury. But it cannot make unreasonable classifications in determining that some persons may have a jury and others may not.

Recognition of the threefold pattern of civil rights in the American system is a prerequisite to a full understanding of the legal problems in the field. Federalism does, indeed, introduce a number of complications into the picture. This fact is particularly to be stressed when one turns to the area of national *protection* of civil rights.

CHAPTER 3

National Protection of Civil Rights

WHEN one is faced with treatment which he considers a violation of some right, it is only natural to look about for a remedy. As pointed out in the first chapter, the remedies are many and varied, and they are not mutually exclusive. Whether the injured person singles out one approach to gaining satisfaction or combines several will depend on the nature of the injury and the degree of irritation which the offended person reaches. One point should be clear, however. The remedy for injuries to person or property or for interference with the ordinary lawful activities of the citizen is normally provided by *state* laws rather than *federal* laws. The usual tort action is brought under state law in state courts. Prosecution for criminal invasion of rights is usually brought under state law and in state courts. Under normal circumstances the laws and the administrative organization for their enforcement provide satisfactory results in the various state systems. The victim of trespass, assault, or improper denial of some license can certainly anticipate fair treatment in the disposition of his claims in the overwhelming bulk of the cases. Thus a careful observer could, with reason, conclude that the state remedies for abridgment of civil rights will normally work reasonably effectively to protect the individual.

There are two situations, however, which might lead this same observer to feel that state remedies alone are inadequate and that additional safeguards in the form of national laws should be added to the picture. The first turns on the character of the person injured and the second the character of the right abridged. If the person is a member of a class subjected to peculiar disabilities, in various communities, then an outside agency may be necessary to ensure equal treatment. This has frequently been pointed out with respect to minority racial or national groups or minority religious sects. The Negro, the Indian, the Puerto Rican, the Jehovah's Witness, or even the white Protestant may in certain areas and in certain periods be accorded heavy-handed treatment by local officials as compared with the treatment of the majority class. Many people have concluded that some sort of national legislation is necessary which can be employed, albeit sparingly and selectively, to push in the direction of equality of treatment.

As to the second situation, there are those who argue that the exercise of certain rights is so vital to the preservation of the democratic system that national safeguards must be provided to guarantee them against interference. Thus the rights of speech, press, assembly, and voting are placed in a preferred position in comparison with other rights. The theory here is that the system can tolerate (although not encourage) a noticeable margin of error in the disposition of ordinary criminal cases or ordinary civil suits to redress wrongs, but to permit abridgments of the rights of speech, press, assembly, and voting is to endanger the entire democratic fabric. Two of the most frequently criticized facets of state judicial systems are the incompetency of inferior court judges and the incompetency or bias of petit jurors. However exaggerated some of these allegations may be, there is no avoiding the conclusion that in both these institutions a great deal of improvement could be made. In practical terms this is the same as saying that the product turned out in many inferior state courts is sometimes pretty shoddy merchandise. Yet no serious drive is under way to adopt an amendment to the national Constitution which would either prescribe or give Congress the authority to prescribe the qualifications of state judges and jurors. Apparently the feeling is that the tolerance is fairly great for the disposition of cases involving what might be considered ordinary personal and property rights. By comparison, the subject of voting rights has received considerable attention at the national level for almost a hundred years. And the only national laws on civil rights to be adopted in this century, down to 1960, were laws to protect voting rights.

In addition to legislative action, the judicial and executive branches can also play a part in the protection of civil rights. Where the United States Constitution applies, the United States Supreme Court can, in appropriate cases, review the decisions of state courts and reverse aberrant interpretations of the Constitution. As pointed out earlier, obtaining such review requires a dogged litigant, a very careful handling of the issues from the trial court on up the ladder, and even an ample portion of luck in hitting the Court with a timely issue in terms of the Court's current emphasis. Nonetheless, a single, clear-cut decision of the Court on a point of constitutional interpretation will normally make itself felt in the state and federal courts throughout the country. The fact, therefore, that the Supreme Court cannot, as a practical matter, correct all the erroneous decisions of all the courts of the nation should not lead one to minimize the impact of the decisions which it does make.

The executive branch has powers which may also be employed very effectively to ensure equality of treatment in specialized areas and to afford protection for certain of the individual's rights. In personnel policies for federal employees, in awarding government contracts, in disbursing federal monies, in laying down enforcement policy for the Department of Justice, and even in general public statements of principle, the President can exercise considerable influence in the field of civil rights.

The major weapons available to the judicial branch have been discussed in earlier chapters. The area of civil rights authority of the federal legislative and executive branches will be taken up separately. Because of the complexities of defining the scope of Congress' powers, however, much the greater portion of the chapter will be devoted to that branch.

NATIONAL LEGISLATION TO PROTECT CIVIL RIGHTS

Laying aside the question of how far the Congress *should* go in the civil rights field, the first problem to consider is the question of how far Congress *can* constitutionally act in this area. And this question presents some of the most difficult and controversial issues in the whole field of constitutional law. Thus forewarned, the student should proceed carefully through the cases and analysis, making certain to grasp the fundamental principles involved.

With respect to domestic matters, the basic fact of Congress' legislative power is that every act passed by the Congress must be tied to some grant of authority in the Constitution. This tie may be somewhat indirect (thus the power may be spoken of as an "implied power"), but it still must be traceable to one or another of the delegated powers. It is not enough, then, that a proposed measure be a worthwhile or useful policy; it must be within that now rather broad list of powers which the Constitution, either directly or by implication, states that Congress can exercise. It is clear that one should not equate wisdom with constitutionality. Congress can constitutionally do a great many foolish things, such as declaring war on Canada, or adding one inch to the official measure of the yard, or abolishing paper money. Conversely, there are policies which might be considered useful to put into operation on the national level, but for which there is no constitutional authority. A national law on divorce or on disposition of property by will would fall into this category. Similarly, in the case of civil rights, there is much that Congress can do, but there are areas which thus far it cannot effectively reach for lack of constitutional authorization.

Delegations of power to Congress are scattered about through the Constitution, but the bulk of such powers are to be found in Article I. The first grant of power to be found which could be applied to civil rights deals with elections. And the matter of voting rights is a particularly good vehicle for examining the basic concepts in federal protection of civil rights. Article I, Section 4, provides:

The Times, Places and Manner of holding Elections for Senators and Representatives, shall be prescribed in each State by the Legislature thereof; but the Congress may at any time by Law make or alter such Regulations, except as to the Places of choosing Senators.

To reduce this clause to its most substantial grant of power, it says that Congress can regulate the *manner* of holding elections for candidates for Congress. If to this we join the stipulation in Article I, Section 2, that electors for the national house of representatives "shall have the qualifications requisite for Electors of the most numerous branch of the State Legislature," then it can be argued that the *qualified elector* has a constitutional right to vote for representatives to Congress, and that Congress has the constitutional power to protect that right by appropriate laws.

It is important even at this stage to delineate carefully the scope of the so-called "right" to vote. To make distinctions based on whether voting is a "right" or a "privilege" is really no particular help. The important questions relate to two aspects of voting: the qualifications for voting and the constitutional and statutory safeguards against interference with the exercise of the franchise by qualified persons. And without some guarantee in either the national and state constitutions or in the statutes of the two governments, there is no right. The problem, then, is to separate the various kinds of elections and to recognize the scope of the guarantees which apply to each of these. Election of federal officers and election of state officers stand on two different grounds.

Nothing in the United States Constitution explicitly sets out the qualifications necessary to vote. Article I, Section 2, indicates by its terms that such matters are left to the individual states to determine. The second section of the Fourteenth Amendment could be construed to grant the franchise to all male citizens twenty-one years of age, unless convicted of crime, but this section is the deadest letter in the Constitution. The states are not given absolutely free rein, however, in setting voting requirements. Certain prohibitions contained in the Constitution impose limits. The Fourteenth Amendment states that no state shall "deny to any person within its jurisdiction the equal protection of the laws." This does not keep the states from setting up reasonable requirements, or classifications, but the basis for the classification must bear some relationship to ability to vote. Thus the state can set an age requirement, but it could not constitutionally bar persons from voting on the basis of color of hair. Second, the Fifteenth Amendment prohibits the states from abridging the right to vote "on account of race, color, or previous condition of servitude." Third, the Nineteenth Amendment prohibits the states from abridging the right to vote on account of sex. Further, each of these amendments contains a clause granting Congress authority to enforce the provisions "by appropriate legislation." Can Congress constitutionally limit the states' discretion any further in prescribing qualifications? The answer to this question lies in the scope accorded to the word "manner" in Article I, Section 4. But keep in mind that this clause relates to the election of *federal* officials and does not empower Congress to regulate the manner of electing *state* officials. If prescribing voter qualifications is a proper regulation of the "manner of holding Elections for Senators and Representatives," then the Congress has the authority to add to or modify the states' requirements for voting for such officials. Such authority would not, however, extend to changing the states' requirements for voting for *state* officials. Just how far Congress' powers extend under Article I, Section 4, still remains open to conjecture. Congress thus far has acted to require a written ballot in federal elections, to punish for fraudulent conduct of such elections, and to limit campaign expenditures and contributions. With the exception of the limited application of the Voting Rights Act of 1965 to the subject, specific laws relative to voter qualifications have not been adopted. At present, then, the states set requirements for voting in both state and federal elections, within the limits imposed by the Fourteenth, Fifteenth, and Nineteenth Amendments, but the Congress has some yet undefined powers to "make or alter" such regulations as they apply to the election of federal officers.

Once the citizen has satisfied the voter requirements of his state, the problem then is to determine what national safeguards can be provided to protect his exercise of the franchise. To the extent that his right to vote is protected by the national Constitution or laws it is a *federal* right. To the extent that such participation is protected only by the state constitution or laws it is a *state* right. The heart of the constitutional problem is the proper distinction between these two rights.

Is there a federal right for qualified voters to vote for senators and representatives? Can Congress safeguard participation in such elections? These were the questions presented in *Ex parte Yarbrough,* decided by the United States Supreme Court in 1884. Yarbrough and others were members of the Ku Klux Klan. They were charged under federal criminal sections for conspiring to intimidate a Negro in the exercise of his right to vote for a member of the United States Congress. It was alleged by Yarbrough that these laws were unconstitutional as being outside the scope of delegated congressional authority. Review of their convictions was sought on petitions for writs of habeas corpus and certiorari.

EX PARTE YARBROUGH
110 U.S. 651 (1884)

Mr. Justice Miller delivered the opinion of the Court....

... That a government whose essential character is republican, whose executive head and legislative body are both elective, whose most numerous and powerful branch of the legislature is elected by the people directly, has no power by appropriate laws to secure this election from the influence of violence, of corruption, and of fraud, is a proposition so startling as to arrest attention and demand the gravest consideration. If this government is anything more than a mere aggregation of delegated agents of other states and governments, each of which is superior to the general government, it must have the power to protect the elections on which its existence depends from violence and corruption. If it has not this power, it is left helpless before the two great natural and historical enemies of all republics, open violence and insidious corruption.

The proposition that it has no such power is supported by the old argument often heard, often repeated, and in this court never assented to, that when a question of the power of Congress arises the advocate of the power must be able to place his finger on words which expressly grant it. The brief of counsel before us, though directed to the authority of that body to pass criminal laws, uses the same language. Because there is no *express* power to provide for preventing violence exercised on the voter as a means of controlling his vote, no such law can be enacted. It destroys at one blow, in construing the Constitution of the United States, the doctrine universally applied to all instruments of writing, that what is implied is as much a part of the instrument as what is expressed. This principle, in its application to the Constitution of the United States, more than to almost any other writing, is a necessity, by reason of the inherent inability to put into words all derivative powers, —a difficulty which the instrument itself recognizes by conferring on Congress the authority to pass all laws necessary and proper to carry into execution the powers expressly granted, and all other powers vested in the government or any branch of it by the Constitution. Article I, section 8, clause 18.

We know of no express authority to pass laws to punish theft or burglary of the treasury of the United States. Is there therefore no power in the Congress to protect the treasury by punishing such theft and burglary? Are the mails of the United States, and the money carried in them, to be left at the mercy of robbers and of thieves who may handle the mail, because the Constitution contains no express words of power in Congress to enact laws for the punishment of those offenses? The principle, if sound, would abolish the entire criminal jurisdiction of the courts of the United States, and the laws which confer that jurisdiction. It is said that the states can pass the necessary law on this subject, and no necessity exists for such action by Congress. But the existence of state laws punishing the counterfeiting of the coin of the United States has never been held to supersede the acts of Congress passed for that purpose, or to justify the United States in failing to enforce its own laws to protect the circulation of the coin which it issues. . . .

Now, the day fixed for electing members of Congress has been established by Congress without regard to the time set for election of state officers in each state, and but for the fact that the state legislatures have, for their own accommodation, required state elections to be held at the same time, these elections would be held for congressmen alone at the time fixed by the act of Congress. Will it be denied that it is in the power of that body to provide laws for the proper conduct of those elections? To provide, if necessary, the officers who shall conduct them and make return of the result? And especially to provide, in an election held under its own authority, for security of life and limb to the voter while in the exercise of this function? Can it be doubted that Congress can, by law, protect the act of voting, the place where it is done, and the man who votes from personal violence or intimidation, and the election itself from corruption or fraud? If this be so, and it is not doubted, are such powers annulled because an election for state officers is held at the same time and place? Is it any less important that the election of members of Congress should be the free choice of all the electors, because state officers are to be elected at the same time? . . . These questions answer themselves; and it is only because the Congress of the United States, through long habit and long years of forbearance, has, in deference and respect to the states, refrained from the exercise of these powers, that they are now doubted. But when, in the pursuance of a new demand for action, that body, as it did in the cases just enumerated, finds it necessary to make additional laws for the free, the pure, and the safe exercise of this right of voting, they stand upon the same ground, and are to be upheld for the same reasons.

It is said that the parties assaulted in these cases are not officers of the United States, and their protection in exercising the right to vote by Congress does not stand on the same ground. But the distinction is not well taken. The power in either case arises out of the circumstance that the function in which the party is engaged or the right which he is about to exercise is dependent on the laws of the United States. In both cases it is the duty of that government to see that he may exercise this right freely, and to protect him from violence while so doing, or on account of so doing. This duty does not arise solely from the interest of the party concerned, but from the necessity of the government itself that its service shall be free from the adverse influence of force and fraud practiced on its agents, and that the votes by which its members of Congress and its President are elected shall be the *free* votes of the electors, and the officers thus chosen the free and uncorrupted choice of those who have the right to take part in that choice.

This proposition answers, also, another objection to the constitutionality of the laws under consideration, namely, that the right to vote for a member of Congress is not dependent upon the Constitution or laws of the United States, but is governed by the law of each state respectively. If this were conceded, the importance to the general government of having the actual election—the voting for those members— free from force and fraud is not diminished by the circumstance that the qualification of the voter is determined by the law of the state where he votes. It equally affects the government; it is as indispensable to the proper discharge of the great function of legislating for that government, that those who are to control this legislation shall not owe their election to bribery or violence, whether the class of persons who shall vote is determined by the law of the state, or by the laws of the United States, or by their united result. But it is not correct to say that the right to vote for a member of Congress does not depend on the Constitution of the United States. The office, if it be properly called an office, is created by that Constitution, and by that alone. It also declares how it shall be filled, namely, by election. Its language is: "The House of Representatives shall be composed of members chosen every second year by the people of the several States; and the electors in each State shall have the same qualifications requisite for electors of the most numerous branch of the State legislature." Article I, section 2. The states, in prescribing the qualifications of voters for the most numerous branch of their own legislatures, do not do this with reference to the election for members of Congress. Nor can they prescribe the qualification for voters for those *eo nomine*. They define who are to vote for the popular branch of their own legislature, and the Constitution of the United States says the same persons shall vote for members of Congress in that state. It adopts the qualification thus furnished as the qualification of its own electors for members of Congress. It is not true, therefore, that electors for members of Congress owe their right to vote to the state law, in any sense which makes the exercise of the right to depend exclusively on the law of the state. . . .

The rule is discharged, and the writ of habeas corpus is denied.

In a more recent case, *Burroughs* v. *United States*, 290 U.S. 534 (1934), the Court upheld the Federal Corrupt Practices Act of 1925 requiring the disclosure of facts as to contributions made to presidential campaigns. The opinion stated that the act sought to preserve the purity of presidential and vice-presidential elections, and "to say that Congress is without power to pass appropriate legislation to safeguard such an election from the improper use of money to influence the result is to deny to the nation in a vital particular the power of self protection."

Taking the *Yarbrough* and *Burroughs* cases together, it is clear that the right of a qualified voter to participate in the election of members of Congress and presidential electors is a federal right, and one which the Congress can protect against interference by any person, official or private.

Does the power to regulate elections extend to *primaries* in which federal candidates are merely nominated? In *Newberry* v. *United States*, 256 U.S. 232 (1921), the Court faced this issue in reviewing the conviction of Senator Newberry of Michigan under a Federal Corrupt Practices Act of 1910. The Act provided penalties for spending more than a prescribed maximum in congressional election campaigns. Senator Newberry spent considerably more than this amount in winning the Republican nomination from Henry Ford. The Supreme Court set the conviction aside, but on the question of congressional power over primaries, the vote was split four-to-four. Thus no definitive holding on this point was obtained. The issue was not settled until 1941 when *United States* v. *Classic* was decided.

Classic and others, election commissioners, were charged with altering and falsely counting the ballots in a Democratic primary in Louisiana at which a candidate for representative in Congress was being nominated. The indictment was brought in a federal district court under Sections 19 and 20 of the United States Criminal Code. Section 19 makes criminal any conspiracy to injure a citizen in the exercise "of any right or privilege secured to him by the Constitution or laws of the United States." Section 20 makes it a crime for anyone "acting under color of any law" willfully to subject any person to the deprivation of any rights protected by the Constitution and laws of the United States. Since the *Yarbrough* case had already declared that the qualified elector has a right to participate in a general election at which candidates for Congress are chosen, the issue in the *Classic* case was whether this right extended to the *primary* at which such candidates were merely nominated. While the vote was split five-to-three in affirming the conviction, the three dissenters disagreed only to the extent of whether Congress *intended* to punish such acts committed in primaries, not whether Congress had the power.

UNITED STATES *v.* CLASSIC

313 U.S. 299 (1941)

Mr. Justice Stone delivered the opinion of the Court....

... [T]he practical operation of the primary in Louisiana, is and has been since the primary election was established in 1900 to secure the election of the Democratic primary nominee for the Second Congressional District of Louisiana.

Interference with the right to vote in the congressional primary in the Second Congressional District for the choice of Democratic candidate for Congress is thus as a matter of law and in fact an interference with the effective choice of the voters at the only stage of the election procedure when their choice is of significance, since it is at the only stage when such interference could have any practical effect on the ultimate result, the choice of the Congressman to represent the district. The primary in Louisiana is an integral part of the procedure for the popular choice of Congressman. The right of qualified voters to vote at the congressional primary in Louisiana and to have their ballots counted is thus the right to participate in that choice.

We come then to the question whether that right is one secured by the Constitution. Section 2 of Article I commands that Congressmen shall be chosen by the people of the several states by electors, the qualifications of which it prescribes. The right of the people to choose, whatever its appropriate constitutional limitations, where in other respects it is defined, and the mode of its exercise is prescribed by state action in conformity to the Constitution, is a right established and guaranteed by the Constitution and hence is one secured by it to those citizens and inhabitants of the state entitled to exercise the right. *Ex parte Yarbrough,* 110 U.S. 651.... While, in a loose sense, the right to vote for representatives in Congress is sometimes spoken of as a right derived from the states, see *Minor* v. *Happersett,* 21 Wall. 162, ... this statement is true only in the sense that the states are authorized by the Constitution, to legislate on the subject as provided by Section 2 of Article I, to the extent that Congress has not restricted state action by the exercise of its powers to regulate elections under Section 4 and its more general power under Article I, Section 8, clause 18 of the Constitution "to make all laws which shall be necessary and proper for carrying into execution the foregoing powers.". . .

Obviously included within the right to choose, secured by the Constitution, is the right of qualified voters within a state to cast their ballots and have them counted at congressional elections. This Court has consistently held that this is a right secured by the Constitution.... And since the constitutional command is without restriction or limitation, the right, unlike those guaranteed by the Fourteenth and Fifteenth Amendments, is secured against the action of individuals as well as of states. *Ex parte Yarbrough.* . . .

. . . The right to participate in the choice of representatives for Congress includes, as we have said, the right to cast a ballot and to have it counted at the general election whether for the successful candidate or not. Where the state law has made the primary an integral part of the procedure of choice, or where in fact the primary effectively controls the choice, the right of the elector to have his ballot counted at the primary, is likewise included in the right protected by Article I, Section 2. And this right of participation is protected just as is the right to vote at the election, where the primary is by law made an integral part of the election machinery, whether the voter exercises his right in a party primary which invariably, sometimes or never determines the ultimate choice of the representatives. . . .

. . . The words of Sections 2 and 4 of Article I, read in the sense which is plainly permissible and in the light of the constitutional purpose, require us to hold that a primary election which involves a necessary step in the choice of candidates for election as representatives in Congress, and which in the circumstances of this case controls that choice, is an election within the meaning of the constitutional provision and is subject to congressional regulation as to the manner of holding it. . . .

[The holding of the Court of Appeals reversing the convictions was reversed.]

The collective results of these voting cases permit us to state that the qualified voter has a federal right to participate in the election of presidential electors, senators, and representatives; he has a similar right to vote in a primary election at which such candidates are being nominated; and the Congress has constitutional authority to adopt legislation to protect this right against interference *by either state officials or private persons.*

But what is the rule when the election is solely to fill state and local offices, with no federal candidates on the ballot? Does Congress have protective powers here? To what extent is there a federal right to vote in a purely state election? It should be clear that Sections 2 and 4 of Article I do not extend congressional authority to such elections. If Congress has any power in this area, it must be derived from other parts of the Constitution. The only other provisions of the Constitution which pertain to the question are the Fourteenth, Fifteenth, and Nineteenth Amendments, referred to earlier. Congress is granted the power to enforce the provisions of each of these amendments. But the reach of congressional power goes no further than the substantive prohibitions contained in the amendments. A careful reading of the three amendments will reveal the key limitation on congressional power in this area—the fact that there is no bar to *private* interference with the right to vote in a state election! The Fourteenth Amendment provides that no *state* shall deny equal protection of the laws; the Fifteenth Amendment prohibits abridgment "by the United States or by any State"; and the Nineteenth Amendment uses this identical phrase. Thus Congress can protect the qualified voter's right to participate in state elections from improper interference by government officials, but it has no authority to punish private persons for such interference. Looking back to the *Classic* and *Yarbrough* cases, Congress has the power to punish both officials and private individuals who hinder another in his right to vote for federal candidates. But when Congress passed a rather loosely worded statute which could have been construed to punish private interference with the right to vote in *both* federal and state elections, the Court held it unconstitutional. The case was *James* v. *Bowman,* 190 U.S. 127 (1903).

Bowman and another were indicted in a federal proceeding for intimidating certain Negroes and preventing them from voting in a federal election in Kentucky. The defendants were private persons. The indictment was based upon Section 5507 of the Revised Statutes (Section 5 of the Act of May 31, 1870) which provided:

Every person who prevents, hinders, controls or intimidates another from exercising, or in exercising the right of suffrage, to whom that right is guaranteed by the Fifteenth Amendment to the Constitution of the United States, by means of bribery or threats of depriving such person of employment or occupation, or of ejecting such person from a rented house, lands, or other property, or by threats of refusing to renew leases or contracts for labor, or by threats of violence to himself or family, shall be punished as provided in the preceding section.

Bowman sued out a writ of habeas corpus on the ground of the unconstitutionality of the section. The district judge granted the writ, and from that judgment the government appealed. The Supreme Court held the section unconstitutional. Despite the fact that the Negroes' right to vote in this particular election *could* have been protected by Congress, the section under question was held to be fatally defective because by its terms it was also directed against private action in state elections, which Congress could not constitutionally punish. In addition, the Fifteenth Amendment prohibits only abridgments "on account of race, color, or previous condition of servitude," and the government nowhere alleged that the bribery or intimidation was *because* of the Negroes' race or color. Thus if the interference with a Negro's right to vote is based on his occupation or religion, rather than his race, there is no violation of the Fifteenth Amendment. And, as the Court stated in a similar election case, also in Kentucky:

It would certainly be dangerous if the legislature could set a net large enough to catch all possible offenders, and leave it to the courts to step inside and say who could be rightfully detained, and who should be set at large. This would, to some extent, substitute the judicial for the legislative department of the government. [*U.S.* v. *Reese,* 92 U.S. 214, 221 (1876).]

To summarize, for our purposes there are four possible combinations of interference with the right of the qualified person to vote: official interference with the right to vote in federal elections, private interference with the right to vote in federal elections, official interference with the right to vote in state elections, and, finally, private interference with the right to vote in state elections. Sections 2 and 4 of Article I have been held to support congressional enactments to protect against the first and second situations; the Fourteenth, Fifteenth, and Nineteenth Amendments collectively support a broad power to protect against the third category of impediments; but there is *no* constitutional power in Congress to protect against purely private abridgment of the voter's participation in a state election. It should be apparent from this analysis of voting rights that in our *federal* system a citizen has, as pointed out in the previous chapter, *federal* rights and he has *state* rights. The former are those protected by the Constitution and laws of the United States, and the latter are those protected only by the constitutions and laws of the states. The distinction between these two categories of rights is crucial to the task of defining congressional powers to protect civil rights.

The next step in the analysis is to understand clearly that neither state nor federal rights are static. New rights can be created, and, under many circumstances, old rights can be modified or destroyed. The United States Constitution does not of its own terms describe rights which are enforceable against abridgment by private persons. To put the matter another way, private action might violate laws, but it cannot violate the Constitution. The only exception to this statement is to be found in the Thirteenth Amendment which states flatly that neither slavery nor involuntary servitude shall exist within the United States. Presumably the victim of such treatment could obtain judicial relief even if Congress had never passed enforcement legislation. But the Constitution does describe rights, albeit vaguely, which are enforceable by appropriate judicial action against abridgment by state and federal officials. Even these, however, are not static. As already indicated, the Fourteenth Amendment has undergone tremendous expansion through judicial interpretation in the past half-century. As newer constructions have been given the "due process" and "equal protection" clauses of that Amendment, to that extent new federal rights have been created. Thus the United States Supreme Court can play an important role in creating new federal rights.

A second source of innovation is congressional enactments. Under its delegated powers Congress can not only provide protection for the rights set up by the Constitution, but it can also add new rights, and congressionally created rights normally run against private as well as official abridgment. For example, Article IV, Section 3, of the Constitution states that, "The Congress shall have Power to dispose of and make all needful Rules and Regulations respecting the Territory or other Property belonging to the United States." With this authority, Congress passed the Homestead Act of 1862, under which millions of acres of public lands were parceled out among pioneering home-seekers. By this Act the Congress created a federal right in such homesteaders to use the land thus obtained free from improper interference by any person. While normally trespassers must be dealt with under state law (since the right to ordinary use of one's property is a state right), Congress can provide punishment for those who interfere with the exercise of a right which Congress creates. In *United States* v. *Waddell,* 112 U.S. 76 (1884), defendants were charged with using violence to drive a homesteader off his land which he had settled pursuant to the Federal Homestead Act. The Court held that the defendants' actions deprived the homesteader of rights secured to him by the laws of the United States and affirmed the application of congressional criminal provisions to the case. Similarly, the Court has held that when Congress enacts a criminal law, there is created a right in the individual to report violations of that law to a federal agent. Thus in *Motes* v. *United States,* 178 U.S. 458 (1900), the Court affirmed the conviction in a federal proceeding of defendants who had murdered a person who had informed federal revenue agents of the illegal operation of a still in Alabama. Thus when the claim of a privilege or immunity or right stems from some special relationship between the individual and the national government, there is a federal right. The cited cases demonstrate this relationship in the matters of voting in a federal election, lawful use of federal homestead property, and reporting a federal crime to a federal agent. Other illustrations will spring to mind where congressional action affords some special protection or bounty. In addition to this category, there is a federal right where the privilege or immunity is set up by the United States Constitution, even in the absence of any special relationship between the individual and the national government. The Fourteenth Amendment "due process" clause has been held to bar the use of coerced confessions in state criminal prosecutions. This means that there is a federal right against state use of such confessions. More broadly, there is a federal right not to be deprived of one's life by the state without due process of law. But since the Fourteenth Amendment limits only the actions of state officials and does not reach the acts of purely private persons, there is *no* federal right abridged when the private person takes the life of another. Just as was shown in the matter of voting, so it is with the other rights enjoyed by the individual in the United States: some federal rights run against abridgment by any person; other federal rights run only against abridgment by officials; and a great many rights are not federal at all, but must depend upon state law for their protection.

A third category of national rights would be those created by treaty action. The right to engage in ordinary lawful business is generally a state right only, but after a treaty was ratified between the United States and China there was created in Chinese aliens in this country a federal right to reside in the state of their choice and to engage in business there on equal terms with American citizens. Since Congress can pass appropriate laws to enforce the terms of treaty agreements, legislation could have been adopted to protect this right against encroachment even by private persons. In *Baldwin* v. *Franks,* 120 U.S. 678 (1887), the United States Supreme Court reviewed in habeas corpus proceedings the arrest of the petitioner for assaulting Chinese citizens and driving them out of a California town. The charge was made under Section 2 of the Act of April 20, 1871, which prohibited conspiracies to deprive another of equal protection of the laws or equal privileges or immunities under the laws. The Court directed petitioner's release, holding the section unconstitutional. The fact that the Chinese citizens were protected under a treaty might have afforded authority for congressional legislation, the Court held, but the provision of the 1871 law was so broadly worded that it covered action beyond the scope of congressional power.

The leading decision in the United States Supreme Court on the subject of congressional authority to protect civil rights came in the *Civil Rights Cases* in 1883. The cases were brought under Sections 1 and 2 of the Civil Rights Act of March 1, 1875, which provided as follows:

Sec. 1: That all persons within the jurisdiction of the United States shall be entitled to the full and equal enjoyment of the accommodations, advantages, facilities and privileges of inns, public conveyances on land or water, theaters and other places of public amusement; subject only to the conditions and limitations established by law and applicable alike to citizens of every race and color, regardless of any previous condition of servitude.

Sec. 2: That any person who shall violate the foregoing section by denying to any citizen, except for reasons by law applicable to citizens of every race and color, . . . the full enjoyment of any of the accommodations . . . or privileges in said section enumerated, . . . shall for every such offense forfeit and pay the sum of $500 to the person aggrieved thereby, . . . and shall also, for every such offense, be deemed guilty of a misdemeanor and, upon conviction thereof, shall be fined not less than $500 nor more than $1,000, or shall be imprisoned not less than thirty days nor more than one year.

Several cases arose in various courts, and these were handled together in the United States Supreme Court under the title *Civil Rights Cases.* They involved denial of accommodations because of race in a hotel, a theater, an opera house, and a railroad.

CIVIL RIGHTS CASES
109 U.S. 3 (1883)

Mr. Justice Bradley delivered the opinion of the Court. . . .

. . . Has Congress constitutional power to make such a law? Of course, no one will contend that the power to pass it was contained in the Constitution before the adoption of the last three Amendments. . . . [But in the brief for the Negro litigants William Randolph stated (27 L. ed. 837): "Our case involves the rights of a citizen of one State traveling 'by a public conveyance by land' through another State, for the purpose of reaching a place in a third State. We maintain that so far as the Act of Congress applies to such a case, the power to pass it is beyond question. Independently of the 'power to enforce by appropriate legislation' the 14th Amendment, there are, as we conceive, at least two other clauses of the Constitution on either of which the Act may rest. The first is the power in Congress to regulate commerce with foreign Nations and among the several States . . . and the other is the provision that 'The citizens of each State shall be entitled to all the privileges and immunities of citizens in the several States.' " And the Solicitor-General, S. F. Phillips, stated in his brief (27 L. ed. 837): "Inns are provided for the accommodation of travelers; for those passing from place to place. They are essential instrumentalities of commerce, which it was the province of the United States to regulate even prior to the recent Amendments to the Constitution."]

The first section of the Fourteenth Amendment, which is the one relied on, after declaring who shall be citizens of the United States, and of the several States, is prohibitory in its character, and prohibitory upon the States. It declares that: "No State shall make or enforce any law which shall abridge the privileges or immunities of citizens of the United States; nor shall any State deprive any person of life, liberty or property without due process of law; nor deny to any person within its jurisdiction the equal protection of the laws." It is State action of a particular character that is prohibited. Individual invasion of individual rights is not the subject-matter of the Amendment. It has a deeper and broader scope. It nullifies and makes void all State legislation, and State action of every kind, which impairs the privileges and immunities of citizens of the United States, or which injures them in life, liberty or property without due process of law, or which denies to any of them the equal protection of the laws. It not only does this, but, in order that the national will, thus declared, may not be a mere *brutum fulmen,* the last section of the Amendment invests Congress with power to enforce it by appropriate legislation. To enforce what? To enforce the prohibition. To adopt appropriate legislation for correcting the effects of such prohibited State laws and State Acts, and thus to render them effectually null, void and innocuous. This is the legislative power conferred upon Congress, and this is the whole of it. It does not invest Congress with power to legislate upon subjects which are within the domain of State legislation; but to provide modes of relief against State legislation, or State action, of the kind referred to. It does not authorize Congress to create a code of municipal law for the regulation of private rights; but to provide modes of redress against the operation of State laws, and the action of State officers executive or judicial, when these are subversive of the fundamental rights specified in the Amendment. Positive rights and privileges are undoubtedly secured by the Fourteenth Amendment; but they are secured by way of prohibition against State laws and State proceedings affecting those rights and privileges, and by power given to Congress to legislate for the purpose of carrying such prohibition into effect; and such legislation must, necessarily, be predicated upon such supposed State laws or State proceedings, and be directed to the correction of their operation and effect. . . .

An apt illustration of this distinction may be found in some of the provisions of the original Constitution. Take the subject of contracts, for example; the Constitution prohibited the States from passing any law impairing the obligation of contracts. This did not give to Congress power to provide laws for the general enforcement of contracts; nor power to invest the courts of the United States with jurisdiction over contracts, so as to enable parties to sue upon them in those courts. It did, however, give the power to provide remedies by which the impairment of contracts by State legislation might be counteracted and corrected; and this power was exercised. The remedy which Congress actually provided was that contained in the 25th section of the Judiciary Act of 1789, 1 Stat. 85, giving to the Supreme Court of the United States jurisdiction by writ of error to review the final decisions of State courts whenever they should sustain the validity of a State statute or authority alleged to be repugnant to the Constitution or laws of the United States. By this means, if a State law was passed impairing the obligation of a contract, and the State tribunals sustained the validity of the law, the mischief could be corrected in this court. The legislation of Congress, and the proceedings provided for under it, were corrective in their character. No attempt was made to draw into the United States courts the litigation of contracts generally; and no such attempt would have been sustained. . . .

And so in the present case, until some State law has been passed, or some State action through its officers or agents has been taken, adverse to the rights of citizens sought to be protected by the Fourteenth Amendment, no legislation of the United States under said Amendment, nor any proceedings under such legislation, can be called into activity; for the prohibitions of the Amendment are against State laws and acts done under State authority. Of course, legislation may and should be provided in advance to meet the exigency when it arises; but it should be adapted to the mischief and wrong which the Amendment was intended to provide against; and that is, State laws, or State action of some kind, adverse to the rights of the citizen secured by the Amendment. Such legislation cannot properly cover the whole domain of rights appertaining to life, liberty and property, defining them and providing for their vindication. That would be to establish a code of municipal law regulative of all private rights between man and man in society. It would be to make Congress take the place of the State Legislatures and to supersede them. It is absurd to affirm that, because the rights of life, liberty and property, which include all civil rights that men have, are, by the Amendment, sought to be protected against invasion on the part of the State without due process of law, Congress may, therefore, provide due process of law for their vindication in every case; and that, because the denial by a State to any persons, of the equal protection of the laws, is prohibited by the Amendment, therefore Congress may establish laws for their equal protection. . . .

An inspection of the law shows that it makes no reference whatever to any supposed or apprehended violation of the Fourteenth Amendment on the part of the States. It is not predicated on any such view. It proceeds *ex directo* to declare that certain acts committed by individuals shall be deemed offenses, and shall be prosecuted and punished by proceedings in the courts of the United States. It does not profess to be corrective of any constitutional wrong committed by the States; it does not make its operation to depend upon any such wrong committed. It applies equally to cases arising in States which have the justest laws respecting the personal rights of citizens, and whose authorities are ever ready to enforce such laws, as to those which arise in States that may have violated the prohibition of the Amendment. In other words, it steps into the domain of local jurisprudence, and lays down rules for the conduct of individuals in society towards each other, and imposes sanctions for the enforcement of those rules, without referring in any manner to any supposed action of the State or its authorities. . . .

In this connection it is proper to state that civil rights, such as are guaranteed by the Constitution against State aggression, cannot be impaired by the wrongful acts of individuals, unsupported by State authority in the shape of laws, customs or judicial or executive proceedings. The wrongful act of an individual, unsupported by any such authority, is simply a private wrong, or a crime of that individual; an invasion of the rights of the injured party, it is true, whether they affect his person, his property or his reputation; but if not sanctioned in some way by the State, or not done under State authority, his rights remain in full force, and may presumably be vindicated by resort to the laws of the State for redress. . . .

Of course, these remarks do not apply to those cases in which Congress is clothed with direct and plenary powers of legislation over the whole subject, accompanied with an express or implied denial of such power to the States, as in the regulation of commerce with foreign Nations, . . . the coining of money, the establishment of post offices and post-roads, the declaring of war, etc. In these cases, Congress has power to pass laws for regulating the subjects specified in every detail, and the conduct and transactions of individuals in respect thereof. But where a subject is not submitted to the general legislative power of Congress, but is only submitted thereto for the purpose of rendering effective some prohibition against particular State legislation or State action in reference to that subject, the power given is limited by its object, and any legislation by Congress in the matter must necessarily be corrective in its character, adapted to counteract and redress the operation of such prohibited State laws or proceedings of State officers. . . .

[The opinion then states that denials of accommodations do not constitute slavery or involuntary servitude, and therefore the Thirteenth Amendment, which does apply to private acts, would not cover the particular wrongs complained of. "It would be running the slavery argument into the ground, to make it apply to every act of discrimination which a person may see fit to make as to the guests he will entertain," or deal with in business.]

On the whole we are of opinion, that no countenance of authority for the passage of the law in question can be found in either the Thirteenth or Fourteenth Amendment of the Constitution; and no other ground of authority for its passage being suggested, it must necessarily be declared void, at least so far as its operation in the several States is concerned.

Justice Harlan dissenting. . . .

I am of the opinion that such discrimination practiced by corporations and individuals in the exercise of their public or *quasi*-public functions is a badge of servitude, the imposition of which Congress may prevent under its power, by appropriate legislation, to enforce the Thirteenth Amendment. . . .

[Justice Harlan then stated that if this is not sufficient, the Fourteenth Amendment adds even more to Congress' power: "All persons born or naturalized in the United States . . . are citizens of the United States and of the State wherein they reside." Congress may enforce this section. It may thus guarantee the interstate citizenship clause in Article IV, which would support the instant act.]

In every material sense applicable to the practical enforcement of the Fourteenth Amendment, railroad corporations, keepers of inns and managers of places of public amusement are agents or instrumentalities of the State, because they are charged with duties to the public, and are amenable, in respect of their duties and functions, to government regulation. It seems to me that, within the principle settled in *Ex parte Virginia,* a denial, by these instrumentalities of the State, to the citizen, because of his race, of that equality of civil rights secured to him by law, is a denial by the State, within the meaning of the Fourteenth Amendment. . . .

[Justice Harlan then stated that, at least with respect to railroads, the act could be sustained as to interstate commerce under the power of Congress to regulate commerce. The fact that the act did not state that it was a regulation of commerce should not foreclose inspection under that power if it could thereby be upheld.]

The general principles enunciated by Justice Bradley in his opinion for the majority are still followed by the Court today. There have been substantial developments in the coverage of what he referred to as "State action," but the opinion is no less important for its fundamental distinction between the reach of congressional power under its "direct and plenary powers" and the lesser grant of authority in the Fourteenth Amendment. Since it is exactly this Fourteenth Amendment delegation of power which is so important in the rights field and which is so difficult to define, a substantial portion of the remainder of this chapter will be devoted to marking out the scope of legislative authority under the Fourteenth Amendment.

It was pointed out earlier that the restrictive interpretation which the Court, in the *Slaughter-House Cases,* gave to the Fourteenth Amendment "privileges and immunities" clause made the task of legislative enforcement of the amendment a difficult one. One of Congress' solutions to this problem was to adopt a provision which was rather general in its wording. It was declared unlawful for persons acting under color of law to deprive any person of rights "secured or protected by the Constitution *or* laws of the United States." Now such a provision is clearly not limited to the bare coverage of the Fourteenth Amendment. For example, applied to voting in federal elections, this would be a perfectly proper exercise of congressional power even without the presence of the Fourteenth Amendment. It should be equally clear, however, that all Fourteenth Amendment violations could be construed as crimes under such a statute. Thus, in a sense, in applying the statute to a variety of deprivations one must engage in a bit of constitutional hopscotch: jumping from one section of the Constitution to another, depending on the particular right involved, to see what authority there might be for applying the law to the specific invasion alleged.

To confine ourselves to the coverage of the Fourteenth Amendment, however, there are two basic tests which must be met before there can be held to be a violation of the amendment. First, to use Justice Bradley's words in the *Civil Rights Cases*, "It is State action of a particular character that is prohibited. Individual invasion of individual rights is not the subject-matter of the Amendment." Second, the right claimed must be one which is protected by the Fourteenth Amendment. The absence of *either* of these facets in the case is fatal to a holding of Fourteenth Amendment violation. For example, the right to life is protected by the amendment, but only against improper deprivation by the *state*. A private lynching or murder would not fit the requirements. Similarly, there is no violation if the state bars persons from practicing medicine without a license, since even though the requisite state action is present, the Fourteenth Amendment does not set up a right in every person to practice medicine on his own terms.

The enumeration of the rights protected by the Fourteenth Amendment is in large part the subject matter of the remainder of this book and cannot be encompassed in a single chapter. Thus the emphasis here will be on the elaboration of the concept of "state action," and the Fourteenth Amendment *rights* will be taken up category by category in the following chapters.

The Court rather early began the extension of the term state action to cover not only legislative action (indicated by the use of "law" in the privileges and immunities clause) but also action of the judicial and executive branches as well. And there was a vertical extension to include all governmental units subordinate to the state. The Court has found violations of the Amendment by the state courts [*Ex parte Virginia*, 100 U.S. 339 (1880)], legislatures [*Strauder* v. *West Virginia*, 100 U.S. 303 (1880)], executives [*Sterling* v. *Constantin*, 287 U.S. 378 (1932)], tax boards [*Raymond* v. *Chicago Union Traction Co.*, 207 U.S. 20 (1907)], boards of education [*West Virginia Board of Education* v. *Barnette*, 319 U.S. 624 (1943)], counties [*Ward* v. *Love County*, 253 U.S. 17 (1920)], and cities [*Home Telephone & Telegraph Co.* v. *Los Angeles*, 227 U.S. 278 (1913)], among others. When any officer or employee of the state or any of its subordinate governmental units acts in pursuance of his official function as required by law, then there is state action within the meaning of the Fourteenth Amendment. The more complex questions concerning state action have arisen with respect to either operations not strictly classified as government operations, or acts of state agents which are not a part of their statutory duties. [See Glenn Abernathy, "Expansion of the State Action

Concept Under the Fourteenth Amendment," 43 *Cornell L.Q.* 375 (1958); Thomas P. Lewis, "The Meaning of State Action," 60 *Colum. L. Rev.* 1083 (1960); and Jerre S. Williams, "The Twilight of State Action," 41 *Texas L. Rev.* 347 (1963).]

A question was raised very soon after the adoption of the Fourteenth Amendment, and even before the decision in the *Civil Rights Cases,* concerning the applicability of the Amendment to the act of a state judge in discriminating racially in the process of selecting jurors. Such discrimination was neither authorized nor prohibited by state law, but Judge Cole, of Virginia, on his own initiative excluded Negroes from jury service. The judge was indicted under Section 4 of the Act of Congress of March 1, 1875, which penalized officials for discriminating on grounds of race or color in the choosing of jurors. While in custody, he petitioned the United States Supreme Court for habeas corpus, alleging that the Act could not constitutionally be applied to him. The question, then, was whether the federal criminal law passed under authority of the "equal protection" clause of the Fourteenth Amendment could constitutionally be applied to official acts of a state judge who acted in his own discretion and not under statutory direction. In *Ex parte Virginia,* 100 U.S. 339 (1880), the Court held that such acts were within the prohibitions of the Fourteenth Amendment and the enforcement act passed under it. Justice Strong, speaking for the majority, stated:

... Whoever, by virtue of public position under a State government, deprives another of property, life, or liberty, without due process of law, or denies or takes away the equal protection of the laws, violates the constitutional inhibition; and as he acts in the name and for the State, and is clothed with the State's power, his act is that of the State. This must be so, or the constitutional prohibition has no meaning. Then the State has clothed one of its agents with power to annul or to evade it.

Suppose, however, that instead of merely acting where state law is silent, the official actually *violates* the law of his state while acting in his official capacity. Would such a situation come within the purview of the Fourteenth Amendment? In early cases dealing with attempts to obtain civil remedies against this type of official action, the Supreme Court vacillated, first saying "no," and then saying "sometimes." As Justice Roberts pointed out in *Screws* v. *United States,* 325 U.S. 91, 148 (1945), discussed below:

Although action taken under such circumstances has been deemed to be deprivation by a "State" of rights guaranteed by the Fourteenth Amendment for purposes of federal jurisdiction, the doctrine has had a fluctuating and dubious history. Compare *Barney* v. *City of New York,* 193 U.S. 430, with *Raymond* v. *Chicago Traction Co.,* 207 U.S. 20.

In *United States* v. *Classic,* discussed earlier, state officers were convicted of willfully miscounting ballots in a federal election. And, of course, this sort of activity was a violation of Louisiana law as well. But the case does not squarely meet the issue as stated here, because Congress has broad powers to punish for federal election frauds even without the Fourteenth Amendment. Here the question is restricted to those rights for which the Fourteenth Amendment alone supports congressional legislation. It was not until 1945 that the United States Supreme Court squarely faced and answered the question with respect to federal criminal penalties. The case was *Screws* v. *United States,* a classic example of police brutality.

Screws, sheriff of Baker County, Georgia, aided by a local police officer and a deputy sheriff, arrested Hall, a Negro citizen of the United States, on a warrant charging theft of a tire. Hall was handcuffed and driven to the courthouse. There he was dragged from the car, and, while still handcuffed, beaten by all three men with their fists and with a two-pound solid-bar blackjack. The beating continued for fifteen to thirty minutes. Hall was then dragged, feet first, through the courthouse yard into the jail and thrown upon the floor, dying. An ambulance was called, but Hall died shortly afterward without regaining consciousness.

An indictment was returned against the three men charging, on one count, violation of Section 20 of the Criminal Code, 18 U.S.C. Section 242. This section provides:

Whoever, under color of any law, statute, ordinance, regulation, or custom, willfully subjects, or causes to be subjected, any inhabitant of any State, Territory, or District to the deprivation of any rights, privileges, or immunities secured or protected by the Constitution and laws of the United States, or to different punishments, pains, or penalties, on account of such inhabitant being an alien, or by reason of his color, or race, than are prescribed for the punishment of citizens, shall be fined not more than $1,000 or imprisoned not more than one year, or both.

Convictions were obtained, and the United States Supreme Court reviewed the case on certiorari. Several constitutional issues were presented, but probably the most important dealt with the question of whether Congress, in enforcing the Fourteenth Amendment, could punish state acts which violated state laws. The answer to the question is complicated by the fact that when the Court applies a statute, it may not consider just the matter of constitutional power, but may have a second problem of determining the exact reach of the statute involved. Congress ordinarily does not exhaust the full scope of a constitutional grant of power when it gives effect to that grant by legislation. The key phrase in the section in question is "under color of any law." It might not have been designed by Congress to cover state acts in violation of state law, but certainly if it *were* so intended, the Fourteenth Amendment must justify such inclusion for it to be constitutional.

Another issue presented in the case was whether the section was a violation of the Fifth Amendment "due process" clause because it subjected persons to criminal penalties under vague and general phrases which did not adequately define just what sort of conduct was made criminal. The majority on the Court held against both claims, although the members were so badly split that there is no "opinion for the Court."

SCREWS v. UNITED STATES
325 U.S. 91 (1945)

Mr. Justice Douglas announced the judgment of the Court and delivered the following opinion, in which the Chief Justice, Mr. Justice Black and Mr. Justice Reed concur....

I

We are met at the outset with the claim that Section 20 is unconstitutional, insofar as it makes criminal acts in violation of the due process clause of the Fourteenth Amendment. The argument runs as follows: It is true that this Act as construed in *United States* v. *Classic* ... was upheld in its application to certain ballot box frauds committed by state officials. But in that case the constitutional rights protected were the rights to vote specifically guaranteed by Art. I, Sections 2 and 4 of the Constitution. Here there is no ascertainable standard of guilt. There have been conflicting views in the Court as to the proper construction of the due process clause. The majority have quite consistently construed it in broad general terms. ... In *Snyder* v. *Massachusetts* ... it was said that due process prevents state action which "offends some principle of justice so rooted in the traditions and conscience of our people as to be ranked as fundamental." The same standard was expressed in *Palko* v. *Connecticut* ... in terms of a "scheme of ordered liberty.". ...

It is said that the Act must be read as if it contained those broad and fluid definitions of due process and that if it is so read it provides no ascertainable standard of guilt. ... In the instant case the decisions of the courts are, to be sure, a source of reference for ascertaining the specific content of the concept of due process. But even so the Act would incorporate by reference a large body of changing and uncertain law. That law is not always reducible to specific rules, is expressible only in general terms, and turns many times on the facts of a particular case. Accordingly, it is argued that such a body of legal principles lacks the basic specificity necessary for criminal statutes under our system or government. ...

... Under that test a local law enforcement officer violates Section 20 and commits a federal offense for which he can be sent to the penitentiary if he does an act which some court later holds deprives a person of due process of law. And he is a criminal though his motive was pure and though his purpose was unrelated to the disregard of any constitutional guarantee. ... Those who enforced local law today might not know for many months (and meanwhile could not find out) whether what they did deprived some one of due process of law. The enforcement of a criminal statute so construed would indeed cast law enforcement agencies loose at their own risk on a vast uncharted sea. ...

We hesitate to say that when Congress sought to enforce the Fourteenth Amendment in this fashion it did a vain thing. We hesitate to conclude that for 80 years this effort of Congress, renewed several times, to protect the important rights of the individual guaranteed by the Fourteenth Amendment has been an idle gesture. ... Only if no construction can save the Act from this claim of unconstitutionality are we willing to reach that result. We do not reach it, for we are of the view that if Section 20 is confined more narrowly than the lower courts confined it, it can be preserved as one of the sanctions to the great rights which the Fourteenth Amendment was designed to secure.

II

We recently pointed out that "willful" is a word "of many meanings, its construction often being influenced by its context.". . . But "when used in a criminal statute it generally means an act done with a bad purpose.". . . In that event something more is required than the doing of the act proscribed by the statute. . . . An evil motive to accomplish that which the statute condemns becomes a constitutent element of the crime. . . . And that issue must be submitted to the jury under appropriate instructions. . . .

An analysis of the cases in which "willfully" has been held to connote more than an act which is voluntary or intentional would not prove helpful as each turns on its own peculiar facts. Those cases, however, make clear that if we construe "willfully" in Section 20 as connoting a purpose to deprive a person of a specific constitutional right, we would introduce no innovation. The Court, indeed, has recognized that the requirement of a specific intent to do a prohibited act may avoid those consequences to the accused which may otherwise render a vague or indefinite statute invalid. The constitutional vice in such a statute is the essential injustice to the accused of placing him on trial for an offense, the nature of which the statute does not define and hence of which it gives no warning. See *United States* v. *Cohen Grocery Co., supra.* But where the punishment imposed is only for an act knowingly done with the purpose of doing that which the statute prohibits, the accused canot be said to suffer from lack of warning or knowledge that the act which he does is a violation of law. The requirement that the act must be willful or purposeful may not render certain, for all purposes, a statutory definition of the crime which is in some respects uncertain. But it does relieve the statute of the objection that it punishes without warning an offense of which the accused was unaware. . . .

Moreover, the history of Section 20 affords some support for that narrower construction. As we have seen, the word "willfully" was not added to the Act until 1909. Prior to that time it may be that Congress intended that he who deprived a person of any right protected by the Constitution should be liable without more. . . . But as we have seen, the word "willfully" was added to make the section "less severe." We think the inference is permissible that its severity was to be lessened by making it applicable only where the requisite bad purpose was present, thus requiring specific intent not only where discrimination is claimed but in other situations as well. We repeat that the presence of a bad purpose or evil intent alone may not be sufficient. We do say that a requirement of a specific intent to deprive a person of a federal right made definite by decision or other rule of law saves the Act from any charge of unconstitutionality on the grounds of vagueness. . . .

It is said, however, that this construction of the Act will not save it from the infirmity of vagueness since neither a law enforcement official nor a trial judge can know with sufficient definiteness the range of rights that are constitutional. But that criticism is wide of the mark. For the specific intent required by the Act is an intent to deprive a person of a right which has been made specific either by the express terms of the Constitution or laws of the United States or by decisions interpreting them. Take the case of a local officer who persists in enforcing a type of ordinance which the Court has held invalid as violative of the guarantees of free speech or freedom of worship. Or a local official continues to select juries in a manner which flies in the teeth of decisions of the Court. If those acts are done willfully, how can the officer possibly claim that he had no fair warning that his acts were prohibited by the statute? He violates the statute not merely because he has a bad purpose but because he acts in defiance of announced rules of law. He who defies a decision interpreting the Constitution knows precisely what he is doing. If sane, he hardly may be heard to say that he knew not what he did. Of course, willful conduct cannot make definite that which is undefined. But willful violators of constitutional requirements, which have been defined, certainly are in no position to say that they had no adequate advance notice that they would be visited with punishment. When they act willfully in the sense in which we use the word, they act in open defiance or in reckless disregard of a constitutional requirement which has been made specific and definite. When they are convicted for so acting, they are not punished for violating an unknowable something. . . .

. . . The fact that the defendants may not have been thinking in constitutional terms is not material where their aim was not to enforce local law but to deprive a citizen of a right and that right was protected by the Constitution. When they so act they at least act in reckless disregard of constitutional prohibitions or guarantees. Likewise, it is plain that basic to the concept of due process of law in a criminal case is a trial—a trial in a court of law, not a "trial by ordeal." *Brown* v. *Mississippi*, 297 U.S. 278, 285. It could hardly be doubted that they who "under color of any law, statute, ordinance, regulation, or custom" act with that evil motive violate Section 20. Those who decide to take the law into their own hands and act as prosecutor, jury, judge, and executioner plainly act to deprive a prisoner of the trial which due process of law guarantees him. And such a purpose need not be expressed; it may at times be reasonably inferred from all the circumstances attendant on the act. . . .

The difficulty here is that this question of intent was not submitted to the jury with the proper instructions. The court charged that petitioners acted illegally if they applied more force than was necessary to make the arrest effectual or to protect themselves from the prisoner's alleged assault. But in view of our construction of the word "willfully" the jury should have been further instructed that it was not sufficient that petitioners had a generally bad purpose. To convict it was necessary for them to find that petitioners had the purpose to deprive the prisoner of a constitutional right, e.g., the right to be tried by a court rather than by ordeal. And in determining whether that requisite bad purpose was present the jury would be entitled to consider all the attendant circumstances—the malice of petitioners, the weapons used in the assault, its character and duration, the provocation, if any, and the like. . . .

III

It is said, however, that petitioners did not act "under color of any law" within the meaning of Section 20 of the Criminal Code. We disagree. We are of the view that petitioners acted under "color" of law in making the arrest of Robert Hall and in assaulting him. They were officers of the law who made the arrest. By their own admissions they assaulted Hall in order to protect themselves and to keep their prisoner from escaping. It was their duty under Georgia law to make the arrest effective. Hence, their conduct comes within the statute.

Some of the arguments which have been advanced in support of the contrary conclusion suggest that the question under Section 20 is whether Congress has made it a federal offense for a state officer to violate the law of his State. But there is no warrant for treating the question in state law terms. The problem is not whether state law has been violated but whether an inhabitant of a State has been deprived of a federal right by one who acts under "color of any law." He who acts under "color" of law may be a federal officer or a state officer. He may act under "color" of federal law or of state law. The statute does not come into play merely because the federal law or the state law under which the officer purports to act is violated. It is applicable when and only when someone is deprived of a federal right by that action. The fact that it is also a violation of state law does not make it any the less a federal offense punishable as such. Nor does its punishment by federal authority encroach on state authority or relieve the state from its responsibility for punishing state offenses.

We agree that when this statute is applied to the action of state officials, it should be construed so as to respect the proper balance between the States and the federal government in law enforcement. Violation of local law does not necessarily mean that federal rights have been invaded. The fact that a prisoner is assaulted, injured, or even murdered by state officials does not necessarily mean that he is deprived of any right protected or secured by the Constitution or laws of the United States. . . . The Fourteenth Amendment did not alter the basic relations between the States and the national government. . . . Our national government is one of delegated powers alone. Under our federal system the administration of criminal justice rests with the states except as Congress, acting within the scope of those delegated powers, has created offenses against the United States. . . . It is only state action of a "particular character" that is prohibited by the Fourteenth Amendment and against which the Amendment authorizes Congress to afford relief. *Civil Rights Cases*, 109 U.S. 3, 11, 13. Thus Congress in Section 20 of the Criminal Code did not undertake to make all torts of state officials federal crimes. It brought within Section 20 only specified acts done "under color" of law and then only those acts which deprived a person of some right secured by the Constitution or laws of the United States. . . .

. . . We are not dealing here with a case where an officer not authorized to act nevertheless takes action. Here the state officers were authorized to make an arrest and to take such steps as were necessary to make the arrest effective. They acted without authority only in the sense that they used excessive force in making the arrest effective. It is clear that under "color" of law means under "pretense" of law. Thus acts of officers in the ambit of their personal pursuits are plainly excluded. Acts of officers who undertake to perform their official duties are included whether they hew to the line of their authority or overstep it. If, as suggested, the statute was designed to embrace only action which the State in fact authorized, the words "under color of any law" were hardly apt words to express the idea. . . .

Since there must be a new trial, the judgment below is

Reversed.

Mr. Justice Rutledge, concurring in the result.

For the compelling reason stated at the end of this opinion I concur in reversing the judgment and remanding the cause for further proceedings. But for that reason, my views would require that my vote be cast to affirm the judgment, for the reasons stated by Mr. Justice Murphy and others I feel forced, in the peculiar situation, to state.

The case comes here established in fact as a gross abuse of authority by state officers. . . . They do not come . . . as faithful state officers, innocent of crime. Justification has been foreclosed. Accordingly, their argument now admits the offense, but insists it was against the state alone, not the nation. So they have made their case in this Court.

In effect, the position urges it is murder they have done, not deprivation of constitutional right. Strange as the argument is the reason. It comes to this, that abuse of state power creates immunity to federal power. Because what they did violated the state's laws, the nation cannot reach their conduct. It may deprive the citizen of his liberty and his life. But whatever state officers may do in abuse of their official capacity can give this Government and its courts no concern. This, though the prime object of the Fourteenth Amendment and Section 20 was to secure these fundamental rights against wrongful denial by exercise of the power of the states. . . .

There could be no clearer violation of the Amendment or the statute. No act could be more final or complete, to denude the victim of rights secured by the Amendment's very terms. Those rights so destroyed cannot be restored. Nor could the part played by the state's power in causing their destruction be lessened, though other organs were not to repudiate what was done. The state's law might thus be vindicated. If so, the vindication could only sustain, it could not detract from the federal power. Nor could it restore what the federal power shielded. Neither acquittal nor conviction, though affirmed by the state's highest court, could resurrect what the wrongful use of state power has annihilated. There was in this case abuse of state power, which for the Amendment's great purposes was state action, final in the last degree, depriving the victim of his liberty and his life without due process of law. . . .

. . . Section 20 strikes only at abuse of official functions by state officers. It does not reach out for crimes done by men in general. Not murder per se, but murder by state officers in the course of official conduct and done with the aid of state power is outlawed. These facts, inherent in the crime, give all the warning constitutionally required. For one, so situated, who goes so far in misconduct can have no excuse of innocence or ignorance.

Generally state officials know something of the individual's basic legal rights. If they do not, they should, for they assume that duty when they assume their office. Ignorance of the law is no excuse for men in general. It is less an excuse for men whose special duty is to apply it, and therefore to know and observe it. If their knowledge is not comprehensive, state officials know or should know when they pass the limits of their authority, so far at any rate that their action exceeds honest error of judgment and amounts to abuse of their office and its function. When they enter such a domain in dealing with the citizen's rights, they should do so at their peril, whether that be created by state or federal law. . . .

[Mr. Justice Rutledge then states that while his conviction is that the judgment should be affirmed, this would result in a lack of a majority to dispose of the case. "Stalemate should not prevail for any reason, however compelling, in a criminal cause, or, if avoidable, in any other." Accordingly, he concurs in voting to reverse the decision as required by the opinion of Mr. Justice Douglas.]

Mr. Justice Murphy dissenting.´

I dissent. Robert Hall, a Negro citizen, has been deprived not only of the right to be tried by a court rather than by ordeal. He has been deprived of the right to life itself. That right belonged to him not because he was a Negro or a member of any particular race or creed. That right was his because he was an American citizen, because he was a human being. As such, he was entitled to all the respect and fair treatment that befits the dignity of man, a dignity that is recognized and guaranteed by the Constitution. Yet not even the semblance of due process has been accorded him. He has been cruelly and unjustifiably beaten to death by local police officers acting under color of authority derived from the state. It is difficult to believe that such an obvious and necessary right is indefinitely guaranteed by the Constitution or is foreign to the knowledge of local police officers so as to cast any reasonable doubt on the conviction under Section 20 of the Criminal Code of the perpetrators of this "shocking and revolting episode in law enforcement.". . .

It is axiomatic, of course, that a criminal statute must give a clear and unmistakable warning as to the acts which will subject one to criminal punishment. And courts are without power to supply that which Congress has left vague. But this salutary principle does not mean that if a statute is vague as to certain criminal acts but definite as to others the entire statute must fall. Nor does it mean that in the first case involving the statute to come before us we must delineate all the prohibited acts that are obscure and all those that are explicit. . . .

It is an illusion to say that the real issue in this case is the alleged failure of Section 20 fully to warn the state officials that their actions were illegal. The Constitution, Section 20 and their own consciences told them that. They knew that they lacked any mandate or authority to take human life unnecessarily or without due process of law in the course of their duties. They knew that their excessive and abusive use of authority would only subvert the ends of justice. The significant question, rather, is whether law enforcement officers and those entrusted with authority shall be allowed to violate with impunity the clear constitutional rights of the inarticulate and the friendless. Too often unpopular minorities, such as Negroes, are unable to find effective refuge from the cruelties of bigoted and ruthless authority. States are undoubtedly capable of punishing their officers who commit such outrages. But where, as here, the states are unwilling for some reason to prosecute such crimes the federal government must step in unless constitutional guarantees are to become atrophied. . . .

. . . We should therefore affirm the judgment.

Mr. Justice Roberts, Mr. Justice Frankfurter and Mr. Justice Jackson, dissenting . . .

Of course the petitioners are punishable. The only issue is whether Georgia alone has the power and duty to punish, or whether this patently local crime can be made the basis of a federal prosecution. The practical question is whether the States should be relieved from responsibility to bring their law officers to book for homicide, by allowing prosecutions in the federal courts for a relatively minor offense carrying a short sentence. The legal question is whether, for the purpose of accomplishing this relaxation of State responsibility, hitherto settled principles for the protection of civil liberties shall be bent and tortured. . . .

The Fourteenth Amendment prohibited a State from so acting as to deprive persons of new federal rights defined by it. Section 5 of the Amendment specifically authorized enabling legislation to enforce that prohibition. Since a State can act only through its officers, Congress provided for the prosecution of any officer who deprives others of their guaranteed rights and denied such an officer the right to defend by claiming the authority of the State for his action. In short, Congress said that no State can empower an officer to commit acts which the Constitution forbade the State from authorizing, whether such unauthorized command be given for the State by its legislative or judicial voice, or by a custom contradicting the written law. . . . The present prosecution is not based on an officer's claim that that for which the United States seeks his punishment was commanded or authorized by the law of his State. On the contrary, the present prosecution is based on the theory that Congress made it a federal offense for a State officer to violate the explicit law of his State. We are asked to construe legislation which was intended to effectuate prohibitions against States for defiance of the Constitution, to be equally applicable where a State duly obeys the Constitution, but an officer flouts State law and is unquestionably subject to punishment by the State for his disobedience. . . .

Such a distortion of federal power devised against recalcitrant State authority never entered the minds of the proponents of the legislation. [The opinion then discusses some of the legislative history of Section 20.]

Were it otherwise it would indeed be surprising. It was natural to give the shelter of the Constitution to those basic human rights for the vindication of which the successful conduct of the Civil War was the end of a long process. And the extension of federal authority so as to guard against evasion by any State of these newly created federal rights was an obvious corollary. But to attribute to Congress the making overnight of a revolutionary change in the balance of the political relations between the National Government and the States without reason, is a very different thing. And to have provided for the National Government to take over the administration of criminal justice from the States to the extent of making every lawless act of the policeman on the beat or in the station house, whether by way of third degree or the illegal ransacking for evidence in a man's house'. . . , a federal offense, would have constituted a revolutionary break with the past overnight. The desire for such a dislocation in our federal system plainly was not contemplated by the Lyman Trumbulls and the John Shermans, and not even by the Thaddeus Stevenses. . . .

. . . It may well be that Congress could, within the bounds of the Fourteenth Amendment, treat action taken by a State official even though in defiance of State law and not condoned by ultimate State authority as the action of "a State." It has never been satisfactorily explained how a State can be said to deprive a person of liberty or property without due process of law when the foundation of the claim is that a minor official has disobeyed the authentic command of his State. . . . Although action taken under such circumstances has been deemed to be deprivation by a "State" of rights guaranteed by the Fourteenth Amendment for purposes of federal jurisdiction, the doctrine has had a fluctuating and dubious history. . . .

But assuming unreservedly that conduct such as that now before us, perpetrated by State officers in flagrant defiance of State law, may be attributed to the State under the Fourteenth Amendment, this does not make it action under "color of any law." Section 20 is much narrower than the power of Congress. Even though Congress might have swept within the federal criminal law any action that could

NATIONAL PROTECTION OF CIVIL RIGHTS

be deemed within the vast reach of the Fourteenth Amendment, Congress did not do so. The presuppositions of our federal system, the pronouncements of the statesmen who shaped this legislation, and the normal meaning of language powerfully counsel against attributing to Congress intrusion into the sphere of criminal law traditionally and naturally reserved for the States alone. . . . In the absence of clear direction by Congress we should leave to the States the enforcement of their criminal law, and not relieve States of the responsibility for vindicating wrongdoing that is essentially local or weaken the habits of local law enforcement by tempting reliance on federal authority for an occasional unpleasant task of local enforcement. . . .

Since the majority of the Court do not share this conviction that the action of the Georgia peace officers was not perpetrated under color of law, we, too, must consider the constitutionality of Section 20. . . . [F]our members of the Court are of the opinion that this plain constitutional principle of definiteness in criminal statutes may be replaced by an elaborate scheme of constitutional exegesis whereby that which Congress has not defined the courts can define from time to time, with varying and conflicting definiteness in the decisions, and that, in any event, an undefined range of conduct may become sufficiently definite if only such undefined conduct is committed "willfully."

In subjecting to punishment "deprivation of any rights, privileges, or immunities secured or protected by the Constitution and laws of the United States," Section 20 on its face makes criminal deprivation of the whole range of undefined appeals to the Constitution. Such is the true scope of the forbidden conduct. Its domain is unbounded and therefore too indefinite. Criminal statutes must have more or less specific contours. This has none.

To suggest that the "right" deprivation of which is made criminal by Section 20 "has been made specific either by the express terms of the Constitution or by decisions interpreting it" hardly adds definiteness beyond that of the statute's own terms. . . . The illustrations given in the Court's opinion underline the inescapable vagueness due to the doubts and fluctuating character of decisions interpreting the Constitution.

This intrinsic vagueness of the terms of Section 20 surely cannot be removed by making the statute applicable only where the defendant has the "requisite bad purpose." Does that not amount to saying that the black heart of the defendant enables him to know what are the constitutional rights deprivation of which the statute forbids, although we as judges are not able to define their classes or their limits, or, at least, are not prepared to state what they are unless it be to say that Section 20 protects whatever rights the Constitution protects? . . .

. . . It is not denied that the Government's contention would make a potential offender against this act of any State official who as a judge admitted a confession of crime, or who as judge of a State court of last resort sustained admission of a confession, which we should later hold constitutionally inadmissible, or who as a public service commissioner issued a regulatory order which we should later hold denied due process or who as a municipal officer stopped any conduct we later should hold to be constitutionally protected. The Due Process Clause of the Fourteenth Amendment has a content the scope of which this Court determines only as cases come here from time to time and then not without close division and reversals of position. Such a dubious construction of a criminal statute should not be made unless language compels. . . .

We are told local authorities cannot be relied upon for courageous and prompt action, that often they have personal or political reasons for refusing to prosecute. If it be significantly true that crimes against local law cannot be locally prosecuted, it is an ominous sign indeed. In any event, the cure is a reinvigoration of State responsibility. It is not an undue incursion of remote federal authority into local duties with consequent debilitation of local responsibility....

Admittedly, with four different opinions discussing two hard legal questions, the *Screws* case is not easy to decipher. Approaching it from the position of looking for similarities rather than differences, however, certain conclusions stand out. At least six of the justices agreed that the Fourteenth Amendment permitted Congress to punish state officials acting in defiance of state law in depriving one of rights protected by the Amendment. Although Justice Roberts did not specifically agree, he did say that "It may well be that Congress could, within the bounds of the Fourteenth Amendment," provide punishment for such action. Six of the justices held, further, that in adopting the "color of law" statute Congress in fact intended to cover illegal state acts such as that of Sheriff Screws. On the issue of vagueness, six justices held that the statute gave adequate notice, even though the exact scope of the due process and equal protection clauses is not clearly defined and even changes from time to time. This was the main thrust of Justice Douglas' stress on the word "willfully." He indicated that this saved the statute from indefiniteness simply because it put the burden on the prosecution to prove that the right involved in any given case was one of which state officials should be aware, and that the deprivation was to this extent a knowing deprivation of right. This was in answer to the very objection made by Justice Roberts, that a judge who admits a confession of crime, later held by the United States Supreme Court to be constitutionally inadmissible, would be a potential offender against the statute. If the claim of right has not yet been recognized in the laws of Congress or in the Supreme Court's interpretations of the Constitution, then the state official who denies the claim cannot have "willfully" deprived the claimant of any right. Thus there is a crucial difference between merely doing an act intentionally and doing the same act, *knowing* that it will deprive another of a constitutional right. The judge in the confession case would fall in the former category, and there would be no "willful" deprivation of right in the statutory sense. Once a clear-cut decision has been rendered by the Supreme Court on the admissibility of such confessions, however, subsequent judges who render decisions contrary to that holding might well be subject to prosecution on the ground that they could be charged with a *willful* act to deprive the claimant of a constitutional right.

Justice Douglas, in his opinion, stated that acts of officers "in the ambit of their personal pursuits are plainly excluded" from the coverage of the statute, or, presumably, the Fourteenth Amendment. And this would seem to be an eminently reasonable delineation of the extent of coverage. To hold differently and consider every act of a state officer or employee to be "state action" subject to the Fourteenth Amendment would appear to place an intolerable burden upon both the individual employee and the state. But this raises the question of where the line is drawn between the private and the official acts of state officials. Few cases are available to illustrate the judicial view of how the distinction is to be made. The extremes of the two categories are, of course, apparent. It is the part official, part private, act which presents the difficulty.

Where an officer's acts are performed while on duty or in response to a citizen's request for some official performance of duty, it would appear that the officer's acts certainly constitute "state action." In *Catlette* v. *United States* this situation was presented in a peculiarly distasteful fashion. Two Jehovah's Witnesses went to Richwood, West Virginia, to distribute religious literature, seek converts, and get a petition signed. After having been warned by Deputy Sheriff Catlette and others to get out of town, the two men and two companions went to the city hall to request the mayor to furnish them police protection while carrying on their religious activities in the city. The mayor was absent, and their request was made to Chief of Police Stewart. Thereupon Catlette and Stewart took the men into the mayor's office. Catlette then said that what "is done from hereon will not be done in the name of the law," and removed his badge. The officers forced three of the men to drink eight ounces of castor oil each, and the fourth, because of his protests, was forced to drink sixteen ounces. These and other members of the sect were then tied in file, marched to their cars, and given their personal property, which had been covered with castor oil and uncomplimentary inscriptions, and advised never to return.

Catlette was prosecuted under Section 20 of the Criminal Code for deprivations of constitutional rights while acting under color of law. He defended on the ground that in view of his statement and the removal of his badge, the acts were committed in his private and not his official capacity, and that therefore such acts were not "under color of any law." The trial court was not impressed with this argument, and he was convicted by the jury. On appeal, Judge Dobie, speaking for the Court of Appeals in *Catlette* v. *United States*, 132 F.2d 902, 906 (4th Cir. 1943), stated on this point:

We must condemn this insidious suggestion that an officer may thus lightly shuffle off his official role. To accept such a legalistic dualism would gut the constitutional safeguards and render law enforcement a shameful mockery.

In a later case involving essentially the same question, the Court of Appeals for another circuit held in similar fashion. In this case the Government obtained the conviction of Tom Crews, a Florida county constable, on the charge of violating the same Section 20, now 18 U.S.C. 242. Crews "arrested" a Negro farmhand on the grounds of drunkenness, proceeded to beat him with a bullwhip, and ultimately forced him to jump into the Suwanee River where he was drowned. Crews appealed his conviction, claiming that his act was purely one of personal vengeance and was devoid of official character and authority, in that he was off duty and out of uniform. In *Crews* v. *United States*, 160 F.2d 746, 750 (5th Cir. 1947), the three judges of the Court of Appeals unanimously rejected this argument, stating, through Judge Waller:

An officer of the law should not be permitted to divest himself of his official authority in actions taken by him wherein he acts, or purports, or pretends, to act pursuant to his authority, and where one, known by another to be an officer, takes the other into custody in a manner which appears on its face to be in the exercise of authority of law, without making to the other any disclosure to the contrary, such officer thereby justifies the conclusion that he was acting under color of law in making such an arrest.

Thus, as Professor Robert Carr so ably stated the rule, "When an officer uses his official position as a means of gaining physical control over his victim, further evidence that his actions were in good part unofficial cannot interfere with the conclusion that he acted under color of law." [Robert Carr, *Federal Protection of Civil Rights* (Ithaca: Cornell University Press, 1947), p. 175.]

Suppose, however, that an officer takes an off-duty job as investigator or guard over private property. Would his acts in such related police capacity constitute "state action"? The answer is less easily determined than in the *Catlette* and *Crews* cases and seems to hinge on the specific facts in each case. The most notable case in this area to reach the United States Supreme Court is *Williams* v. *United States*, 341 U.S. 97 (1951). A Florida lumber company, having suffered numerous thefts, hired Williams, who operated a detective agency, to find the thieves. He held a special police officer's card issued by the City of Miami and had taken an oath and qualified as a special police officer. Williams and others over a period of three days took four men to a paint shack on the company's premises and used brutal methods to obtain a confession from each of them. One Ford, a policeman, was sent by his superior to lend authority to the proceedings. And Williams, who committed the assaults, went about flashing his badge.

The indictment charged a violation of Section 20 (now 18 U.S.C. 242) in that Williams, acting under color of law, used force to make each victim confess and that the victims were denied the right to be tried by due process of law. He was found guilty by a jury under instructions which conformed with the ruling of the Court in *Screws* v. *United States*. On certiorari, the Court affirmed the conviction. Justice Douglas, speaking for the majority, stated:

[T] his was an investigation conducted under the aegis of the state, as evidenced by the fact that a regular police officer was detailed to attend it. . . . There was, therefore, evidence that he acted under authority of Florida law; and the manner of his conduct of the interrogations makes clear that he was asserting the authority granted him and not acting in the role of a private person. In any event the charge to the jury drew the line between official and unofficial conduct which we explored in *Screws* v. *United States* ..., and gave petitioner all of the protection which "color of law" as used in Section 20 offers.

The opinion then pointed out that while the right involved might be doubtful in other situations, no such difficulty was presented in the instant case. "It is as plain as a pikestaff that the present confessions would not be allowed in evidence whatever the school of thought concerning the scope and meaning of the Due Process Clause." On the issue of whether the deprivation was "willful," Justice Douglas quoted with approval the trial judge's charge to the jury:

The trial judge charged in part on this phase of the case: "The law denies to anyone acting under color of law ... the right to try a person by ordeal; that is, for the officer himself to inflict such punishment upon the person as he thinks the person should receive. Now in determining whether this requisite of willful intent was present in this case as to these counts, you gentlemen are entitled to consider all the attendant circumstances; the malice, if any, of the defendants toward these men; the weapon used in the assault, if any; and the character and duration of the investigation, if any, of the assault, and the time and manner in which it was carried out. All these facts and circumstances may be taken into consideration from the evidence that has been submitted for the purpose of determining whether the acts of the defendants were willful and for the deliberate and willful purpose of depriving these men of their Constitutional rights to be tried by a jury just like everyone else."

Another facet of the problem of delineating state action appears in the classification of the privately owned and managed operation which receives direct financial aid from the state. Is the act of such an agency an act of the state or is it a private act for purposes of the Fourteenth Amendment? Obviously, a categorical answer to the question is impossible. It would be a rather far-fetched doctrine which would consider as state agents all people on relief, unemployed persons benefiting under state compensation plans, persons on state retirement pensions, or all companies which profit from ordinary contract arrangements with the state. On the other hand, there are operations which might have begun as purely private, but which have become so enmeshed with the agencies of state government through grants or other special governmental treatment that they take on the character of state institutions. These, perhaps, should be considered as state agencies for the purposes of the Fourteenth Amendment.

In 1945 a question was raised concerning the status of the Enoch Pratt Free Library of Baltimore. Kerr, a Negro, sued for damages and an injunction on complaint that she was refused admission to a library training class conducted by the library to prepare persons for staff positions in the central library and its branches. She charged that the library was performing a governmental function, that she was rejected solely because of race, and that such rejection constituted state action prohibited by the Fourteenth Amendment. The library defended on the ground that it was a private corporation.

The library was established by Pratt in 1882. He erected a building and established a fund and gave them to the City of Baltimore on condition that the city would create a perpetual annuity of $50,000 for maintaining the library and branches. In giving legal effect to the terms of the gift, the Maryland legislature passed a statute and the city passed three ordinances. The real and personal property vested in the city by virtue of the act, as well as later acquisitions, were exempted from state and city taxes. In addition to the $50,000 annually appropriated, much greater sums were required to meet demands for increased services. In 1943 and 1944 more than half a million dollars were appropriated. In addition, the city paid large sums for bond interest, bond retirement, and the retirement funds for the library's employees. Salary checks were issued by the city's payroll officer and charged against the library's appropriation. The library budget was included in the regular city budget, and library employees were included within the municipal employees' retirement system.

In *Kerr* v. *Enoch Pratt Free Library*, 149 F.2d 212 (4th Cir. 1945) [*cert. denied*, 326 U.S. 721 (1945)], the Court of Appeals held that the library's action was state action within the meaning of the Fourteenth Amendment. The two criteria stressed by the court were control by the state over the library's activities and the volume or importance of governmental financial assistance afforded. The opinion indicated no line of demarcation to aid in determining how far along the spectrum from zero to complete control or complete financial support the state must go before the activity becomes that of the state. Nor is it easy to see where such a line can be drawn.

The state may aid a private operation in various ways other than by direct financial assistance. It may give the organization the power of eminent domain, it may grant tax exemptions, or it may give it a monopolistic status for certain purposes. Does the receipt of such assistance convert the organization into a state agency? According to Justice Harlan, in his dissent in the *Civil Rights Cases*, it would, especially if the state acquired special control powers in return.

One of the most thoroughly argued cases on the point to date is the case of *Dorsey* v. *Stuyvesant Town Corporation*, 299 N.Y. 512, 87 N.E.2d 541 (1949) [*cert. denied*, 339 U.S. 981 (1950)], decided by the New York Court of Appeals. Stuyvesant Town was built as an apartment housing development pursuant to a contract between the City of New York, Metropolitan Insurance Company, and its wholly owned subsidiary, Stuyvesant. Stuyvesant was organized under the state's Redevelopment Companies Law of 1942, as amended. The purpose of the law was to encourage private companies to enter the housing field. Under that law, the City of New York, by eminent domain, brought under one good title an area of eighteen blocks in the city, the area having been declared one of substandard housing. Stuyvesant acquired the property, including certain streets which the city had agreed to close, by paying to the city the cost of acquiring land

and buildings. The agreement provided that Stuyvesant would demolish the old buildings and construct new ones without expense to the city, and the city granted the corporation a twenty-five year tax exemption to the extent of the enhanced value to be created by the project. Certain writers estimated the total tax exemption to reach approximately $50,000,000. [See Walter J. Blum and Norman Bursler, "Tax Subsidies for Rental Housing," 15 *U. Chi. L. Rev.* 255, 269, n.22 (1948).] The project represented an investment of about $90,000,000 of private funds by the Metropolitan Insurance Company. No state law barred the owner or operator of this project from discriminating, racially or otherwise, in his choice of tenants. While repeated attempts had been made in the state legislature to amend the redevelopment law to bar racial discrimination, all had failed as of that time. Although the matter was discussed in the city council, the agreement reached contained no bar to practice of racial discrimination by the landlord. When finally completed, the project housed approximately twenty-five thousand persons. The contract gave the city the right to regulate rents and certain auditing privileges, and prohibited the mortgage or sale of the property.

Dorsey, a Negro, was refused tenancy because of race and sued to enjoin Stuyvesant from denying accommodations because of race on the ground that to do so was in violation of the Fourteenth Amendment. The issue presented was whether the city's assistance in the form of eminent domain and tax exemptions and its reserved control over the housing operation made the Stuyvesant Corporation a state instrumentality within the meaning of the Fourteenth Amendment. By the narrow margin of four-to-three the New York Court of Appeals held that Stuyvesant was not a state agency for purposes of the Fourteenth Amendment. The United States Supreme Court denied certiorari. The majority opinion stated that to argue that the housing development was barred from racial discrimination "on the ground that helpful co-operation between the State and the respondents transforms the activities of the latter into state action, comes perilously close to asserting that any State assistance to an organization which discriminates necessarily violates the Fourteenth Amendment." The dissenters argued that the degree of involvement by the city in the project was such that the requisite state action was present to invoke the prohibitions of the Fourteenth Amendment.

Burton v. *Wilmington Parking Authority*, 365 U.S. 715 (1961), dealt tangentially with the question of whether a lessee of state property who opens his business to the public comes within the Fourteenth Amendment's bar to racial discrimination. A parking building was owned and operated by the Parking Authority, an agency of the State of Delaware. It leased a portion of the building to a private corporation for the establishment of a restaurant. Plaintiff brought an action for declaratory and injunctive relief on the ground that the restaurant's racially discriminatory policy was state action barred by the Fourteenth Amendment. The Delaware Supreme Court held that the restaurant was operating in a purely private capacity and denied the relief. The United States Supreme Court reversed. Justice Clark, speaking for the majority, examined the lease arrangements and concluded:

Addition of all these activities, obligations and responsibilities of the Authority, the benefits mutually conferred, together with the obvious fact that the restaurant is operated as an integral part of a public building devoted to a public parking service, indicates that degree of state participation and involvement in discriminatory action which it was the design of the Fourteenth Amendment to condemn. It is irony amounting to grave injustice that in one part of a single building, erected and maintained with public funds by an agency of the State to serve a public purpose, all persons have equal rights, while in another portion, also serving the public, a Negro is a second-class citizen, offensive because of his race. . . . [N]o State may effectively abdicate its responsibilities by either ignoring them or by merely failing to discharge them whatever the motive may be. . . . By its inaction, the Authority, and through it the State, has not only made itself a party to the refusal of service, but has elected to place its power, property and prestige behind the admitted discrimination. . . .

The opinion went on to state, however, that the conclusions drawn from this case were by no means "universal truths on the basis of which every state leasing agreement is to be tested."

Yet another question concerning the application of the Fourteenth Amendment is whether it can properly reach deprivations of rights which occur because of the *inaction* of a state official. An affirmative answer was indicated in the *Burton* opinion, above, as well as in some of the white primary cases, e.g., *Terry* v. *Adams*, 345 U.S. 461 (1953). But the Court has not squarely ruled on this specific point. Good illustrations are to be found in some of the cases reaching federal courts of appeals, however. In *Catlette* v. *United States*, discussed earlier, a group of Jehovah's Witnesses were refused the police protection they requested while engaged in religious activities. On the issue of whether the Fourteenth Amendment and 18 U.S.C. Section 52 (now Section 242) could apply to inaction of state officials the opinion stated:

And since the failure of Catlette to protect the victims from group violence or to arrest the members of the mob who assaulted the victims constituted a violation of his common law duty, his dereliction in this respect comes squarely within the provisions of 18 U.S.C.A. Section 52.

It is true that a denial of equal protection has hitherto been largely confined to affirmative acts of discrimination. The Supreme Court, however, has already taken the position that culpable official State inaction may also constitute a denial of equal protection.

In *Lynch* v. *United States*, 189 F.2d 476 (5th Cir. 1951), a federal court of appeals reviewed the conviction of a Georgia sheriff who had allowed

Negro prisoners in his custody to be kidnapped and beaten by a Ku Klux Klan local. The sheriff claimed that he had been overpowered, but evidence was introduced which was sufficient to convince the jury that even if he didn't cooperate, he did nothing to apprehend or punish the offenders. The court of appeals upheld the conviction unanimously, the opinion stating, "There was a time when the denial of equal protection of the laws was confined to affirmative acts, but the law now is that culpable official inaction may also constitute a denial of equal protection."

It may be seen from the previous analysis that the concept of what constitutes state action is a broad one. And intentional denial by state action of the rights protected by the Fourteenth Amendment can be the subject of remedial legislation by Congress, as provided by the enforcement section of that amendment. Yet even today, despite the importance of recent civil rights acts, the century-old "color of law" statute, Section 242 of Title 18, remains as one of the most important federal criminal provisions applicable to state deprivations of civil rights. Congress is not restricted to criminal provisions in protecting rights, of course, and may offer appropriate civil remedies as well. As a companion piece to Section 242 there are civil provisions applicable to "color of law" deprivations in Section 1983 of Title 42 of the United States Code.

Section 1983. Civil action for deprivation of rights

Every person who, under color of any statute, ordinance, regulation, custom, or usage, of any State or Territory, subjects or causes to be subjected, any citizen of the United States or other person within the jurisdiction thereof to the deprivation of any rights, privileges, or immunities secured by the Constitution and laws, shall be liable to the party injured in an action at law, suit in equity, or other proper proceeding for redress.

Since this section provides for suits for damages, injunctions, or special orders appropriate to the occasion, it is the key jurisdictional basis for litigation in federal courts seeking relief for state deprivations of federal rights. Most of the important segregation questions initiated in the federal courts, for example, have been partially or wholly Section 1983 actions. While normally the suit is for an injunction to halt the objectionable practice, the plaintiff may choose to sue for money damages under the section. In *Monroe* v. *Pape*, 365 U.S. 167 (1961), the Court examined the application of Section 1983 to an illegal search and seizure committed by municipal police. The complaint alleged that thirteen Chicago police officers broke into petitioners' home in the early morning, routed them from bed, made them stand naked in the living room, and ransacked every room, emptying drawers and ripping mattress covers. It further alleged that Mr. Monroe was then taken to the police station, detained for ten hours, interrogated about a recent murder, refused permission to call his family or his attorney, and finally released without charges preferred against him. A suit for damages was brought against the thirteen officers and the City of Chicago under Section 1983. The district court dismissed the complaint, and the court of appeals affirmed. The United States Supreme Court held that Congress did not intend in this act to make municipalities liable for injuries caused by their officers, but it further held that the section did provide remedies against the kind of state action alleged in the complaint, and thus the trial court should not have dismissed.

In addition to the sections already discussed, in the period following the Civil War Congress passed a number of other statutes designed to protect civil rights. The Thirteenth Amendment was ratified in 1865, the Fourteenth in 1868, and the Fifteenth in 1870, all three containing enforcement clauses. During the years 1866–1875 Congress adopted seven broad civil rights statutes with a variety of sections outlining specific rights. These ranged from antipeonage provisions to prohibitions against denial of equal accommodations in inns—the section involved in the *Civil Rights Cases*. In less than thirty years after the passage of the last act, the program had ended in failure. [See Eugene Gressman, "The Unhappy History of Civil Rights Legislation," 50 *Mich. L. Rev.* 1323 (1952).] This failure was attributable to three causes: (1) Several key provisions were held unconstitutional by the United States Supreme Court. (2) Congress repealed a number of other provisions. (3) Administrative officers charged with enforcement were reluctant to use the authority remaining to them after the action of the Court and Congress.

The antipeonage provisions still remain, as 18 U.S.C. Sections 1581, 1583, and 1584. [See Sydney Brodie, "The Federally Secured Right to be Free from Bondage." 40 *Geo. L. J.* 367 (1952).] In addition to these, there are only three important criminal sections which survive. Section 242 has been discussed in some detail. Another, Section 243 of Title 18, makes it a criminal offense "for any officer or any person charged with any duty in the selection or summoning of jurors" to discriminate on grounds of race or color in the summoning of any citizen for service on federal or state juries. This is the section which was used in the prosecution of a Virginia judge in the case leading to *Ex parte Virginia*. The third remaining provision is Section 241 of Title 18, formerly Section 19 of the Criminal Code. In its present form it states:

Section 241. Conspiracy against rights of citizens.

If two or more persons conspire to injure, oppress, threaten, or intimidate any citizen in the free exercise or enjoyment of any right or privilege secured to him by the Constitution or laws of the United States, or because of his having so exercised the same; or

If two or more persons go in disguise on the highway, or on the premises of another, with intent to prevent or hinder his free exercise or enjoyment of any right or privilege so secured—

They shall be fined not more than $5,000 or imprisoned not more than ten years, or both.

It should be noted that Section 241 defines a felony with considerably stiffer penalties than are provided in Section 242, which defines a misdemeanor. Further, Section 241 does not require a finding of official action or action taken "under color of law." It is clear, then, that it was intended to reach certain kinds of acts of private persons. Two questions remain, however. First, what kinds of private acts are prohibited by the section? Second, can the section be employed against *officials* who engage in the proscribed conduct?

As to the first question, the previous analysis has already shown that the only kind of private action which can constitutionally be reached by the Congress is the interference with a federal right. As indicated, such rights are those created by Congress or arising out of the special relationship of national government to the individual. Thus private interference with an ordinary lawful speech or assembly could not be punishable under Section 241, but private interference with the attempt to vote in a federal election could properly be brought under its coverage, as in *Ex parte Yarbrough,* above.

The second question presents somewhat greater difficulties. There appear to be three possible approaches to the application of Section 241 to official action: (1) since Section 242 specifically covers acts "under color of law," to avoid duplication Section 241 logically should apply *only* to private acts; (2) Section 241 *can* be applied to officials, but since the primary purpose of the section was to reach private acts, it can reach only the kinds of interference for which Congress can punish private persons and does not extend to the full range of rights protected by the due process and equal protection clauses; or (3) Section 241 may be employed against official action as well as private action, and with respect to the former it extends to any deprivation for which Congress may constitutionally punish state officers. In effect, this last approach would mean that with respect to conspiracies including state officers, Section 241 would overlap Section 242 completely and offer substantially greater penalties in the bargain.

This question was discussed at length in *United States* v. *Williams,* 341 U.S. 70 (1951), but on this issue the Court split four-to-four and the question remained unresolved. This was a companion case to *Williams* v. *United States,* discussed earlier (arising out of a Section 242 prosecution), and was a prosecution for violation of Section 241. Justice Frankfurter, speaking for himself and three others, examined the legislative history of Section 241 and concluded that the rights which it protects "are those which Congress can beyond doubt constitutionally secure against interference by private individuals." He further examined the previous cases making the distinction between "rights that flow from the substantive powers of the Federal Government and may clearly be protected from private interference, and interests which the Constitution only guarantees from interference by States." He concluded that Section 241 does not extend "to rights which the Federal Constitution merely guarantees against abridgment by the States."

Four other members of the Court, taking the "plain words" approach to interpreting the statute, found no basis for making the differentiation stated by Justice Frankfurter. They felt that since the language was so similar the rights guarded by Sections 241 and 242 were identical when state officials were involved in the deprivation.

The definitive answer to the question was not given until 1966 when the Court handed down decisions in two important cases involving prosecutions under Sections 241 and 242. The first case was *United States* v. *Guest,* 383 U.S. 745 (1966), involving a Section 241 prosecution of six private persons. The second case was *United States* v. *Price,* 383 U.S. 787 (1966), involving prosecutions under both Section 241 and Section 242 of a group of eighteen persons, some of whom were private persons and some of whom were state officials.

The *Guest* case held that Section 241, as applied to private defendants only, may be construed to reach deprivation of Fourteenth Amendment rights, as well as those running against private interference, if the finding is made that state involvement was present leading to the constitutional violation. The *Price* case held that (1) where a conspiracy between private persons and state officials is charged, Secton 241 may properly be applied to both categories of defendants, and (2) in such case the measure of the rights protected by the section is the broader coverage of rights guaranteed against interference by state officials, on the ground that the joint state-private action makes the conduct of all defendants state action, and (3) on the same theory, Section 242 may properly be applied to all such defendants as acting "under color of law."

In *United States* v. *Guest,* six private persons were indicted, under Section 241, for a conspiracy to deprive Negro citizens of the free exercise and enjoyment of (1) the right to accommodations of motion picture theaters, restaurants, and other such places of public accommodation; (2) the right to equal utilization of public facilities operated by the state or any subdivision thereof; (3) the right to the use on the same terms as white citizens of the public streets and highways in the state; and (4) the right to travel freely to and from the state. Upon motion of the defendants the district court dismissed the indictment. Upon appeal, the Supreme Court held that it had no jurisdiction to review the first paragraph on direct appeal (because the dismissal was rested on defective pleading) but reversed the judgment as to the other paragraphs. As to the second paragraph of the indictment, it was argued that since there exist no "equal protection" clause rights against wholly private action, the judgment of the district court on this phase of the case must be affirmed. Speaking for the majority, Justice Stewart said, "On its face, the argument is unexceptionable. The Equal Protection Clause speaks to the State or to those acting under the color of its authority." He stated that from the beginning, it has been the view of the Court that the Fourteenth Amendment protects the individual against *state action,* not against wrongs done by *individuals,* and "It remains the Court's view today." But he stated further:

This is not to say, however, that the involvement of the State need be either exclusive or direct. In a variety of situations the Court has found state action of a nature sufficient to create rights under the Equal Protection Clause even though the participation of the State was peripheral, or its action was only one of several co-operative forces leading to the constitutional violation. . . .

This case, however, requires no determination of the threshold level that state action must attain in order to create rights under the Equal Protection Clause. This is so because, contrary to the argument of the litigants, the indictment in fact contains an express allegation of state involvement sufficient at least to require the denial of a motion to dismiss. One of the means of accomplishing the object of the conspiracy, according to the indictment, was "By causing the arrest of Negroes by means of false reports that such Negroes had committed criminal acts.". . . [T]he allegation is broad enough to cover a charge of active connivance by agents of the State in the making of the "false reports," or other conduct amounting to official discrimination clearly sufficient to constitute denial of rights protected by the Equal Protection Clause. Although it is possible that a bill of particulars, or the proofs if the case goes to trial, would disclose no co-operative action of that kind by officials of the State, the allegation is enough to prevent dismissal of this branch of the indictment.

The opinion combined the third and fourth paragraphs for discussion of the right to travel in interstate commerce. Justice Stewart stated that it was a right that has been "firmly established and repeatedly recognized" as a basic right under the Constitution. And in a footnote to his discussion of the previous cases on the point, he said, "Although these cases in fact involved governmental interference with the right of free interstate travel, their reasoning fully supports the conclusion that the constitutional right of interstate travel is a right secured against interference from any source whatever, whether governmental or private." He pointed out, however, that "A specific intent to interfere with the federal right must be proved, and at a trial the defendants are entitled to a jury instruction phrased in those terms."

Justice Clark filed a concurring opinion, joined by Justices Black and Fortas. He stated that the Court's opinion "clearly avoids the question whether Congress, by appropriate legislation, has the power to punish private conspiracies that interfere with Fourteenth Amendment rights, such as the right to utilize public facilities." In order to clear up any doubts on this point relative to his position he stated that it was "both appropriate and necessary under the circumstances here to say that there now can be no doubt that the specific language of Section 5 [of the Fourteenth Amendment] empowers the Congress to enact laws punishing all conspiracies—with or without state action—that interfere with Fourteenth Amendment rights."

Justice Brennan, joined by the Chief Justice and Justice Douglas, concurred in part and dissented in part. He stated that he did not agree with that part of the opinion dealing with the second paragraph "which holds, as I read the opinion, that a conspiracy to interfere with the exercise of the right to equal utilization of state facilities is not, within the meaning of Section 241, a conspiracy to interfere with the exercise of a 'right ... secured ... by the Constitution' unless discriminatory conduct by state officers is involved in the alleged conspiracy." He stated that a majority of six members of the Court agreed that Section 5 empowers Congress to enact laws punishing *all* conspiracies to interfere with the exercise of Fourteenth Amendment rights, whether or not state officers or others acting under the color of state law are implicated in the conspiracy. (He included those joining his opinion and those concurring with Justice Clark's opinion.) In brief, he argued that a given right having been set up by the Fourteenth Amendment, it could be protected against interference by anyone, even though the terms of the Amendment limit its application to state acts. He seemingly argued that it was permissible to limit *judicial* enforcement of the Fourteenth Amendment to the area of state action, but that Congress under Section 5 of the same Amendment could reach private interference with these rights as well.

The ramifications of this approach are of substantial import, for it could point to the eclipse of the state action doctrine as a meaningful limitation on Congress' power to protect civil rights. The result would be a very substantial broadening of national legislative power in this area.

In the *Price* case, decided on the same day as the *Guest* case, the Court considered on direct appeal the dismissal of federal indictments arising out of the notorious murders of three civil rights workers in the state of Mississippi in 1964.

UNITED STATES *v.* PRICE

383 U.S. 787 (1966)

Mr. Justice Fortas delivered the opinion of the Court.

These are direct appeals from the dismissal in part of two indictments returned by the United States Grand Jury for the Southern District of Mississippi. The indictments allege assaults by the accused persons upon the rights of the asserted victims to due process of law under the Fourteenth Amendment. The indictment in No. 59 charges 18 persons with violations of 18 USC Section 241 (1964 ed.). In No. 60, the same 18 persons are charged with offenses based upon 18 USC Section 242 (1964 ed.). These are among the so-called civil rights statutes which have come to us from Reconstruction days....

The sole question presented in these appeals is whether the specified statutes make criminal the conduct for which the individuals were indicted. It is an issue of construction, not of constitutional power....

The events upon which the charges are based, as alleged in the indictments, are as follows: On June 21, 1964, Cecil Ray Price, the Deputy Sheriff of Neshoba County, Mississippi, detained Michael Henry Schwerner, James Earl Chaney and

Andrew Goodman in the Neshoba County jail located in Philadelphia, Mississippi. He released them in the dark of that night. He then proceeded by automobile on Highway 19 to intercept his erstwhile wards. He removed the three men from their automobile, placed them in an official automobile of the Neshoba County Sheriff's office, and transported them to a place on an unpaved road.

[The indictment further alleged that these acts were a part of a conspiracy on the part of the 18 defendants to "punish" the three men, and that the three were unlawfully assaulted, shot and killed. The bodies were then transported to an earthen dam some five miles from Philadelphia, Mississippi.]

These are federal and not state indictments. They do not charge as crimes the alleged assaults or murders. The indictments are framed to fit the stated federal statutes, and the question before us is whether . . . the indictments charge offenses against the various defendants which may be prosecuted under the designated federal statutes. . . .

The indictment in No. 60 contains four counts, each of which names as defendants the three officials and 15 nonofficial persons. The First Count charges, on the basis of allegations substantially as set forth above, that all of the defendants conspired "to wilfully subject" Schwerner, Chaney and Goodman "to the deprivation of their right, privilege and immunity secured and protected by the Fourteenth Amendment of the Constitution of the United States not to be summarily punished without due process of law by persons acting under color of the laws of the State of Mississippi." This is said to constitute a conspiracy to violate Section 242, and therefore an offense under 18 USC Section 371. The latter section, the general conspiracy statute, makes it a crime to conspire to commit any offense against the United States. The penalty for violation is the same as for direct violation of Section 242—that is, it would be a misdemeanor.

On a motion to dismiss, the District Court sustained this First Count as to all defendants. As to the sheriff, deputy sheriff and patrolman, the court recognized that each was clearly alleged to have been acting "under color of law" as required by Section 242. As to the private persons, the District Court held that "[I]t is immaterial to the conspiracy that these private individuals were not acting under color of law" because the count charges that they were conspiring with persons who were so acting. . . .

No appeal was taken by the defendants from the decision of the trial court with respect to the First Count and it is not before us for adjudication.

The Second, Third and Fourth Counts of the indictment in No. 60 charge all of the defendants, not with conspiracy, but with substantive violations of Section 242. Each of these counts charges that the defendants, acting "under color of the laws of the State of Mississippi," "did wilfully assault, shoot and kill" Schwerner, Chaney and Goodman, respectively, "for the purpose and with the intent" of punishing each of the three and that the defendants "did thereby wilfully deprive" each "of rights, privileges and immunities secured and protected by the Constitution and the laws of the United States"—namely, due process of law.

The District Court held these counts of the indictment valid as to the sheriff, deputy sheriff and patrolman. But it dismissed them as against the nonofficial defendants because the counts do not charge that the latter were "officers in fact, or de facto in anything allegedly done by them 'under color of law.' "

We note that by sustaining these counts against the three officers, the court again necessarily concluded that an offense under Section 242 is properly stated by allegations of willful deprivation, under color of law, of life and liberty without due process of law. We agree. No other result would be permissible under the decisions of this Court. *Screws* v. *United States.* ...

But we cannot agree that the Second, Third or Fourth Counts may be dismissed as against the nonofficial defendants. Section 242 applies only where a person indicted has acted "under color" of law. Private persons, jointly engaged with state officials in the prohibited action, are acting "under color" of law for purposes of the statute. To act "under color" of law does not require that the accused be an officer of the State. It is enough that he is a willful participant in joint activity with the State or its agents.

In the present case, according to the indictment, the brutal joint adventure was made possible by state detention and calculated release of the prisoners by an officer of the State. ... Those who took advantage of participation by state officers in accomplishment of the foul purpose alleged must suffer the consequences of that participation. In effect, if the allegations are true, they were participants in official lawlessness, acting in willful concert with state officers and hence under color of law. ...

Accordingly, we reverse the dismissal of the Second, Third and Fourth Counts of the indictment in No. 60 and remand for trial.

No. 59 charges each of the 18 defendants with a felony—a violation of Section 241. This indictment is in one count. It charges that the defendants "conspired together ... to injure, oppress, threaten and intimidate" Schwerner, Chaney and Goodman "in the free exercise and enjoyment of the right and privilege secured to them by the Fourteenth Amendment to the Constitution of the United States not to be deprived of life or liberty without due process of law by persons acting under color of the laws of Mississippi." ... The penalty under Section 241 is a fine of not more than $5,000 or imprisonment for not more than 10 years, or both. ...

The District Court dismissed the indictment as to all defendants. In effect, although Section 241 includes "rights or privileges secured by the Constitution or laws of the United States" without qualification or limitation, the Court held that it does not include rights protected by the Fourteenth Amendment. ...

But the District Court purported to read the statutes with the gloss of *Williams I* [341 U.S. 70 (1951)]. In that case, the only case in which this Court has squarely confronted the point at issue, the Court did in fact sustain dismissal of an indictment under Section 241. But it did not, as the District Court incorrectly assumed, hold that Section 241 is inapplicable to Fourteenth Amendment rights. The Court divided equally on the issue. Four Justices, in an opinion by Mr. Justice Frankfurter, were of the view that Section 241 "only covers conduct which interferes with rights arising from the substantive powers of the Federal Government" —rights "which Congress can beyond doubt constitutionally secure against interference by private individuals." ... Four other Justices, in an opinion by Mr. Justice Douglas, found no support for Mr. Justice Frankfurter's view in the language of the section, its legislative history, or its judicial interpretation up to that time. They read the statute as plainly covering conspiracies to injure others in the exercise of Fourteenth Amendment rights. ... *Williams I* thus left the proper construction of Section 241, as regards its applicability to protect Fourteenth Amendment rights, an open question.

... On the basis of an extensive re-examination of the question, we conclude that the District Court erred; that Section 241 must be read as it is written—to reach conspiracies "to injure . . . any citizen in the free exercise or enjoyment of any right or privilege secured to him by the Constitution or laws of the United States . . ."; that this language includes rights or privileges protected by the Fourteenth Amendment; that whatever the ultimate coverage of the section may be, it extends to conspiracies otherwise within the scope of the section, participated in by officials alone or in collaboration with private persons; and that the indictment in No. 59 properly charges such a conspiracy in violation of Section 241. . . .

[Here follows an examination of the language and the purposes of the statute.]

In this context, it is hardly conceivable that Congress intended Section 241 to apply only to a narrow and relatively unimportant category of rights. We cannot doubt that the purpose and effect of Section 241 was to reach assaults upon rights under the entire Constitution, including the Thirteenth, Fourteenth and Fifteenth Amendments, and not merely under part of it. . . .

The present application of the statutes at issue does not raise fundamental questions of federal-state relationships. We are here concerned with allegations which squarely and indisputably involve state action in direct violation of the mandate of the Fourteenth Amendment—that no State shall deprive any person of life or liberty without due process of law. . . . In any event, the problem, being statutory and not constitutional, is ultimately, as it was in the beginning, susceptible of congressional disposition.

Reversed and remanded.

[Mr. Justice Black concurs in the judgment and opinion of the Court except insofar as the opinion relies upon the *Williams* cases.]

It has been seen that Section 242 of the Criminal Code has its civil counterpart in Section 1983 of Title 42 of the United States Code. Similarly, there is a civil provision, Section 1985 (3) of Title 42, which is drawn in somewhat the same language as Section 241 of the Criminal Code. It is not really a twin section, however, since the types of deprivations covered are not identical. Both Section 241 and Section 1985 (3) refer to conspiracies, but they are conspiracies to accomplish somewhat different purposes.

Section 1985 (3). Conspiracies: to deprive citizens of rights or privileges.

If two or more persons in any State or Territory conspire or go in disguise on the highway or on the premises of another, for the purpose of depriving, either directly or indirectly, any person or class of persons of the equal protection of the laws, or of equal privileges and immunities under the laws; or for the purpose of preventing or hindering the constituted authorities of any State or Territory from giving or securing to all persons within such State or Territory the equal protection of the laws; or if two or more persons conspire to prevent by force, intimidation, or threat, any citizen who is lawfully entitled to vote, from giving his support or advocacy in a legal manner, toward or in favor of the election of any lawfully qualified person as an elector for President or Vice President, or as a Member of Congress of the United States; or to injure any citizen in person or property on account of such support or advocacy; in any case of conspiracy set forth in this section, if one or more persons engaged therein do, or cause to be done, any act in furtherance of the object of such conspiracy, whereby another is injured in his person or property, or deprived of having and exercising any right or privilege of a citizen of the United States, the party so injured or deprived may have an action for the recovery of damages occasioned by such injury or deprivation, against any one or more of the conspirators.

It should be noted that the section is narrower in scope than Section 241. Except for those clauses dealing with voting rights, Section 1985(3) is limited to deprivations of "equal protection of the laws" or "equal privileges and immunities under the law." It is harder to determine liability under such language than it is to find deprivation of "any right or privilege" secured by the Constitution or laws of the United States, as provided in Section 241. Further, Section 1985(3) provides only for an action to recover damages, and not equitable relief. In *Collins* v. *Hardyman*, 341 U.S. 641 (1951), the Court construed the statute as reaching only conspiracies under color of state law. In *Griffin* v. *Breckenridge*, 403 U.S. 88 (1971), the Court extended its application to purely private conspiracies aimed at invidiously discriminatory deprivation of the equal enjoyment of rights secured to all by law. Petitioners, Negro citizens of Mississippi, alleged that while travelling on the highway in an automobile driven by one Grady, a citizen of Tennessee, the white respondents, pursuant to a conspiracy, blocked the travellers' passage on the public highways, forced them from the car, held them at bay with firearms, and amidst threats of murder clubbed them, inflicting serious physical injury. They sued for damages under Section 1985(3). The District Court and the Court of Appeals, relying on *Collins* v. *Hardyman*, held that the complaint should be dismissed for failure to allege state action. The Supreme Court unanimously reversed. Justice Stewart, speaking for the Court, stated:

. . . On their face, the words of the statute fully encompass the conduct of private persons. The provision speaks simply of "two or more persons in any State or Territory" who "conspire or go in disguise on the highway or on the premises of another." Going in disguise, in particular, is in this context an activity so little associated with official action and so commonly connected with private marauders that this clause could almost never be applicable under the artificially restrictive construction of *Collins*. And since the "going in disguise" aspect must include private action, it is hard to see how the conspiracy aspect, joined by a disjunctive, could be read to require the involvement of state officers. . . . [The opinion then examines the section's companion statutory provisions, concluding that to read into 1985(3) a state action requirement would be unwarranted, since it would result in simply duplicating the coverage of one or more of the companion provisions. It further examined the legislative history of the section and concluded that Congress intended coverage of private action.]
It is thus evident that all indicators—text, companion provisions, and legislative history—point unwaveringly to §1985(3)'s coverage of private conspiracies. That

the statute was meant to reach private action does not, however, mean that it was intended to apply to all tortious, conspiratorial interferences with the rights of others. . . . The language requiring intent to deprive of *equal* protection, or *equal* privileges and immunities, means that there must be some racial, or perhaps otherwise class-based, invidiously discriminatory animus behind the conspirators' action. The conspiracy, in other words, must aim at a deprivation of the equal enjoyment of rights secured by the law to all. . . . .

As for the constitutional basis for the remedy against private conspiracies to deny Negroes their equal rights, the Court stated that the Thirteenth Amendment afforded ample power to Congress. Further, there was the allegation that one member was from another state, and the Court has "firmly established that the right of interstate travel is constitutionally protected, does not necessarily rest on the Fourteenth Amendment, and is assertable against private as well as governmental interference."

It would appear that the *Griffin* decision offers an important new weapon for identifiable minority groups to attempt to redress injuries inflicted by private action and motivated by "invidiously discriminatory animus."

The two criminal and two civil sections discussed represent the most important statutory provisions in the federal code applicable to the general field of civil rights down to the year 1957. Many complaints were voiced that additional federal remedies were needed, particularly in the area of voting. It was pointed out that the federal government could initiate action only in the criminal sections. The civil provisions could be brought to bear only upon the initiative of private persons, many of whom could not bear the expense involved in long and complicated litigation. It was urged that at the very least a new law be adopted to permit the United States government to file an action to obtain appropriate remedies against voting abridgments. The first civil rights legislation to be passed since 1875 was enacted in 1957 in response to these demands. This was the Civil Rights Act of 1957 (71 Stat. 634). Further safeguards to voting rights were added in the Civil Rights Act of 1960, the Civil Rights Act of 1964, and culminating in the broad provisions of the Voting Rights Act of 1965. (The provisions of these acts dealing with voting are treated separately in Chapter 8, "Voting and Apportionment." The provisions of the Civil Rights Act of 1964 which apply to rights other than voting are discussed in Chapter 7, "Equal Protection of the Law.")

To summarize briefly the legislative powers of the national government to protect civil rights, the Congress can act to protect only those rights which derive in some fashion from the United States Constitution, or federal laws, or treaties adopted by the United States. The catalog of these federal rights is not static, and rights may be modified or expanded or new rights created by constitutional amendment, by legislation, or by entering into new treaty arrangements. And Congress may, by appropriate legislation, provide remedies for interference with any of these federal rights. The constitutional basis for congressional activity may vary with either the right involved or the source of the interference, however, and some care must be exercised in the remedies provided in order to deal precisely with a given deprivation. Potential sources of interference are state officers, private persons, and federal officers. The Fourteenth Amendment authorizes legislation protecting against deprivations of rights committed by the first group but not the others. Separate support must be found in the Constitution for remedies directed solely toward the latter sources. The broad delegated powers in Article I of the Constitution may be applied to any persons, official or private, and Congress has in these grants a rich source of authority to create new rights or provide stronger protections for older rights. Primarily grounded in the commerce power, the Civil Rights Act of 1964 for the first time set up a federal right not to be discriminated against on the basis of race or color in the enjoyment of various kinds of recreational and restaurant accommodations. Since the Fourteenth Amendment had already been construed to bar such discrimination on the part of state officials, the law is primarily directed toward private interference, but the "supremacy" clause dictates that state agencies as well as private persons are bound by the congressional enactments if the provisions of the laws apply to both. As to interference occasioned by federal administrators, Congress has ample power to provide remedies since it creates the positions and may clearly define the limits under which federal agencies may exercise their powers. As an illustration, the Post Office Department has on occasion, as one of several censorship devices, used a mail-block sanction (prohibiting the delivery of all mail to offending sources of allegedly obscene publications). Under a law passed by Congress in 1960, the mail-block sanction may not be used without an order from a federal court.

Finally, the treaty power may be employed to create new federal rights. The United States can constitutionally enter into a treaty agreement with Japan, for example, setting up reciprocal rights in the nationals of each country to enter lawful business pursuits while a legal resident of the other country. And this right of the resident Japanese alien in the United States could then be protected by Congress in giving effect to the terms of the treaty.

All nonfederal rights, however, stem from state laws and constitutions, and it is up to the states to provide remedies for interference with these rights. To repeat an earlier statement, the crucial problem in defining congressional powers to safeguard rights is the careful distinction between federal rights and state rights.

EXECUTIVE PROTECTION OF CIVIL RIGHTS

The general powers available to the federal judicial and legislative branches to protect civil rights have been discussed. It should not be overlooked, however, that the President of the United States has certain areas, albeit limited, in which he, too, can serve as a protector of rights.

In the first place, the President and Vice-President are the only elected federal officials who have as their constituency the whole of the nation. Senators and Representatives in Congress represent states or districts. In a real sense, then, the President is our only official national spokesman. In such position he can speak both for and to the American public. In periods of tension or crisis where there are potential dangers to the enjoyment of rights, the President can, by public statements and actions, serve as the conscience of the nation. As Franklin D. Roosevelt wrote shortly after his first election [quoted in Richard P. Longaker, *The Presidency and Individual Liberties* (Ithaca: Cornell University Press, 1961), p. 31]:

The Presidency is not merely an administrative office. That is the least of it. . . . It is preeminently a place of moral leadership. All of our great Presidents were leaders of thought at times when certain historic ideas in the life of the nation had to be clarified. . . . That is what the office is . . . a superb opportunity for re-applying, applying in new conditions, the simple rules of human conduct to which we always go back.

As chief legislator, the President has considerable influence from time to time on the programs which Congress will consider. Of course legislative suggestions, no matter from what source, must obtain approval of the Congress, but the President, by a variety of devices, can bring to bear appreciable pressures to gain support for his proposals. The Civil Rights Act of 1964 and the Voting Rights Act of 1965 are cases in point.

As chief administrator, the President has very substantial powers to protect the individual against federal abridgment of rights. In the areas of loyalty checks on federal employees, passport interference, instigation of deportation proceedings against aliens—in short, the entire range of federal administrative activity—the direction of activity and the energy with which it proceeds are largely under the control of the President. Of course the agencies and administrators must work within the statutory authority granted by Congress and within the congressional allocations of money. But despite these important boundaries, there is a vast area of discretion remaining to the President to determine how the congressional mandate will be carried out. Even taking into account the limitations of control over a giant bureaucracy, a President sensitive to the rights of the individual can exercise surveillance over the policies and procedures of the administrative agencies to ensure that at least in broad outline the executive branch will not become a source of unwarranted interference with individual liberty. His appointive and removal powers can be substantial weapons in guaranteeing performance in accordance with his policies. Thus in 1934 President Roosevelt appointed Huntington Cairns as special legal adviser to the Treasury Department. In administering the law barring importation of obscene literature, the Customs Bureau appeared to be following too restrictive an approach to decisions on exclusion of books and art from abroad. Mr. Cairns spent considerable time investigating the standards employed by customs inspectors, and his subsequent recommendations and influence were clearly in the direction of lessening censorship. [See Zechariah Chafee, *Government and Mass Communications* (Chicago: University of Chicago Press, 1947), pp. 254-275.]

In view of the limited corrective capacity of the judicial branch, such policies of restraint by the executive are of particular note in periods of pressure for conformity. During wartime, for example, overzealous United States attorneys might well be able to obtain indictments and even convictions under the sedition laws against persons who merely express public discontent with the handling of military operations. Firm statements of presidential policy, normally through the Attorney General, exhorting restraint in the enforcement of such laws can have a beneficial effect in stemming the excesses of overenthusiastic prosecutors. On Attorney General Francis Biddle's insistence, for example, sedition cases during World War II were given very close scrutiny, in order to avoid the shotgun prosecutions which were all too common during World War I. In a directive to all United States Attorneys, he stated: [1]

This Department will oppose any curtailment of those rights beyond that absolutely necessary to the efficient conduct of the military and the war effort of the United States. Indeed, a further disregard for civil rights can only be viewed as distinctly injurious to national morale and subversive of the democratic ideals which the nation is seeking to defend.

Similarly, it appears that the Truman Administration followed a conscious policy of restraint in its treatment of conscientious objectors who refused to register, only rarely invoking the criminal process.

One of the clearest illustrations of the executive decision to withhold the full enforcement power, and thereby avoid causing undue hardship, occurred in 1959. In companion cases, *Bartkus* v. *Illinois*, 359 U.S. 121 (1959), and *Abbate* v. *United States*, 359 U.S. 187 (1959), the United States Supreme Court reaffirmed an old doctrine that there is no violation of the prohibition against double jeopardy in the separate state and federal criminal prosecutions for offenses against both jurisdictions even though they arise out of a single act. Immediately following the decision, Attorney General William P. Rogers announced for the Department of Justice a

[1] Department of Justice Circular 3356, May 21, 1940, quoted in Richard P. Longaker, *The Presidency and Individual Liberties* (Ithaca: Cornell University Press, 1961), p. 134.

policy that no federal prosecution would be initiated following a state prosecution on a charge arising out of the same act unless unusual circumstances appeared. Even here, the Attorney General himself would have to approve the decision to prosecute. He recognized that whatever the arguments in support of the Court's decision, there would obviously be situations in which multiple prosecutions would be altogether severe. His statement is open recognition of the fact that one should not equate constitutionality with wisdom. In his own words, "The mere existence of a power does not mean that it should necessarily be exercised."

In other circumstances the protection of individual freedom might call for greater energy, rather than less, in the enforcement of the law. The various civil rights sections of the code lay dormant for most of the period since 1875. While it would appear obvious that federal prosecutions against state officers should not be casually initiated (and to this extent some restraint is called for), at the same time, there are enough serious abridgments of rights by state officers to indicate that a policy of complete nonenforcement of these sections is not the proper one either. In recent years the Congress and the President have shown increasing concern over denial of voting rights. As previously indicated, there is considerable legislation already on the books dealing with the subject at the national level. A President who is keenly interested in protecting the right to participate in elections has substantial statutory weapons and the weight of the whole Department of Justice, if he wishes to employ it, to bring to bear on the matter. It should be kept in mind that executive energy in such instances cannot necessarily be measured in terms of the number of prosecutions brought. In the first place, even a slight increase in cases initiated can serve as a warning signal and can have a salutary effect in diminishing violations. In the second place, the goal may be equally well attained in many areas merely by inspection, field investigation, and surveillance without a formal prosecution. The important factor is that the point be brought home, to persons in position to use official powers to abridge rights, that the President means business. The public statements and the general activity displayed in the executive branch, as well as the formal suits initiated, are influential indicators in accomplishing the purpose of protection of rights.

In yet a different direction the President has substantial control over such matters as personnel policies and other internal rules and regulations for the conduct of federal agencies. An illustration of the way this control can be employed to protect rights is the influence of the President in ending segregation in the armed forces. President Franklin Roosevelt initiated the moves in this direction, followed by increased pressures by Presidents Truman and Eisenhower. Desegregation was accomplished in the military in Korea and, by 1955, in the entire armed forces. Coupled with these moves was the decision to end segregation in schools on military posts and in federal facilities generally.

By executive order, Presidents Truman, Eisenhower, and Kennedy have pushed out even further to press for nondiscrimination in employment. In awarding government contracts the United States has the power to impose various conditions on the contracting parties. In 1941 President Roosevelt issued an executive order establishing a Committee on Fair Employment Practices and requiring that all federal defense contracts contain a stipulation obligating the contractor "not to discriminate against any worker because of race, creed, color, or national origin." [2] Under various titles and with varying effectiveness a committee for this purpose has been continued. Whatever the actual enforcement policy of these committees might be, it is clear that such a power of "government by contract" has enormous potential impact.

Since the President is also commander-in-chief of the national military arm, there is at least the possibility that under appropriate conditions he has ultimately at his disposal the armed might of the nation to guarantee the effectuation of national law and policy. Laying aside the question of presidential power to deploy troops outside the continental United States, these are important constitutional questions involved in the President's use of military force in the domestic United States.

One approach to the question of presidential power to use the military is to require that it be done within the limits of statutory authorization. Thus the President would be able to call out the military forces for domestic use only in situations spelled out by Congress. At least some adherence to this viewpoint is implicit in the fact that various authorizing statutes of this kind have been adopted by Congress almost from the beginning of the nation. As early as 1792, Congress authorized the President to call out the militia "whenever the laws of the United States shall be opposed or the execution thereof obstructed, in any state by combinations too powerful to be suppressed by the ordinary course of judicial proceedings or by the power vested in the marshals." The famous Whisky Rebellion was quenched under this provision in 1794.

The present version of this section is Section 332 of Title 10 of the United States Code:

> Whenever the President considers that unlawful obstructions, combinations, or assemblages, or rebellion against the authority of the United States, make it impracticable to enforce the laws of the United States in any State or Territory by the ordinary course of judicial proceedings, he may call into Federal service such of the militia of any State, and use such of the armed forces, as he considers necessary to enforce those laws or to suppress the rebellion.

It was essentially in accordance with the authority given by this section that President Eisenhower in 1957 issued Executive Order No. 10730, ordering the Secretary of Defense to take appropriate steps to maintain order in the integration crisis in Little Rock, Arkansas. Within hours, Central

---

[2] See Richard P. Longaker, op. cit., pp. 120–125, for an account of the handling of the nondiscrimination clause under the different administrations.

High School in that city was under guard by the paratroopers of the 101st Airborne Division.

Another, and broader, approach to presidential power to call out the military for maintaining domestic order lies in the view that the President has not only the power but also the duty of enforcing acts of Congress, treaties, and the rights, duties, and obligations growing out of the Constitution itself. In the execution of this duty, the President has such powers and may utilize such agencies as are necessary to see that the national peace is maintained. In this view, no congressional enabling legislation is necessary. The power is in the President irrespective of such support.

An important statement of national power is to be found in the opinion in the case of *In re Debs*, 158 U.S. 564 (1895). A strike against the Pullman Company in Chicago had led to a stoppage of almost all trains out of the city. An injunction was obtained against Eugene Debs, leader of the union, forbidding the strikers from interfering with the mails or interstate commerce in any way. The injunction was ignored, and considerable violence occurred. The federal marshal informed the Attorney General that he was unable to enforce the order, and President Cleveland ordered federal troops into the city. Debs and others were arrested for contempt and received sentences ranging from three to six months. The Supreme Court unanimously upheld the President's action and refused to issue a writ of habeas corpus. In the course of the opinion, Justice Brewer stated:

... The entire strength of the nation may be used to enforce in any part of the land the full and free exercise of all national powers and the security of all rights entrusted by the Constitution to its care. The strong arm of the national government may be put forth to brush away all obstructions to the freedom of interstate commerce or the transportation of the mails. If the emergency arises, the army of the nation, and all its militia, are at the service of the nation to compel obedience to its laws.

Probably the best answer to the question of presidential power to employ force inside the United States is given (although in a different context) by Professor Corwin, with his fine sense of the historical development of the office of the President. [See E. S. Corwin, *The President, Office and Powers*, 4th ed. (New York: New York University Press, 1957), p. 157.] He states that just as nature abhors a vacuum, so does a period of emergency. Something will be done in a crisis which demands action. If Congress has legislated, then probably the President will act within that authorization. If it has not, the President may act anyhow in preserving the "peace of the United States," to use the phrase of Justice Miller in *In re Neagle*, 135 U.S. 1 (1890). Casuistic arguments about presidential power to uphold the laws, the federal courts, and the Constitution of the United States will find little sympathy either in public opinion or, in all probability, in the federal courts.

Presidential powers to promote or protect civil rights are admittedly more elusive of understanding than are those of Congress. Further, the "visibility" with which the President or the executive agencies operate is much lower than is the case with Congress. When Congress passes, or fails to pass, important civil rights bills, a great deal of publicity and comment may be expected to follow. But executive decisions, particularly agency policy decisions, are less visible to the public, and it is considerably more difficult to arrive at a clear picture of just what the President and his subordinates in the executive branch are doing in the civil rights area at any given time. The mere fact that the picture relative to executive powers is cloudy, however, should not lead the observer to conclude that they are therefore minimal. It is hoped that the brief discussion and illustrations given will indicate sufficiently that there are tremendous weapons available to the President both for internal policing of federal practices and procedures and for external pressures on private and state action inimical to individual freedom.

CHAPTER 4

The Rights of the Accused

ONE of the hardest tasks for the nonlawyer is the full appreciation of the value of procedural regularity. A commonly heard criticism of appellate courts is that they reverse criminal convictions "because of some technicality." Procedural requirements are sometimes viewed impatiently as mere obstructions to the efficient administration of criminal justice. What is being overlooked in these attacks on procedural "technicalities" is the realization that over the long pull of centuries these requirements have served as the gradually accumulating building blocks to form our most effective barrier against arbitrary governmental deprivation of life and liberty. As Justice Frankfurter succinctly stated it, "The history of liberty has largely been the history of observance of procedural safeguards." [*McNabb* v. *United States*, 318 U.S. 332, 347 (1943).]

The primary constitutionally guaranteed procedures in federal prosecutions are fairly explicitly stated in Article I, Section 9, and in the Bill of Rights. But the Fifth Amendment also contains the broad guarantee that no one can be deprived of life or liberty "without due process of law." The primary constitutionally guaranteed procedures in state prosecutions are contained in the "due process" and "equal protection" clauses of the Fourteenth Amendment. The Court has time and time again been faced with the task of giving content to the nebulous phrase "due process of law" in testing the validity of criminal procedures employed by the state or the federal government. In *Davidson* v. *New Orleans*, 96 U.S. 97, 104 (1877), Justice Miller said that if it were possible to define with precision the exact requirements of due process, "no more useful construction could be furnished to any part of the fundamental law." Since the courts of the nation have uniformly agreed that no such definition is possible, they have followed a course of defining the phrase, to quote Justice Miller again, "by the gradual process of judicial inclusion and exclusion, as the cases presented for decision shall require." In recognition of this practice, the approach here is to break up the criminal process into the more or less successive stages through which an accused may travel and examine the constitutional requirements at each stage. It will be seen that despite the absence of a precise definition of procedural due process, there is in the concept a general requirement that the procedures used at each stage must meet the test of "fundamental fairness."

In *Twining* v. *New Jersey*, 211 U.S. 78 (1908), the United States Supreme Court, through Justice Moody, made a tentative effort to point the way in approaching due process questions:

> The essential elements of due process of law ... are singularly few, though of wide application and deep significance. ... Due process requires that the court which assumes to determine the rights of parties shall have jurisdiction ... and that there shall be notice and opportunity for hearing given the parties. ... Subject to these two fundamental conditions, which seem to be universally prescribed in all systems of law established by civilized countries, this court has, up to this time, sustained all state laws, statutory or judicially declared, regulating procedure, evidence, and methods of trial, and held them to be consistent with due process of law.

We have in this statement what might be called the "hard core of due process"—jurisdiction, notice, and hearing. Taking these essential elements, along with the concept of fundamental fairness, the Court has over the years gradually elaborated the rules and principles which are followed today. At the same time, it must be noted that decisions expressing new requirements are often merely the bases for still further developments. Due process is by no means a static concept. Every term of Court sees refinements, modifications, and even reversals of former positions.

The process of "incorporation" of the Bill of Rights guarantees into the Fourteenth Amendment was treated earlier in Chapter 2. It was pointed out that although many of the rights are now so incorporated, the Court has not yet imposed the identical procedural standards on states that the Bill of Rights requires in federal proceedings. In addition, federal statutes and Supreme Court rules may lay down requirements for federal prosecutions which do not apply in state proceedings. In the examination of the various stages of administration of criminal justice an attempt will be made to illustrate the differences between federal standards and state standards as imposed by the United States Constitution or as result from federal statutes or rules of court. It should be kept in mind, of course, that the states are free to adjust their procedures to furnish *more* protection to the accused than the bare minimum required by the Fourteenth Amendment.

NOTICE OF WHAT CONDUCT IS MADE CRIMINAL

THE "VOID FOR VAGUENESS" RULE

To begin with the law which defines a crime, fairness demands that the law spell out with sufficient clarity just what it is that the legislature is trying to prohibit. Without this basic notice, the citizen surely should not be held accountable in a criminal prosecution which may result in a forfeiture of life, liberty, or property. In *Connally* v. *General Construction Company*, 269 U.S. 385 (1926), the United States Supreme Court had occasion to examine an Oklahoma statute making it a crime to pay "less than the current rate of per diem wages in the locality where the work is performed. . . ." The Court found that such vague directions as "current rate" and "locality where the work is performed" were not sufficiently clear to apprise an employer of just what rates of pay would be so low as to violate the law. Prosecutions under such a law, then, would be in violation of the "due process" clause because insufficient notice was given.

The Court followed *Connally* in holding invalid a New Jersey law in *Lanzetta* v. *New Jersey*, 306 U.S. 451 (1939). The law made it a crime to be a "gangster," and conviction was punishable by a fine not exceeding $10,000 or imprisonment not exceeding 20 years or both. The definition of "gangster" was stated as "Any person not engaged in any lawful occupation, known to be a member of any gang consisting of two or more persons, who has been convicted at least three times of being a disorderly person, or who has been convicted of any crime in this or in any other State." Justice Butler, for the Court, stated the rule:

No one may be required at peril of life, liberty or property to speculate as to the meaning of penal statutes. All are entitled to be informed as to what the State commands or forbids. The applicable rule is stated in *Connally* v. *General Construction Co.* . . . : "That the terms of a penal statute creating a new offense must be sufficiently explicit to inform those who are subject to it what conduct on their part will render them liable to its penalties, is a well-recognized requirement, consonant alike with ordinary notions of fair play and the settled rules of law. And a statute which either forbids or requires the doing of an act in terms so vague that men of common intelligence must necessarily guess at its meaning and differ as to its application, violates the first essential of due process of law."

Justice Butler concluded that the statute was too ambiguous and "the terms it employs to indicate what it purports to denounce are so vague, indefinite and uncertain that it must be condemned as repugnant to the due process clause of the Fourteenth Amendment." [See generally, Note, "The Void-for-Vagueness Doctrine in the Supreme Court," 109 *U. Pa. L. Rev.* 67 (1960).]

In applying statutes in particular cases the courts must of necessity interpret those statutes. In so doing, the judges are not restricted to mere explanations of what the words mean. If they feel that the phraseology is somewhat ambiguous or rather too loose to meet the test of definiteness, they may add a gloss in the interpretation which will serve to tighten up the statute. If such modifications are made by the highest court of the jurisdiction involved, they become officially a part of the statute, just as though the legislature added them initially. In the case to follow, the Court of Appeals of New York made just such a modification in order to try to save a criminal section from the vice of vagueness.

WINTERS *v.* NEW YORK

333 U.S. 507 (1948)

Mr. Justice Reed delivered the opinion of the Court.

Appellant is a New York City bookdealer, convicted, on information, of a misdemeanor for having in his possession with intent to sell certain magazines charged to violate subsection 2 of Section 1141 of the New York Penal Law. It reads as follows:

"Section 1141. Obscene prints and articles

1. A person . . . who,

2. Prints, utters, publishes, sells, lends, gives away, distributes or shows, or has in his possession with intent to sell, lend, give away, distribute or show or otherwise offers for sale, loan, gift or distribution, any book, pamphlet, magazine, newspaper or other printed paper devoted to the publication, and principally made up of criminal news, police reports, or accounts of criminal deeds, or pictures, or stories of deeds of bloodshed, lust or crime; . . .

Is guilty of a misdemeanor, . . ."

. . . The appellant contends that the subsection violates the right of free speech and press because it is vague and indefinite. It is settled that a statute so vague and indefinite, in form and as interpreted, as to permit within the scope of its language the punishment of incidents fairly within the protection of the guarantee of free speech is void, on its face, as contrary to the Fourteenth Amendment. . . . Where the alleged vagueness of a state statute had been cured by an opinion of the state court, confining a statute punishing the circulation of publications "having a tendency to encourage or incite the commission of any crime" to "encouraging an actual breach of law," this Court affirmed a conviction under the stated limitation of meaning. The accused publication was read as advocating the commission of the crime of indecent exposure. *Fox* v. *Washington,* 236 U.S. 273, 277. . . .

On its face, the subsection here involved violates the rule of the Stromberg and Herndon cases that statutes which include prohibitions of acts fairly within the protection of a free press are void. It covers detective stories, treatises on crime, reports of battle carnage, et cetera. In recognition of this obvious defect, the New York Court of Appeals limited the scope by construction. Its only interpretation of the meaning of the pertinent subsection is that given in this case. After pointing out that New York statutes against indecent or obscene publications have generally been construed to refer to sexual impurity, it interpreted the section here in question to forbid these publications as "indecent or obscene" in a different manner. The Court held that collections of criminal deeds of bloodshed or lust "can be so massed as to become vehicles for inciting violent and depraved crimes against the person and in that case such publications are indecent or obscene in an admissible sense, . . ." The Court of Appeals by this authoritative interpretation made the subsection applicable to publications that, besides meeting the other particulars of the statute, so massed their collection of pictures and stories of bloodshed and of lust "as to become vehicles for inciting violent and depraved crimes against the person." Thus, the statute forbids the massing of stories of bloodshed and lust in such a way as to incite to crime against the person. This construction fixes the meaning of the statute for this case. The interpretation by the Court of Appeals puts these words in the statute as definitely as if it had been so amended by the legislature. . . . We assume that the defendant, at the time he acted, was chargeable with knowledge of the scope of subsequent interpretation. . . . As lewdness in publications is punishable under Section 1141(1) and the usual run of stories of bloodshed, such as detective stories, are excluded, it is the massing as an incitation to crime that becomes the important element. . . .

. . . [E]ven considering the gloss put upon the literal meaning by the Court of Appeals' restriction of the statute . . . , we find the specification of publications, prohibited from distribution, too uncertain and indefinite to justify the conviction of this petitioner. Even though all detective tales and treatises on criminology are not forbidden, and though publications made up of criminal deeds not characterized by bloodshed or lust are omitted from the interpretation of the Court of Appeals, we think fair use of collections of pictures and stories would be interdicted because of the utter impossibility of the actor or the trier to know where this new standard of guilt would draw the line between the allowable and the forbidden publications. No intent or purpose is required—no indecency or obscenity in any sense heretofore known to the law. "So massed as to incite to crime" can become meaningful only by concrete instances. This one example is not enough. The clause proposes to punish the printing and circulation of publications that courts or juries may think influence generally persons to commit crimes of violence against the person. No conspiracy to commit a crime is required. . . . It is not an effective notice of new crime. The clause has no technical or common law meaning. . . . The statute as construed by the Court of Appeals does not limit punishment to the indecent and obscene, as formerly understood. When stories of deeds of bloodshed, such as many in the accused magazines, are massed so as to incite to violent crimes, the statute is violated. It does not seem to us that an honest distributor of publications could know when he might be held to have ignored such a prohibition. Collections of tales of war horrors, otherwise unexceptionable, might well be found to be "massed" so as to become "vehicles for exciting violent and depraved crimes." Where a statute is so vague as to make criminal an innocent act, a conviction under it cannot be sustained. . . .

Reversed.

Mr. Justice Frankfurter, joined by Mr. Justice Jackson and Mr. Justice Burton, dissenting. . . .

Fundamental fairness of course requires that people be given notice of what to avoid. If the purpose of a statute is undisclosed, if the legislature's will has not been revealed, it offends reason that punishment should be meted out for conduct which at the time of its commission was not forbidden to the understanding of those who wished to observe the law. This requirement of fair notice that there is a boundary of prohibited conduct not to be overstepped is included in the conception of "due process of law." The legal jargon for such failure to give forewarning is to say that the statute is void for "indefiniteness."

But "indefiniteness" is not a quantitative concept. It is not even a technical concept of definite components. It is itself an indefinite concept. There is no such thing as "indefiniteness" in the abstract, by which the sufficiency of the requirements expressed by the term may be ascertained. The requirement is fair notice that conduct may entail punishment. But whether notice is or is not "fair" depends upon the subject matter to which it relates. Unlike the abstract stuff of mathematics, or the quantitatively ascertainable elements of much of natural science, legislation is greatly concerned with the multiform psychological complexities of individual and social conduct. Accordingly, the demands upon legislation, and its responses, are variable and multiform. That which may appear to be too vague and even meaningless as to one subject matter may be as definite as another subject matter of legislation permits, if the legislative power to deal with such a subject is not to be altogether denied. The statute books of every State are full of instances of what may look like unspecific definitions of crime, of the drawing of wide circles of prohibited conduct. . . .

At one point in the opinion for the majority it was stated that the phrase "so massed as to incite to crime" had no "technical or common law meaning." The point here is that words or phrases which may appear somewhat vague have in some instances become reasonably definite as a result of many years—even centuries—of application by the courts. What this really means, it appears, is that while the layman might be confused by the terms, the judges know what they mean, and therefore they are not vague or uncertain. Even so, ancient common-law crimes may, in particular cases, be given so broad a construction as to run afoul of the prohibition against vagueness. The crime of breach of the peace has roots in early common law. But when a Georgia court applied its breach of the peace statute to convict six young Negroes for peacefully playing basketball in a public park customarily used only by whites, the United States Supreme Court, in *Wright* v. *Georgia*, 373 U.S. 284 (1963), unanimously held that such a construction of the statute failed to afford adequate notice that their conduct was prohibited thereby.

The Prohibition Against Ex Post Facto Laws

While ex post facto laws are normally considered separately from due process questions, the basic defect inherent in such laws is the failure to give adequate notice. To apply a criminal law retroactively, to the disadvantage of the accused, is to violate the most fundamental notions of fairness. Thus even without the prohibitions against ex post facto laws in Article I, Sections 9 and 10 of the Constitution, the "due process" clauses of the Fifth and Fourteenth Amendments might be considered adequate to bar the application of such laws.

Whatever the framers of the Constitution might have intended, the Court has consistently held that only criminal laws can come within the meaning of ex post facto prohibitions. Retroactive civil laws, then, do not run afoul of this provision of the Constitution. The leading case on the subject is *Calder* v. *Bull*, decided in 1798 and still ruling law.

CALDER *v.* BULL

3 Dallas 386 (1798)

[In March, 1793, the Court of Probate of Hartford disapproved a certain will under which Bull claimed. Bull failed to appeal within the statutory limit of eighteen months and therefore lost his right of appeal under the existing statute.

In May, 1795, the Connecticut legislature passed a law setting aside the decree of the probate court and granting a new hearing, as a result of which the property went to Bull. Calder and wife, whose claims were set aside by the second decree, appealed to the state Supreme Court, which affirmed the decree. On writ of error the United States Supreme Court examined the claim that application of the revised law was violative of the prohibition against ex post facto laws.]

Mr. Justice Chase. . . .

. . . The sole inquiry is, whether this resolution or law of Connecticut, having such operation, is an ex post facto law within the prohibition of the Federal Constitution? . . .

I shall endeavor to show what law is to be considered an ex post facto law, within the words and meaning of the prohibition in the Federal Constitution. The prohibition, "that no state shall pass any ex post facto law," necessarily requires some explanation; for, naked and without explanation, it is unintelligible, and means nothing. Literally, it is only that a law shall not be passed concerning, and after the fact, or thing done, or action committed. I would ask, what fact; of what nature, or kind; and by whom done? That Charles 1st, king of England, was beheaded; that Oliver Cromwell was Protector of England; that Louis XVI, late king of France, was guillotined,—are all facts, that have happened; but it would be nonsense to suppose, that the states were prohibited from making any law after either of these events, and with reference thereto. The prohibition, in the letter, is not to pass any law concerning and after the fact; but the plain and obvious meaning and intention of the prohibition is this: that the Legislatures of the several states shall not pass laws, after a fact done by a subject or citizen, which shall have relation to such fact, and shall punish him for having done it. The prohibition considered in this light, is an additional bulwark in favor of the personal security of the subject, to protect his person from punishment by legislative acts, having a retrospective operation. I do not think it was inserted to secure the citizen in his private rights, of either property, or contracts. The prohibition not to make anything but gold and silver coin a tender in payment of debts, and not to pass any law impairing the obligation of contracts, were inserted to secure private rights; but the restriction not to pass any ex post facto law, was to secure the person of the subject from injury, or punishment, in consequence of such law. If the prohibition against making ex post facto laws was intended to secure personal rights from being affected, or injured, by such laws, and the prohibition is sufficiently extensive for that object, the other restraints I have enumerated, were unnecessary, and therefore improper; for both of them are retrospective.

I will state what laws I consider ex post facto laws, within the words and the intent of the prohibition. 1st. Every law that makes an action done before the passing of the law, and which was innocent when done, criminal; and punishes such action. 2d. Every law that aggravates a crime, or makes it greater than it was, when committed. 3d. Every law that changes the punishment, and inflicts a greater punishment, than the law annexed to the crime, when committed. 4th. Every law that alters the legal rules of evidence, and receives less, or different, testimony, than the law required at the time of the commission of the offense, in order to convict the offender. All these, and similar laws, are manifestly unjust and oppressive. In my opinion, the true distinction is between ex post facto laws, and retrospective laws. Every ex post facto law must necessarily be retrospective; but every retrospective law is not an ex post facto law; the former, only, are prohibited. Every law that takes away or impairs rights vested, agreeably to existing laws, is retrospective, and is generally unjust, and may be oppressive; and it is a good general rule that a law should have no retrospect; but there are cases in which laws may justly, and for the benefit of the community, and also of individuals, relate to a time antecedent to their commencement; as statutes of oblivion, or of pardon. They are certainly retrospective, and literally both concerning, and after, the facts committed. But I do not consider any law ex post facto, within the prohibition, that mollifies the rigor of the criminal law; but only those that create, or aggravate, the crime; or increase the punishment, or change the rules of evidence, for the purpose of conviction. Every law that is to have an operation before the making thereof, as to commence at an antecedent time, or to save time from the Statute of Limitations, or to excuse acts which were unlawful, and before committed, and the like, is retrospective. But such laws may be proper or necessary, as the case may be. There is a great and apparent difference between making an unlawful act lawful, and the making an innocent action criminal, and punishing it as a crime. The expressions "ex post facto laws" are technical; they had been in use long before the Revolution, and had acquired an appropriate meaning by legislators, lawyers, and authors. The celebrated and judicious Sir William Blackstone, in his Commentaries, considers an ex post facto law precisely in the same light I have done. His opinion is confirmed by his successor, Mr. Wooddeson, and by the author of the "Federalist," whom I esteem superior to both, for his extensive and accurate knowledge of the true principles of government.

I also rely greatly on the definition, or explanation of ex post facto laws, as given by the convention, of Massachusetts, Maryland, and North Carolina, in their several constitutions, or forms of government. . . .

Judgment affirmed.

[Mr. Justice Paterson, Mr. Justice Iredell, and Mr. Justice Cushing each delivered concurring opinions.]

In determining whether a particular retroactive criminal law is ex post facto, within the rule of *Calder* v. *Bull,* the Court requires a showing that the new law will disadvantage defendants generally, as a class, rather than merely a particular defendant. Thus to reduce the size of the criminal jury from twelve to eight, and apply the reduction retroactively, was held to come within the bar against ex post facto laws in *Thompson* v. *Utah,* 170 U.S. 343 (1898). This was on the theory that defendants generally could be convicted more easily with eight jurors than twelve under a requirement of unanimity. But in the same year, in *Thompson* v. *Missouri,* 171 U.S. 380 (1898), the Court held that a change in the rules of evidence, to permit admission of letters written by the accused to his wife, was not ex post facto, despite the fact that a comparison of the handwriting showed that Thompson wrote a prescription for strychnine used to commit murder. The conviction was sustained on the ground that under the new rule both the state and the defendant were allowed to avail themselves of this additional evidence, and it would not uniformly operate to the disadvantage of the accused. [See Oliver P. Field, "Ex Post Facto in the Constitution," 20 *Mich. L. Rev.* 315 (1922).]

NOTICE TO THE ACCUSED OF THE OFFENSE
CHARGED AGAINST HIM

In addition to the general requirement that a statute be sufficiently clear to warn the citizenry of what the legislature is prohibiting, there is a more specific requirement of due process that the accused in a criminal proceeding be notified of the charge placed against him. Fairness demands that he know in advance just what the prosecution is for, in order that he may adequately attempt a defense. At an earlier stage in America this rule was carried to such extremes that indictments could be quashed unless the most minute details of the alleged crime were set forth—the manufacturer, the caliber, the color, and the model of the gun used to commit a murder, for example, and the physical location of the wound which was caused. The courts of today no longer require such lengthy descriptive essays in the indictments, but there must still appear a charge of sufficient clarity to apprise the accused of the nature of the offense charged. A good statement of the matter is found in *State* v. *Popolos,* 103 A.2d 511 (Me., 1954), where the defendant questioned the adequacy of his indictment for perjury:

> The essentials of an indictment for *perjury* in this State are set forth in a prescribed form by the legislature. But such a form is subject to constitutional restrictions and must be in compliance therewith. The statutes prescribing forms of indictment have removed many of the niceties of technical pleading and the indictment is made little more than a simple statement of the offense couched in ordinary language and with due regard for the rights of the accused. But they cannot change the requirements that the indictment must, as at common law, contain every averment that is necessary to inform the defendant of the particular circumstances of the charge against him. . . .
>
> Under the Constitution of the United States and by provision of the Constitution of Maine the accused is entitled to be informed of the nature and cause of the accusation against him. These provisions are based on the presumption of innocence and require such certainty in indictments as will enable an innocent man to prepare for trial. But no greater particularity of allegation that may be of service to the accused in understanding the charge and preparing his defense is necessary. However, all the elements or facts necessary to the crime charged must be set out fully and clearly. . . .

The issue of adequate notice was brought to the United States Supreme Court in 1948 in a rather curious case. As the case appeared to that Court, the Supreme Court of Arkansas held that a conviction under one section of a law could not be sustained, but it was affirmed, nonetheless, since there appeared to be sufficient evidence to convict under another section, even though the defendant was never charged with the latter violation.

COLE *v.* ARKANSAS

333 U.S. 196 (1948)

[Arkansas adopted a law in 1943 making it a felony to interfere in specified ways with one's right to work. The two key sections provided, in part:

Section 1. It shall be unlawful for any person by the use of force or violence . . . to prevent or attempt to prevent any person from engaging in any lawful vocation within this State. . . .

Section 2. It shall be unlawful for any person acting in concert with one or more other persons, to assemble at or near any place where a "labor dispute" exists and by force or violence prevent . . . any person from engaging in any lawful vocation, or for any person acting . . . in concert with one or more other persons, to promote, encourage or aid any such unlawful assemblage.]

Mr. Justice Black delivered the opinion of the Court.

The petitioners were convicted of a felony in an Arkansas state court and sentenced to serve one year in the state penitentiary. . . . We granted certiorari because the record indicated that at least one of the questions presented was substantial. That question, in the present state of the record, is the only one we find it appropriate to consider. The question is: "Were the petitioners denied due process of law . . . in violation of the Fourteenth Amendment by the circumstance that their convictions were affirmed under a criminal statute for violation of which they had not been charged?"

The present convictions are under an information. The petitioners urge that the information charged them with a violation of Section 2 of Act 193 of the 1943 Arkansas Legislature and that they were tried and convicted of violating only Section 2. The State Supreme Court affirmed their convictions on the ground that the information had charged and the evidence had shown that the petitioners had violated Section 1 of the Arkansas Act which describes an offense separate and distinct from the offense described in Section 2. . . .

We therefore have this situation. The petitioners read the information as charging them with an offense under Section 2 of the Act, the language of which the information had used. The trial judge construed the information as charging an offense under Section 2. He instructed the jury to that effect. He charged the jury that petitioners were on trial for the offense of promoting an unlawful assemblage, not for the offense "of using force and violence." Without completely ignoring the judge's charge, the jury could not have convicted petitioner for having committed the separate, distinct, and substantially different offense defined in Section 1. Yet the State Supreme Court refused to consider the validity of the convictions under Section 2, for violation of which petitioners were tried and convicted. It affirmed their convictions as though they had been tried for violating Section 1, an offense for which they were neither tried nor convicted.

No principle of procedural due process is more clearly established than that notice of the specific charge, and a chance to be heard in a trial of the issues raised by that charge, if desired, are among the constitutional rights of every accused in a criminal proceeding in all courts, state or federal. . . . If, as the State Supreme Court held, petitioners were charged with a violation of Section 1, it is doubtful both that the information fairly informed them of that charge and that they sought to defend themselves against such a charge; it is certain that they were not tried for or found guilty of it. It is as much a violation of due process to send an accused to prison following conviction of a charge on which he was never tried as it would be to convict him upon a charge that was never made. . . .

We are constrained to hold that the petitioners have been denied safeguards guaranteed by due process of law—safeguards essential to liberty in a government dedicated to justice under law.

In the present state of the record we cannot pass upon those contentions which challenge the validity of Section 2 of the Arkansas Act. The judgment is reversed and remanded to the State Supreme Court for proceedings not inconsistent with this opinion.

Reversed and remanded.

UNREASONABLE SEARCHES AND SEIZURES

The Fourth Amendment to the United States Constitution begins with the phrase, "The right of the people to be secure in their persons, houses, papers, and effects, against unreasonable searches and seizures, shall not be violated . . ." The clear purport of the phrase is that not all seizures or searches are prohibited; it is only those which are *unreasonable* which are barred. The second part of the sentence states, "and no warrants shall issue, but upon probable cause, supported by oath or affirmation, and particularly describing the place to be searched, and the persons or things to be seized."

The phraseology of the Fourth Amendment raises two important questions of interpretation. First, what kinds of searches and seizures are "unreasonable"? Second, what sorts of information or observations are sufficient to constitute "probable cause" to believe that an offense was committed and that the things sought are in the place specified? The general bounds of the "probable cause" requirement become additionally important because of the fact that not all searches require a warrant, but even the exceptions demand that the officer meet this same test before proceeding, just as though he were attempting to obtain a warrant.

SEARCH WITH A VALID WARRANT

The two main procedural points involved in obtaining a warrant are: first, the warrant issues from a judicial officer in order to guarantee a somewhat more detached and neutral view of the matter, and second, the place to be searched, and the persons or things to be seized, must be specifically described. The latter requirement is a response to the despised "writs of assistance" under which the British made general searches during the colonial period.

Some of the basic aspects of Fourth Amendment application are treated in *Boyd* v. *United States,* decided in 1886.

BOYD *v.* UNITED STATES
116 U.S. 616 (1886)

Mr. Justice Bradley delivered the opinion of the Court:

This was an information filed by the District Attorney of the United States in the District Court for the Southern District of New York in July, 1884, in a case of seizure and forfeiture of property, against thirty-five cases of plate glass, seized by the collector as forfeited to the United States, under the 12th section of the "Act to Amend the Customs Revenue Laws," etc., passed June 22, 1874, 18 Stat. at L. 186.

It is declared by that section that any owner, importer, consignee, etc., who shall, with intent to defraud the revenue, make or attempt to make any entry of imported merchandise, by means of any fraudulent or false invoice ... shall for each offense be fined in any sum not exceeding $5,000 nor less than $50, or be imprisoned for any time not exceeding two years, or both; and, in addition to such fine, such merchandise shall be forfeited.

The charge was that the goods in question were imported into the United States to the Port of New York, subject to the payment of duties; and that the owners or agents of said merchandise, or other person unknown, committed the alleged fraud, which was described in the words of the statute. The plaintiffs in error entered a claim for the goods, and pleaded that they did not become forfeited in manner and form as alleged. On the trial of the cause it became important to show the quantity and value of the glass contained in twenty-nine cases previously imported. To do this the district attorney offered in evidence an order made by the district judge under the fifth section of the same Act of June 22, 1874, directing notice under seal of the court to be given to the claimants, requiring them to produce the invoice of the twenty-nine cases. The claimants, in obedience to the notice, but objecting to its validity and to the constitutionality of the law, produced the invoice; and when it was offered in evidence by the district attorney they objected to its reception, on the ground that in a suit for forfeiture no evidence can be compelled from the claimants themselves, and also that the statute, so far as it compels production of evidence to be used against the claimants, is unconstitutional and void.

The evidence being received and the trial closed, the jury found a verdict for the United States, condemning the thirty-five cases of glass which were seized, and judgment of forfeiture was given. This judgment was affirmed by the circuit court, and the decision of that court is now here for review. ...

The clauses of the Constitution, to which it is contended that these laws are repugnant, are the Fourth and Fifth Amendments. The Fourth declares: "The right of the people to be secure in their persons, houses, papers and effects, against unreasonable searches and seizures, shall not be violated; and no warrants shall issue, but upon probable cause, supported by oath or affirmation, and particularly describing the place to be searched, and the persons or things to be seized." The fifth article, amongst other things, declares that no person "shall be compelled in any criminal case to be a witness against himself."

But, in regard to the Fourth Amendment, it is contended that, whatever might have been alleged against the constitutionality of the Acts of 1863 and 1867, that of 1874, under which the order in the present case was made, is free from constitutional objection, because it does not authorize the search and seizure of books and papers, but only requires the defendant or claimant to produce them. That is so; but it declares that if he does not produce them, the allegations which it is affirmed they will prove shall be taken as confessed. This is tantamount to compelling their production; for the prosecuting attorney will always be sure to state the evidence expected to be derived from them as strongly as the case will admit of. It is true that certain aggravating incidents of actual search and seizure, such as forcible entry into a man's house and searching amongst his papers, are wanting; and to this extent the proceeding under the Act of 1874 is a mitigation of that which was authorized by the former Acts; but it accomplishes the substantial object of those Acts in forcing from a party evidence against himself. It is our opinion, therefore, that a compulsory production of a man's private papers to establish a criminal charge against him or to forfeit his property is within the scope of the Fourth Amendment to the Constitution, in all cases in which a search and seizure would be; because it is a material ingredient and effects the sole object and purpose of search and seizure.

The principal question, however, remains to be considered. Is a search and seizure or, what is equivalent thereto, a compulsory production of a man's private papers, to be used in evidence against him in a proceeding to forfeit his property for alleged fraud against the revenue laws—is such a proceeding for such a purpose an *"unreasonable* search and seizure" within the meaning of the Fourth Amendment of the Constitution? Or is it a legitimate proceeding? It is contended by the counsel for the Government that it is a legitimate proceeding, sanctioned by long usage and the authority of judicial decision. No doubt long usage, acquiesced in by the courts, goes a long way to prove that there is some plausible ground or reason for it, in the law or in the historical facts which have imposed a particular construction of the law favorable to such usage. . . . But we do not find any long usage or any contemporary construction of the Constitution which would justify any of the Acts of Congress now under consideration. As before stated, the Act of 1863 was the first Act in this country, and we might say either in this country or in England, so far as we have been able to ascertain, which authorized the search and seizure of a man's private papers or the compulsory production of them, for the purpose of using them in evidence against him in a criminal case, or in a proceeding to enforce the forfeiture of his property. Even the Act under which the obnoxious writs of assistance were issued did not go as far as this, but only authorized the examination of ships and vessels and persons found therein, for the purpose of finding goods prohibited to be imported or exported, or on which the duties were not paid; and to enter into and search any suspected vaults, cellars or warehouses for such goods. The search for and seizure of stolen or forfeited goods or goods liable to duties and concealed to avoid the payment thereof are totally different things from a search for and seizure of a man's private books and papers for the purpose of obtaining information therein contained, or of using them as evidence against him. The two things differ *toto coelo.* In the one case, the Government is entitled to the possession of the property; in the other it is not. The seizure of stolen goods is authorized by the common law; and the seizure of goods forfeited for a breach of the revenue laws, or concealed to avoid the duties payable on them, has been authorized by English statutes for at least two centuries past; and the like seizures have been authorized by our own Revenue Acts from the commencement of Government. . . . So also the supervision authorized to be exercised by officers of the revenue over the manufacture or custody of excisable articles, and the entries thereof in books required by law to be kept for their inspection, are necessarily excepted out of the category of unreasonable searches and seizures. So also the laws which provide for the search and seizure of articles and things which it is unlawful for a person to have in his possession for the purpose of issue or disposition, such as counterfeit coin, lottery tickets, implements of gambling, etc., are not within this category. . . .

[The opinion here discusses the colonial experience with writs of assistance and quotes extensively from Lord Camden's opinion in *Entick* v. *Carrington*, 19 Howell State Trials, 1029, arising out of the controversy between the English Government and John Wilkes.]

The principles laid down in this opinion affect the very essence of constitutional liberty and security. They reach farther than the concrete form of the case then before the court, with its adventitious circumstances; they apply to all invasions, on the part of the Government and its employees, of the sanctity of a man's home and the privacies of life. It is not the breaking of his doors and the rummaging of his drawers that constitutes the essence of the offense; but it is the invasion of his indefeasible right of personal security, personal liberty and private property, where that right has never been forfeited by his conviction of some public offense; it is the invasion of this sacred right which underlies and constitutes the essence of Lord Camden's judgment. Breaking into a house and opening boxes and drawers are circumstances of aggravation; but any forcible and compulsory extortion of a man's own testimony or of his private papers to be used as evidence to convict him of crime or to forfeit his goods is within the condemnation of that judgment. In this regard the Fourth and Fifth Amendments run almost into each other. . . .

We have already noticed the intimate relation between the two Amendments. They throw great light on each other. For the "unreasonable searches and seizures" condemned in the Fourth Amendment are almost always made for the purpose of compelling a man to give evidence against himself, which in criminal cases is condemned in the Fifth Amendment; and compelling a man "in a criminal case to be a witness against himself," which is condemned in the Fifth Amendment, throws light on the question as to what is an "unreasonable search and seizure" within the meaning of the Fourth Amendment. And we have been unable to perceive that the seizure of a man's private books and papers to be used in evidence against him is substantially different from compelling him to be a witness against himself. We think it is within the clear intent and meaning of those terms. We are also clearly of opinion that proceedings instituted for the purpose of declaring the forfeiture of a man's property by reason of offenses committed by him, though they may be civil in form, are in their nature criminal. In this very case, the ground of forfeiture as declared in the twelfth section of the Act of 1874, on which the information is based, consists of certain acts of fraud committed against the public revenue in relation to imported merchandise, which are made criminal by the statute; and it is declared that the offender shall be fined not exceeding $5,000 . . . ; and in addition to such fine merchandise shall be forfeited. . . . If the government prosecutor elects to waive an indictment and to file a civil information against the claimants (that is, civil in form) can he by this device take from the proceeding its criminal aspect and deprive the claimants of their immunities as citizens, and extort from them a production of their private papers, or, as an alternative, a confession of guilt? This cannot be. The information, though technically a civil proceeding, is in substance and effect a criminal one. . . . As, therefore, suits for penalties and forfeitures, incurred by the commission of offenses against the law, are of this quasi criminal nature, we think that they are within the reason of criminal proceedings for all the purposes of the Fourth Amendment of the Constitution, and of that portion of the Fifth Amendment which declares that no person shall be compelled in any criminal case to be a witness against himself; and we are further of opinion that a compulsory production of the private books and papers of the owner of goods sought to be forfeited in such a suit is compelling him to be a witness against himself, within the meaning of the Fifth Amendment to the Constitution; and is the equivalent of a search and seizure, and an unreasonable search and seizure, within the meaning of the Fourth Amendment. . . .

We are of opinion, therefore, that the judgment of the Circuit Court should be reversed, and the cause remanded, with directions to award a trial; and it is so ordered.

[Mr. Justice Miller wrote a concurring opinion, joined by Chief Justice Waite.]

The *Boyd* case thus distinguished between stolen goods or goods liable to duties, on the one hand, and private books and papers, on the other. The former categories of property have long been subject to seizure, while the latter are not *lawfully* subject to seizure under the Fourth Amendment if they are of purely evidentiary value. It was here that the Court's opinion noted that the "Fourth and Fifth Amendments run almost into each other," since the obvious reason for taking the private papers would be to introduce them as evidence against the owner. The fact that an article of stolen property might later be introduced as evidence after having been seized should be differentiated from the situation in *Boyd,* for the stolen item is contraband, not legally the property of the possessor, and therefore there is technically no *self*-incrimination as might be the case with personal writings and papers.

This joinder of the Fourth and Fifth Amendments has been the occasion for some confusion in later cases. It seems to indicate that the Fourth Amendment is somehow connected to the question of admissibility of evidence. And it does not on the surface appear to be a grossly improper construction of the Fourth Amendment to suggest that it would bar illegally obtained evidence in a criminal prosecution. However, *Boyd* did not go so far, and neither did the Court in later cases, until very recently. *Boyd* should be read as indicating that when a search and seizure is made of material which would be barred as evidence under the self-incrimination rule, then it thereby becomes an *unreasonable* search and seizure, thus violating the Fourth Amendment. It also holds that *purely* evidentiary material is outside the scope of a lawful search and seizure. This aspect of the holding is sort of a logical loose end, but until 1967 it was ruling law. The difficulty with drawing the Fifth Amendment into the picture is that the self-incrimination clause is now held to be limited to protection against *testimonial* compulsion, and may well not apply to papers, books, or physical items which are not considered to be "evidence of a testimonial or communicative nature." [See the majority opinion in *Schmerber* v. *California*, 384 U.S. 757 (1966), laying down this rule.] The two facets of the *Boyd* case are seen more sharply in examining specific items. Suppose a valid search is undertaken in a suspect's room, in the course of which is found (1) his personal diary which gives detailed accounts of how various crimes were committed, and (2) a letter from an accomplice describing in complimentary terms the same crimes of the accused and congratulating him on the ingenious planning and executing of these crimes. Would seizure be proper? If neither item was stolen or used in committing crimes or unlawful to possess, then they would be of "purely evidentiary" value and the

Boyd rule would bar seizure. In the case of the diary, the entries might be considered "evidence of a testimonial or communicative nature," and thus the Fifth Amendment nexus might be considered as an appropriate rationale for such a bar. But in the case of the letter, what has the Fifth Amendment protection against self-incrimination to do with a letter written by another? The logic of the holding is not altogether flawless, although the rule may still commend itself, as a straight Fourth Amendment rule, to staunch supporters of protection against seizures. [See generally, Nelson B. Lasson, *The History and Development of the Fourth Amendment to the United States Constitution* (Baltimore: The Johns Hopkins University Press, 1937).]

The so-called "mere evidence" rule of *Boyd* v. *United States* was reexamined and discarded in *Warden* v. *Hayden,* 387 U.S. 294 (1967), with only one dissent, officially, but with two other justices objecting to the broad repudiation of the rule.

WARDEN *v.* HAYDEN

387 U.S. 294 (1967)

[Following the armed robbery of a cab company in Baltimore, Maryland, two cab drivers, attracted by shouts of "Holdup," followed a man who fled the company premises, and watched him enter a residence. One driver notified the company dispatcher by radio that the man was a Negro about 5'8" tall, wearing a light cap and dark jacket, and that he had entered the house on Cocoa Lane. The dispatcher relayed the information to police. Within minutes, police arrived at the house in a number of patrol cars. They searched the first and second floors and the cellar for the suspect. Hayden was found in an upstairs bedroom, and he was arrested when the officers on the first floor reported that no other man was in the house. One officer discovered a shotgun and a pistol in a flush tank in a bathroom adjoining the bedroom. Another officer, who was searching the cellar for "a man or the money" found, in a washing machine, a jacket and trousers of the type the fleeing man was said to have worn. A clip of ammunition for the pistol and a cap were found under the mattress of Hayden's bed. All these items of evidence were introduced against him at his trial.]

Mr. Justice Brennan delivered the opinion of the Court.

We review in this case the validity of the proposition that there is under the Fourth Amendment a "distinction between merely evidentiary materials, on the one hand, which may not be seized either under the authority of a search warrant or during the course of a search incident to arrest, and on the other hand, those objects which may validly be seized including the instrumentalities and means by which a crime is committed, the fruits of crime such as stolen property, weapons by which escape of the person arrested might be effected, and property the possession of which is a crime.". . .

We agree with the Court of Appeals that neither the entry without warrant to search for the robber, nor the search for him without warrant was invalid. . . . The police . . . acted reasonably when they entered the house and began to search for a man of the description they had been given and for weapons which he had used in the robbery or might use against them. The Fourth Amendment does not require police officers to delay in the course of an investigation if to do so would gravely endanger their lives or the lives of others. Speed here was essential, and only a thorough search of the house for persons and weapons could have insured that Hayden was the only man present and that the police had control of all weapons which could be used against them or to effect an escape. . . .

It is argued that, while the weapons, ammunition, and cap may have been seized in the course of a search for weapons, the officer who seized the clothing was searching neither for the suspect nor for weapons when he looked into the washing machine in which he found the clothing. . . .

We come, then, to the question whether, even though the search was lawful, the Court of Appeals was correct in holding that the seizure and introduction of the items of clothing violated the Fourth Amendment because they are "mere evidence.". . . We today reject the distinction as based on premises no longer accepted as rules governing the application of the Fourth Amendment. . . .

Nothing in the language of the Fourth Amendment supports the distinction between "mere evidence" and instrumentalities, fruits of crime, or contraband. On its face, the provision assures the "right of the people to be secure in their persons, houses, papers, and effects . . . ," without regard to the use to which any of these things are applied. This "right of the people" is certainly unrelated to the "mere evidence" limitation. Privacy is disturbed no more by a search directed to a purely evidentiary object than it is by a search directed to an instrumentality, fruit, or contraband. . . . Indeed, the distinction is wholly irrational, since, depending on the circumstances, the same "papers and effects" may be "mere evidence" in one case and "instrumentality" in another. See Comment, 20 U. Chi. L. Rev. 319, 320–322 (1953).

In *Gouled* v. *United States* . . . the Court said that search warrants "may not be used as a means of gaining access to a man's house or office and papers solely for the purpose of making search to secure evidence to be used against him in a criminal or penal proceeding. . . ." The Court derived from *Boyd* v. *United States, supra*, the proposition that warrants "may be resorted to only when a primary right to such search and seizure may be found in the interest which the public or the complainant may have in the property to be seized, or in the right to the possession of it, or when a valid exercise of the police power renders possession of the property by the accused unlawful and provides that it may be taken.". . .

The items of clothing involved in this case are not "testimonial" or "communicative" in nature, and their introduction therefore did not compel respondent to become a witness against himself in violation of the Fifth Amendment. *Schmerber* v. *California*, 384 U.S. 757. This case thus does not require that we consider whether there are items of evidential value whose very nature precludes them from being the object of a reasonable search and seizure. . . .

The premise in *Gouled* that government may not seize evidence simply for the purpose of proving crime has . . . been discredited. The requirement that the Government assert in addition some property interest in material it seizes has long been a fiction, obscuring the reality that government has an interest in solving crime. *Schmerber* settled the proposition that it is reasonable, within the terms of the Fourth Amendment, to conduct otherwise permissible searches for the purpose of obtaining evidence which would aid in apprehending and convicting criminals. The requirements of the Fourth Amendment can secure the same protection of privacy whether the search is for "mere evidence" or for fruits, instrumentalities or contraband. There must, of course, be a nexus—automatically provided in the case of fruits, instrumentalities or contraband—between the item to be seized and criminal behavior. Thus in the case of "mere evidence," probable cause must be examined in terms of cause to believe that the evidence sought will aid in a particular apprehension or conviction. . . . The clothes found in the washing machine matched the description of those worn by the robber and the police therefore could reasonably believe that the items would aid in the identification of the culprit. . . .

The judgment of the Court of Appeals is

Reversed.

Mr. Justice Black concurs in the result.

Mr. Justice Fortas, with whom the Chief Justice joins, concurring. .

Mr. Justice Douglas, dissenting. . . .

Another question arising under searches with a warrant is: what things are subject to seizure? Since the warrant must describe the articles to be seized, it would seem reasonable to conclude that *only* such items described are subject to seizure. Generally speaking, this appears to be the rule that is followed, but officers may also seize other property if such property is related to the things described in the warrant, or if it is contraband. [See Ernest W. Machen, Jr., *The Law of Search and Seizure* (Chapel Hill: Institute of Government, University of North Carolina, 1950), pp. 37–41.] Thus in *Cofer* v. *United States,* 37 F.2d 677 (C.A. 5th, 1930), officers were held to have exceeded their power when they seized gun shells from a locked trunk while searching defendant's premises under a warrant directing a seizure of liquor. But in *Bennett* v. *United States,* 145 F.2d 270 (C.A. 4th, 1944), a seizure of counterfeit ration coupons was held reasonable under a warrant the affidavit for which mentioned only counterfeit apparatus. The ration coupons were considered to be "related objects" and therefore properly seized.

Although the law is not completely clear, it should be noted that the rule with respect to seizures under a search warrant is not necessarily identical to that concerning searches and seizures incident to a lawful arrest. The latter appears to give officers somewhat broader powers and is discussed separately below.

Search and Seizure Without a Warrant

The Fourth Amendment prohibits unreasonable searches and seizures and seems to suggest, as a generalization, that searches or seizures without a warrant are unreasonable. There are certain important exceptions to such a generalization, however. An arrest is, of course, a seizure, and an illegal arrest is an unconstitutional seizure under the Fourth Amendment, as indicated in *Henry* v. *United States,* 361 U.S. 98 (1959). But the Fourth Amendment does not demand a warrant in every case for the arrest to be lawful. Most arrests are made without warrants. At common law a warrant was required to arrest for any *misdemeanor* except a breach of the peace committed in the presence of the officer, and continuing at the time of the arrest. An arrest could be made for a *felony* without a warrant if the officer had reasonable ground to believe that a felony had been committed and the arrested person committed it. These rules have been modified by statute in most of the states. The general rule today is that an officer may arrest without warrant for *all* offenses committed in the presence of the officer, and may arrest a person for a *felony* without a warrant when he has reasonable cause to believe that a felony has been committed and reasonable cause to believe that such person has committed it. These are the exceptions, then, to a general requirement of a warrant prior to an *arrest*. [See Ernest W. Machen, Jr., *The Law of Arrest* (Chapel Hill: Institute of Government, University of North Carolina, 1950); Wayne R. LaFave, *Arrest* (Boston: Little, Brown, 1965).]

As to *searches,* there are two important exceptions to the general requirement of a warrant. The first is a search conducted as an incident to a lawful arrest, and the second is a search of a movable vehicle based upon "probable cause" sufficient to have justified issuance of a warrant had it been requested. In these two situations a search without warrant is not *ipso facto* unreasonable, although the officers may by various improper procedures turn it into an unreasonable search. This would be the case, for example, if the extent of the search is too far-ranging or if the manner in which it is carried out is altogether improper.

The first of these exceptions is of ancient origin. For one reason, the officer should search the person of the accused and the immediate vicinity at least to be certain that there are no weapons by which the arrestee can effect an escape. In addition, the courts are agreed that an officer has the authority, following a lawful arrest, to make such a search in order to prevent the destruction or loss of the fruits of the crime or the instruments by which it was committed. It is important to keep in mind, however, that for such a search to be justified without warrant, the arrest must be lawful on grounds independent of what the search turns up. The protection against unreasonable searches would be for the most part undermined if the arrest could be justified on the basis of evidence turned up by the search. Thus in *Johnson* v. *United States,* 333 U.S. 10 (1948), experienced narcotics officers, after a tip from an informer, went to a hotel room and immediately recognized the odor of burning opium emanating from the room. The officers knocked, and when a woman opened the door, one of the officers said, "I want you to consider yourself under arrest because we are going to search the room." On appeal after conviction, the United States Supreme Court held that at this point the officers had no ground for making the arrest, since they could not have known who was committing the crime. The Court held that the identification of the odor would have been "probable cause" sufficient to obtain a warrant, but that the arrest was invalid and the subsequent search, which indicated that no one else was present but the accused, could not validate the arrest. The government "is obliged to justify the arrest by the search and at the same time to justify the search by the arrest. This will not do. An officer gaining access to private living quarters under color of his office and of the law which he personifies must then have some valid basis in law for the intrusion. Any other rule . . . would obliterate one of the most fundamental distinctions between our form of government, where officers are under the law, and the police-state where they are the law."

Two other questions concerning search incident to arrest were dealt with in *United States* v. *Rabinowitz,* 339 U.S. 56 (1950). These were the issues of the legitimate extent of such a search and also the legality of a search without a warrant which goes beyond the person of the accused to include his room, where the police have time to obtain a search warrant but fail to do so. The majority held that a thorough search of desk, safe and file cabinets in a one-room office following arrest on a valid arrest warrant was not an unreasonable search within the bar of the Fourth Amendment. It further held that the fact that the police had ample time to procure a search warrant but failed to do so did not make the search unreasonable. Contradictions and vacillations in the line of decisions on these points led the Court to make yet another attempt at resolution in 1969.

CHIMEL *v.* CALIFORNIA
395 U.S. 752 (1969)

Mr. Justice Stewart delivered the opinion of the Court.

This case raises basic questions concerning the permissible scope under the Fourth Amendment of a search incident to a lawful arrest.

The relevant facts are essentially undisputed. Late in the afternoon of September 13, 1965, three police officers arrived at the Santa Ana, California, home of the petitioner with a warrant authorizing his arrest for the burglary of a coin shop. The officers knocked on the door, identified themselves to the petitioner's wife, and asked if they might come inside. She ushered them into the house, where they waited 10 or 15 minutes until the petitioner returned home from work. When the petitioner entered the house, one of the officers handed him the arrest warrant and asked for permission to "look around." The petitioner objected, but was advised that "on the basis of the lawful arrest," the officers would nonetheless conduct a search. No search warrant had been issued.

Accompanied by the petitioner's wife, the officers then looked through the entire three-bedroom house, including the attic, the garage, and a small workshop. In some rooms the search was relatively cursory. In the master bedroom and sewing room, however, the officers directed the petitioner's wife to open drawers and "to physically move contents of the drawers from side to side so that [they] might view any items that would have come from [the] burglary." After completing the search, they seized numerous items—primarily coins, but also several medals, tokens, and a few other objects. The entire search took between 45 minutes and an hour.

At the petitioner's subsequent state trial on two charges of burglary, the items taken from his house were admitted into evidence against him, over his objection that they had been unconstitutionally seized. He was convicted, and the judgments of conviction were affirmed by both the California District Court of Appeal . . . and the California Supreme Court.

Without deciding the question, we proceed on the hypothesis that the California courts were correct in holding that the arrest of the petitioner was valid under the Constitution. This brings us directly to the question whether the warrantless search of the petitioner's entire house can be constitutionally justified as incident to that arrest. The decisions of this Court bearing upon that question have been far from consistent, as even the most cursory review makes evident.

Approval of a warrantless search incident to a lawful arrest seems first to have been articulated by the Court in 1914 as dictum in *Weeks* v. *United States*, 232 U.S. 383. . . .

[Here the opinion traces the decisions, and their inconsistencies, from *Weeks* v. *U.S.* to *Harris* v. *U.S.*]

In [*Harris* v. *United States*, 331 U.S. 145 (1947)] officers had obtained a warrant for Harris' arrest on the basis of his alleged involvement with the cashing and interstate transportation of a forged check. He was arrested in the living room of his four-room apartment, and in an attempt to recover two canceled checks thought to have been used in effecting the forgery, the officers undertook a thorough search of the entire apartment. . . . The Court rejected Harris' Fourth Amendment claim, sustaining the search as "incident to arrest." . . .

Only a year after Harris, however, the pendulum swung again. In *Trupiano* v. *United States*, 334 U.S. 699 (1948), agents raided the site of an illicit distillery, saw one of several conspirators operating the still, and arrested him, contemporaneously "seizing the illicit distillery." . . . The Court held that the arrest and others made subsequently had been valid, but that the unexplained failure of the agents to procure a search warrant—in spite of the fact that they had had more than enough time before the raid to do so—rendered the search unlawful. . . .

In 1950, two years after Trupiano, came *United States* v. *Rabinowitz*, 339 U.S. 56, the decision upon which California primarily relies in the case now before us. In Rabinowitz, federal authorities had been informed that the defendant was dealing in stamps bearing forged overprints. On the basis of that information they secured a warrant for his arrest, which they executed at his one-room business office. At the time of the arrest, the officers "searched the desk, safe, and file cabinets in the office for about an hour and a half," . . . and seized 573 stamps with forged overprints. The stamps were admitted into evidence at the defendant's trial, and this Court affirmed his conviction, rejecting the contention that the warrantless search had been unlawful. The Court held that the search in its entirety fell within the principle giving law enforcement authorities "[t]he right 'to search the place where the arrest is made in order to find and seize things connected with the crime. . . .'" Harris was regarded as "ample authority" for that conclusion. . . .

Rabinowitz has come to stand for the proposition, inter alia, that a warrantless search "incident to a lawful arrest" may generally extend to the area that is considered to be in the "possession" or under the "control" of the person arrested. And it was on the basis of that proposition that the California courts upheld the search of the petitioner's entire house in this case. That doctrine, however, at least in the broad sense in which it was applied by the California courts in this case, can withstand neither historical nor rational analysis.

Even limited to its own facts, the Rabinowitz decision was, as we have seen, hardly founded on an unimpeachable line of authority. As Mr. Justice Frankfurter commented in dissent in that case, the "hint" contained in Weeks was, without persuasive justification, "loosely turned into dictum and finally elevated to a decision." ...

Only last Term in *Terry* v. *Ohio*, 392 U.S. 1, we emphasized that "the police must, whenever practicable, obtain advance judicial approval of searches and seizures through the warrant procedure," ... and that "[t]he scope of [a] search must be 'strictly tied to and justified by' the circumstances which rendered its initiation permissible." ... The search undertaken by the officer in that "stop and frisk" case was sustained under that test, because it was no more than a "protective ... search for weapons." ... But in a companion case, *Sibron* v. *New York*, 392 U.S. 40, we applied the same standard to another set of facts and reached a contrary result, holding that a policeman's action in thrusting his hand into a suspect's pocket had been neither motivated by nor limited to the objective of protection. Rather, the search had been made in order to find narcotics, which were in fact found.

A similar analysis underlies the "search incident to arrest" principle, and marks its proper extent. When an arrest is made, it is reasonable for the arresting officer to search the person arrested in order to remove any weapons that the latter might seek to use in order to resist arrest or effect his escape. Otherwise, the officer's safety might well be endangered, and the arrest itself frustrated. In addition, it is entirely reasonable for the arresting officer to search for and seize any evidence on the arrestee's person in order to prevent its concealment or destruction. And the area into which an arrestee might reach in order to grab a weapon or evidentiary items must, of course, be governed by a like rule. A gun on a table or in a drawer in front of one who is arrested can be as dangerous to the arresting officer as one concealed in the clothing of the person arrested. There is ample justification, therefore, for a search of the arrestee's person and the area "within his immediate control"—construing that phrase to mean the area from within which he might gain possession of a weapon or destructible evidence.

There is no comparable justification, however, for routinely searching rooms other than that in which an arrest occurs—or, for that matter, for searching through all the desk drawers or other closed or concealed areas in that room itself. Such searches, in the absence of well-recognized exceptions, may be made only under the authority of a search warrant. The "adherence to judicial processes" mandated by the Fourth Amendment requires no less. ...

The petitioner correctly points out that one result of decisions such as Rabinowitz and Harris is to give law enforcement officials the opportunity to engage in searches not justified by probable cause, by the simple expedient of arranging to arrest suspects at home rather than elsewhere. We do not suggest that the petitioner is necessarily correct in his assertion that such a strategy was utilized here, but the fact remains that had he been arrested earlier in the day, at his place of employment rather than at home, no search of his house could have been made without a search warrant. In any event, even apart from the possibility of such police tactics, the general point so forcefully made by Judge Learned Hand in *United States* v. *Kirchenblatt*, 16 F.2d 202, remains:

"After arresting a man in his house, to rummage at will among his papers in search of whatever will convict him, appears to us to be indistinguishable from what might be done under a general warrant; indeed, the warrant would give more protection, for presumably it must be issued by a magistrate. True, by hypothesis the power would not exist, if the supposed offender were not found on the premises; but it is small consolation to know that one's papers are safe only so long as one is not at home." Id., at 203.

Rabinowitz and Harris have been the subject of critical commentary for many years, and have been relied upon less and less in our own decisions. It is time, for the reasons we have stated, to hold that on their own facts, and insofar as the principles they stand for are inconsistent with those that we have endorsed today, they are no longer to be followed.

Application of sound Fourth Amendment principles to the facts of this case produces a clear result. The search here went far beyond the petitioner's person and the area from within which he might have obtained either a weapon or something that could have been used as evidence against him. There was no constitutional justification, in the absence of a search warrant, for extending the search beyond that area. The scope of the search was, therefore, "unreasonable" under the Fourth and Fourteenth Amendments, and the petitioner's conviction cannot stand.

Reversed.

Mr. Justice Harlan, concurring. . . .
Mr. Justice White, with whom Mr. Justice Black joins, dissenting. . . .

In *Terry* v. *Ohio,* 392 U.S. 1 (1968), and *Sibron* v. *New York,* 392 U.S. 40 (1968), the Court examined the validity of "stop and frisk" practices in two discrete situations. The first involved an experienced officer's observation of three men, his conclusion that they were contemplating a daylight robbery of a store, and his "patting down" procedure which revealed that two of the men carried guns. The second involved an officer's suspicion that Sibron possessed narcotics, and the officer's subsequent search of Sibron's pocket, revealing heroin. Petitioners in each case claimed that the evidence was seized unconstitutionally and sought review of their convictions. The Court held that such warrantless searches had to meet the Fourth Amendment's requirements of probable cause and had to be based on reasonable grounds to believe the suspect to be armed and dangerous. It further distinguished between "patting down" the suspect and actually searching his pockets. Using these tests, the *Terry* evidence was held admissible, but the *Sibron* evidence was held to have been illegally seized. [See Paul G. Chevigny, "Police Abuses in Connection with the Law of Search and Seizure," 5 *Crim. L. Bull.* 3 (1969).]

The second general exception to the requirement of a warrant prior to search is in the situation of movable vehicles, such as automobiles, airplanes, or boats. The leading United States Supreme Court decision on the subject is *Carroll* v. *United States,* 267 U.S. 132 (1925), involving the admissibility of bottles of liquor seized from an automobile by federal prohibition agents without a warrant. Chief Justice Taft, after examining various federal statutes, stated for the Court:

> We have made a somewhat extended reference to these statutes to show that the guaranty of freedom from unreasonable searches and seizures by the Fourth Amendment has been construed, practically since the beginning of the government, as recognizing a necessary difference between a search of a store, dwelling house, or other structure in respect of which a proper official warrant readily may be obtained, and a search of a ship, motor boat, wagon, or automobile for contraband goods, where it is not practicable to secure a warrant because the vehicle can be quickly moved out of the locality or jurisdiction in which the warrant must be sought.

It was brought out in that same opinion, however, that such an exception should not be construed by the police as carte blanche to search movable vehicles out of curiosity or mere suspicion: "In cases where seizure is impossible except without warrant, the seizing officer acts unlawfully and at his peril unless he can show the court probable cause."

In *Brinegar* v. *United States,* in 1949, the Court reaffirmed the principle announced in *Carroll* and also gave some attention to the matter of defining "probable cause."

BRINEGAR *v.* UNITED STATES
338 U.S. 160 (1949)

[Federal officers were patrolling a highway leading from known sources of liquor supply in Joplin, Missouri, to a probable illegal market in "dry" Oklahoma. They observed a car driven by a person whom one of the officers had arrested about five months previously for illegally transporting liquor and whom he knew to have a reputation for hauling liquor. On two prior occasions he had seen the same man loading liquor into his car in large quantities in Joplin, Missouri. The officers pursued the car at high speed and forced it off the road. The driver admitted he was transporting liquor. The liquor was seized and used as evidence at a trial in which the driver was convicted of violating federal liquor laws. At the trial the court denied a motion to suppress the evidence on the claim that there was no probable cause to believe that he was carrying liquor, and therefore the chase and detention were illegal, and the liquor was unlawfully seized.]

Mr. Justice Rutledge delivered the opinion of the Court....

... The evidence here is undisputed, is admissible on the issue of probable cause, and clearly establishes that the agent had good ground for believing that Brinegar was engaged regularly throughout the period in illicit liquor running and dealing....

Guilt in a criminal case must be proved beyond a reasonable doubt and by evidence confined to that which long experience in the common-law tradition, to some extent embodied in the Constitution, has crystallized into rules of evidence consistent with that standard....

However, if those standards were to be made applicable in determining probable cause for an arrest or for search and seizure, more especially in cases such as this involving moving vehicles used in the commission of crime, few indeed would be the situations in which an officer, charged with protecting the public interest by enforcing the law, could take effective action toward that end. Those standards have seldom been so applied.

In dealing with probable cause, however, as the very name implies, we deal with probabilities. These are not technical; they are the factual and practical considerations of everyday life on which reasonable and prudent men, not legal technicians, act. The standard of proof is accordingly correlative to what must be proved.

"The substance of all the definitions" of probable cause "is a reasonable ground for belief of guilt.". . . And this "means less than evidence which would justify condemnation" or conviction, as Marshall, Ch. J., said for the Court more than a century ago. . . . Since Marshall's time, at any rate, it has come to mean more than bare suspicion: Probable cause exists where "the facts and circumstances within their [the officers'] knowledge, and of which they had reasonably trustworthy information, [are] sufficient in themselves to warrant a man of reasonable caution in the belief that" an offense has been or is being committed. *Carroll* v. *United States*, 267 U.S. 132, 162.

The rule of probable cause is a practical, non-technical conception affording the best compromise that has been found for accommodating . . . often opposing interests. Requiring more would unduly hamper law enforcement. To allow less would be to leave law-abiding citizens at the mercy of the officers' whim or caprice. . . .

Accordingly the judgment is   *Affirmed.*

Mr. Justice Jackson, joined by Justices Frankfurter and Murphy, dissenting.
. . . Undoubtedly the automobile presents peculiar problems for law enforcement agencies, is frequently a facility for the perpetration of crime and an aid in the escape of criminals. But if we are to make judicial exceptions to the Fourth Amendment for these reasons, it seems to me they should depend somewhat upon the gravity of the offense. If we assume, for example, that a child is kidnaped and the officers throw a roadblock about the neighborhood and search every outgoing car, it would be a drastic and undiscriminating use of the search. The officers might be unable to show probable cause for searching any particular car. However, I should candidly strive hard to sustain such an action, executed fairly and in good faith, because it might be reasonable to subject travelers to that indignity if it was the only way to save a life and detect a vicious crime. But I should not strain to sustain such a roadblock and universal search to salvage a few bottles of bourbon and catch a bootlegger. . . .

In *Draper* v. *United States*, 358 U.S. 307 (1959), the Court affirmed a conviction for illegal transportation of narcotics, and the crucial question was whether the arresting officer had "probable cause" to believe the petitioner was committing a crime when the arrest was made, thus permitting the narcotics turned up by the subsequent search to be introduced as evidence. It was established that the federal narcotics agent had some twenty-nine years experience, that one Hereford had been engaged as a "special employee" of the Bureau of Narcotics for about six months and from time to time gave tips to the agent regarding narcotics violations, and that the agent had always found such tips to be accurate and reliable. Hereford told the agent that Draper had moved to a specified address, "was peddling narcotics to several addicts," that he had gone to Chicago to buy heroin and would return on either the morning of September 8th or of September 9th by train. He also gave the agent a detailed physical description of Draper and of the clothing he was wearing, and said that he would be carrying a tan zipper bag, and that he habitually "walked real fast." On the morning of September 9th agents saw a person alight from an incoming Chicago train. He had the exact physical attributes and wore the precise clothing described by Hereford. He walked rapidly and carried a tan zipper bag. The agent arrested him, searched him, and found two envelopes containing heroin. The trial court denied a motion to suppress the evidence, and Draper was convicted.

With one dissent, the Court affirmed the conviction. The petitioner contended that the information given to the agent was "hearsay" and, since it could not have been legally competent evidence in a criminal trial, could not be used in assessing "probable cause." He argued further that even if it could have been considered, it was insufficient to constitute "probable cause" justifying the arrest. Citing *Brinegar* v. *United States*, the Court rejected petitioner's contentions and held the arrest, and therefore the subsequent search, lawful.

In *Beck* v. *Ohio*, 379 U.S. 89 (1964), however, the Court reversed a conviction for unlawful possession of gambling slips, where the officers stopped petitioner while driving his car, arrested him without a warrant, searched his car, and finally found clearing house slips "beneath the sock of his leg." The only bases for the arrest were the statements of one of the officers that petitioner had "a record in connection with clearing house and scheme of chance," and that he had "information" and that he had "heard reports." The majority of six distinguished the case from *Draper* in that the record nowhere showed what information the officer had received or what the source of such information was, and held that "the Constitution demands a greater showing of probable cause than can be found in the present record."

It should not be assumed that informers must be identified in court, however, to meet the requirements of probable cause or of the right of confrontation. In *McCray* v. *Illinois*, 386 U.S. 300 (1967), the Court held that in the circumstances of the case, the police did not have to reveal their informer's identity. The informer told police that petitioner "was selling narcotics and had narcotics on his person and that he could be found in the vicinity of 47th and Calumet at this particular time." The officers proceeded to that vicinity, found petitioner, arrested him, and in the ensuing search found heroin on his person. The officers had known the informant for more than a year, in which time, according to one officer, he had given information concerning narcotics "20 or 25 times" and that the information had resulted in convictions. The majority of five distinguished the case from *Beck* v. *Ohio*, and held that as in *Draper* v. *United States* there was probable cause to sustain the arrest and incidental search.

In addition to the two well-recognized exceptions to the requirement of a search warrant (and the obvious one of consent), another situation was considered by the Court in 1959—the right of a health inspector to examine private premises without a warrant. The case was *Frank* v. *Maryland*, 359 U.S. 360 (1959), holding that conviction and fine for refusal to permit a health inspector to inspect the premises for rat infestation did not violate the Fourteenth Amendment. The majority opinion, through Justice Frankfurter, first stressed the point that the inspection was conducted solely to determine whether there were conditions existing which were forbidden by ordinance—not to gather evidence for a criminal prosecution. He further pointed to the long history of administrative inspections:

Inspection without a warrant, as an adjunct to a regulatory scheme for the general welfare of the community and not as a means of enforcing the criminal law, has antecedents deep in our history. For more than 200 years Maryland has empowered its officers to enter upon ships, carriages, shops, and homes in the service of the common welfare. . . .

Justice Douglas, joined by three others, filed a vigorous dissent. The close vote of five-to-four suggested a tenuous status for the Court's holding. Justice Frankfurter had indicated that as the complexities and problems of urban life increased, so would the need for freer governmental right to inspect. Others, however, argued that for the same reasons the government should be more severely limited in order to forestall mounting invasions of privacy without some probable cause requirement as included in the issuance of a search warrant. The controversy culminated in a reexamination of the question in 1967 and the overruling of *Frank* v. *Maryland*.

CAMARA *v.* MUNICIPAL COURT OF SAN FRANCISCO
387 U.S. 523 (1967)

[An inspector of the Division of Housing Inspection of the San Francisco Department of Public Health entered an apartment building to make a routine annual inspection for possible violations of the city's Housing Code. The building's manager informed the inspector that appellant, lessee of the ground floor, was using the rear of his leasehold as a personal residence. Claiming that the building's occupancy permit did not allow residential use of the ground floor, the inspector confronted appellant and demanded that he permit an inspection of the premises. Appellant refused to allow the inspection because the inspector lacked a search warrant. The inspector returned two days later, again without a warrant, and appellant again refused to allow an inspection. A citation was then mailed ordering appellant to appear at the district attorney's office. When appellant failed to appear, two inspectors returned to his apartment and informed him that he was required to permit an inspection under §503 of the Housing Code, which set up a right of entry for authorized city employees "at reasonable times" for the purpose of performing any duty imposed upon them by the Municipal Code. Appellant still refused to permit the search without a warrant. Thereafter he was arrested and charged with refusing to permit a lawful inspection. When his demurrer to the criminal complaint was denied, appellant filed this petition for a writ of prohibition.]

Mr. Justice White delivered the opinion of the Court. . . .

In *Frank* v. *Maryland*, this Court upheld the conviction of one who refused to permit a warrantless inspection of private premises for the purposes of locating and abating a suspected public nuisance. Although *Frank* can arguably be distinguished from these cases on its facts, the *Frank* opinion has generally been interpreted as carving out an additional exception to the rule that warrantless searches are unreasonable under the Fourth Amendment. . . . The District Court of Appeal so interpreted *Frank* in this case, and that ruling is the core of appellant's challenge here. We proceed to a re-examination of the factors which persuaded the *Frank* majority to adopt this construction of the Fourth Amendment's prohibition against unreasonable searches.

To the *Frank* majority, municipal fire, health, and housing inspection programs "touch at most upon the periphery of the important interests safeguarded by the Fourteenth Amendment's protection against official intrusions,". . . because the inspections are merely to determine whether physical conditions exist which do not comply with minimum standards prescribed in local regulatory ordinances. Since the inspector does not ask that the property owner open his doors to a search for "evidence of criminal action" which may be used to secure the owner's criminal conviction, historic interests of "self-protection" jointly protected by the Fourth and Fifth Amendments are said not to be involved. . . .

We may agree that a routine inspection of the physical condition of private property is a less hostile intrusion than the typical policeman's search for the fruits and instrumentalities of crime. . . . But we cannot agree that the Fourth Amendment interests at stake in these inspection cases are merely "peripheral.". . . [E]ven the most law-abiding citizen has a very tangible interest in limiting the circumstances under which the sanctity of his home may be broken by official authority, for the possibility of criminal entry under the guise of official sanction is a serious threat to personal and family security. And even accepting *Frank*'s rather remarkable premise, inspections of the kind we are here considering do in fact jeopardize "self-protection" interests of the property owner. Like most regulatory laws, fire, health, and housing codes are enforced by criminal processes. In some cities, discovery of a violation by the inspector leads to a criminal complaint. . . .

The final justification suggested for warrantless administrative searches is that the public interest demands such a rule: it is vigorously argued that the health and safety of entire urban populations is dependent upon enforcement of minimum fire, housing, and sanitation standards, and that the only effective means of enforcing such codes is by routine systematized inspection of all physical structures. . . . But we think this argument misses the mark. The question is not, at this stage at least, whether these inspections may be made, but whether they may be made without a warrant. . . . It has nowhere been urged that fire, health, and housing code inspection programs could not achieve their goals within the confines of a reasonable search warrant requirement. . . .

In summary, we hold that administrative searches of the kind at issue here are significant intrusions upon the interests protected by the Fourth Amendment, that such searches when authorized and conducted without a warrant procedure lack the traditional safeguards which the Fourth Amendment guarantees to the individual, and that the reasons put forth in *Frank* v. *Maryland* and in other cases for upholding these warrantless searches are insufficient to justify so substantial a weakening of the Fourth Amendment's protections. Because of the nature of the municipal programs under consideration, however, these conclusions must be the beginning, not the end of our inquiry. . . .

[The opinion then discusses the "probable cause" requirement of the Fourth Amendment, and the conclusion is reached that this requirement would not necessarily be the same for municipal code inspection programs as for criminal investigations. The standard of reasonableness is weighed in terms of the needs and goals of code enforcement. Thus "area inspections" would not be justified in a search for stolen goods, but in the enforcement of fire, sanitation and housing codes, "such programs have a long history of judicial and public acceptance."]

Having concluded that the area inspection is a "reasonable" search of private property within the meaning of the Fourth Amendment, it is obvious that "probable cause" to issue a warrant to inspect must exist if reasonable legislative or administrative standards for conducting an area inspection are satisfied with respect to a particular dwelling. Such standards, which will vary with the municipal program being enforced, may be based upon the passage of time, the nature of the building (*e.g.*, a multi-family apartment house), or the condition of the entire area, but they will not necessarily depend upon specific knowledge of the condition of the particular dwelling. It has been suggested that so to vary the probable cause test from the standard applied in criminal cases would be to authorize a "synthetic search warrant" and thereby to lessen the overall protections of the Fourth Amendment. *Frank* v. *Maryland*. . . . But we do not agree. The warrant procedure is designed to guarantee that a decision to search private property is justified by a reasonable governmental interest. But reasonableness is still the ultimate standard. If a valid public interest justifies the intrusion contemplated, then there is probable cause to issue a suitably restricted search warrant. . . .

Since our holding emphasizes the controlling standard of reasonableness, nothing we say today is intended to foreclose prompt inspections, even without a warrant, that the law has traditionally upheld in emergency situations. . . . (seizure of unwholesome food) . . . (compulsory small pox vaccination) . . . (health quarantine) . . . (summary destruction of tubercular cattle). On the other hand, in the case of most routine area inspections, there is no compelling urgency to inspect at a particular time or on a particular day. Moreover, most citizens allow inspections of their property without a warrant. Thus, as a practical matter and in light of the Fourth Amendment's requirement that a warrant specify the property to be searched, it seems likely that warrants should normally be sought only after entry is refused unless there has been a citizen complaint or there is other satisfactory reason for securing immediate entry. . . .

The judgment is vacated and the case is remanded for further proceedings not inconsistent with this opinion.

It is so ordered.

[In the companion case of *See* v. *Seattle*, 387 U.S. 541 (1967), the Court held that the *Camara* rule applied to commercial structures as well as private residences.]

Mr. Justice Clark, with whom Mr. Justice Harlan and Mr. Justice Stewart join, dissenting. . . .

. . . As I read it, the Fourth Amendment guarantee of individual privacy is, by its language, specifically qualified. It prohibits only those searches that are "unreasonable." The majority seem to recognize this for they set up a new test for the long-recognized and enforced Fourth Amendment's "probable cause" requirement for the issuance of warrants. They would permit the issuance of paper warrants, in area inspection programs, with probable cause based on area inspection standards as set out in municipal codes, and with warrants issued by the rubber stamp of a willing magistrate. In my view, this degrades the Fourth Amendment.

Moreover, history supports the *Frank* disposition. Over 150 years of city *in rem* inspections for health and safety purposes have continuously been enforced. In only one case during all that period have the courts denied municipalities this right....

... The majority seems to hold that warrants may be obtained after a refusal of initial entry; I can find no such constitutional distinction or command. This boxcar warrant will be identical as to every dwelling in the area, save the street number itself. I daresay they will be printed up in pads of a thousand or more—with space for the street number to be inserted—and issued by magistrates in broadcast fashion as a matter of course.

I ask: Why go through such an exercise, such a pretense? As the same essentials are being followed under present procedures, I ask: Why the ceremony, the delay, the expense, the abuse of the search warrant? In my view this will not only destroy its integrity but will degrade the magistrate issuing them and soon bring disrepute not only upon the practice but upon the judicial process. It will be very costly to the city in paperwork incident to the issuance of the paper warrants, in loss of time of inspectors and waste of the time of magistrates and will result in more annoyance to the public. It will also be more burdensome to the occupant of the premises to be inspected. Under a search warrant the inspector can enter any time he chooses. Under the existing procedures he can enter only at reasonable times and invariably the convenience of the occupant is considered. I submit that the identical grounds for action elaborated today give more support—both legal and practical— to the present practice as approved in *Frank* v. *Maryland, supra,* than it does to this legalistic facade that the Court creates....

A peculiar aspect of the administrative search is the unannounced late-night "bedcheck" by welfare agencies to ensure that deserted wives who are recipients of family support payments are not being visited by their husbands and thus forfeiting benefit rights. No warrant is used, but failure of the recipient to permit the search in itself is sufficient to withdraw support payments. In *Wyman* v. *James,* 400 U.S. 309 (1971), the Court held that such searches, with the coercive aspect of threatened termination of benefits, did not violate Fourth Amendment protections. [For criticism of the practice, see Albert M. Bendich, "Privacy, Poverty, and the Constitution," 54 *Calif. L. Rev.* 407 (1966), and Charles A. Reich, "Midnight Welfare Searches and the Social Security Act," 72 *Yale L. J.* 1347

WYMAN *v.* JAMES

400 U.S. 309 (1971)

Mr. Justice Blackmun delivered the opinion of the Court.

This appeal presents the issue whether a beneficiary of the program for Aid to

Families with Dependent Children (AFDC) may refuse a home visit by the case-worker without risking the termination of benefits.

The New York State and City social services commissioners appeal from a judgment and decree of a divided three-judge District Court holding invalid and un-constitutional in application §134 of the New York Social Services Law ... and granting injunctive relief ... The beneficiary's thesis, and that of the District Court majority, is that home visitation is a search and, when not consented to or when not supported by a warrant based on probable cause, violates the beneficiary's Fourth and Fourteenth Amendment rights. . . .

When a case involves a home and some type of official intrusion into that home, as this case appears to do, an immediate and natural reaction is one of concern about Fourth Amendment rights and the protection which that Amendment is intended to afford. . . .

This natural and quite proper protective attitude, however, is not a factor in this case, for the seemingly obvious and simple reason that we are not concerned here with any search by the New York social service agency in the Fourth Amendment meaning of that term. It is true that the governing statute and regulations appear to make mandatory the initial home visit and the subsequent periodic "contacts" (which may include home visits) for the inception and continuance of aid. It is also true that the caseworker's posture in the home visit is perhaps, in a sense, both rehabilitative and investigative. But this latter aspect, we think, is given too broad a character and far more emphasis than it deserves if it is equated with a search in the traditional criminal law context. We note, too, that the visitation in itself is not forced or compelled, and that the beneficiary's denial of permission is not a criminal act. If consent to the visitation is withheld, no visitation takes place. The aid then never begins or merely ceases, as the case may be. There is no entry of the home and there is no search. . . .

There are a number of factors which compel us to conclude that the home visit proposed for Mrs. James is not unreasonable:

1. The public's interest in this particular segment of the area of assistance to the unfortunate is protection and aid for the dependent child whose family requires such aid for that child. The focus is on the *child* and, further, it is on the child who is *dependent*. There is no more worthy object of the public's concern. The dependent child's needs are paramount, and only with hesitancy would we relegate those needs, in the scale of comparative values, to a position secondary to what the mother claims as her rights.

2. The agency, with tax funds provided from federal as well as from state sources, is fulfilling a public trust. The State, working through its qualified wel-fare agency, has appropriate and paramount interest and concern in seeing and assuring that the intended and proper objects of that tax-produced assistance are the ones who benefit from the aid it dispenses. Surely it is not unreasonable, in the Fourth Amendment sense or in any other sense of that term, that the State have at its command a gentle means, of limited extent and of practical and considerate application, of achieving that assurance.

3. One who dispenses purely private charity naturally has an interest in and expects to know how his charitable funds are utilized and put to work. The public, when it is the provider, rightly expects the samee. It might well expect more, be-cause of the trust aspect of public funds, and the recipient, as well as the case-worker, has not only an interest but an obligation. . . .

7. Mrs. James, in fact, on this record presents no specific complaint of any

unreasonable intrusion of her home and nothing which supports an inference that the desired home visit had as its purpose the obtaining of information as to criminal activity. She complains of no proposed visitation at an awkward or retirement hour. She suggests no forcible entry. She refers to no snooping. . . . What Mrs. James appears to want from the agency which provides her and her infant son with the necessities for life is the right to receive those necessities upon her own informational term, to utilize the Fourth Amendment as a wedge for imposing those terms, and to avoid questions of any kind. . . .

Mr. Justice Douglas, dissenting. . . .

Mr. Justice Marshall, whom Mr. Justice Brennan joins, dissenting. . . .

Although the Court does not agree with my conclusion that the home visit is an unreasonable search, its opinion suggests that even if the visit were unreasonable, appellee has somehow waived her right to object. Surely the majority cannot believe that valid Fourth Amendment consent can be given under the threat of the loss of one's sole means of support. . . .

In deciding that the homes of AFDC recipients are not entitled to protection from warrantless searches by welfare caseworkers, the Court declines to follow prior case law and employs a rationale that, if applied to the claims of all citizens, would threaten the vitality of the Fourth Amendment. . . . I find no little irony in the fact that the burden of today's departure from principled adjudication is placed upon the lowly poor. Perhaps the majority has explained why a commercial warehouse deserves more protection than does this poor woman's home. I am not convinced; and therefore, I must respectfully dissent.

In *Griswold* v. *Connecticut,* 381 U.S. 479 (1965), a majority of the Court indicated that the Constitution creates "zones of privacy" which are beyond the scope of any legitimate search, and held invalid the Connecticut law barring the use of any drug or instrument for contraceptive purposes. Justice Douglas, for the majority, said: "Would we allow the police to search the sacred precincts of marital bedrooms for telltale signs of the use of contraceptives? The very idea is repulsive to the notions of privacy surrounding the marriage relationship." The constitutional basis for this right of privacy was seemingly found in the Fourth Amendment. The Justice stated: "We recently referred in *Mapp* v. *Ohio* . . . to the Fourth Amendment as creating a 'right to privacy, no less important than any other right carefully and particularly reserved to the people.' See Beaney, The Constitutional Right to Privacy, 1962 *Sup. Ct. Rev.* 212; Griswold, The Right to be Let Alone, 55 *Nw. U. L. Rev.* 216 (1960)."

Justice Goldberg, joined by the Chief Justice and Justice Brennan, concurred, but he referred to a different source for the "right of marital privacy." He stated that the Ninth Amendment was designed to protect additional fundamental rights not enumerated in the first eight amendments, and that a right of marital privacy was so "basic and fundamental and so deep-rooted in our society" that it could not be abridged without violating the Ninth Amendment. The ramifications of opening up broad construction of the Ninth Amendment to judicial review of state and federal legislation were pointedly criticized by dissenting Justices Black and Stewart.

In view of the enormous refinements in electronic surveillance and the increase in various forms of psychological testing for attitudes, habits, prejudices and beliefs, the developing law in the area of a constitutional right to privacy compels particular attention for the next few years. It is somewhat early at this point to state firm rules of law on the matter. [See Alan F. Westin, "Science, Privacy, and Freedom: Issues and Proposals for the 1970's," 66 *Colum. L. Rev.* 1003 (1966).]

ADMISSIBILITY OF EVIDENCE OBTAINED ILLEGALLY

The distinction between the question of unreasonable searches and the question of admissibility of illegally obtained evidence is important, because in *Weeks* v. *United States*, 232 U.S. 383 (1914), the Court held that the Fourth Amendment did not of its own force bar from a criminal prosecution the use of items seized illegally. The Fourth Amendment did not, according to the rule of *Weeks*, constitute a rule of evidence. The Court went on to state, however, that unless such evidence were excluded, the Fourth Amendment would present no effective bar to improper searches and seizures. Thus *Weeks* held that as a federal rule of evidence, which in its supervisory function the Supreme Court can lay down for all federal courts, evidence illegally obtained by federal officers could not be used in a federal prosecution. (A majority of the Court, however, has now construed the *Weeks* rule as a Fourth Amendment requirement.)

At this point the complications of the federal system again enter the picture. Fourth Amendment limitations do not necessarily spell out the coverage of Fourteenth Amendment due process limitations on the states. And federal exclusionary rules are not applicable to the states' criminal procedures unless they rise to the level of constitutional requirements. The Fourteenth Amendment test, in the words of Justice Cardozo in *Palko* v. *Connecticut*, is whether a particular procedure or safeguard is "of the very essence of a scheme of ordered liberty." In 1949, the United States Supreme Court in *Wolf* v. *Colorado*, 338 U.S. 25, held that for the states to permit the use of evidence obtained illegally in a criminal prosecution was not a violation of the Fourteenth Amendment. Justice Frankfurter's opinion for the majority adverted to the *Weeks* doctrine, pointing out that as of 1949, thirty states rejected the *Weeks* doctrine, while seventeen states were in agreement with it. In view of this survey, he stated:

The jurisdictions which have rejected the *Weeks* doctrine have not left the right of privacy without other means of protection. Indeed, the exclusion of evidence is a remedy which directly serves only to protect those upon whose person or premises something incriminating has been found. We cannot, therefore, regard it as a departure from basic standards to remand such persons, together with those who emerge scatheless from a search, to the remedies of private action and such protection as the internal discipline of the police, under the eyes of an alert public opinion, may afford. Granting that in practice the exclusion of evidence may be an effective way of deterring unreasonable searches, it is not for this Court to condemn as falling below the minimal standards assured by the Due Process Clause a State's reliance upon other methods which, if consistently enforced, would be equally effective. . . .

We hold, therefore, that in a prosecution in a State court for a State crime the Fourteenth Amendment does not forbid the admission of evidence obtained by an unreasonable search and seizure.

Despite the holding that illegally obtained evidence was not barred in a subsequent prosecution, Justice Frankfurter's opinion pointed out that "were a State affirmatively to sanction such police incursion into privacy it would run counter to the guaranty of the Fourteenth Amendment violation." Thus the majority held that arbitrary and illegal searches and seizures by the state constituted a Fourteenth Amendment violation, but this did not bar the introduction of the evidence so obtained in a prosecution. The apparent contradiction can be resolved in one way by making such conduct on the part of state officers actionable under the civil or criminal provisions of the Civil Rights Acts. This, of course, is exactly what the Court held in 1961 in the case of *Monroe* v. *Pape*, discussed earlier.

Justice Murphy, in one of the three dissenting opinions in the *Wolf* case, said:

The conclusion is inescapable that but one remedy exists to deter violations of the search and seizure clause. That is the rule which excludes illegally obtained evidence. Only by exclusion can we impress upon the zealous prosecutor that violation of the Constitution will do him no good. And only when that point is driven home can the prosecutor be expected to emphasize the importance of observing constitutional demands in his instructions to the police.

The frustrations experienced by some members of the Court, occasioned by adherence to the *Wolf* rule, were sharply brought to focus in the case of *Irvine* v. *California*, 374 U.S. 128 (1954). In *Irvine* the police, after having made a key to fit the door, made repeated illegal entries into the home of a suspected bookmaker. They installed a secret microphone in the home and moved it from room to room, including the Irvines' bedroom. For over a month the police eavesdropped on conversations in this way, and on the basis of information thus obtained Irvine was tried and convicted. The United States Supreme Court affirmed, on authority of the *Wolf* rule, but Justice Jackson, who announced the judgment of the Court and wrote the principal opinion, thoroughly excoriated the behavior of the police. He stated that what was done "would be almost incredible if it were not admitted. Few police measures have come to our attention that more flagrantly, deliberately, and persistently violated the fundamental principle declared by the Fourth Amendment as a restriction on the Federal Government." Justice Jackson made a novel suggestion in the case, indicating his strong feeling that the officers should not escape unscathed, even though the evidence was admissible:

If the officials have willfully deprived a citizen of the United States of a right or privilege secured to him by the Fourteenth Amendment, that being the right to be secure in his home against unreasonable searches, as defined in *Wolf* v. *Colorado*, their conduct may constitute a federal crime. . . . We believe the Clerk of this Court should be directed to forward a copy of the record in this case, together with a copy of this opinion, for attention of the Attorney General of the United States.

The dissatisfaction with *Wolf*'s bifurcation of the Fourth Amendment culminated in 1961 in a landmark case in the area of searches and seizures. The case was *Mapp* v. *Ohio,* and a majority of the Court officially adopted the conclusion expressed by Justice Murphy in his dissent in the *Wolf* case.

MAPP *v.* OHIO
367 U.S. 643 (1961)

Mr. Justice Clark delivered the opinion of the Court.

Appellant stands convicted of knowingly having had in her possession and under her control certain lewd and lascivious books, pictures, and photographs in violation of . . . Ohio's Revised Code. As officially stated in the syllabus to its opinion, the Supreme Court of Ohio found that her conviction was valid though "based primarily upon the introduction in evidence of lewd and lascivious books and pictures unlawfully seized during an unlawful search of defendant's home. . . ."

[Three Cleveland police officers had come to appellant's residence in 1957, demanding entry on information that "a person was hiding out in the home who was wanted for questioning in connection with a recent bombing" and that policy paraphernalia was hidden in the home. Appellant, after phoning her attorney, refused to admit them without a search warrant. They returned later with several additional officers and forcibly broke into the house. Mrs. Mapp demanded to see a warrant. A paper, claimed to be a warrant, was held up by one of the officers. She grabbed the "warrant" and placed it in her bosom. A struggle ensued in which the officers recovered the piece of paper and handcuffed appellant because she had been "belligerent" in resisting their official rescue of the "warrant" from her person. The entire first and second floors of the house were thoroughly searched, and the search spread to the basement. In a trunk in the basement officers found the obscene material, for possession of which she was ultimately convicted. At the trial no search warrant was produced by the prosecution, nor was the failure to produce one explained or accounted for. The Ohio Supreme Court stated that there was "considerable doubt as to whether there ever was any warrant for the search of defendant's home." That court, however, followed *Wolf* v. *Colorado* in holding that despite the illegal seizure, the evidence obtained was admissible.]

I

Seventy-five years ago, in *Boyd* v. *United States* . . . , considering the Fourth and Fifth Amendments as running "almost into each other" on the facts before it, this Court held that the doctrines of those Amendments "apply to all invasions on the part of the government and its employees of the sanctity of a man's home and the privacies of life. . . .

The Court noted that "constitutional provisions for the security of person and property should be liberally construed. . . . It is the duty of courts to be watchful for the constitutional rights of the citizen, and against any stealthy encroachments thereon.". . .

Less than 30 years after *Boyd*, this Court, in *Weeks* v. *United States*, . . . stated that "the Fourth Amendment . . . put the courts of the United States and Federal officials, in the exercise of their power and authority, under limitations and restraints [and] . . . forever secure[d] the people, their persons, houses, papers and effects against all unreasonable searches and seizures under the guise of law . . . and the duty of giving to it force and effect is obligatory upon all entrusted under our Federal system with the enforcement of the laws.". . .

Finally, the Court in that case clearly stated that use of the seized evidence involved "a denial of the constitutional rights of the accused." At p. 398. Thus, in the year 1914, in the *Weeks* case, this Court "for the first time" held that "in a federal prosecution the Fourth Amendment barred the use of evidence secured through an illegal search and seizure." *Wolf* v. *Colorado* . . . This Court has ever since required of federal law officers a strict adherence to that command which this Court has held to be a clear, specific, and constitutionally required—even if judicially implied—deterrent safeguard without insistence upon which the Fourth Amendment would have been reduced to "a form of words." *Holmes, J., Silverthorne Lumber Co.* v. *United States.* . . .

II

In 1949, 35 years after *Weeks* was announced, this Court, in *Wolf* v. *Colorado* . . . , again for the first time, discussed the effect of the Fourth Amendment upon the States through the operation of the Due Process Clause of the Fourteenth Amendment. It said:

"We have no hesitation in saying that were a State affirmatively to sanction such police incursion into privacy it would run counter to the guaranty of the Fourteenth Amendment." At p. 28.

Nevertheless, after declaring that the "security of one's privacy against arbitrary intrusion by the police" is "implicit in the 'concept of ordered liberty' and as such enforceable against the States through the Due Process Clause,". . . and announcing that it "stoutly adhere[d]" to the *Weeks* decision, the Court decided that the *Weeks* exclusionary rule would not then be imposed upon the States as "an essential ingredient of the right.". . . The Court's reasons for not considering essential to the right to privacy, as a curb imposed upon the States by the Due Process Clause, that which decades before had been posited as part and parcel of the Fourth Amendment's limitation upon federal encroachment of individual privacy, were bottomed on factual considerations.

While they are not basically relevant to a decision that the exclusionary rule is an essential ingredient of the Fourth Amendment as the right it embodies is vouchsafed against the States by the Due Process Clause, we will consider the current validity of the factual grounds upon which *Wolf* was based. . . .

. . . While in 1949, prior to the *Wolf* case, almost two-thirds of the States were opposed to the exclusionary rule, now, despite the *Wolf* case, more than half of those since passing upon it, by their own legislative or judicial decision, have wholly or partly adopted or adhered to the *Weeks* rule. . . . Significantly, among those now following the rule is California which, according to its highest court, was "compelled to reach that conclusion because other remedies have completely failed to secure compliance with the constitutional provisions. . . ." In connection with this California case, we note that the second basis elaborated in *Wolf* in support of its failure to enforce the exclusionary doctrine against the States was that "other means of protection" have been afforded "the right to privacy.". . . The experience of California that such other remedies have been worthless and futile is buttressed by the experience of other States. The obvious futility of relegating the Fourth Amendment to the protection of other remedies has, moreover, been recognized by this Court since *Wolf*. See *Irvine* v. *California*. . . .

Likewise, time has set its face against what *Wolf* called the "weighty testimony" of *People* v. *Defore*. . . . There Justice (then Judge) Cardozo, rejecting adoption of the *Weeks* exclusionary rule in New York, had said that "[t]he Federal rule as it stands is either too strict or too lax.". . . However, the force of that reasoning has been largely vitiated by later decisions of this Court. These include the recent discarding of the "silver platter" doctrine which allowed federal judicial use of evidence seized in violation of the Constitution by state agents, *Elkins* v. *United States*, 364 U.S. 206, *supra*; the relaxation of the formerly strict requirements as to standing to challenge the use of evidence thus seized, so that now the procedure of exclusion, "ultimately referable to constitutional safeguards," is available to anyone even "legitimately on [the] premises" unlawfully searched, *Jones* v. *United States*, 362 U.S. 257 (1960); and, finally, the formulation of a method to prevent state use of evidence unconstitutionally seized by federal agents, *Rea* v. *United States*, 350 U.S. 214 (1956). . . .

It, therefore, plainly appears that the factual considerations supporting the failure of the *Wolf* Court to include the *Weeks* exclusionary rule when it recognized the enforceability of the right to privacy against the States in 1949, while not basically relevant to the constitutional consideration, could not, in any analysis, now be deemed controlling.

III

. . . And only last Term, after again carefully re-examining the *Wolf* doctrine in *Elkins* v. *United States* . . . the Court pointed out that "the controlling principles" as to search and seizure and the problem of admissibility "seemed clear" until the announcement in *Wolf* "that the Due Process Clause of the Fourteenth Amendment does not itself require state courts to adopt the exclusionary rule" of the *Weeks* case. . . . At the same time the Court pointed out, "the underlying constitutional doctrine which Wolf established . . . that the Federal Constitution . . . prohibits unreasonable searches and seizures by state officers" had undermined the "foundation upon which the admissibility of state-seized evidence in a federal trial originally rested. . . ." The Court concluded that it was therefore obliged to hold, although it chose the narrower ground on which to do so, that all evidence obtained by an unconstitutional search and seizure was inadmissible in a federal court regardless of its source. Today we once again examine *Wolf*'s constitutional documentation of the right to privacy free from unreasonable state intrusion, and, after its dozen years on our books, are led by it to close the only courtroom door remaining open to evidence secured by official lawlessness in flagrant abuse of that basic right, reserved to all persons as a specific guarantee against that very same unlawful conduct. We hold that all evidence obtained by searches and seizures in violation of the Constitution is, by that same authority, inadmissible in a state court. . . .

V

. . . Moreover, our holding that the exclusionary rule is an essential part of both the Fourth and Fourteenth Amendments is not only the logical dictate of prior cases, but it also makes very good sense. There is no war between the Constitution and common sense. Presently, a federal prosecutor may make no use of evidence illegally seized, but a State's attorney across the street may, although he supposedly is operating under the enforceable prohibitions of the same Amendment. Thus, the State, by admitting evidence unlawfully seized, serves to encourage disobedience to the Federal Constitution which it is bound to uphold. Moreover, as was said in *Elkins*, "[t]he very essence of a healthy federalism depends upon the avoidance of needless conflict between state and federal courts.". . . Such a conflict, hereafter needless, arose this very Term, in *Wilson* v. *Schnettler, 365* U.S. 381 (1961), in which, and in spite of the promise made by *Rea,* we gave full recognition to our practice in this regard by refusing to restrain a federal officer from testifying in a state court as to evidence unconstitutionally seized by him in the performance of his duties. Yet the double standard recognized until today hardly put such a thesis into practice. In nonexclusionary States, federal officers, being human, were by it invited to and did, as our cases indicate, step across the street to the State's attorney with their unconstitutionally seized evidence. Prosecution on the basis of that evidence was then had in a state court in utter disregard of the enforceable Fourth Amendment. If the fruits of an unconstitutional search had been inadmissible in both state and federal courts, this inducement to evasion would have been sooner eliminated. There would be no need to reconcile such cases as *Rea* and *Schnettler,* each pointing up the hazardous uncertainties of our heretofore ambivalent approach. . . .

There are those who say, as did Justice (then Judge) Cardozo that under our constitutional exclusionary doctrine "[t]he criminal is to go free because the constable has blundered.". . . In some cases this will undoubtedly be the result. But, as was said in *Elkins*, "there is another consideration—the imperative of judicial integrity.". . . The criminal goes free, if he must, but it is the law that sets him free. Nothing can destroy a government more quickly than its failure to observe its own laws, or worse, its disregard of the charter of its own existence. . . .

The judgment of the Supreme Court of Ohio is reversed and the cause remanded for further proceedings not inconsistent with this opinion.

Reversed and Remanded.

Mr. Justice Black, concurring.

. . . I am still not persuaded that the Fourth Amendment, standing alone, would be enough to bar the introduction into evidence against an accused of papers and effects seized from him in violation of its commands. For the Fourth Amendment does not itself contain any provision expressly precluding the use of such evidence, and I am extremely doubtful that such a provision could properly be inferred from nothing more than the basic command against unreasonable searches and seizures. Reflection on the problem, however, in the light of cases coming before the Court since *Wolf,* has led me to conclude that when the Fourth Amendment's ban against unreasonable searches and seizures is considered together with the Fifth Amendment's ban against compelled self-incrimination, a constitutional basis emerges which not only justifies but actually requires the exclusionary rule. . . .

Mr. Justice Douglas, concurring. . . .

Mr. Justice Harlan, whom Mr. Justice Frankfurter and Mr. Justice Whittaker join, dissenting.

In overruling the *Wolf* case the Court, in my opinion, has forgotten the sense of judicial restraint which, with due regard for *stare decisis,* is one element that should enter into deciding whether a past decision of this Court should be overruled. Apart from that I also believe the *Wolf* rule represents sounder Constitutional doctrine than the new rule which now replaces it.

I

From the Court's statement of the case one would gather that the central, if not controlling, issue on this appeal is whether illegally state-seized evidence is Constitutionally admissible in a state prosecution, an issue which would of course face us with the need for re-examining *Wolf*. However, such is not the situation. For, although that question was indeed raised here and below among appellant's subordinate points, the new and pivotal issue brought to the Court by this appeal is whether Section 2905.34 of the Ohio Revised Code making criminal the *mere* knowing possession or control of obscene material, and under which appellant has been convicted, is consistent with the rights of free thought and expression assured against state action by the Fourteenth Amendment. That was the principal issue which was decided by the Ohio Supreme Court, which was tendered by appellant's Jurisdictional Statement, and which was briefed and argued in this Court.

In this posture of things, I think it fair to say that five members of this Court have simply "reached out" to overrule *Wolf*. With all respect for the views of the majority, and recognizing that *stare decisis* carries different weight in Constitutional adjudication than it does in nonconstitutional decision, I can perceive no justification for regarding this case as an appropriate occasion for re-examining *Wolf*....

The occasion which the Court has taken here is in the context of a case where the question was briefed not at all and argued only extremely tangentially....

I would think that our obligation to the States, on whom we impose this new rule, as well as the obligation of orderly adherence to our own processes would demand that we seek that aid which adequate briefing and argument lends to the determination of an important issue....

The preservation of a proper balance between state and federal responsibility in the administration of criminal justice demands patience on the part of those who might like to see things move faster among the States in this respect. Problems of criminal law enforcement vary widely from State to State.... For us the question remains, as it has always been, one of state power, not one of passing judgment on the wisdom of one state course or another. In my view this Court should continue to forbear from fettering the States with an adamant rule which may embarrass them in coping with their own peculiar problems in criminal law enforcement....

[Memorandum of Mr. Justice Stewart concurring in the reversal on the ground that the conviction was not consistent with "the rights of free thought and expression" guaranteed by the Fourteenth Amendment].

Ker v. *California*, 374 U.S. 23 (1963), held that "the standard of reasonableness is the same under the Fourth and Fourteenth Amendments," thus clearly "incorporating" the Fourth Amendment.

Reference was made in *Mapp* v. *Ohio* to the "silver platter" doctrine. This doctrine, as applied earlier, permitted *federal* judicial use of evidence seized illegally by state agents and without any collusion by federal agents in the illegal seizure. Conversely, state courts, under earlier approaches, could use evidence illegally seized by federal officers without violating either the Constitution or judicially imposed restrictions. Even prior to the *Mapp* case, however, the "silver platter" doctrine was being eaten away. In *Rea* v. *United States,* 350 U.S. 214 (1956), the Court held that a federal law enforcement agent who seized evidence on the basis of an invalid search warrant could be enjoined from turning over such evidence to state authorities for use in a state prosecution and from giving testimony concerning the evidence. Justice Douglas, writing for the majority, stated, "The only relief asked is against a federal agent, who obtained the property as a result of the abuse of process issued by a United States Commissioner. . . . In this posture we have then a case that raises not a constitutional question but one concerning our supervisory powers over federal law enforcement agencies."

In *Elkins* v. *United States,* 364 U.S. 206 (1960), the other aspect of the doctrine was overturned. It held that evidence illegally seized by state officers and turned over to federal authorities could not be used in a federal prosecution. Justice Stewart, speaking for the majority, pointed out that "What is here invoked is the Court's supervisory power over the administration of criminal justice in the federal courts, under which the Court has 'from the very beginning of its history, formulated rules of evidence to be applied in federal criminal prosecutions.' " He stated further:

> Free and open cooperation between state and federal law enforcement officers is to be commended and encouraged. Yet that kind of cooperation is hardly promoted by a rule that implicitly invites federal officers to withdraw from such association and at least tacitly to encourage state officers in the disregard of constitutionally protected freedom. If on the other hand, it is understood that the fruit of an unlawful search by state agents will be inadmissible in a federal trial, there can be no inducement to subterfuge and evasion with respect to federal-state cooperation in criminal investigation. Instead, forthright cooperation under constitutional standards will be promoted and fostered.

It should be noted that *Rea, Elkins,* and *Mapp* dealt with evidence obtained illegally by *official* action. Do they also operate to bar the use of evidence obtained illegally by *private* persons and handed over to state or federal officers? Nothing in the opinions of those cases would indicate a change in the rule laid down in *Burdeau* v. *McDowell,* 256 U.S. 465 (1921), which held that evidence stolen by private individuals and turned over to federal officers was admissible in a criminal prosecution. The Fourth and Fourteenth Amendments prohibit official action only, and do not represent barriers to private misconduct.

As pointed out earlier, the First Amendment's safeguards have been fully "incorporated" into the Fourteenth Amendment, and the measure of the First Amendment's protections against national abridgment is equally the measure of the Fourteenth Amendment's protection against action by states. Until 1961, however, this was the only portion of the Bill of Rights which had been fully reproduced in the Fourteenth Amendment. With the decisions in *Mapp* v. *Ohio* and *Ker* v. *California* it would appear that the Fourth Amendment's standards have also been elevated to the "incorporated" status.

The opinion in *Mapp*, however, left unanswered the question of whether the bar to admission of illegally obtained evidence should be applied retroactively and thus open the way for those in prison to attack their convictions where such evidence was used by the prosecution. The Court did not reach this issue until four years later, in *Linkletter* v. *Walker*, 381 U.S. 618 (1965), and by a seven-to-two vote held that the *Mapp* rule did not operate retrospectively upon cases finally decided prior to the *Mapp* case. Justice Clark, for the Court, pointed out that while the various federal courts of appeals had split on the issue, the "state courts which have considered the question have almost unanimously decided against application to cases finalized prior to *Mapp*." The petitioner contended that prior cases demonstrated that an absolute rule of retroaction prevails in the area of constitutional adjudication. Justice Clark gave a brief but instructive "outline of the history and theory of the problem presented" and concluded that "the Constitution neither prohibits nor requires retrospective effect." The doctrine of "void *ab initio*" was well stated in *Norton* v. *Shelby Co.*, 118 U.S. 425 (1886), in which the Court held that unconstitutional action "confers no rights; it imposes no duties; it affords no protection; it creates no office; it is, in legal contemplation, as inoperative as though it had never been passed." This Blackstonian view was opposed by the Austinian view that judges do more than merely discover law; they make law. And thus one cannot deny the existence of an overruled law as a juridical fact. Justice Clark stated "We believe that the existence of the *Wolf* doctrine prior to *Mapp* is 'an operative fact and may have consequences which cannot justly be ignored. The past cannot always be erased by a new judicial declaration.'" He pointed out that the purpose in *Mapp* was to deter the lawless action of the police, and that purpose would not be served at this late date by the wholesale release of the guilty victims. He further suggested that retrospective application "would tax the administration of justice to the utmost." He concluded:

Finally, in each of the three areas in which we have applied our rule retrospectively the principle that we applied went to the fairness of the trial—the very integrity of the fact-finding process. Here, as we have pointed out, the fairness of the trial is not under attack. All that petitioner attacks is the admissibility of evidence, the reliability and relevancy of which is not questioned, and which may well have had no effect on the outcome.

[Justice Black, joined by Justice Douglas, dissented. He stated "I am at a loss to understand why those who suffer from the use of evidence secured by a search and seizure in violation of the Fourth Amendment should be treated differently from those who have been denied other guarantees of the Bill of Rights."]

[See generally, Oliver P. Field, *The Effect of an Unconstitutional Statute* (Minneapolis: University of Minnesota Press, 1935); Paul Freund, "New Vistas in Constitutional Law," 112 *U. Pa. L. Rev.* 631 (1964); Note, "Prospective Overruling and Retroactive Application in the Federal Courts," 71 *Yale L. J.* 907 (1962); Thomas S. Currier, "Time and Change in Judge-Made Law: Prospective Overruling," 51 *Va. L. Rev.* 201 (1965); Annotation, "Retroactive or Prospective Overruling," 14 L ed 2d 992.]

WIRETAPPING

Following the logic of the decisions to date in the area of wiretapping and eavesdropping presents substantial difficulties. The constitutional issue was taken up in *Olmstead* v. *United States*, 277 U.S. 438 (1928). By a five-to-four vote the United States Supreme Court held that phone taps by federal officers did not violate the Fourth Amendment. Chief Justice Taft, speaking for the majority, stated:

The well known historical purpose of the Fourth Amendment, directed against general warrants and writs of assistance, was to prevent the use of governmental force to search a man's house, his person, his papers, and his effects, and to prevent their seizure against his will. . . .

The Amendment itself shows that the search is to be of material things—the person, the house, his papers or his effects. The description of the warrant necessary to make the proceeding lawful is that it must specify the place to be searched and the person or *things* to be seized. . . .

The United States takes no such care of telegraph or telephone messages as of mailed sealed letters. The Amendment does not forbid what was done here. There was no searching. There was no seizure. The evidence was secured by the use of the sense of hearing and that only. There was no entry of the houses or offices of the defendants. . . .

Congress may, of course, protect the secrecy of telephone messages by making them, when intercepted, inadmissible in evidence in Federal criminal trials, by direct legislation, and thus depart from the common law of evidence. But the courts may not adopt such a policy by attributing an enlarged and unusual meaning to the Fourth Amendment. The reasonable view is that one who installs in his house a telephone instrument with connecting wires intends to project his voice to those quite outside, and that the wires beyond his house and messages while passing over them are not within the protection of the Fourth Amendment. Here those who intercepted the projected voices were not in the house of either party to the conversation. . . .

A standard which would forbid the reception of evidence if obtained by other than nice ethical conduct by government officials would make society suffer and give criminals greater immunity than has been known heretofore. In the absence of controlling legislation by Congress, those who realize the difficulties in bringing offenders to justice may well deem it wise that the exclusion of evidence should be confined to cases where rights under the Constitution would be violated by admitting it. . . .

[Justice Holmes gave a vigorous dissenting opinion, in the course of which he said:]

. . . It is desirable that criminals should be detected, and to that end that all available evidence should be used. It also is desirable that the government should not itself foster and pay for other crimes, when they are the means by which the evidence is to be obtained. If it pays its officers for having got evidence by crime I do not see why it may not as well pay them for getting it in the same way, and I can attach no importance to protestations of disapproval if it knowingly accepts and pays and announces that in the future it will pay for the fruits. We have to choose, and for my part I think it a less evil that some criminals should escape than that the government should play an ignoble part.

For those who agree with me, no distinction can be taken between the government as prosecutor and the government as judge. If the existing code does not permit district attorneys to have a hand in such dirty business, it does not permit the judge to allow such iniquities to succeed. . . . And if all that I have said so far be accepted, it makes no difference that in this case wire tapping is made a crime by the law of the state, not by the law of the United States. It is true that a state cannot make rules of evidence for courts of the United States, but the state has authority over the conduct in question, and I hardly think that the United States would appear to greater advantage when paying for an odious crime against state law than when inciting to the disregard of its own. . . .

[Justice Brandeis, also dissenting, made some prophetic statements about the "progress" of the various sciences in the art of prying into private lives:]

. . . The progress of science in furnishing the government with means of espionage is not likely to stop with wire-tapping. Ways may some day be developed by which the government, without removing papers from secret drawers, can reproduce them in court, and by which it will be enabled to expose to a jury the most intimate occurrences of the home. Advances in the psychic and related sciences may bring means of exploring unexpressed beliefs, thoughts and emotions. . . . Can it be that the Constitution affords no protection against such invasions of individual security? . . .

Decency, security, and liberty alike demand that government officials shall be subjected to the same rules of conduct that are commands to the citizen. In a government of laws, existence of the government will be imperiled if it fails to observe the law scrupulously. Our government is the potent, the omnipresent, teacher. For good or for ill, it teaches the whole people by its example. Crime is contagious. If the government becomes a law-breaker, it breeds contempt for law; it invites every man to become a law unto himself; it invites anarchy. To declare that in the administration of the criminal law the end justifies the means—to declare that the government may commit crimes in order to secure the conviction of a private criminal—would bring terrible retribution. Against that pernicious doctrine this Court should resolutely set its face.

[For an interesting treatment of the *Olmstead* case—"its genesis, its unfolding, and its impact"—see Walter F. Murphy, *Wiretapping on Trial: A Case Study in the Judicial Process* (New York: Random House, 1965).]

In his opinion for the majority, Chief Justice Taft suggested that if Congress so desired, it could bar the admission of intercepted telephone messages in federal criminal trials. Congress adopted the suggestion in passing the Federal Communications Act of 1934. The relevant portion of the Act is Section 605:

Unauthorized publication or use of communications. No person receiving or assisting in receiving, or transmitting, . . . any interstate or foreign communication by wire or radio shall divulge or publish the existence, contents, substance, purport, effect, or meaning thereof, . . . to any person other than the addressee . . . ; and no person not being authorized by the sender shall intercept any communication and divulge or publish the existence, contents, substance, purport, effect, or meaning of such intercepted communication to any person; . . . and no person having received such intercepted communication or having become acquainted with the contents, . . . or meaning of the same or any part thereof, knowing that such information was so obtained, shall divulge or publish the existence, contents, . . . or meaning of the same or any part thereof, or use the same . . . for his own benefit or for the benefit of another not entitled thereto. . . .

Section 501 of the Act made the willful and knowing violation of this section punishable by a fine of not more than $10,000 or by imprisonment for a term of not more than two years or both.

The Court faced the problem of interpreting the impact of Section 605 on admissibility of evidence in *Nardone* v. *United States*, 302 U.S. 379 (1937). The defendants, under indictment for smuggling alcohol, objected to the testimony of federal agents to the substance of telephone conversations by defendants which the agents had overheard by means of wiretaps. The trial judge rejected their contention, and they were convicted. On appeal, the Court reversed the conviction, holding that Section 605 comprehended federal agents in the phrase "no person" shall intercept and divulge communications by wire, and also holding that the prohibition against divulging the communication "to any person" barred the agents' testimony in court relative to the intercepted communication.

In a new trial following the first decision, Nardone and his codefendants were again convicted. On appeal, the defendants raised the issue of whether they could be barred from examining the prosecution to see whether it used the information obtained by the wiretap to acquire evidence. The Court of Appeals affirmed the trial judge's refusal to allow the examination. The Supreme Court, however, reversed in *Nardone* v. *United States*, 308 U.S. 338 (1939). It pointed out that merely to bar the testimony concerning conversations and at the same time to permit such illegally obtained information to be used to run down leads for evidence which *could* be admitted would be to "stultify the policy which compelled" the decision in the first *Nardone* case. It went on to say that the trial judge must allow to the accused an opportunity to prove, in wiretap situations, that "a substantial portion of the case against him was a fruit of the poisonous tree."

In *Weiss* v. *United States*, 308 U.S. 321 (1939), the Court examined the question of whether Section 605 operated to bar testimony as to an *intrastate* conversation which was tapped by a state officer. The wires tapped, however, were cables of both intrastate and interstate communications, and calls of both types were intercepted. The Court held that under such circumstances Section 605 barred the introduction in federal proceedings of conversations which were intrastate as well as those interstate.

The Department of Justice and the Federal Bureau of Investigation have taken the position that both wiretapping *and* divulgence must take place before a violation of Section 605 occurs. Thus wiretapping alone for purposes of keeping abreast of criminal activities, but not for purposes of bringing specific charges against the persons involved, would not be considered as barred by the statute. This view has been expressed by former Attorney General Herbert Brownell. [See Herbert Brownell, "The Public Security and Wiretapping," 39 *Cornell L. Q.* 195, 197 (1954).] He pointed out that except for a short period during 1940, every Attorney General since 1932 has favored and authorized wiretapping by federal officers in security cases and in particularly atrocious crimes such as kidnapping. And numerous bills have been introduced in Congress over the past quarter of a century which would provide certain kinds of exceptions to the rule of inadmissibility of wiretap evidence, especially in cases involving national security. [For a collection of such bills, see Hearings before the Subcommittee on Constitutional Rights of the Committee on the Judiciary, United States Senate, *Wiretapping, Eavesdropping, and the Bill of Rights*, 86th Cong., 1st Sess. (1959), Part 4, pp. 781–1032.]

During the course of hearings before the Senate Judiciary Subcommittee on Constitutional Rights in 1959, Chairman Thomas Hennings, Jr., wrote to Attorney General William Rogers asking him to appear before the subcommittee. Shortly thereafter the following letter was sent to Chairman Hennings from the Attorney General (Hearings, *supra*, p. 1036):

OFFICE OF THE ATTORNEY GENERAL
Washington, D.C., July 2, 1959.

Honorable THOMAS C. HENNINGS, JR.,
U.S. Senate, Washington, D.C.

DEAR SENATOR: It was most pleasant to talk with you today about some of the problems of law enforcement and constitutional rights in which we have mutual interests and responsibilities.

With regard to your inquiry concerning wiretapping, let me refer to testimony given by the Director of the Federal Bureau of Investigation, Mr. J. Edgar Hoover, before the House Appropriations Subcommittee on February 5, 1959:

MR. ROONEY. Mr. Director, how many telephone taps do you presently have in existence, and for what purposes are these taps used?

MR. HOOVER. Mr. Chairman, we have at the present time 74 telephone taps. Any request to tap a telephone by the FBI is submitted in writing and personally approved in advance by the Attorney General. They are utilized only in cases involving the internal security of the Nation or where a human life may be imperiled, such as kidnaping. We do not use telephone taps in any other types of investigation performed by the FBI.

Except as indicated by Mr. Hoover this procedure, which has been consistently followed for many years, is not otherwise employed by the Department of Justice. There is, of course, no divulgence of the information obtained as proscribed by section 605 of the Communications Act.

With best personal regards,
   Sincerely,

WILLIAM P. ROGERS,
Attorney General.

Another problem in the wiretap cases has been occasioned by the factor of federal-state relations. In 1952 the Court considered the question of whether Section 605 barred the use of state-gathered wiretap evidence in a state prosecution. In *Schwartz* v. *Texas,* 344 U.S. 199 (1952), the Court, relying on *Wolf* v. *Colorado,* held such evidence admissible. Justice Douglas was the lone dissenter. Justice Minton, speaking for the majority, stated:

> ... Although the intercepted calls would be inadmissible in a federal court, it does not follow that such evidence is inadmissible in a state court. Indeed, evidence obtained by a state officer by means which would constitute an unlawful search and seizure under the Fourth Amendment to the Federal Constitution is nonetheless admissible in a state court, *Wolf* v. *Colorado* ... while such evidence, if obtained by a federal officer, would be clearly inadmissible.... The problem under Section 605 is somewhat different because the introduction of the intercepted communications would itself be a violation of the statute, but in the absence of an expression by Congress, this is simply an additional factor for a state to consider in formulating a rule of evidence for use in its own courts. Enforcement of the statutory prohibition in Section 605 can be achieved under the penal provisions of Section 501....
>
> ... If Congress is authorized to act in a field, it should manifest its intention clearly. It will not be presumed that a federal statute was intended to supersede the exercise of the power of the state unless there is a clear manifestation of intention to do so. The exercise of federal supremacy is not lightly to be presumed....

The Court thus indicated that for state officers to wiretap and divulge the intercepted communications was a violation of Section 605, but this fact alone did not require that a state conviction based on such evidence be set aside. The suggested remedy was a federal prosecution of the offending officers based on Section 501. In view of the letter from Attorney General Rogers, above, outlining FBI wiretap procedures, it might be suspected that to anticipate any such prosecution would be unrealistic.

On the matter of using state-gathered wiretap evidence in a *federal* prosecution, however, the Court gave a straightforward denunciation. In *Benanti* v. *United States,* 355 U.S. 96 (1957), Chief Justice Warren, speaking for the Court stated:

[C]onfronted as we are by this clear statute, and resting our decision on its provisions, it is neither necessary nor appropriate to discuss by analogy distinctions suggested to be applicable to the Fourth Amendment. Section 605 contains an express, absolute prohibition against the divulgence of wiretapping.

Since the Court in *Schwartz* relied heavily on *Wolf* v. *Colorado*, and since *Mapp* v. *Ohio* overrules *Wolf*, it strongly suggests that *Schwartz* is no longer a valid rule. There are possible approaches to distinguish the holding in *Schwartz* and thereby retain it, but at the very least that rule is on tenuous ground.

Finally, it should be noted that other types of mechanical devices for eavesdropping do not necessarily fall under the proscriptions against wiretaps. Concealed microphones, long-range parabolic microphones, detectaphones, and other newer electronic devices may be treated differently if they do not "intercept" communications "by wire or radio." Section 605 is not necessarily violated by such listening devices, and the result is that distinctions have been made in determining admissibility of information obtained by mechanical eavesdropping reminiscent of the warnings voiced by Justice Brandeis in *Olmstead* in 1928. Even in situations where Section 605 does not apply, however, there may still be a violation of the Fourth or Fourteenth Amendments if improper methods are used in installing such devices—as for instance illegal entry into the home to set up listening equipment.

In *Goldman* v. *United States*, 316 U.S. 129 (1942), the Court considered the applicability of Section 605 to the use of a detectaphone placed against an office wall in order to listen to conversations taking place in the office next door. Conversations overheard in this manner were used in a subsequent trial, even though they consisted in part of words uttered by the defendant over the telephone. By a five-to-three vote the Court held that such evidence was not barred by Section 605 because there had been no "interception" of the telephone conversation, and the Act did not guarantee the secrecy of telephone conversations as such. "The listening in the next room to the words of [the petitioner] as he talked into the telephone receiver was no more the interception of a wire communication, within the meaning of the Act, than would have been the overhearing of the conversation by one sitting in the same room." The Court pointed out also that there had been no physical trespass, and therefore no improper search and seizure within the provisions of the Fourth Amendment.

A similar view was expressed in *On Lee* v. *United States*, 343 U.S. 747 (1952), involving a federal agent who was "wired for sound" with a microphone and transmitter concealed on his person. He went to the laundry of defendant, his former employer, and engaged On Lee in friendly conversation about his role in the illegal narcotics traffic. On Lee made damaging admissions, which were picked up by another federal agent stationed outside the shop with a receiving set. At the subsequent trial, the admissions

were introduced against On Lee. These circumstances were held not to constitute a violation of his Fourth Amendment rights since On Lee had voluntarily admitted the agent to his premises, and thus there was no trespass.

In 1961 the Court was asked to re-examine its positions in *Goldman* and
On Lee, and even the basic rationale of *Olmstead* v. *United States.* The case
was *Silverman* v. *United States,* 366 U.S. 505 (1961), involving the use of
a listening device called a "spike mike." Petitioners were convicted of gambling offenses in the District Court for the District of Columbia. At the
trial police officers were permitted to describe incriminating conversations
engaged in by the petitioners and overheard by the officers by means of an
instrument called a "spike mike." The instrument was a microphone with
a spike about a foot long attached to it, together with an amplifier, a power
pack, and earphones. The officers inserted the spike under a baseboard in a
second-floor room of a vacant, adjoining row house into the party wall, until it made contact with a heating duct. This converted the entire heating
system into a conductor of sound, and conversations on both floors of the
house were audible to the officers. Testimony regarding these conversations,
admitted at the trial over timely objection, played a substantial part in the
petitioners' convictions.

The Court unanimously reversed the convictions on the ground that "the
eavesdropping was accomplished by means of an unauthorized physical
penetration into the premises occupied by the petitioners." Counsel urged
that a re-examination of the rationale of *Olmstead* v. *United States* "is now
essential in the light of recent and projected developments in the science
of electronics." Justice Stewart stated for the Court, however, that "We
need not here contemplate the Fourth Amendment implications of these
and other frightening paraphernalia which the vaunted marvels of an electronic age may visit upon human society." He stated that eavesdropping
accomplished by means of such a physical intrusion was clearly illegal, and
testimony obtained thereby could not be admitted. Thus it was unnecessary to re-examine earlier decisions.

In *Berger* v. *New York,* 388 U.S. 41 (1967), the Court considered the
validity of New York's permissive eavesdrop statute which permitted certain courts to issue "an ex parte order for eavesdropping," upon oath or
affirmation of a district attorney or ranking police officers that there was
reasonable ground to believe that evidence of crime might be thus obtained,
and particularly describing the person whose communications, conversations, or discussions were to be overheard or recorded and the purpose
thereof. The order would be effective for a period of no more than two
months unless extended by the judge who signed the original order. In view
of the rather widespread support for a "middle position" of outlawing
eavesdrop testimony instigated by the government, except for that obtained
under a special court order, the decision in *Berger* v. *New York* was awaited
with more than usual interest. When it was announced, the square holding
of the majority was that the New York statute was violative of the Fourth

and Fourteenth Amendments. The vote was five-to-four, however, on this point, although Justice Stewart joined the majority on other grounds. With six separate opinions in the case, the Court was too badly split to draw firm generalizations.

BERGER *v.* NEW YORK

388 U.S. 41 (1967)

Mr. Justice Clark delivered the opinion of the Court.

This writ tests the validity of New York's permissive eavesdrop statute.... We have concluded that the language of New York's statute is too broad in its sweep resulting in a trespassory intrusion into a constitutionally protected area and is, therefore, violative of the Fourth and Fourteenth Amendments....

[Berger, the petitioner, was convicted on two counts of conspiracy to bribe the Chairman of the New York State Liquor Authority. The case arose out of a complaint by one Pansini, a bar owner, to the District Attorney that agents of the Authority had harassed him for his failure to pay a bribe for a liquor license. The District Attorney's office directed that Pansini, equipped with a recording device, interview an employee of the Authority. The employee advised Pansini that the price for a license was $10,000 and suggested that he contact one Neyer, an attorney. Neyer admitted having worked with the Authority employee, apparently concerning liquor licenses.

On the basis of this evidence an eavesdrop order was obtained permitting the installation of a recording device in Neyer's office. On the basis of leads obtained from this eavesdrop, a second order was obtained to plant a recorder in the office of one Steinman. After some two weeks of eavesdropping, a conspiracy was uncovered involving petitioner as "a go-between" for the principal conspirators and concerning the issuance of liquor licenses for the Playboy and Tenement Clubs of New York City. The parties stipulated that the State had no information on which to base its case except that obtained by the use of the eavesdrop evidence. Relevant portions of the recordings were received in evidence at the trial and were played to the jury, and petitioner was convicted.]

Sophisticated electronic devices have now been developed (commonly known as "bugging") which are capable of eavesdropping on anyone in most any given situation....

As science developed these detection techniques, lawmakers, sensing the resulting invasion of individual privacy, have provided some statutory protection for the public. Seven States, California, Illinois, Maryland, Massachusetts, Nevada, New York, and Oregon, prohibit surreptitious eavesdropping by mechanical or electronic device. However, all, save Illinois, permit official court-ordered eavesdropping. Some 36 States prohibit wiretapping. But of these, 27 permit "authorized" interception of some type. Federal law, as we have seen, prohibits interception and divulging or publishing of the content of wiretaps without exception. In sum, it is fair to say that wiretapping on the whole is outlawed, except for permissive use by law enforcement officials in some States; while electronic eavesdropping is—save for seven States—permitted both officially and privately. And, in six of the seven States electronic eavesdropping ("bugging") is permissible on court order....

The Court was faced with its first wiretap case in 1928, *Olmstead* v. *United States.* ... There the interception of Olmstead's telephone line was accomplished without entry upon his premises and was, therefore, found not to be proscribed by the Fourth Amendment. The basis of the decision was that the Constitution did not forbid the obtaining of evidence by wiretapping unless it involved actual unlawful entry into the house. . . .

The first "bugging" case reached the Court in 1942 in *Goldman* v. *United States*. . . . There the Court found that the use of a detectaphone placed against an office wall in order to hear private conversations in the office next door did not violate the Fourth Amendment because there was no physical trespass in connection with the relevant interception. And in *On Lee* v. *United States* . . . (1952), we found that since "no trespass was committed" a conversation between Lee and a federal agent, occurring in the former's laundry and electronically recorded, was not condemned by the Fourth Amendment. Thereafter in *Silverman* v. *United States* . . . (1961), the Court found "that the eavesdropping was accomplished by means of an unauthorized physical penetration into the premises occupied by the petitioners.". . .

While New York's statute satisfies the Fourth Amendment's requirement that a neutral and detached authority be interposed between the police and the public, . . . the broad sweep of the statute is immediately observable. . . .

The Fourth Amendment commands that a warrant issue not only upon probable cause supported by oath or affirmation, but also "particularly describing the place to be searched, and the persons or things to be seized." New York's statute lacks this particularization. It merely says that a warrant may issue on reasonable ground to believe that evidence of crime may be obtained by the eavesdrop. It lays down no requirement for particularity in the warrant as to what specific crime has been or is being committed, nor "the place to be searched," or "the persons or things to be seized" as specifically required by the Fourth Amendment. The need for particularity and evidence of reliability in the showing required when judicial authorization of a search is sought is especially great in the case of eavesdropping. By its very nature eavesdropping involves an intrusion on privacy that is broad in scope. As was said in *Osborn* v. *United States*, 385 U.S. 323 (1966), the "indiscriminate use of such devices in law enforcement raises grave constitutional questions under the Fourth and Fifth Amendments," and imposes "a heavier responsibility on this Court in its supervision of the fairness of procedures. . . ." . . . There, two judges acting jointly authorized the installation of a device on the person of a prospective witness to record conversations between him and an attorney for a defendant then on trial in the United States District Court. The judicial authorization was based on an affidavit of the witness setting out in detail previous conversations between the witness and the attorney concerning the bribery of jurors in the case. The recording device was, as the Court said, authorized "under the most precise and discriminate circumstances, circumstances which fully met the 'requirement of particularity' " of the Fourth Amendment. . . . Among other safeguards, the order described the type of conversation sought with particularity, thus indicating the specific objective of the Government in entering the constitutionally protected area and the limitations placed upon the officer executing the warrant. Under it the officer could not search unauthorized areas; likewise, once the property sought, and for which the order was issued, was found the officer could not use the order as a passkey to further search. In addition, the order authorized one limited intrusion rather than a series or a continuous surveillance. And, we note that a new order was issued when the officer sought to resume the search and probable cause was shown for the succeeding one. Moreover, the order was executed by the officer with dispatch, not over a prolonged and extended period. In this manner no greater invasion of privacy was permitted than was necessary under the circumstances. Finally the officer was required to and did make a return on the order showing how it was executed and what was seized. Through these strict precautions the danger of an unlawful search and seizure was minimized.

On the contrary, New York's statute lays down no such "precise and discriminate" requirements. . . . New York's broadside authorization rather than being "carefully circumscribed" so as to prevent unauthorized invasions of privacy actually permits general searches by electronic devices, the truly offensive character of which was first condemned in *Entick* v. *Carrington, supra,* and which were then known as "general warrants.". . .

We believe the statute here is equally offensive. First . . . eavesdropping is authorized without requiring belief that any particular offense has been or is being committed; nor that the property sought, the conversations, be particularly described. . . . Secondly, authorization of eavesdropping for a two-month period is the equivalent of a series of intrusions, searches, and seizures pursuant to a single showing of probable cause. . . . During such . . . period the conversations of any and all persons coming into the area covered by the device will be seized indiscriminately and without regard to their connection to the crime under investigation . . . Third, the statute places no termination date on the eavesdrop once the conversation sought is seized. This is left entirely in the discretion of the officer. Finally, the statute's procedure, necessarily because its success depends on secrecy, has no requirement for notice as do conventional warrants, nor does it overcome this defect by requiring some showing of special facts. . . . In short, the statute's blanket grant of permission to eavesdrop is without adequate judicial supervision or protective procedures. . . .

It is said with fervor that electronic eavesdropping is a most important technique of law enforcement and that outlawing it will severely cripple crime detection. . . .

In any event we cannot forgive the requirements of the Fourth Amendment in the name of law enforcement. This is no formality that we require today but a fundamental rule that has long been recognized as basic to the privacy of every home in America. . . . Few threats to liberty exist which are greater than that posed by the use of eavesdropping devices. . . .

It is said that neither a warrant nor a statute authorizing eavesdropping can be drawn so as to meet the Fourth Amendment's requirements. If that be true then the "fruits" of eavesdropping devices are barred under the Amendment. On the other hand this Court has in the past, under specific conditions and circumstances, sustained the use of eavesdropping devices. See *Goldman* v. *United States, supra; On Lee* v. *United States, supra;* . . . and *Osborn* v. *United States, supra.* . . . Our concern with the statute here is whether its language permits a trespassory invasion of the home, by general warrant, contrary to the command of the Fourth Amendment. As it is written, we believe that it does.

Reversed.

Mr. Justice Douglas, concurring.

I join the opinion of the Court because at long last it overrules *sub silentio Olmstead* v. *United States* . . . and its offspring and brings wiretapping and other electronic eavesdropping fully within the purview of the Fourth Amendment. . . .

Mr. Justice Stewart, concurring in the result. . . .

I think that "electronic eavesdropping, *as such,* or as it is permitted by this statute, is not an unreasonable search and seizure." The statute contains many provisions more stringent than the Fourth Amendment generally requires, as Mr. Justice Black has so forcefully pointed out. . . .

I would hold that the affidavits on which the judicial order issued in this case did not constitute a showing of probable cause adequate to justify the authorizing order. . . .

Accordingly, I would reverse the judgment.

Mr. Justice White, dissenting. . . .

Mr. Justice Harlan, dissenting.

The Court in recent years has more and more taken to itself sole responsibility for setting the pattern of criminal law enforcement throughout the country. . . .

Today's decision is in this mold. Despite the fact that the use of electronic eavesdropping devices as instruments of criminal law enforcement is currently being comprehensively addressed by the Congress and various other bodies in the country, the Court has chosen, quite unnecessarily, to decide this case in a manner which will seriously restrict, if not entirely thwart, such efforts, and will freeze further progress in this field, except as the Court may itself act or a Constitutional Amendment may set things right.

In my opinion what the Court is doing is very wrong, and I must respectfully dissent. . . .

Mr. Justice Black, dissenting. . . .

. . . [W]hile the Court faintly intimates to the contrary, it seems obvious to me that its holding, by creating obstacles that cannot be overcome, makes it completely impossible for the State or the Federal Government ever to have a valid eavesdropping statute. All of this is done, it seems to me, in part because of the Court's hostility to eavesdropping as "ignoble" and "dirty business" and in part because of fear that rapidly advancing science and technology is making eavesdropping more and more effective. . . . Neither of these, nor any other grounds that I can think of, are sufficient in my judgment to justify a holding that the use of evidence secured by eavesdropping is barred by the Constitution. . . .

[See Chap. 9, *infra,* for the more recent decisions in *Katz* v. *United States,* 389 U.S. 347 (1967), and *United States* v. *White,* 401 U.S. 745 (1971). On wiretapping and eavesdropping generally, see Alan F. Westin, *Privacy and Freedom* (New York: Atheneum, 1967); Samuel Dash, Richard F. Schwartz, and Robert Knowlton, *The Eavesdroppers* (New Brunswick: Rutgers University Press, 1959); R. Kent Greenawalt, "The Consent Problem in Wiretapping and Eavesdropping," 68 *Colum. L. Rev.* 189 (1968); Gerald A. Novack, "Electronic Surveillance: The New Standards," 35 *Brooklyn L. Rev.* 49 (1968); Ralph S. Spritzer, "Electronic Surveillance by Leave of the Magistrate: The Case in Opposition," 118 *U. Pa. L. Rev.* 169 (1969).]

SELF-INCRIMINATION

The privilege against self-incrimination is generally accepted as a landmark in the development of procedural guarantees. It became established in the common law as a revolt against procedures in which accused persons were questioned under oath by judges, both to get evidence and to obtain confessions. Immunity from such interrogation was written into the Fifth Amendment of the Constitution and provides that "no person . . . shall be compelled in any criminal case to be a witness against himself."

While it is sometimes suggested that the purpose of the privilege was simply to prevent torture, there is another reason as well. It lies in the general feeling that the concept of fair play demands that the individual not be required to accuse and convict himself out of his own mouth. The case against him must be built by the government without requiring of the accused that he make their case for them by his own testimony. This aspect of the privilege has important consequences. It is not confined, for example, merely to cases of criminal prosecution, but extends to all sorts of proceedings where testimony might be required and where the divulgences might lead to a later criminal prosecution of the witness. Thus the privilege can operate in civil cases and in legislative investigations, as well as in a criminal prosecution. The first case to rule squarely on the application of the privilege to testimony before congressional investigating committees was *Quinn* v. *United States*, 349 U.S. 155 (1955). In the opinion of the Court, upholding the application of the privilege, Chief Justice Warren said:

The privilege against self-incrimination is a right that was hard-earned by our forefathers. The reasons for its inclusion in the Constitution—and the necessities for its preservation—are to be found in the lessons of history. As early as 1650, remembrance of the horror of Star Chamber proceedings a decade before had firmly established the privilege in the common law of England. Transplanted to this country as part of our legal heritage, it soon made its way into various state constitutions and ultimately in 1791 into the federal Bill of Rights. The privilege, this Court has stated, "was generally regarded then, as now, as a privilege of great value, a protection to the innocent though a shelter to the guilty, and a safeguard against heedless, unfounded or tyrannical prosecutions." Coequally with our other constitutional guarantees, the Self-Incrimination Clause "must be accorded liberal construction in favor of the right it was intended to secure." Such liberal construction is particularly warranted in a prosecution of a witness for a refusal to answer, since the respect normally accorded the privilege is then buttressed by the presumption of innocence accorded a defendant in a criminal trial. To apply the privilege narrowly or begrudgingly—to treat it as an historical relic, at most merely to be tolerated—is to ignore its development and purpose.

THE INVOCATION OF THE PRIVILEGE

In the case of a criminal defendant, invocation of the privilege is a very simple matter—he merely refuses to take the stand. By so doing, he precludes the prosecution from asking him any questions at all, incriminating or not. The defendant's counsel must weigh this advantage against the disadvantage that the jury may interpret such failure to defend himself as a sign of guilt, but the privilege is there if he chooses to use it. One problem which has arisen on this point is the constitutionality of permitting the trial judge to comment to the jury on the defendant's failure to take the stand. In *Twining* v. *New Jersey,* 211 U.S. 78 (1908), the Court held that it was not violative of the Fourteenth Amendment's privilege against self-incrimination for a state judge to charge the jury: "Because a man does not go upon the stand you are not necessarily justified in drawing an inference of guilt. But you have a right to consider the fact that he does not go upon the stand where a direct accusation is made against him." No case involving the Fifth Amendment's application directly to such a comment has been decided, since Congress by statute has required that federal judges specifically instruct juries that failure to take the stand should *not* be considered as evidence of guilt. But it was generally presumed that the Fifth Amendment would bar adverse comment in federal courts. In *Malloy* v. *Hogan,* 378 U.S. 1 (1964), the Court "incorporated" the Fifth Amendment privilege into the Fourteenth Amendment, thus imposing the federal standard upon the states. This inevitably led to the re-examination of the *Twining* rule, and in *Griffin* v. *California,* 380 U.S. 609 (1965), the Court held that "the Fifth Amendment, in its direct application to the federal government and its bearing on the States by reason of the Fourteenth Amendment, forbids either comment by the prosecution on the accused's silence or instructions by the court that such silence is evidence of guilt."

Suppose the person who is to be questioned is not a criminal defendant, but is instead a witness before a grand jury or a congressional committee. If he is under subpoena, he does not have the choice of refusing to "take the stand." How, then, does he invoke the privilege? The answer is that he must make a decision on each question as it is asked, as to whether he thinks his answer might incriminate him. If he concludes that it might do so, then he can refuse to answer, but he must in some way indicate that his refusal is based on the privilege. This leads to two questions. First, is a set formula necessary to invoke the privilege? Second, is the investigating body bound to accept the witness' conclusion that the answer would be incriminating?

As to the manner in which the witness claims his privilege, this was the principal issue in *Quinn* v. *United States,* above. The witness had refused to answer certain questions put to him by a subcommittee of the House Committee on Un-American Activities. He stated that his refusal was based on "the first and fifth amendments." In a subsequent trial for contempt, the government contended that by coupling the First Amendment with the Fifth as his basis for refusal, the petitioner was not really invoking the privilege. Quinn was convicted and appealed. Reversing the conviction the Court, through Chief Justice Warren, said:

It is agreed by all that a claim of the privilege does not require any special combination of words. Plainly a witness need not have the skill of a lawyer to invoke the protection of the Self-Incrimination Clause. If an objection to a question is made in any language that a committee may reasonably be expected to understand as an attempt to invoke the privilege, it must be respected both by the committee and by a court in a prosecution under Section 192. . . .

. . . [T]he fact that a witness expresses his intention in vague terms is immaterial so long as the claim is sufficiently definite to apprise the committee of his intention. As everyone agrees, no ritualistic formula is necessary in order to invoke the privilege. In the instant case, Quinn's references to the Fifth Amendment were clearly sufficient to put the committee on notice of an apparent claim of the privilege. It then became incumbent on the committee either to accept the claim or to ask petitioner whether he was in fact invoking the privilege. Particularly is this so if it is true, as the Government contends, that petitioner feared the stigma that might result from a forthright claim of his constitutional right to refuse to testify. It is precisely at such times—when the privilege is under attack by those who wrongly conceive of it as merely a shield for the guilty—that governmental bodies must be most scrupulous in protecting its exercise.

As to whether the questioning body is absolutely bound by the witness' answer that his response might incriminate him, the answer is a qualified "No." If the refusal is followed by a citation for contempt, and the question is before a court, the judge must make some sort of judgment as to whether there is any basis for fearing that an answer might incriminate the witness. The problem was discussed by Chief Justice Marshall while on circuit in the treason trial of Aaron Burr in 1807. During the course of the trial the attorney for the United States offered in evidence a paper in code. Burr's secretary was asked whether he understood the paper and declined to answer on the ground that he might incriminate himself. The court was asked to decide whether the excuse offered was sufficient to prevent his answering. In *United States* v. *Burr* [In re *Willie*], 25 Fed. Cas. 38, No. 14,692e (C.C.D. Va. 1807), the Chief Justice said:

When a question is propounded, it belongs to the court to consider and to decide whether any direct answer to it can implicate the witness. If this be decided in the negative, then he may answer it without violating the privilege which is secured to him by law. If a direct answer to it may criminate himself, then he must be the sole judge what his answer would be. The court cannot participate with him in this judgment, because they cannot decide on the effect of his answer without knowing what it would be; and a disclosure of that fact to the judges would strip him of the privilege which the law allows, and which he claims. It follows necessarily then, from this statement of things, that if the question be of such a description that an answer to it may or may not criminate the witness, according to the purport of that answer, it must rest with himself, who alone can tell what it would be, to answer the question or not. . . .

On examination of the question, the Chief Justice concluded that it could be answered without implicating the witness.

A similar approach was taken by Justice Clark, for the Court, in *Hoffman* v. *United States*, 341 U.S. 479 (1951), who stated: "The witness is not exonerated from answering merely because he declares that in so doing he would incriminate himself—his say-so does not of itself establish the hazard of incrimination. It is for the court to say whether his silence is justified . . . and to require him to answer if 'it clearly appears to the court that he is mistaken.' " He went on to say, however, just as did Chief Justice Marshall, that the witness cannot be required to make a complete revelation to prove his contention, or else the privilege is lost. By way of instruction, he stated: "[T]o sustain the privilege, it need only be evident from the implications of the question, in the setting in which it is asked, that a responsive answer to the question or an explanation of why it cannot be answered might be dangerous because injurious disclosure could result."

On occasion witnesses seem to plead the Fifth Amendment privilege when there would appear to be no basis whatever for a prosecution irrespective of the answer given. The general rule is that for the privilege to be invoked, there must be a real possibility of incrimination. However, this sometimes leaves the witness with the difficult problem of deciding when to stop answering questions after he has already answered several of them in a particular line of questioning. This was the problem presented in *Blau* v. *United States*, 340 U.S. 159 (1950). In response to questions by a grand jury about her employment by the Communist Party, the witness refused to answer and invoked the privilege. The government contended that it is not a crime merely to be an employee of the Party, and that she could not properly invoke the privilege. Petitioner was upheld in her refusal to answer:

At the time petitioner was called before the grand jury, the Smith Act was on the statute books making it a crime among other things to advocate knowingly the desirability of overthrow of the Government by force or violence. . . . These provisions made future prosecution of petitioner far more than "a mere imaginary possibility. . . ." Whether such admissions by themselves would support a conviction under a criminal statute is immaterial. Answers to the questions asked by the grand jury would have furnished a link in the chain of evidence needed in a prosecution.

While in *Blau* the witness was charged with having invoked the privilege before it was necessary, in a subsequent case the question presented was whether the witness had waited too long to permit its invocation, thereby in effect waiving it by already answering incriminating questions. The case was *Rogers* v. *United States*, 340 U.S. 367 (1951), arising out of a federal grand jury investigation in Colorado. Petitioner testified that she had held the position of Treasurer of the Communist Party of Denver and had been in possession of the membership lists and dues records of the Party. At the time of the investigation she no longer held such position and denied having possession of the records. But she refused to identify the person to whom she had given the Party's books, stating to the court as her only reason: "I don't feel that I should subject a person or persons to the same thing that

I'm going through." She later repeated her refusal, asserting this time the privilege against self-incrimination.

She was sentenced for contempt, the court of appeals affirmed, and the United States Supreme Court affirmed, three justices dissenting. Chief Justice Vinson, for the majority, first pointed out that the petitioner had no privilege with respect to the books of the Party. "Books and records kept 'in a representative rather than in a personal capacity cannot be the subject of the personal privilege against self-incrimination, even though production of the papers might tend to incriminate [their keeper] personally.'" He stated further that the *Blau* rule did not apply since she had already freely described her membership, activities, and office in the Party. "Since the privilege against self-incrimination presupposes a real danger of legal detriment arising from the disclosure, petitioner cannot invoke the privilege where response to the specific question in issue here would not further incriminate her. Disclosure of a fact waives the privilege as to details." Thus after admitting to office-holding in the Party, disclosure of acquaintance with her successor "presents no more than 'a mere imaginary possibility' of increasing the danger of prosecution."

THE SCOPE OF THE PRIVILEGE

While the privilege "must be accorded liberal construction" and is "of great value," it does not extend to every divulgence which might have injurious consequences. In the first place, as the Court pointed out in *Rogers* v. *United States,* above, the privilege is purely personal and cannot be invoked to protect others. Similarly, the privilege can be claimed only by natural persons and not by corporations or other organizations. As was stated in *United States* v. *White,* 322 U.S. 694 (1944):

[T]he papers and effects which the privilege protects must be the private property of the person claiming the privilege, or at least in his possession in a purely personal capacity.... But individuals, when acting as representatives of a collective group, cannot be said to be exercising their personal rights and duties nor to be entitled to their purely personal privileges.... In their official capacity, therefore, they have no privilege against self-incrimination. And the official records and documents of the organization that are held by them in a representative rather than in a personal capacity cannot be the subject of the personal privilege against self-incrimination, even though production of the papers might tend to incriminate them personally.

Ullmann v. *United States,* 350 U.S. 422 (1956), dealt with three questions which are of special note in defining the scope and limits of the privilege. The case arose out of an application of the Immunity Act of 1954, 68 Stat. 833. The relevant portions of the Act provide:

Section 3486. Compelled testimony tending to incriminate witnesses; immunity

(a) In the course of any investigation relating to any interference with or endangering of, or any plans or attempts to interfere with or endanger the national security or defense of the United States by treason, sabotage, espionage, sedition, seditious conspiracy or the overthrow of its Government by force or violence, no witness shall be excused from testifying or from producing books, papers, or other evidence before either House, or before any committee of either House, or before any joint committee of the two Houses of Congress on the ground that the testimony or evidence required of him may tend to incriminate him or subject him to a penalty or forfeiture, when the record shows that—

(1) in the case of proceedings before one of the Houses of Congress, that a majority of the members present of that House; or

(2) in the case of proceedings before a committee, that two-thirds of the members of the full committee shall by affirmative vote have authorized such witness to be granted immunity under this section with respect to the transactions, matters, or things concerning which he is compelled, after having claimed his privilege against self-incrimination to testify or produce evidence by direction of the presiding officer and that an order of the United States district court for the district wherein the inquiry is being carried on has been entered into the record requiring said person to testify or produce evidence. Such an order may be issued by a United States district court judge upon application by a duly authorized representative of the Congress or of the committee concerned. But no such witness shall be prosecuted or subjected to any penalty or forfeiture for or on account of any transaction, matter, or thing concerning which he is so compelled, after having claimed his privilege against self-incrimination, to testify or produce evidence, nor shall testimony so compelled be used as evidence in any criminal proceeding [except prosecutions for perjury or contempt committed while giving testimony] against him in any court.

[Another subsection provided for similar immunity in the event of testimonial compulsion "in any case or proceeding before any grand jury or court of the United States" involving similar offenses, except that certain additional specific acts of Congress were named.]

Leaving aside a procedural question involved in the case, *Ullmann* v. *United States* raised three important questions concerning the application of the Immunity Act of 1954. In so doing, the reach of the protection offered by the privilege was also under consideration. The three questions were: (1) Is the immunity provided by the Act sufficiently broad to displace the protection afforded by the privilege against self-incrimination? (2) Does the Act provide immunity from state prosecution for crime, and, if so, can Congress constitutionally do so? (3) Does the Fifth Amendment prohibit compulsion of what would otherwise be self-incriminating testimony no matter what the scope of the immunity statute?

ULLMANN v. UNITED STATES
350 U.S. 422 (1956)

Mr. Justice Frankfurter delivered the opinion of the Court.

[On November 10, 1954, the United States Attorney for the Southern District of New York filed an application under the Immunity Act of 1954, for an order requiring petitioner to testify before a grand jury. The District Court granted the application but petitioner refused to answer the questions and was convicted of contempt.]

It is relevant to define explicitly the spirit in which the Fifth Amendment's privilege against self-incrimination should be approached. This command of the Fifth Amendment . . . registers an important advance in the development of our liberty—"one of the great landmarks in man's struggle to make himself civilized." Time has not shown that protection from the evils against which this safeguard was directed is needless or unwarranted. This constitutional protection must not be interpreted in a hostile or niggardly spirit. Too many, even those who should be better advised, view this privilege as a shelter for wrongdoers. They too readily assume that those who invoke it are either guilty of crime or commit perjury in claiming the privilege. Such a view does scant honor to the patriots who sponsored the Bill of Rights as a condition to acceptance of the Constitution by the ratifying States. The Founders of the Nation were not naive or disregardful of the interests of justice. . . .

As no constitutional guarantee enjoys preference, so none should suffer subordination or deletion. . . . To view a particular provision of the Bill of Rights with disfavor inevitably results in a constricted application of it. This is to disrespect the Constitution.

It is in this spirit of strict, not lax, observance of the constitutional protection of the individual that we approach the claims made by petitioner in this case. The attack on the Immunity Act as violating the Fifth Amendment is not a new one. Sixty years ago this Court considered, in *Brown* v. *Walker*, 161 U.S. 591, the constitutionality of a similar Act. . . . In that case, Brown, auditor for a railroad company, had been subpoenaed to testify before a grand jury which was investigating charges that officers and agents of the company had violated the Interstate Commerce Act. Invoking the privilege against self-incrimination, he refused to answer certain questions concerning the operations and the rebate policy of the railroad. On an order to show cause before the United States District Court . . . he was adjudged in contempt. . . . Petitioner appealed to this Court, urging that the 1893 immunity statute was unconstitutional.

The Court considered and rejected petitioner's arguments, holding that a statute which compelled testimony but secured the witness against a criminal prosecution which might be aided directly or indirectly by his disclosures did not violate the Fifth Amendment's privilege against self-incrimination and that the 1893 statute did provide such immunity. . . .

Petitioner, however, attempts to distinguish *Brown* v. *Walker*. He argues that this case is different from *Brown* v. *Walker* because the impact of the disabilities imposed by federal and state authorities and the public in general—such as loss of job, expulsion from labor unions, state registration and investigation statutes, passport eligibility, and general public opprobrium—is so oppressive that the statute does not give him true immunity. This, he alleges, is significantly different from the impact of testifying on the auditor in *Brown* v. *Walker*, who could the next day resume his job with reputation unaffected. But, as this Court has often held, the immunity granted need only remove those sanctions which generate the fear justifying invocation of the privilege: "The interdiction of the Fifth Amendment operates only where a witness is asked to incriminate himself—in other words, to give testimony which may possibly expose him to a criminal charge. But if the criminality has already been taken away, the Amendment ceases to apply." *Hale* v. *Henkel*, 201 U.S. 43, 67....

Petitioner questions the constitutional power of Congress to grant immunity from state prosecution. Congressional abolition of state power to punish crimes committed in violation of state law presents a more drastic exercise of congressional power than that which we considered in *Adams*. In that case, only the use of the compelled testimony, not prosecution itself, was prohibited. Here the State is forbidden to prosecute. But it cannot be contested that Congress has power to provide for national defense and the complementary power "To make all Laws which shall be necessary and proper for carrying into Execution the foregoing Powers, and all other Powers vested by this Constitution in the Government of the United States, or in any Department or Officer thereof." U.S. Const., Art. I, Sec. 8, cl. 18. The Immunity Act is concerned with the national security. It reflects a congressional policy to increase the possibility of more complete and open disclosure by removal of fear of state prosecution. We cannot say that Congress' paramount authority in safeguarding national security does not justify the restriction it has placed on the exercise of state power for the more effective exercise of conceded federal power....

Petitioner also urges that if *Brown* v. *Walker* is found nondistinguishable and controlling, then that case should be reconsidered and overruled. He also urges upon us a "return" to a literal reading of the Fifth Amendment. *Brown* v. *Walker* was the second case to deal with an immunity statute. Four years previously in *Counselman* v. *Hitchcock*, 142 U.S. 547, a unanimous Court had found constitutionally inadequate the predecessor to the 1893 statute because the immunity granted was incomplete, in that it merely forbade the use of the testimony given and failed to protect a witness from future prosecution based on knowledge and sources of information obtained from the compelled testimony. It was with this background that the 1893 statute, providing complete immunity from prosecution, was passed and that *Brown* v. *Walker* was argued and decided. As in *Counselman* . . . , numerous arguments were presented.... The Court was closely divided in upholding the statute, and the opinions reflect the thoroughness with which the issues were considered. Since that time the Court's holding in *Brown* v. *Walker* has never been challenged; the case and the doctrine it announced have consistently and without question been treated as definitive by this Court, in opinions written, among others, by Holmes and Brandeis....

We are not dealing here with one of the vague, undefinable, admonitory provisions of the Constitution whose scope is inevitably addressed to changing circumstances. The privilege against self-incrimination is a specific provision of which it is peculiarly true that "a page of history is worth a volume of logic."... For the history of the privilege establishes not only that it is not to be interpreted literally, but also that its sole concern is, as its name indicates, with the danger to a witness forced to give testimony leading to the infliction "of penalties affixed to the criminal acts. . . ." *Boyd* v. *United States*, 116 U.S. 616, 634. We leave *Boyd* v. *United States* unqualified, as it was left unqualified in *Brown* v. *Walker*. Immunity displaces the danger. Once the reason for the privilege ceases, the privilege ceases. We reaffirm *Brown* v. *Walker*, and in so doing we need not repeat the answers given by that case to the other points raised by petitioner.

The judgment of the Court of Appeals is

Affirmed.

Mr. Justice Reed concurs in the opinion and judgment of the Court except as to the statement that no constitutional guarantee enjoys preference. . . .

Mr. Justice Douglas, with whom Mr. Justice Black concurs, dissenting.

I would reverse the judgment of conviction. I would base the reversal on *Boyd* v. *United States*, 116 U.S. 616, or, in the alternative, I would overrule the five-to-four decision of *Brown* v. *Walker*, 161 U.S. 591, and adopt the view of the minority in that case that the right of silence created by the Fifth Amendment is beyond the reach of Congress.

First, as to the *Boyd* case. There are numerous disabilities created by federal law that attach to a person who is a Communist. These disabilities include ineligibility for employment in the Federal Government and in defense facilities, disqualification for a passport, the risk of internment, the risk of loss of employment as a longshoreman—to mention only a few. These disabilities imposed by federal law are forfeitures within the meaning of our cases and as much protected by the Fifth Amendment as criminal prosecution itself. But there is no indication that the Immunity Act . . . grants protection against those disabilities. The majority will not say that it does. I think, indeed, that it must be read as granting only partial, not complete, immunity for the matter disclosed under compulsion. Yet, as the Court held in *Counselman* v. *Hitchcock*, 142 U.S. 547, 586, an immunity statute to be valid must "supply a complete protection from all the perils against which the constitutional prohibition was designed to guard. . . .". . .

There is great infamy involved in the present case, apart from the loss of rights of citizenship under federal law which I have already mentioned. The disclosure that a person is a Communist practically excommunicates him from society. School boards will not hire him. . . . A lawyer risks exclusion from the bar . . . ; a doctor, the revocation of his license to practice. . . . If an actor, he is on a black list. . . . And he will be able to find no employment in our society except at the lowest level, if at all. . . .

It is no answer to say that a witness who exercises his Fifth Amendment right of silence and stands mute may bring himself into disrepute. If so, that is the price he pays for exercising the right of silence granted by the Fifth Amendment. The critical point is that the Constitution places the right of silence *beyond the reach of government*. The Fifth Amendment stands between the citizen and his government. When public opinion casts a person into the outer darkness, as happens today when a person is exposed as a Communist, the Government brings infamy on the head of the witness when it compels disclosure. That is precisely what the Fifth Amendment prohibits. . . .

The majority opinion in the *Ullmann* case makes it clear that the privilege is not a broad guarantee of a right to silence. Even where injurious consequences may clearly follow the divulgence of information requested by a congressional committee or a grand jury, the privilege cannot protect the witness' refusal to answer questions unless those answers would tend to *incriminate* the witness. The majority held that the privilege does not extend to other kinds of anticipated injury, such as loss of job or reputation. Thus when Congress or a United States attorney offers immunity from criminal prosecution (under the terms of the statute), *Ullmann* v. *United States* holds that such offer covers the full reach of the privilege, and the

witness is then bound to answer relevant questions under penalty of citation for contempt.

THE PROBLEM OF IMMUNITY AND FEDERALISM

Both the states and the federal government have statutes trading immunity for information, and these date back more than a century. Some
of the provisions apply to specific kinds of crimes, while others are more
broadly drawn to cover any criminal offense. It is not uncommon to find a
multiplicity of statutes in a single state dealing with the matter of immunity. New York, for example, has more than twoscore provisions under
which witnesses may obtain immunity in return for giving testimony.

Since a single act can constitute both a federal and a state crime, the
familiar complications of federalism arise in connection with immunity
granted by one but not both jurisdictions. Does a grant of immunity by one
jurisdiction carry with it insulation against prosecutions by the other based
on the testimony? If not, is that fact sufficient to support a refusal to
testify grounded on fear of incrimination?

As stated earlier, it was not until the decision in *Malloy* v. *Hogan*, 378
U.S. 1 (1964), that the Court fully incorporated the Fifth Amendment
privilege into the Fourteenth Amendment. Justice Brennan, for the majority, stated: "The Fourteenth Amendment secures against state invasion
the same privilege that the Fifth Amendment guarantees against federal
infringement—the right of a person to remain silent unless he chooses to
speak in the unfettered exercise of his own will, and to suffer no penalty,
as held in *Twining*, for such silence." In so holding, the Court reversed a
contempt conviction for petitioner's refusal to answer questions relating
to gambling activities, and held that the *Twining* rule can no longer be
accepted as the appropriate standard for the exercise of the privilege.
Under the double standard of Fifth and Fourteenth Amendment self-
incrimination protection, a form of legalized coerced confession had been
supported by the Court where the federal government could force testimony by extending immunity and subsequently the state government could
prosecute for state crimes revealed. Conversely, the federal prosecutor could
use testimony exacted by state officials in return for the limited immunity
from state prosecution. These cases were reconsidered, and overruled, in
light of *Malloy* v. *Hogan*, in a decision rendered on the same day as that
case, in *Murphy* v. *Waterfront Commission of New York Harbor*, 378
U.S. 52 (1964). Petitioners were subpoenaed to testify at a hearing conducted by the Waterfront Commission of New York Harbor concerning
a work stoppage at the Hoboken piers. After refusing to respond to certain
questions on the ground that the answers might tend to incriminate them,
petitioners were granted immunity from prosecution under the laws of New
Jersey and New York. Notwithstanding this grant of immunity, they still
refused to respond to the questions on the ground that the answers might
tend to incriminate them under *federal* law, to which the grant of im-

munity did not purport to extend. Petitioners were thereupon held in civil and criminal contempt of court. The New Jersey Supreme Court affirmed the civil contempt judgments, holding that a state may constitutionally compel a witness to give testimony which might be used in a federal prosecution against him. The United States Supreme Court unanimously reversed, although there was some disagreement on the grounds for the decision. Justice Goldberg, speaking for five members of the Court, referred to *Malloy* v. *Hogan* in stating:

We have held today that the Fifth Amendment privilege against self-incrimination must be deemed fully applicable to the States through the Fourteenth Amendment. . . . This case presents a related issue: whether one jurisdiction within our federal structure may compel a witness, whom it has immunized from prosecution under its laws, to give testimony which might then be used to convict him of a crime against another such jurisdiction. . . .

Respondent contends . . . that we should adhere to the "established rule" that the constitutional privilege against self-incrimination does not protect a witness in one jurisdiction against being compelled to give testimony which could be used to convict him in another jurisdiction. This "rule" has three decisional facets: *United States* v. *Murdock,* 284 U.S. 141 [1931], held that the Federal Government could compel a witness to give testimony which might incriminate him under state law; *Knapp* v. *Schweitzer,* 357 U.S. 371 [1958], held that a State could compel a witness to give testimony which might incriminate him under federal law; and *Feldman* v. *United States,* 322 U.S. 487 [1944], held that testimony thus compelled by a State could be introduced into evidence in the federal courts.

Our decision today in *Malloy* v. *Hogan, supra,* necessitates a reconsideration of this rule. Our review of the pertinent cases in this Court and of their English antecedents reveals that *Murdock* did not adequately consider the relevant authorities and has been significantly weakened by subsequent decisions of this Court, and, further, that the legal premises underlying *Feldman* and *Knapp* have since been rejected. . . .

[Quoting from the dissenting opinion of Justice Black in the *Knapp* case, Justice Goldberg stated that most of the policies and purposes of the privilege are defeated when a witness "can be whipsawed into incriminating himself under both state and federal law" even though the privilege against self-incrimination is applicable to each. "This has become especially true in our age of 'cooperative federalism,' where th Federal and State Governments are waging a united front against many types of criminal activity." He concluded:]

[W]e hold the constitutional rule to be that a state witness may not be compelled to give testimony which may be incriminating under federal law unless the compelled testimony and its fruits cannot be used in any manner by federal officials in connection with a criminal prosecution against him. We conclude, moreover, that in order to implement this constitutional rule and accommodate the interests of the State and Federal Governments in investigating and prosecuting crime, the Federal Government must be prohibited from making any such use of compelled testimony and its fruits. . . .

It follows that petitioners here may now be compelled to answer the questions propounded to them. . . . We have now overruled *Feldman* and held that the Federal

Government may make no such use of the answers. Fairness dictates that petitioners should now be afforded an opportunity, in light of this development, to answer the questions.

As Justice Goldberg stated in a footnote, "the basic issue is the same whether the testimony is compelled by the Federal Government and used by a State, or compelled by a State and used by the Federal Government." Thus a grant of immunity by either jurisdiction now gives full protection against use of testimony or information by the other to initiate a prosecution.

THE PRIVILEGE, REGISTRATION LAWS, AND COMPULSORY FILING

Following the Kefauver Crime Committee investigation into crime and racketeering, Congress enacted the Gamblers' Occupational Tax Act in 1951. The Act levied a tax on persons engaged in the business of accepting wagers and required that they register with the Collector of Internal Revenue. In *United States* v. *Kahriger*, 345 U.S. 22 (1953), the Court, by a six-to-three vote, upheld the registration requirement against the claim that it violated the protection against self-incrimination. The majority reasoned that the privilege "has relation only to past acts, not to future acts that may or may not be committed." In dissenting, Justice Black said he was sure that the Act "creates a squeezing device contrived to put a man in federal prison if he refuses to confess himself into a state prison as a violator of state gambling law."

In *Marchetti* v. *United States*, 390 U.S. 39 (1968), and *Grosso* v. *United States*, 390 U.S. 62 (1968), the Court overruled *Kahriger*. Justice Harlan, writing for the majority in both cases, stated:

Substantial hazards of incrimination as to past or present acts plainly may stem from the requirements to register and to pay the occupational tax. . . . In the first place, satisfaction of those requirements increases the likelihood that any past or present gambling offenses will be discovered and successfully prosecuted. It both centers attention upon the registrant as a gambler, and compels "injurious disclosures" which may provide or assist in the collection of evidence admissible in a prosecution for past or present offenses. . . .

In *Haynes* v. *United States*, 390 U.S. 85 (1968), the Court held void the registration requirements of the National Firearms Act of 1934. The defendant had been convicted for knowingly possessing a sawed-off shotgun which had not been registered with the Secretary of the Treasury. The Court held that a proper claim of the privilege against self-incrimination provides a full defense to prosecutions either for failure to register a firearm or for possession of an unregistered firearm under the Firearms Act.

In *Leary* v. *United States*, 395 U.S. 6 (1969), the Court held, without dissent, that the elaborate registration provisions of the Marihuana Tax

Act violated the defendant's privilege against self-incrimination. There was a "real and appreciable" risk where the law required an order form which issued only upon identification as a transferee of marijuana, and further provided for notification of such status to state law officers.

In the context of Communist activities controls the Court has considered other federal registration requirements. The Subversive Activities Control Act of 1950 required Communist-action organizations, as defined by the statute, to register with the Attorney General, such registration to include a list of individual members. The Act further provided that if the officers of a Communist-action organization failed to register, then the individual members become criminally liable if they fail to register themselves within sixty days after the registration order issued. After lengthy litigation, the self-incrimination issues were substantially settled by the Court. The cases are treated at some length in Chapter 6 and will only briefly be reviewed here. In *Communist Party of the United States* v. *Subversive Activities Control Board*, 367 U.S. 1 (1961), the Court held that as to the officers of the Communist Party, the issue of whether the registration order violated the privilege against self-incrimination was premature. Justice Frankfurter, for the Court, stated:

We cannot know now that the Party's officers will ever claim the privilege. . . . If a claim of privilege is made, it may or may not be honored by the Attorney General. We cannot, on the basis of supposition that the privilege will be claimed and not honored, proceed now to adjudicate the constitutionality under the Fifth Amendment of the registration provisions.

In *Albertson* v. *Subversive Activities Control Board*, 382 U.S. 70 (1965), however, the Court faced the issue squarely and ruled that as to the individual member of a Communist-action organization required to register, the requirement violated the privilege against self-incrimination. Justice Brennan, for the Court, noted that the Act had an immunity provision applicable to registrants, but he found that the immunity offered was incomplete. "It does not preclude the use of the admission as an investigatory lead, a use which is barred by the privilege."

SELF-INCRIMINATION: COERCED CONFESSIONS

While a confession is clearly a way in which one can incriminate himself, our present rules with respect to the use of confessions are not simply applications of the privilege to the subject of confessions. The privilege and the rule barring coerced confessions are different both in point of historical development and in the way they are applied. The privilege was firmly established by the latter seventeenth century, but the rule barring forced confessions did not come until the latter eighteenth century. In barring such confessions in federal proceedings, the Court did not rely on the Fifth Amendment privilege, but, instead, adopted a rule of evidence binding on the lower federal courts to accomplish the purpose. The phraseology of the

privilege indicates strongly that it is to operate in official proceedings only
—"in any criminal case." Such an interpretation would permit the use
of a confession so long as it was obtained outside the formal proceedings
of the court, grand jury, or legislative hearing. Thus a different basis than
the privilege was considered necessary to afford the desired protection
against coerced confessions. The federal bar to admission of coerced confessions originated, therefore, simply as a rule of evidence. Both this bar
and the privilege against self-incrimination point in the same direction, of
course, of guaranteeing to the accused fair play in the proceedings against
him. As will be seen in the cases to follow, the prohibition against the use
of coerced confessions has now been elevated to constitutional status as a
requirement of due process of law.

Although the practice of barring coerced confessions in federal trials is
an old one, it was not until 1936 that the Court held that the introduction
of coerced confessions in state prosecutions violated the Fourteenth Amendment's "due process" clause. The case was *Brown* v. *Mississippi,* and the
Court was faced with the problem of qualifying an earlier statement made
in *Twining* v. *New Jersey* relative to self-incrimination and due process. In
Twining the Court had held that in a state criminal case, judicial comment
to the jury concerning defendant's refusal to take the stand in his defense
was not a violation of due process of law. In the last sentence of his opinion
for the Court, Justice Moody had stated "We think that the exemption
from compulsory self-incrimination in the courts of the States is not secured by any part of the Federal Constitution." In *Brown* v. *Mississippi*
the state used this statement to support their argument that coerced confessions were within the holding of the *Twining* case and thus their admission as evidence did not violate the "due process" clause.

BROWN *v.* MISSISSIPPI
297 U.S. 278 (1936)

[Three Negroes were arrested on March 30, 1934, for the murder of one
Raymond Stewart. Testimony indicated that police officers administered sustained
and brutal whippings to all three men until they confessed to the crime. They
were then told that if they changed their story at any time, additional beatings
would be given. They were indicted on April 4, 1934, and were then arraigned
and pleaded not guilty. Counsel were appointed by the court to defend them, and
trial was begun the next morning. Aside from the confessions, there was no evidence
sufficient to warrant the submission of the case to the jury. Testimony as to the
confessions was received over the objection of defendants' counsel. Defendants then
testified that the confessions were false and had been procured by physical torture.
The case went to the jury with instructions, upon the request of defendants'
counsel, that if the jury had reasonable doubt as to the confessions having resulted
from coercion, *and that they were not true,* they were not to be considered as
evidence. The jury found the three defendants guilty, and they were sentenced
to death. The Mississippi Supreme Court affirmed the judgment.]

Mr. Chief Justice Hughes delivered the opinion of the Court.

The question in this case is whether convictions, which rest solely upon confessions shown to have been extorted by officers of the state by brutality and violence, are consistent with the due process of law required by the Fourteenth Amendment of the Constitution of the United States. . . .

The grounds of the decision were (1) that immunity from self-incrimination is not essential to due process of law; and (2) that the failure of the trial court to exclude the confessions after the introduction of evidence showing their incompetency, in the absence of a request for such exclusion, did not deprive the defendants of life or liberty without due process of law; and that even if the trial court had erroneously overruled a motion to exclude the confessions, the ruling would have been mere error reversible on appeal, but not a violation of constitutional right. . . .

1. The state stresses the statement in *Twining* v. *New Jersey*, 211 U.S. 78, 114, that "exemption from compulsory self-incrimination in the courts of the states is not secured by any part of the Federal Constitution," and the statement in *Snyder* v. *Massachusetts*, 291 U.S. 97, 105, that "the privilege against self-incrimination may be withdrawn and the accused put upon the stand as a witness for the state." But the question of the right of the state to withdraw the privilege against self-incrimination is not here involved. The compulsion to which the quoted statements refer is that of the processes of justice by which the accused may be called as a witness and required to testify. Compulsion by torture to extort a confession is a different matter.

The state is free to regulate the procedure of its courts in accordance with its own conceptions of policy, unless in so doing it "offends some principle of justice so rooted in the traditions and conscience of our people as to be ranked as fundamental." *Synder* v. *Massachusetts, supra.* . . . The state may abolish trial by jury. It may dispense with indictment by a grand jury and substitute complaint or information. *Walker* v. *Sauvinet*, 92 U.S. 90; *Hurtado* v. *California*, 110 U.S. 516; *Snyder* v. *Massachusetts, supra.* But the freedom of the state in establishing its policy is the freedom of constitutional government and is limited by the requirement of due process of law. Because a state may dispense with a jury trial, it does not follow that it may substitute trial by ordeal. The rack and torture chamber may not be substituted for the witness stand. The state may not permit an accused to be hurried to conviction under mob domination—where the whole proceeding is but a mask—without supplying corrective process. *Moore* v. *Dempsey*, 261 U.S. 86. The state may not deny to the accused the aid of counsel. *Powell* v. *Alabama*, 287 U.S. 45. Nor may a state, through the action of its officers, contrive a conviction through the pretense of a trial which in truth is "but used as a means of depriving a defendant of liberty through a deliberate deception of court and jury by the presentation of testimony known to be perjured." *Mooney* v. *Holohan* 294 U.S. 103. And the trial equally is a mere pretense where the state authorities have contrived a conviction resting solely upon confessions obtained by violence. The due process clause requires "that state action, whether through one agency or another, shall be consistent with the fundamental principles of liberty and justice which lie at the base of all our civil and political institutions." *Hebert* v. *Louisiana*, 272 U.S. 312. It woud be difficult to conceive of methods more revolting to the sense of justice than those taken to procure the confessions of these petitioners, and the use of the confessions thus obtained as the basis for conviction and sentence was a clear denial of due process.

2. It is in this view that the further contention of the State must be considered. That contention rests upon the failure of counsel for the accused, who had objected to the admissibility of the confessions, to move for their exclusion after they had been introduced and the fact of coercion had been proved. It is a contention which proceeds upon a misconception of the nature of petitioners' complaint. That complaint is not of the commission of mere error, but of a wrong so fundamental that it made the whole proceeding a mere pretense of a trial and rendered the conviction and sentence wholly void. . . .

In the instant case, the trial court was fully advised by the undisputed evidence of the way in which the confessions had been procured. The trial court knew that there was no other evidence upon which conviction and sentence could be based. Yet it proceeded to permit conviction and to pronounce sentence. . . . The court thus denied a federal right fully established and specially set up and claimed, and the judgment must be reversed.

It is so ordered.

The Court has further made it clear that even though a coerced confession be considered truthful and reliable, its admission into evidence will void a conviction. Justice Frankfurter, speaking for the Court in *Rogers* v. *Richmond*, 365 U.S. 534 (1961), said:

Our decisions under [the Fourteenth] Amendment have made clear that convictions following the admission into evidence of confessions which are involuntary . . . cannot stand. This is so not because such confessions are unlikely to be true but because the methods used to extract them offend an underlying principle in the enforcement of our criminal law: that ours is an accusatorial and not an inquisitorial system—a system in which the State must establish guilt by evidence independently and freely secured and may not by coercion prove its charge against an accused out of his own mouth. . . .

From a fair reading of [expressions of the courts below], we cannot but conclude that the question whether Rogers' confessions were admissible into evidence was answered by reference to a legal standard which took into account the circumstance of probable truth or falsity. And this is not a permissible standard under the Due Process Clause of the Fourteenth Amendment.

In addition, in *Malinski* v. *New York*, 324 U.S. 401 (1945), the Court held that a conviction must be set aside where a coerced confession was admitted into evidence, even though other evidence was presented sufficient to sustain a conviction. As to the question of who determines whether a confession is voluntary, the New York rule, followed also in some other jurisdictions, required that the trial judge make a preliminary determination and exclude the confession if in no circumstances it could be deemed voluntary. But if the evidence presented a fair question as to its voluntariness, the judge was required to submit to the jury the determination of the voluntariness and truthfulness of the confession. In *Jackson* v. *Denno*, 378 U.S. 368 (1964), the Court, relying heavily on *Rogers* v. *Richmond* and *Malinski* v. *New York*, held that where a jury is returning a general verdict, it cannot be assumed that the jury could reliably distinguish the issue of voluntariness from the question of truthfulness, and the procedure thus violates Fourteenth Amendment due process. Justice White, for the majority, said "The overall determination of the voluntariness of a confession has thus become an exceedingly sensitive task, one that requires facing the issue squarely, in illuminating isolation and unbeclouded by other issues and the effect of extraneous but prejudicial evidence." He also suggested the difficulty of ignoring a confession even after it has been found to be involuntary. "[T]he fact of a defendant's confession is solidly implanted in the jury's mind, for it has not only heard the confession, but it has been instructed to consider and judge its voluntariness and is in position to assess whether it is true or false." Thus the rule now imposed requires that a separate determination on voluntariness be made before the jury is brought into the picture.

As the Court settled the issue of the use of confessions obtained by physical torture, it moved on to take up the more difficult issue of the admissibility of confessions obtained after lengthy interrogation. [As will be seen, this aspect of the coerced confession problem moves ineluctably into conjunction with the question of the stage at which the right to counsel accrues, and is largely disposed of by the recent decision in *Miranda* v. *Arizona*, 384 U.S. 436 (1966), discussed below.] It has been a not uncommon practice for the police to take suspects to the police station "for investigation" in order to see whether interrogation will uncover additional information bearing on the commission of the crime. The wide variety of such situations which have come to the Court for appraisal has led to a group of decisions in which the members of the Court have been badly split on the rationale of the cases. *Ashcraft* v. *Tennessee*, 322 U.S. 143 (1944), involved a claim of coercion in the extraction of a confession after a 36-hour period of practically continuous questioning, under powerful electric lights, by relays of officers, experienced investigators, and highly trained lawyers. At the end of this period of interrogation, Ashcraft confessed to hiring another person to murder his wife. Justice Black, speaking for the majority, stated that the confession was "not voluntary but compelled." He stated further that the detention incommunicado and the 36-hour questioning were "so inherently coercive that its very existence is irreconcilable with the possession of mental freedom by a lone suspect against whom its full coercive force is brought to bear." Justice Jackson, with whom two other justices concurred, dissented vigorously. He stated:

A confession is wholly and incontestably voluntary only if a guilty person gives himself up to the law and becomes his own accuser. The Court bases its decision on the premise that custody and examination of a prisoner for 36 hours is "inherently coercive." Of course it is. And so is custody and examination for one hour. Arrest itself is inherently coercive, and so is detention.... Of course such acts put pressure upon the prisoner to answer questions, to answer them truthfully, and to confess if guilty.

But does the Constitution prohibit use of all confessions made after arrest because questioning, while one is deprived of freedom, is "inherently coercive"? The Court does not quite say so, but it is moving far and fast in that direction. The step it now takes is to hold this confession inadmissible because of the time taken in getting it.

... Always heretofore the ultimate question has been whether the confessor was in possession of his own will and self-control at the time of confession. For its bearing on this question the Court always has considered the confessor's strength or weakness, whether he was educated or illiterate, intelligent or moronic, well or ill, Negro or white....

Although the vote has been close in subsequent decisions, the Court has invalidated a number of confessions since *Ashcraft* on the ground of mental coercion. The vote was five-to-four in four cases decided in the five years following *Ashcraft*. [*Malinski* v. *New York*, 324 U.S. 401 (1945); *Haley* v. *Ohio*, 332 U.S. 596 (1948); *Turner* v. *Pennsylvania*, 338 U.S. 62 (1949); *Harris* v. *South Carolina*, 338 U.S. 68 (1949).] In another, *Watts* v. *Indiana*, 338 U.S. 49 (1949), the petitioner was arrested on a charge of criminal assault and was also questioned about a murder which occurred in the same location as the assault. For six nights, Sunday excepted, petitioner was questioned from late in the afternoon until almost dawn by relays of officers. At three o'clock on the final morning he confessed to the crime. During the period he was under the exclusive control of the officers, without aid of counsel, and without advice as to his constitutional rights. Announcing the judgment of the Court reversing the conviction, Justice Frankfurter stated:

A confession by which life becomes forfeit must be the expression of free choice. A statement to be voluntary of course need not be volunteered. But if it is the product of sustained pressure by the police it does not issue from a free choice. When a suspect speaks because he is overborne, it is immaterial whether he has been subjected to a physical or mental ordeal. Eventual yielding to questioning under such circumstances is plainly the product of the suction process of interrogation and therefore the reverse of voluntary. We would have to shut our minds to the plain significance of what here transpired to deny that this was a calculated endeavor to secure a confession through the pressure of unrelenting interrogation. The very relentlessness of such interrogation implies that it is better for the prisoner to answer than to persist in the refusal of disclosure which is his constitutional right. To turn the detention of an accused into a process of wrenching from him evidence which could not be extorted in open court with all its safeguards, is so grave an abuse of the power of arrest as to offend the procedural standards of due process.

In still another case of mental pressure, *Leyra* v. *Denno*, 347 U.S. 556 (1954), the Court set aside a conviction based on a confession obtained by a state-employed psychiatrist. A man suspected of murder was questioned intensively for three days. When he complained of sinus pains, a state-employed psychiatrist was brought in to talk to him. After a further period of questioning by the doctor, during which it was suggested that the accused would feel better if he told the whole story, a confession was made to the doctor. He then called in the police, and the accused repeated the confession which was introduced at the trial. The Court held that both confessions were to be viewed together and that sufficient mental coercion was present to invalidate them. It was considered by the Court to be one continuous process, during which "an already physically and emotionally exhausted suspect's ability to resist interrogation was broken to almost trancelike submission by use of the arts of a highly skilled psychiatrist."

It is not possible to state a clear-cut rule of decision in the mental coercion cases. Each case must be examined separately on its own facts. Thus in *Fikes* v. *Alabama,* 352 U.S. 191 (1957), two confessions obtained from a mentally retarded, and, perhaps, mentally ill Negro and relied upon to convict him of burglary with intent to rape were held to have been involuntary. Detained in a prison far from his home, denied a preliminary hearing required under Alabama law, and held incommunicado, except for one visit from his father, defendant was interrogated intermittently over a period of eleven days. After the second confession, on the tenth day, he was arraigned. The Court stressed the detention incommunicado, the delay in arraignment, and the protracted questioning, but said that the acceptability of a confession was to be determined "by a weighing of the circumstances of pressure against the power of resistance of the person confessing. What would be overpowering to the weak of will or mind might be utterly ineffective against an experienced criminal." In concurring, Justice Frankfurter pointed out that while none of the facts in *Fikes* standing alone would justify a reversal, "in combination they bring the result below the Plimsoll line of 'due process'."

The difficulty in maintaining consistency in the coerced confession decisions was well stated in *Culombe* v. *Connecticut,* 367 U.S. 568 (1961), reversing the conviction based on a confession of a mental defective who was subjected to psychological pressure during a four-day question period. The Court pointed out that it was impossible "precisely to delimit, or to surround with specific, all-inclusive restrictions, the power of interrogation allowed to state law enforcement officers in obtaining confessions. No single litmus-paper test for constitutionally impermissible interrogation has been evolved. . . ." [For an analysis of the cases on coerced confessions, see *The Constitution of the United States of America,* 88th Cong., 1st Sess., Sen. Doc. No. 39 (U.S. Government Printing Ofc., 1964), pp. 1233–1251. An extensive bibliography and case analysis on police interrogation and coerced confessions is included in Justice Frankfurter's opinion in *Culombe.*] Justices Douglas and Black concurred, but they would have reversed the conviction solely on the ground of denial of counsel. Justice Douglas stated:

I find this case a simple one. . . . It is . . . controlled by the principle some of us have urged upon the Court in several prior cases. . . . That principle is that any accused—whether rich or poor—has the right to consult a lawyer before talking with the police. . . .

It is said that if we enforced the guarantee of counsel by allowing a person, who is arrested, to obtain legal advice before talking with the police, we "would effectively preclude police questioning" . . . and "would constrict police activities in a manner that in many cases might impair their ability to solve crimes.". . . It is said that "any lawyer worth his salt will tell the suspect in no uncertain terms to make no statement to the police under any circumstances." *Watts* v. *Indiana*, . . . In other words an attorney is likely to inform his client, clearly and unequivocally, that "No person . . . shall be compelled in any criminal case to be a witness against himself," as provided in the Fifth Amendment. This is the "evil" to be feared from contact between a police suspect and his lawyer.

Justice Douglas' remarks show clearly the conjunction of the privilege and the right to counsel at the interrogation stage. He and Justice Black waged a long campaign for acceptance of this view, culminating in success in *Miranda* v. *Arizona* in 1966.

Before proceeding further, a brief look should be taken at federal practice regarding admissibility of confessions. The Court has held coerced confessions inadmissible as a rule of evidence in federal prosecutions. In *McNabb* v. *United States*, 318 U.S. 332 (1943), the Court took another step and held inadmissible a confession obtained by federal authorities who had not promptly taken the accused before a committing officer (as required by Rule 5 of the Federal Rules of Criminal Procedure). Thus the rule laid down was that a confession was inadmissible in a federal prosecution if secured during a period of unlawful detention. In *Upshaw* v. *United States*, 335 U.S. 410 (1948), the Court held that such confessions are inadmissible even though there is no proof of improper pressures brought to bear in obtaining the confessions. This was not construed as a requirement of the Constitution, but was in the exercise of the Court's supervisory power over the lower federal courts. The rule was followed in the highly controversial decision in *Mallory* v. *United States*, 354 U.S. 449 (1957), which reversed a conviction and death sentence for rape in a federal case. Washington, D.C., police had apprehended petitioner and others around two-thirty one afternoon. Petitioner was questioned for some forty-five minutes by four officers and strenuously denied his guilt. Around four o'clock the suspects were asked to submit to "lie detector" tests, and they agreed. Petitioner's questioning began at about eight o'clock, and after an hour and a half of interrogation he stated that he had committed the crime. At ten o'clock that evening the police attempted to reach a United States Commissioner for the purpose of arraignment. Failing in this, they had petitioner examined by a deputy coroner, who noted no indications of physical or psychological coercion, and around midnight he dictated his confession to a typist. Not until the following morning was he brought before a commissioner, although, as the Court stated, "arraignment could easily have been made in the same building in which the police headquarters were housed."

Justice Frankfurter, speaking for the Court, cited Rule 5(a), requiring that officers take an arrested person "without unnecessary delay before the nearest available commissioner," and 5(b) relative to the commissioner's function:

The commissioner shall inform the defendant of the complaint against him, of his right to retain counsel and of his right to have a preliminary examination. He shall also inform the defendant that he is not required to make a statement and that any statement made by him may be used against him. The commissioner shall allow the defendant reasonable time and opportunity to consult counsel and shall admit the defendant to bail as provided in these rules.

Again we see, this time in congressional legislation, the juxtaposition of the privilege and the right to counsel. In pointing out the purpose of Rule 5(a) and (b), Justice Frankfurter said, "Not until he had confessed, when any judicial caution had lost its purpose, did the police arraign him." Thus the Court followed the *McNabb* rule in holding the confession inadmissible as a device to force the police to follow the congressional requirement of prompt arraignment and avoid the "tempting utilization of intensive interrogation, easily gliding into the evils of 'the third degree'."

A great deal of criticism from a variety of sources was leveled at the Court following both the *McNabb* and the *Mallory* decisions, and bills were introduced in Congress after each decision to protect the admissibility of voluntary confessions. Exhaustive hearings were conducted on the matter by a Senate subcommittee, and the published material contains a wealth of information on problems of confessions and police detention, proposed legislation, and journal articles. [See Hearings before the Subcommittee on Constitutional Rights of the Committee on the Judiciary, United States Senate, 85th Cong., 2nd Sess., *Confessions and Police Detention* (U.S. Government Printing Ofc., 1958).]

It has been pointed out by many writers that the *McNabb-Mallory* rule would not necessarily bar the use of damaging *admissions* (as opposed to confessions, or complete acknowledgment of guilt), such as the names of witnesses or a hidden weapon or the location of a buried body. [See, e.g., M. C. Slough, "Confessions and Admissions," 28 *Fordham L. Rev.* 96 (1959).] Rather than abandon the rule because of such weakness, however, the Court has moved to strengthen it in an attempt to close the loophole. *Gideon* v. *Wainwright*, 372 U.S. 335 (1963), had held that the Sixth Amendment's right to counsel was "incorporated" into the Fourteenth Amendment. But the key counsel decision in the context of the privilege against self-incrimination during police interrogation came in *Escobedo* v. *Illinois*, 378 U.S. 478 (1964).

Petitioner was arrested at 2:30 A.M. without a warrant and interrogated. He was released that afternoon pursuant to a writ of habeas corpus obtained by his lawyer. Several days later, he was again arrested and interrogated further. He asked to see his lawyer, who had arrived shortly thereafter at police headquarters, but the police refused. The lawyer asked permission to see Escobedo, and this request was refused. Notwithstanding repeated requests by each, the petitioner and his retained lawyer were afforded no opportunity to consult with each other during the course of the entire interrogation. During the course of the interrogation the petitioner made several damaging admissions implicating himself in the crime, and these statements were introduced into evidence. At no time was he advised of his constitutional right to remain silent. In reversing the conviction, Justice Goldberg stated for the majority of the Court:

> We hold . . . that where, as here, the investigation is no longer a general inquiry into an unsolved crime but has begun to focus on a particular suspect, the suspect has been taken into police custody, the police carry out a process of interrogations that lends itself to eliciting incriminating statements, the suspect has requested and been denied an opportunity to consult with his lawyer, and the police have not effectively warned him of his absolute constitutional right to remain silent, the accused has been denied "the Assistance of Counsel" in violation of the Sixth Amendment to the Constitution as "made obligatory upon the States by the Fourteenth Amendment," *Gideon* v. *Wainwright,* and that no statement elicited by the police during the interrogation may be used against him at a criminal trial.

The logical conclusion suggested by *Escobedo* came in *Miranda* v. *Arizona,* 384 U.S. 436 (1966). Four cases were brought together for decision, and without specific concentration on the facts of these cases, the Court sought to lay down the governing principles concerning interrogation and the Fifth Amendment privilege. Chief Justice Warren, speaking for the majority of five, referred to the *Escobedo* case at the outset, saying that "This case has been the subject of judicial interpretation and spirited legal debate since it was decided two years ago." He continued, "We granted certiorari in these cases . . . in order further to explore some facets of the problems, thus exposed, of applying the privilege against self-incrimination to in-custody interrogation, and to give concrete constitutional guidelines for law enforcement agencies and courts to follow." The rule was stated as follows:

> Our holding will be spelled out with some specificity in the pages which follow but briefly stated it is this: the prosecution may not use statements, whether exculpatory or inculpatory, stemming from custodial interrogation of the defendant unless it demonstrates the use of procedural safeguards effective to secure the privilege against self-incrimination. By custodial interrogation, we mean questioning initiated by law enforcement officers after a person has been taken into custody or otherwise deprived of his freedom of action in any significant way. As for the procedural safeguards to be employed, unless other fully effective means are devised to inform accused persons of their right of silence and to assure a continuous opportunity to exercise it, the following measures are required. Prior to any questioning, the person must be warned that he has a right to remain silent, that any statement he does make may be used as evidence against him, and that he has a right to the presence

of an attorney, either retained or appointed. The defendant may waive effectuation of these rights, provided the waiver is made voluntarily, knowingly and intelligently. If, however, he indicates in any manner and at any stage of the process that he wishes to consult with an attorney before speaking there can be no questioning. Likewise, if the individual is alone and indicates in any manner that he does not wish to be interrogated, the police may not question him. The mere fact that he may have answered some questions or volunteered some statements on his own does not deprive him of the right to refrain from answering any further inquiries until he has consulted with an attorney and thereafter consents to be questioned.

In as simple and nontechnical language as he could muster, the Chief Justice then proceeded to elaborate the specific requirements under which the police must operate. A mere warning is not sufficient to protect the privilege; "the right to have counsel present at the interrogation is indispensable to the protection of the Fifth Amendment privilege." An indigent must not only be warned, but he must also be advised that he has a right to an appointed attorney to represent him. In the case of a waiver of the right to counsel and the privilege, "a heavy burden rests on the Government to demonstrate that the defendant knowingly and intelligently waived" his privilege and the right to counsel. The police may still "seek out evidence in the field," question persons not under restraint, and make general on-the-scene inquiry as to facts surrounding a crime. The Chief Justice stated further:

[W]e do not purport to find all confessions inadmissible. . . . There is no requirement that police stop a person who enters a police station and states that he wishes to confess to a crime, or a person who calls the police to offer a confession or any other statement he desires to make. Volunteered statements of any kind are not barred by the Fifth Amendment and their admissibility is not affected by our holding today.

Justice Clark, in dissenting, pointed out that custodial interrogation has long been recognized as an essential tool in effective law enforcement. With respect to the majority's position he stated:

Such a strict constitutional specific inserted at the nerve center of crime detection may well kill the patient. Since there is at this time a paucity of information and an almost total lack of empirical knowledge on the practical operation of requirements, truly comparable to those announced by the majority, I would be more restrained lest we go too far too fast.

Justice Harlan delivered a trenchant criticism of the majority's position. He argued that in terms of the history of the Fifth Amendment privilege, in the carrying of the right to counsel "into the station house," and as an expression of desirable public policy, the majority was absolutely wrong. He stated that the "Court is taking a real risk with society's welfare in imposing its new regime on the country." He described the facts in the

Miranda case, involving the kidnapping and forcible rape of an 18-year-old girl. Miranda was later arrested, picked out of a lineup by the victim, and then interrogated by two police officers for two hours or less during the daytime. He gave an oral and then a written confession, "unmarked by any of the traditional indicia of coercion." Justice Harlan concluded:

They assured a conviction for a brutal and unsettling crime, for which the police had and quite possibly could obtain little evidence other than the victim's identifications, evidence which is frequently unreliable. There was, in sum, a legitimate purpose, no perceptible unfairness, and certainly little risk of injustice in the interrogation. Yet the resulting confessions, and the responsible course of police practice they represent, are to be sacrificed to the Court's own finespun conception of fairness which I seriously doubt is shared by many thinking citizens in this country.

In *Johnson* v. *New Jersey*, 384 U.S. 719 (1966), the Court held that *Miranda* and *Escobedo* would not be applied retroactively, and thus the rules of those cases would apply prospectively from the dates the decisions were handed down.

Another problem which is sometimes treated in the context of coerced confessions, although not involving testimonial utterances in any way, is the question of the legality of obtaining evidence from the actual person of the accused. Use of the person for identification purposes has long been sanctioned. The point was discussed by Justice Holmes in *Holt* v. *United States* (218 U.S. 245, 252-253) in 1910:

Another objection is based upon an extravagant extension of the Fifth Amendment. A question arose as to whether a blouse belonged to the prisoner. A witness testified that the prisoner put it on and it fitted him. It is objected that he did this under the same duress that made his statements inadmissible, and that it should be excluded for the same reasons. But the prohibition of compelling a man in a criminal court to be witness against himself is a prohibition of the use of physical or moral compulsion *to extort communications from him*, not an exclusion of his body as evidence when it may be material. The objection in principle would forbid a jury to look at a prisoner and compare his features with a photograph in proof. (Italics added.)

As Justice Holmes stated, the person may even be used in supplying evidentiary proof over and above mere identification—as in trying on a blouse found at the scene of the crime. The problem is really one of coerced *evidence* rather than coerced confessions, although it is frequently put in the latter category. The question of how far the police can go in obtaining evidence from the person of the accused is thus better viewed as simply a due process question rather than in the context of self-incrimination. In this framework it is easier to distinguish the holdings in the two cases to follow: *Rochin* v. *California* and *Breithaupt* v. *Abram*.

ROCHIN v. CALIFORNIA
342 U.S. 165 (1952)

Mr. Justice Frankfurter delivered the opinion of the Court.

Having "some information that [the petitioner] was selling narcotics," three deputy sheriffs of the County of Los Angeles, on the morning of July 1, 1949, made for the two-story dwelling house in which Rochin lived with his mother, his common-law wife, brothers and sisters. Finding the outside door open, they entered and then forced open the door to Rochin's room on the second floor. Inside they found petitioner sitting partly dressed on the side of the bed, upon which his wife was lying. On a "night stand" beside the bed the deputies spied two capsules. When asked "Whose stuff is this?" Rochin seized the capsules and put them in his mouth. A struggle ensued, in the course of which the three officers "jumped upon him" and attempted to extract the capsules. The force they applied prove unavailing against Rochin's resistance. He was handcuffed and taken to a hospital. At the direction of one of the officers a doctor forced an emetic solution through a tube into Rochin's stomach against his will. This "stomach pumping" produced vomiting. In the vomited matter were found two capsules which proved to contain morphine.

Rochin was brought to trial before a California Superior Court, sitting without a jury, on the charge of possessing "a preparation of morphine".... Rochin was convicted and sentenced to sixty days' imprisonment. The chief evidence against him was the two capsules. They were admitted over petitioner's objection, although the means of obtaining them was frankly set forth in the testimony by one of the deputies, substantially as here narrated.

On appeal, the District Court of Appeal affirmed the conviction, despite the finding that the officers "were guilty of unlawfully breaking into and entering defendant's room and were guilty of unlawfully assaulting and battering, torturing and falsely imprisoning the defendant at the alleged hospital."... The Supreme Court of California denied without opinion Rochin's petition for a hearing. Two justices dissented from this denial....

This Court granted certiorari... because a serious question is raised as to the limitations which the Due Process Clause of the Fourteenth Amendment imposes on the conduct of criminal proceedings by the States....

... Regard for the requirements of the Due Process Clause "inescapably imposes upon this Court an exercise of judgment upon the whole course of the proceedings [resulting in a conviction] in order to ascertain whether they offend those canons of decency and fairness which express the notions of justice of English-speaking peoples even toward those charged with the most heinous offenses." *Malinski* v. *New York*.... These standards of justice are not authoritatively formulated anywhere as though they were specifics. Due process of law is a summarized constitutional guarantee of respect for those personal immunities which, as Mr. Justice Cardozo twice wrote for the Court, are "so rooted in the traditions and conscience of our people as to be ranked as fundamental," *Snyder* v. *Massachusetts*, 291 U.S. 97, 105, or are "implicit in the concept of ordered liberty." *Palko* v. *Connecticut*, 302 U.S. 319, 325....

Applying these general considerations to the circumstances of the present case, we are compelled to conclude that the proceedings by which this conviction was

obtained do more than offend some fastidious squeamishness or private senti-
mentalism about combatting crime too energetically. It is conduct that shocks the
conscience. Illegally breaking into the privacy of the petitioner, the struggle to
open his mouth and remove what was there, the forcible extraction of his stomach's
contents—this course of proceeding by agents of government to obtain evidence
is bound to offend even hardened sensibilities. They are methods too close to the
rack and the screw to permit of constitutional differention.

It has long since ceased to be true that due process of law is heedless of the
means by which otherwise relevant and credible evidence is obtained. Even before
the series of recent cases enforced the constitutional principle the States could not
base convictions upon confessions, however much verified, but obtained by coercion.
These decisions are not arbitrary exceptions to the comprehensive right of States
to fashion their own rules of evidence for criminal trials. They are not sports in
our constitutional law but applications of a general principle. They are only
instances of the general requirement that States in their prosecutions respect certain
decencies of civilized conduct. Due process of law, as a historic and generative
principle, precludes defining, and thereby confining, these standards of conduct
more precisely than to say that convictions cannot be brought about by methods
that offend "a sense of justice." See Mr. Chief Justice Hughes, speaking for a
unanimous Court in *Brown* v. *Mississippi*, 297 U.S. 278, 285, 286. It would be
a stultification of the responsibility which the course of constitutional history has
cast upon this Court to hold that in order to convict a man the police cannot
extract by force what is in his mind but can extract what is in his stomach.

To attempt in this case to distinguish what lawyers call "real evidence" from
verbal evidence is to ignore the reasons for excluding coerced confessions. Use of
involuntary verbal confessions in State criminal trials is constitutionally obnoxious
not only because of their unreliability. They are inadmissible under the Due Process
Clause even though statements contained in them may be independently established
as true. Coerced confessions offend the community's sense of fair play and decency.
So here, to sanction the brutal conduct which naturally enough was condemned
by the court whose judgment is before us, would be to afford brutality the cloak
of law. Nothing would be more calculated to discredit law and thereby to brutalize
the temper of a society. . . .

We are not unmindful that hypothetical situations can be conjured up shading
imperceptibly from the circumstances of this case and by gradations producing
practical differences despite seemingly logical extensions. But the Constitution is
"intended to preserve practical and substantial rights, not to maintain theories."
Davis v. *Mills*, 194 U.S. 451, 457.

On the facts of this case the conviction of the petitioner has been obtained by
methods that offend the Due Process Clause. The judgment below must be

Reversed.

Mr. Justice Minton took no part in the consideration or decision of this case.
Mr. Justice Black, concurring.

Adamson v. *California*, 332 U.S. 46, 68-123, sets out reasons for my belief that
state as well as federal courts and law enforcement officers must obey the Fifth
Amendment's command that "No person . . . shall be compelled in any criminal
case to be a witness against himself." I think a person is compelled to be a witness
against himself not only when he is compelled to testify, but also when as here,

incriminating evidence is forcibly taken from him by a contrivance of modern science. Cf. *Boyd* v. *United States*, 116 U.S. 616; ... California convicted this petitioner by using against him evidence obtained in this manner, and I agree with Mr. Justice Douglas that the case should be reversed on this ground. ...

Mr. Justice Douglas, concurring. ...

As an original matter it might be debatable whether the provision in the Fifth Amendment that no person "shall be compelled in any criminal case to be a witness against himself" serves the ends of justice. Not all civilized legal procedures recognize it. But the choice was made by the Framers, a choice which sets a standard for legal trials in this country. The Framers made it a standard of due process for prosecutions by the Federal Government. If it is a requirement of due process for a trial in the federal court house, it is impossible for me to say it is not a requirement of due process for a trial in the state court house. ... Of course an accused can be compelled to be present at the trial, to stand, to sit, to turn this way or that, and to try on a cap or a coat. See *Holt* v. *United States*, 218 U.S. 245, 252, 253. But I think that words taken from his lips, capsules taken from his stomach, blood taken from his veins are all inadmissible provided they are taken from him without his consent. They are inadmissible because of the command of the Fifth Amendment. ...

In his concurring opinion, Justice Douglas put "blood taken from his veins" in the same area of constitutional protection as capsules taken from the stomach. He stated that in either case they are inadmissible if taken from the accused without his consent. Five years later the Court was faced with this exact question in *Breithaupt* v. *Abram*. Differences in approach among the justices which were indicated in *Rochin* resulted in a sharp split in the vote in *Breithaupt*.

BREITHAUPT *v.* ABRAM
352 U.S. 432 (1957)

Mr. Justice Clark delivered the opinion of the Court.

Petitioner, while driving a pickup truck on the highways of New Mexico, was involved in a collision with a passenger car. Three occupants of the car were killed and petitioner was seriously injured. A pint whiskey bottle, almost empty, was found in the glove compartment of the pickup truck. Petitioner was taken to a hospital and while lying unconscious in the emergency room the smell of liquor was detected on his breath. A state patrolman requested that a sample of petitioner's blood be taken. An attending physician, while petitioner was unconscious, withdrew a sample of about 20 cubic centimeters of blood by use of a hypodermic needle. This sample was delivered to the patrolman and subsequent laboratory analysis showed this blood to contain about .17 per cent alcohol.

Petitioner was thereafter charged with involuntary manslaughter. Testimony regarding the blood test and its result was admitted into evidence at trial over petitioner's objection. This included testimony of an expert that a person with .17 per cent alcohol in his blood was under the influence of intoxicating liquor. Petitioner was convicted and sentenced for involuntary manslaughter. He did not appeal the conviction. Subsequently, however, he sought release from his imprisonment by a petition for a writ of habeas corpus to the Supreme Court of New Mexico.

That court, after argument, denied the writ. . . . Petitioner contends that his conviction, based on the result of the involuntary blood test, deprived him of his liberty without that due process of law guaranteed him by the Fourteenth Amendment to the Constitution. We granted certiorari. . . .

It has been clear since *Weeks* v. *United States*, 232 U.S. 383, that evidence obtained in violation of rights protected by the Fourth Amendment to the Federal Constitution must be excluded in federal criminal prosecutions. There is argument on behalf of petitioner that the evidence used here, the result of the blood test, was obtained in violation of the Due Process Clause of the Fourteenth Amendment in that the taking was the result of an unreasonable search and seizure violative of the Fourth Amendment. Likewise, he argues that by way of the Fourteenth Amendment there has been a violation of the Fifth Amendment in that introduction of the test result compelled him to be a witness against himself. Petitioner relies on the proposition that "the generative principles" of the Bill of Rights should extend the protections of the Fourth and Fifth Amendments to his case through the Due Process Clause of the Fourteenth Amendment. But *Wolf* v. *Colorado* . . . answers this contention in the negative. . . . New Mexico has rejected, as it may, the exclusionary rule set forth in *Weeks*. . . . Therefore, the rights petitioner claims afford no aid to him here for the fruits of the violations, if any, are admissible in the State's prosecution.

Petitioner's remaining and primary assault on his conviction is not so easily unhorsed. He urges that the conduct of the state officers here offends that "sense of justice" of which we spoke in *Rochin* v. *California*. . . . But we see nothing comparable here to the facts in *Rochin*.

Basically the distinction rests on the fact that there is nothing "brutal" or "offensive" in the taking of a sample of blood when done, as in this case, under the protective eye of a physician. To be sure, the driver here was unconscious when the blood was taken, but the absence of conscious consent, without more, does not necessarily render the taking a violation of a constitutional right; and certainly the test as administered here would not be considered offensive by even the most delicate. Furthermore, due process is not measured by the yardstick of personal reaction or the sphygmogram of the most sensitive person, but by that whole community sense of "decency and fairness" that has been woven by common experience into the fabric of acceptable conduct. It is on this bedrock that this Court has established the concept of due process. The blood test procedure has become routine in our everyday life. It is a ritual for those going into the military service as well as those applying for marriage licenses. Many colleges require such tests before permitting entrance and literally millions of us have vountarily gone through the same, though a longer routine, in becoming blood donor. Likewise, we note that a majority of our States have either enacted statutes in some form authorizing tests of this nature or permit findings so obtained to be admitted in evidence. We therefore conclude that a blood test taken by a skilled technician is not such "conduct that shocks the conscience," *Rochin, supra*, . . . nor such a method of obtaining evidence that it offends a "sense of justice," *Brown* v. *Mississippi*. . . . This is not to say that the indiscriminate taking of blood under different conditions, or by those not competent to do so may not amount to such "brutality" as would come under the *Rochin* rule. The chief law-enforcement officer of New Mexico, while at the Bar of this Court, assured us that every proper medical precaution is afforded an accused from whom the blood is taken.

The test upheld here is not attacked on the ground of any basic deficiency or of injudicious application, but admittedly is a scientifically accurate method of detecting alcoholic content in the blood, thus furnishing an exact measure upon which to base a decision as to intoxication. Modern community living requires modern scientific methods of crime detection lest the public go unprotected. The increasing slaughter on our highways, most of which should be avoidable, now reaches the astounding figures only heard of on the battlefield. The States, through safety measures, modern scientific methods, and strict enforcement of traffic laws, are using all reasonable means to make automobile driving less dangerous.

As against the right of an individual that his person be held inviolable, even against so slight an intrusion as is involved in applying a blood test of the kind to which millions of Americans submit as a matter of course nearly every day, must be set the interests of society in the scientific determination of intoxication, one of the great causes of the mortal hazards of the road. And the more so since the test likewise may establish innocence, thus affording protection against the treachery of judgment based on one or more of the senses. Furthermore, since our criminal law is to no small extent justified by the assumption of deterrence, the individual's right to immunity from such invasion of the body as is involved in a properly safeguarded blood test is far outweighed by the value of its deterrent effect due to public realization that the issue of driving while under the influence of alcohol can often by this method be taken out of the confusion of conflicting contentions.

For these reasons the judgment is

Affirmed.

Mr. Chief Justice Warren, with whom Mr. Justice Black and Mr. Justice Douglas join, dissenting:

The judgment in this case should be reversed if *Rochin* v. *California* ... is to retain its vitality and stand as more than an instance of personal revulsion against particular police methods. I cannot agree with the Court when it says, "We see nothing comparable here to the facts in *Rochin.*" It seems to me the essential elements of the cases are the same and the same result should follow.

There is much in the Court's opinion concerning the hazards on our nation's highways, the efforts of the States to enforce the traffic laws and the necessity for the use of modern scientific methods in the detection of crime. Everybody can agree with these sentiments, and yet they do not help us particularly in determining whether this case can be distinguished from *Rochin*. That case grew out of police efforts to curb the narcotics traffic, in which there is surely a state interest of at least as great magnitude as the interest in highway law enforcement....

... Of course, one may consent to having his blood extracted or his stomach pumped and thereby waive any due process objection.... But where there is no affirmative consent, I cannot see that it should make any difference whether one states unequivocally that he objects or resorts to physical violence in protest or is in such condition that he is unable to protest. The Court, however, states that "the absence of conscious consent, without more, does not necessarily render the taking a violation of a constitutional right." This implies that a different result might follow if petitioner had been conscious and had voiced his objection. I reject the distinction.... I cannot accept an analysis that would make physical resistance by a prisoner a prerequisite to the existence of his constitutional rights. ...

Only personal reaction to the stomach pump and the blood test distinguish them. To base the restriction which the Due Process Clause imposes on state criminal procedures upon such reactions is to build on shifting sands. We should, in my opinion, hold that due process means at least that law enforcement officers in their efforts to obtain evidence from persons suspected of crime must stop short of bruising the body, breaking skin, puncturing tissue or extracting body fluids, whether they contemplate doing it by force or by stealth.

Viewed according to this standard the judgment should be reversed.

Mr. Justice Douglas, with whom Mr. Justice Black joins, dissenting. . . .

As I understood today's decision there would be a violation of due process if the blood had been withdrawn from the accused after a struggle with the police. But the sanctity of the person is equally violated and his body assaulted where the prisoner is incapable of offering resistance as it would be if force were used to overcome his resistance. In both cases evidence is used to convict a man which had been obtained from him on an involuntary basis. I would not draw a line between the use of force on the one hand and trickery, subterfuge, or any police technique which takes advantage of the inability of the prisoner to resist on the other. Nor would I draw a line between involuntary extraction of words from his lips, the involuntary extraction of the contents of his stomach, and the involuntary extraction of fluids of his body when the evidence obtained is used to convict him. Under our system of government, police cannot compel people to furnish the evidence necessary to send them to prison. Yet there is compulsion here, following the violation by the police of the sanctity of the body of an unconscious man. . . .

In *Schmerber* v. *California*, 384 U.S. 757 (1966), the Court ruled on the admissibility of a blood test report on intoxication where the blood sample was taken from the injured petitioner despite his refusal, on the advice of counsel, to consent to the test. He contended that the admission of such evidence violated due process under the Fourteenth Amendment, his privilege against self-incrimination under the Fifth Amendment, his right to counsel under the Sixth Amendment, and the prohibitions against unreasonable searches and seizures under the Fourth Amendment, as these have been incorporated into the Fourteenth Amendment. The Court stated that in view of the important decisions rendered since *Breithaupt* v. *Abram* (*viz., Escobedo* v. *Illinois, Malloy* v. *Hogan,* and *Mapp* v. *Ohio*), certiorari was granted to reconsider the questions. Justice Brennan, speaking for a majority of five, stated: "We hold that the privilege protects an accused only from being compelled to testify against himself, or otherwise provide the State with evidence of a testimonial or communicative nature, and that the withdrawal of blood and use of the analysis in question in this case did not involve compulsion to these ends." The due process contention was rejected squarely on the basis of *Breithaupt,* and the majority concluded that no substantial right to counsel issue was presented. On the Fourth Amendment claim, the Court stated that there was probable cause to believe petitioner to be intoxicated, that the officer therefore made a lawful arrest, and that the ordering of the blood test without a warrant was "an appropriate incident to petitioner's arrest" in order to prevent the "destruction of evidence" by normal physiological elimination of blood alcohol. Justices Harlan and Stewart concurred, with the only additional comment that "While agreeing with the Court that the taking of this blood test involved no testimonial compulsion, I would go further and hold that apart from this consideration the case in no way implicates the Fifth Amendment." Chief Justice Warren and Justices Black and Douglas dissented, following their views expressed in *Breithaupt*.

THE RIGHT TO COUNSEL

One of the most important rights of one accused of crime is the right to be represented by counsel. At common law a defendant had the right to employ counsel when charged with a misdemeanor, but not in cases of treason or felony. The theory apparently was that the Crown might err in petty offenses, but in the graver charges no case would be brought unless the evidence was so clear that guilt was evident. Therefore no lawyer was necessary, and the judge would see that procedures were fair. Full right of counsel was not extended by Parliament until 1836, much later than in the United States. Congress provided for the assistance of counsel in the original Judiciary Act of 1789, and in most of the original states the right was granted to accused persons whether in misdemeanor or felony cases.

It should be noted, however, that the original meaning of the right to counsel extended only to permission for the accused to employ and bring in to the trial a lawyer of his choosing. No general provision was made for the indigent defendant who might want and even badly need counsel, but who was too poor to employ a lawyer. Thus the Sixth Amendment provision for "assistance of counsel for his defense" in "all criminal prosecutions" was permissive only. It imposed no duty on the government to provide free counsel. The Federal Crimes Act of 1790, however, provided that counsel must be appointed in all capital cases at the request of the defendant. And Delaware, Pennsylvania, and South Carolina by 1789 had similar provisions. Connecticut apparently went further and the judges appointed counsel upon request if they felt that the accused needed it. With these exceptions, the "right to counsel" only gave the accused the right to hire a lawyer. In construing the federal requirement under the Sixth Amendment and under the Act of 1790, the Court held that neither the Constitution nor the statutes made court-appointed counsel mandatory in noncapital cases. Referring to the 1790 statute, which required counsel in all capital cases, the Court said, "There would appear to be a negative pregnant here." *United States* v. *Van Duzee*, 140 U.S. 169, 173 (1891). Thus it concluded that no appointment need be made in any other type of cases. It did leave the trial court with discretion to appoint counsel in noncapital cases if the judge saw fit, but it held that there was neither constitutional nor statutory duty to do so. As recently as 1931 this interpretation received official recognition. The Wickersham Commission, appointed by

President Hoover to investigate law enforcement, stated in its report in that year: "[T]he right guaranteed is one of employing counsel, not one of having counsel provided by the Government." [U.S. National Commission on Law Observance and Enforcement, *Report on Prosecution* 30 (U.S. Government Printing Ofc., 1931). See generally, William M. Beaney, *The Right of Counsel in American Courts* (Ann Arbor: University of Michigan Press, 1955); J. A. C. Grant, "Our Common Law Constitution," 40 *B. U. L. Rev.* 1, 5-10 (1960); David Fellman, *The Defendant's Rights* (New York: Rinehart, 1958) Chap. 7.]

The landmark case on the scope of the Sixth Amendment right to counsel is *Johnson* v. *Zerbst*. While the famous Scottsboro case of *Powell* v. *Alabama* preceded it by six years, the latter case dealt with Fourteenth Amendment right to counsel and will be taken up below.

JOHNSON *v.* ZERBST

304 U.S. 458 (1938)

Mr. Justice Black delivered the opinion of the Court.

Petitioner, while imprisoned in a Federal penitentiary, was denied habeas corpus by the District Court. . . .

Petitioner is serving sentence under a conviction in a United States District Court for possessing and uttering counterfeit money. It appears from the opinion of the District Judge denying habeas corpus that he believed petitioner was deprived, in the trial court, of his constitutional right under the provision of the Sixth Amendment that "In all criminal prosecutions, the accused shall enjoy the right . . . to have the Assistance of Counsel for his defence." However, he held that proceedings depriving petitioner of his constitutional right to assistance of Counsel were not sufficient "to make the trial void and justify its annulment in a habeas corpus proceeding, but that they constituted trial errors or irregularities which could only be corrected on appeal."

The Court of Appeals affirmed and we granted certiorari due to the importance of the questions involved.

[The opinion then recites the facts from the record. In November, 1934, petitioner and another were arrested for possessing and uttering counterfeit notes and were kept in jail for failure to give bail. In January they were indicted, and two days later were given notice of the indictment. They were immediately arraigned, tried, convicted and sentenced that day to four and one-half years in the penitentiary. While counsel had represented them in the preliminary hearing before the commissioner, the accused were unable to employ counsel for their trial. Upon arraignment, both pleaded guilty, said that they had no lawyer, and—in response to an inquiry of the court—stated that they were ready for trial. They were then tried, convicted and sentenced for a felony, without assistance of counsel.

Four months later petitioners filed applications for appeal which were denied because filed too late. The time for filing a motion for new trial and for taking an appeal is limited to three and five days, respectively.]

One. . . . The Sixth Amendment stands as a constant admonition that if the constitutional safeguards it provides be lost, justice will not "still be done." It embodies a realistic recognition of the obvious truth that the average defendant does not have the professional legal skill to protect himself when brought before a tribunal with power to take his life or liberty, wherein the prosecution is presented by experienced and learned Counsel. That which is simple, orderly and necessary to the lawyer—to the untrained layman—may appear intricate, complex and mysterious. Consistently with the wise policy of the Sixth Amendment and other parts of our fundamental charter, this Court has pointed to ". . . the humane policy of the modern criminal law . . ." which now provides that a defendant ". . . if he be poor, . . . may have counsel furnished him by the state . . . not infrequently . . . more able than the attorney for the state." [*Patton* v. *United States*, 281 U.S. 276, 308.]

The ". . . right to be heard would be, in many cases, of little avail if it did not comprehend the right to be heard by counsel. . . ." [*Powell* v. *Alabama*, 287 U.S. 45, 68, 69.] The Sixth Amendment withholds from Federal Courts, in all criminal proceedings, the power and authority to deprive an accused of his life or liberty unless he has or waives the assistance of Counsel.

Two. There is insistence here that petitioner waived this constitutional right. The District Court did not so find. It has been pointed out that "courts indulge every reasonable presumption against waiver" of fundamental constitutional rights and that we "do not presume acquiescence in the loss of fundamental rights." A waiver is ordinarily an intentional relinquishment or abandonment of a known right or privilege. The determination of whether there has been an intelligent waiver of the right to Counsel must depend, in each case, upon the particular facts and circumstances surrounding that case, including the background, experience, and conduct of the accused. . . .

The constitutional right of an accused to be represented by Counsel invokes, of itself, the protection of a trial court, in which the accused—whose life or liberty is at stake—is without Counsel. This protecting duty imposes the serious and weighty responsibility upon the trial judge of determining whether there is an intelligent and competent waiver by the accused. While an accused may waive the right to Counsel, whether there is a proper waiver should be clearly determined by the trial court, and it would be fitting and appropriate for that determination to appear upon the record.

Three. The District Court, holding petitioner could not obtain relief by habeas corpus, said:

"It is unfortunate, if petitioners lost their right to a new trial through ignorance or negligence, but such misfortune cannot give this Court jurisdiction in a habeas corpus case to review and correct the errors complained of.". . .

. . . Of the contention that the law provides no effective remedy for such a deprivation of rights affecting life and liberty, it may well be said—as in *Mooney* v. *Holohan*, 294 U.S. 103, 113—that it "falls with the premise." To deprive a citizen of his only effective remedy would not only be contrary to the "rudimentary demands of justice" but destructive of a constitutional guaranty specifically designed to prevent injustice.

Since the Sixth Amendment constitutionally entitles one charged with crime to the assistance of Counsel, compliance with this constitutional mandate is an essential jurisdictional prerequisite to a Federal court's authority to deprive an accused of his life or liberty. When this right is properly waived, the assistance of Counsel is no longer a necessary element of the court's jurisdiction to proceed to conviction and sentence. If the accused, however, is not represented by Counsel and has not competently and intelligently waived his constitutional right, the Sixth Amendment stands as a jurisdictional bar to a valid conviction and sentence depriving him of his life or his liberty. A court's jurisdiction at the beginning of trial may be lost "in the course of the proceedings" due to failure to complete the court—as the Sixth Amendment requires—by providing Counsel for an accused who is unable to obtain Counsel, who has not intelligently waived this constitutional guaranty, and whose life or liberty is at stake. If this requirement of the Sixth Amendment is not complied with, the court no longer has jurisdiction to proceed. The judgment of conviction pronounced by a court without jurisdiction is void, and one imprisoned thereunder may obtain release by habeas corpus. A judge of the United States—to whom a petition for habeas corpus is addressed—should be alert to examine "the facts for himself when if true as alleged they make the trial absolutely void.". . .

The cause is reversed and remanded to the District Court for action in harmony with this opinion.

Reversed.

Mr. Justice Reed concurs in the reversal.

Mr. Justice McReynolds is of opinion that the judgment of the court below should be affirmed.

Mr. Justice Butler is of the opinion that the record shows that petitioner waived the right to have counsel, that the trial court had jurisdiction, and that the judgment of the Circuit Court of Appeals should be affirmed.

Mr. Justice Cardozo took no part in the consideration or decision of this case.

With no support from historical analysis, from the writings of the proponents of the Amendment, or from precedent, then, the majority, almost casually, held that the Sixth Amendment right to counsel extends to the *appointment* of counsel for indigent defendants in federal proceedings. *Johnson* v. *Zerbst* contains two important subsidiary points. First, the defendant may waive counsel, but such waiver must be "intelligent and competent." The duty placed on the trial judge is clear; he must make certain that under the circumstances of the charge, the possible penalties, and the capabilities of the accused, that a request to proceed without counsel would not result in serious disability to the accused. Second, failure to meet the Sixth Amendment requirement with respect to counsel is a jurisdictional defect, and therefore the collateral remedy of habeas corpus may properly be employed.

The application of the Fourteenth Amendment to the question of counsel in state criminal proceedings has now arrived at the same position as that of the Sixth Amendment in federal proceedings, but the course was far more tortuous. As mentioned earlier, the leading case in this area is *Powell* v. *Alabama,* decided in 1932.

POWELL *v.* ALABAMA
287 U.S. 45 (1932)

Mr. Justice Sutherland delivered the opinion of the Court.

These cases were argued together and submitted for decision as one case.

The petitioners, hereafter referred to as defendants, are negroes charged with the crime of rape, committed upon the persons of two white girls. The crime is said to have been committed on March 25, 1931. The indictment was returned in a state court of first instance on March 31, and the record recites that on the same day the defendants were arraigned and entered pleas of not guilty. There is a further recital to the effect that upon the arraignment they were represented by counsel. But no counsel had been employed, and aside from a statement made by the trial judge several days later during a colloquy immediately preceding the trial, the record does not disclose when, or under what circumstances, an appointment of counsel was made, or who was appointed. During the colloquy referred to, the trial judge, in response to a question, said that he had appointed all the members of the bar for the purpose of arraigning the defendants and then of course anticipated that the members of the bar would continue to help the defendants if no counsel appeared. Upon the argument here both sides accepted that as a correct statement of the facts concerning the matter.

There was a severance upon the request of the state, and the defendants were tried in three several groups, as indicated above. As each of the three cases was called for trial, each defendant was arraigned, and, having the indictment read to him, entered a plea of not guilty. Whether the original arraignment and pleas were regarded as ineffective is not shown. Each of the three trials was completed within a single day. Under the Alabama statute the punishment for rape is to be fixed by the jury, and in its discretion may be from ten years' imprisonment to death. The juries found defendants guilty and imposed the death penalty upon all. The trial court overruled motions for new trials and sentenced the defendants in accordance with the verdicts. The judgments were affirmed by the state supreme court. . . .

. . . It is perfectly apparent that the proceedings, from beginning to end, took place in an atmosphere of tense, hostile and excited public sentiment. During the entire time, the defendants were closely confined or were under military guard. The record does not disclose their ages, except that one of them was nineteen; but the record clearly indicates that most, if not all, of them were youthful, and they are constantly referred to as "the boys." They were ignorant and illiterate. All of them were residents of other states, where alone members of their families or friends resided.

However guilty defendants, upon due inquiry, might prove to have been, they were, until convicted, presumed to be innocent. It was the duty of the court having their cases in charge to see that they were denied no necessary incident of a fair trial. . . . The sole inquiry which we are permitted to make is whether the federal Constitution was contravened . . . whether the defendants were in substance denied the right of counsel, and if so, whether such denial infringes the due process clause of the Fourteenth Amendment. . . .

It is hardly necessary to say that, the right to counsel being conceded, a defendant should be afforded a fair opportunity to secure counsel of his own choice. Not only was that not done here, but such designation of counsel as was attempted was either so indefinite or so close upon the trial as to amount to a denial of effective and substantial aid in that regard. This will be amply demonstrated by a brief review of the record.

[The opinion then quotes from the record, indicating clearly that no specific designation of counsel was made until the time of trial, and even then on the basis of a volunteer who stated, "I will go ahead and help do anything I can do."]

And in this casual fashion the matter of counsel in a capital case was disposed of. . . .

... In any event, the circumstance lends emphasis to the conclusion that during perhaps the most critical period of the proceedings against these defendants, that is to say, from the time of their arraignment until the beginning of their trial, when consultation, thorough-going investigation and preparation were vitally important, the defendants did not have the aid of counsel in any real sense, although they were as much entitled to such aid during that period as at the trial itself. . . .

... The defendants, young, ignorant, illiterate, surrounded by hostile sentiment, haled back and forth under guard of soldiers, charged with an atrocious crime regarded with especial horror in the community where they were to be tried, were thus put in peril of their lives within a few moments after counsel for the first time charged with any degree of responsibility began to represent them. . . .

It never has been doubted by this court, or any other so far as we know, that notice and hearing are preliminary steps essential to the passing of an enforceable judgment, and that they, together with a legally competent tribunal having jurisdiction of the case, constitute basic elements of the constitutional requirement of due process of law. . . .

What, then, does a hearing include? Historically and in practice, in our own country at least, it has always included the right to the aid of counsel when desired and provided by the party asserting the right. The right to be heard would be, in many cases, of little avail if it did not comprehend the right to be heard by counsel. Even the intelligent and educated layman has small and sometimes no skill in the science of law. If charged with crime, he is incapable, generally, of determining for himself whether the indictment is good or bad. He is unfamiliar with the rules of evidence. Left without the aid of counsel he may be put on trial without a proper charge, and convicted upon incompetent evidence, or evidence irrelevant to the issue or otherwise inadmissible. He lacks both the skill and knowledge adequately to prepare his defense, even though he have a perfect one. He requires the guiding hand of counsel at every step in the proceedings against him. Without it, though he be not guilty, he faces the danger of conviction because he does not know how to establish his innocence. If that be true of men of intelligence, how much more true is it of the ignorant and illiterate, or those of feeble intellect. If in any case, civil or criminal, a state or federal court were arbitrarily to refuse to hear a party by counsel, employed by and appearing for him, it reasonably may not be doubted that such a refusal would be a denial of a hearing, and, therefore, of due process in the constitutional sense. . . .

In the light of the facts outlined in the forepart of this opinion—the ignorance and illiteracy of the defendants, their youth, the circumstances of public hostility, the imprisonment and the close surveillance of the defendants by the military forces, the fact that their friends and families were all in other states and communication with them necessarily difficult, and above all that they stood in deadly peril of their lives—we think the failure of the trial court to give them reasonable time and opportunity to secure counsel was a clear denial of due process.

But passing that, and assuming their inability, even if opportunity had been given to employ counsel, as the trial court evidently did assume, we are of opinion that, under the circumstances just stated, the necessity of counsel was so vital and imperative that the failure of the trial court to make an effective appointment of counsel was likewise a denial of due process within the meaning of the Fourteenth

Amendment. Whether this would be so in other criminal prosecutions, or under other circumstances, we need not determine. All that it is necessary now to decide, as we do decide, is that in a capital case, where the defendant is unable to employ counsel, and is incapable adequately of making his own defense because of ignorance, feeble-mindedness, illiteracy, or the like, it is the duty of the court, whether requested or not, to assign counsel for him as a necessary requisite of due process of law; and that duty is not discharged by an assignment at such a time or under such circumstances as to preclude the giving of effective aid in the preparation and trial of the case.... In a case such as this, whatever may be the rule in other cases, the right to have counsel appointed, when necessary, is a logical corollary from the constitutional right to be heard by counsel. ...

The judgments must be reversed and the causes remanded for further proceedings not inconsistent with this opinion.

Judgments reversed.

[Justice Butler, joined by Justice McReynolds, dissented.]

Justice Sutherland was careful in stating the decision to confine the ruling to the peculiar facts of the case. At the same time, there was dictum which could give encouragement to those who wished to see the Fourteenth Amendment right to counsel for the indigent defendant broadened. In 1942, however, the majority made it clear that they did not intend to equate the Fourteenth Amendment requirement with that of the Sixth Amendment. The case was *Betts* v. *Brady*, 316 U.S. 455 (1942), and dealt with a trial for robbery in the state court of Maryland. Petitioner was too poor to employ counsel, so informed the judge at his arraignment, and requested that counsel be appointed for him. The judge refused, pointing out that counsel was appointed for indigent defendants only in prosecutions for murder and rape. The trial proceeded, without a jury, and the judge found him guilty. The sentence imposed was eight years. Relief having been denied under habeas corpus proceeding in the state court of appeals, petitioner applied to the United States Supreme Court for certiorari, which was granted. The majority held that under the circumstances of the case, no denial of a fair trial could be inferred. Thus counsel was not a constitutional necessity. Justice Roberts, for the majority, reviewed the history of common law practice and found that provisions that defendant should be "allowed" counsel or should have a right "to be heard by himself and his counsel," were intended to do away with the rule which *denied* representation, but were not "aimed to compel the State to provide counsel for a defendant." The opinion stated further that "the due process clause of the Fourteenth Amendment does not incorporate, as such, the specific guarantees found in the Sixth Amendment," namely, the right to counsel.

Justice Black, joined by Justices Douglas and Murphy, dissented, and thus began a sustained campaign by a minority of the justices to equate the Fourteenth Amendment rule with that of the Sixth Amendment as announced in *Johnson* v. *Zerbst*. The campaign culminated in victory in 1963, when *Betts* v. *Brady* was squarely overruled in the case of *Gideon* v. *Wainwright,* to be discussed later. In his dissent in the *Betts* case Justice Black stated:

A practice cannot be reconciled with "common and fundamental ideas of fairness and right," which subjects innocent men to increased dangers of conviction merely because of their poverty. Whether a man is innocent cannot be determined from a trial in which, as here, denial of counsel has made it impossible to conclude, with any satisfactory degree of certainty, that the defendant's case was adequately presented.

He stated further, "I believe that the Fourteenth Amendment made the Sixth applicable to the states."

One additional case out of the host of cases between *Powell* and *Gideon* is worthy of note because of the peculiar twist it gave to the rule announced by Justice Sutherland in *Powell* v. *Alabama.* The case is *Bute* v. *Illinois,* 333 U.S. 640 (1948). Roy Bute, a fifty-seven-year-old man, pleaded guilty and was convicted of "taking indecent liberties with children." He was sentenced to one to twenty years in jail. The record was silent as to whether petitioner had desired to be represented by counsel or had been able to procure counsel. After he had served eight years in jail, in 1946, he filed a writ of error in the Supreme Court of Illinois, claiming that he had been denied representation by counsel. His writ was denied, and the United States Supreme Court granted certiorari. In a five-to-four decision the denial was affirmed. The majority could find no fundamental unfairness in the trial and nothing unusual in the status of the defendant which would have demanded counsel. Justice Burton, for the majority, stated:

On the facts thus before us in these records, which must be our sole guides in these cases, there is no good reason to doubt either the due process or the propriety of the procedure followed by the trial court. There is nothing in the records on which to base a claim that the petitioner's conduct did not fit the charges made against him. There is nothing in them on which to base a claim of abnormality, intoxication, or insanity on the part of the petitioner or on which to base a claim that there was any indignation, prejudice or emotional influence affecting the conduct or thought of anyone connected with these trials.

Justice Sutherland had stated in *Powell* that the accused must have appointed counsel if it is a capital case *and* if the accused is ignorant, feeble-minded, illiterate, "or the like." Justice Burton in the *Bute* case changed this "and" to "or." The result was two rules. Counsel must be furnished in every capital case and in every other case where special facts seem to make it mandatory for a fair trial. His statement was:

[T]his Court repeatedly has held that failure to appoint counsel to assist a defendant or to give a fair opportunity to the defendant's counsel to assist him in his defense where charged with a capital crime is a violation of due process of law under the Fourteenth Amendment. . . .

In a noncapital state felony case, this Court has recognized the constitutional right of the accused to the assistance of counsel for his defense when there are special circumstances showing that, otherwise, the defendant would not enjoy that fair notice and adequate hearing which constitute the foundation of due process of law in the trial of any criminal charge.

The dissenters, Justice Douglas, joined by the Justices Black, Murphy and Rutledge, continued the fight for reversing the "ill-starred decision" in *Betts* v. *Brady*. The point was stressed that in every capital case counsel was required, simply because the guilty as well as the innocent are entitled to a fair trial. "Those considerations are equally germane though liberty rather than life hangs in the balance. Certainly due process shows no less solicitude for liberty than for life. A man facing a prison term may, indeed, have as much at stake as life itself."

As more and more "special circumstances" requiring counsel impressed themselves upon the majority of the Court (such as youth, inability to speak English, complexity of the issues involved in the case, "loaded" suggestions by officers of the state to plead guilty), the pressures both of argument and case-load pushed almost inexorably in the direction of a more clear-cut rule. The decision was unanimous when it finally came in 1963 in *Gideon* v. *Wainwright*.

GIDEON *v.* WAINWRIGHT
372 U.S. 335 (1963)

Mr. Justice Black delivered the opinion of the Court.

Petitioner was charged in a Florida state court with having broken and entered a poolroom with intent to commit a misdemeanor. This offense is a felony under Florida law. Appearing in court without funds and without a lawyer, petitioner asked the court to appoint counsel for him, [a request denied by the court on the ground that the law of Florida required appointment only in capital cases].

Put to trial before a jury, Gideon conducted his defense about as well as could be expected from a layman. He made an opening statement to the jury, cross-examined the State's witnesses, presented witnesses in his own defense, declined to testify himself, and made a short argument "emphasizing his innocence to the charge contained in the Information filed in this case." The jury returned a verdict of guilty, and petitioner was sentenced to serve five years in the state prison. Later, petitioner filed in the Florida Supreme Court this habeas corpus petition attacking his conviction and sentence on the ground that the trial court's refusal to appoint counsel for him denied him rights "guaranteed by the Constitution and the Bill of Rights by the United States Government." Treating the petition for habeas corpus as properly before it, the State Supreme Court, "upon consideration thereof" but without an opinion, denied all relief. Since 1942, when *Betts* v. *Brady*, 316 U.S. 455, was decided by a divided Court, the problem of a defendant's federal constitutional right to counsel in a state court has been a continuing source of controversy and litigation in both state and federal courts. To give this problem another review here, we granted certiorari. . . . Since Gideon was proceeding *in forma pauperis*, we appointed counsel to represent him and requested both sides to discuss in their briefs and oral arguments the following: "Should this Court's holding in *Betts* vs. *Brady* . . . be reconsidered?"

I

The facts upon which Betts claimed that he had been unconstitutionally denied the right to have counsel appointed to assist him are strikingly like the facts upon which Gideon here bases his federal constitutional claim. . . . Since the facts and circumstances of the two cases are so nearly indistinguishable, we think the *Betts* v. *Brady* holding if left standing would require us to reject Gideon's claim that the Constitution guarantees him the assistance of counsel. Upon full reconsideration we conclude that *Betts* v. *Brady* should be overruled.

II

. . . We accept *Betts* v. *Brady*'s assumption, based as it was on our prior cases, that a provision of the Bill of Rights which is "fundamental and essential to a fair trial" is made obligatory upon the States by the Fourteenth Amendment. We think the Court in *Betts* was wrong, however, in concluding that the Sixth Amendment's guarantee of counsel is not one of these fundamental rights. Ten years before *Betts* v. *Brady,* this Court, after full consideration of all the historical data examined in *Betts,* had unequivocally declared that "the right to the aid of counsel is of this fundamental character." *Powell* v. *Alabama,* 287 U.S. 45, 68, (1932). While the Court at the close of its *Powell* opinion did by its language, as this Court frequently does, limit its holding to the particular facts and circumstances of that case, its conclusions about the fundamental nature of the right to counsel are unmistakable. Several years later, in 1936, the Court reemphasized what it had said about the fundamental nature of the right to counsel in this language:

"We concluded that certain fundamental rights, safeguarded by the first eight amendments against federal action, were also safeguarded against state action by the due process clause of the Fourteenth Amendment, and among them the fundamental right of the accused to the aid of counsel in a criminal prosecution." *Grosjean* v. *American Press Co.,* 297 U.S. 233, 243, 244 (1936).

And again in 1938 this Court said:

"[The assistance of counsel] is one of the safeguards of the Sixth Amendment deemed necessary to insure fundamental human rights of life and liberty. . . . The Sixth Amendment stands as a constant admonition that if the constitutional safeguards it provides be lost, justice will not 'still be done.' " *Johnson* v. *Zerbst,* 304 U.S. 458, 462 (1938). . . .

In light of these and many other prior decisions of this Court, it is not surprising that the *Betts* Court, when faced with the contention that "one charged with crime, who is unable to obtain counsel, must be furnished counsel by the State," conceded that "expressions in the opinions of this court lend color to the argument. . . ." 316 U.S., at 462, 463. The fact is that in deciding as it did—that "appointment of counsel is not a fundamental right, essential to a fair trial"— the Court in *Betts* v. *Brady* made an abrupt break with its own well-considered precedents. In returning to these old precedents, sounder we believe than the new, we but restore constitutional principles established to achieve a fair system of justice. Not only these precedents but also reason and reflection require us to recognize that in our adversary system of criminal justice, any person haled into court, who is too poor to hire a lawyer, cannot be assured a fair trial unless counsel is provided for him. This seems to us to be an obvious truth. Governments, both state and federal, quite properly spend vast sums of money to establish machinery to try defendants accused of crime. Lawyers to prosecute are everywhere deemed essential to protect the public's interest in an orderly society. Similarly, there are few defendants charged with crime, few indeed, who fail to hire the best lawyers they can get to prepare and present their defenses. That government hires lawyers to prosecute and defendants who have the money hire lawyers to defend are the strongest indications of the widespread belief that lawyers in criminal courts are necessities, not luxuries. The right of one charged with crime to counsel may not be deemed fundamental and essential to fair trials in some countries, but it is in ours. From the very beginning, our state and national constitutions and laws have laid great emphasis on procedural and substantive safeguards designed to assure fair trials before impartial tribunals in which every defendant stands equal before the law. This noble ideal cannot be realized if the poor man charged with crime has to face his accusers without a lawyer to assist him. A defendant's need for a lawyer is nowhere better stated than in the moving words of Mr. Justice Sutherland in *Powell* v. *Alabama.* . . .

The Court in *Betts* v. *Brady* departed from the sound wisdom upon which the Court's holding in *Powell* v. *Alabama* rested. Florida, supported by two other States, has asked that *Betts* v. *Brady* be left intact. Twenty-two States, as friends of the Court, argue that *Betts* was "an anachronism when handed down" and that it should now be overruled. We agree.

The judgment is reversed and the cause is remanded to the Supreme Court of Florida for further action not inconsistent with this opinion.

Reversed.

[Justices Douglas, Clark, and Harlan each filed separate concurring opinions.]

Another aspect of the right to counsel to be considered is the minimal offense to which it applies. Since the Sixth Amendment extends the right "in all criminal prosecutions," it presumably is a right enforceable even in cases involving petty offenses. But in several earlier cases dealing with the Sixth Amendment right of jury trial (also extending to "all criminal prosecutions"), the Court has held that the right extends only to the more serious crimes and not to "petty offenses." The first statement to this effect was in *Callan* v. *Wilson*, 127 U.S. 540 (1888), holding, however, that a conspiracy to invade the rights of another was a "grave offense." In *District of Columbia* v. *Clawans*, 300 U.S. 617 (1937), the Court held that the offense of engaging in a business without a license, the maximum penalty for which was $300 or 90 days in jail, was a "petty offense" not requiring a jury trial. But in *District of Columbia* v. *Colts*, 282 U.S. 63 (1930), the Court held that a charge of reckless driving so as to endanger life and property, even though carrying a maximum penalty of only $100 fine and 30 days in jail, was too serious an offense to be regarded as "petty," and thus required application of the right to a jury trial.

From the opinions in *Cheff* v. *Schnackenberg*, 384 U.S. 373 (1966), dealing with a sentence of six months in a case of criminal contempt tried without a jury, it would appear that a majority of the Court adheres to the view that certain classes of lesser offenses would not demand jury trial.

The rationale for defining the scope of the right of jury trial is not, of course, analogous to that of the right to counsel, but the same phrase of the Constitution is involved, and the cases are, therefore, relevant. Further, Congress, in 18 U.S.C. 3006A, provided:

Each United States district court, with the approval of the judicial council of the circuit, shall place in operation throughout the district a plan for furnishing representation for defendants charged with felonies or misdemeanors, *other than petty offenses as defined in section 1 of this title,* who are financially unable to obtain an adequate defense. (Italics added.)

Section 1 of Title 18 defines petty offenses as those for which the penalty does not exceed a sentence of six months or a fine of $500 or both. It should be noted, however, that Section 3006A is part of an overall provision to set up *compensation* plans for appointed counsel, and is not necessarily coextensive with the Sixth Amendment's requirements for appointment of counsel for the indigent defendant. At this date further litigation seems to be necessary to clear up the question of whether the indigent defendant has a right to appointed counsel in prosecutions for petty offenses.

A landmark decision was rendered in 1967 which extended the right to counsel to juvenile court proceedings where delinquency is charged. The case was *In re Gault,* 387 U.S. 1 (1967), and the decision will presumably have a marked impact on the organization and procedures of juvenile courts in the nation. (The majority opinion is excerpted in the section, "The Right to a Fair Hearing.")

STAGE AT WHICH THE RIGHT TO COUNSEL ACCRUES

The Sixth Amendment refers to "prosecutions," but makes no mention of detention, interrogation, preliminary hearings, or the other pretrial stages which an accused must face. Then when does the right to counsel accrue? In 1932, in *Powell* v. *Alabama,* Justice Sutherland stated that the defendant "requires the guiding hand of counsel at every step in the proceedings against him." It was not until the decision in *Miranda* v. *Arizona* in 1966, however, that the Court officially adopted the view that the right extends to the interrogation stage.

Prior to the decision in *Gideon,* the primary thrust of litigation in the counsel cases was to broaden the categories of cases in which appointed counsel was guaranteed at the *trial stage.* Even so, the issue of when the right first obtained in the chronology of criminal procedure began to appear in some of the pre-*Gideon* cases. In *Hamilton* v. *Alabama,* 368 U.S. 52 (1961), for example, the Court held that appointment of counsel for indigent defendants must be made as early as the arraignment stage if this is "a critical stage in a criminal proceeding." Petitioner was convicted of the capital crime of breaking and entering a dwelling at night with intent to ravish, and was not afforded counsel until the trial stage. In reversing, the Court pointed out that under Alabama law the arraignment was the only stage at which the defense of insanity could be pleaded, that pleas in abatement could be made, or that motions to quash based on the ground that the grand jury was improperly drawn could be made.

In the traditional judicial manner of fashioning a new rule, then, *Hamilton* represented a cautious first step, limited to the facts of that case. As recently as 1958, in *Crooker* v. *California*, 357 U.S. 433 (1958), the Court had held that a confession could be admitted even though obtained by interrogation after denial of petitioner's request to contact his lawyer. While the Court agreed that some kinds of deprivation of pretrial counsel might violate the "fundamental fairness" rule, they held that in this case no such defect was present. The accused was a college graduate with one year of law school and certainly was aware of his right to remain silent. Justice Douglas, for the four dissenters, stated categorically, "The demands of our civilization expressed in the Due Process Clause require that the accused who wants a counsel should have one at any time after the moment of arrest."

As pointed out in the previous section, *Escobedo* v. *Illinois*, 378 U.S. 478 (1964), overturned *Crooker* and held that where a suspect has been taken into police custody and requests an opportunity to consult with his lawyer, a denial of this request and a failure to effectively warn him of his absolute right to remain silent is a violation of the constitutional right to assistance of counsel. The logical conclusion suggested by *Escobedo* came in *Miranda* v. *Arizona*, 384 U.S. 436 (1966), in which the Court held that prior to any questioning the person taken into custody must be warned that he has a right to remain silent, and that he has a right to the presence of an attorney, either retained or appointed. The right to counsel was superimposed on the Fifth Amendment privilege, and the Chief Justice, for the Court, stated that "the right to have counsel present at the interrogation is indispensable to the protection of the Fifth Amendment privilege." (See the previous section on Coerced Confessions for further treatment of the case.)

EFFECTIVE REPRESENTATION BY COUNSEL

In the majority opinion in *Powell* it was pointed out that "the failure of the trial court to make an effective appointment of counsel" was a denial of due process. Appointment must be made in time to be of some assistance to the accused. "That duty is not discharged by an assignment at such time or under such circumstances as to preclude the giving of effective aid in the preparation and trial of the case." *Miranda* held that assignment must be made at the interrogation stage if the right is not waived. And in the case where the police feel that evidence is sufficient that no interrogation is necessary, *Hamilton* v. *Alabama* indicates that assignment must be made early enough to protect the interests of the defendant fully. A second interpretation of the requirement of "effective" representation raises the question of the competence of counsel handling the case. A losing defendant may protest that, through inefficiency or neglect, counsel appointed by the court was so incompetent that the conviction was obtained without due process of law. Obviously, appellate courts will be reluctant to overturn convictions under such a claim, both out of consideration for the orderly disposition of cases and also out of concern for the lawyer's standing as a professional man, heavily dependent upon his reputation. In retrospect, most trials could probably have been conducted more effectively had certain changes in strategy been made. But such a conclusion standing alone is insufficient to support a claim of denial of due process. The deficiencies must be so glaring and gross that the appellate court can see that on its face the trial was patently unfair. Thus in *Sanchez* v. *Indiana,* 199 Ind. 235, 157 N.W. 1 (1927), reversal was obtained where counsel, hired by friends of an eighteen-year-old illiterate Mexican, was unaware of forcible process for obtaining witnesses, failed to object to obviously incompetent evidence, failed to submit instructions, and failed to produce character witnesses for the defendant, who had no previous criminal record.

It has been held that proper representation is not satisfied by the appointment of nonlawyers, even though they are law students, in *Jones* v. *Georgia,* 57 Ga. App. 344, 195 S.E. 316 (1938). And if the court appoints a single lawyer to represent two or more defendants being tried jointly, there must not be a conflict of interest as to the defendants which would result in a deprivation of fair representation. On the whole, however, the burden on the claimant of proving gross incompetence of counsel has only rarely been successfully met.

THE RIGHT TO APPOINTED COUNSEL ON APPEAL

In 1956 the Court held in *Griffin* v. *Illinois,* 351 U.S. 12, that indigent defendants have a constitutional right to a free transcript on appeal: "destitute defendants must be afforded as adequate appellate review as defendants who have money enough to buy transcripts." This case was followed later in *Eskridge* v. *Washington State Board,* 357 U.S. 214 (1958), with the statement that "a State denies a constitutional right guaranteed by the Fourteenth Amendment if it allows all convicted defendants to have appellate review except those who cannot afford to pay for the records of their trials." These cases obviously suggested litigation on the issue of whether an indigent defendant also has a constitutional right to appointment of counsel to prosecute an appeal. The issue was determined in 1963 in *Douglas* v. *California.*

DOUGLAS *v.* CALIFORNIA
372 U.S. 353 (1963)

Mr. Justice Douglas delivered the opinion of the Court.

Petitioners, Bennie Will Meyes and William Douglas, were jointly tried and convicted in a California court on an information charging them with 13 felonies....

Although several questions are presented in the petition for certiorari, we address ourselves to only one of them. The record shows that petitioners requested, and were denied, the assistance of counsel on appeal, even though it plainly appeared they were indigents. In denying petitioners' requests, the California District Court of Appeal stated that it had "gone through" the record and had come to the conclusion that "no good whatever could be served by appointment of counsel." . . . The District Court of Appeal was acting in accordance with a California rule of criminal procedure which provides that state appellate courts, upon the request of an indigent for counsel, may make "an independent investigation of the record and determine whether it would be of advantage to the defendant or helpful to the appellate court to have counsel appointed. . . . After such investigation, appellate courts should appoint counsel if in their opinion it would be helpful to the defendant or the court, and should deny the appointment of counsel only if in their judgment such appointment would be of no value to either the defendant or the court.". . .

We agree, however, with Justice Traynor of the California Supreme Court, who said that the "[d]enial of counsel on appeal to an indigent would seem to be a discrimination at least as invidious as that condemned in *Griffin* v. *Illinois*. . . ." . . . In *Griffin* v. *Illinois*, . . . we held that a State may not grant appellate review in such a way as to discriminate against some convicted defendants on account of their poverty. There, as in *Draper* v. *Washington*, 372 U.S. 487, the right to a free transcript on appeal was in issue. Here the issue is whether or not an indigent shall be denied the assistance of counsel on appeal. In either case the evil is the same: discrimination against the indigent. For there can be no equal justice where the kind of an appeal a man enjoys "depends on the amount of money he has." *Griffin* v. *Illinois, supra.* . . .

In spite of California's forward treatment of indigents, under its present practice the type of an appeal a person is afforded in the District Court of Appeal hinges upon whether or not he can pay for the assistance of counsel. If he can the appellate court passes on the merits of his case only after having the full benefit of written briefs and oral argument by counsel. If he cannot the appellate court is forced to prejudge the merits before it can even determine whether counsel should be provided. At this stage in the proceedings only the barren record speaks for the indigent, and, unless the printed pages show that an injustice has been committed, he is forced to go without a champion on appeal. Any real chance he may have had of showing that his appeal has hidden merit is deprived him when the court decides on an *ex parte* examination of the record that the assistance of counsel is not required.

We are not here concerned with problems that might arise from the denial of counsel for the preparation of a petition for discretionary or mandatory review beyond the stage in the appellate process at which the claims have once been presented by a lawyer and passed upon by an appellate court. We are dealing only with the *first appeal*, granted as a matter of right to rich and poor alike . . . , from a criminal conviction. We need not now decide whether California would have to provide counsel for an indigent seeking a discretionary hearing from the California Supreme Court after the District Court of Appeals had sustained his conviction . . . , or whether counsel must be appointed for an indigent seeking review of an appellate affirmance of his conviction in this Court by appeal as of right or by petition for a writ of certiorari which lies within the Court's discretion. But it is appropriate to observe that a State can, consistently with the Fourteenth Amendment, provide for differences so long as the result does not amount to a denial of due process or an "invidious discrimination.". . . . Absolute equality is not required; lines can be and are drawn and we often sustain them. . . . But where the merits of *the one and only appeal* an indigent has as of right are decided without benefit of counsel, we think an unconstitutional line has been drawn between rich and poor.

When an indigent is forced to run this gantlet of a preliminary showing of merit, the right to appeal does not comport with fair procedure. In the federal courts, on the other hand, an indigent must be afforded counsel on appeal whenever he challenges a certification that the appeal is not taken in good faith. *Johnson* v. *United States,* 352 U.S. 565. The federal courts must honor his request for counsel regardless of what they think the merits of the case may be; and "representation in the role of an advocate is required." *Ellis* v. *United States,* 356 U.S. 674, 675. In California, however, once the court has "gone through" the record and denied counsel, the indigent has no recourse but to prosecute his appeal on his own, as best he can, no matter how meritorious his case may turn out to be. The present case, where counsel was denied petitioners on appeal, shows that the discrimination is not between "possibly good and obviously bad cases," but between cases where the rich man can require the court to listen to argument of counsel before deciding on the merits, but a poor man cannot. There is lacking that equality demanded by the Fourteenth Amendment where the rich man, who appeals as of right, enjoys the benefit of counsel's examination into the record, research of the law, and marshalling of arguments on his behalf, while the indigent, already burdened by a preliminary determination that his case is without merit, is forced to shift for himself. The indigent, where the record is unclear or the errors are hidden, has only the right to a meaningless ritual, while the rich man has a meaningful appeal.

We vacate the judgment of the District Court of Appeal and remand the case to that court for further proceedings not inconsistent with this opinion.

It is so ordered.

Mr. Justice Clark, dissenting.

I adhere to my vote in *Griffin* v. *Illinois* . . . , but, as I have always understood that case, it does not control here. It had to do with the State's obligation to furnish a record to an indigent on appeal. There we took pains to point out that the State was free to "find other means of affording adequate and effective appellate review to indigent defendants.". . . Here California has done just that in its procedure for furnishing attorneys for indigents on appeal. We all know that the overwhelming percentage of *in forma pauperis* appeals are frivolous. Statistics of this Court show that over 96% of the petitions filed here are of this variety. California, in the light of a like experience, has provided that upon the filing of an application for the appointment of counsel the District Court of Appeal shall make "an independent investigation of the record and determine whether it would be of advantage to the defendant or helpful to the appellate court to have counsel appointed.". . . California's courts did that here and after examining the record certified that such an appointment would be neither advantageous to the petitioners nor helpful to the court. It, therefore, refused to go through the useless gesture of appointing an attorney. In my view neither the Equal Protection Clause nor the Due Process Clause requires more. I cannot understand why the Court says that this procedure afforded petitioners "a meaningless ritual." To appoint an attorney would not only have been utter extravagance and a waste of the State's funds but as surely "meaningless" to petitioners.

With this new fetish for indigency the Court piles an intolerable burden on the State's judicial machinery. Indeed, if the Court is correct it may be that we should first clean up our own house. We have afforded indigent litigants much less protection than has California. Last Term we received over 1,200 *in forma pauperis* applications in none of which had we appointed attorneys or required a record. Some were appeals of right. Still we denied the petitions or dismissed the appeals on the moving papers alone.

At the same time we had hundreds of paid cases in which we permitted petitions or appeals to be filed with not only records but briefs by counsel, after which they were disposed of in due course. On the other hand, California furnishes the indigent a complete record and if counsel is requested requires its appellate courts either to (1) appoint counsel or (2) make an independent investigation of that record and determine whether it would be of advantage to the defendant or helpful to the court to have counsel appointed. . . .

Mr. Justice Harlan, whom Mr. Justice Stewart joins, dissenting. . . .

THE RIGHT TO A FAIR HEARING

In addition to the guarantees already discussed, there are other requirements of the Sixth Amendment, and of due process generally, which are held to be requirements of a fair hearing. The Sixth Amendment guarantees the accused in a federal prosecution the right to a "public trial." The "due process" clause of the Fourteenth Amendment also assures this right in state proceedings. The Court so ruled in *In re Oliver,* 333 U.S. 257 (1948), holding invalid the criminal contempt conviction of a witness before a Michigan judge, sitting as a "one-man grand jury," and conducting the proceeding in secret. The Court stated:

The traditional Anglo-American distrust for secret trials has been variously ascribed to the notorious use of this practice by the Spanish Inquisition, to the excesses of the English Court of Star Chamber, and to the French monarchy's abuse of the *lettre de cachet*. All of these institutions obviously symbolized a menace to liberty.

Further, since publicity may be given to the proceedings, both witnesses and officials may tend to operate in more honest and trustworthy fashion. [See Max Radin, "The Right to a Public Trial," 6 *Temp. L. Q.* 381 (1932); Charles W. Quick, "A Public Criminal Trial," 60 *Dick. L. Rev.* 21 (1955).]

Due process also includes the right of the accused to be present at his trial in order to face his accusers and advise with his lawyer. Thus trials *in absentia* would seem normally to be unconstitutional in the United States. But in *Illinois* v. *Allen,* 397 U.S. 337 (1970), the Court held that the removal of a disruptive defendant from the courtroom during a criminal trial was not violative of his constitutional right to be present at trial. (See Chap. 9 for the case cutting.) The Court held that, alternatively, the trial judge could bind and gag the defendant or cite him for contempt.

The mere fact that the superficial formalities of a trial are adhered to is not sufficient to meet the test of due process, if the result is dictated by external pressures. In *Moore* v. *Dempsey*, 261 U.S. 86 (1923), the Court reviewed the conviction of five Negroes in an Arkansas court for the murder of a white man. The trial court and the neighborhood were "thronged with an adverse crowd that threatened the most dangerous consequences to anyone interfering with the desired result." The trial lasted about forty-five minutes, and in less than five minutes the jury brought in a verdict of guilty of murder. According to the allegations and affidavits "no jury-man could have voted for an acquittal and continued to live in Phillips County and if any prisoner by any chance had been acquitted by a jury he could not have escaped the mob." In reversing the denial of habeas corpus, Justice Holmes, for the Court, quoted from an earlier case, stating that "if the State, supplying no corrective process, carries into execution a judgment of death or imprisonment based upon a verdict thus produced by mob domination, the State deprives the accused of his life or liberty without due process of law."

Due process also demands that the trial be conducted by an unbiased judge. The best-known case on the point is *Tumey* v. *Ohio*, 273 U.S. 510 (1927), involving a conviction for violation of the liquor laws of the state. The mayor was authorized to try such offenses without a jury, and he received, in addition to his salary, the costs imposed on the defendant in case of conviction. Further, also in the event of conviction, the municipality received half the fine levied. In reversing, Chief Justice Taft stated for the Court:

> All questions of judicial qualification may not involve constitutional validity. Thus matters of kinship, personal bias, state policy, remoteness of interest would seem generally to be matters merely of legislative discretion.... But it certainly violates the Fourteenth Amendment and deprives a defendant in a criminal case of due process of law to subject his liberty or property to the judgment of a court, the judge of which has a direct, personal, substantial pecuniary interest in reaching a conclusion against him in his case....
> ...Every procedure which would offer a possible temptation to the average man as a judge to forget the burden of proof required to convict the defendant, or which might lead him not to hold the balance nice, clear, and true between the state and the accused denies the latter due process of law.

In *Dugan* v. *Ohio*, 277 U.S. 61 (1928), however, the Court, in refusing to reverse a conviction, emphasized that the judge's pecuniary interest had to be "direct, personal, and substantial" in order to disqualify him under the *Tumey* rule. It held that the interest was too remote in this case, which involved a mayor-judge on a fixed salary, who was a member of the city commission and was paid from the city's general fund, into which one-half of the fines of convicted persons was paid. [See generally, John P. Frank, "Disqualification of Judges," 56 *Yale L. J.* 605 (1947).]

The Sixth Amendment guarantees the accused a right "to be confronted with the witnesses against him," and, as a corollary thereto, the right to cross-examine them. In fact, the right of "confrontation" is intended primarily to afford to the accused an opportunity to cross-examine. The policy behind this requirement is well stated in Wigmore's *Textbook on the Law of Evidence* (Brooklyn: Foundation Press, 1935), Sec. 242:

> [It is insisted upon because] the experience of the last three centuries of judicial trials has demonstrated convincingly that in disputed issues one cannot depend on the mere assertion of anybody, however plausible, without scrutiny into its bases. All the weaknesses that may affect a witness' trustworthiness—observation, memory, bias, interest, and the like—may otherwise lurk unrevealed; modifying circumstances omitted in his tale may give his facts an entirely different effect, if disclosed; and cross-examination is the best way to get at these.

In *Jencks* v. *United States*, 353 U.S. 657 (1957), the Court held that when the government calls its informers to the stand as witnesses in a criminal prosecution, it cannot refuse to produce the statements and reports of such informers in the possession of the government, if requested by the defendant as necessary aids to adequate cross-examination. The decision was criticized on the ground that it would open up the confidential and secret files of the government to general inspection by criminals, but the Court stated that the government must make the choice of either granting defendants full rights of cross-examination or proceeding without the desired testimony. [See Robert B. McKay, "The Right of Confrontation," 1959 *Wash. U. L. Q.* 122 (1959); Barrie M. Karen, "The Right to Production for Inspection of Documents in Possession of the Government: Guaranteed by the Due Process Clause?" 31 *So. Calif. L. Rev.* 78 (1957).]

In *Pointer* v. *Texas*, 380 U.S. 400 (1965), the Court "incorporated" the Sixth Amendment right of confrontation into the Fourteenth Amendment "due process" clause. At the defendant's trial in a state court on a charge of robbery, the state, over defendant's objections, introduced the transcript of a witness' testimony given at the preliminary hearing, at which defendant was not represented by counsel and had no opportunity to cross-examine the witness. The state showed that the witness had moved out of Texas with no intention of returning. Defendant was convicted, and his conviction affirmed by the appellate court. On certiorari, the United States Supreme Court reversed. Justice Black, for the Court, stated:

> It cannot seriously be doubted at this late date that the right of cross-examination is included in the right of an accused in a criminal case to confront the witnesses against him. And probably no one, certainly no one experienced in the trial of lawsuits, would deny the value of cross-examination in exposing falsehood and bringing out the truth in the trial of a criminal case. . . .
>
> There are few subjects, perhaps, upon which this Court and other courts have been more nearly unanimous than in their expressions of belief that the right of confrontation and cross-examination is an essential and fundamental requirement for the kind of fair trial which is this country's constitutional goal. . . .
>
> . . . We hold that petitioner was entitled to be tried in accordance with the

protection of the confrontation guarantee of the Sixth Amendment, and that that guarantee, like the right against compelled self-incrimination, is "to be enforced against the States under the Fourteenth Amendment according to the same standards that protect those personal rights against federal encroachment." *Malloy* v. *Hogan.* . . .

The Court followed *Pointer* in *Douglas* v. *Alabama,* 380 U.S. 415 (1965). Defendant was charged with assault with intent to murder. An accomplice, who had been tried separately and found guilty, was called as a witness by the state but invoked his privilege against self-incrimination because he planned to appeal his conviction. The solicitor then produced a confession purportedly signed by the witness and, under the guise of cross-examination to refresh the witness' recollection, read from the document, pausing after every few sentences to ask him, before the jury, "Did you make that statement?" Each time, the witness invoked the privilege. Defendant's counsel objected to the reading, but defendant was convicted and the state supreme court affirmed. The Court unanimously reversed, holding that in the circumstances, petitioner's inability to cross-examine the witness as to the alleged confession "plainly denied him the right of cross-examination secured by the Confrontation Clause."

In *Washington* v. *Texas,* 388 U.S. 14 (1967), the Court "incorporated" the Sixth Amendment right to have compulsory process for obtaining witnesses in his favor into the Fourteenth Amendment. It further held that this right was denied by Texas statutes which provided that persons charged or convicted as coparticipants in the same crime could not testify for one another, although there was no bar to their testifying for the state. The witness Washington wished to call had previously been convicted of the same crime, sentenced to fifty years in prison, and was confined in the Dallas County jail. On the basis of the statutes, the trial judge refused to allow the witness to testify. The United States Supreme Court unanimously reversed. Chief Justice Warren, for eight of the members, stated:

The right to offer the testimony of witnesses, and to compel their attendance, if necessary, is in plain terms the right to present a defense, the right to present the defendant's version of the facts as well as the prosecution's to the jury so it may decide where the truth lies. Just as an accused has the right to confront the prosecution's witnesses for the purpose of challenging their testimony, he has the right to present his own witnesses to establish a defense. This right is a fundamental element of due process of law.

It was argued that such witnesses should be disqualified on the ground that they are particularly likely to commit perjury. The Chief Justice pointed out that "the absurdity of the rule" is demonstrated by the fact that the accused accomplice could testify for the prosecution. It was further suggested that such witnesses would be more apt to lie for their coparticipants. The response by the Chief Justice was: "To think that criminals will lie to save their fellows but not to obtain favors from the prosecution for themselves is indeed to clothe the criminal class with more nobility than one might expect to find in the public at large."

One of the most important decisions of recent years involving criminal procedure came in 1967 in *In re Gault*, 387 U.S. 1 (1967). In that case the Court held that juvenile delinquency proceedings which may lead to commitment in state institutions must measure up to the essentials of due process and fair treatment. An Arizona juvenile court had committed a fifteen-year-old boy to the state industrial school for the period of his minority, unless officially discharged sooner. The boy was taken into custody by the county sheriff, without notice to his parents, on a complaint charging the defendant with making an obscene telephone call. The juvenile judge held a hearing at which the boy, his mother, his older brother, and two probation officers appeared. No transcript or recording was made, the complainant was not present, and no one was sworn. Later testimony by the juvenile judge was to the effect that the judge questioned the defendant at this hearing and that he admitted making lewd statements over the telephone. Neither the boy nor his parents was advised of his right to counsel or to remain silent. At a second hearing the following week, still without transcript or recording, the defendant and another boy, charged with participating in the same telephone call, were questioned further. Witnesses differed in their recollections of the defendant's testimony at this hearing. His parents recalled that he admitted only to having dialed the number, and that the other boy had made the remarks. The mother asked that the complainant be present to testify as to which boy had done the talking. The judge stated that she did not have to be present. At the conclusion of the hearing the defendant was committed to the state industrial school. Since no appeal was permitted by statute, the commitment was attacked by habeas corpus. The trial court dismissed, and the Arizona Supreme Court affirmed. The United States Supreme Court considered the case on appeal and reversed.

IN RE GAULT
387 U.S. 1 (1967)

Mr. Justice Fortas delivered the opinion of the Court. . . .

[Appellants] urge that we hold the Juvenile Code of Arizona invalid on its face or as applied in this case because, contrary to the Due Process Clause of the Fourteenth Amendment, the juvenile is taken from the custody of his parents and committed to a state institution pursuant to proceedings in which the Juvenile Court has virtually unlimited discretion, and in which the following basic rights are denied:

1. Notice of the charges;
2. Right to counsel;
3. Right to confrontation and cross-examination;
4. Privilege against self-incrimination;
5. Right to a transcript of the proceedings; and
6. Right to appellate review. . . .

We do not in this opinion consider the impact of these constitutional provisions upon the totality of the relationship of the juvenile and the state. . . . We consider only the problems presented to us by this case. These relate to the proceedings by which a determination is made as to whether a juvenile is a "delinquent" as a result of alleged misconduct on his part, with the consequence that he may be committed to a state institution. . . .

From the inception of the juvenile court system, wide differences have been tolerated—indeed insisted upon—between the procedural rights accorded to adults and those of juveniles. . . .

The early reformers were appalled by adult procedures and penalties, and by the fact that children could be given long prison sentences and mixed in jails with hardened criminals. . . . The apparent rigidities, technicalities, and harshness which they observed in both substantive and procedural criminal law were therefore to be discarded. The idea of crime and punishment was to be abandoned. The child was to be "treated" and "rehabilitated" and the procedures, from apprehension through institutionalization, were to be "clinical" rather than punitive.

These results were to be achieved, without coming to conceptual and constitutional grief, by insisting that the proceedings were not adversary, but that the State was proceeding as *parens patriae*. The Latin phrase proved to be a great help to those who sought to rationalize the exclusion of juveniles from the constitutional scheme; but its meaning is murky and its historic credentials are of dubious relevance. . . .

Accordingly, the highest motives and most enlightened impulses led to a peculiar system for juveniles, unknown to our law in any comparable context. The constitutional and theoretical basis for this peculiar system is—to say the least—debatable. And in practice . . . the results have not been entirely satisfactory. Juvenile court history has again demonstrated that unbridled discretion, however benevolently motivated, is frequently a poor substitute for principle and procedure. In 1937, Dean Pound wrote: "The powers of the Star Chamber were a trifle in comparison with those of our juvenile courts. . . ." The absence of substantive standards has not necessarily meant that children receive careful, compassionate, individualized treatment. The absence of procedural rules based upon constitutional principle has not always produced fair, efficient, and effective procedures. Departures from established principles of due process have frequently resulted not in enlightened procedure, but in arbitrariness. . . .

It is claimed that juveniles obtain benefits from the special procedures applicable to them which more than offset the disadvantages of denial of the substance of normal due process. As we shall discuss, the observance of due process standards, intelligently and not ruthlessly administered, will not compel the States to abandon or displace any of the substantive benefits of the juvenile process. . . .

. . . For example, the commendable principles relating to the processing and treatment of juveniles separately from adults are in no way involved or affected by the procedural issues under discussion. Further, we are told that one of the important benefits of the special juvenile court procedures is that they avoid classifying the juvenile as a "criminal." The juvenile offender is now classed as a "delinquent." There is, of course, no reason why this should not continue. It is disconcerting, however, that this term has come to involve only slightly less stigma than the term "criminal" applied to adults. . . .

Beyond this, it is frequently said that juveniles are protected by the process from disclosure of their deviational behavior. . . . This claim of secrecy, however, is more rhetoric than reality. Disclosure of court records is discretionary with the judge in most jurisdictions. . . .

In any event, there is no reason why, consistently with due process, a State cannot continue, if it deems it appropriate, to provide and to improve provision for the confidentiality of records of police contacts and court action relating to juveniles. . . .

Further, it is urged that the juvenile benefits from informal proceedings in the court. The early conception of the juvenile court proceeding was one in which a fatherly judge touched the heart and conscience of the erring youth by talking over his problems, by paternal advice and admonition, and in which, in extreme situations, benevolent and wise institutions of the State provided guidance and help "to save him from a downward career.". . . But recent studies have, with surprising unanimity, entered sharp dissent as to the validity of this gentle conception. They suggest that the appearance as well as the actuality of fairness, impartiality and orderliness—in short, the essentials of due process may be a more impressive and more therapeutic attitude so far as the juvenile is concerned. . . .

Ultimately, however, we confront the reality of that portion of the juvenile court process with which we deal in this case. A boy is charged with misconduct. The boy is committed to an institution where he may be restrained of liberty for years. . . .

In view of this, it would be extraordinary if our Constitution did not require the procedural regularity and the exercise of care implied in the phrase "due process." Under our Constitution, the condition of being a boy does not justify a kangaroo court. . . .

If Gerald had been over 18, he would not have been subject to Juvenile Court proceedings. For the particular offense immediately involved, the maximum punishment would have been a fine of $5 to $50, or imprisonment in jail for not more than two months. Instead, he was committed to custody for a maximum of six years. If he had been over 18 and had committed an offense to which such a sentence might apply, he would have been entitled to substantial rights under the Constitution of the United States as well as under Arizona's laws and constitution. . . . So wide a gulf between the State's treatment of the adult and of the child requires a bridge sturdier than mere verbiage, and reasons more persuasive than cliche can provide. . . .

Notice of Charges

. . . The applicable Arizona statute provides for a petition to be filed in Juvenile Court, alleging in general terms that the child is "neglected, dependent, or delinquent." The statute explicitly states that such a general allegation is sufficient, "without alleging the facts.". . .

We cannot agree with the court's conclusion that adequate notice was given in this case. . . . Due process of law requires notice of the sort we have described— that is, notice which would be deemed constitutionally adequate in a civil or criminal proceeding. . . .

Right to Counsel

Appellants charge that the Juvenile Court proceedings were fatally defective because the court did not advise Gerald or his parents of their right to counsel, and proceeded with the hearing, the adjudication of delinquency and the order of commitment in the absence of counsel for the child and his parents or an express waiver of the right thereto. . . . The court argued that "The parent and the probation officer may be relied upon to protect the infant's interests." Accordingly it rejected the proposition that "due process requires that an infant have a right to counsel." . . . We do not agree. . . . The child "requires the guiding hand of counsel at every step in the proceedings against him.". . .

Confrontation, Self-Incrimination, Cross-Examination

Appellants urge that the writ of habeas corpus should have been granted because of the denial of the rights of confrontation and cross-examination in the Juvenile Court hearings, and because the privilege against self-incrimination was not observed. The Juvenile Court Judge testified at the habeas corpus hearing that he had proceeded on the basis of Gerald's admissions at the two hearings. . . .

It would indeed be surprising if the privilege against self-incrimination were available to hardened criminals but not to children. The language of the Fifth Amendment, applicable to the States by operation of the Fourteenth Amendment, is unequivocal and without exception. And the scope of the privilege is comprehensive. . . .

Against the application to juveniles of the right to silence, it is argued that juvenile proceedings are "civil" and not "criminal," and therefore the privilege should not apply. . . .

. . . For this purpose, at least, commitment is a deprivation of liberty. It is incarceration against one's will, whether it is called "criminal" or "civil.". . .

We conclude that the constitutional privilege against self-incrimination is applicable in the case of juveniles as it is with respect to adults. . . .

. . . Apart from the "admission," there was nothing upon which a judgment or finding might be based. There was no sworn testimony. Mrs. Cook, the complainant, was not present. . . .

. . . We now hold that, absent a valid confession, a determination of delinquency and an order of commitment to a state institution cannot be sustained in the absence of sworn testimony subjected to the opportunity for cross-examination in accordance with our law and constitutional requirements. . . .

[Justices Black and White concurred. Justice Harlan concurred in part and dissented in part. Justice Stewart dissented.]

In *Re Winship*, 397 U.S. 358 (1970), the Court examined the New York rule permitting conviction in juvenile delinquency proceedings based on a "preponderance of evidence." The Court reversed, holding that the due process clause protected an accused juvenile in a criminal prosecution against conviction except upon proof beyond a reasonable doubt. But in *McKeiver* v. *Pennsylvania*, 403 U.S. 528 (1971), in a badly fragmented set of opinions, the Court held that the Fourteenth Amendment does not require a jury trial in criminal proceedings in juvenile courts.

DOUBLE JEOPARDY

Protection against double jeopardy was firmly grounded in the common law well before the addition of the Fifth Amendment provision that no person shall be "subject for the same offence to be twice put in jeopardy of life or limb." In fact the English rule today, embodying the common law principle, is tighter than our own, since the law does not even permit English appellate courts to send criminal cases back for new trials. The choice is between correction of errors below, if possible, or simply vacating the judgment of conviction, so rigidly is the rule against double jeopardy construed.

Since jeopardy means the danger of conviction, *indictment* for crime does not put a person in jeopardy, and therefore repeated indictments do not constitute double jeopardy. Jeopardy does not attach until the trial actually begins. If trial is without a jury, jeopardy commonly attaches when the first witness is sworn or when the court has begun to hear evidence. If the case is tried to a jury, jeopardy begins when the jury is impaneled and sworn. The general rule is that only under exceptional circumstances can the trial be halted after this stage and the accused subjected later to a second trial. Such would be the case where a juror is disqualified or the jury fails to reach a verdict. The latter situation was involved in *United States* v. *Perez,* 9 Wheat. 579 (1824), in which the Court stated: "The prisoner has not been convicted or acquitted, and may again be put upon his defense. We think, that in all cases of this nature, the law has invested courts of justice with the authority to discharge a jury from giving any verdict, whenever, in their opinion, taking all the circumstances into consideration, there is a manifest necessity for the act, or the ends of public justice would otherwise be defeated."

The double jeopardy clause would bar having the government secure a mistrial solely to afford the prosecution a chance to improve its preparation of the case. In *Brock* v. *North Carolina,* 344 U.S. 424 (1953), however, the Court held that the Fourteenth Amendment did not preclude the state's second trial of the defendant after the first trial was declared a mistrial on motion of the prosecution when two of the state's key witnesses, apparently without warning, refused to answer incriminating questions. The witnesses had already been convicted, but were awaiting word on an appeal and refused to talk in the interim. They lost their appeals and were then willing to testify in the later trial.

In a federal case with a somewhat similar question presented, the Court held differently. The opinion for the Court gives a résumé of some of the cases involving the effect of discharging the jury on subsequent prosecutions.

DOWNUM *v.* UNITED STATES

372 U.S. 734 (1963)

Mr. Justice Douglas delivered the opinion of the Court.

This case, involving a federal prosecution for stealing from the mail and forging and uttering checks so stolen, presents a question under the Double Jeopardy Clause of the Fifth Amendment. . . . The claim of double jeopardy arose as follows:

On the morning of April 25, 1961, the case was called for trial and both sides announced ready. A jury was selected and sworn and instructed to return at 2 P.M.

When it returned, the prosecution asked that the jury be discharged because its key witness on Counts 6 and 7 [of an eight-count indictment] was not present— one Rutledge, who was the payee on the checks involved in those counts. Petitioner moved that Counts 6 and 7 be dismissed for want of prosecution and asked that the trial continue on the rest of the counts. This motion was denied and the judge discharged the jury over petitioner's objection. Two days later when the case was called again and a second jury impaneled, petitioner pleaded former jeopardy. His plea was overruled, a trial was had, and he was found guilty. The Court of Appeals affirmed, 300 F.2d 137; and we granted the petition for certiorari because of the seeming conflict between this decision and *Cornero* v. *United States,* 48 F.2d 69, from the Ninth Circuit. . . .

The present case was one of a dozen set for call during the previous week, and those cases involved approximately 100 witnesses. Subpoenas for all of them including Rutledge had been delivered to the marshal for service. The day before the case was first called, the prosecutor's assistant checked with the marshal and learned that Rutledge's wife was going to let him know where her husband was, if she could find out. No word was received from her and no follow-up was made. The prosecution allowed the jury to be selected and sworn even though one of its key witnesses was absent and had not been found.

From *United States* v. *Perez,* 9 Wheat. 579, decided in 1824, to *Gori* v. *United States,* 367 U.S. 364, decided in 1961, it has been agreed that there are occasions where a second trial may be had although the jury impaneled for the first trial was discharged without reaching a verdict and without the defendant's consent. The classic example is a mistrial because the jury is unable to agree. *United States* v. *Perez.* . . . In *Wade* v. *Hunter,* 336 U.S. 684, the tactical problems of an army in the field were held to justify the withdrawal of a court-martial proceeding and the commencement of another one on a later day. Discovery by the judge during a trial that a member or members of the jury were biased pro or con one side has been held to warrant discharge of the jury and direction of a new trial. . . . At times the valued right of a defendant to have his trial completed by the particular tribunal summoned to sit in judgment on him may be subordinated to the public interest— when there is an imperious necessity to do so. *Wade* v. *Hunter, supra* (336 U.S. 690). Differences have arisen as to the application of the principle. See *Brock* v. *North Carolina,* 344 U.S. 424. . . . Harassment of an accused by successive prosecutions or declaration of a mistrial so as to afford the prosecution a more favorable opportunity to convict are examples when jeopardy attaches. *Gori* v. *United States, supra* (367 U.S. 369). But those extreme cases do not mark the limits of the guarantee. The discretion to discharge the jury before it has reached a verdict is to be exercised "only in very extraordinary and striking circumstances," to use the words of Mr. Justice Story in *United States* v. *Coolidge* (CC Mass) 2 Gall 364, F. Cas. No. 14858. For the prohibition of the Double Jeopardy Clause is "not against being punished twice; but against being twice put in jeopardy." *United States* v. *Ball,* 163 U.S. 662, 669.

The jury first selected to try petitioner and sworn was discharged because a prosecution witness had not been served with a summons and because no other arrangements had been made to assure his presence. That witness was essential only for two of the six counts concerning petitioner. Yet the prosecution opposed petitioner's motion to dismiss those two counts and to proceed with a trial on the other four counts—a motion the court denied. Here as in *Wade* v. *Hunter, supra,* we refuse to say that the absence of witnesses "can never justify discontinuance of a trial." Each case must turn on its facts. On this record, however, we think what was said in *Cornero* v. *United States* (Ca 9 Cal) 48 F.2d 69, *supra,* states the governing principle. There a trial was first continued because prosecution witnesses were not present and when they had not been found at the time the case was again called, the jury was discharged. A plea of double jeopardy was sustained when a second jury was selected, the court saying:

"The fact is that, when the district attorney impaneled the jury without first ascertaining whether or not his witnesses were present, he took a chance. . . . The situation presented is simply one where the district attorney entered upon the trial of the case without sufficient evidence to convict. This does not take the case out of the rule with reference to former jeopardy. There is no difference in principle between a discovery by the district attorney immediately after the jury was impaneled that his evidence was insufficient and a discovery after he had called some or all of his witnesses." 48 F.2d, at 71.

That view, which has some support in the authorities, is in our view the correct one. We resolve any doubt "in favor of the liberty of the citizen, rather than exercise what would be an unlimited, uncertain and arbitrary judicial discretion." This means that the judgment below must be and is

Reversed.

Mr. Justice Clark, with whom Mr. Justice Harlan, Mr. Justice Stewart and Mr. Justice White join, dissenting.

I adhere to *Wade* v. *Hunter,* which in short holds that "a trial can be discontinued when particular circumstances manifest a necessity for so doing, and when failure to discontinue would defeat the ends of justice.". . .

The conclusions of the trial court and the Court of Appeals indicate that they viewed the circumstances in which the prosecutor found himself as having resulted from excusable oversight. There is no indication that the prosecutor's explanation was a mere cover for negligent preparation or that his action was in any way deliberate. There is nothing in the record that even suggests that the circumstances were used by the prosecutor for the purpose of securing a more favorable jury or in any way to take advantage of or to harass the petitioner. Indeed, it appears to be just one of those circumstances which often creep into a prosecutor's life as a result of inadvertence when many cases must be handled during a short trial period. . . .

As I see the problem, the issue is whether the action of the prosecutor in failing to check on the presence of his witness before allowing a jury to be sworn was of such moment that it constituted a deprival of the petitioner's rights and entitled him to a verdict of acquittal without any trial on the merits. Obviously under the facts here he suffered no such deprivation. Ever since *Perez* this Court has recognized that the "ends of public justice" must be considered in determining such a question. . . . In this light I cannot see how this Court finds that the trial judge abused his discretion in affording the Government a two-day period in which to bring forward its key witness who, to its surprise, was found to be temporarily absent. I believe that the "ends of public justice," to which Mr. Justice Story referred in *Perez,* require that the Government have a fair opportunity to present the people's case and obtain adjudication on the merits, rather than that the criminal be turned free because of the harmless oversight of the prosecutor.

DOUBLE JEOPARDY AND CRIMINAL APPEALS

The federal law is clear that the government has no right to appeal after a verdict of acquittal, since the protection against double jeopardy encompasses such an action. Such was the holding in *Kepner* v. *United States,* 195 U.S. 100 (1904). This reaffirmed a similar holding based on common law considerations in *United States* v. *Sanges,* 144 U.S. 310, 323 (1892). Since jeopardy does not attach merely upon indictment, however, a judgment to quash an indictment is appealable by the Government. The old Fourteenth Amendment rule (no longer valid) was laid down in *Palko* v. *Connecticut,* 302 U.S. 319 (1937). The Court held there that where errors of law, to the prejudice of the State, were committed in the trial court, the State could appeal for a new trial. In *Benton* v. *Maryland,* 395 U.S. 784 (1969), however, the Court incorporated the Fifth Amendment's protection against double jeopardy into the Fourteenth Amendment and overruled *Palko.*

At the common law, and still in England, the appellate court was barred from ordering a retrial following conviction, even if material error was found in the trial proceedings. American courts have followed a practice of ordering a wholly new trial if the convicted defendant appealed and "reversible errors" were found to have occurred in the first trial. In *United States* v. *Keen,* 6 Fed. Cas. 686 (1839), Justice McLean, on circuit, vigorously rejected the view that the constitutional provision prohibited a new trial on the defendant's motion after a conviction, or that it "guarantees to him the right of being hung, to protect him from the danger of a second trial." The theory followed here seems to be that since the request is made by the defendant, the claim of double jeopardy is implicitly waived. There is no particular difficulty with this approach if the defendant obtains a new trial on the same charge for which conviction resulted in the first trial. A problem arises, however, if the conviction is for a lesser included offense of the original charge and on subsequent retrial the defendant again faces the more serious original charge. In *Palko,* for example, the defendant was tried for first degree murder. He was convicted of second degree murder. At the new trial he was again tried, and convicted, of *first* degree murder. The Court held in 1957, in *Green* v. *United States,* that such a procedure in the federal courts would violate the Fifth Amendment's protection against double jeopardy.

GREEN *v.* UNITED STATES

335 U.S. 184 (1957)

Opinion of the Court by Mr. Justice Black, announced by Mr. Justice Douglas.

This case presents a serious question concerning the meaning and application of that provision of the Fifth Amendment to the Constitution which declares that no person shall

"... be subject for the same offence to be twice put in jeopardy of life or limb. ..."

The petitioner, Everett Green, was indicted by a District of Columbia grand jury in two counts. The first charged that he had committed arson by maliciously setting fire to a house. The second accused him of causing the death of a woman by this alleged arson which if true amounted to murder in the first degree punishable by death. Green entered a plea of not guilty to both counts and the case was tried by a jury. After each side had presented its evidence the trial judge instructed the jury that it could find Green guilty of arson under the first count and of either (1) first degree murder or (2) second degree murder under the second count. The trial judge treated second degree murder, which is defined by the District Code as the killing of another with malice aforethought, and is punishable by imprisonment for a term of years or for life, as an offense included within the language charging first degree murder in the second count of the indictment.

The jury found Green guilty of arson and of second degree murder but did not find him guilty on the charge of murder in the first degree. Its verdict was silent on that charge. The trial judge accepted the verdict, entered the proper judgments and dismissed the jury. Green was sentenced to one to three years' imprisonment for arson and five to twenty years' imprisonment for murder in the second degree. He appealed the conviction of second degree murder. The Court of Appeals reversed that conviction because it was not supported by evidence and remanded the case for a new trial. . . .

On remand Green was tried again for first degree murder under the original indictment. At the outset of this second trial he raised the defense of former jeopardy but the court overruled his plea. This time a new jury found him guilty of first degree murder and he was given the mandatory death sentence. Again he appealed. Sitting *en banc,* the Court of Appeals rejected his defense of former jeopardy . . . and affirmed the conviction. . . .

The constitutional prohibition against "double jeopardy" was designed to protect an individual from being subjected to the hazards of trial and possible conviction more than once for an alleged offense. . . .

The underlying idea, one that is deeply ingrained in at least the Anglo-American system of jurisprudence, is that the State with all its resources and power should not be allowed to make repeated attempts to convict an individual for an alleged offense, thereby subjecting him to embarrassment, expense and ordeal and compelling him to live in a continuing state of anxiety and insecurity, as well as enhancing the possibility that even though innocent he may be found guilty.

In accordance with this philosophy it has long been settled under the Fifth Amendment that a verdict of acquittal is final, ending a defendant's jeopardy, and even when "not followed by any judgment, is a bar to a subsequent prosecution for the same offence." *United States* v. *Ball,* . . . Thus it is one of the elemental principles of our criminal law that the Government cannot secure a new trial by means of an appeal even though an acquittal may appear to be erroneous. . . .

At common law a convicted person could not obtain a new trial by appeal except in certain narrow instances. As this harsh rule was discarded courts and legislatures provided that if a defendant obtained the reversal of a conviction by his own appeal he could be tried again for the same offense. Most courts regarded the new trial as a second jeopardy but justified this on the ground that the appellant had "waived" his plea of former jeopardy by asking that the conviction be set aside. Other courts viewed the second trial as continuing the same jeopardy which had attached at the first trial by reasoning that jeopardy did not come to an end until the accused was acquitted or his conviction became final. But whatever the rationalization, this Court has also held that a defendant can be tried a second time for an offense when his prior conviction for that same offense had been set aside on appeal. *United States* v. *Ball*, 163 U.S. 662.

In this case, however, we have a much different question. . . . For the reasons stated hereafter, we conclude that this second trial for first degree murder placed Green in jeopardy twice for the same offense in violation of the Constitution.

Green was in direct peril of being convicted and punished for first degree murder at his first trial. He was forced to run the gantlet once on that charge and the jury refused to convict him. When given the choice between finding him guilty of either first or second degree murder it chose the latter. In this situation the great majority of cases in this country have regarded the jury's verdict as an implicit acquittal on the charge of first degree murder. . . . In brief, we believe this case can be treated no differently, for purposes of former jeopardy, than if the jury had returned a verdict which expressly read: "We find the defendant not guilty of murder in the first degree but guilty of murder in the second degree."

After the original trial, but prior to his appeal, it is indisputable that Green could not have been tried again for first degree murder for the death resulting from the fire. A plea of former jeopardy would have absolutely barred a new prosecution even though it might have been convincingly demonstrated that the jury erred in failing to convict him of that offense. And even after appealing the conviction of second degree murder he still could not have been tried a second time for first degree murder had his appeal been unsuccessful.

Nevertheless the Government contends that Green "waived" his constitutional defense of former jeopardy to a second prosecution on the first degree murder charge by making a *successful appeal* of his improper conviction of second degree murder. We cannot accept this paradoxical contention. . . .

Reduced to plain terms, the Government contends that in order to secure the reversal of an erroneous conviction of one offense, a defendant must surrender his valid defense of former jeopardy not only on that offense but also on a different offense for which he was not convicted and which was not involved in his appeal. . . . The law should not, and in our judgment does not, place the defendant in such an incredible dilemma. Conditioning an appeal of one offense on a coerced surrender of a valid plea of former jeopardy on another offense exacts a forfeiture in plain conflict with the constitutional bar against double jeopardy. . . .

Reversed.

Mr. Justice Frankfurter, whom Mr. Justice Burton, Mr. Justice Clark and Mr. Justice Harlan join, dissenting. . . .

In 1969, in *Benton* v. *Maryland,* the Court incorporated the Fifth Amendment's protection against double jeopardy into the Fourteenth Amendment. Following the federal rule announced in *Green* v. *United States,* the Court held that due process barred the State from subjecting a defendant to charges on retrial other than those for which he was convicted at the initial trial. *Palko* and, by implication, *Brock* v. *North Carolina* were overruled.

BENTON *v.* MARYLAND

395 U.S. 784 (1969)

Mr. Justice Marshall delivered the opinion of the Court.

[In a Maryland state court trial on charges of burglary and larceny, the jury found the defendant not guilty of larceny, but convicted him on the burglary count, for which he was sentenced to ten years in prison. Because both the grand and petit juries in the case had been unconstitutionally selected, the Maryland Court of Appeals remanded the case to the trial court, where the defendant was given the option of demanding reindictment and retrial, which he did. At the second trial, again for both larceny and burglary, the defendant's motion to dismiss the larceny charge as subjecting him to double jeopardy was denied, he was found guilty of both offenses, and he was given concurrent sentences of fifteen years on the burglary count and five years for larceny. The newly created Maryland Court of Special Appeals rejected the defendant's double jeopardy claim on the merits, and the Maryland Court of Appeals denied discretionary review.]

In 1937, this Court decided the landmark case of *Palko* v. *Connecticut.* . . . Palko, although indicted for first-degree murder, had been convicted of murder in the second degree after a jury trial in a Connecticut state court. The State appealed and won a new trial. Palko argued that the Fourteenth Amendment incorporated, as against the States, the Fifth Amendment requirement that no person "be twice put in jeopardy of life or limb." The Court disagreed. Federal double jeopardy standards were not applicable against the States. Only when a kind of jeopardy subjected a defendant to "a hardship so acute and shocking that our polity will not endure it," . . . . did the Fourteenth Amendment apply. The order for a new trial was affirmed. In subsequent appeals from state courts, the Court continued to apply this lesser Palko standard. See, e.g., *Brock* v. *North Carolina.* . . .

. . . [W]e today find that the double jeopardy prohibition of the Fifth Amendment represents a fundamental ideal in our constitutional heritage, and that it should apply to the States through the Fourteenth Amendment. Insofar as it is inconsistent with this holding, *Palko* v. *Connecticut* is overruled. . . . The validity of petitioner's larceny conviction must be judged, not by the watered-down standard enunciated in Palko, but under this Court's interpretations of the Fifth Amendment double jeopardy provision.

It is clear that petitioner's larceny conviction cannot stand once federal double jeopardy standards are applied. Petitioner was acquitted of larceny in his first trial. Because he decided to appeal his burglary conviction, he is forced to suffer retrial on the larceny count as well. As this Court held in *Green* v. *United States.* . . , "[c]onditioning an appeal of one offense on a coerced surrender of a valid plea of former jeopardy on another offense exacts a forfeiture in plain conflict with the constitutional bar against double jeopardy.". . .

Mr. Justice White, concurring. . . .

Mr. Justice Harlan, whom Mr. Justice Stewart joins, dissenting. . . .

In *North Carolina* v. *Pearce*, 395 U.S. 711 (1969), the Court examined another double jeopardy issue—the problem of the successful appellant who is given a more severe sentence upon retrial than at the first trial. The Court held that while such sentences were not *ipso facto* unconstitutional, any punishment already exacted must be "fully credited," and where more severe punishment is given, the judge's reasons for doing so must affirmatively appear, and the factual data upon which the increased sentence is based must be made a part of the record for the purpose of reviewing the constitutionality of such sentence.

TRIAL FOR MULTIPLE RELATED OFFENSES

Double jeopardy issues of a special sort may be presented when an accused is tried on multiple counts—entirely in a single trial or in successive trials—arising out of the execution of a single criminal plot. Three facets of this situation occur, each presenting separate problems. (1) The criminal law has developed in a fashion which results in a great deal of overlapping, and consequently a single criminal *act* may in fact be chargeable as two or more *offenses*. In defining criminal offenses the law has operated like the pathologist's knife in splitting the total transaction into several discrete parts, each of which constitutes a separate crime. Thus a burglary might actually be broken down into the separate charges of conspiracy to commit burglary, possession of burglar's tools with intent to commit burglary, and burglary. (2) A criminal may commit several crimes on a single occasion, as, for example, by robbing five different customers in a tavern. In so doing, he has committed five separate crimes and may be so charged. The problem arises when he is tried *seriatim* on these charges, rather than in one trial. (3) A third double jeopardy issue stems from the fact that we live under a federal system, and a single act may constitute both a state crime and a federal crime.

The constitutionality of trying a defendant on closely related charges is usually determined by whether additional facts must be proved in the additional charges. If so, then there is no double jeopardy. If the same facts would support a conviction on the additional charges, then double jeopardy occurs. Thus it is permissible to try an accused both for conspiracy to commit a crime and for the substantive crime. It is also permissible to try for breaking and entering with intent to commit larceny and, additionally, for committing the larceny. But if the additional charge is an *included* offense the situation is different. Bank robbery and conspiracy to commit bank robbery are capable of separate treatment and may even be tried at different trials, since either crime may take place without the other. But murder includes the lesser crime of manslaughter, and if trial is had on either charge, a later trial on the other is precluded.

When a criminal robs several persons on a single occasion, he has committed multiple crimes of an identical nature. The question then arises of whether he can be tried in a series of trials under these circumstances or whether the prohibition against double jeopardy limits the government to a single trial. Two cases involving this issue under the Fourteenth Amendment were decided in 1958. They were *Hoag* v. *New Jersey,* 356 U.S. 464 (1958), and *Ciucci* v. *Illinois,* 356 U.S. 571 (1958).

The *Hoag* case involved the robbery of five persons one evening in a

New Jersey tavern. Hoag was indicted separately for robbery of three of the victims, and the indictments were joined for trial. At this trial acquittal resulted. All five victims were called as witnesses in the trial. Subsequently, Hoag was indicted, tried and convicted for robbing a fourth person at the tavern. The same issues of identification of Hoag as a participant in the robbery and the credibility of Hoag's alibi were presented at the second trial. Hoag argued that in these circumstances his second trial was in violation of the due process protection against double jeopardy. The Supreme Court of New Jersey sustained the conviction, and on certiorari the United States Supreme Court affirmed by a five-to-three vote. The majority took into account the fact that several of the witnesses, to the surprise of the State, failed to identify Hoag as one of the robbers after having done so during the police investigation, and concluded that this was not an attempt on the part of the State to wear the accused out by a multitude of cases with accumulated trials. The dissenters argued that "Hoag is made to run the gantlet twice," since the only contested issue was whether he was one of the robbers. This they felt clearly violated the constitutional protection against double jeopardy.

In the same term of Court, a similar holding followed in *Ciucci* v. *Illinois*, 356 U.S. 571 (1958). In this case the vote was five-to-four, with Mr. Justice Brennan participating and voting with the dissenters. Ciucci's wife and three children were found dead with bullet wounds in their heads in a burning building. Ciucci was charged on four separate murder indictments and tried three successive times, first for the murder of his wife, and then for the murder of two of the three children. At each of the trials the prosecution introduced into evidence details of all four deaths. Under Illinois law, the jury fixed the penalty for first degree murder. Ciucci was convicted in each of the three trials. The sentences by the three different juries increased successively from 20 years for the wife, to 45 years for the first child, to death for the second child. The same majority as in *Hoag*, in a per curiam opinion, affirmed the judgment on authority of *Hoag* and *Palko*. In 1970, in the wake of *Benton* v. *Maryland*, the Court overruled this position in *Ashe* v. *Swenson*.

ASHE *v.* SWENSON

397 U.S. 436 (1970)

Mr. Justice Stewart delivered the opinion of the Court.

[Six men engaged in a poker game were robbed by three or four masked gunmen. Six weeks after being acquitted in a state trial for the robbery of one of the players, the defendant was tried for the robbery of another of the players and was convicted. The witnesses in the two trials were for the most part the same, and the State's evidence establishing the facts of the robbery was uncontradicted, but the testimony identifying the defendant as one of the robbers was substantially stronger at the second trial. The Supreme Court of Missouri affirmed the conviction, holding that the "plea of former jeopardy must be denied." A collateral attack upon the conviction in the state courts five years later was also unsuccessful. The defendant then brought a habeas corpus proceeding in the United States District Court, claiming that the second prosecution had violated his right not to be twice put in jeopardy. The District Court denied the writ, the Court of Appeals affirmed, and the Supreme Court granted certiorari.]

As the District Court and the Court of Appeals correctly noted, the operative facts here are virtually identical to those of *Hoag* v. *New Jersey.* . . . Viewing the question presented solely in terms of Fourteenth Amendment due process—whether the course that New Jersey had pursued had "led to fundamental unfairness," . . . —this Court declined to reverse the judgment of conviction, because "in the circumstances shown by this record, we cannot say that petitioner's later prosecution and conviction violated due process." . . . The Court found it unnecessary to decide whether "collateral estoppel"—the principle that bars relitigation between the same parties of issues actually determined at a previous trial—is a due process requirement in a state criminal trial. . . . And in the view the Court took of the issues presented, it did not, of course, even approach consideration of whether collateral estoppel is an ingredient of the Fifth Amendment guarantee against double jeopardy.

The doctrine of *Benton* v. *Maryland* . . . puts the issues in the present case in a perspective quite different from that in which the issues were perceived in *Hoag* v. *New Jersey.* The question is no longer whether collateral estoppel is a requirement of due process, but whether it is a part of the Fifth Amendment's guarantee against double jeopardy. . . .

"Collateral estoppel" is an awkward phrase, but it stands for an extremely important principle in our adversary system of justice. It means simply that when an issue of ultimate fact has once been determined by a valid and final judgment, that issue cannot again be litigated between the same parties in any future lawsuit. . . . The federal decisions have made clear that the rule of collateral estoppel in criminal cases is not to be applied with the hypertechnical and archaic approach of a 19th century pleading book, but with realism and rationality. Where a previous judgment of acquittal was based upon a general verdict, as is usually the case, this approach requires a court to "examine the record of a prior proceeding, taking into account the pleadings, evidence, charge, and other relevant matter, and conclude whether a rational jury could have grounded its verdict upon an issue other than that which the defendant seeks to foreclose from consideration." . . .

Straightforward application of the federal rule to the present case can lead to but one conclusion. . . . The single rationally conceivable issue in dispute before the jury was whether the petitioner had been one of the robbers. And the jury by its verdict found that he had not. . . .

The ultimate question to be determined, then, in the light of *Benton* v. *Maryland, supra,* is whether this established rule of federal law is embodied in the Fifth Amendment guarantee against double jeopardy. We do not hesitate to hold that it is. For whatever else that constitutional guarantee may embrace, . . . it surely protects a man who has been acquitted from having to "run the gantlet" a second time. . . .

The question is not whether Missouri could validly charge the petitioner with six separate offenses for the robbery of the six poker players. It is not whether he could have received a total of six punishments if he had been convicted in a single trial of robbing the six victims. It is simply whether, after a jury determined by its verdict that the petitioner was not one of the robbers, the State could constitutionally hale him before a new jury to litigate that issue again. . . .

The judgment is reversed, and the case is remanded to the Court of Appeals for the Eighth Circuit for further proceedings consistent with this opinion.

[Separate concurring opinions were written by Justice Black, Justice Harlan, and Justice Brennan, who was joined by Justices Douglas and Marshall. Chief Justice Burger dissented.]

Another multiple offense problem arises when a single act constitutes a crime under state law and also under municipal ordinance. The question of whether dual prosecution in such situations constitutes double jeopardy was considered in *Waller* v. *Florida,* decided on the same day as *Ashe.*

WALLER *v.* FLORIDA
397 U.S. 387 (1970)

Mr. Chief Justice Burger delivered the opinion of the Court....

Petitioner was one of a number of persons who removed a canvas mural which was affixed to a wall inside the City Hall of St. Petersburg, Florida. After the mural was removed, the petitioner and others carried it through the streets of St. Petersburg until they were confronted by police officers. After a scuffle, the officers recovered the mural, but in a damaged condition.

The petitioner was charged by the City of St. Petersburg with the violation of two ordinances: first, destruction of city property; and second, disorderly breach of the peace. He was found guilty in the municipal court on both counts, and a sentence of 180 days in the county jail was imposed.

Thereafter an information was filed against the petitioner by the State of Florida charging him with grand larceny. It is conceded that this information was based on the same acts of the petitioner as were involved in the violation of the two city ordinances.... Thereafter petitioner was tried in the Circuit Court of Florida by a jury and was found guilty of the felony of grand larceny....

On appeal, the District Court of Appeal of Florida considered and rejected petitioner's claim that he had twice been put in jeopardy because prior to his conviction of grand larceny, he had been convicted by the municipal court of an included offense of the crime of grand larceny.... [The District Court of Appeal quoted the Florida Supreme Court saying:]

" 'This double jeopardy argument has long been settled contrary to the claims of the petitioner. We see no reason to recede from our established precedent on the subject. Long ago it was decided that an act committed within municipal limits may be punished by city ordinance even though the same act is also proscribed as a crime by a state statute. An offender may be tried for the municipal offense in the city court and for the crime in the proper state court. Conviction or acquittal in either does not bar prosecution in the other.' "...

... Whether in fact and law petitioner committed separate offenses which could support separate charges was not decided by the Florida courts, nor do we reach that question. What is before us is the asserted power of the two courts within one State to place petitioner on trial for the same alleged crime.

In *Benton* v. *Maryland* ... this Court declared the double jeopardy provisions of the Fifth Amendment applicable to the States.... Here, as in *North Carolina* v. *Pearce* ... *Benton* should be applied to test petitioner's conviction....

Florida does not stand alone in treating municipalities and the State as separate sovereign entities, each capable of imposing punishment for the same alleged crime. Here, respondent State of Florida seeks to justify this separate sovereignty theory by asserting that the relationship between a municipality and the state is analogous to the relationship between a State and the Federal Government. Florida's chief reliance is placed upon this Court's holdings in *Bartkus* v. *Illinois* ... and *Abbate* v. *United States* ... which permitted successive prosecutions by the Federal and State Governments as separate sovereigns. ...

[The] provisions of the Florida Constitution demonstrate that the judicial power to try petitioner on the first charges in municipal court springs from the same organic law that created the state court of general jurisdiction in which petitioner was tried and convicted for a felony. Accordingly, the apt analogy to the relationship between municipal and state governments is to be found in the relationship between the government of a Territory and the Government of the United States. The legal consequence of that relationship was settled in *Grafton* v. *United States,* 206 U.S. 333 (1907), where this Court held that a prosecution in a court of the United States is a bar to a subsequent prosecution in a territorial court, since both are arms of the same sovereign. ...

Thus *Grafton*, not *Fox* v. *Ohio, supra,* or its progeny, *Bartkus* v. *Illinois* ... or *Abbate* v. *United States* ... controls, and we hold that on the basis of the facts upon which the Florida District Court of Appeal relied petitioner could not lawfully be tried both by the municipal government and by the State of Florida. In this context a "dual sovereignty" theory is an anachronism, and the second trial constituted double jeopardy violative of the Fifth and Fourteenth Amendments to the United States Constitution. ... [Judgment in the second trial vacated, and the cause remanded for further proceedings in accord with this opinion.]

[Justices Black and Brennan wrote concurring opinions.]

The final aspect of the multiple offense problems to be considered is that of trial by both federal and state authority where a single act constitutes a crime against both jurisdictions. Beginning in 1852 in *Moore* v. *Illinois,* 14 How. 13, the Court has indicated in a number of cases that trials by both jurisdictions in such instances would not violate the prohibitions against double jeopardy. While the most recent decision to date on the point, *Bartkus* v. *Illinois,* follows this rule, the opinions in *Benton, Ashe,* and *Waller* suggest that it is now on very tenuous ground.

BARTKUS *v.* ILLINOIS

359 U.S. 121 (1959)

Mr. Justice Frankfurter delivered the opinion of the Court.

Petitioner was tried in the Federal District Court for the Northern District of Illinois on December 18, 1953, for robbery of a federally insured savings and loan association ... in violation of 18 U.S.C. Sec. 2113. The case was tried to a jury and resulted in an acquittal. On January 8, 1954, an Illinois grand jury indicted Bartkus. The facts recited in the Illinois indictment were substantially identical to those contained in the prior federal indictment. The Illinois indictment charged that these facts constituted a violation of Illinois Revised Statutes, 1951 c. 38, Sec. 501, a robbery statute. Bartkus was tried and convicted in the Criminal Court of Cook County and was sentenced to life imprisonment under the Illinois Habitual Criminal Statute. ...

The Illinois trial court considered and rejected petitioner's plea of *autrefois acquit*. That ruling and other alleged errors were challenged before the Illinois Supreme Court which affirmed the conviction. . . .

The state and federal prosecutions were separately conducted. It is true that the agent of the Federal Bureau of Investigation who had conducted the investigation on behalf of the Federal Government turned over to the Illinois prosecuting officials all the evidence he had gathered against the petitioner. Concededly, some of that evidence had been gathered after acquittal in the federal court. The only other connection between the two trials is to be found in a suggestion that the federal sentencing of the accomplices who testified against petitioner in both trials was purposely continued by the federal court until after they testified in the state trial. The record establishes that the prosecution was undertaken by state prosecuting officials within their discretionary responsibility and on the basis of evidence that conduct contrary to the penal code of Illinois had occurred within their jurisdiction. It establishes also that federal officials acted in cooperation with state authorities, as is the conventional practice between the two sets of prosecutors throughout the country. It does not support the claim that the State of Illinois in bringing its prosecution was merely a tool of the federal authorities, who thereby avoided the prohibition of the Fifth Amendment against a retrial of a federal prosecution after an acquittal. It does not sustain a conclusion that the state prosecution was a sham and a cover for a federal prosecution, and thereby in essential fact another federal prosecution. . . .

Constitutional challenge to successive state and federal prosecutions based upon the same transaction or conduct is not a new question before the Court though it has now been presented with conspicuous ability. The Fifth Amendment's proscription of double jeopardy has been invoked and rejected in over twenty cases of real or hypothetical successive state and federal prosecution cases before this Court. While *United States* v. *Lanza*, 260 U.S. 377 [1922], was the first case in which we squarely held valid a federal prosecution arising out of the same facts which had been the basis of a state conviction, the validity of such a prosecution by the Federal Government has not been questioned by this Court since the opinion in *Fox* v. *State of Ohio*, 5 How. 410, more than one hundred years ago. . . .

In a dozen cases decided by this Court [before *United States* v. *Lanza*] this Court had occasion to reaffirm the principle first enunciated in *Fox* v. *State of Ohio*. Since *Lanza* the Court has five times repeated the rule that successive state prosecutions are not in violation of the Fifth Amendment. Indeed Mr. Justice Holmes once wrote of this rule that it "is too plain to need more than statement.". . .

The experience of state courts in dealing with successive prosecutions by different governments is obviously also relevant in considering whether or not the Illinois prosecution of Bartkus violated due process of law. Of the twenty-eight States which have considered the validity of successive state and federal prosecutions as against a challenge of violation of either a state constitutional double-jeopardy provision or a common-law evidentiary rule of *autrefois acquit* and *autrefois convict,* twenty-seven have refused to rule that the second prosecution was or would be barred. These States were not bound to follow this Court and its interpretation of the Fifth Amendment. The rules, constitutional, statutory, or common law which bound them drew upon the same experience as did the Fifth Amendment, but were and are of separate and independent authority. . . .

With this body of precedent as irrefutable evidence that state and federal courts have for years refused to bar a second trial even though there had been a prior trial by another government for a similar offense, it would be disregard of a long, unbroken, unquestioned course of impressive adjudication for the Court now to rule that due process compels such a bar. A practical justification for rejecting such a reading of due process also commends itself in aid of this interpretation of the Fourteenth Amendment. In *Screws* v. *United States*, 325 U.S. 91, defendants were tried and convicted in a federal court under federal statutes with maximum sentences of a year and two years respectively. But the state crime there involved was a capital offense. Were the federal prosecution of a comparatively minor offense to prevent state prosecution of so grave an infraction of state law, the result would be a shocking and untoward deprivation of the historic right and obligation of the States to maintain peace and order within their confines. It would be in derogation of our federal system to displace the reserved power of States over state offenses by reason of prosecution of minor federal offenses by federal authorities beyond the control of the States. . . .

Precedent, experience, and reason all support the conclusion that Alphonse Bartkus has not been deprived of due process of law by the State of Illinois.

Affirmed.

Mr. Justice Black, with whom the Chief Justice and Mr. Justice Douglas concur, dissenting. . . .

The Court's holding further limits our already weakened constitutional guarantees against double prosecutions. *United States* v. *Lanza* . . . allowed federal conviction and punishment of a man who had been previously convicted and punished for the identical acts by one of our States. Today, for the first time in its history, this Court upholds the state conviction of a defendant who had been *acquitted* of the same offense in the federal courts. I would hold that a federal trial following either state acquittal or conviction is barred by the Double Jeopardy Clause of the Fifth Amendment. *Abbate* v. *United States*, 359 U.S. 187 (dissenting opinion). And, quite apart from whether that clause is as fully binding on the States as it is on the Federal Government, . . . I would hold that Bartkus' conviction cannot stand. For I think double prosecutions for the same offense are so contrary to the spirit of our free country that they violate even the prevailing view of the Fourteenth Amendment, expressed in *Palko* v. *Connecticut*. . . .

The Court apparently takes the position that a second trial for the same act is somehow less offensive if one of the trials is conducted by the Federal Government and the other by a State. Looked at from the standpoint of the individual who is being prosecuted, this notion is too subtle for me to grasp. If double punishment is what is feared, it hurts no less for two "Sovereigns" to inflict it than for one. If danger to the innocent is emphasized, that danger is surely no less when the power of State and Federal Governments is brought to bear on one man in two trials, than when one of these "Sovereigns" proceeds alone. In each case, inescapably, a man is forced to face danger twice for the same conduct.

The Court, without denying the almost universal abhorrence of such double prosecutions, nevertheless justifies the practice here in the name of "federalism." This, it seems to me, is a misuse and desecration of the concept. Our Federal Union was conceived and created "to establish Justice" and to "secure the Blessings of Liberty," not to destroy any of the bulwarks on which both freedom and justice depend. We should, therefore, be suspicious of any supposed "requirements" of "federalism" which result in obliterating ancient safeguards. I have been shown nothing in the history of our Union, in the writings of its Founders, or elsewhere, to indicate that individual rights deemed essential by both State and Nation were to be lost through the combined operations of the two governments. Nor has the Court given any sound reason for thinking that the successful operation of our dual system of government depends in the slightest on the power to try people twice for the same act.

Implicit in the Court's reliance on "federalism" is the premise that failure to allow double prosecutions would seriously impair law enforcement in both State and Nation. For one jurisdiction might provide minor penalties for acts severely punished by the other and by accepting pleas of guilty shield wrongdoers from justice. I believe this argument fails on several grounds. In the first place it relies on the unwarranted assumption that State and Nation will seek to subvert each other's laws. It has elsewhere been persuasively argued that most civilized nations do not and have not needed the power to try people a second time to protect themselves even when dealing with foreign lands. . . .

Ultimately the Court's reliance on federalism amounts to no more than the notion that, somehow, one act becomes two because two jurisdictions are involved. Hawkins, in his Pleas of the Crown, long ago disposed of a similar contention made to justify two trials for the same offense by different counties as "a mere Fiction or Construction of Law, which shall hardly take Place against a Maxim made in Favour of Life." It was discarded as a dangerous fiction then, it should be discarded as a dangerous fiction now. . . .

I would reverse.

[Mr. Justice Brennan, joined by Chief Justice Warren and Mr. Justice Douglas, dissented on the ground that the unusual extent of federal assistance and participation in the state trial made it "actually a second federal prosecution" barred by the double jeopardy provisions of the Fifth Amendment.]

Immediately following the decisions in *Bartkus* and *Abbate*, in 1959, the then Attorney General, William P. Rogers, announced for the Department of Justice a policy that no federal prosecution would be initiated following a state prosecution on a charge arising out of the same act unless unusual circumstances appeared. Even here, it was stated, the Attorney General himself would have to approve the decision to prosecute.

The majority and dissenting opinions in *Bartkus*, taken together with the action of Attorney General Rogers, raise the interesting question of the degree to which official discretion can be permitted, in order to retain flexibility, in the face of our traditional repugnance to double punishment. They are also illustrative of the point that care must be exercised in erecting any rule to the level of a constitutional requirement, since this tends to remove any "play at the joints" in the application of the rule.

[See J. A. C. Grant, "Successive Prosecutions by State and Nation," 4 *U.C.L.A. L. Rev.* 1 (1956); Walter T. Fisher, "Double Jeopardy, Two Sovereignties and the Intruding Constitution," 28 *U. Chi. L. Rev.* 591 (1961).]

TRIAL BY JURY

Trial by jury in criminal cases has been probably the most venerated and often praised of any of the procedural guarantees of the Constitution. It has undergone a slow erosion, however, and is only used in the more important cases in England. In the United States a similar trend is evident, and increasingly the jury trial is being waived. In addition, several states have reduced the number of jurors required or changed the unanimity requirement or both. But in federal trials the right to a jury is specifically guaranteed, and this has been held to mean the common law requirements of a unanimous verdict of a jury composed of twelve persons. The guarantee of jury trial in criminal cases is found both in Article III and in the Sixth Amendment of the Constitution. Article III, Section 2, Clause 3 states:

The trial of all crimes, except in cases of impeachment, shall be by jury; and such trial shall be held in the State where the said crimes shall have been committed; but when not committed within any State, the trial shall be at such place or places as the Congress may by law have directed.

The Sixth Amendment states:

In all criminal prosecutions the accused shall enjoy the right to a speedy and public trial, by an impartial jury of the State and district wherein the crime shall have been committed. . . .

The questions of what kind of jury and whether the jury trial is mandatory or merely a privilege of the accused were explored fully in *Patton* v. *United States* in 1930.

PATTON *v.* UNITED STATES

281 U.S. 276 (1930)

Mr. Justice Sutherland delivered the opinion of the Court.

The defendants (plaintiffs in error) were indicted in a Federal district court, charged with conspiring to bribe a Federal prohibition agent, a crime punishable by imprisonment in a Federal penitentiary for a term of years. A jury of twelve men was duly empaneled. The trial began on October 19, 1927, and continued before the jury of twelve until October 26 following, at which time one of the jurors, because of severe illness, became unable to serve further as a juror. Thereupon it was stipulated in open court by the government and counsel for defendants, defendants personally assenting thereto, that the trial should proceed with the remaining eleven jurors. . . .

The trial was concluded on the following day, and a verdict of guilty was rendered by the eleven jurors. . . . An appeal was taken to the circuit court of appeals upon the ground that the defendants had no power to waive their constitutional right to a trial by a jury of twelve persons.

The court below, being in doubt as to the law applicable to the situation thus presented, and desiring the instruction of this court, has certified the following question:

"After the commencement of a trial in a Federal court before a jury of twelve men upon an indictment charging a crime, punishment for which may involve a penitentiary sentence, if one juror becomes incapacitated and unable to further proceed with his work as a juror, can defendant or defendants and the government, through its official representative in charge of the case, consent to the trial proceeding to a finality with eleven jurors, and can defendant or defendants thus waive the right to a trial and verdict by a constitutional jury of twelve men?"....

... [W]e first inquire what is embraced by the phrase "trial by jury." That it means a trial by jury as understood and applied at common law, and includes all the essential elements as they were recognized in this country and England when the Constitution was adopted, is not open to question. Those elements were: (1) That the jury should consist of twelve men, neither more nor less; (2) that the trial should be in the presence and under the superintendence of a judge having power to instruct them as to the law and advise them in respect of the facts; and (3) that the verdict should be unanimous. [In support of these points the Court cites three cases: (1) *Thompson* v. *Utah*, 170 U.S. 343 (1898), where the Court reversed a conviction by a jury of eight men in the Territory of Utah, saying that the Constitution demanded a jury of not less than twelve persons; (2) *Capital Traction Co.* v. *Hof*, 174 U.S. 1 (1899), which held the superintendence of a judge necessary to jury trial; and *American Publishing Co.* v. *Fisher*, 166 U.S. 464 (1897), which held that the verdict must be unanimous.]

A constitutional jury means twelve men as though that number had been specifically named; and it follows that, when reduced to eleven, it ceases to be such a jury quite as effectively as though the number had been reduced to a single person. . . .

We come, then, to the crucial inquiry: Is the effect of the constitutional provisions in respect of trial by jury to establish a tribunal as a part of the frame of government, or only to guarantee to the accused the right to such a trial? If the former, the question certified by the lower court must, without more, be answered in the negative. . . .

The record of English and colonial jurisprudence antedating the Constitution will be searched in vain for evidence that trial by jury in criminal cases was regarded as a part of the structure of government, as distinguished from a right or privilege of the accused. On the contrary, it uniformly was regarded as a valuable privilege bestowed upon the person accused of crime for the purpose of safeguarding him against the oppressive power of the king and the arbitrary or partial judgment of the court. Thus Blackstone, who held trial by jury both in civil and criminal cases in such esteem that he called it "the glory of the English law," nevertheless looked upon it as a "privilege," albeit "the most transcendent privilege which any subject can enjoy." Book III, p. 379. . . .

In the light of the foregoing it is reasonable to conclude that the framers of the Constitution simply were intent upon preserving the right of trial by jury primarily for the protection of the accused. . . . That this was the purpose of the third article is rendered highly probable by a consideration of the form of expression used in the Sixth Amendment. . . .

Upon this view of the constitutional provisions we conclude that Article 3,

Section 2, is not jurisdictional, but was meant to confer a right upon the accused which he may forego at his election. To deny his power to do so is to convert a privilege into an imperative requirement. . . .

In *Singer* v. *United States*, 380 U.S. 24 (1965), however, the Court carefully confined the *Patton* case to the precise facts of proceeding to a verdict with eleven instead of twelve jurors, with the consent of the parties. Rule 23 (a) of the Federal Rules of Criminal Procedure provides:

Cases required to be tried by jury shall be so tried unless the defendant waives a jury trial in writing with the approval of the court and the consent of the government.

Singer was charged with violations of the mail fraud statute and offered to waive a trial by jury. The trial court approved, but the government refused to give its consent. Petitioner was subsequently convicted by a jury, and the Court granted certiorari to consider his claim that the Sixth Amendment affords an unconditional right in a federal criminal case for the defendant to have his case decided by a judge alone if he considers it to be to his advantage. The Court unanimously denied this interpretation and held Rule 23 (a) to be valid. "The ability to waive a constitutional right does not ordinarily carry with it the right to insist upon the opposite of that right. . . . [A]lthough he can waive his right to be confronted by the witnesses against him, it has never been seriously suggested that he can thereby compel the Government to try the case by stipulation." The Chief Justice pointed out that if the consent of the judge or prosecutor to waiver is withheld, "the result is simply that the defendant is subject to an impartial trial by jury—the very thing that the Constitution guarantees him."

While the Sixth Amendment guarantees the right of jury trial "in all criminal prosecutions," and Article III states that the trial "of all Crimes" shall be by jury, the Court has uniformly held that the Constitution does not require that petty offenses be tried to a jury. This, too, is a common-law feature of jury trial. The rule was stated in *District of Columbia* v. *Colts*, 282 U.S. 63 (1930). Colts was charged with having operated a motor vehicle in the district at a greater rate of speed than twenty-two miles an hour (the legal limit) recklessly, "in such manner and condition so as to endanger property and individuals." He demanded trial by jury but was refused. In reviewing his conviction the court of appeals reversed the judgment, holding that the offense went beyond the character of a petty offense, and therefore the accused was constitutionally entitled to trial by jury. The United States Supreme Court affirmed this decision. Justice Sutherland, for a unanimous Court, stated:

It will be seen that the respondent is not charged merely with the comparatively slight offense of exceeding the twenty-two mile limit of speed . . . or merely with driving recklessly . . . ; but with the grave offense of having driven at the forbidden rate of speed and recklessly, "so as to endanger property and individuals."

By section 165 of title 18 of the D.C. Code, . . . the Constitution is made the test—as, of course, it must be—to determine whether the accused be entitled to a jury trial. Article 3, Section 2, Cl. 3, of the Constitution provides that, "The Trial of all Crimes, except in Cases of Impeachment, shall be by Jury." This provision is to be interpreted in the light of common law, according to which petty offenses might be proceeded against summarily before a magistrate sitting without a jury. See *Callan* v. *Wilson*, 127 U.S. 540, 557. That there may be many offenses called "petty offenses" which do not rise to the degree of crimes within the meaning of Article 3, and in respect of which Congress may dispense with a jury trial, is settled. ...

Whether a given offense is to be classed as a crime, so as to require a jury trial, or as a petty offense, triable summarily without a jury, depends primarily upon the nature of the offense. The offense here charged is not merely *malum prohibitum*, but in its very nature is *malum in se*. It was an indictable offense at common law ... when horses, instead of gasoline, constituted the motive power. The New Jersey Court of Errors and Appeals, in *State* v. *Rodgers, supra,* has discussed the distinction between traffic offenses of a petty character, subject to summary proceedings without indictment and trial by jury, and those of a serious character, amounting to public nuisances indictable at common law; and its examination of the subject makes clear that the offense now under review is of the latter character.

Until 1968 the Court followed the *Palko* rule of "fundamental fairness" with respect to the use of jury trials in state prosecutions and even indicated in several cases that the State could abolish the criminal jury altogether without violating the Fourteenth Amendment. In *Duncan* v. *Louisiana*, 391 U.S. 145 (1968), however, the Court incorporated the Sixth Amendment jury trial guarantee into the Fourteenth. It was then assumed that the old rule of *Maxwell* v. *Dow*, 176 U.S. 681 (1900), that the State could provide for a jury of eight instead of twelve, and of *Jordan* v. *Massachusetts*, 225 U.S. 167 (1912), that the State could dispense with the requirement of unanimity without violating the Fourteenth Amendment, had fallen also. But in *Williams* v. *Florida*, 399 U.S. 78 (1970), the Court held that the Sixth Amendment did *not* require the common-law jury of twelve members, and that therefore neither the federal courts nor the state courts were *constitutionally* bound to provide juries of twelve. (See Chapter 9 for the opinions in the *Duncan* and *Williams* cases.)

The Sixth Amendment requires that the federal jury, in addition to some of the common-law aspects, must be "impartial." The Court apparently incorporated this requirement into the Fourteenth Amendment in *Parker* v. *Gladden*, 385 U.S. 363 (1966). In so doing it reversed a conviction following a trial during which a bailiff, assigned to shepherd the sequestered jury, had stated to one of the jurors, in the presence of others, that the defendant was guilty. As in *Turner* v. *Louisiana*, 379 U.S. 466 (1965), where a similar situation occurred, the Court held this to be a denial of the right of confrontation also.

There are three stages at which issues of partiality may occur in connection with jury trial: (1) when the general jury panel is drawn for a term of court; (2) when the jurors are drawn from the general panel for a specific case; and (3) during the course of the trial. Problems at the first stage result from improper exclusions in either the law or the administration of the juror qualification law. The problem at the second stage is basically that of eliminating jurors who have an improper bias in the specific case on which they might serve. At the third stage the issue is presented if jurors are improperly influenced, as by bribery or other illegal persuasion, during the course of the trial.

The first of these stages presents the most difficult constitutional problem, and is the one to be treated here. The second stage can normally be handled by the method of examining prospective jurors under oath and removing ("for cause") those found to be unduly prejudiced or to have an interest in the case. (In addition, each side is allowed a specified number of "peremptory" challenges for which no reason need be assigned.) On occasion, because of unusual notoriety, it may be impossible to impanel an impartial jury in the locality in which the crime occurred. In such instances the guarantee of impartiality can only be met by granting a continuance or a change of venue to allow the trial to take place in another location. [The problem of "trial by newspaper" is treated at some length in Chapter 6, in the section "Free Press v. Fair Administration of Justice."]

The third problem is partially avoided by careful admonition of jurors in advance by the judge and, frequently, by close guard during the course of the trial. Violators are dealt with severely, and tampering with the jury is ground for declaring a mistrial (if the trial is still in progress) or vacating the judgment (if the trial has been concluded).

One problem concerning the "impartial jury" was presented by the fact that government employees served on juries in criminal cases brought by the United States in the District of Columbia. In *Crawford* v. *United States*, 212 U.S. 183 (1909), the Court decided, on common-law grounds, that such employees were disqualified in federal criminal proceedings. As the number of government employees in the district increased and jury panels became more difficult to fill, Congress in 1935 removed the disqualification by statute. The act was held valid in *United States* v. *Wood*, 299 U.S. 123 (1936). By a narrow majority the Court in *Frazier* v. *United States*, 335 U.S. 497 (1948), held that government employees as a class are not disqualified by an implied bias against defendants. Of course, individual employees may be disqualified if shown to have actual bias.

As to the composition of juries, federal statutes have required that federal jurors be selected in accordance with the laws of the state where the trial is held. The state laws must, however, meet the Fourteenth Amendment tests of due process and equal protection. In addition, the Supreme Court can exercise special supervisory power over federal juries, which permits the Court to impose extra requirements with regard to these which it cannot impose on state juries. In *Thiel* v. *Southern Pacific Company* the Court examined an allegation that day laborers were systematically excluded from jury service.

THIEL *v.* SOUTHERN PACIFIC COMPANY
328 U.S. 217 (1946)

Mr. Justice Murphy delivered the opinion of the Court.

Petitioner, a passenger, jumped out of the window of a moving train operated by the respondent, the Southern Pacific Company. He filed a complaint in a California state court to recover damages, alleging that the respondent's agents knew that he was "out of his normal mind" and should not be accepted as a passenger or else should be guarded and that, having accepted him as a passenger, they left him unguarded and failed to stop the train before he finally fell to the ground. At respondent's request the case was removed to the federal district court at San Francisco on the ground of diversity of citizenship, respondent being a Kentucky corporation. . . .

After demanding a jury trial, petitioner moved to strike out the entire jury panel, alleging *inter alia* that "mostly business executives or those having the employer's viewpoint are purposely selected on said panel, thus giving a majority representation to one class or occupation and discriminating against other occupations and classes, particularly the employees and those in the poorer classes who constitute, by far, the great majority of citizens eligible for jury service." Following a hearing at which testimony was taken, the motion was denied. Petitioner then attempted to withdraw his demand for a jury trial but the respondent refused to consent. A jury of twelve was chosen. Petitioner thereupon challenged these jurors upon the same grounds previously urged in relation to the entire jury panel and upon the further ground that six of the twelve jurors were closely affiliated and connected with the respondent. The court denied this challenge. The trial proceeded and the jury returned a verdict for the respondent. . . .

. . . The Ninth Circuit Court of Appeals affirmed the judgment in its entirety . . . and we brought the case here on certiorari "limited to the question whether petitioner's motion to strike the jury panel was properly denied." . . .

The American tradition of trial by jury, considered in connection with either criminal or civil proceedings, necessarily contemplates an impartial jury drawn from a cross-section of the community. . . . This does not mean, of course, that every jury must contain representatives of all the economic, social, religious, racial, political and geographical groups of the community; frequently such complete representation would be impossible. But it does mean that prospective jurors shall be selected by court officials without systematic and intentional exclusion of any of these groups. Recognition must be given to the fact that those eligible for jury service are to be found in every stratum of society. Jury competence is an individual rather than a group or class matter. That fact lies at the very heart of the jury system. To disregard it is to open the door to class distinctions and discriminations which are abhorrent to the democratic ideals of trial by jury. . . .

The undisputed evidence in this case demonstrates a failure to abide by the proper rules and principles of jury selection. Both the clerk of the court and the jury commissioner testified that they deliberately and intentionally excluded from the jury lists all persons who work for a daily wage. They generally used the city directory as the source of names of prospective jurors. In the words of the clerk, "If I see in the directory the name of John Jones and it says he is a longshoreman, I do not put his name in, because I have found by experience that that man will not serve as a juror, and I will not get people who will qualify. The minute that a juror is called into court on a venire and says he is working for $10 a day and cannot afford to work for four, the Judge has never made one of those men serve, and so in order to avoid putting names of people in who I know won't become jurors in the court, won't qualify as jurors in this court, I do leave them out.... Where I thought the designation indicated that they were day laborers, I mean they were people who were compensated solely when they were working by the day, I leave them out." The jury commissioner corroborated this testimony.... The evidence indicated, however, that laborers who were paid weekly or monthly wages were placed on the jury lists, as well as the wives of daily wage earners....

This exclusion of all those who earn a daily wage cannot be justified by federal or state law....

...Wage earners, including those who are paid by the day, constitute a very substantial portion of the community, a portion that cannot be intentionally and systematically excluded in whole or in part without doing violence to the democratic nature of the jury system. Were we to sanction an exclusion of this nature we would encourage whatever desires those responsible for the selection of jury panels may have to discriminate against persons of low economic and social status. We would breathe life into any latent tendencies to establish the jury as the instrument of the economically and socially privileged. That we refuse to do.

It is clear that a federal judge would be justified in excusing a daily wage earner for whom jury service would entail an undue financial hardship. But that fact cannot support the complete exclusion of all daily wage earners regardless of whether there is actual hardship involved....

It follows that we cannot sanction the method by which the jury panel was formed in this case. The trial court should have granted petitioner's motion to strike the panel. That conclusion requires us to reverse the judgment below in the exercise of our power of supervision over the administration of justice in the federal courts....

Reversed.

Mr. Justice Jackson took no part in the consideration or decision of this case.

[Mr. Justice Frankfurter, with whom Mr. Justice Reed concurred, wrote a dissenting opinion.]

The *Thiel* holding was followed shortly thereafter in *Ballard* v. *United States*, 329 U.S. 187 (1946). The case involved the indictment and conviction of Mrs. Ballard for conspiring to use and using the mails to defraud. It was conceded by the government that women were eligible for jury service under California law, that women were not included in the panel of grand and petit jurors in the Southern District of California, and that they were intentionally and systematically excluded from the panel. The Court held that this was reversible error. Justice Douglas, for the majority, stated:

We conclude that the purposeful and systematic exclusion of women from the panel in this case was a departure from the scheme of jury selection which Congress adopted and that, as in the *Thiel* case, we should exercise our power of supervision over the administration of justice in the federal courts ... to correct an error which permeated this proceeding.

It is said, however, that an all male panel drawn from the various groups within a community will be as truly representative as if women were included. The thought is that the factors which tend to influence the action of women are the same as those which influence the action of men—personality, background, economic status —and not sex. Yet it is not enough to say that women when sitting as jurors neither act nor tend to act as a class. Men likewise do not act as a class. But, if the shoe were on the other foot, who would claim that a jury was truly representative of the community if all men were intentionally and systematically excluded from the panel? The truth is that the two sexes are not fungible; a community made up of one is different from a community composed of both; the subtle interplay of influence one on the other is among the imponderables. To insulate the courtroom from either may not in a given case make an iota of difference. Yet a flavor, a distinct quality is lost if either sex is excluded. The exclusion of one may indeed make the jury less representative of the community than would be true if an economic or racial group were excluded. . . .

Four justices dissented in the *Ballard* case, but their arguments were not directed to the issue of exclusion itself. In 1948 Congress revised the law relative to federal proceedings to prescribe uniform standards for jurors in federal courts instead of making qualifications depend on state laws. Now all local citizens are qualified if they have reached twenty-one years of age and are not incompetent under state law to serve. In addition, a change was made by the Civil Rights Act of 1957 which had the effect of admitting qualified women to service on federal juries, irrespective of whether state law disqualifies them from state jury service.

While the Sixth and Seventh Amendments guarantee the right of jury trial in both criminal cases and civil cases at law in the federal courts, the Fourteenth Amendment has been construed to allow states broad powers to modify common-law jury requirements or even to abolish the jury altogether. If the state retains jury trial, however, even though modifications are permissible, it cannot deny equal protection in the administration of the jury provisions. Thus it was held as early as 1880 in *Strauder* v. *West Virginia,* 100 U.S. 303, that trial of a Negro defendant by a jury from which all Negroes were excluded by law was a denial of equal protection guaranteed by the Fourteenth Amendment. A long series of subsequent cases have uniformly followed this rule. One of the more recent cases, *Avery* v. *Georgia,* 345 U.S. 559 (1953), presented a novel process for exclusion of Negroes. Prospective jurors had their names printed on tickets, with white persons on white tickets and Negroes on yellow tickets. The tickets were placed in a box, and a judge drew out the required number. These were given to the sheriff, who in turn handed them to the clerk, who typed up the final list for the panel. In the *Avery* case not a single Negro was selected to serve on a panel of sixty. The Supreme Court concluded that such a procedure established a prima facie case of discrimination, which the state failed to overcome. In *Hernandez* v. *Texas,* 347 U.S. 475 (1954), the Court reversed the conviction of Hernandez upon a finding that no person with a Mexican or Latin-American name had served on a jury in that county for twenty-five years. As the Court has often pointed out, however, there is no constitutional requirement of proportional representation or even that a particular jury have members of the race or economic class of the defendant. Carried to such an extreme, a bank robber would be able to claim one or more of his trade on the jury trying him. For the state to exclude any category, however, it must show reasons relevant to the function which the jury is required to perform, and not exclude merely on grounds of race or occupation.

On the exclusion from jury service by statute, women are still placed in a special category for purposes of Fourteenth Amendment application. As of this date, Alabama and Mississippi still bar women altogether from state juries. In addition, eighteen states, as well as the District of Columbia, have accorded women an absolute exemption based solely on their sex and exercisable in one form or another. The validity under the Fourteenth Amendment of one of these latter statutes, and, indirectly, the total disqualification, was discussed in *Hoyt* v. *Florida*, 368 U.S. 57 (1961). Appellant, a woman, was convicted by an all-male jury in Florida for the second degree murder of her husband. Under Florida law both men and women are eligible for jury duty, but women are given an absolute exemption and are not put on the jury list unless they voluntarily register for such service. Appellant claimed that the nature of the crime of which she was convicted "peculiarly demanded the inclusion of persons of her own sex on the jury." According to the prosecution there was a marital upheaval involving the suspected infidelity of the husband, the husband's final rejection of his wife's efforts at reconciliation, and the culmination of the argument was the wife's assault on the husband with a baseball bat. As Justice Harlan stated the matter for the Court, "It is claimed, in substance, that women jurors would have been more understanding or compassionate than men in assessing the quality of appellant's act and her defense of 'temporary insanity.' " She thus challenged the constitutionality of the jury law both on its face and as applied. By a unanimous vote the Court affirmed.

Justice Harlan stated:

Of course, these premises misconceive the scope of the right to an impartially selected jury assured by the Fourteenth Amendment. That right does not entitle one accused of crime to a jury tailored to the circumstances of the particular case, whether relating to the sex or other condition of the defendant, or to the nature of the charges to be tried. It requires only that the jury be indiscriminately drawn from among those eligible in the community for jury service, untrammeled by any arbitrary and systematic exclusions. . . . The result of this appeal must therefore depend on whether such an exclusion of women from jury service has been shown.

The Court specifically refused to reconsider the dictum in *Strauder* v. *West Virginia* to the effect that a state could confine jury duty to males. "This constitutional proposition has gone unquestioned for more than eighty years in the decisions of the Court . . . and had been reflected, until 1957, in congressional policy respecting jury service in the federal courts themselves." Justice Harlan then stated that the differential classification of male and female jurors was not so unreasonable as to be "thus infected with unconstitutionality." Women can be treated differently, since "Despite the enlightened emancipation of women from the restrictions and protections of bygone years, and their entry into many parts of community life formerly considered to be reserved to men, woman is still regarded as the center of home and family life."

The Court further concluded that there was no showing of "arbitrary, systematic exclusionary purpose" in the fact that the county jury list of some 10,000 inhabitants qualified to be jurors contained only about 220 women. "It is sufficiently evident from the record that the presence on the jury list of no more than ten or twelve women in the earlier years, and the failure to add in 1957 more women to those already on the list, are attributable not to any discriminatory motive, but to a purpose to put on the list only those women who might be expected to be qualified for service if actually called."

A more difficult question of discrimination was presented by the "blue ribbon" jury system as practiced in New York. Two companion cases were decided by the Supreme Court in 1947, with the system being upheld by the narrow margin of five to four.

FAY *v.* NEW YORK

BOVE *v.* NEW YORK

332 U.S. 261 (1947)

Mr. Justice Jackson delivered the opinion of the Court.

These cases present the same issue, a challenge to the constitutionality of the special or so-called "blue ribbon" jury as used by state courts in the State and County of New York.

Such a jury found Fay and Bove guilty of conspiracy to extort and of extortion. [Appellants were officers in certain building trades unions. The City of New York awarded various construction contracts, and appellants collected from the contractors some $300,000. The defense claimed that the payments were voluntary—bribes, perhaps, but not extortion—in return for assistance offered the contractors in avoiding labor trouble and strikes. Appellants did not challenge the general jury qualification statutes whereby the population of New York County, numbering some 1,800,000, was "sifted to produce a general jury panel of about 60,000," either as to the provisions of the statutes or their administration. They did focus their attack, however, upon the statutes and sifting procedures through which the general panel was shrunk to the special or "blue ribbon" panel of about 3,000.]

Special jurors are selected from those accepted for the general panel by the county clerk, but only after each has been subpoenaed for personal appearance and has testified under oath as to his qualification and fitness. The statute prescribes standards for their selection by declaring ineligible and directing elimination of these classes: (1) All who have been disqualified or who claim and are allowed exemption from general service. (2) All who have been convicted of a criminal offense, or found guilty of fraud or misconduct by judgment of any civil court. (3) All who possess such conscientious opinions with regard to the death penalty as would preclude their finding a defendant guilty if the crime charged be punishable with death. (4) All who doubt their ability to lay aside an opinion or impression formed from newspaper reading or otherwise, or to render an impartial verdict upon the evidence uninfluenced by any such opinion or impression, or whose opinion of circumstantial evidence is such as would prevent their finding a verdict of guilty upon such evidence, or who avow such a prejudice against any law of the State as would preclude finding a defendant guilty of a violation of such law, or who avow such a prejudice against any particular defense to a criminal charge as would prevent giving a fair and impartial trial upon the merits of such defense, or who avow that they cannot in all cases give to a defendant who fails to testify as a witness in his own behalf the full benefit of the statutory provision that such defendant's neglect or refusal to testify as a witness in his own behalf shall not create any presumption against him.

The special jury panel is not one brought into existence for this particular case nor for any special class of offenses or type of accused. It is part of the regular machinery of trial in counties of one million or more inhabitants. In its sound discretion the court may order trial by special jury on application of either party in a civil action and by either the prosecution or defense in criminal cases. The motion may be granted only on a showing that "by reason of the importance or intricacy of the case, a special jury is required" or "the issue to be tried has been so widely commented upon . . ." or that for any other reason "the due, efficient and impartial administration of justice in the particular case would be advanced by the trial of such an issue by a special jury.". . .

We fail to perceive on its face any constitutional offense in the statutory standards prescribed for the special panel. The Act does not exclude, or authorize the clerk to exclude, any person or class because of race, creed, color or occupation. It imposes no qualification of an economic nature beyond that imposed by the concededly valid general panel statute. Each of the grounds of elimination is reasonably and closely related to the juror's suitability for the kind of service the special panel requires or to his fitness to judge the kind of cases for which it is most frequently utilized. Not all of the grounds of elimination would appear relevant to the issues of the present case. But we know of no right of defendants to have a specially constituted panel which would include all persons who might be fitted to hear their particular and unique case. This panel is for service in a wide variety of cases and its eliminations must be judged in that light. We cannot overlook that one of the features which has tended to discredit jury trials is interminable examination and rejection of prospective jurors. In a metropolis with notoriously congested court calendars we cannot find it constitutionally forbidden to set up administrative procedures in advance of trial to eliminate from the panel those who, in a large proportion of cases, would be rejected by the court after its time had been taken in examination to ascertain the disqualifications. Many of the standards of elimination which the clerk is directed to apply in choice of the panel are those the court would have to apply to excuse a juror on challenge for cause. . . .

The allegations of fact upon which defendants ask us to hold these special panels unconstitutional come to three: (1) That laborers, operatives, craftsmen, foremen and service employees were systematically, intentionally and deliberately excluded from the panel. (2) That women were in the same way excluded. (3) That the special panel is so composed as to be more prone to convict than the general panel.

(1) The proof that laborers and such were excluded consists of a tabulation of occupations as listed in the questionnaires filed with the clerk. . . .

. . . [T]he two tables do not afford statistical proof that the jury percentages are the result of discrimination. Such a conclusion would be justified only if we knew whether the application of the proper jury standards would affect all occupations alike, of which there is no evidence and which we regard as improbable. . . .

. . . It is impossible from the defendants' evidence in this case to find that the distribution of the jury panel among occupations is not the result of the application of legitimate standards of disqualification.

On the other hand, the evidence that there has been no discrimination as to occupation in selection of the panel, while from interested witnesses, whose duty it was to administer the law, is clear and positive and is neither contradicted nor improbable. The testimony of those in charge of the selection, offered by the defendants themselves, is that without occupational discrimination they applied the standards of the statute to all whom they examined. We are unable to find that this evidence is untrue.

(2) As to the exclusion of women, it will be remembered that the law of New York gives to women the privilege to serve but does not impose service as a duty. . . . But the evidence does not show that women are excluded from the special jury. In this case three women talesmen were examined. One was pronounced "satisfactory" by both sides and served on the jury. . . .

(3) A more serious allegation against the special jury panel is that it is more inclined than the general panel to convict. . . .

If it were proved that in 1945 an inequality between the special jury's record of convictions and that of the ordinary jury continued as it was found by the Judicial Council to have prevailed in 1933–34, some foundation would be laid for a claim of unequal treatment. . . .

But the defendants have failed to show by any evidence whatever that this disparity in ratio of conviction existed in 1945 when they were tried. . . .

We hold, therefore, that defendants have not carried the burden of showing that the method of their trial denied them equal protection of the law.

The defendants' other objection is grounded on [the due process clause of the Fourteenth Amendment.] . . .

These defendants rely heavily on arguments drawn from our decisions in *Glasser* v. *United States*, . . . *Thiel* v. *Southern Pacific Company*, . . . and *Ballard* v. *United States*. . . . But those decisions were not constrained by any duty of deference to the authority of the State over local administration of justice. They dealt only with juries in federal courts. Over federal proceedings we may exert a supervisory power with greater freedom to reflect our notions of good policy than we may constitutionally exert over proceedings in state courts, and those expressions of policy are not necessarily embodied in the concept of due process. . . .

. . . Undoubtedly a system of exclusions could be so manipulated as to call a jury before which defendants would have so little chance of a decision on the evidence that it would constitute a denial of due process. A verdict on the evidence, however, is all an accused can claim; he is not entitled to a set-up that will give a chance of escape after he is properly proven guilty. Society also has a right to a fair trial. The defendant's right is a neutral jury. He has no constitutional right to friends on the jury. . . .

The other objection which petitioners urge under the due process clause is that the special jury panel was invalidated by exclusion of an economic group comprising such specified classifications as laborers, craftsmen and service employees. They argue that the jury panel was chosen "with a purpose to obtain persons of conservative views, persons of the upper economic and social stratum in New York County, persons having a tendency to convict defendants accused of crime, and to exclude those who might understand the point of view of the laboring man." As we have pointed out, there is no proof of exclusion of these. At most, the proof shows lack of proportional representation and there is an utter deficiency of proof that this was the result of a purpose to discriminate against this group as such. The uncontradicted evidence is that no person was excluded because of his occupation or economic status. . . . A fair application of literacy, intelligence and other tests would hardly act with proportional equality on all levels of life. . . .

Affirmed.

Mr. Justice Murphy, dissenting. . . .

. . . Whatever may be the standards erected by jury officials for distinguishing between those eligible for such a "blue ribbon" panel and those who are not, the distinction itself is an invalid one. It denies the defendant his constitutional right to be tried by a jury fairly drawn from a cross-section of the community. It forces upon him a jury drawn from a panel chosen in a manner which tends to obliterate the representative basis of the jury. . . .

. . . [A] cross-section of the community includes persons with varying degrees of training and intelligence and with varying economic and social positions. . . . It is a democratic institution, representative of all qualified classes of people. . . . To the extent that a "blue ribbon" panel fails to reflect this democratic principle, it is constitutionally defective. . . .

Mr. Justice Black, Mr. Justice Douglas and Mr. Justice Rutledge join in this dissent.

In a more recent case, *Brown* v. *Allen,* 344 U.S. 443 (1953), the Court examined the contention of a Negro petitioner that the state's method of selecting jurors from lists of taxpayers was a violation of the "equal protection" and "due process" clauses of the Fourteenth Amendment. The majority of the Court held that such a procedure was not invalid, despite the fact that the lists contained a higher proportion of whites than Negroes. Justice Reed, for the majority, stated:

We recognize the fact that these lists have a higher proportion of white citizens than of colored, doubtless due to inequality of educational and economic opportunities. While those who chose the names for the jury lists might have included names other than taxpayers, such action was not mandatory under state law. . . . We do not think a use, nondiscriminatory as to race, of the tax lists violates the Fourteenth Amendment, nor can we conclude on the evidence adduced that the results of the use require a conclusion of unconstitutionality.

As stated earlier, even though the general panel and the specific jury are chosen in accordance with statutory and constitutional requirements, subjection of the jury to improper pressures during the course of a trial may be sufficient to violate the accused's right to an impartial jury. This was the claim made in *Turner* v. *Louisiana*, 379 U.S. 466 (1965), in challenging a conviction for murder. During the three-day trial, two deputy sheriffs, who were the two principal prosecution witnesses, were charged with the supervision of the jurors. Thus they were in continuous company with the jurors. They drove the jurors to a restaurant for each meal, and to their lodgings each night. The deputies ate with them, conversed with them, and did errands for them.

Defendant's counsel moved for a mistrial when the deputies testified, but the court denied the motions on the ground that there was no showing that either deputy had talked with any member of the jury about the case itself. Defendant was convicted and sentenced to death, and the Louisiana Supreme Court affirmed.

On certiorari, the United States Supreme Court reversed, with Justice Clark filing the only dissenting vote. Justice Stewart, for the majority, discussed the due process problem:

In the constitutional sense, trial by jury in a criminal case necessarily implies at the very least that the "evidence developed" against a defendant shall come from the witness stand in a public courtroom where there is full judicial protection of the defendant's right of confrontation, of cross-examination, and of counsel. What happened in this case operated to subvert these basic guarantees of trial by jury.... [T]he credibility which the jury attached to the testimony of these two key witnesses must inevitably have determined whether Wayne Turner was to be sent to his death. To be sure, their credibility was assailed by Turner's counsel through cross-examination in open court. But the potentialities of what went on outside the courtroom during the three days of the trial may well have made these courtroom proceedings little more than a hollow formality....

... We deal here not with a brief encounter, but with a continuous and intimate association throughout a three-day trial—an association which gave these witnesses an opportunity, as [one deputy] put it, to renew old friendships and make new acquaintances among the members of the jury.... [T]he relationship was one which could not but foster the jurors' confidence in those who were their official guardians during the entire period of the trial. And Turner's fate depended upon how much confidence the jury placed in these two witnesses.

Justice Clark "with regret" dissented. In view of the fact that "no prejudice whatever is shown," and in view of the widespread acceptance of the practice of permitting an officer who testifies in a case also to be in charge of the jury, he felt that it could not be considered violative of the Fourteenth Amendment's "due process" clause.

[See generally, James Bradley Thayer, *A Preliminary Treatise on Evidence at the Common Law* (Boston: Little, Brown, 1898); Sir Patrick Devlin, *Trial by Jury* (London: Stevens, 1956); Felix Frankfurter and Thomas G. Corcoran, "Petty Federal Offenses and the Constitutional Guaranty of Trial by Jury," 39 *Harv. L. Rev.* 917 (1926); Lester B. Orfield, "Trial by Jury in Federal Criminal Procedure," 1962 *Duke L. J.* 29 (1962); on jury trial in contempt proceedings see Ronald L. Goldfarb and Stephen Kurzman, "Civil Rights v. Civil Liberties: The Jury Trial Issue," 12 *U.C.L.A. L. Rev.* 486 (1965).]

HABEAS CORPUS

There are several varieties of writs of habeas corpus. The one which is commonly referred to, however, as "the" writ, when the shorthand title is employed, is *habeas corpus ad subjiciendum et recipiendum*. It stems from the common law, with certain important extensions made by the famous Habeas Corpus Act adopted by Parliament in 1679. The writ is purely procedural in character. Its primary function is to provide a procedure whereby a speedy inquiry may be made by a judge into the legality of a detention on a criminal charge. More broadly, however, it can be used to test the legality of any restraint of person.

Since the writ is available to test the legality of detentions, it may be brought into play either before trial or after conviction and sentence. In the latter situation, however, it should be noted that habeas corpus is not a substitute for appeal. Allegations of error may be properly considered on appeal which are outside the scope of attack by habeas corpus. As a generalization, habeas corpus represents only a collateral attack on the detention, and concerns contentions which mainly reach questions of the jurisdiction of the committing court or agency. The Court has, however, tended to broaden the category of issues which it will accept as "jurisdictional questions." Under older approaches, a showing in a return to a writ that the prisoner was held under final process based upon a judgment of a court of competent jurisdiction closed the inquiry. This same rule was carried over into the Judiciary Act of 1789. But in 1867 Congress made a major change in the law. It extended the availability of the writ to state as well as federal prisoners, and made it applicable to restraints of liberty "in violation of the constitution, or of any treaty or law of the United States."

It should be clear that a court could have jurisdiction over a specific party and cause of action, but that procedures might be employed in the course of the trial "in violation of the constitution." Thus the act of 1867 opened the way for a much broader scope of "review" than was formerly the case. It still, however, does not permit the use of habeas corpus to reach ordinary assignments of error, such as an erroneous charge to the jury or the admission of improper evidence, where such claims do not rise to the status of constitutional rights. Thus appellate review should not be neglected under the mistaken belief that habeas corpus can serve the same purposes. While there is no time limit on the availability of the writ, unlike the situation with respect to appeals, the writ is narrower in its application. At the same time, there are procedural aspects of the use of the writ which afford more flexibility than is the case with appeal. Appeals are normally carried to a specified court, while any coordinate trial court may entertain a petition for habeas corpus.

That the scope of the writ is not confined to common-law rules or even, for that matter, to earlier American judicial interpretation, was made clear in *Johnson* v. *Zerbst*, 304 U.S. 458 (1938), discussed earlier in this chapter. In holding that habeas corpus was an appropriate remedy for attacking a federal conviction denying the Sixth Amendment right to counsel, the majority, through Justice Black, stated:

> The scope of inquiry in habeas corpus proceedings has been broadened—not narrowed—since the adoption of the Sixth Amendment. . . . A court's jurisdiction at the beginning of trial may be lost "in the course of the proceedings" due to failure to complete the court—as the Sixth Amendment requires—by providing Counsel for an accused who is unable to obtain Counsel, who has not intelligently waived this constitutional guaranty, and whose life or liberty is at stake. If this requirement of the Sixth Amendment is not complied with, the court no longer has jurisdiction to proceed. The judgment of conviction pronounced by a court without jurisdiction is void, and one imprisoned thereunder may obtain release by habeas corpus.

More recently, a majority of the Court asserted the right to expand the writ by judicial interpretation and to permit its use for a purpose unknown to the common law, to bring a prisoner into court to argue his own appeal. Justice Murphy, for the majority, in *Price* v. *Johnston*, 334 U.S. 266, 282 (1948), stated:

> [W]e do not conceive that a circuit court of appeals, in issuing a writ of *habeas corpus* under Section 262 of the Judicial Code, is necessarily confined to the precise forms of that writ in vogue at the common law or in the English judicial system. Section 262 says that the writ must be agreeable to the usages and principles of "law," a term which is unlimited by the common law or the English law. And since "law" is not a static concept, but expands and develops as new problems arise, we do not believe that the forms of the *habeas corpus* writ authorized by Section 262 are only those recognized in this country in 1789, when the original Judiciary Act containing the substance of this section came into existence.

A dramatic use for habeas corpus is illustrated by cases in which the evidence or testimony indicates that the whole trial proceedings are infected with basic unfairness. Such a case was *Moore* v. *Dempsey*, 261 U.S. 86 (1923), discussed earlier, where evidence showed the entire trial to have been under mob domination. Justice Holmes, for the majority, stated:

> We assume . . . that the corrective process supplied by the state may be so adequate that interference by habeas corpus ought not to be allowed. It certainly is true that mere mistakes of law in the course of a trial are not to be corrected in that way. But if the case is that the whole proceeding is a mask,—that counsel

jury, and judge were swept to the fatal end by an irresistible wave of public passion, and that the state courts failed to correct the wrong,—neither perfection in the machinery for correction nor the possibility that the trial court and counsel saw no other way of avoiding an immediate outbreak of the mob can prevent this court from securing to the petitioners their constitutional rights.

The general rule is that the writ of habeas corpus is unavailable unless the petitioner is under detention or in custody in some fashion. Thus in *Parker* v. *Ellis*, 362 U.S. 574 (1960), where the petition attacking the conviction on constitutional grounds was properly filed, but where the Court's review of denial of the writ came after the prisoner had completed the sentence, the Court dismissed on the ground that the case had become moot. Four justices dissented, with Chief Justice Warren vigorously contending that the "in custody" requirement was met at the time of filing the application for habeas corpus, and that no such requirement was relevant to the Court's ability to *grant relief* when the proper case was made out. "Rather, the federal courts are given a broad grant of authority to 'dispose of the matter as law and justice require.'" Petitioner had spent three years—out of a five-year sentence—attacking his conviction in state and federal courts. "Now that petitioner has dutifully fulfilled the requirement that he exhaust—an apt word—all other remedies, he is told that it is too late for the Court to act."

Although under this requirement habeas corpus would not have been available, in *United States* v. *Morgan*, 346 U.S. 502 (1954), the Court held that the writ of error *coram nobis* was available to petition the federal courts to set aside a conviction and sentence for a federal crime, even though petitioner had served the full term for which he had been sentenced. In that case Morgan was in state prison and serving a longer sentence as a second offender, and thus hoped to have this sentence reduced by having the judgment of conviction on the first crime (a federal offense) vacated.

In *Jones* v. *Cunningham*, 371 U.S. 236 (1963), the Court faced the question of whether the "in custody" requirement of 28 U.S.C. 2241 was sufficiently met in the supervisory control exercised over a parolee by the state parole board. Petitioner had been sentenced as a recidivist in state court and filed a petition for habeas corpus in federal district court alleging the invalidity of his conviction on the ground of denial of right to counsel. The superintendent of the prison was named as respondent. The petition was dismissed and appeal was taken. Before the appeal was argued, the prisoner was paroled, and he moved to add the parole board as respondents. The court of appeals refused on the ground that the board did not have physical custody of the prisoner and dismissed the petition on the ground that the case was moot because the petitioner was out of prison. On certiorari, the United States Supreme Court unanimously reversed. The Court agreed that the case was moot as to the prison superintendent, but it held that the stringent controls over the parolee exercised by the parole board met the "in custody" requirement of the statute necessary to the issuance of habeas corpus. The lower courts were thus ordered to proceed to a decision on the merits of petitioner's case.

For federal courts to intervene in state criminal process through the device of habeas corpus is, of course, to raise delicate questions of federal-state relations. For this reason, the federal code requires that state prisoners exhaust their state remedies, including habeas corpus, prior to petitioning federal courts for the writ. The normal appellate route for state prisoners is to proceed through the state courts as far as allowable, and then, if a federal question is presented, to petition the United States Supreme Court for certiorari. Since the writ of certiorari issues only in the sound discretion of the Supreme Court, most petitions are denied by the Court. Assuming that in a given case appellant is denied certiorari by the United States Supreme Court, petitions the state court for habeas corpus and has his petition dismissed, but still believes his claim to be valid, can he then petition the federal district court for the writ? The answer is yes, but there is a very slender chance of success. The technical aspects of the use of the writ in such cases are rather too complex for discussion in a generalized treatment of this sort, but they are taken up in some detail in *Brown* v. *Allen,* 344 U.S. 443 (1953). The Court decided a case in 1961, however, which illustrates some of the involved procedural gantlet through which a petitioner may have to travel and also the effect of issuance of the writ and discharge. The case was *Irvin* v. *Dowd,* involving a claim of jury partiality in a conviction for murder.

IRVIN *v.* DOWD
366 U.S. 717 (1961)

Mr. Justice Clark delivered the opinion of the Court.

This is a habeas corpus proceeding brought to test the validity of petitioner's conviction for murder and sentence of death in the Circuit Court of Gibson County, Indiana. The Indiana Supreme Court affirmed the conviction in Irvin v. State . . . , and we denied direct review by certiorari "without prejudice to filing for federal habeas corpus after exhausting state remedies." 353 U.S. 98. Petitioner immediately sought a writ of habeas corpus, under 28 USC Section 2241, in the District Court for the Northern District of Indiana, claiming that his conviction had been obtained in violation of the Fourteenth Amendment in that he did not receive a fair trial. That court dismissed the proceeding on the ground that petitioner had failed to exhaust his state remedies. 153 F. Supp. 531. On appeal, the Court of Appeals for the Seventh Circuit affirmed the dismissal. 251 F. 2d 548. We granted certiorari, 356 U.S. 948, and remanded to the Court of Appeals for decision on the merits or remand to the District Court for reconsideration. 359 U.S. 394. The Court of Appeals retained jurisdiction and decided the claim adversely to petitioner. 271 F. 2d 552. We granted certiorari, 361 U.S. 959.

As stated in the former opinion, 359 U.S., at 396, 397:

"The constitutional claim arises in this way. Six murders were committed in the vicinity of Evansville, Indiana, two in December 1954, and four in March

1955. The crimes, extensively covered by news media in the locality, aroused great excitement and indignation throughout Vanderburgh County, where Evansville is located, and adjoining Gibson County, a rural county of approximately 30,000 inhabitants. The petitioner was arrested on April 8, 1955. Shortly thereafter, the Prosecutor of Vanderburgh County and Evansville police officials issued press releases, which were intensively publicized, stating that the petitioner had confessed to the six murders. The Vanderburgh County Grand Jury soon indicted the petitioner for the murder which resulted in his conviction. This was the murder of Whitney Wesley Kerr allegedly committed in Vanderburgh County on December 23, 1954. Counsel appointed to defend petitioner immediately sought a change of venue from Vanderburgh County, which was granted, but to adjoining Gibson County. [Petitioner's motion for a change of venue alleged that the awaited trial of petitioner had become the cause célébre of this small community—so much so that curbstone opinions, not only as to petitioner's guilt but even as to what punishment he should receive, were solicited and recorded on the public streets by a roving reporter, and later were broadcast over the local stations.] Alleging that the widespread and inflammatory publicity had also highly prejudiced the inhabitants of Gibson County against the petitioner, counsel ... sought another change of venue, from Gibson County to a county sufficiently removed from the Evansville locality that a fair trial would not be prejudiced. The motion was denied, apparently because the pertinent Indiana statute allows only a single change of venue." During the course of the *voir dire* examination, which lasted some four weeks, petitioner filed two more motions for continuances. All were denied. . . .

[The Court then held that petitioner had not been tried by the impartial jury guaranteed by the Fourteenth Amendment.]

Petitioner's detention and sentence of death pursuant to the void judgment is in violation of the Constitution of the United States and he is therefore entitled to be freed therefrom. The judgments of the Court of Appeals and the District Court are vacated and the case remanded to the latter. However, petitioner is still subject to custody under the indictment filed by the State of Indiana in the Circuit Court of Gibson County charging him with murder in the first degree and may be tried on this or another indictment. The District Court has power, in a habeas corpus proceeding, to "dispose of the matter as law and justice require." 28 U.S.C. 2243. Under the predecessors of this section, "this Court has often delayed the discharge of the petitioner for such reasonable time as may be necessary to have him taken before the court where the judgment was rendered, that defects which render discharge necessary may be corrected." *Mahler* v. *Eby*, 264 U.S. 32, 46. Therefore, on remand, the District Court should enter such orders as are appropriate and consistent with this opinion ... which allow the State a reasonable time in which to retry petitioner. . . .

Vacated and remanded.

Mr. Justice Frankfurter, concurring. . . .

[See generally, Zechariah Chafee, "The Most Important Human Right in the Constitution," 32 *B. U. L. Rev.* 144 (1952); David Fellman, *The Defendant's Rights* (New York: Rinehart, 1958) Chap. 5; William J. Brennan, Jr., "Federal Habeas Corpus and State Prisoners: An Exercise in Federalism," 7 *Utah L. Rev.* 423 (1961); Curtis R. Reitz, "Federal Habeas

Corpus: Impact of an Abortive State Proceeding," 74 *Harv. L. Rev.* 1315 (1961); Paul M. Bator, "Finality in Criminal Law and Federal Habeas Corpus for State Prisoners," 76 *Harv. L. Rev.* 441 (1963).]

A specialized use of habeas corpus is its function as a narrow form of civil court review of military detention. Many of the procedural requirements of the Bill of Rights are made inapplicable to military trials. Article I of the Constitution authorizes Congress "to make rules for the government and regulation of the land and naval forces," and the Fifth Amendment, either specifically or by implication, exempts courts-martial from the requirements of grand jury indictment and jury trial. Under the Uniform Code of Military Justice, adopted by Congress in 1950, substantial guarantees in favor of the accused were added to the old provisions, and careful appellate review procedures are set out *within* the military establishment. The long-established rule, however, is that there is no ordinary appellate review by the civil courts over the judgments of courts-martial. [See Earl Warren, "The Bill of Rights and the Military," 37 *N.Y.U. L. Rev.* 181 (1962); James Snedeker, "Habeas Corpus and Court-Martial Prisoners," 6 *Vand. L. Rev.* 288 (1953).] For this reason, the writ of habeas corpus occupies an exceptional place in the relationship of the two systems. It is the single judicial remedy by which any civil collateral attack can be made on a military detention. And its application is severely limited to the single question of whether the sentencing court had jurisdiction.

As the Court said in *Hiatt* v. *Brown*, 339 U.S. 103 (1950), "It is well settled that 'by habeas corpus the civil courts exercise no supervisory or correcting power over the proceedings of a court-martial. . . . The single inquiry, the test, is jurisdiction.' *Re Grimley*, 137 U.S. 147 (1890)." A case illustrative of the utility of habeas corpus to test military court jurisdiction is that of *Toth* v. *Quarles*, decided in 1955.

UNITED STATES *ex rel.* TOTH *v.* QUARLES

350 U.S. 11 (1955)

Mr. Justice Black delivered the opinion of the Court.

After serving with the United States Air Force in Korea, Robert W. Toth was honorably discharged. He returned to his home in Pittsburgh and went to work in a steel plant. Five months later he was arrested by military authorities on charges of murder and conspiracy to commit murder while an airman in Korea. At the time of arrest he had no relationship of any kind with the military. He was taken to Korea to stand trial before a court-martial under authority of a 1950 Act of Congress. The Court of Appeals sustained the Act, rejecting the contention that civilian ex-servicemen like Toth could not constitutionally be subjected to trial by court-martial. . . . We granted certiorari to pass upon this important constitutional question. . . .

This Court has held that the Article I clause just quoted authorizes Congress to subject persons actually in the armed service to trial by court-martial for military and naval offenses. Later it was held that court-martial jurisdiction could be exerted over a dishonorably discharged soldier then a military prisoner serving a sentence imposed by a prior court-martial. It has never been intimated by this Court, however, that Article I military jurisdiction could be extended to civilian ex-soldiers who had severed all relationship with the military and its institutions. To allow this extension of military authority would require an extremely broad construction of the language used in the constitutional provision relied on. For given its natural meaning, the power granted Congress "To make Rules" or regulate "the land and naval Forces" would seem to restrict court-martial jurisdiction to persons who are actually members or part of the armed forces. There is a compelling reason for construing the clause this way: any expansion of court-martial jurisdiction like that in the 1950 Act necessarily encroaches on the jurisdiction of federal courts set up under Article III of the Constitution where persons on trial are surrounded with more constitutional safeguards than in military tribunals.

Article III provides for the establishment of a court system as one of the separate but coordinate branches of the National Government. It is the primary, indeed the sole business of these courts to try cases and controversies between individuals and between individuals and the Government. This includes trial of criminal cases. These courts are presided over by judges appointed for life, subject only to removal by impeachment. Their compensation cannot be diminished during their continuance in office. The provisions of Article III were designed to give judges maximum freedom from possible coercion or influence by the executive or legislative branches of the Government. But the Constitution and the Amendments in the Bill of Rights show that the Founders were not satisfied with leaving determination of guilt or innocence to judges, even though wholly independent. They further provided that no person should be held to answer in those courts for capital or other infamous crimes unless on the presentment or indictment of a grand jury drawn from the body of the people. Other safeguards designed to protect defendants against oppressive governmental practices were included. . . .

We find nothing in the history or constitutional treatment of military tribunals which entitles them to rank along with Article III courts as adjudicators of the guilt or innocence of people charged with offenses for which they can be deprived of their life, liberty or property. Unlike courts, it is the primary business of armies and navies to fight or be ready to fight wars should the occasion arise. But trial of soldiers to maintain discipline is merely incidental to an army's primary fighting function. To the extent that those responsible for performance of this primary function are diverted from it by the necessity of trying cases, the basic fighting purpose of armies is not served. And conceding to military personnel that high degree of honesty and sense of justice which nearly all of them undoubtedly have, it still remains true that military tribunals have not been and probably never can be constituted in such way that they can have the same kind of qualifications that the Constitution has deemed essential to fair trials of civilians in federal courts. For instance, the Constitution does not provide life tenure for those performing judicial functions in military trials. They are appointed by military commanders and may be removed at will. Nor does the Constitution protect their salaries as it does judicial salaries. Strides have been made toward making courts-martial less subject to the will of the executive department which appoints, supervises and ultimately controls them. But from the very nature of things, courts have more independence in passing on the life and liberty of people than do military tribunals. . . .

Fear has been expressed that if this law is not sustained discharged soldiers may escape punishment altogether for crimes they commit while in the service. But that fear is not warranted and was not shared by the Judge Advocate General of the Army who made a strong statement against passage of the law. He asked Congress to "confer jurisdiction upon Federal courts to try any person for an offense denounced by the [military] code if he is no longer subject thereto. This would be consistent with the fifth amendment of the Constitution.". . . It is conceded that it was wholly within the constitutional power of Congress to follow this suggestion and provide for federal district court trials of discharged soldiers accused of offenses committed while in the armed services. This concession is justified. U.S. Const., Art. III, Section 2. . . . There can be no valid argument, therefore, that civilian ex-servicemen must be tried by court-martial or not tried at all. If that is so it is only because Congress has not seen fit to subject them to trial in federal district courts.

None of the other reasons suggested by the Government are sufficient to justify a broad construction of the constitutional grant of power to Congress to regulate the armed forces. That provision itself does not empower Congress to deprive people of trials under Bill of Rights safeguards, and we are not willing to hold that power to circumvent those safeguards should be inferred through the Necessary and Proper Clause. It is impossible to think that the discipline of the Army is going to be disrupted, its morale impaired, or its orderly processes disturbed, by giving ex-servicemen the benefit of a civilian court trial when they are actually civilians. And we are not impressed by the fact that some other countries which do not have our Bill of Rights indulge in the practice of subjecting civilians who were once soldiers to trials by courts-martial instead of trials by civilian courts.

Determining the scope of the constitutional power of Congress to authorize trial by court-martial presents another instance calling for limitation to *"the least possible power adequate to the end proposed."* We hold that Congress cannot subject civilians like Toth to trial by court-martial. They, like other civilians, are entitled to have the benefit of safeguards afforded those tried in the regular courts authorized by Article III of the Constitution.

[Justice Reed, joined by Justices Burton and Minton, dissented. Justice Minton, joined by Justice Burton, dissented.]

See Chapter 9 for *O'Callahan* v. *Parker*, 395 U.S. 258 (1969), involving court-martial jurisdiction over nonservice-connected crimes of soldiers.)

A final aspect of the writ of habeas corpus concerns the form and the procedure accompanying its use. The prisoner or his lawyer or a friend petitions an appropriate judge to issue the writ. While there is no rigid requirement of a particular form, there are certain essential allegations and statements of fact which must be presented in order for consideration to be given the petition. Illustrative of the general pattern is the following type of petition to a federal District Court Judge:

To the Honorable _____ Judge, of the United States District Court, for the District of _____, _____ Division.

Your petitioner [name] alleges that he is unlawfully imprisoned and detained by _____ in the [institution] in the city of _____, county of _____ under and by virtue of a pretended writ or warrant issued by [identity of judge or officer issuing warrant or commitment, if known]. His imprisonment and detention are unlawful in that [statement of facts showing illegality]. The petitioner has exhausted all other remedies before filing this petition. [Statement of facts showing what federal, state or administrative remedies, as the case may be, have been sought and the disposition of such requests.]

Wherefore _____, your petitioner, prays that a Writ of Habeas Corpus issue out of this court to _____, commanding him forthwith to have the body of this petitioner before the court together with the cause of his detention and to abide the further order of the court herein.

_____,
Petitioner

Dated _____, 19__

Upon receipt of such a petition alleging facts which would support a charge of illegal detention, the judge issues the writ, directed to the warden or other person detaining the petitioner, ordering him to bring the prisoner before the judge for hearing. While the judge may doubt the authenticity of the claims of petitioner, if a proper statement is made, the writ issues. However, as Justice Jackson pointed out in *Brown* v. *Allen,* 344 U.S. 443, 547 (1953), "Unless it state facts which, if proved, would warrant relief, the applicant is not entitled as of right to a hearing." This factor normally presents no problem to the prisoner, however, since most penitentiaries have among the inmates at least one expert on drawing petitions for habeas corpus. Judges have often complained, however, that since the issuance of the writ is very nearly automatic and since there is no limit on the number of petitions a prisoner may file, that the writ is all too often used merely as a device to get a few days vacation from the prison. Justice Jackson, again in *Brown* v. *Allen,* stated:

[T]his Court has sanctioned progressive trivialization of the writ until floods of stale, frivolous and repetitious petitions inundate the docket of the lower courts and swell our own. Judged by our own disposition of habeas corpus matters, they have, as a class, become peculiarly undeserving. It must prejudice the occasional meritorious application to be buried in a flood of worthless ones. He who must search a haystack for a needle is likely to end up with the attitude that the needle is not worth the search. Nor is it any answer to say that few of these petitions in any court really result in the discharge of the petitioner. That is condemnation of the procedure which has encouraged frivolous cases.

The "needle" referred to by Justice Jackson turns out to represent between 1 percent and 2 percent of the total petitions handled in federal courts. Many people, especially the prisoners concerned, feel that even this small return on the time invested is worth the effort.

The writ itself, as in the case of the petition, follows no ritualistic formula. In federal proceedings it issues in the name of the President of the

United States, is directed to the jailer, and commands him to bring both the prisoner and an explanation of the cause of his detention. A sample form is the following:

[Title of court.]

In the Matter of _____, On Habeas Corpus,

No. _____.

The President of the United States of America

To: _____, or any other person having the body of _____ in custody.

Greeting:

We command you, that you have the body of _____, by you imprisoned and detained, as it is said, with the time and cause of such imprisonment and detention, before me, or one of the other judges sitting at a term of this court for the hearing of motions, to be held at room _____, _____ Building, City of _____, County of _____, on the _____ day of _____, 19__, at [time], to do and receive what shall then and there be considered concerning him and have you then and there this writ.

Witness, Honorable _____, United States District Judge, _____ District of _____ the _____ day of _____, One Thousand Nine Hundred and _____.

_____,
                                                                       Clerk.

Allowed: _____

_____,
U.S.D.J.

At the hearing following the writ, petitioner is then required to prove his allegations, either from the record or by witnesses or both. If he does so, the court issues an order discharging the prisoner. If he fails, the court issues an order dismissing the writ, and the prisoner is remanded to the custody of the jailer for return to prison. It should be recalled, however, that under the federal code, as indicated in *Irvin* v. *Dowd,* above, the court has the power in habeas corpus proceedings to "dispose of the matter as law and justice require." Thus if the petitioner's allegations merely entitle him to a new trial and not outright freedom, the court may, as in *Irvin* v. *Dowd,* vacate his judgment of conviction but return him to custody to await retrial.

CRUEL AND UNUSUAL PUNISHMENTS

The Eighth Amendment provides that "cruel and unusual punishments" shall not be inflicted. The phraseology derives from the English Bill of Rights of 1689, and similar provisions were found in colonial records in this country. Presumably the guarantee bars such ancient practices as branding, drawing and quartering, burning alive, or crucifixion. But the death penalty as such has not been held to violate the provision as long as it is carried out without unnecessary cruelty. In upholding execution by a firing squad, in *Wilkerson* v. *Utah,* 99 U.S. 130 (1879), the Court stated, "Difficulty would attend the effort to define with exactness the extent of the constitutional provision which provides that cruel and unusual punishments shall not be inflicted, but it is safe to affirm that punishments of torture,... and all others in the same line of unnecessary cruelty, are forbidden by that Amendment to the Constitution."

Not only the *manner* of punishment but also the severity of the penalty in relation to the crime has been considered an appropriate issue within the scope of the guarantee. In *Weems* v. *United States,* 217 U.S. 349 (1910), the Court held invalid a Philippine statute prescribing fine and imprisonment in irons from twelve to twenty years for entry of a known false statement in a public record, on the ground that the gross disparity between this punishment and that imposed for other more serious crimes violated the prohibition against cruel and unusual punishments.

In *Louisiana ex rel. Francis* v. *Resweber,* 329 U.S. 459 (1947), four members of the Court assumed, "but without so deciding," that the Eighth Amendment's prohibition was binding on the states through the Fourteenth Amendment. The case involved a claim of cruel and unusual punishment where petitioner had been placed in the electric chair and the switch thrown, without consequent death, and the subsequent setting of a second date for execution. The state contended that the failure was due to a mechanical defect, that it was unintended, and that a subsequent execution would not be a denial of due process. The petitioner contended that to force him to undergo the strain of preparing for execution, actually to place him in the electric chair and throw the switch, and then to send him back to prison to be subjected to the whole process again, was a cruel and unusual punishment even if unintentional. By a five-to-four vote the Court upheld the state's position, stressing that it was an unforeseeable accident with "no purpose to inflict unnecessary pain." Four justices dissented, pointing out that the intent of the executioner was immaterial to the issue of cruel and unusual punishment, and protesting "death by installments."

In *Trop* v. *Dulles,* 356 U.S. 86 (1958), the Court held invalid the denationalization of a native-born citizen convicted by a court-martial of desertion from the military or naval forces in time of war and dismissed or dishonorably discharged. One of the grounds for invalidation was that divestiture of citizenship in such case was a cruel and unusual punishment. Chief Justice Warren, speaking for four members of the Court, said "This Court has had little occasion to give precise content to the Eighth Amendment," but the scope of the Amendment "is not static. The Amendment must draw its meaning from the evolving standards of decency that mark the progress of a maturing society."

On the merits, the Chief Justice stated that denationalization in this case was a violation of the Eighth Amendment:

There may be involved no physical mistreatment, no primitive torture. There is instead the total destruction of the individual's status in organized society. It is a form of punishment more primitive than torture, for it destroys for the individual the political existence that was centuries in the development. . . . His very existence is at the sufferance of the country in which he happens to find himself. . . . In short, the expatriate has lost the right to have rights.

Concurring separately, Justice Brennan agreed that such punishment was unduly severe in relationship to the power Congress was exercising, but he stopped short of holding it violative of the Eighth Amendment.

More recently, in *Robinson* v. *California*, 370 U.S. 660 (1962), the Court held invalid a California statute making it a misdemeanor for a person to "be addicted to the use of narcotics," subject to a mandatory jail term of not less than 90 days. Justice Stewart, speaking for five members of the Court, pointed out that the statute was not the usual one which punished for the use, purchase, sale, or possession of narcotics, but it was rather a statute "which makes the 'status' of narcotic addiction a criminal offense, for which the offender may be prosecuted 'at any time before he reforms.' " He concluded:

We hold that a state law which imprisons a person thus afflicted as a criminal, even though he has never touched any narcotic drug within the State or been guilty of any irregular behavior there, inflicts a cruel and unusual punishment in violation of the Fourteenth Amendment. To be sure, imprisonment for ninety days is not, in the abstract, a punishment which is either cruel or unusual. But the question cannot be considered in the abstract. Even one day in prison would be a cruel and unusual punishment for the "crime" of having a common cold.

In concurring, Justice Douglas elaborated further the reasons why the statute was violative of the prohibition against cruel and unusual punishments.

A dissenting opinion to a memorandum decision of the Court denying a petition for certiorari is an unusual place for a new constitutional issue to be raised. But three justices took such an occasion to express themselves in *Rudolph* v. *Alabama*, 375 U.S. 889 (1963). Justice Goldberg, joined by Justice Douglas and Justice Brennan, dissented from the denial of certiorari:

I would grant certiorari in this case . . . to consider whether the Eighth and Fourteenth Amendments to the United States Constitution permit the imposition of the death penalty on a convicted rapist who has neither taken nor endangered human life.

The following questions, *inter alia,* seem relevant and worthy of argument and consideration:

(1) In light of the trend both in this country and throughout the world against punishing rape by death, does the imposition of the death penalty by those States

which retain it for rape violate "evolving standards of decency that mark the progress of [our] maturing society," or "standards of decency more or less universally accepted?"

(2) Is the taking of human life to protect a value other than human life consistent with the constitutional proscription against "punishments which by their excessive ... severity are greatly disproportioned to the offenses charged?"

(3) Can the permissible aims of punishment (e.g., deterrence, isolation, rehabilitation) be achieved as effectively by punishing rape less severely than by death (e.g., by life imprisonment); if so, does the imposition of the death penalty for rape constitute "unnecessary cruelty?"

Several years have now passed without a decision to date on the questions raised by Justice Goldberg, but they nonetheless raise interesting Eighth Amendment considerations. Certainly the Court has taken a somewhat more active interest in the applications of this Amendment in the past decade, and it may be anticipated that litigation in this area will probably increase.

[On cruel and unusual punishments generally, see David Fellman, *The Defendant's Rights* (New York: Rinehart, 1958) Chap. 11; Note, "The Constitutional Prohibition against Cruel and Unusual Punishment—Its Present Significance," 4 *Vand. L. Rev.* 680 (1951); Arthur E. Sutherland, Jr., "Due Process and Cruel Punishment," 64 *Harv. L. Rev.* 271 (1950); James S. Campbell, "Revival of the Eighth Amendment: Development of Cruel Punishment Doctrine by the Supreme Court," 16 *Stan. L. Rev.* 996 (1964).]

CHAPTER 5

Religious Freedom

THE part played by religious enthusiasts in the settlement and development of America is an oft-told story. What is sometimes overlooked, however, is the fact that religious liberty did not reach fruition with the landing of the Pilgrims. On the contrary, the attainment of the present broad measure of religious freedom in America is a story of long, and sometimes bitter, struggle extending over more than three centuries. Even today, there are controverted areas of policy and practice in which various minority sects are claiming abridgment of their constitutional guarantees of religious liberty.

The Puritans brought with them to New England the conviction that men have a right and a duty to associate voluntarily for religious purposes. For this group, however, religious freedom meant only freedom to practice the true faith—Puritanism. They not only did not accept the principle of religious toleration; they went further and used the arm of government both to prosecute dissenters and to enforce observance of certain of the church laws. Thus we have depicted in the history of the Massachusetts Bay Colony two of the primary enemies of religious freedom—active support of religion by the government and governmental suppression of certain religious exercises.

In Massachusetts Bay Puritanism was the official faith. In the Virginia charter of 1609 the doctrine and rites of the Church of England were established by law. While most other faiths were apparently to be tolerated, the charter particularly excluded "persons who affected the 'superstitions of the Church of Rome.'" In New Netherlands the Dutch Reformed Church had the exclusive right of public worship. And in the Spanish colonies the Inquisition was imported to guarantee the repression of non-Catholic heresies.

At the midseventeenth century only two of the English colonies, Rhode Island and Maryland, offered substantial religious freedom. Not until almost the outbreak of the Revolutionary War did the attitude on religious liberty begin to soften and governmental policy toward minority sects show signs of easing. Changes in the law followed, with Virginia leading the way by its adoption of religious toleration in the Declaration of Rights accompanying its 1776 constitution. Pennsylvania in the same year and Massachusetts in 1780 guaranteed to all faiths the freedom to worship publicly. These were measures directed to *one* of the problems of religious freedom—that of *free exercise* of religion. And while they were important gains, they represented actually only a strong start along a long road. Some of the most important developments, in fact, have come in the period since 1940.

Another major hurdle to overcome in the advance toward religious freedom was disestablishment and the abolition of taxation for religious purposes. These problems arise from the presence of *active government support* of religion, especially where the support is for a specific religion. Modifications were made in the latter years of the Revolution, and in 1785 Jefferson's famous Act for Establishing Religious Freedom passed the Virginia legislature. Other states followed, although New England was much slower to succumb to the trend. The Connecticut constitution of 1818 provided for separation of church and state, but this chapter of the struggle was not closed until the last state, Massachusetts, adopted a constitutional amendment in 1833 to remove the state from active promotion of a particular religion.

Since 1833, and particularly since the end of World War II, the problem of governmental support of religion has broadened, and the controversies have presented issues more difficult of logical resolution. There is probably fairly general agreement in the United States that government should not actively show a preference for one religious sect. But suppose government promotes all religious sects equally. Does this present a threat to religious freedom? Does the fact that the overwhelming majority of people in the United States profess a preference for Christianity justify Sunday Closing Laws? Is religious liberty endangered by either promoting or permitting religious exercises in the public schools? Does government act improperly if it includes religious schools among the beneficiaries of aid-to-education appropriation bills? These questions are less easily disposed of than those involving the clear-cut issue of preferential treatment.

The theory behind the argument for virtually complete separation of church and state is fairly easy to state. It rests on a view that religious liberty is best protected when government remains absolutely neutral on matters of religion. The problem, however, is that one man's neutrality is another man's hostility. To some, government is neutral toward religion if it does not support or even permit religious exercises in public schools during the school day. It is neither promoting sectarian religion nor is it prohibiting the child from engaging in religious observance, so long as it takes place outside the ambit of public school activities. To others, the denial of permission to use a portion of the school day for religious exercises is to *interfere* with religious freedom and therefore is outright governmental hostility. The newer cases raising the separation issue have presented questions which are more and more difficult of logical resolution. The result has frequently been more readily defensible as simply a convenient place to draw the line, rather than the logical necessities of applying the broad principle of "separation of church and state."

The two aspects of religious liberty—freedom from governmental establishment of religion and the free exercise of religion—will be taken up separately in this chapter. In the First Amendment both aspects are covered, in the phrase "Congress shall make no law respecting an establishment of religion, or prohibiting the free exercise thereof."

SEPARATION OF CHURCH AND STATE

The "establishment" clause of the First Amendment has long since been rephrased in the general literature and in the popular mind to become simply a guarantee of "separation of church and state." The controversy over separation in America has its roots in the debate between John Cotton and Roger Williams in Massachusetts Bay Colony in the first half of the seventeenth century. It has continued at intervals ever since. But the first case to reach the United States Supreme Court in which the Court really came to grips with the question of applying the First Amendment's "establishment" clause (albeit through the Fourteenth Amendment) did not arrive until 1947. State courts for some years have been faced with establishment issues, although most of these are of twentieth century vintage. Thus we have the somewhat strange situation of a burgeoning body of relatively new case law on a controversy which in America is as old as the colonial settlements themselves.

Aid to Religious Schools

EVERSON v. BOARD OF EDUCATION
330 U.S. 1 (1947)

Mr. Justice Black delivered the opinion of the Court.

A New Jersey statute authorizes its local school districts to make rules and contracts for the transportation of children to and from schools.* The appellee, a township board of education, acting pursuant to this statute, authorized reimbursement to parents of money expended by them for the bus transportation of their children on regular busses operated by the public transportation system. Part of this money was for the payment of transportation of some children in the community to Catholic parochial schools. These church schools give their students, in addition to secular education, regular religious instruction conforming to the religious tenets and modes of worship of the Catholic Faith. The superintendent of these schools is a Catholic priest.

The appellant, in his capacity as a district taxpayer, filed suit in a State court challenging the right of the Board to reimburse parents of parochial school students. He contended that the statute and the resolution passed pursuant to it violated both the State and the Federal Constitutions. That court held that the legislature was without power to authorize such payment under the State constitution. 132 N.J.L. 98. The New Jersey Court of Errors and Appeals reversed, holding that

* "Whenever in any district there are children living remote from any schoolhouse, the board of education of the district may make rules and contracts for the transportation of such children to and from school, including the transportation of school children to and from school other than a public school, except such school as is operated for profit in whole or in part...."

neither the statute nor the resolution passed pursuant to it was in conflict with the State constitution or the provisions of the Federal Constitution in issue. 133 N.J.L. 350. The case is here on appeal under 28 U.S.C. Section 344(a).

Since there has been no attack on the statute on the ground that a part of its language excludes children attending private schools operated for profit from enjoying State payment for their transportation, we need not consider this exclusionary language; it has no relevancy to any constitutional question here presented. Furthermore, if the exclusion clause had been properly challenged, we do not know whether New Jersey's highest court would construe its statutes as precluding payment of the school transportation of any group of pupils, even those of a private school run for profit. Consequently, we put to one side the question as to the validity of the statute against the claim that it does not authorize payment for the transportation generally of school children in New Jersey.

The only contention here is that the State statute and the resolution, insofar as they authorized reimbursement to parents of children attending parochial schools, violate the Federal Constitution in these two respects, which to some extent overlap. First. They authorize the State to take by taxation the private property of some and bestow it upon others, to be used for their own private purposes. This, it is alleged, violates the due process clause of the Fourteenth Amendment. Second. The statute and the resolution forced inhabitants to pay taxes to help support and maintain schools which are dedicated to, and which regularly teach, the Catholic Faith. This is alleged to be a use of State power to support church schools contrary to the prohibition of the First Amendment which the Fourteenth Amendment made applicable to the states. . . .

It is much too late to argue that legislation intended to facilitate the opportunity of children to get a secular education serves no public purposes. . . . The same thing is no less true of legislation to reimburse needy parents, or all parents, for payment of the fares of their children so that they can ride in public busses to and from schools rather than run the risk of traffic and other hazards incident to walking or "hitch-hiking." . . . Nor does it follow that a law has a private rather than a public purpose because it provided that tax-raised funds will be paid to reimburse individuals on account of money spent by them in a way which furthers a public program. . . . Subsidies and loans to individuals such as farmers and home owners, and to privately owned transportation systems, as well as many other kinds of businesses, have been common-place practice in our state and national history. . . .

Second. The new Jersey statute is challenged as a "law respecting the establishment of religion." The First Amendment, as made applicable to the states by the Fourteenth, *Murdock* v. *Pennsylvania,* 319 U.S. 105, commands that a state "shall make no law respecting an establishment of religion, or prohibiting the free exercise thereof." . . . These words of the First Amendment reflected in the minds of early Americans a vivid mental picture of conditions and practices which they fervently wished to stamp out in order to preserve liberty for themselves and for their posterity. Doubtless their goal has not been entirely reached; but so far has the Nation moved toward it that the expression "law respecting the establishment of religion," probably does not so vividly remind present-day Americans of the evils, fears, and political problems that caused that expression to be written into our Bill of Rights. Whether this New Jersey law is one respecting the "establishment of religion" requires an understanding of the meaning of that language, particularly with respect to the imposition of taxes. Once again, therefore, it is not inappropriate briefly to review the background and environment of the period in which that constitutional language was fashioned and adopted.... [Here the opinion reviews the historical events and concludes with the interpretation that the First Amendment was intended to bar the government from adopting measures to "tax, to support, or otherwise to assist any or all religions...."]

The "establishment of religion" clause of the First Amendment means at least this: Neither a state nor the Federal Government can set up a church. Neither can pass laws which aid one religion, aid all religions, or prefer one religion over another. Neither can force nor influence a person to go to or to remain away from church against his will or force him to profess a belief or disbelief in any religion. No person can be punished for entertaining or professing religious beliefs or disbeliefs, for church attendance or non-attendance. No tax in any amount, large or small, can be levied to support any religious activities or institutions, whatever they may be called, or whatever form they may adopt to teach or practice religion. Neither a state nor the Federal Government can, openly or secretly, participate in the affairs of any religious organizations or groups and vice versa. In the words of Jefferson, the clause against establishment of religion by law was intended to erect "a wall of separation between Church and State." *Reynolds* v. *United States,* 98 U.S. 145, 164.

We must consider the New Jersey statute in accordance with the foregoing limitations imposed by the First Amendment. But we must not strike that state statute down if it is within the State's constitutional power even though it approaches the verge of that power.... New Jersey cannot consistently with the "establishment of religion" clause of the First Amendment contribute tax-raised funds to the support of an institution which teaches the tenets and faith of any church. On the other hand, other language of the amendment commands that New Jersey cannot hamper its citizens in the free exercise of their own religion. Consequently, it cannot exclude individual Catholics, Lutherans, Mohammedans, Baptists, Jews, Methodists, Non-believers, Presbyterians, or the members of any other faith, *because of their faith, or lack of it,* from receiving the benefits of public welfare legislation. While we do not mean to intimate that a state could not provide transportation only to children attending public schools, we must be careful, in protecting the citizens of New Jersey against state-established churches, to be sure that we do not inadvertently prohibit New Jersey from extending its general state law benefits to all its citizens without regard to their religious belief.

Measured by these standards, we cannot say that the First Amendment prohibits New Jersey from spending tax-raised funds to pay the bus fares of parochial school pupils as a part of a general program under which it pays the fares of pupils attending public and other schools. It is undoubtedly true that children are helped to get to church schools. There is even a possibility that some of the children might not be sent to the church schools if the parents were compelled to pay their children's bus fares out of their own pockets when transportation to a public school would have been paid for by the state. The same possibility exists where the state requires a local transit company to provide reduced fares to school children including those attending parochial schools, or where a municipally owned transportation system undertakes to carry all school children free of charge. Moreover, state-paid policemen, detailed to protect children going to and from church schools from the very real hazards of traffic, would serve much the same purpose and accomplish much the same result as state provisions intended to guarantee free transportation of a kind which the state deems to be best for the school children's welfare. And parents might refuse to risk their children to the serious danger of traffic accidents going to and from parochial schools, the approaches to which were not protected by policemen. Similarly, parents might be reluctant to permit their children to attend schools which the state had cut off from such general government services as ordinary police and fire protection, connections for sewage disposal, public highways and sidewalks. Of course, cutting off church schools from these services, so separate and so indisputably marked off from the religious function, would make it far more difficult for the schools to operate. But such is obviously not the purpose of the First Amendment. That Amendment requires the state to be neutral in its relations with groups of religious believers and non-believers; it does not require the state to be their adversary. State power is no more to be used so as to handicap religions than it is to favor them.

This Court has said that parents may, in the discharge of their duty under state compulsory education laws, send their children to a religious rather than a public school if the school meets the secular educational requirements which the state has power to impose. See *Pierce* v. *Society of Sisters*, 268 U.S. 510. It appears that these parochial schools meet New Jersey's requirements. The state contributes no money to the schools. It does not support them. Its legislation, as applied, does no more than provide a general program to help parents get their children, regardless of their religion, safely and expeditiously to and from accredited schools.

The First Amendment has erected a wall between church and state. That wall must be kept high and impregnable. We could not approve the slightest breach. New Jersey has not breached it here.

Affirmed.

Mr. Justice Jackson, dissenting....

Whether the taxpayer constitutionally can be made to contribute aid to parents of students because of their attendance at parochial schools depends upon the nature of those schools and their relation to the Church....

It is no exaggeration to say that the whole historic conflict in temporal policy between the Catholic Church and non-Catholics comes to a focus in their respective school policies. The Roman Catholic Church, counseled by experience in many ages and many lands and with all sorts and conditions of men, takes what, from the viewpoint of its own progress and the success of its mission, is a wise estimate of the importance of education to religion. It does not leave the individual to pick up religion by chance. It relies on early and indelible indoctrination in the faith and order of the Church by the word and example of persons consecrated to the task....

I should be surprised if any Catholic would deny that the parochial school is a vital, if not the most vital, part of the Roman Catholic Church. If put to the choice, that venerable institution, I should expect, would forego its whole service for mature persons before it would give up education of the young, and it would be a wise choice. Its growth and cohesion, discipline and loyalty, spring from its schools. Catholic education is the rock on which the whole structure rests, and to render tax aid to its Church school is indistinguishable to me from rendering the same aid to the Church itself.

It is of no importance in this situation whether the beneficiary of this expenditure of tax-raised funds is primarily the parochial school and incidentally the pupil, or whether the aid is directly bestowed on the pupil with indirect benefits to the school. The state cannot maintain a Church and it can no more tax its citizens to furnish free carriage to those who attend a Church. The prohibition against establishment of religion cannot be circumvented by a subsidy, bonus or reimbursement of expense to individuals for receiving religious instruction and indoctrination. . . .

Mr. Justice Frankfurter joins in this opinion.

Mr. Justice Rutledge, with whom Mr. Justice Frankfurter, Mr. Justice Jackson and Mr. Justice Burton agree, dissenting. . . .

This case forces us to determine squarely for the first time what was "an establishment of religion" in the First Amendment's conception; and by that measure to decide whether New Jersey's action violates its command.

[Here the opinion contains a survey of the "generating history" of the religious clause of the First Amendment.]

In view of this history no further proof is needed that the Amendment forbids any appropriation, large or small, from public funds to aid or support any and all religious exercises. But if more were called for, the debates in the First Congress and this Court's consistent expressions, whenever it has touched on the matter directly, supply it. . . .

Compulsory attendance upon religious exercises went out early in the process of separating church and state, together with forced observance of religious forms and ceremonies. Test oaths and religious qualification for office followed later. These things none devoted to our great tradition of religious liberty would think of bringing back. Hence today, apart from efforts to inject religious training or exercises and sectarian issues into the public schools, the only serious surviving threat to maintaining that complete and permanent separation of religion and civil power which the First Amendment commands is through use of the taxing power to support religion, religious establishments, or establishments having a religious foundation whatever their form or special religious function.

Does New Jersey's action furnish support for religion by use of the taxing power? Certainly it does, if the test remains undiluted as Jefferson and Madison made it, that money taken by taxation from one is not to be used or given to support another's religious training or belief, or indeed one's own. Today as then the furnishing of "contributions of money for the propagation of opinions which he disbelieves" is the forbidden exaction; and the prohibition is absolute for whatever measure brings that consequence and whatever amount may be sought or given to that end.

The funds used here were raised by taxation. The Court does not dispute, nor could it, that their use does in fact give aid and encouragement to religious instruction. It only concludes that this aid is not "support" in law. But Madison and Jefferson were concerned with aid and support in fact, not as a legal conclusion "entangled in precedents.". . . Here parents pay money to send their children to parochial school and funds raised by taxation are used to reimburse them. This not only helps the children to get to school and the parents to send them. It aids them in a substantial way to get the very thing which they are sent to the particular school to secure, namely, religious training and teaching. . . .

Despite the close vote in the case and the controversy aroused by the decision, *Everson* remains as ruling law on the bus transportation issue. However, the earlier cautions concerning the impact of federalism on civil rights must be called to mind here. All the Court held in *Everson* was that the New Jersey bus transportation scheme did not violate the United States Constitution. Obviously the case did not hold that the state was *required* to furnish such transportation. Less obviously, perhaps, it in no way foreclosed a decision by the state courts that such a scheme would violate *state* constitutional provisions relative to separation of church and state. In our federal system the state supreme court is the final judge of the construction of the state constitution. And a practice may be held violative of state constitutional provisions even though it does not offend against the United States Constitution, and even though the constitutional phraseology is identical. In fact, the bus transportation issue was litigated under state constitutional provisions in several states both before and after the *Everson* decision, and the weight of authority among the state courts is against such transportation. [The cases are canvassed in David Fellman, *Religion in American Public Law* (Boston: Boston University Press, 1965), pp. 81–83.]

The most recent controversy involving public assistance to sectarian education concerned the proposed federal grants to elementary and secondary schools. President Kennedy's proposals in 1961 contemplated assistance only to the *public* schools. Pressure developed to extend the assistance to private schools as well, including sectarian schools. President Kennedy stated his belief that federal grants and across-the-board loans to sectarian schools would violate the First Amendment. On March 28, 1961, Secretary of Health, Education and Welfare Abraham Ribicoff submitted to Senate Labor and Public Welfare Education Subcommittee Chairman Wayne Morse a legal brief prepared by the Administration on the constitutionality of federal aid to parochial schools. The brief stated that "the permissible area of legislation which renders incidental benefits to church schools is not clear." But there was a categorical statement that "Federal grants to sectarian schools for general educational purposes would run squarely into the prohibitions of the First Amendment as interpreted in the *Everson*, *McCollum* and *Zorach* cases." [See Note, 50 *Geo. L. J.* 351 (1961).]

The positions of those who opposed and those who supported federal aid to church-related schools were compromised in the passage of the Elementary and Secondary School Improvement Act of 1965. About one-fourth of the more than $1,000,000,000 to be provided was to be earmarked for the purchase of textbooks and for the establishment of supplementary education centers, both of which would be under the control of the public schools but the benefits to be shared by pupils in the parochial schools.

"RELEASED TIME" PROGRAMS

It has been a long-established practice in many public school districts of the United States to include various kinds of religious exercises as a part of the school program. In some of these districts specific times are set aside during the school week when pupils are "released" from regular classes in order to attend some sort of religious program in the school building. An establishment issue is clearly presented by such practices, but the first case on that issue to reach the United States Supreme Court did not arrive until 1948. It dealt with the "released time" program followed in Champaign, Illinois.

ILLINOIS *ex rel.* McCOLLUM *v.* BOARD OF EDUCATION
333 U.S. 203 (1948)

Mr. Justice Black delivered the opinion of the Court.

This case relates to the power of a state to utilize its tax-supported public school system in aid of religious instruction insofar as that power may be restricted by the First and Fourteenth Amendments to the Federal Constitution.

The appellant, Vashti McCollum, began this action for mandamus against the Champaign Board of Education in the Circuit Court of Champaign County, Illinois. Her asserted interest was that of a resident and taxpayer of Champaign and of a parent whose child was then enrolled in the Champaign public schools....

Appellant's petition for mandamus alleged that religious teachers, employed by private religious groups, were permitted to come weekly into the school buildings during the regular hours set apart for secular teaching, and then and there for a period of thirty minutes substitute their religious teaching for the secular education provided under the compulsory education law. The petitioner charged that this joint public-school religious-group program violated the First and Fourteenth Amendments to the United States Constitution. The prayer of her petition was that the Board of Education be ordered to "adopt and enforce rules and regulations prohibiting all instruction in and teaching of religious education in all public schools in Champaign School District Number 71, ... and in all public school houses and buildings in said district when occupied by public schools."...

Although there are disputes between the parties as to various inferences that may or may not properly be drawn from the evidence concerning the religious program, the following facts are shown by the record without dispute. In 1940 interested members of the Jewish, Roman Catholic, and a few of the Protestant faiths formed a voluntary association called the Champaign Council on Religious Education. They obtained permission from the Board of Education to offer classes in religious instruction to public school pupils in grades four to nine inclusive. Classes were made up of pupils whose parents signed printed cards requesting that their children be permitted to attend; they were held weekly, thirty minutes for the lower grades, forty-five minutes for the higher. The council employed the religious teachers at no expense to the school authorities, but the instructors were subject to the approval and supervision of the superintendent of schools. The classes were taught in three separate religious groups by Protestant teachers, Catholic priests, and a Jewish rabbi, although for the past several years there have apparently been no classes instructed in the Jewish religion. Classes were conducted in the regular classrooms of the school building. Students who did not choose to take the religious instruction were not released from public school duties; they were required to leave their classrooms and go to some other place in the school building for pursuit of their secular studies. On the other hand, students who were released from secular study for the religious instructions were required to be present at the religious classes. Reports of their presence or absence were to be made to their secular teachers.

The foregoing facts, without reference to others that appear in the record, show the use of tax-supported property for religious instruction and the close cooperation between the school authorities and the religious council in promoting religious education. The operation of the state's compulsory education system thus assists and is integrated with the program of religious instruction carried on by separate religious sects. Pupils compelled by law to go to school for secular education are released in part from their legal duty upon the condition that they attend the religious classes. This is beyond all question a utilization of the tax-established and tax-supported public school system to aid religious groups to spread their faith. And it falls squarely under the ban of the First Amendment (made applicable to the States by the Fourteenth) as we interpreted it in *Everson* v. *Board of Education,* 330 U.S. 1.... The majority in the *Everson* case, and the minority ..., agreed that the First Amendment's language, properly interpreted, had erected a wall of separation between Church and State. They disagreed as to the facts shown by the record and as to the proper application of the First Amendment's language to those facts.

Recognizing that the Illinois program is barred by the First and Fourteenth Amendments if we adhere to the views expressed both by the majority and the minority in the *Everson* case, counsel for the respondents challenge those views as dicta and urge that we reconsider and repudiate them. They argue that historically the First Amendment was intended to forbid only government preference of one religion over another, not an impartial governmental assistance of all religions. In addition they ask that we distinguish or overrule our holding in the *Everson* case that the Fourteenth Amendment made the "establishment of religion" clause of the First Amendment applicable as a prohibition against the States. After giving full consideration to the arguments presented we are unable to accept either of these contentions.

To hold that a State cannot consistently with the First and Fourteenth Amendments utilize its public school system to aid any or all religious faiths or sects in the dissemination of their doctrines and ideals does not, as counsel urge, manifest a governmental hostility to religion or religious teachings. A manifestation of such hostility would be at war with our national tradition as embodied in the First Amendment's guaranty of the free exercise of religion. For the First Amendment rests upon the premise that both religion and government can best work to achieve their lofty aims if each is left free from the other within its respective sphere. Or, as we said in the *Everson* case, the First Amendment has erected a wall between Church and State which must be kept high and impregnable.

Here not only are the state's tax-supported public school buildings used for the dissemination of religious doctrines. The State also affords sectarian groups an invaluable aid in that it helps to provide pupils for their religious classes through use of the state's compulsory public school machinery. This is not separation of Church and State.

The cause is reversed and remanded to the State Supreme Court for proceedings not inconsistent with this opinion.

Reversed and remanded.

Mr. Justice Frankfurter delivered the following opinion, in which Mr. Justice Jackson, Mr. Justice Rutledge and Mr. Justice Burton join. [Mr. Justice Rutledge and Mr. Justice Burton concurred also in the Court's opinion.]...

Religious education so conducted on school time and property is patently woven into the working scheme of the school. The Champaign arrangement thus presents powerful elements of inherent pressure by the school system in the interest of religious sects. The fact that this power has not been used to discriminate is beside the point. Separation is a requirement to abstain from fusing functions of Government and of religious sects, not merely to treat them all equally. That a child is offered an alternative may reduce the constraint; it does not eliminate the operation of influence by the school in matters sacred to conscience and outside the school's domain. The law of imitation operates, and non-conformity is not an outstanding characteristic of children. The result is an obvious pressure upon children to attend. Again, while the Champaign school population represents only a fraction of the more than two hundred and fifty sects of the nation, not even all the practicing sects in Champaign are willing or able to provide religious instruction. The children belonging to these non-participating sects will thus have inculcated in them a feeling of separatism when the school should be the training ground for habits of community, or they will have religious instruction in a faith which is not that of their parents. As a result, the public school system of Champaign actively furthers inculcation in the religious tenets of some faiths, and in the process sharpens the consciousness of religious differences at least among some of the children committed to its care. These are consequences not amenable to statistics. But they are precisely the consequences against which the Constitution was directed when it prohibited the Government common to all from becoming embroiled, however innocently, in the destructive conflicts of which the history of even this country records some dark pages. . . .

We renew our conviction that "we have staked the very existence of our country on the faith that complete separation between the state and religion is best for the state and best for religion." *Everson* v. *Board of Education*. If nowhere else, in the relation between Church and State, "good fences make good neighbors."

Mr. Justice Jackson, concurring. . . .

Mr. Justice Reed, dissenting. . . .

Mr. Jefferson, as one of the founders of the University of Virginia, a school which from its establishment in 1819 has been wholly governed, managed and controlled by the State of Virginia, was faced with the same problem that is before this Court today: the question of the constitutional limitation upon religious education in public schools. In his annual report as Rector, to the President and Directors of the Literary Fund . . . Mr. Jefferson set forth his views at some length. These suggestions of Mr. Jefferson were adopted and c. II, Section 1, of the Regulations of the University of October 4, 1824, provided that:

"Should the religious sects of this State, or any of them, according to the invitation held out to them, establish within, or adjacent to, the precincts of the University, schools for instruction in the religion of their sect, the students of the University will be free, and expected to attend religious worship at the establishment of their respective sects, in the morning, and in time to meet their school in the University at its stated hour."

Thus, the "wall of separation between church and State" that Mr. Jefferson built at the University which he founded did not exclude religious education from that school. The difference between the generality of his statements on the separation of church and state and the specificity of his conclusions on education are considerable. A rule of law should not be drawn from a figure of speech. . . .

Well-recognized and long-established practices support the validity of the Illinois statute here in question. That statute, as construed in this case, is comparable to those in many states. . . .

The practices of the federal government offer many examples of this kind of "aid" by the state to religion. The Congress of the United States has a chaplain for each House who daily invokes divine blessings and guidance for the proceedings. The armed forces have commissioned chaplains from early days. They conduct the public services in accordance with the liturgical requirements of their respective faiths, ashore and afloat, employing for the purpose property belonging to the United States and dedicated to the services of religion. Under the Servicemen's Readjustment Act of 1944, eligible veterans may receive training at government expense for the ministry in denominational schools. The schools of the District of Columbia have opening eexrcises which "include a reading from the Bible without note or comment, and the Lord's prayer."

In the United States Naval Academy and the United States Military Academy, schools wholly supported and completely controlled by the federal government, there are a number of religious activities. Chaplains are attached to both schools. Attendance at church services on Sunday is compulsory at both the Military and Naval Academies. . . .

. . . Devotion to the great principle of religious liberty should not lead us into a rigid interpretation of the constitutional guarantee that conflicts with accepted habits of our people. This is an instance where, for me, the history of past practices is determinative of the meaning of a constitutional clause not a decorous introduction to the study of its text. The judgment should be affirmed.

The decision in the *McCollum* case was greeted with a storm of protest. One of America's most eminent scholars in constitutional law, Professor E. S. Corwin, argued that the "establishment" clause only barred the government from setting up an official church or showing preference for one religion over another. [See E. S. Corwin, "The Supreme Court as National School Board," 14 *Law & Contemp. Prob.* 3 (1949).] But groups supporting the viewpoint of the majority took encouragement from the decision, and plans were soon under way to initiate suits testing the "released time" programs in other parts of the nation. The New York City program was brought before the Court for examination only four years after *McCollum*. In *Zorach* v. *Clauson* the Court beat a strategic retreat and upheld this "dismissed time" program in which the pupils were permitted to leave the school grounds during the school day for their religious instruction.

ZORACH *v.* CLAUSON
343 U.S. 306 (1952)

Mr. Justice Douglas delivered the opinion of the Court.

New York City has a program which permits its public schools to release students during the school day so that they may leave the school buildings and school grounds and go to religious centers for religious instruction or devotional exercises. A student is released on written request of his parents. Those not released stay in the classrooms. The churches make weekly reports to the schools, sending a list of children who have been released from public school but who have not reported for religious instruction.

This "released time" program involves neither religious instruction in public school classrooms nor the expenditure of public funds. All costs, including the application blanks, are paid by the religious organizations. The case is therefore unlike *McCollum* v. *Board of Education*, 333 U.S. 203, which involved a "released time" program from Illinois. In that case the classrooms were turned over to religious instructors. We accordingly held that the program violated the First Amendment which (by reason of the Fourteenth Amendment) prohibits the states from establishing religion or prohibiting its free exercise.

Appellants, who are taxpayers and residents of New York City and whose children attend its public schools, challenge the present law, contending it is in essence not different from the one involved in the *McCollum* case. Their argument, stated elaborately in various ways, reduces itself to this: the weight and influence of the school is put behind a program for religious instruction; public school teachers police it, keeping tab on students who are released; the classroom activities come to a halt while the students who are released for religious instruction are on leave; the school is a crutch on which the churches are leaning for support in their religious training; without the cooperation of the schools this "released time" program, like the one in the *McCollum* case, would be futile and ineffective. The New York Court of Appeals sustained the law against this claim of unconstitutionality. . . .

There is a suggestion that the system involves the use of coercion to get public school students into religious classrooms. There is no evidence in the record before us that supports that conclusion. The present record indeed tells us that the school authorities are neutral in this regard and do no more than release students whose parents so request. If in fact coercion were used, if it were established that any one or more teachers were using their office to persuade or force students to take the religious instruction, a wholly different case would be presented. Hence we put aside the claim of coercion both as respects the "free exercise" of religion and "an establishment of religion" within the meaning of the First Amendment. . . .

. . . There cannot be the slightest doubt that the First Amendment reflects the philosophy that Church and State should be separated. And so far as interference with the "free exercise" of religion and an "establishment" of religion are concerned, the separation must be complete and unequivocal. The First Amendment within the scope of its coverage permits no exception; the prohibition is absolute. The First Amendment, however, does not say that in every and all respects there shall be a separation of Church and State. Rather, it studiously defines the manner, the specific ways, in which there shall be no concert or union or dependency one on the other. That is the common sense of the matter. Otherwise the state and religion would be aliens to each other—hostile, suspicious, and even unfriendly. Churches could not be required to pay even property taxes. Municipalities would not be permitted to render police or fire protection to religious groups. Policemen who helped parishioners into their places of worship would violate the Constitution. Prayers in our legislative halls; the appeals to the Almighty in the messages of the Chief Executive; the proclamations making Thanksgiving Day a holiday; "so help me God" in our courtroom oaths—these and all other references to the Almighty that run through our laws, our public rituals, our ceremonies would be flouting the First Amendment. A fastidious atheist or agnostic could even object to the supplication with which the Court opens each session: "God save the United States and this Honorable Court."

We would have to press the concept of separation of Church and State to these extremes to condemn the present law on constitutional grounds. The nullification of this law would have wide and profound effects. A Catholic student applies to his teacher for permission to leave the school during hours on a Holy Day of Obligation to attend a mass. A Jewish student asks his teacher for permission to be excused for Yom Kippur. A Protestant wants the afternoon off for a family baptismal ceremony. In each case the teacher requires parental consent in writing. In each case the teacher, in order to make sure the student is not a truant, goes further and requires a report from the priest, the rabbi, or the minister. The teacher in other words cooperates in a religious program to the extent of making it possible for her students to participate in it. Whether she does it occasionally for a few students, regularly for one, or pursuant to a systematized program designed to further the religious needs of all the students does not alter the character of the act.

We are a religious people whose institutions presuppose a Supreme Being. We guarantee the freedom to worship as one chooses. We make room for as wide a variety of beliefs and creeds as the spiritual needs of man deem necessary. We sponsor an attitude on the part of government that shows no partiality to any one group and that lets each flourish according to the zeal of its adherents and the appeal of its dogma. When the state encourages religious instruction or cooperates with religious authorities by adjusting the schedule of public events to sectarian needs, it follows the best of our traditions. For it then respects the religious nature of our people and accommodates the public service to their spiritual needs. To hold that it may not would be to find in the Constitution a requirement that the government show a callous indifference to religious groups. That would be preferring those who believe in no religion over those who do believe. Government may not finance religious groups nor undertake religious instruction nor blend secular and sectarian education nor use secular institutions to force one or some religion on any person. But we find no constitutional requirement which makes it necessary for government to be hostile to religion and to throw its weight against efforts to widen the effective scope of religious influence. The government must be neutral when it comes to competition between sects. It may not thrust any sect on any person. It may not make a religious observance compulsory. It may not coerce anyone to attend church, to observe a religious holiday, or to take religious instruction. But it can close its doors or suspend its operations as to those who want to repair to their religious sanctuary for worship or instruction. No more than that is undertaken here.

This program may be unwise and improvident from an educational or a community viewpoint. That appeal is made to us on a theory, previously advanced, that each case must be decided on the basis of "our own prepossessions.".... Our individual preferences, however, are not the constitutional standard. The constitutional standard is the separation of Church and State. The problem, like many problems in constitutional law, is one of degree....

In the *McCollum* case the classrooms were used for religious instruction and the force of the public school was used to promote that instruction. Here as we have said, the public schools do no more than accommodate their schedules to a program of outside religious instruction. We follow the *McCollum* case. But we cannot expand it to cover the present released time program unless separation of Church and State means that public institutions can make no adjustments of their schedules to accommodate the religious needs of the people. We cannot read into the Bill of Rights such a philosophy of hostility to religion.

Affirmed.

Mr. Justice Black, dissenting. . . .

I see no significant difference between the invalid Illinois system and that of New York here sustained. Except for the use of the school buildings in Illinois, there is no difference between the systems which I consider even worthy of mention. In the New York program, as in that of Illinois, the school authorities release some of the children on the condition that they attend the religious classes, get reports on whether they attend, and hold the other children in the school building until the religious hour is over. . . . *McCollum* . . . held that Illinois could not constitutionally manipulate the compelled classroom hours of its compulsory school machinery so as to channel children into sectarian classes. Yet that is exactly what the Court holds New York can do. . . .

Difficulty of decision in the hypothetical situations mentioned by the Court, but not now before us, should not confuse the issues in this case. Here the sole question is whether New York can use its compulsory education laws to help religious sects get attendants presumably too unenthusiastic to go unless moved to do so by the pressure of this state machinery. That this is the plan, purpose, design and consequence of the New York program cannot be denied. The state thus makes religious sects beneficiaries of its power to compel children to attend secular schools. Any use of such coercive power by the state to help or hinder some religious sects or to prefer all religious sects over nonbelievers or vice versa is just what I think the First Amendment forbids. In considering whether a state has entered this forbidden field the question is not whether it has entered too far but whether it has entered at all. New York is manipulating its compulsory education laws to help religious sects get pupils. This is not separation but combination of Church and State. . . .

Mr. Justice Frankfurter, dissenting. . . .

Mr. Justice Jackson, dissenting.

This released time program is founded upon a use of the State's power of coercion, which, for me, determines its unconstitutionality. Stripped to its essentials, the plan has two stages: first, that the State compel each student to yield a large part of his time for public secular education; and, second, that some of it be "released" to him on condition that he devote it to sectarian religious purposes.

No one suggests that the Constitution would permit the State directly to require this "released" time to be spent "under the control of a duly constituted religious body." This program accomplishes that forbidden result by indirection. If public education were taking so much of the pupils' time as to injure the public or the students' welfare by encroaching upon their religious opportunity, simply shortening everyone's school day would facilitate voluntary and optional attendance at Church classes. But that suggestion is rejected upon the ground that if they are made free many students will not go to the Church. Hence, they must be deprived of freedom for this period, with Church attendance put to them as one of the two permissible ways of using it.

The greater effectiveness of this system over voluntary attendance after school hours is due to the truant officer who, if the youngster fails to go to the Church school, dogs him back to the public schoolroom. Here schooling is more or less suspended during the "released time" so the nonreligious attendants will not forge ahead of the churchgoing absentees. But it serves as a temporary jail for a pupil who will not go to Church. It takes more subtlety of mind than I possess to deny that this is governmental constraint in support of religion. It is as unconstitutional, in my view, when exerted by indirection as when exercised forthrightly.

As one whose children, as a matter of free choice, have been sent to privately supported Church schools, I may challenge the Court's suggestion that opposition to this plan can only be antireligious, atheistic, or agnostic. My evangelistic brethren confuse an objection to compulsion with an objection to religion. It is possible to hold a faith with enough confidence to believe that what should be rendered to God does not need to be decided and collected by Caesar.

The day that this country ceases to be free for irreligion it will cease to be free for religion—except for the sect that can win political power. The same epithetical jurisprudence used by the Court today to beat down those who oppose pressuring children into some religion can devise as good epithets tomorrow against those who object to pressuring them into a favored religion. And, after all, if we concede to the State power and wisdom to single out "duly constituted religious" bodies as exclusive alternatives for compulsory secular instruction, it would be logical to also uphold the power and wisdom to choose the true faith among those "duly constituted." We start down a rough road when we begin to mix compulsory public education with compulsory godliness.

A number of Justices just short of a majority of the majority that promulgates today's passionate dialectics joined in answering them in *Illinois* ex rel. *McCollum* v. *Board of Education*, 333 U.S. 203. The distinction attempted between that case and this is trivial, almost to the point of cynicism, magnifying its nonessential details and disparaging compulsion which was the underlying reason for invalidity. A reading of the Court's opinion in that case along with its opinion in this case will show such difference of overtones and undertones as to make clear that the *McCollum* case has passed like a storm in a teacup. The wall which the Court was professing to erect between Church and State has become even more warped and twisted than I expected. Today's judgment will be more interesting to students of psychology and of the judicial processes than to students of constitutional law.

As pointed out in the majority opinion, the New York courts refused to consider plaintiff's offers of proof of coercion. [A description of some of the practices under the released time program in New York City, with quotations from affidavits filed in the Supreme Court, Kings County, is given in Note, "Released Time Reconsidered: The New York Plan is Tested," 61 *Yale L. J.* 405 (1952).] In one of the affidavits, for example, it was alleged that in one sixth grade classroom the students who did not attend the religious programs were given very difficult long division arithmetic problems during every released time hour, while those who went to their religious exercises were excused from this work. [On the released time issue generally, see George E. Reed, "Church-State and the Zorach Case," 27 *Notre Dame Law.* 529 (1952); Paul G. Kauper, "Church, State and Freedom: A Review," 52 *Mich. L. Rev.* 829 (1954); Leo Pfeffer, "Released Time and Religious Liberty: A Reply," 53 *Mich. L. Rev.* 91 (1954).]

Some indication of the importance of the retention in school of nonparticipants is shown in the finding of one investigator that several such programs of religious instruction collapsed from nonattendance when they were shifted to the time immediately after school hours and the nonparticipating student was free to go home or play as the alternative to a religious program. [See Gordon Patric, "The Impact of a Court Decision: Aftermath of the McCollum Case," 6 *Journal of Public Law* 455 (1957).]

The Bible and Prayer in Public Schools

The decisions by the United States Supreme Court on the use of Bible-reading and prayer in the public schools have stirred protest and controversy to an extent rarely equaled in the history of the Court. It should not be forgotten, however, that litigation on these issues is by no means new. While these decisions were the first in which the Court ruled on the validity of such practices under the United States Constitution, the issues have been litigated in various forms under *state* constitutional provisions for over a hundred years, and in the appellate courts of nearly half the states. The earliest reported case is a Maine case, *Donahoe* v. *Richards*, 38 Me. 376 (1854), in which the court held that a regulation adopting the King James version of the Bible as a textbook, binding upon all pupils, was not a violation of the rights of conscience or religion guaranteed by the state constitution. Of the twenty-three state appellate courts which have considered the issue of Bible-reading in the public schools, seventeen held that the practices challenged did not violate state or federal constitutional provisions, but the courts of six states held the practices invalid under state constitutional provisions. A Wisconsin decision, *State ex rel. Weiss* v. *District Board of Edgerton*, 76 Wis. 177, 44 N.W. 967 (1890), was the earliest of these decisions ruling against Bible-reading, and this was in 1890. [The cases are canvassed in David Fellman, *Religion in American Public Law* (Boston: Boston University Press, 1965), pp. 98–99. See also, Robert E. Cushman, "The Holy Bible and the Public Schools," 40 *Cornell L. Q.* 475 (1955).] Thus the issue was already a very old one even in the judicial arena by the time it reached the United States Supreme Court, and, further, twenty-five percent of the twenty-three states ruling on the question had ruled *against* the validity of Bible-reading in the public schools. The first decision to come from the Supreme Court did not come off until 1962, however, and involved the so-called Regents' prayer in the state of New York.

ENGEL *v.* VITALE

370 U.S. 421 (1962)

Mr. Justice Black delivered the opinion of the Court.

The respondent Board of Education of Union Free School District No. 9, New Hyde Park, New York, acting in its official capacity under state law, directed the School District's principal to cause the following prayer to be said aloud by each class in the presence of a teacher at the beginning of each school day:

"Almighty God, we acknowledge our dependence upon Thee, and we beg Thy blessings upon us, our parents, our teachers and our country."

This daily procedure was adopted on the recommendation of the State Board of Regents, a governmental agency created by the State Constitution to which the New York Legislature has granted broad supervisory, executive, and legislative powers over the State's public school system. These state officials composed the prayer which they recommended and published as a part of their "Statement on Moral and Spiritual Training in the Schools," saying: "We believe that this Statement will be subscribed to by all men and women of good will, and we call upon all of them to aid in giving life to our program."

Shortly after the practice of reciting the Regents' prayer was adopted by the School District, the parents of ten pupils brought this action in a New York State Court insisting that use of this official prayer in the public schools was contrary to the beliefs, religions, or religious practices of both themselves and their children. ... The New York Court of Appeals ... sustained an order of the lower state courts which had upheld the power of New York to use the Regents' prayer as a part of the daily procedures of its public schools so long as the schools did not compel any pupil to join in the prayer over his or his parents' objection. We granted certiorari to review this important decision involving rights protected by the First and Fourteenth Amendments.

We think that by using its public school system to encourage recitation of the Regents' prayer, the State of New York has adopted a practice wholly inconsistent with the Establishment Clause. There can, of course, be no doubt that New York's program of daily classroom invocation of God's blessings as prescribed in the Regents' prayer is a religious activity. It is a solemn avowal of divine faith and supplication for the blessings of the Almighty. The nature of such a prayer has always been religious, none of the respondents has denied this and the trial court expressly so found. ...

The petitioners contend among other things that the state laws requiring or permitting use of the Regents' prayer must be struck down as a violation of the Establishment Clause because that prayer was composed by governmental officials as a part of a governmental program to further religious beliefs. For this reason, petitioners argue, the State's use of the Regents' prayer in its public school system breaches the constitutional wall of separation between Church and State. We agree with that contention since we think that the constitutional prohibition against laws respecting an establishment of religion must at least mean that in this country it is no part of the business of government to compose official prayers for any group of the American people to recite as a part of a religious program carried on by government.

It is a matter of history that this very practice of establishing governmentally composed prayers for religious services was one of the reasons which caused many of our early colonists to leave England and seek religious freedom in America. The Book of Common Prayer, which was created under governmental direction and which was approved by Acts of Parliament in 1548 and 1549, set out in minute detail the accepted form and content of prayer and other religious ceremonies to be used in the established, tax-supported Church of England. The controversies over the Book and what should be its content repeatedly threatened to disrupt the peace of that country as the accepted forms of prayer in the established church changed with the views of the particular ruler that happened to be in control at the time. Powerful groups representing some of the varying religious views of the people struggled among themselves to impress their particular views upon the

Government and obtain amendments of the Book more suitable to their respective notions of how religious services should be conducted in order that the official religious establishment would advance their particular religious beliefs. Other groups, lacking the necessary political power to influence the Government on the matter, decided to leave England and its established church and seek freedom in America from England's governmentally ordained and supported religion. ...

... The First Amendment was added to the Constitution to stand as a guarantee that neither the power nor the prestige of the Federal Government would be used to control, support or influence the kinds of prayer the American people can say— that the people's religions must not be subjected to the pressures of government for change each time a new political administration is elected to office. Under that Amendment's prohibition against governmental establishment of religion, as reinforced by the provisions of the Fourteenth Amendment, government in this country, be it state or federal, is without power to prescribe by law any particular form of prayer which is to be used as an official prayer in carrying on any program of governmentally sponsored religious activity.

There can be no doubt that New York's state prayer program officially establishes the religious beliefs embodied in the Regents' prayer. The respondents' argument to the contrary, which is largely based upon the contention that the Regents' prayer is "non-denominational" and the fact that the program, as modified and approved by state courts, does not require all pupils to recite the prayer but permits those who wish to do so to remain silent or be excused from the room, ignores the essential nature of the program's constitutional defects. Neither the fact that the prayer may be denominationally neutral, nor the fact that its observance on the part of the students is voluntary can serve to free it from the limitations of the Establishment Clause, as it might from the Free Exercise Clause, of the First Amendment, both of which are operative against the States by virtue of the Fourteenth Amendment. Although these two clauses may in certain instances overlap, they forbid two quite different kinds of governmental encroachment upon religious freedom. The Establishment Clause, unlike the Free Exercise Clause, does not depend upon any showing of direct governmental compulsion and is violated by the enactment of laws which establish an official religion whether those laws operate directly to coerce nonobserving individuals or not. This is not to say, of course, that laws officially prescribing a particular form of religious worship do not involve coercion of such individuals. When the power, prestige and financial support of government is placed behind a particular religious belief, the indirect coercive pressure upon religious minorities to conform to the prevailing officially approved religion is plain. But the purposes underlying the Establishment Clause go much further than that. Its first and most immediate purpose rested on the belief that a union of government and religion tends to destroy government and to degrade religion. The history of governmentally established religion, both in England and in this country, showed that whenever government had allied itself with one particular form of religion, the inevitable result had been that it had incurred the hatred, disrespect and even contempt of those who held contrary beliefs. That same history showed that many people had lost their respect for any religion that had relied upon the support of government to spread its faith. The Establishment Clause thus stands as an expression of principle on the part of the Founders of our Constitution that religion is too personal, too sacred, too holy, to permit its "unhallowed perversion" by a civil magistrate. ... The New York laws officially prescribing the Regents' prayers are inconsistent with both the purposes of the Establishment Clause and with the Establishment Clause itself.

It has been argued that to apply the Constitution in such a way as to prohibit state laws respecting an establishment of religious services in public schools is to indicate a hostility toward religion or toward prayer. Nothing, of course, could be more wrong. . . . It is neither sacrilegious nor antireligious to say that each separate government in this country should stay out of the business of writing or sanctioning official prayers and leave that purely religious function to the people themselves and to those the people choose to look to for religious guidance. . . .

The judgment of the Court of Appeals of New York is reversed and the cause remanded for further proceedings not inconsistent with this opinion.

Reversed and remanded.

Mr. Justice Frankfurter took no part in the decision of this case.

Mr. Justice White took no part in the consideration or decision of this case.

Mr. Justice Douglas, concurring. . . .

Mr. Justice Stewart, dissenting. . . .

The Court today decides that in permitting this brief non-denominational prayer the school board has violated the Constitution of the United States. I think this decision is wrong.

The Court does not hold, nor could it, that New York has interfered with the free exercise of anybody's religion. For the state courts have made clear that those who object to reciting the prayer must be entirely free of any compulsion to do so, including any "embarrassments and pressures . . ." But the Court says that in permitting school children to say this simple prayer, the New York authorities have established "an official religion."

With all respect, I think the Court has misapplied a great constitutional principle. I cannot see how an "official religion" is established by letting those who want to say a prayer say it. On the contrary, I think that to deny the wish of these school children to join in reciting this prayer is to deny them the opportunity of sharing in the spiritual heritage of our Nation.

The Court's historical review of the quarrels over the Book of Common Prayer in England throws no light for me on the issue before us in this case. . . . What is relevant to the issue here is not the history of an established church in sixteenth century England or in eighteenth century America, but the history of the religious traditions of our people, reflected in countless practices of the institutions and officials of our government.

At the opening of each day's Session of the Court we stand, while one of our officials invokes the protection of God. Since the days of John Marshall our Crier has said, "God save the United States and this Honorable Court." Both the Senate and the House of Representatives open their daily Sessions with prayer. Each of our Presidents, from George Washington to John F. Kennedy, has upon assuming his office asked the protection and help of God.

The Court today says that the state and federal governments are without constitutional power to prescribe any particular form of words to be recited by any group of the American people on any subject touching religion. The third stanza of "The Star-Spangled Banner," made our National Anthem by Act of Congress in 1931, contains these verses:

"Blest with victory and peace, may the heav'n rescued land
Praise the Pow'r that hath made and preserved us a nation!
Then conquer we must, when our cause it is just,
And this to be our motto 'In God is our Trust.' "

In 1954 Congress added a phrase to the Pledge of Allegiance to the Flag so that it now contains the words "one Nation *under God* indivisible, with liberty and justice for all." In 1952 Congress enacted legislation calling upon the President each year to proclaim a National Day of Prayer. Since 1865 the words, "IN GOD WE TRUST" have been impressed on our coins.

Countless similar examples could be listed, but there is no need to belabor the obvious. It was all summed up by this Court just ten years ago in a single sentence: "We are a religious people whose institutions presuppose a Supreme Being." *Zorach* v. *Clauson*, 343 U.S. 306, 313.

I do not believe that this Court, or the Congress, or the President has by the actions and practices I have mentioned established an "official religion" in violation of the Constitution. And I do not believe the State of New York has done so in this case. What each has done has been to recognize and to follow the deeply entrenched and highly cherished spiritual traditions of our Nation—traditions which come down to us from those who almost two hundred years ago avowed their "firm reliance on the Protection of Divine Providence" when they proclaimed the freedom and independence of this brave new world.

I dissent.

The criticism which the Court received after the *McCollum* decision was mild by comparison with the tempest which blew up following *Engel* v. *Vitale*. Fresh charges were leveled that the members of the majority were atheistic or even Communist-inspired. And another round of proposals was aired calling for mass impeachments. Much of the initial anger was dispelled, however, as more people actually read the opinions, and officials of a number of different religious organizations issued public statements pointing out that the decision gave constitutional status to what they had long argued—that the church and the home, rather than the public schools, should be the primary centers of religious instruction. On legal grounds, however, Professor Sutherland of the Harvard Law School criticized the decision on the ground that the *de minimis* rule should have been employed by the Court to avoid ruling on such a small religious exercise. [Arthur E. Sutherland, Jr., "Establishment According to Engel," *76 Harv. L. Rev.* 25 (1962).] And Dean Erwin Griswold of the Harvard Law School criticized Justice Black for what he considered to be an extreme absolutist position in barring all religion from public activity. [Erwin Griswold, "Absolute Is in the Dark," 8 *Utah L. Rev.* 167 (1963).]

Despite the fact that the opinion was carefully written to apply only to governmentally written prayers, it was not difficult to make the necessary extension to predict the treatment to be accorded Bible-reading and the recitation of the Lord's Prayer as officially sponsored exercises in the public schools. One year later, almost to the day, the Court decided companion cases from Pennsylvania and Maryland and held such exercises unconstitutional.

SCHOOL DISTRICT OF ABINGTON TOWNSHIP *v.* SCHEMPP (NO.142)

MURRAY *v.* CURLETT (NO. 119)

374 U.S. 203 (1963)

Mr. Justice Clark delivered the opinion of the Court.

Once again we are called upon to consider the scope of the provision of the First Amendment to the United States Constitution which declares that "Congress shall make no law respecting an establishment of religion or prohibiting the free exercise thereof. . . ." These companion cases present the issues in the context of state action requiring that schools begin each day with readings from the Bible. While raising the basic questions under slightly different factual situations, the cases permit of joint treatment. In light of the history of the First Amendment and of our cases interpreting and applying its requirements, we hold that the practices at issue and the laws requiring them are unconstitutional under the Establishment Clause, as applied to the states through the Fourteenth Amendment. . . .

I

The Facts in Each Case: No. 142. The Commonwealth of Pennsylvania by law . . . requires that "At least ten verses from the Holy Bible shall be read, without comment, at the opening of each public school on each school day. Any child shall be excused from such Bible reading, or attending such Bible reading, upon the written request of his parent or guardian.". . .

On each school day at the Abington High School between 8:15 and 8:30 A.M., while the pupils are attending their home rooms or advisory sections, opening exercises are conducted pursuant to the statute. The exercises are broadcast into each room in the school building through an intercommunications system and are conducted under the supervision of a teacher by students attending the school's radio and television workshop. Selected students from this course gather each morning in the school's workshop studio for the exercises, which include readings by one of the students of 10 verses of the Holy Bible, broadcast to each room in the building. This is followed by the recitation of the Lord's Prayer, likewise over the intercommunications system, but also by the students in the various classrooms, who are asked to stand and join in repeating the prayer in unison. The exercises are closed with the flag salute and such pertinent announcements as are of interest to the students. Participation in the opening exercises, as directed by the statute, is voluntary. The student reading the verses from the Bible may select the passages and read from any version he chooses, although the only copies furnished by the school are the King James version, copies of which were circulated to each teacher by the school district. During the period in which the exercises have been conducted the King James, the Douay and the Revised Standard versions of the Bible have been used, as well as the Jewish Holy Scriptures. There are no prefatory statements, no questions asked or solicited, no comments or explanations made and no interpretations given at or during the exercises. The students and parents are advised that the student may absent himself from the classroom or, should he elect to remain, not participate in the exercises.

It appears from the record that in schools not having an intercommunications system the Bible reading and the recitation of the Lord's Prayer were conducted by the homeroom teacher, who chose the text of the verses and read them herself or had students read them in rotation or by volunteers. This was followed by a standing recitation of the Lord's Prayer, together with the Pledge of Allegiance to the flag by the class in unison and a closing announcement of routine school items of interest.

At the first trial Edward Schempp and the children testified as to specific religious doctrines purveyed by a literal reading of the Bible "which were contrary to the religious beliefs which they held and to their familial teaching.". . . The children testified that all of the doctrines to which they referred were read to them at various times as part of the exercises. Edward Schempp testified at the second trial that he had considered having Roger and Donna excused from attendance at the exercises but decided against it for several reasons, including his belief that the children's relationships with their teachers and classmates would be adversely affected.

Expert testimony was introduced by both appellants and appellees at the first trial, which testimony was summarized by the trial court as follows:

"Dr. Solomon Grayzel testified that there were marked differences between the Jewish Holy Scriptures and the Christian Holy Bible, the most obvious of which was the absence of the New Testament in the Jewish Holy Scriptures. Dr. Grayzel testified that portions of the New Testament were offensive to Jewish tradition and that, from the standpoint of Jewish faith, the concept of Jesus Christ as the Son of God was 'practically blasphemous.' He cited instances in the New Testament which, assertedly, were not only sectarian in nature but tended to bring the Jews into ridicule or scorn. . . .

"Dr. Luther A. Weigle, an expert witness for the defense, testified in some detail as to the reasons for and the methods employed in developing the King James and the Revised Standard Versions of the Bible. On direct examination, Dr. Weigle stated that the Bible was nonsectarian within the Christian faiths.". . .

No. 119. In 1905 the Board of School Commissioners of Baltimore City adopted a rule. . . . The rule provided for the holding of opening exercises in the schools of the city consisting primarily of the "reading, without comment, of a chapter of the Holy Bible and/or the use of the Lord's Prayer." The petitioners, Mrs. Madalyn Murray and her son, William J. Murray, III, are both professed atheists. Following unsuccessful attempts to have the respondent school board rescind the rule this suit was filed for mandamus to compel its rescission or cancellation. It was alleged that William was a student in a public school of the city and Mrs. Murray, his mother, was a taxpayer therein; that it was the practice under the rule to have a reading on each school morning from the King James version of the Bible; that at petitioners' insistence the rule was amended to permit children to be excused from the exercise on request of the parent and that William had been excused pursuant thereto; that nevertheless the rule as amended was in violation of the petitioners' rights "to freedom of religion under the First and Fourteenth Amendments" and in violation of "the principle of separation between church and state, contained therein. . . ." The petition particularized the petitioners' atheistic beliefs and stated that the rule, as practiced, violated their rights "in that it threatens their religious liberty by placing a premium on belief as against non-belief and subjects their freedom of conscience to the rule of the majority; it pronounces belief in God as the source of all moral and spiritual values, equating these values with religious values, and thereby renders sinister, alien and suspect the beliefs and ideals of. . . . Petitioners, promoting doubt and question of their morality, good citizenship and good faith."

The respondents demurred and the trial court, recognizing that the demurrer admitted all facts well pleaded, sustained it without leave to amend. The Maryland Court of Appeals affirmed, the majority of four justices holding the exercise not in violation of the First and Fourteenth Amendments, with three justices dissenting. . . .

"The government is neutral, and, while protecting all, it prefers none, and it disparages none."

Before examining this "neutral" position in which the Establishment and Free Exercise Clauses of the First Amendment place our government it is well that we discuss the reach of the Amendment under the cases of this Court.

[The opinion here contains numerous quotations from the various previous cases on religious freedom.]

The wholesome "neutrality" of which this Court's cases speak thus stems from a recognition of the teachings of history that powerful sects or groups might bring about a fusion of governmental and religious functions or a concert or dependency of one upon the other to the end that official support of the State or Federal Government would be placed behind the tenets of one or of all orthodoxies. This the Establishment Clause prohibits. And a further reason for neutrality is found in the Free Exercise Clause, which recognizes the value of religious training, teaching and observance and, more particularly, the right of every person to freely choose his own course with reference thereto, free of any compulsion from the state. This the Free Exercise Clause guarantees. Thus, as we have seen, the two clauses may overlap. As we have indicated, the Establishment Clause has been directly considered by this Court eight times in the past score of years and, with only one Justice dissenting on the point, it has consistently held that the clause withdrew all legislative power respecting religious belief or the expression thereof. The test may be stated as follows: what are the purpose and the primary effect of the enactment? If either is the advancement or inhibition of religion then the enactment exceeds the scope of legislative power as circumscribed by the Constitution. That is to say that to withstand the strictures of the Establishment Clause there must be a secular legislative purpose and a primary effect that neither advances nor inhibits religion. . . . The Free Exercise Clause, likewise considered many times here, withdraws from legislative power, state and federal, the exertion of any restraint on the free exercise of religion. Its purpose is to secure religious liberty in the individual by prohibiting any invasions thereof by civil authority. Hence it is necessary in a free exercise case for one to show the coercive effect of the enactment as it operates against him in the practice of his religion. The distinction between the two clauses is apparent—a violation of the Free Exercise Clause is predicated on coercion while the Establishment Clause violation need not be so attended.

Applying the Establishment Clause principles to the cases at bar, we find that the States are requiring the selection and reading at the opening of the school day of verses from the Holy Bible and the recitation of the Lord's Prayer by the students in unison. These exercises are prescribed as part of the curricular activities of students who are required by law to attend school. They are held in the school buildings under the supervision and with the participation of teachers employed in those schools. None of these factors, other than compulsory school attendance, was present in the program upheld in *Zorach* v. *Clauson*. The trial court in No. 142

has found that such an opening exercise is a religious ceremony and was intended by the State to be so. We agree with the trial court's finding as to the religious character of the exercises. Given that finding the exercises and the law requiring them are in violation of the Establishment Clause.

There is no such specific finding as to the religious character of the exercises in No. 119, and the State contends (as does the State in No. 142) that the program is an effort to extend its benefits to all public school children without regard to their religious belief. Included within its secular purposes, it says, are the promotion of moral values, the contradiction to the materialistic trends of our times, the perpetuation of our institutions and the teaching of literature. The case came up on demurrer, of course, to a petition which alleged that the uniform practice under the rule had been to read from the King James version of the Bible and that the exercise was sectarian. The short answer, therefore, is that the religious character of the exercise was admitted by the State. But even if its purpose is not strictly religious, it is sought to be accomplished through readings, without comment, from the Bible. Surely the place of the Bible as an instrument of religion cannot be gainsaid, and the State's recognition of the pervading religious character of the ceremony is evident from the rule's specific permission of the alternative use of the Catholic Douay version as well as the recent amendment permitting nonattendance at the exercises. None of these factors is consistent with the contention that the Bible is here used either as an instrument for nonreligious moral inspiration or as a reference for the teaching of secular subjects.

The conclusion follows that in both cases the laws require religious exercises and such exercises are being conducted in direct violation of the rights of the appellees and petitioners. Nor are these required exercises mitigated by the fact that individual students may absent themselves upon parental request, for that fact furnishes no defense to a claim of unconstitutionality under the Establishment Clause. See *Engel* v.*Vitale, supra* (370 U.S. at 430). Further, it is no defense to urge that the religious practices here may be relatively minor encroachments on the First Amendment. The breach of neutrality that is today a trickling stream may all too soon become a raging torrent and, in the words of Madison, "it is proper to take alarm at the first experiment on our liberties." Memorial and Remonstrance Against Religious Assessments, quoted in *Everson, supra,* 330 U.S. at 65.

It is insisted that unless these religious exercises are permitted a "religion of secularism" is established in the schools. ... We do not agree, however, that this decision in any sense has that effect. In addition, it might well be said that one's education is not complete without a study of comparative religion or the history of religion and its relationship to the advancement of civilization. It certainly may be said that the Bible is worthy of study for its literary and historic qualities. Nothing we have said here indicates that such study of the Bible or of religion, when presented objectively as part of a secular program of education, may not be effected consistent with the First Amendment. But the exercises here do not fall into those categories. They are religious exercises, required by the States in violation of the command of the First Amendment that the Government maintain strict neutrality, neither aiding nor opposing religion.

Finally, we cannot accept that the concept of neutrality, which does not permit a State to require a religious exercise even with the consent of the majority of those affected, collides with the majority's right to free exercise of religion. While the Free Exercise Clause clearly prohibits the use of state action to deny the rights of free exercise to *anyone,* it has never meant that a majority could use the machinery of the State to practice its beliefs. Such a contention was effectively answered by Mr. Justice Jackson for the Court in *West Virginia State Board of Education* v. *Barnette,* 319 U.S. 624, 638 (1943):

"The very purpose of a Bill of Rights was to withdraw certain subjects from the vicissitudes of political controversy, to place them beyond the reach of majorities and officials and to establish them as legal principles to be applied by the courts. One's right to . . . freedom of worship . . . and other fundamental rights may not be submitted to vote; they depend on the outcome of no elections.". . .

[Judgment in No. 142 affirmed. Judgment in No. 119 reversed and the cause remanded.]

Mr. Justice Douglas, concurring. . . .

Mr. Justice Brennan, concurring. . . .

Attendance at the public schools has never been compulsory; parents remain morally and constitutionally free to choose the academic environment in which they wish their children to be educated. The relationship of the Establishment Clause of the First Amendment to the public school system is preeminently that of reserving such a choice to the individual parent, rather than vesting it in the majority of voters of each State or school district. The choice which is thus preserved is between a public secular education with its uniquely democratic values, and some form of private, or sectarian education, which offers values of its own. In my judgment the First Amendment forbids the State to inhibit that freedom of choice by diminishing the attractiveness of either alternative—either by restricting the liberty of the private schools to inculcate whatever values they wish, or by jeopardizing the freedom of the public school from private or sectarian pressures. . . .

The line between permissible and impermissible forms of involvement between government and religion has already been considered by the lower federal and state courts. I think a brief survey of certain of these forms of accommodation will reveal that the First Amendment commands not official hostility toward religion, but only a strict neutrality in matters of religion. Moreover, it may serve to suggest that the scope of our holding today is to be measured by the special circumstances under which these cases have arisen, and by the particular dangers to church and state which religious exercises in the public schools present. It may be helpful for purposes of analysis to group these other practices and forms of accommodation into several rough categories.

A. *The Conflict Between Establishment and Free Exercise.*—There are certain practices, conceivably violative of the Establishment Clause, the striking down of which might seriously interfere with certain religious liberties also protected by the First Amendment. Provisions for churches and chaplains to military establishments for those in the armed services may afford one such example. The like provision by state and federal governments for chaplains in penal institutions may afford another example. It is argued that such provisions may be assumed to contravene the Establishment Clause, yet be sustained on constitutional grounds as necessary to secure to the members of the Armed Forces and prisoners those rights of worship guaranteed under the Free Exercise Clause. Since government has deprived such persons of the opportunity to practice their faith at places of their choice, the argument runs, government may, in order to avoid infringing the free exercise guarantees, provide substitutes where it requires such persons to be. . . .

The State must be steadfastly neutral in all matters of faith, and neither favor nor inhibit religion. In my view, government cannot sponsor religious exercises in the public schools without jeopardizing that neutrality. On the other hand, hostility, not neutrality, would characterize the refusal to provide chaplains and places of worship for prisoners and soldiers cut off by the State from all civilian opportunities for public communion, the withholding of draft exemptions for ministers and conscientious objectors, or the denial of the temporary use of an empty public building to a congregation whose place of worship has been destroyed by fire or flood. I do not say that government *must* provide chaplains or draft exemptions, or that the courts should intercede if it fails to do so.

B. *Establishment and Exercises in Legislative Bodies.*—The saying of invocational prayers in legislative chambers, state or federal, and the appointment of legislative chaplains, might well represent no involvements of the kind prohibited by the Establishment Clause. Legislators, federal and state, are mature adults who may presumably absent themselves from such public and ceremonial exercises without incurring any penalty, direct or indirect. . . .

C. *Non-Devotional Use of the Bible in the Public Schools.*—The holding of the Court today plainly does not foreclose teaching *about* the Holy Scriptures or about the differences between religious sects in classes in literature or history. Indeed, whether or not the Bible is involved, it would be impossible to teach meaningfully many subjects in the social sciences or the humanities without some mention of religion. To what extent, and at what points in the curriculum religious materials should be cited, are matters which the courts ought to entrust very largely to the experienced officials who superintend our Nation's public schools. They are experts in such matters, and we are not. . . .

D. *Uniform Tax Exemptions Incidentally Available to Religious Institutions.*— Nothing we hold today questions the propriety of certain tax deductions or exemptions which incidentally benefit churches and religious institutions, along with many secular charities and nonprofit organizations. If religious institutions benefit, it is in spite of rather than because of their religious character. For religious institutions simply share benefits which government makes generally available to educational, charitable, and eleemosynary groups. There is no indication that taxing authorities have used such benefits in any way to subsidize worship or foster belief in God. And as among religious beneficiaries, the tax exemption or deduction can be truly non-discriminatory, available on equal terms to small as well as large religious bodies, to popular and unpopular sects, and to those organizations which reject as well as those which accept a belief in God. . . .

F. *Activities Which, Though Religious in Origin, Have Ceased to Have Religious Meaning.*—As we noted in our Sunday Law decision, nearly every criminal law on the books can be traced to some religious principle or inspiration. But that does not make the present enforcement of the criminal law in any sense an establishment of religion, simply because it accords with widely held religious principles. As we said in *McGowan* v. *Maryland*, 366 U.S. 420, 442, "the 'Establishment' clause does not ban federal or state regulation of conduct whose reason or effect merely happens to coincide or harmonize with the tenets of some or all religions." This rationale suggests that the use of the motto "In God We Trust" on currency, on documents and public buildings and the like may not offend the clause. It is not that the use of those four words can be dismissed as *"de minimis"*—for I suspect there would be intense opposition to the abandonment of that motto. The truth is that we have simply interwoven the motto so deeply into the fabric of our civil polity that its present use may well not present that type of involvement which the First Amendment prohibits.

This general principle might also serve to insulate the various patriotic exercises and activities used in the Public schools and elsewhere which, whatever may have been their origins, no longer have a religious purpose or meaning. The reference to divinity in the revised pledge of allegiance, for example, may merely recognize the historical fact that our Nation was believed to have been founded "under God." Thus reciting the pledge may be no more of a religious exercise than the reading aloud of Lincoln's Gettysburg Address, which contains an allusion to the same historical fact. . . .

Mr. Justice Goldberg, with whom Mr. Justice Harlan joins, concurring. . . .

Mr. Justice Stewart, dissenting. . . .

It might . . . be argued that parents who want their children exposed to religious influences can adequately fulfill that wish off school property and outside school time. With all its surface persuasiveness, however, this argument seriously misconceives the basic constitutional justification for permitting the exercises at issue in these cases. For a compulsory state educational system so structures a child's life that if religious exercises are held to be an impermissible activity in schools, religion is placed at an artificial and state-created disadvantage. Viewed in this light, permission of such exercises for those who want them is necessary if the schools are truly to be neutral in the matter of religion. And a refusal to permit religious exercises thus is seen, not as the realization of state neutrality, but rather as the establishment of a religion of secularism, or at the least, as government support of the beliefs of those who think that religious exercises should be conducted only in private. . . .

Our decisions make clear that there is no constitutional bar to the use of government property for religious purposes. On the contrary, this Court has consistently held that the discriminatory barring of religious groups from public property is itself a violation of First and Fourteenth Amendment guarantees. *Fowler* v. *Rhode Island*, 345 U.S. 67; *Niemotko* v. *Maryland*, 340 U.S. 268. . . .

It is clear that the dangers of coercion involved in the holding of religious exercises in a schoolroom differ qualitatively from those presented by the use of similar exercises or affirmations in ceremonies attended by adults. Even as to children, however, the duty laid upon government in connection with religious exercises in the public schools is that of refraining from so structuring the school environment as to put any kind of pressure on a child to participate in those exercises; it is not that of providing an atmosphere in which children are kept scrupulously insulated from any awareness that some of their fellows may want to open the school day with prayer, or of the fact that there exist in our pluralistic society differences of religious belief. . . .

. . . [R]eligious exercises are not constitutionally invalid if they simply reflect differences which exist in the society from which the school draws its pupils. They become constitutionally invalid only if their administration places the sanction of secular authority behind one or more particular religious or irreligious beliefs. . . .

Viewed in this light, it seems to me clear that the records in both of the cases before us are wholly inadequate to support an informed or responsible decision. Both cases involve provisions which explicitly permit any student who wishes, to be excused from participation in the exercises. There is no evidence in either case as to whether there would exist any coercion of any kind upon a student who did not want to participate. . . .

What our Constitution indispensably protects is the freedom of each of us, be he Jew or Agnostic, Christian or Atheist, Buddhist or Free-thinker, to believe or disbelieve, to worship or not worship, to pray or keep silent, according to his own conscience, uncoerced and unrestrained by government. It is conceivable that these school boards, or even all school boards, might eventually find it impossible to administer a system of religious exercises during school hours in such a way as to meet this constitutional standard—in such a way as completely to free from any kind of official coercion those who do not affirmatively want to participate. But I think we must not assume that school boards so lack the qualities of inventiveness and good will as to make impossible the achievement of that goal.

I would remand both cases for further hearings.

Opposition to the prayer decisions led to an enormous mail campaign demanding that members of Congress introduce constitutional amendments to permit prayer and Bible-reading in the public schools. During the 88th Congress, through the third week of March 1964, 146 proposals for such constitutional amendments were introduced in the House and sent to the House Judiciary. A group of House members supporting amendment met to join forces behind a single proposal. The result was the "Becker Amendment," named for representative Frank Becker of New York who had sponsored the first prayer amendment bill in the 88th Congress. The text was as follows: (H. J. Res. 693):

Sec. 1. Nothing in this Constitution shall be deemed to prohibit the offering, reading from, or listening to prayers or Biblical Scriptures, if participation therein is on a voluntary basis, in any governmental or public school, institution or place.

Sec. 2. Nothing in this Constitution shall be deemed to prohibit making reference to belief in, reliance upon, or invoking the aid of God or a Supreme Being in any governmental or public document, proceeding, activity, ceremony, school, institution, or place, or upon any coinage, currency, or obligation of the United States.

Sec. 3. Nothing in this Article shall constitute an establishment of religion.

Although the House Judiciary Committee held hearings on the proposals, action was delayed sufficiently long until supporters of the Court's decisions mounted strong counter pressures, and no amendment proposal has passed the Congress to date. [For an account of the legislative history of the proposals, the stands taken by various church groups, and testimony before the Judiciary Committee, see *Congressional Quarterly Weekly Report*, No. 18 (May 1, 1964), pp. 881–885.]

An interesting aspect of the Bible in the public schools was presented in New Jersey in litigation involving the free distribution of Gideon Bibles at a group of public schools. One of the primary methods of operation of the Gideons International is the placing of Bibles in hotels, hospitals, and schools. A local chapter of the organization asked the Board of Education of the Borough of Rutherford for permission to distribute copies to public school children in the municipality. The volume contained the Book of Psalms, Proverbs, and the New Testament, all in the King James version. At a meeting of the Board of Education to consider the request, objections were voiced by a Catholic priest and a Jewish rabbi, on the grounds that the Gideons' New Testament was sectarian and forbidden to Catholic and Jewish children under the laws of their respective religions. The proposal passed, however, with only one dissenting vote.

Arrangements were made for forms to be sent to school by parents who wished their children to receive the free copies of the Bible. It was ordered that the distribution was to take place after school, and no other pupils were to be in the room when the Bibles were distributed.

Two plaintiffs, one Jewish and one Catholic, sought an injunction in a New Jersey Court to restrain the Board of Education from carrying out its plan for Bible distribution. Each contended that the Gideon Bible is "a sectarian work of peculiar religious value and significance to members of the Protestant faith," and that its distribution to children of their faiths violated the teachings, tenets and principles of their respective religions. Prior to the case, however, the Catholic child transferred schools and his issue became moot. In *Tudor* v. *Board of Education of Rutherford*, 14 N.J. 31 (1953), the New Jersey Supreme Court held the proposal unconstitutional. Chief Justice Vanderbilt, for the court, said in part:

This brings us to the heart of our problem here—namely, whether the resolution of the Board of Education displays that favoritism that is repugnant to our constitution. By permitting the distribution of the Gideon Bible, has the Board of Education established one religious sect in preference to another? Although as to the Catholic plaintiff this action has become moot due to the withdrawal of his child from the public schools of Rutherford, some testimony was presented at the trial as to his claim of sectarianism so we will at times refer to such testimony in our opinion. Our decision, however, is based upon the claim of the Jewish plaintiff that the resolution of the Rutherford Board of Education constitutes a preference of one religion over the Hebrew faith.

A review of the testimony at the trial convinces us that the King James version or Gideon Bible is unacceptable to those of the Jewish faith. In this regard Rabbi Joachim Prinz testified:

"The New Testament is in profound conflict with the basic principles of Judaism. It is not accepted by the Jewish people as a sacred book. The Bible of the Jewish people is the Old Testament. The New Testament is not recognized as part of the Bible. The teachings of the New Testament are in complete and profound conflict with what Judaism teaches. It presupposes the concept of Jesus of Nazareth as a divinity, a concept which we do not accept." . . .

. . . Nor is there any doubt that the King James version of the Bible is as unacceptable to Catholics as the Douay version is to Protestants. According to the testimony in this case the canon law of the Catholic Church provides that "Editions of the original text of the sacred scriptures published by non-Catholics are forbidden *ipso jure*." . . .

We find from the evidence presented in this case that the Gideon Bible is a sectarian book, and that the resolution of the defendant Board of Education to permit its distribution through the public school system ... was in violation of the First Amendment of the United States Constitution, as incorporated into the Fourteenth Amendment, and of Article 1, paragraph 4, of the New Jersey Constitution. It therefore must be set aside. ...

[The Chief Justice then quoted from certain of the expert testimony elicited from a psychologist and a professor of education to the effect that the student is not really free to make a choice but will feel that "he will be something of an outcast and a pariah if he does not go along with this procedure," and also that the distribution would create tensions among the religious groups and divide the children in terms of receiving or not receiving Bibles.]

We cannot accept the argument that here, as in the *Zorach* case, the State is merely "accommodating" religion. It matters little whether the teachers themselves will distribute the Bibles or whether that will be done by members of the Gideons International. The same vice exists, that of preference of one religion over another. This is all the more obvious when we realize the motive of the Gideons. ... The society is engaged in missionary work, accomplished in part by placing the King James version of the Bible in the hands of public school children throughout the United States. To achieve this end it employs the public school system as the medium of distribution. It is at the school that the pupil receives the request slip to take to his parents for signature. It is at the school that the pupil actually receives his Gideon Bible. In other words, the public school machinery is used to bring about the distribution of these Bibles to the children of Rutherford. In the eyes of the pupils and their parents the Board of Education has placed its stamp of approval upon this distribution, and in fact, upon the Gideon Bible itself. ... Dr. William Heard Kilpatrick stated:

"The Protestants would feel that the school is getting behind this thing; the Catholics would feel that the school is getting behind a Protestant affair; the Jews would feel that the school is getting behind the Protestant religion as opposed to their religion; and the people who don't accept any religion would feel that the school is actually trying to teach the religion through this means."

This is more than mere "accommodation" of religion permitted in the *Zorach* case. The school's part in this distribution is an active one and cannot be sustained on the basis of a mere assistance to religion.

... To permit the distribution of the King James version of the Bible in the public schools of this state would be to cast aside all the progress made in the United States and throughout New Jersey in the field of religious toleration and freedom. We would be renewing the ancient struggles among the various religious faiths to the detriment of all. This we must decline to do. ...

More recently some groups, particularly some of the Jewish organizations, have raised questions concerning the propriety of so-called Christological observances in the public schools—Easter programs, Christmas programs, nativity scenes, and other programs or activities specifically associated with Christian beliefs. As of this date the attempts to resolve such issues have taken place primarily in the lower level political arenas—representations before school boards, principals, or city councils—rather than in the courts. One such attack was carried forward in the courts of Florida, however. Suit was brought against the Dade County Board of Instruction challenging Bible-reading, prayer, baccalaureate exercises, religious census for students, and alleged religious tests for the employment and promotion of teachers in the public schools. The Florida Supreme Court upheld the Board on all counts, *Chamberlin* v. *Dade County Board of Public Instruction*, 143 So.2d 21 (1963). On appeal, the United States Supreme Court vacated the judgment and remanded the case for reconsideration in the light of the *Murray* and *Schempp* cases. [374 U.S. 487 (1963).] The Florida Supreme Court then reaffirmed its judgment, 160 So.2d 97 (1964), and the case went back to the United States Supreme Court on appeal. In *Chamberlin* v. *Dade County Board of Public Instruction*, 377 U.S. 402 (1964), the Court rendered the following *per curiam* opinion reversing the Florida Supreme Court:

...The judgment of the Florida Supreme Court is reversed with respect to the issues of the constitutionality of prayer, and of devotional Bible reading...in the public schools of Dade County.... As to the other questions raised, the appeal is dismissed for want of properly presented federal questions....

Mr. Justice Douglas, with whom Mr. Justice Black agrees, concurring in part.

I join in reversing the Supreme Court of Florida on the main issue in the case.

The "other questions raised" which the Court refuses to consider...involve the constitutionality under the First and Fourteenth Amendments of baccalaureate services in the schools, a religious census among pupils, and a religious test for teachers. The Florida Supreme Court disposed of those issues on the authority of *Doremus* v. *Board of Education*...which held that a taxpayer lacks standing to challenge religious exercises in the public schools....I think it is arguable that appellant-taxpayers do have standing to challenge these practices.

I think, however, that two of those "other questions"—the baccalaureate services and the religious census—do not present substantial federal questions, and so I concur in the dismissal of the appeal as to them. As to the religious test for teachers, I think a substantial question is presented....

Mr. Justice Stewart would note probable jurisdiction of this appeal and set it down for argument on the merits.

SUNDAY CLOSING LAWS AND THE "ESTABLISHMENT" CLAUSE

One of the clearest legacies bequeathed to us by the American Puritans is the Sunday Blue Law. Whatever the errors perpetuated concerning the Puritan's capacity for sin and pleasure—and the adjective "puritanical" is illustrative of such error—the accounts of his rigid and sober Sabbath observance are grounded in solid fact. Now, more than three hundred years later, we still retain laws which bar many kinds of mercantile and manufacturing operations on Sunday. For those persons whose Sabbath observance is on Sunday this is a congenial arrangement. For others, it may introduce a certain conflict in accommodating their religious and business interests to the Sunday Closing Law. At the very least, they may feel that the state is adopting punitive legislation which favors certain religious sects and penalizes others. Despite the clear indication that Sunday Laws were originally adopted as a means of promoting Christian observance, the earlier court decisions have uniformly upheld such laws, as in the case of *Petit* v. *Minnesota*, 177 U.S. 164 (1900), where a state law forbidding Sunday labor except works of necessity or charity was upheld. The first detailed examination of Sunday Laws by the United States Supreme Court under the claims of establishment of religion and abridgment of free exercise of religion did not occur, however, until 1961. In that year four cases involving the Sunday Laws of Massachusetts, Pennsylvania, and Maryland were decided, and in each case the laws were upheld against the claims of violation of religious liberty. The Maryland case, *McGowan* v. *Maryland*, covers the establishment arguments most thoroughly and will be presented as illustrative of the Court's view on that issue. (Since the Sunday laws contain a myriad of exceptions and exemptions from the closing requirement, the question of improper classification under the "equal protection" clause naturally arises, but this issue has been omitted from the cutting below since it does not relate directly to the matter of religious liberty.)

McGOWAN *v.* MARYLAND

366 U.S. 420 (1961)

Mr. Chief Justice Warren delivered the opinion of the Court.

The issues in this case concern the constitutional validity of Maryland criminal statutes, commonly known as Sunday Closing Laws or Sunday Blue Laws. . . .

Appellants are seven employees of a large discount department store located on a highway in Anne Arundel County, Maryland. They were indicted for the Sunday sale of a three-ring loose-leaf binder, a can of floor wax, a stapler and staples, and a toy submarine in violation of Md. Ann. Code, Art. 27 §521. Generally, this section prohibited, throughout the State, the Sunday sale of all merchandise except the retail sale of tobacco products, confectioneries, milk, drugs and medicines, and newspapers and periodicals. Recently amended, this section also now excepts from the general prohibition the retail sale in Anne Arundel County of all foodstuffs, automobile and boating accessories, flowers, toilet goods, hospital supplies and souvenirs. It now further provides that any retail establishment in Anne Arundel County which does not employ more than one person other than the owner may operate on Sunday.

Although appellants were indicted only under §521, in order properly to consider several of the broad constitutional contentions, we must examine the whole body of Maryland Sunday laws. Several sections of the Maryland statutes are particularly relevant to evaluation of the issues presented. . . .

The remaining statutory sections concern a myriad of exceptions for various counties, districts of counties, cities, and towns throughout the State. Among the activities allowed in certain areas on Sunday are such sports as football, baseball, golf, tennis, bowling, croquet, basketball, lacrosse, soccer, hockey, swimming, softball, boating, fishing, skating, horseback riding, stock car racing and pool or billiards. Other immunized activities permitted in some regions of the State include group singing or playing of musical instruments; the exhibition of motion pictures; dancing; the operation of recreation centers, picnic grounds, swimming pools, skating rinks and miniature golf courses. . . .

. . . Appellants were convicted and each was fined five dollars and costs. . . .

III

The final questions for decision are whether the Maryland Sunday Closing laws conflict with the Federal Constitution's provisions for religious liberty. . . . But appellants allege only economic injury to themselves; they do not allege any infringement of their own religious freedoms due to Sunday closing. In fact, the record is silent as to what appellants' religious beliefs are. Since the general rule is that "a litigant may only assert his own constitutional rights or immunities," *United States* v. *Raines,* 362 U.S. 17, 22, we hold that appellants have no standing to raise this contention. . . .

Secondly, appellants contend that the statutes violate the guarantee of separation of church and state in that the statutes are laws respecting an establishment of religion contrary to the First Amendment, made applicable to the states by the Fourteenth Amendment. . . . Appellants here concededly have suffered direct economic injury, allegedly due to the imposition on them of the tenets of the Christian religion. We find that, in these circumstances, these appellants have standing to complain that the statutes are laws respecting an establishment of religion.

The essence of appellant's "establishment" argument is that Sunday is the Sabbath day of the predominant Christian sects; that the purpose of the enforced stoppage of labor on that day is to facilitate and encourage church attendance; that the purpose of setting Sunday as a day of universal rest is to induce people with no religion or people with marginal religious beliefs to join the predominant Christian sects; that the purpose of the atmosphere of tranquility created by Sunday closing is to aid the conduct of church services and religious observance of the sacred day. In subtantiating their "establishment" argument, appellants rely on the wording of the present Maryland statutes, on earlier versions of the current Sunday laws and on prior judicial characterizations of these laws by the Maryland Court of Appeals. Although only the constitutionality of §521, of the section under which appellants have been convicted, is immediately before us in this litigation, inquiry into the history of Sunday Closing Laws in our country, in addition to an examination of the Maryland Sunday closing statutes in their entirety and of their history, is relevant to the decision of whether the Maryland Sunday Law in question is one respecting an establishment of religion. There is no dispute that the original laws which dealt with Sunday labor were motivated by religious forces. But what we must decide is whether present Sunday legislation having undergone extensive changes from the earliest forms, still retains its religious character.

Sunday Closing Laws go far back into American history having been brought to the colonies with a background of English legislation dating to the thirteenth century. . . . The law of the colonies to the time of the Revolution and the basis of the Sunday laws in the States was 29 Charles II, c. 7 (1677). It provided, in part:

"For the better observation and keeping holy the Lord's day, commonly called Sunday: be it enacted . . . that all the laws enacted and in force concerning the observation of the Lord's day, *and repairing to the church thereon,* be carefully put in execution; and that all and every person and persons whatsoever shall upon every Lord's day apply themselves to the observation of the same, by exercising themselves thereon in the duties of piety and true religion, publicly and privately; and that no tradesman, artificer, workman, laborer, or other person whatsoever, *shall do or exercise any worldly labor or business or work* of their ordinary callings upon the Lord's day, . . ." (Emphasis added.)

Observation of the above language, and of that of the prior mandates, reveals clearly that the English Sunday legislation was in aid of the established church.

The American colonial Sunday restrictions arose soon after settlement. Starting in 1650, the Plymouth Colony proscribed servile work, unnecessary travelling, sports, and the sale of alcoholic beverages on the Lord's day and enacted laws concerning church attendance. . . .

But, despite the strongly religious origin of these laws, beginning before the eighteenth century, nonreligious arguments for Sunday closing began to be heard more distinctly and the statutes began to lose some of their totally religious flavor. In the middle 1700's, Blackstone wrote, "[T]he keeping one day in the seven holy, as a time of relaxation and refreshment as well as for public worship, is of admirable service to a state considered merely as civil institution. It humanizes, by the help of conversation and society, the manners of the lower classes; which would otherwise degenerate into a sordid ferocity and savage selfishness of spirit; it enables the industrious workman to pursue his occupation in the ensuing week with health and cheerfulness." 4 Bl. Comm. 63. . . . With the advent of the First Amendment, the colonial provisions requiring church attendance were soon repealed. . . .

More recently, further secular justifications have been advanced for making Sunday a day of rest, a day when people may recover from the labors of the week just passed and may physically and mentally prepare for the week's work to come. In England, during the First World War, a committee investigating the health conditions of munitions workers reported that "if the maximum output is to be secured and maintained for any length of time, a weekly period of rest must be allowed. . . . On economic and social grounds alike this weekly period of rest is best provided on Sunday."

The proponents of Sunday closing legislation are no longer exclusively representatives of religious interests. Recent New Jersey Sunday legislation was supported by labor groups and trade associations. . . .

. . . Some of our States now enforce their Sunday legislation through Departments of Labor, e.g., SC Code Ann (1952), §64-5. Thus have Sunday laws evolved from the wholly religious sanctions that originally were enacted.

Moreover, litigation over Sunday closing laws is not novel. Scores of cases may be found in the state appellate courts relating to sundry phases of Sunday enactments. Religious objections have been raised there on numerous occasions but sustained only once, in *Ex parte Newman,* 9 Cal 502 (1858); and that decision was overruled three years later, in *Ex parte Andrews,* 18 Cal. 678. . . .

However, it is equally true that the "Establishment" Clause does not ban federal or state regulation of conduct whose reason or effect merely happens to coincide or harmonize with the tenets of some or all religions. In many instances, the Congress or state legislatures conclude that the general welfare of society, wholly apart from any religious considerations, demands such regulation. Thus, for temporal purposes, murder is illegal. And the fact that this agrees with the dictates of the Judaeo-Christian religions while it may disagree with others does not invalidate the regulation. So too with the questions of adultery and polygamy. . . .

In light of the evolution of our Sunday Closing Laws through the centuries, and of their more or less recent emphasis upon secular considerations, it is not difficult to discern that as presently written and administered, most of them, at least, are of a secular rather than of a religious character, and that presently they bear no relationship to establishment of religion as those words are used in the Constitution of the United States.

Throughout this century and longer, both the federal and state governments have oriented their activities very largely toward improvement of the health, safety, recreation and general well-being of our citizens. Numerous laws affecting public health, safety factors in industry, laws affecting hours and conditions of labor of women and children, week-end diversion at parks and beaches, and cultural activities of various kinds, now point the way toward the good life for all. Sunday Closing Laws, like those before us, have become part and parcel of this great governmental concern wholly apart from their original purposes or connotations. The present purpose and effect of most of them is to provide a uniform day of rest for all citizens; the fact that this day is Sunday, a day of particular significance for the dominant Christian sects, does not bar the State from achieving its secular goals. To say that the States cannot prescribe Sunday as a day of rest for these purposes solely because centuries ago such laws had their genesis in religion would give a constitutional interpretation of hostility to the public welfare rather than one of mere separation of church and state.

We now reach the Maryland statutes under review. . . .

Considering the language and operative effect of the current statutes, we no longer find the blanket prohibition against Sunday work or bodily labor. To the contrary, we find . . . the Sunday sale of tobaccos and sweets and a long list of sundry articles which we have enumerated above. . . . the Sunday operation of bathing beaches, amusement parks and similar facilities; . . . the Sunday sale of alcoholic beverages, . . . Sunday bingo and the Sunday playing of pin-ball machines and slot machines, activities generally condemned by prior Maryland Sunday legislation. Certainly, these are not works of charity or necessity. . . . These provisions, along with those which permit various sports and entertainments on Sunday, seem clearly to be fashioned for the purpose of providing a Sunday atmosphere of recreation, cheerfulness, repose and enjoyment. Coupled with the general proscription against other types of work, we believe that the air of the day is one of relaxation rather than one of religion. . . .

But, this does not answer all of appellants' contentions. We are told that the State has other means at its disposal to accomplish its secular purpose, other courses that would not even remotely or incidentally give state aid to religion. . . . It is true that if the State's interest were simply to provide for its citizens a periodic respite from work, a regulation demanding that everyone rest one day in seven, leaving the choice of the day to the individual, would suffice.

However, the State's purpose is not merely to provide a one-day-in-seven work stoppage. In addition to this, the State seeks to set one day apart from all others as a day of rest, repose, recreation and tranquility—a day which all members of the family and community have the opportunity to spend and enjoy together, a day in which there exists relative quiet and disassociation from the everyday intensity of commercial activities, a day in which people may visit friends and relatives who are not available during working days.

Obviously, a State is empowered to determine that a rest-one-day-in-seven statute would not accomplish this purpose; that it would not provide for a general cessation of activity, a special atmosphere of tranquility, a day which all members of the family or friends and relatives might spend together. Furthermore, it seems plain that the problems involved in enforcing such a provision would be exceedingly more difficult than those in enforcing a common-day-of-rest provision.

Moreover, it is common knowledge that the first day of the week has come to have special significance as a rest day in this country.... Sunday is a day apart from all others. The cause is irrelevant; the fact exists. It would seem unrealistic for enforcement purposes and perhaps detrimental to the general welfare to require a State to choose a common-day-of-rest other than that which most persons would select of their own accord. For these reasons, we hold that the Maryland statutes are not laws respecting an establishment of religion. ...

Accordingly, the decision is

Affirmed.

Separate opinion of Mr. Justice Frankfurter, whom Mr. Justice Harlan joins.... Mr. Justice Douglas, dissenting.

The question is not whether one day out of seven can be imposed by a State as a day of rest. The question is not whether Sunday can by force of custom and habit be retained as a day of rest. The question is whether a State can impose criminal sanctions on those who, unlike the Christian majority that make up our society, worship on a different day or do not share the religious scruples of the majority....

With that as my starting point I do not see how a State can make protesting citizens refrain from doing innocent acts on Sunday because the doing of those acts offends sentiments of their Christian neighbors....

... The "establishment" clause protects citizens also against any law which selects any religious custom, practice, or ritual, puts the force of government behind it, and fines, imprisons, or otherwise penalizes a person for not observing it. The Government plainly could not join forces with one religious group and decree a universal and symbolic circumcision. Nor could it require all children to be baptized or give tax exemptions only to those whose children were baptized.

Could it require a fast from sunrise to sunset throughout the Moslem month of Ramadan? I should think not. Yet why then can it make criminal the doing of other acts, as innocent as eating, during the day that Christians revere? ...

The issue of these cases would therefore be in better focus if we imagined that a state legislature controlled by orthodox Jews and Seventh Day Adventists, passed a law making it a crime to keep a shop open on Saturdays. Would a Baptist, Catholic, Methodist, or Presbyterian be compelled to obey that law or go to jail or pay a fine? Or suppose Moslems grew in political strength here and got a law through a state legislature making it a crime to keep a shop open on Fridays? Would the rest of us have to submit under the fear of criminal sanctions? ....

It seems to me plain that by these laws the States compel one, under sanction of law, to refrain from work or recreation on Sunday because of the majority's religious views about that day. The State by law makes Sunday a symbol of respect or adherence. Refraining from work or recreation in deference to the majority's religious feelings about Sunday is within every person's choice. By what authority can government compel it?

Cases are put where acts that are immoral by our standards but not by the standards of other religious groups are made criminal. That category of cases, until today, has been a very restricted one confined to polygamy . . . and other extreme situations. . . . None of the actions made constitutionally criminal today involves the doing of any act that any society has deemed to be immoral. . . .

The State can of course require one day of rest a week: one day when every shop or factory is closed. Quite a few States make that requirement. Then the "day of rest" becomes purely and simply a health measure. But the Sunday laws operate differently. They force minorities to obey the majority's religious feelings of what is due and proper for a Christian community; they provide a coercive spur to the "weaker brethren," to those who are indifferent to the claims of a Sabbath through apathy or scruple. Can there be any doubt that Christians, now aligned vigorously in favor of these laws, would be as strongly opposed, if they were prosecuted under a Moslem law that forbade them from engaging in secular activities on days that violated Moslem scruples?

There is an "establishment" of religion in the constitutional sense if any practice of any religious group has the sanction of law behind it. There is an interference with the "free exercise" of religion if what in conscience one can do or omit doing is required because of the religious scruples of the community. Hence I would declare each of those laws unconstitutional as applied to the complaining parties, whether or not they are members of a sect which observes as their Sabbath a day other than Sunday.

When these laws are applied to Orthodox Jews . . . or to Sabbatarians their vice is accentuated. If the Sunday laws are constitutional, Kosher markets are on a five-day week. Thus those laws put an economic penalty on those who observe Saturday rather than Sunday as the Sabbath. For the economic pressures on these minorities, created by the fact that our communities are predominantly Sunday-minded, there is no recourse. When, however, the State uses its coercive powers—here the criminal law—to compel minorities to observe a second Sabbath, not their own, the State undertakes to aid and "prefer one religion over another" contrary to the commands of the Constitution. . . .

THE "FREE EXERCISE" OF RELIGION

As previously pointed out, the First Amendment contains two clauses designed to safeguard religious liberty—the "establishment" clause and the "free exercise" clause. These are, of course, but complementary facets of the overall protection for religious freedom. While the one shades off into the other, it is still useful to separate the two facets for analysis. As Justice Frankfurter stated in his concurring opinion in *McGowan* v. *Maryland*:

Within the discriminating phraseology of the First Amendment, distinction has been drawn between cases raising "establishment" and "free exercise" questions. Any attempt to formulate a bright-line distinction is bound to founder. In view of the competition among religious creeds, whatever "establishes" one sect disadvantages another, and vice versa. But it is possible historically, and therefore helpful analytically—no less for problems arising under the Fourteenth Amendment, illuminated as that Amendment is by our national experience, than for problems arising under the First—to isolate in general terms the two largely overlapping areas of concern reflected in the two constitutional phrases, "establishment" and "free exercise.". . .

Religious minorities were too busy struggling for their existence during the earlier period of American development to feel that they could turn to the courts for protection against majority rules which merely pinched but did not destroy. As the major battles were won in the political arena—freedom to engage in public worship, freedom from taxes to support religion, and freedom from the onus of an established religion—the climate was prepared for settling the secondary sources of friction by the calmer method of litigation. Thus it was not until the latter quarter of the nineteenth century that the first major case on religious liberty reached the United States Supreme Court. The case was *Reynolds* v. *United States,* decided in 1879, and it dealt with the constitutionality of a law prohibiting polygamous marriages as applied to a Mormon whose religion encouraged such a practice.

PERMISSIBLE AREAS OF RESTRAINT—
PROTECTION OF MORALS, HEALTH, AND SAFETY

REYNOLDS v. UNITED STATES
98 U.S. 145 (1879)

[Reynolds was convicted in a district court of the Territory of Utah of the crime of bigamy, in violation of Section 5352, Revised Statutes of the United States, which prohibited bigamy in any place under exclusive jurisdiction of the United States. He admitted to having entered into a second marriage, but alleged that as a Mormon "That it was the duty of male members of said Church, circumstances permitting, to practice polygamy: ... that the failing or refusing to practice polygamy by such male members of said Church, when circumstances would admit, would be punished, and that the penalty for such failure and refusal would be damnation in the life to come."]

Mr. Chief Justice Waite delivered the opinion of the Court....

[T]he question is raised, whether religious belief can be accepted as a justification of an overt act made criminal by the law of the land. The inquiry is not as to the power of Congress to prescribe criminal laws for the Territories, but as to the guilt of one who knowingly violates a law which has been properly enacted, if he entertains a religious belief that the law is wrong.

Congress cannot pass a law for the government of the Territories which shall prohibit the free exercise of religion. The First Amendment to the Constitution expressly forbids such legislation. Religious freedom is guaranteed everywhere throughout the United States, so far as congressional interference is concerned. The question to be determined is, whether the law now under consideration comes within this prohibition.

The word "religion" is not defined in the Constitution. We must go elsewhere, therefore, to ascertain its meaning, and nowhere more appropriately, we think, than to the history of the times in the midst of which the provision was adopted. The precise point of the inquiry is, what is the religious freedom which has been guaranteed?

Before the adoption of the Constitution, attempts were made in some of the Colonies and States to legislate not only in respect to the establishment of religion, but in respect to its doctrines and precepts as well. The people were taxed, against their will, for the support of religion, and sometimes for the support of particular sects to whose tenets they could not and did not subscribe. Punishments were prescribed for a failure to attend upon public worship, and sometimes for entertaining heretical opinions. The controversy upon this general subject was animated in many of the States, but seemed at last to culminate in Virginia. In 1784, the House of Delegates of that State having under consideration "A bill establishing provision for teachers of the Christian religion," postponed it until the next session, and directed that the bill should be published and distributed, and that the People be requested "to signify their opinion respecting the adoption of such a bill at the next session of Assembly."

This brought out a determined opposition. Amongst others, Mr. Madison prepared a "Memorial and Remonstrance," which was widely circulated and signed, and in which he demonstrated "that religion, or the duty we owe the Creator," was not within the cognizance of civil government. At the next session the proposed bill was not only defeated, but another, "for establishing religious freedom," drafted by Mr. Jefferson, was passed. In the preamble of this Act religious freedom is defined; and after a recital "That to suffer the civil magistrate to intrude his powers into the field of opinion, and to restrain the profession of propagation of principles on supposition of their ill tendency, is a dangerous fallacy which at once destroys all religious liberty," it is declared "that it is time enough for the rightful purposes of civil government for its officers to interfere when principles break out into overt acts against peace and good order." In these two sentences is found the true distinction between what properly belongs to the Church and what to the State.

[The opinion then gives a brief account of the pressures for adoption of an amendment to the United States Constitution which would guarantee religious liberty. It includes the statement of Thomas Jefferson with respect to the First Amendment's "wall of separation between Church and State." Continuing Jefferson's statement, "Adhering to this expression of the Supreme will of the Nation in behalf of the rights of conscience, I shall see, with sincere satisfaction, the progress of those sentiments which tend to restore man to all his natural rights, convinced he has no natural right in opposition to his social duties."] Coming as this does from an acknowledged leader of the advocates of the measure, it may be accepted almost as an authoritative declaration of the scope and effect of the amendment thus secured. Congress was deprived of all legislative power over mere opinion, but was left free to reach actions which were in violation of social duties or subversive of good order.

Polygamy has always been odious among the Northern and Western Nations of Europe and, until the establishment of the Mormon Church, was almost exclusively a feature of the life of Asiatic and African people. At common law, the second marriage was always void, and from the earliest history of England polygamy has been treated as an offense against society. After the establishment of the ecclesiastical courts, and until the time of James I., it was punished through the instrumentality of those tribunals, not merely because ecclesiastical rights had been violated, but because upon the separation of the ecclesiastical courts from the civil, the ecclesiastical were supposed to be the most appropriate for the trial of matrimonial causes and offenses against the rights of marriage; just as they were for testamentary causes and the settlement of the estates of deceased persons.

By the Statute of 1 James I., ch. 11, the offense, if committed in England or

Wales, was made punishable in the civil courts, and the penalty was death. As this statute was limited in its operation to England and Wales, it was at a very early period re-enacted, generally with some modifications, in all the Colonies. In connection with the case we are now considering, it is a significant fact that on the 8th of December 1788, after the passage of the Act establishing religious freedom, and after the convention of Virginia had recommended as an amendment to the Constitution of the United States the declaration in a Bill of Rights that "All men have an equal, natural and unalienable right to the free exercise of religion, according to the dictates of conscience," the Legislature of that State substantially enacted the Statute of James I., death penalty included, because as recited in the preamble, "It hath been doubted whether bigamy or polygamy be punishable by the laws of this Commonwealth." From that day to this we think it may safely be said there never has been a time in any State of the Union when polygamy has not been an offense against society, cognizable by the civil courts and punishable with more or less severity. In the face of all this evidence, it is impossible to believe that the constitutional guaranty of religious freedom was intended to prohibit legislation in respect to this most important feature of social life. Marriage, while from its very nature a sacred obligation, is, nevertheless, in most civilized nations, a civil contract, and usually regulated by law.... There cannot be a doubt that, unless restricted by some form of constitution, it is within the legitimate scope of the power of every civil government to determine whether polygamy or monogamy shall be the law of social life under its dominion.

In our opinion the statute immediately under consideration is within the legislative power of Congress. It is constitutional and valid as prescribing a rule of action for all those residing in the Territories, and in places over which the United States have exclusive control. This being so, the only question which remains is, whether those who make polygamy a part of their religion are excepted from the operation of the statute. If they are, then those who do not make polygamy a part of their religious belief may be found guilty and punished, while those who do must be acquitted and go free. This would be introducing a new element into criminal law. Laws are made for the government of actions, and while they cannot interfere with mere religious belief and opinions, they may with practices. Suppose one believed that human sacrifices were a necessary part of religious worship would it be seriously contended that the civil government under which he lived could not interfere to prevent a sacrifice? Or if a wife religiously believed it was her duty to burn herself upon the funeral pile of her dead husband, would it be beyond the power of the civil government to prevent her carrying her belief into practice?

So here, as a law of the organization of society under the exclusive dominion of the United States, it is provided that plural marriages shall not be allowed. Can a man excuse his practices to the contrary because of his religious belief? To permit this would be to make the professed doctrines of religious belief superior to the law of the land, and in effect to permit every citizen to become a law unto himself. Government could exist only in name under such circumstances....

Affirmed.

As the *Reynolds* opinion makes clear, the First Amendment was not intended, and has not been so construed, to set up an absolute right to engage in a course of action just because one's religion happens to dictate it. Reasonable restrictions adopted by governments in furtherance of the health, safety, and convenience of the community may be enforced even against claims of violation of religious freedom.

The state has a well-recognized interest in the proper care and maintenance of children, and every state has laws charging parents with due attention to the health needs of their minor children. Issues have arisen, however, as a result of parental decisions to rely on prayer or special religious ceremony rather than normal medical assistance for the cure of sick children. There is no question but that a competent adult may freely choose whether to submit to medical treatment or not. The question arises, however, whether the parent is constitutionally free to make the same choices on religious grounds for his minor children. Typical of the general view of state courts is that expressed in *Craig* v. *State of Maryland*, decided by the Maryland Supreme Court.

CRAIG v. STATE OF MARYLAND
220 Md. 590, 155 A.2d 684 (1959)

[Defendants, father and mother, refused, on religious grounds, to call for medical care for their child, afflicted with pneumonia. As members of the Church of God they based their belief in divine healing on the Epistle of James 5:14, 15—"If there be any sick among you, let him call in the Elders of the Church." The child died and the parents were tried and convicted of involuntary manslaughter, on the theory that they were grossly negligent in failing to provide medical care. Appellants claim that such statutes as Maryland's requiring medical care for children violate their free exercise of religion protected by the Constitution of the United States.]

[The opinion by Justice Prescott first points out that the holding in *Regina* v. *Wagstaffe*, to the effect that parents of a sick child who omit to call in medical assistance because of their religious belief are not guilty of manslaughter, is irrelevant because it is a common law decision, and Maryland has by statute charged parents with medical care for their children.]

Appellants claim that such statutes violate their free exercise of religion protected by the Constitution of the United States.

The authorities are practically unanimous in holding to the contrary of the appellants' contention here. . . .

In prosecutions for the breach of a duty imposed by statute to furnish necessary medical aid to a minor child, the particular religious belief of the person charged with the offense constitutes no defense. . . . *People* v. *Pierson*, 176 N.Y. 201, 68 N.E. 243, 63 L.R.A. 187, seems to be a leading case upon the subject. After a most interesting and enlightening discourse upon the origin of medical science, the growth of legends of miracles and the intertwining of religion into the treating of sickness, the court held that a statute making the failure to furnish medical attention to a child a misdemeanor as applied to a person believing that prayer was the proper cure for illness was not violative of a New York constitutional provision guaranteeing the freedom of religious worship, since the religious belief secured by the Constitution did not extend to practices inconsistent with the peace or safety of the State, which involved the protection of the lives and health of its children and in the obedience of its citizens to its laws. The appellants were, and are, at perfect liberty to believe in the religion of their selection; they may pray, anoint and call in the Elders of their church in case of sickness of their minor children; but they, like all parents, must also obey the mandate of Article 72A, Section 1, by providing medical aid when the circumstances properly call for the same. . . .

The appellants' contention that they were denied "equal protection of the laws". . . is likewise without merit. It is based upon . . . Article 43, Section 140, which provides that "[N]othing in this subtitle . . . shall prevent any Christian Science practitioner duly registered in the Christian Science Journal . . . from treating human ills in accordance with the tenets of Christian Science or from making an adequate charge for services performed." They complain that they were prosecuted for treating human ills by prayer, when the above section permits Christian Scientists to render such treatment legally. They were, however, not prosecuted because they prayed, but for their alleged negligent failure to provide medical care. While Section 140 *permits* the treating of human ills in accordance with the tenets of Christian Science, it does not, in any manner, render such treatment the legal equivalent of medical care; hence Christian Science parents find themselves under the same duty to provide medical care for their minor children under the provisions of Article 72A, Section 1, when the circumstances require such care, as do all other parents. There is no discrimination here that violates the equal protection clause.

[The judgments were reversed, however, and the cases remanded for new trials. No testimony was entered to show that the parents were aware of the seriousness of the disease until two or three days prior to death. Testimony of doctors was that at that stage antibiotics probably would not have helped. Thus the evidence was insufficient to sustain a finding that gross negligence was the proximate cause of death.]

The only case thus far to reach the United States Supreme Court involving a conflict between child care laws and the claim of free exercise of religion is *Prince* v. *Massachusetts*, 321 U.S. 158 (1944). It concerned the validity of the application of the state's child labor law to the guardian of a nine-year-old girl, who was permitted by the guardian to engage in "preaching work" and the sale and distribution of religious literature on the public streets after school hours. The defendant objected on the ground of interference with her religious freedom. By a five-to-four vote the Court held the application of such a criminal law valid as a reasonable police regulation designed to protect the welfare of children, even against the competing claim of religious exercise. The Court noted that the authority of the State as *parens patriae* "is not nullified merely because the parent grounds his claim to control the child's course of conduct on religion or conscience." The Court stated further:

The state's authority over children's activities is broader than over like actions of adults. This is peculiarly true of public activities and in matters of employment. A democratic society rests, for its continuance, upon the healthy, well-rounded growth of young people into full maturity as citizens, with all that implies. It may secure this against impeding restraints and dangers within a broad range of selection. Among evils most appropriate for such action are the crippling effects of child employment, more especially in public places, and the possible harms arising from other activities subject to all the diverse influences of the street. It is too late now to doubt that legislation appropriately designed to reach such evils is within the state's police power, whether against the parent's claim to control of the child or one that religious scruples dictate contrary action.

Justice Murphy dissented on the ground that the particular prohibition of religious activities by children in this case was unreasonable, suggesting that "the reasonableness that justifies the prohibition of the ordinary distribution of literature in the public streets by children is not necessarily the reasonableness that justifies such a drastic restriction when the distribution is part of their religious faith."

Where religious practices endanger the health or safety of others in the community, the courts have had no difficulty applying the normal police power regulations to such practices. As one illustration, a number of state supreme courts have dealt with claims of violation of religious freedom in the convictions of persons who engage in handling poisonous snakes as a part of their religious ritual. Such convictions have uniformly been upheld against claims of violation of the free exercise clauses of state constitutions. Illustrative of the cases is *Harden* v. *State of Tennessee,* 188 Tenn. 17, 216 S.W.2d 708 (1949).

Harden and others were convicted of violating a statute making it unlawful for any person to handle or display any poisonous or dangerous snake in such manner as to endanger the life or health of any person. They were members of a religious denomination believing that the handling of poisonous snakes was a test of the sincerity of their faith and, further, that nonbelievers would be converted to their faith upon witnessing this miracle of safely handling such snakes. The Tennessee Supreme Court, in upholding the conviction, pointed out:

Aside from the fact that such handling of a rattlesnake is commonly known to be fraught with danger, there is in this record affirmative evidence that at this particular church at least one worshipper was bitten by a poisonous snake and died from the effects thereof within a few hours.

Reasonable minds must agree that the aforementioned practice of so handling poisonous snakes as a part of the religious services of this Church is dangerous to the life and health of people.

The court stated further that the statute did not interfere with the conscience of the defendants, or their beliefs concerning snakes, but that society had a right to protection of life and health which was equally as precious as defendants' right to free exercise of religion.

The courts of the states have also upheld state laws which require affirmative action to prevent disease, as well as the requirements of caring for ill minor children. The compulsory vaccination laws have been upheld in general in *Jacobson* v. *Massachusetts,* 197 U.S. 11 (1905), and convictions for failure to vaccinate children as a condition for admission to public school have been upheld against religious challenge, as in *Anderson* v. *State,* 84 Ga. App. 259, 65 S.E. 2d 848 (1951). Fluoridation has been upheld against the challenge from members of religious sects opposed to medication that such a program violates their religious liberty, as in *Baer* v. *City of Bend,* 206 Ore. 221, 292 P. 2d 134 (1956). It is interesting to note that such groups do not normally oppose *chlorination* of water although they do oppose *fluoridation.* The distinction apparently is drawn on the basis that chlorination merely kills certain bacteria, while fluoridation specifically is designed to serve as a caries preventive and is therefore a form of medication.

Another area in which the police power has been deemed to take precedence over claims of religious liberty is protection against fraud. Spiritual healing and faith healing have probably been with us since the earliest case of illness. Since normal physiological processes will rectify three-fourths of all illness, and psychosomatic disorders may respond to readjustment of mental state, the reportable "cures" of healers may reach impressive percentage figures. Claimants of special supernatural powers to heal the sick have often been sincerely convinced that they possessed such talents. Others have formed religious sects which included as an article of faith the belief that participation in certain kinds of religious ritual would result in curing illness. Where there is a clear nexus between religious belief or practice and the attempts to heal the sick, government denies religious freedom if it attempts actively to intervene. On the other hand, there are those who, without any prompting of religious conviction, set up healing enterprises with all the panoply and trappings of religion and play upon the credulity of the ignorant and the desperation of the incurably ill solely for financial gain. The general view is that the latter category of healers can properly be made the object of prosecutions for fraud, although there are strong dissents from this view.

The United States Supreme Court in 1944 considered the issue of the constitutionality under the First Amendment of prosecution of faith healers for mail fraud. The "I Am" cult was established in California by one Guy Ballard. The founders and leaders of the movement were subjected to a mail fraud prosecution. Guy Ballard claimed that he and his wife Edna and their child had been selected by St. Germain (dead since A.D. 488) as earthly representatives of the true religion. As a consequence of such divine designation Guy Ballard could heal incurable diseases and take spots off clothing, or at least so their doctrine taught. Funds were received from believers to carry on the work of the cult, and the mails were used for this purpose, as well as for the sale of various types of printed matter describing the doctrines of the cult. Very substantial profits were made on the printed material.

The federal government charged that the mails had been used to defraud.

The major question throughout was just what the jury was supposed to decide: whether the Ballards could cure the incurable, or whether the Ballards *believed* that they could cure the incurable. The trial judge decided that the jury could only examine the latter, that is the question of whether the Ballards honestly believed what they taught.

Before the case was concluded Guy Ballard died, following an operation, but his wife and child were convicted, fined, and given suspended prison sentences. The Court of Appeals reversed on the ground that the trial judge improperly charged the jury as to the defendants' sincerity. This decision was appealed, and the United States Supreme Court, agreeing with the view of the trial judge, reversed the decision of the Court of Appeals. Justice Douglas, speaking for the Court in *United States* v. *Ballard*, 322 U.S. 78 (1944), stated that this approach was in line with the First Amendment protection of religious freedom. Clearly, he said, the Constitution did not countenance an examination into the truth or falsity of beliefs, for then any religious group could be brought into court to prove the validity of its teachings, and religious freedom would be at an end. The majority, however, voted to remand the case for the disposition of other issues, with three justices dissenting. Justice Jackson was the lone dissenter on the question of the government's right to try the Ballards. He was by no means impressed with what he called "humbug, untainted by any trace of truth," but he felt that a jury simply would not be able to distinguish the beliefs of the Ballards from the credibility of such beliefs in reaching their verdict. In view of this difficulty he felt that the only safe course from the standpoint of religious freedom was to rule out such trials altogether. Even the more orthodox ministers or clergymen might be hard pressed on occasion if they were subjected to a sincerity test for everything said in the pulpit before the collection plate was passed. [For an interesting treatment of *Ballard*, see David Fellman, *The Limits of Freedom* (New Brunswick: Rutgers University Press, 1959), pp. 6–19.]

COMPULSORY PATRIOTIC EXERCISES AND RELIGIOUS FREEDOM

In the public schools of many states there are compulsory exercises which include the salute to the flag and the recitation of the pledge of allegiance. The Jehovah's Witnesses sect believes that such a gesture of respect for the flag as saluting is forbidden by the commands of Scripture. Reliance is especially placed on the third, fourth, and fifth verses of Chapter 20 of Exodus prohibiting false gods, graven images, and bowing down to such images. In 1940 the United States Supreme Court faced the issue of whether children in the public schools could be expelled for refusal on religious grounds to participate in the flag salute exercises. In *Minersville School District* v. *Gobitis*, 310 U.S. 586 (1940), the Court held that such provisions did not unconstitutionally abridge religious liberty. Justice Frankfurter, for the majority, stated:

We are dealing with an interest inferior to none in the hierarchy of legal values. National unity is the basis of national security.... To stigmatize legislative judgment in providing for this universal gesture of respect for the symbol of our national life in the setting of the common school as a lawless inroad on that freedom of conscience which the Constitution protects, would amount to no less than the pronouncement of pedagogical and psychological dogma in a field where courts possess no marked and certainly no controlling competence. The influences which help toward a common feeling for the common country are manifold. Some may seem harsh and others no doubt are foolish. Surely, however, the end is legitimate. And the effective means for its attainment are still so uncertain and so unauthenticated by science as to preclude us from putting the widely prevalent belief in flag-saluting beyond the pale of legislative power. It mocks reason and denies our whole history to find in the allowance of a requirement to salute our flag on fitting occasions the seeds of sanction for obeisance to a leader.... Where all the effective means of inducing political changes are left free from interference, education in the abandonment of foolish legislation is itself a training in liberty. To fight out the wise use of legislative authority in the forum of public opinion and before legislative assemblies rather than to transfer such a contest to the judicial arena, serves to vindicate the self-confidence of a free people.

Justice Stone was the only dissenter in the case. In a vigorous dissent he stated:

... [B]y this law the state seeks to coerce these children to express a sentiment which, as they interpret it, they do not entertain, and which violates their deepest religious convictions.... History teaches us that there have been but few infringements of personal liberty by the state which have not been justified, as they are here, in the name of righteousness and the public good, and few which have not been directed, as they are now, at politically helpless minorities.... I cannot conceive that in prescribing, as limitations upon the powers of government, the freedom of the mind and spirit secured by the explicit guarantees of freedom of speech and religion, [the framers] intended or rightly could have left any latitude for a legislative judgment that the compulsory expression of belief which violates religious convictions would better serve the public interest than their protection.

The *Minersville* decision was subjected to wide criticism. In an unusual step, three justices took the occasion of a dissenting opinion in a case arising in 1942 to announce that they felt the *Minersville* case was "wrongly decided." With Justice Stone, this made four members opposing that decision. Justice Byrnes, a member of the *Minersville* majority, resigned and was replaced by Justice Rutledge in 1943. In that same year the issue was relitigated in the case of *West Virginia State Board of Education* v. *Barnette*.

WEST VIRGINIA STATE BOARD OF EDUCATION *v.* BARNETTE
319 U.S. 624 (1943)

Mr. Justice Jackson delivered the opinion of the Court....

The Board of Education on January 9, 1942, adopted a resolution containing recitals taken largely from the Court's *Gobitis* opinion and ordering that the salute to the flag become "a regular part of the program of activities in the public schools," that all teachers and pupils "shall be required to participate in the salute honoring the Nation represented by the Flag; provided, however, that refusal to salute the Flag be regarded as an Act of insubordination, and shall be dealt with accordingly.". . .

Failure to conform is "insubordination" dealt with by expulsion. Readmission is denied by statute until compliance. Meanwhile the expelled child is "unlawfully absent" and may be proceeded against as a delinquent. His parents or guardians are liable to prosecution, and if convicted are subject to fine not exceeding $50 and jail term not exceeding thirty days.

Appellees, citizens of the United States and of West Virginia, brought suit in the United States District Court for themselves and others similarly situated asking its injunction to restrain enforcement of these laws and regulations against Jehovah's Witnesses. The Witnesses are an unincorporated body teaching that the obligation imposed by law of God is superior to that of laws enacted by temporal government. Their religious beliefs include a literal version of Exodus, Chapter 20, verses 4 and 5, which says: "Thou shalt not make unto thee any graven image, or any likeness of anything that is in heaven above, or that is in the earth beneath, or that is in the water under the earth; thou shalt not bow down thyself to them, nor serve them." They consider that the flag is an "image within this command." For this reason they refuse to salute it.

Children of this faith have been expelled from school and are threatened with exclusion for no other cause. Officials threaten to send them to reformatories maintained for criminally inclined juveniles. Parents of such children have been prosecuted and are threatened with prosecutions for causing delinquency.

. . . The cause was submitted on the pleadings to a District Court of three judges. It restrained enforcement as to the plaintiffs and those of that class. The Board of Education brought the case here by direct appeal.

This case calls upon us to reconsider a precedent decision, as the Court throughout its history often has been required to do. Before turning to the *Gobitis* case, however, it is desirable to notice certain characteristics by which this controversy is distinguished.

The freedom asserted by these appellees does not bring them into collision with rights asserted by any other individual. It is such conflicts which most frequently require intervention of the State to determine where the rights of one end and those of another begin. . . . The sole conflict is between authority and rights of the individual. The State asserts power to condition access to public education on making a prescribed sign and profession and at the same time to coerce attendance by punishing both parent and child. The latter stand on a right of self-determination in matters that touch individual opinion and personal attitude. . . .

There is no doubt that, in connection with the pledges, the flag salute is a form of utterance. . . .

. . . To sustain the compulsory flag salute we are required to say that a Bill of Rights which guards the individual's right to speak his own mind, left it open to public authorities to compel him to utter what is not in his mind. . . .

Nor does the issue as we see it turn on one's possession of particular religious views or the sincerity with which they are held. While religion supplies appellees' motive for enduring the discomforts of making the issue in this case, many citizens who do not share these religious views hold such a compulsory rite to infringe constitutional liberty of the individual. It is not necessary to inquire whether non-conformist beliefs will exempt from the duty to salute unless we first find power to make the salute a legal duty.

The *Gobitis* decision, however, *assumed,* as did the argument in that case and in this, that power exists in the State to impose the flag salute discipline upon school children in general. The Court only examined and rejected a claim based on religious beliefs of immunity from an unquestioned general rule. The question which underlies the flag salute controversy is whether such a ceremony so touching matters of opinion and political attitude may be imposed upon the individual by official authority under powers committed to any political organization under our Constitution. We examine rather than assume existence of this power and, against this broader definition of issues in this case, re-examine specific grounds assigned for the *Gobitis* decision. . . .

3. The *Gobitis* opinion reasoned that this is a field "where courts possess no marked and certainly no controlling competence," that it is committed to the legislatures as well as the courts to guard cherished liberties and that it is constitutionally appropriate to "fight out the wise use of legislative authority in the forum of public opinion and before legislative assemblies rather than to transfer such a contest to the judicial arena," since all the "effective means of inducing political changes are left free."

The very purpose of a Bill of Rights was to withdraw certain subjects from the vicissitudes of political controversy, to place them beyond the reach of majorities and officials and to establish them as legal principles to be applied by the courts. One's rights to life, liberty, and property, to free speech, a free press, freedom of worship and assembly, and other fundamental rights may not be submitted to vote; they depend on the outcome of no elections. . . .

4. Lastly, and this is the very heart of the *Gobitis* opinion, it reasons that "national unity is the basis of national security," that the authorities have "the right to select appropriate means for its attainment," and hence reaches the conclusion that such compulsory measures toward "national unity" are constitutional. Upon the verity of this assumption depends our answer in this case.

National unity as an end which officials may foster by persuasion and example is not in question. The problem is whether under our Constitution compulsion as here employed is a permissible means for its achievement.

Struggles to coerce uniformity of sentiment in support of some end thought essential to their time and country have been waged by many good as well as by evil men. Nationalism is a relatively recent phenomenon but at other times and places the ends have been racial or territorial security, support of a dynasty or regime, and particular plans for saving souls. As first and moderate methods to attain unity have failed, those bent on its accomplishment must resort to an ever increasing severity. As governmental pressure toward unity becomes greater, so strife becomes more bitter as to whose unity it shall be. Probably no deeper division of our people could proceed from any provocation than from finding it necessary to choose what doctrine and whose program public educational officials shall compel youth to unite in embracing. Ultimate futility of such attempts to compel coherence is the lesson of every such effort from the Roman drive to stamp out Christianity as a disturber of its pagan unity, the Inquisition, as a means to religious and dynastic unity, the Siberian exiles as a means to Russian unity, down to the fast failing efforts of our present totalitarian enemies. Those who begin coercive elimination of dissent soon find themselves exterminating dissenters. Compulsory unification of opinion achieves only the unanimity of the graveyard.

It seems trite but necessary to say that the First Amendment to our Constitution was designed to avoid those ends by avoiding these beginnings. There is no mysticism in the American concept of the State or of the nature or origin of its authority. We set up government by consent of the governed, and the Bill of Rights denies those in power any legal opportunity to coerce that consent. Authority here is to be controlled by public opinion, not public opinion by authority.

The case is made difficult not because the principles of its decision are obscure but because the flag involved is our own. Nevertheless, we apply the limitations of the Constitution with no fear that freedom to be intellectually and spiritually diverse or even contrary will disintegrate the social organization. To believe that patriotism will not flourish if patriotic ceremonies are voluntary and spontaneous instead of a compulsory routine is to make an unflattering estimate of the appeal of our institutions to free minds. We can have intellectual individualism and the rich cultural diversities that we owe to exceptional minds only at the price of occasional eccentricity and abnormal attitudes. When they are so harmless to others or to the State as those we deal with here, the price is not too great. But freedom to differ is not limited to things that do not matter much. That would be a mere shadow of freedom. The test of its substance is the right to differ as to things that touch the heart of the existing order.

If there is any fixed star in our constitutional constellation, it is that no official, high or petty, can prescribe what shall be orthodox in politics, nationalism, religion, or other matters of opinion or force citizens to confess by word or act their faith therein. If there are any circumstances which permit an exception, they do not now occur to us.

We think the action of the local authorities in compelling the flag salute and pledge transcends constitutional limitations on their power and invades the sphere of intellect and spirit which it is the purpose of the First Amendment to our Constitution to reserve from all official control.

The decision of this Court in *Minersville School District* v. *Gobitis* and the holdings of those few *per curiam* decisions which preceded and foreshadowed it are overruled, and the judgment enjoining enforcement of the West Virginia Regulation is   *Affirmed.*

Mr. Justice Roberts and Mr. Justice Reed adhere to the views expressed by the Court in *Minersville School District* v. *Gobitis* . . . and are of the opinion that the judgment below should be reversed.

Mr. Justice Black and Mr. Justice Douglas concurring. . . .

Mr. Justice Murphy concurring. . . .

Mr Justice Frankfurter, dissenting.

One who belongs to the most vilified and persecuted minority in history is not likely to be insensible to the freedoms guaranteed by our Constitution. Were my purely personal attitude relevant I should wholeheartedly associate myself with the general libertarian views in the Court's opinion, representing as they do the thought and action of a lifetime. But as judges we are neither Jew nor Gentile, neither Catholic nor agnostic. We owe equal attachment to the Constitution and are equally bound by our judicial obligations whether we derive our citizenship from the earliest or the latest immigrants to these shores. As a member of this Court I am not justified in writing my private notions of policy into the Constitution, no matter how deeply I may cherish them or how mischievous I may deem their disregard. The duty of a judge who must decide which of two claims before the Court shall prevail, that of a State to enact and enforce laws within its general competence or that of an individual to refuse obedience because of the demands of his conscience, is not that of the ordinary person. It can never be emphasized too much that one's own opinion about the wisdom or evil of a law should be excluded altogether when one is doing one's duty on the bench. The only opinion of our own even looking in that direction that is material is our opinion of whether legislators could in reason have enacted such a law. In the light of all the circumstances, including the history of this question in this Court, it would require more daring than I possess to deny that reasonable legislators could have taken the action which is before us for review. Most unwillingly, therefore, I must differ from my brethren with regard to legislation like this. I cannot bring my mind to believe that the "liberty" secured by the Due Process Clause gives this Court authority to deny to the State of West Virginia the attainment of that which we all recognize as a legitimate legislative end, namely, the promotion of good citizenship, by employment of the means here chosen. . . .

The reason why from the beginning even the narrow judicial authority to nullify legislation has been viewed with a jealous eye is that it serves to prevent the full play of the democratic process. The fact that it may be an undemocratic aspect of our scheme of government does not call for its rejection or its disuse. But it is the best of reasons, as this Court has frequently recognized, for the greatest caution in its use. . . .

Under our constitutional system the legislature is charged solely with civil concerns of society. If the avowed or intrinsic legislative purpose is either to promote or to discourage some religious community or creed, it is clearly within the constitutional restrictions imposed on legislatures and cannot stand. But it by no means follows that legislative power is wanting whenever a general non-discriminatory civil regulation in fact touches conscientious scruples or religious beliefs of an individual or a group. Regard for such scruples or beliefs undoubtedly presents one of the most reasonable claims for the exertion of legislative accommodation. It is, of course, beyond our power to rewrite the State's requirement, by providing exemptions for those who do not wish to participate in the flag salute or by making some other accommodations to meet their scruples. That wisdom might suggest the making of such accommodations and that school administration would not find it too difficult to make them and yet maintain the ceremony for those not refusing to conform, is outside our province to suggest. Tact, respect, and generosity toward variant views will always commend themselves to those charged with the duties of legislation so as to achieve a maximum of good will and to require a minimum of unwilling submission to a general law. But the real question is, who is to make such accommodations, the courts or the legislature? . . .

Conscientious scruples, all would admit, cannot stand against every legislative compulsion to do positive acts in conflict with such scruples. We have been told that such compulsions override religious scruples only as to major concerns of the state. But the determination of what is major and what is minor itself raises questions of policy. For the way in which men equally guided by reason appraise importance goes to the very heart of policy. Judges should be very diffident in setting their judgment against that of a state in determining what is and what is not a major concern, what means are appropriate to proper ends, and what is the total social cost in striking the balance of imponderables. . . .

. . . I think I appreciate fully the objections to the law before us. But to deny that it presents a question upon which men might reasonably differ appears to me to be intolerance. And since men may so reasonably differ, I deem it beyond my constitutional power to assert my view of the wisdom of this law against the view of the state of West Virginia. . . .

Of course patriotism cannot be enforced by the flag salute. But neither can the liberal spirit be enforced by judicial invalidation of illiberal legislation. Our constant preoccupation with the constitutionality of legislation rather than with its wisdom tends to preoccupation of the American mind with a false value. The tendency of focussing attention on constitutionality is to make constitutionality synonymous with wisdom, to regard a law as all right if it is constitutional. Such an attitude is a great enemy of liberalism. Particularly in legislation affecting freedom of thought and freedom of speech much which should offend a free-spirited society is constitutional. Reliance for the most precious interests of civilization, therefore, must be found outside of their vindication in courts of law. Only a persistent positive translation of the faith of a free society into the convictions and habits and actions of a community is the ultimate reliance against unabated temptations to fetter the human spirit.

[For a thorough treatment of the flag salute cases, see David Manwaring, *Render Unto Caesar: The Flag Salute Controversy* (Chicago: University of Chicago Press, 1962).]

FREE EXERCISE OF RELIGION AND THE PROBLEMS OF SABBATARIANS

In *McGowan* v. *Maryland,* discussed earlier, Maryland's Sunday Laws were challenged on the ground that they represented an establishment of religion. In companion cases decided on the same day as *McGowan* (*Gallagher* v. *Crown Kosher Super Market of Massachusetts* and *Braunfeld* v. *Brown*) Sunday Closing Laws were challenged by members of the Orthodox Jewish faith on the ground that they were an interference with the free exercise of their religion. The essence of the claim was that their religion required them to remain closed on Saturday, and that if they were compelled to remain closed on Sunday as well, the effect of the law would be to compel them to make a choice between going out of business or violating their religious beliefs and remaining open on Saturday. In *Gallagher,* for example, it was testified that the market had been conducting about one-third of its weekly business on Sunday, and that to close on that day would be ruinous.

BRAUNFELD *v.* BROWN
366 U.S. 599 (1961)

Mr. Chief Justice Warren announced the judgment of the Court and an opinion in which Mr. Justice Black, Mr. Justice Clark, and Mr. Justice Whittaker concur.

This case concerns the constitutional validity of the application to appellants of the Pennsylvania criminal statute, enacted in 1959, which proscribes the Sunday retail sale of certain enumerated commodities. Among the questions presented are whether the statute is a law respecting an establishment of religion and whether the statute violates equal protection. Since both of these questions, in reference to this very statute, have already been answered in the negative, . . . and since appellants present nothing new regarding them, they need not be considered here. Thus, the only question for consideration is whether the statute interferes with the free exercise of appellants' religion.

Appellants are merchants in Philadelphia who engage in the retail sale of clothing and home furnishings within the proscription of the statute in issue. Each of the appellants is a member of the Orthodox Jewish faith, which requires the closing of their places of business and a total abstention from all manner of work from nightfall each Friday until nightfall each Saturday. They instituted a suit in the court below seeking a permanent injunction against the enforcement of the 1959 statute. . . .

A three-judge court was properly convened and it dismissed the complaint. . . . On appeal brought under 28 USC Section 1253, we noted probable jurisdiction. . . .

Appellants contend that the enforcement against them of the Pennsylvania statute will prohibit the free exercise of their religion because, due to the statute's compulsion to close on Sunday, appellants will suffer substantial economic loss, to the benefit of their non-Sabbatarian competitors, if appellants also continue their Sabbath observance by closing their businesses on Saturday; that this result will either compel appellants to give up their Sabbath observance, a basic tenet of the Orthodox Jewish faith, or will put appellants at a serious economic disadvantage if they continue to adhere to the Sabbath. Appellants also assert that the statute will operate so as to hinder the Orthodox Jewish faith in gaining new adherents. And the corollary to these arguments is that if the free exercise of appellants' religion is impeded, that religion is being subjected to discriminatory treatment by the State. . . .

Concededly, appellants and all other persons who wish to work on Sunday will be burdened economically by the State's day of rest mandate; and appellants point out that their religion requires them to refrain from work on Saturday as well. Our inquiry then is whether, in these circumstances, the First and Fourteenth Amendments forbid application of the Sunday Closing Law to appellants.

Certain aspects of religious exercise cannot, in any way, be restricted or burdened by either federal or state legislation. Compulsion by law of the acceptance of any creed or the practice of any form of worship is strictly forbidden. The freedom to hold religious beliefs and opinions is absolute. . . .

However, the freedom to act, even when the action is in accord with one's religious convictions is not totally free from legislative restrictions. . . . As pointed out in *Reynolds* v. *United States* . . . legislative power over mere opinion is forbidden but it may reach people's actions when they are found to be in violation of important social duties or subversive of good order, even when the actions are demanded by one's religion. . . .

But . . . the statute at bar does not make unlawful any religious practices of appellants; the Sunday law simply regulates a secular activity and, as applied to appellants, operates so as to make the practice of their religious beliefs more expensive. Furthermore, the law's effect does not inconvenience all members of the Orthodox Jewish faith but only those who believe it necessary to work on Sunday. And even these are not faced with as serious a choice as forsaking their religious practices or subjecting themselves to criminal prosecution. Fully recognizing that the alternatives open to appellants and others similarly situated—retaining their present occupations and incurring economic disadvantage or engaging in some other commercial activity which does not call for either Saturday or Sunday labor—may well result in some financial sacrifice in order to observe their religious beliefs, still the option is wholy different than when the legislation attempts to make a religious practice itself unlawful.

To strike down, without the most critical scrutiny, legislation which imposes only an indirect burden on the exercise of religion, i.e., legislation which does not make unlawful the religious practice itself, would radically restrict the operating latitude of the legislature. Statutes which tax income and limit the amount which may be deducted for religious contributions impose an indirect economic burden on the observance of the religion of the citizen whose religion requires him to donate a greater amount to his church; statutes which require the courts to be closed on Saturday and Sunday impose a similar indirect burden on the observance of the religion of the trial lawyer whose religion requires him to rest on a weekday. The list of legislation of this nature is nearly limitless. . . .

Of course, to hold unassailable all legisation regulating conduct which imposes solely an indirect burden on the observance of religion would be a gross oversimplification. If the purpose or effect of a law is to impede the observance of one or all religions or is to discriminate invidiously between religions, that law is constitutionally invalid even though the burden may be characterized as being only indirect. But if the State regulates conduct by enacting a general law within its power, the purpose and effect of which is to advance the State's secular goals, the statute is valid despite its indirect burden on religious observance unless the State may accomplish its purpose by means which do not impose such a burden. . . .

As we pointed out in *McGowan* v. *Maryland* . . . we cannot find a State without power to provide a weekly respite from all labor and, at the same time, to set one day of the week apart from the others as a day of rest, repose, recreation and tranquillity. . . .

However, appellants . . . contend that the State should cut an exception from the Sunday labor proscription for those people who, because of religious conviction, observe a day of rest other than Sunday. By such regulation, appellants contend, the economic disadvantages imposed by the present system would be removed and the State's interest in having all people rest one day would be satisfied.

A number of States provide such an exemption, and this may well be the wiser solution to the problem. But our concern is not with the wisdom of legislation but with its constitutional limitation. Thus, reason and experience teach that to permit the exemption might well undermine the State's goal of providing a day that, as best possible, eliminates the atmosphere of commercial noise and activity. Although not dispositive of the issue, enforcement problems would be more difficult since there would be two or more days to police rather than one and it would be more difficult to observe whether violations were occurring.

Additional problems might also be presented by a regulation of this sort. To allow only people who rest on a day other than Sunday to keep their businesses open on that day might well provide the people with an economic advantage over their competitors who must remain closed on that day; this might cause the Sunday-observers to complain that their religions are being discriminated against. With this competitive advantage existing, there could well be the temptation for some, in order to keep their businesses open on Sunday, to assert that they have religious convictions which compel them to close their businesses on what had formerly been their least profitable day. This might make necessary a state-conducted inquiry into the sincerity of the individual's religious beliefs, a practice which a State might believe would itself run afoul of the spirit of constitutionally protected religious guarantees. Finally, in order to keep the disruption of the day at a minimum, exempted employers would probably have to hire employees who themselves qualified for the exemption because of their own religious beliefs, a practice which a State might feel to be opposed to its general policy prohibiting religious discrimination in hiring. For all of these reasons, we cannot say that the Pennsylvania statute before us is invalid, either on its face or as applied.

Mr. Justice Harlan concurs in the judgment. Mr. Justice Brennan and Mr. Justice Stewart concur in our disposition of appellants' claims under the Establishment Clause and the Equal Protection Clause. Mr. Justice Frankfurter and Mr. Justice Harlan have rejected appellants' claim under the Free Exercise Clause in a separate opinion.

Accordingly, the decision is

Affirmed.

Separate opinion of Mr. Justice Frankfurter, whom Mr. Justice Harlan joins [relating to all four of the Sunday law cases]....

Mr. Justice Brennan, concurring and dissenting.

I agree with the Chief Justice that there is no merit in appellants' establishment and equal-protection claims. I dissent, however, as to the claim that Pennsylvania has prohibited the free exercise of appellants' religion....

[The complaint alleges that] "Plaintiff, Abraham Braunfeld, will be unable to continue in his business if he may not stay open on Sunday and he will thereby lose his capital investment." In other words, the issue in this case—and we do not understand either appellees or the Court to contend otherwise—is whether a State may put an individual to a choice between his business and his religion. The Court today holds that it may. But I dissent, believing that such a law prohibits the free exercise of religion....

What, then, is the compelling state interest which impels the Commonwealth of Pennsylvania to impede appellants' freedom of worship?... It is the mere convenience of having everyone rest on the same day. It is to defend this interest that the Court holds that a State need not follow the alternative route of granting an exemption for those who in good faith observe a day of rest other than Sunday.

It is true, I suppose, that the granting of such an exemption would make Sundays a little noisier, and the task of police and prosecutor a little more difficult. It is also true that a majority—21—of the 34 States which have general Sunday regulations have exemptions of this kind. We are not told that those States are significantly noisier, or that their police are significantly more burdened, than Pennsylvania's. Even England, not under the compulsion of a written constitution, but simply influenced by considerations of fairness, has such an exemption for some activities. The Court conjures up several difficulties with such a system which seem to me more fanciful than real....

In fine, the Court, in my view, has exalted administrative convenience to a constitutional level high enough to justify making one religion economically disadvantageous. . . .

I would reverse this judgment and remand for a trial of appellants' allegations, limited to the free-exercise-of-religion issue.

Mr. Justice Stewart, dissenting.

I agree with substantially all that Mr. Justice Brennan has written. Pennsylvania has passed a law which compels an Orthodox Jew to choose between his religious faith and his economic survival. That is a cruel choice. It is a choice which I think no State can constitutionally demand. For me this is not something that can be swept under the rug and forgotten in the interest of enforced Sunday togetherness. I think the impact of this law upon these appellants grossly violates their constitutional right to the exercise of their religion.

Mr. Justice Douglas, dissenting. [This dissent to the holding in *McGowan* v. *Maryland* applies to all four Sunday Law cases.]

The question is not whether one day out of seven can be imposed by a State as a day of rest. The question is not whether Sunday can by force of custom and habit be retained as a day of rest. The question is whether a State can impose criminal sanctions on those who, unlike the Christian majority that makes up our society, worship on a different day or do not share the religious scruples of the majority. . . .

[The Justice here takes up the "establishment" issue, included in the excerpts quoted earlier in *McGowan* v. *Maryland*.]

When these laws are applied to Orthodox Jews, as they are in [*Gallagher* and *Braunfeld*], or to Sabbatarians their vice is accentuated. If the Sunday laws are constitutional, Kosher markets are on a five-day week. Thus those laws put an economic penalty on those who observe Saturday rather than Sunday as the Sabbath. For the economic pressures on these minorities, created by the fact that our communities are predominantly Sunday-minded, there is no recourse. When, however, the State uses its coercive powers—here the criminal law—to compel minorities to observe a second Sabbath, not their own, the State undertakes to aid and "prefer one religion over another"—contrary to the command of the Constitution. . . .

The reverse side of an "establishment" is a burden on the "free exercise" of religion. Receipt of funds from the state benefits the established church directly; laying an extra tax on nonmembers benefits the established church indirectly. Certainly the present Sunday laws place Orthodox Jews and Sabbatarians under extra burdens because of their religious opinions or beliefs. Requiring them to abstain from their trade or business on Sunday reduces their work-week to five days, unless they violate their religious scruples. This places them at a competitive disadvantage and penalizes them for adhering to their religious beliefs.

. . . The special protection which Sunday laws give the dominant religious groups and the penalty they place on minorities whose holy day is Saturday constitute in my view state interference with the "free exercise" of religion.

An unusual aspect of the problem faced by a Sabbatarian in a Sunday-observing society is the question of eligibility for unemployment compensation in the face of a refusal to accept any job requiring Saturday work.

Does denial by the state agency of such compensation constitute abridgment of religious freedom for the Saturday worshipper? The Court decided the issue in a case arriving from South Carolina in 1963, *Sherbert* v. *Verner*, 374 U.S. 398 (1963).

The appellant in the case became a member of the Seventh-day Adventist Church in 1957 at a time when her employer permitted her to work a five-day week. In 1959 the work week was changed to six days, including Saturday, for all shifts in the mill. Appellant was discharged by her employer because she refused to work on Saturday, the Sabbath Day of her faith. She was unable to obtain other employment for which she was qualified because of her refusal to take Saturday work and filed for unemployment compensation benefits under the state law. The appellee Employment Security Commission found her disqualified for benefits by their interpretation of the provision disqualifying persons who fail to accept "suitable work when offered" by the employment office. The South Carolina Supreme Court sustained this finding.

With two dissenting votes, the United States Supreme Court reversed, holding the decision of the Commission to be an abridgment of the free exercise of religion. Justice Brennan, for the majority, stated:

Here not only is it apparent that appellant's declared ineligibility for benefits derives solely from the practice of her religion, but the pressure upon her to forego that practice is unmistakable. The ruling forces her to choose between following the precepts of her religion and forfeiting benefits, on the one hand, and abandoning one of the precepts of her religion in order to accept work, on the other hand. Governmental imposition of such a choice puts the same kind of burden upon the free exercise of religion as would a fine imposed against appellant for her Saturday worship.

The Court noted further that South Carolina law expressly saves the Sunday worshipper from penalties or from discrimination because of refusal, based on his religion, to work on Sunday. "The unconstitutionality of the disqualification of the Sabbatarian is thus compounded by the religious discrimination which South Carolina's general statutory scheme necessarily effects." The Court could find no strong state interest in enforcing the eligibility provisions against the claim of free exercise of religion. To this extent it found the state interest asserted "is wholly dissimilar to the interests which were found to justify the less direct burden upon religious practices in *Braunfeld* v. *Brown*," namely, the provision of one uniform day of rest for all workers.

Justice Stewart concurred, but he stated that he did not see how the decision could be reconciled with that in *Braunfeld* v. *Brown*, since in both cases the state forced the citizen to make a choice between his religion and his economic welfare. Justice Harlan dissented, joined by Justice White, on the ground that Mrs. Sherbert's denial of benefits was no different from that of "any other claimant . . . denied benefits who was not 'available for work' for personal reasons." Justice Harlan also stated that the decision was inconsistent with that in *Braunfeld* v. *Brown*.

A comparison of the *Braunfeld* and *Sherbert* cases would seem to point to a conclusion that governmental "neutrality" in the religion cases cannot but be a relativistic characterization. Attempts to treat the "establishment" clause purely in terms of governmental neutrality will on occasion lead to situations where, as Justice Stewart pointed out in his opinion in the *Sherbert* case, the "establishment" clause and the "free exercise" clause "will run into head-on collision." South Carolina's "neutrality" in applying its nondiscriminatory unemployment compensation law without regard for its impact upon particular religious minorities was construed by the Court as a kind of *hostility* violative of the "free exercise" clause. Yet for the state to make a specific exception in the application of its law on grounds of religious belief (as the *Sherbert* majority required in order to meet "the governmental obligation of neutrality in the face of religious differences") can also be construed as a kind of governmental *preference* based on religion and thus violative of the establishment clause. If to ignore religious aspects is hostility and to take religious customs or practices into account is aid or preference, then indeed neutrality may be merely chimerical.

To stamp "In God We Trust" on our coins and to insert "under God" in the pledge of allegiance is, in a measure at least, to give governmental support to religion. For the government to strike out these phrases would surely be construed by many Americans as hostility to religion. By such a definition, neutrality is simply the absence of a conscious policy. Once the issue is raised, however, a policy decision is in fact made, whether the proposal is adopted or rejected, and the position of neutrality is then erased. Only a *de minimis* rule circumvents the issue.

Some of the opinions in the religion cases seem to suggest that the establishment clause approaches an absolute prohibition—a real wall of separation—while the free exercise clause involves weighing of interests. Other opinions lay stress on the direct versus indirect effect test. Neither approach solves both the logical and the practical problems presented, nor perhaps would any other. The balancing test can, however, be employed usefully in the mixed free exercise and establishment cases. The *Sunday Law Cases* presented such mixed issues, and the majority and concurring opinions devoted considerable space to such matters as enforcement problems, the interest of the state in a designated day of rest, and the interference with the individual's religion which such laws occasioned. And Justice Brennan stated for the Court in *Sherbert* v. *Verner*, "We must . . . consider whether some compelling state interest . . . justifies the substantial infringement of appellant's First Amendment right." [See Paul Kauper, "Schempp and Sherbert: Studies in Neutrality and Accommodation," 1963 *Religion and the Public Order* 3; Comment, "A Braunfeld v. Brown Test for Indirect Burdens on the Free Exercise of Religion," 48 *Minn. L. Rev.* 1165 (1964);

P. B. Kurland, *Religion and the Law: of Church and State and the Supreme Court* (Chicago: University of Chicago Press, 1962).]

RELIGIOUS OATHS

Whatever may be the constitutional status of formal governmental religious declarations or practices (as in the mottoes on coins or the religious exercises in governmental ceremonies), it is clear that when government requires an affirmation of religious belief, it oversteps the bounds of the First Amendment. The governmental requirement of a religious test oath is thus unconstitutional. The Court dealt with the issue in 1961 in considering the validity of a Maryland constitutional provision held to require a belief in God as a qualification for holding public office.

TORCASO *v.* WATKINS

367 U.S. 488 (1961)

Mr. Justice Black delivered the opinion of the Court.

Article 37 of the Declaration of Rights of the Maryland Constitution provides:

"[N]o religious test ought ever to be required as a qualification for any office of profit or trust in this State, other than a declaration of belief in the existence of God. . . ."

The appellant Torcaso was appointed to the office of Notary Public by the Governor of Maryland but was refused a commission to serve because he would not declare his belief in God. He then brought this action in a Maryland Circuit Court to compel issuance of his commission, charging that the State's requirement that he declare this belief violated "the First and Fourteenth Amendments to the Constitution of the United States. . . ." The Circuit Court rejected these federal constitutional contentions, and the highest court of the State, the Court of Appeals, affirmed, holding that the state constitutional provision is self-executing and requires declaration of belief in God as a qualification for office without need for implementing legislation. The case is therefore properly here on appeal under 28 USC Sec. 1257(2).

There is, and can be, no dispute about the purpose or effect of the Maryland Declaration of Rights requirement before us—it sets up a religious test which was designed to and, if valid, does bar every person who refuses to declare a belief in God from holding a public "office of profit or trust" in Maryland. The power and authority of the State of Maryland thus is put on the side of one particular sort of believers—those who are willing to say they believe in "the existence of God." It is true that there is much historical precedent for such laws. Indeed, it was largely to escape religious test oaths and declarations that a great many of the early colonists left Europe and came here hoping to worship in their own way. It soon developed, however, that many of those who had fled to escape religious test oaths turned out to be perfectly willing, when they had the power to do so, to force dissenters from their faith to take test oaths in conformity with that faith. This brought on a host of laws in the new Colonies imposing burdens and disabilities of various kinds upon varied beliefs depending largely upon what group happened to be politically strong enough to legislate in favor of its own beliefs. The effect of all this was the formal or practical "establishment" of particular religious faiths in most of the Colonies, with consequent burdens imposed on the free exercise of the faiths of nonfavored believers. . . .

When our Constitution was adopted, the desire to put the people "securely beyond the reach" of religious test oaths brought about the inclusion in Article 6 of that document of a provision that "no religious Test shall ever be required as a Qualification to any Office or public Trust under the United States.". . . Not satisfied, however, with Article 6 and other guarantees in the original Constitution, the First Congress proposed and the states very shortly thereafter adopted our Bill of Rights, including the First Amendment. That Amendment broke new constitutional ground in the protection it sought to afford to freedom of religion, speech, press, petition and assembly. Since prior cases in this Court have thoroughly explored and documented the history behind the First Amendment, the reasons for it, and the scope of the religious freedom it protects, we need not cover that ground again. What was said in our prior cases we think controls our decision here. . . .

The Maryland Court of Appeals thought, and it is argued here, that this Court's later holding and opinion in *Zorach* v. *Clauson* . . . had in part repudiated the statement in the *Everson* opinion . . . previously reaffirmed in *McCollum*. But the Court's opinion in *Zorach* specifically stated: "We follow the *McCollum* case.". . . Nothing decided or written in *Zorach* lends support to the idea that the Court there intended to open up the way for government, state or federal, to restore the historically and constitutionally discredited policy of probing religious beliefs by test oaths or limiting public offices to persons who have, or perhaps more properly profess to have, a belief in some particular kind of religious concept.

We repeat and again reaffirm that neither a State nor the Federal Government can constitutionally force a person "to profess a belief or disbelief in any religion." Neither can constitutionally pass laws nor impose requirements which aid all religions as against nonbelievers, and neither can aid those religions based on a belief in the existence of God as against those religions founded on different beliefs.*

In upholding the State's religious test for public office the highest court of Maryland said:

"The petitioner is not compelled to believe or disbelieve, under threat of punishment or other compulsion. True, unless he makes the declaration of belief he cannot hold public office in Maryland, but he is not compelled to hold office."

The fact, however, that a person is not compelled to hold public office cannot possibly be an excuse for barring him from office by state-imposed criteria forbidden by the Constitution. This was settled by our holding in *Wieman* v. *Updegraff*, 344 U.S. 183. We there pointed out that whether or not "an abstract right to public employment exists," Congress could not pass a law providing " '. . . that no federal employee shall attend Mass or take any active part in missionary work.' "

This Maryland religious test for public office unconstitutionally invades the appellant's freedom of belief and religion and therefore cannot be enforced against him.

The judgment of the Supreme Court of Maryland is accordingly reversed and the cause is remanded for further proceedings not inconsistent with this opinion.

Reversed and Remanded.

Mr. Justice Frankfurter and Mr. Justice Harlan concur in the result.

---

* Among religions in this country which do not teach what would generally be considered a belief in the existence of God are Buddhism, Taoism, Ethical Culture, Secular Humanism and others. . . .

Several of the justices in *United States* v. *Ballard* and the *Sunday Law Cases* and *Sherbert* v. *Verner* referred to the delicate ground of governmental inquiry into religious beliefs. *Torcaso* v. *Watkins* held that government may not condition office holding on the affirmation of a belief in the existence of God. A related problem is presented in the draft law exemption granted by statute to conscientious objectors. The constitutional issue of forcing one to perform military service against his religious convictions has not squarely arisen because of the exemption provided in all national conscription laws since the first one in 1917. But draft boards have been faced with the problems of applying the exemptions to claimant conscientious objectors. In so doing, they inquired into the beliefs of the claimant for exemption and the evidence indicating the tenacity with which he held to the principle of nonviolence—e.g., whether he acquired his convictions before or after the outbreak of hostilities. Obviously the claimant cannot be given exemption merely for the asking, and the Court has held, in *Dickinson* v. *United States*, 346 U.S. 389 (1953), that the claim of ministerial exemption is subject to judicial review. A number of cases have reached the Supreme Court since World War II dealing with both the exemption from combatant service for conscientious objectors and the exemption for ordained ministers. In general the cases have dealt with either statutory construction or with the fairness of administrative procedures or findings. [For a collection of the cases dealing with conscientious objectors, see Annotation, "Who Is Entitled to Exemption as a Conscientious Objector Within the Universal Military Training and Service Act," 13 L ed 2d 1186.]

An interesting aspect of the problem was presented in *United States* v. *Seeger*, 380 U.S. 163 (1965), a consolidated group of cases which treats comprehensively the background of legislation as to conscientious objectors. The cases raised the question of the constitutionality, under the First Amendment, of the section of the Universal Military Training and Service Act which defines the term "religious training and belief" (for purposes of the exemption) as "an individual's belief in a relation to a Supreme Being involving duties superior to those arising from any human relation, but [not including] essentially political, sociological, or a merely personal moral code." Seeger stated that he was conscientiously opposed to war in any form by reason of his "religious" belief, but preferred to leave open the question as to his belief in a Supreme Being. He stated further that his was a "belief in and devotion to goodness and virtue for their own sakes, and a religious faith in a purely ethical creed," without belief in God, "except in the remotest sense." His belief was found to be sincere and made in good faith. He was classified 1-A and ordered to report for induction into the armed forces. Upon refusal he was tried and convicted for refusal to submit to induction. The court of appeals reversed, and the government sought review on writ of certiorari. In another of the cases Forest Peter was convicted in a federal district court in California on a charge of refusing to submit to induction. He had stated that he was not a member of a religious sect or organization, but that he conscientiously objected to war, and felt it a violation of his moral code to take human life. As to whether his conviction was religious, he quoted with approval the Reverend John Holmes' definition of religion as "the consciousness of some power manifest in nature which helps man in the ordering of his life in harmony with its demands . . . ; it is man thinking his highest, feeling his deepest, and living his best." As to his belief in a Supreme Being, Peter stated that he supposed "you could call that a belief in the Supreme Being or God. These just do not happen to be the words I use." He was classified 1-A, convicted for failure to report for induction, and the court of appeals affirmed.

The United States Supreme Court unanimously affirmed the reversal of Seeger's conviction and reversed the conviction of Peter, without, however, reaching the constitutional issues raised. The Court concluded that the statutory purpose, in using the expression "Supreme Being" rather than the designation "God," "was merely clarifying the meaning of religious training and belief so as to embrace all religions and to exclude essentially political, sociological, or philosophical views." Justice Clark, for the Court, then formulated the appropriate test: "We believe that under this construction, the test of belief 'in a relation to a Supreme Being' is whether a given belief that is sincere and meaningful occupies a place in the life of its possessor parallel to that filled by the orthodox belief in God of one who clearly qualifies for the exemption." He said further, "This construction avoids imputing to Congress an intent to classify different religious beliefs, exempting some and excluding others, and is in accord with the well-established congressional policy of equal treatment for those whose opposition to service is grounded in their religious tenets." In support of the construction given the Act, various theological authorities and even the Schema of the recent Ecumenical Council were cited to indicate the "ever-broadening understanding of the modern religious community." [For more recent cases, see "Note on War Protestors" in Chap. 9. For further reference, see Francis Heisler, "The Law versus the Conscientious Objector," 20 *U. Chi. L. Rev.* 441 (1953); Selective Service System, *Conscientious Objection* (Special Monograph No. 11, 1950); J. D. Tietz, "Jehovah's Witnesses: Conscientious Objectors," 28 *So. Calif. L. Rev.* 123 (1955).]

COMPULSORY PUBLIC EDUCATION LAWS AND RELIGIOUS FREEDOM

Aside from the Bible and prayer cases, which presented establishment issues primarily, there have been two important areas of conflict between educational policy and religious freedom. The first issue discussed was the flag salute controversy, treated earlier. The second was the attempt by the state of Oregon to require all children to attend *public* schools through the eighth grade in the face of parental choice of private sectarian elementary school education. Although the case, *Pierce* v. *Society of Sisters*, was decided on a purely secular application of the Fourteenth Amendment's protection to the "liberty" of parents and teachers, the religious freedom application is clear.

PIERCE v. SOCIETY OF SISTERS
268 U.S. 510 (1925)

Mr. Justice McReynolds delivered the opinion of the Court.

These appeals are from decrees, based upon undenied allegations, which granted preliminary orders restraining appellants from threatening or attempting to enforce the Compulsory Education Act adopted November 7, 1922, under the initiative provision of her Constitution by the voters of Oregon. They present the same points of law; there are no controverted questions of fact. Rights said to be guaranteed by the Federal Constitution were specially set up, and appropriate prayers asked for their protection.

The challenged act, effective September 1, 1926, requires every parent, guardian, or other person having control or charge or custody of a child between eight and sixteen years to send him "to a public school for the period of time a public school shall be held during the current year" in the district where· the child resides; and failure so to do is declared a misdemeanor. There are exemptions—not specially important here—for children who are not normal, or who have completed the eighth grade, or whose parents or private teachers reside at considerable distances fom any public school, or who hold special permits from the county superintendent. The manifest purpose is to compel general attendance at public schools by normal children, between eight and sixteen, who have not completed the eighth grade. And without doubt enforcement of the statute would seriously impair, perhaps destroy, the profitable features of appellees' business, and greatly diminish the value of their property.

Appellee the Society of Sisters is an Oregon corporation, organized in 1880, with power to care for orphans, educate and instruct the youth, establish and maintain academies or schools, and acquire necessary real and personal property. It has long devoted its property and effort to the secular and religious education and care of children, and has acquired the valuable good will of many parents and guardians. . . . The Compulsory Education Act of 1922 has already caused the withdrawal from its schools of children who would otherwise continue, and their income has steadily declined. The appellants, public officers, have proclaimed their purpose strictly to enforce the statute. . . .

[Appellee Hill Military Academy is a private corporation engaged in operating for profit an elementary, college preparatory, and military training school for boys. The average attendance is one hundred, and the annual fees received for each student amount to some $800.]

No question is raised concerning the power of the state reasonably to regulate all schools, to inspect, supervise, and examine them, their teachers and pupils; to require that all children of proper age attend some school, that teachers shall be of good moral character and patriotic disposition, that certain studies plainly essential to good citizenship must be taught, and that nothing be taught which is manifestly inimical to the public welfare.

The inevitable practical result of enforcing the act under consideration would be destruction of appellees' primary schools, and perhaps all other private primary schools for normal children within the state of Oregon. Appellees are engaged in a kind of undertaking not inherently harmful, but long regarded as useful and meritorious. Certainly there is nothing in the present records to indicate that they have failed to discharge their obligations to patrons, students, or the state. And there are no peculiar circumstances or present emergencies which demand extraordinary measures relative to primary education.

Under the doctrine of *Meyer* v. *Nebraska,* 262 U.S. 390, we think it entirely plain that the Act of 1922 unreasonably interferes with the liberty of parents and guardians to direct the upbringing and education of children under their control. As often heretofore pointed out, rights guaranteed by the Constitution may not be abridged by legislation which has no reasonable relation to some purpose within the competency of the state. The fundamental theory of liberty upon which all governments in this Union repose excludes any general power of the State to standardize its children by forcing them to accept instruction from public teachers only. The child is not the mere creature of the State; those who nurture him and direct his destiny have the right, coupled with the high duty, to recognize and prepare him for additional obligations.

Appellees are corporations and therefore, it is said, they cannot claim for themselves the liberty which the Fourteenth Amendment guarantees. Accepted in the proper sense, this is true. . . . But they have business and property for which they claim protection. These are threatened with destruction through the unwarranted compulsion which appellants are exercising over present and prospective patrons of their schools. And this court has gone very far to protect against loss threatened by such action. . . .

The decrees below are

Affirmed.

It should be noted that *Pierce* v. *Society of Sisters* held only that the state could not constitutionally prohibit parents from sending their children to a nonpublic school. It can, of course, require all children to attend *some* school through a specified grade or until reaching a specified age. And although *Pierce* offers substantial protections to the continued operation of the private school, the state clearly has the power to demand minimum standards in such schools, such as curriculum and teacher accreditation, if the private schools are to be allowed as alternatives to the public schools. [See Fred F. Beach and Robert F. Will, "The State and Non-public Schools" (U.S. Office of Ed., Misc. No. 28, 1958).]

PRIOR RESTRAINTS ON THE FREE EXERCISE OF RELIGION

In many of the previous free exercise cases the judicial approach has been to make a determination of the interest the state may have in maintaining a specific policy and the kind and degree of restraint on the individual's exercise of religion. To say, therefore, that the individual may practice his religion freely so long as he does not violate the criminal laws of the state is too facile a generalization. If the statement were true as given, then no interference which took the form of a penal statute would violate the guarantee of religious freedom. The crux of the problem is the determination of whether the application of a criminal provision in a particular exercise of religion situation is an improper infringement of that exercise. And the weighing of interests involved in each separate fact situation can result in a decision either in favor of the claimed immunity or against it, depending on how a majority of the Court may view the weight of the state's and the individual's interests. Thus in *Reynolds* and *Prince* the Court upheld the application of criminal statutes barring polygamy and certain forms of child labor, respectively, against the claims of religious freedom. But in *West Virginia Board of Education* v. *Barnette* the Court held that to punish the parent and to expel the child who refused on religious grounds to salute the flag in public school exercises was violative of the constitutional protection to free exercise of religion. Whether a particular criminal law can constitutionally be applied to restrict religious exercise will turn on the kind and degree of interference and the value to the state of imposing the restraint.

There is one category of First Amendment restrictions, however, concerning which the Court has taken a virtually absolutist position—those laws or official practices which impose "prior restraints" on First Amendment freedoms. The theory here is that if a course of action is not *malum in se* or *malum prohibita* (is not, for example, in the category of human sacrifice or polygamy or forced child labor of certain kinds) then it is a violation of First Amendment guarantees to require permits or licenses as conditions of engaging in the religious activity. This is in essence the doctrine of "no previous restraints." It does not, of course, halt the application of the ordinary criminal provisions to the conduct of the participants. Delivering a religious sermon is not *per se* unlawful, but the time, the place, and the kind of language used may still be such as to justify criminal penalties. The point of the "no previous restraint" doctrine, however, is that one cannot be barred at the outset the right to participate in an ordinarily lawful religious exercise or have that right conditioned on permission given by some governmental official.

In the setting in which the cases have frequently come to the Court, the crucial question is often whether the *general* course of action engaged in by the religious claimant can properly be declared unlawful by the state. If the decision is that such activity in general cannot be declared unlawful, then no prior permit or license, unless nondiscretionary in nature, can be required for the First Amendment exercise. Specific crimes committed in the course of the normally lawful activity may be punished, but the presence of such illegal aspects in past or similar activity may not be used to justify the attempt to impose prior restraints in the first place. Punishment for these must come under the application of the appropriate criminal laws and represent separate issues.

The cases on religious freedom and prior restraint generally show a clear overlap with free speech issues. Indeed, the prior restraint issues in their most familiar setting involve matters of communication and oral persuasion. But since not all prior restraints of speech are clearly unconstitutional (see, for example, *Prince* v. *Massachusetts,* discussed earlier), the attempt has been made to establish a more generalized rationale for the doctrine. (See Chapter 6 for a more detailed discussion of prior restraints.) The first case to come to the United States Supreme Court involving the prior restraint doctrine as applied to religious freedom was *Cantwell* v. *Connecticut,* decided in 1940.

CANTWELL *v.* CONNECTICUT

310 U.S. 296 (1940)

Mr. Justice Roberts delivered the opinion of the Court.

Newton Cantwell and his two sons, Jesse and Russell, members of a group known as Jehovah's Witnesses, and claiming to be ordained ministers, were arrested in New Haven, Connecticut, and each was charged by information in five counts, with statutory and common-law offenses. After trial in the Court of Common Pleas of New Haven County each of them was convicted on the third count, which charged a violation of Section 6294 of the General Statutes of Connecticut, and on the fifth count, which charged commission of the common-law offenses of inciting a breach of the peace. . . .

The facts adduced to sustain the convictions on the third count follow. On the day of their arrest the appellants were engaged in going singly from house to house on Cassius Street in New Haven. They were individually equipped with a bag containing books and pamphlets on religious subjects, a portable phonograph and a set of records, each of which, when played, introduced, and was a description of, one of the books. Each appellant asked the person who responded to his call for permission to play one of the records. If permission was granted he asked the person to buy the book described and, upon refusal, he solicited such contribution towards the publication of the pamphlets as the listener was willing to make. If a contribution was received, a pamphlet was delivered upon condition that it would be read.

Cassius Street is in a thickly populated neighborhood, where about ninety per cent of the residents are Roman Catholics. A phonograph record, describing a book entitled "Enemies," included an attack on the Catholic religion. None of the persons interviewed were members of Jehovah's Witnesses.

The statute under which the appellants were charged provides:

"No person shall solicit money, services, subscriptions or any valuable thing for any alleged religious, charitable or philanthropic cause, from other than a member of the organization for whose benefit such person is soliciting or within the county in which such person or organization is located unless such cause shall have been approved by the secretary of the public welfare council. Upon application of any person in behalf of such cause, the secretary shall determine whether such cause is a religious one or is a bona fide object of charity or philanthropy and conforms to reasonable standards of efficiency and integrity, and, if he shall so find, shall approve the same and issue to the authority in charge a certificate to that effect. Such certificate may be revoked at any time. Any person violating any provision of this section shall be fined not more than one hundred dollars or imprisoned not more than thirty days or both."

The appellants claimed that their activities were not within the statute but consisted only of distribution of books, pamphlets, and periodicals. The State Supreme Court construed the finding of the trial court to be that "in addition to the sale of the books and the distribution of the pamphlets the defendants were also soliciting contributions or donations of money for an alleged religious cause, and thereby came within the purview of the statute." It overruled the contention that the Act, as applied to the appellants, offends the due process clause of the Fourteenth Amendment, because it abridges or denies religious freedom and liberty of speech and press. The court stated that it was the solicitation that brought the appellants within the sweep of the Act and not their other activities in the dissemination of literature. It declared the legislation constitutional as an effort by the State to protect the public against fraud and imposition in the solicitation of funds for what purported to be religious, charitable, or philanthropic causes.

The facts which were held to support the conviction of Jesse Cantwell on the fifth count were that he stopped two men in the street, asked, and received, permission to play a phonograph record, and played the record "Enemies," which attacked the religion and church of the two men, who were Catholics. Both were incensed by the contents of the record and were tempted to strike Cantwell unless he went away. On being told to be on his way he left their presence. There was no evidence that he was personally offensive or entered into any argument with those he interviewed.

The court held that the charge was not assault or breach of the peace or threats on Cantwell's part, but invoking or inciting others to breach of the peace, and that the facts supported the conviction of that offense.

First. We hold that the statute, as construed and applied to the appellants, deprives them of their liberty without due process of law in contravention of the Fourteenth Amendment. The fundamental concept of liberty embodied in that Amendment embraces the liberties guaranteed by the First Amendment.... No one would contest the proposition that a State may not, by statute, wholly deny the right to preach or to disseminate religious views. Plainly such a previous and absolute restraint would violate the terms of the guarantee. It is equally clear that a State may by general and non-discriminatory legislation regulate the times, the places, and the manner of soliciting upon its streets, and of holding meeting thereon; and may in other respects safeguard the peace, good order and comfort of the community, without unconstitutionally invading the liberties protected by the Fourteenth Amendment. The appellants are right in their insistence that the Act in question is not such a regulation. If a certificate is procured, solicitation is permitted without restraint but, in the absence of a certificate, solicitation is altogether prohibited.

The appellants urge that to require them to obtain a certificate as a condition of soliciting support for their views amounts to a prior restraint on the exercise of their religion within the meaning of the Constitution. The State insists that the Act, as construed by the Supreme Court of Connecticut, imposes no previous restraint upon the dissemination of religious views or teaching but merely safeguards against the perpetration of frauds under the cloak of religion. Conceding that this is so, the question remains whether the method adopted by Connecticut to that end transgresses the liberty safeguarded by the Constitution.

The general regulation, in the public interest, of solicitation, which does not involve any religious test and does not unreasonably obstruct or delay the collection of funds, is not open to any constitutional objection, even though the collection be for a religious purpose. Such regulation would not constitute a prohibited previous restraint on the free exercise of religion or interpose an inadmissible obstacle to its exercise.

It will be noted, however, that the Act requires an application to the secretary of the public welfare council of the State; that he is empowered to determine whether the cause is a religious one, and that the issue of a certificate depends upon his affirmative action. If he finds that the cause is not that of religion, to solicit for it becomes a crime. He is not to issue a certificate as a matter of course. His decision to issue or refuse it involves appraisal of facts, the exercise of judgment, and the formation of an opinion. He is authorized to withhold his approval if he determines that the cause is not a religious one. Such a censorship of religion as the means of determining its right to survive is a denial of liberty protected by the First Amendment and included in the liberty which is within the protection of the Fourteenth.

Nothing we have said is intended even remotely to imply that, under the cloak of religion, persons may, with impunity, commit frauds upon the public. Certainly penal laws are available to punish such conduct. Even the exercise of religion may be at some slight inconvenience in order that the state may protect its citizens from injury. Without doubt a State may protect its citizens from fraudulent solicitation by requiring a stranger in the community, before permitting him publicly to solicit funds for any purpose, to establish his identity and his authority to act for the cause which he purports to represent. The State is likewise free to regulate the time and manner of solicitation generally, in the interest of public safety, peace, comfort or convenience. But to condition the solicitation of aid for the perpetuation of religious views or systems upon a license, the grant of which rests in the exercise of a determination by state authority as to what is a religious cause, is to lay a forbidden burden upon the exercise of liberty protected by the Constitution.

Second. We hold that, in the circumstances disclosed, the conviction of Jesse Cantwell on the fifth count must be set aside. Decision as to the lawfulness of the conviction demands the weighing of two conflicting interests. The fundamental law declares the interest of the United States that the free exercise of religion be not prohibited and that freedom to communicate information and opinion be not abridged. The State of Connecticut has an obvious interest in the preservation and protection of peace and good order within her borders. We must determine whether the alleged protection of the State's interest, means to which end would, in the absence of limitation by the Federal Constitution, lie wholly within the State's discretion, has been pressed, in this instance, to a point where it has come into fatal collision with the overriding interest protected by the federal compact. . . .

Having these considerations in mind, we note that Jesse Cantwell, on April 25, 1938, was upon a public street, where he had a right to be, and where he had a right peacefully to impart his views to others. There is no showing that his deportment was noisy, truculent, overbearing or offensive. He requested of two pedestrians permission to play to them a phonograph record. The permission was granted. It is not claimed that he intended to insult or affront the hearers by playing the record. It is plain that he wished only to interest them in his propaganda. The sound of the phonograph is not shown to have disturbed residents of the street, to have drawn a crowd, or to have impeded traffic. Thus far he had invaded no right or interest of the public or of the men accosted.

The record played by Cantwell embodies a general attack on all organized religious systems as instruments of Satan and injurious to man; it then singles out the Roman Catholic Church for strictures couched in terms which naturally would offend not only persons of that persuasion, but all others who respect the honestly held religious faith of their fellows. The hearers were in fact highly offended. One of them said he felt like hitting Cantwell and the other that he was tempted to throw Cantwell off the street. . . .

Cantwell's conduct, in the view of the court below, considered apart from the effect of his communication upon his hearers, did not amount to a breach of the peace. One may, however, be guilty of the offense if he commit acts or make statements likely to provoke violence and disturbance of good order, even though no such eventuality be intended. Decisions to this effect are many, but examination discloses that, in practically all, the provocative language which was held to amount to a breach of the peace consisted of profane, indecent, or abusive remarks directed to the person of the hearer. Resort to epithets or personal abuse is not in any proper sense communication of information or opinion safeguarded by the Constitution, and its punishment as a criminal act would raise no question under that instrument. . . .

Although the contents of the record not unnaturally aroused animosity, we think that, in the absence of a statute narrowly drawn to define and punish specific conduct as constituting a clear and present danger to a substantial interest of the State, the petitioner's communication, considered in the light of the constitutional guarantees, raised no such clear and present menace to public peace and order as to render him liable to conviction of the common law offense in question.

The judgment affirming the convictions on the third and fifth counts is reversed and the cause is remanded for further proceedings not inconsistent with this opinion.

Reversed.

It should be noted that the holding of *Cantwell* v. *Connecticut* reaches only those discretionary practices on the part of officials which would allow them to make distinctions between what is and what is not a religious cause. The Court did not hold that every requirement of obtaining a permit prior to embarking on religious solicitation would be unconstitutional. It did, however, point out that such requirements would have to be rather severely limited to such purposes as identification and notification in order to protect against fraud to escape the strictures of the First Amendment's protections to speech and religion.

Another case illustrating the firmness with which the Court's majority has applied its rule regarding permit requirements is *Kunz* v. *New York*, decided in 1951. As in *Cantwell*, the case presents concurrently questions of free speech and religious freedom.

KUNZ *v.* NEW YORK

340 U.S. 290 (1951)

Mr. Chief Justice Vinson delivered the opinion of the Court.

New York City has adopted an ordinance which makes it unlawful to hold public worship meetings on the streets without first obtaining a permit from the city police commissioner. Appellant, Carl Jacob Kunz, was convicted and fined $10 for violating this ordinance by holding a religious meeting without a permit. The conviction was affirmed by the . . . New York Court of Appeals, three judges dissenting. . . . The case is here on appeal, it having been urged that the ordinance is invalid under the Fourteenth Amendment.

Appellant is an ordained Baptist minister who speaks under the auspices of the

"Outdoor Gospel Work," of which he is the director. He has been preaching for about six years, and states that it is his conviction and duty to "go out on the highways and byways and preach the word of God." In 1946, he applied for and received a permit under the ordinance in question, there being no question that appellant comes within the classes of persons entitled to receive permits under the ordinance.* This permit, like all others, was good only for the calendar year in which issued. In November, 1946, his permit was revoked after a hearing by the police commissioner. The revocation was based on evidence that he had ridiculed and denounced other religious beliefs in his meetings.

Although the penalties of the ordinance apply to anyone who "ridicules and denounces other religious beliefs," the ordinance does not specify this as a ground for permit revocation. Indeed, there is no mention in the ordinance of any power of revocation. However, appellant did not seek judicial or administrative review of the revocation proceedings, and any question as to the propriety of the revocation is not before us in this case. In any event, the revocation affected appellant's rights to speak in 1946 only. Appellant applied for another permit in 1947, and again in 1948, but was notified each time that his application was "disapproved," with no reason for the disapproval being given. On September 11, 1948, appellant was arrested for speaking at Columbus Circle in New York City without a permit. It is from the conviction which resulted that this appeal has been taken.

Appellant's conviction was thus based upon his failure to possess a permit for 1948. We are here concerned only with the propriety of the action of the police commissioner in refusing to issue that permit. Disapproval of the 1948 permit application by the police commissioner was justified by the New York courts on the ground that a permit had previously been revoked "for good reasons." It is noteworthy that there is no mention in the ordinance of reasons for which such a permit application can be refused. This interpretation allows the police commissioner, an administrative official, to exercise discretion in denying subsequent permit applications on the basis of his interpretation, at that time, of what is deemed to be conduct condemned by the ordinance. We have here, then, an ordinance which gives an administrative official discretionary power to control in advance the right of citizens to speak on religious matters on the streets of New York. As such, the ordinance is clearly invalid as a prior restraint on the exercise of First Amendment rights.

In considering the right of a municipality to control the use of public streets for the expression of religious views, we start with the words of Mr. Justice Roberts that "Wherever the title of streets and parks may rest, they have immemorially been held in trust for the use of the public and, time out of mind, have been used for purposes of assembly, communicating thoughts between citizens, and discussing public questions." *Hague* v. *C.I.O.,* 307 U.S. 496, 515. Although this Court has recognized that a statute may be enacted which prevents serious interference with normal usage of streets and parks, *Cox* v. *New Hampshire,* 312 U.S. 569, we have consistently condemned licensing systems which vest in an administrative official discretion to grant or withhold a permit upon broad criteria unrelated to proper regulation of public places. In *Cantwell* v. *Connecticut,* 310 U.S. 296 (1940), this Court held invalid an ordinance which required a license for soliciting money for religious causes. Speaking for a unanimous Court, Mr. Justice Roberts said: "But

* The New York Court of Appeals has construed the ordinance to require that all initial requests for permits by eligible applicants must be granted. 300 N.Y. at 276.

to condition the solicitation of aid for the perpetuation of religious views or systems upon a license, the grant of which rests in the exercise of a determination by state authority as to what is a religious cause, is to lay a forbidden burden upon the exercise of liberty protected by the Constitution." 310 U.S. at 307. . . .

The court below has mistakenly derived support for its conclusion from the evidence produced at the trial that appellant's religious meetings had, in the past, caused some disorder. There are appropriate public remedies to protect the peace and order of the community if appellant's speeches should result in disorder or violence. "In the present case, we have no occasion to inquire as to the permissible scope of subsequent punishment." *Near* v. *Minnesota,* 283 U.S. 697, 715. We do not express any opinion on the propriety of punitive remedies which the New York authorities may utilize. We are here concerned with suppression—not punishment. It is sufficient to say that New York cannot vest restraining control over the right to speak on religious subjects in an administrative official where there are no appropriate standards to guide his action.

Reversed.

Mr. Justice Black concurs in the result.

Mr. Justice Frankfurter, concurring in the result. . . .

Mr. Justice Jackson, dissenting. . . .

At these meetings, Kunz preached, among many other things of like tenor, that "The Catholic Church makes merchandise out of souls," that Catholicism is "a religion of the devil," and that the Pope is "the anti-Christ." The Jews he denounced as "Christ-killers," and he said of them, "All the garbage that didn't believe in Christ should have been burnt in the incinerators. It's a shame they all weren't.". . .

This Court today initiates the doctrine that language such as this, in the environment of the street meeting, is immune from prior municipal control. We would have a very different question if New York had presumed to say that Kunz could not speak his piece in his own pulpit or hall. But it has undertaken to restrain him only if he chooses to speak at street meetings. There is a world of difference. The street preacher takes advantage of people's presence on the streets to impose his message upon what, in a sense, is a captive audience. A meeting on private property is made up of an audience that has volunteered to listen. The question, therefore, is not whether New York could, if it tried, silence Kunz, but whether it must place its streets at his service to hurl insults at the passerby. . . .

Of course, as to the press, there are the best of reasons against any licensing or prior restraint. Decisions such as *Near* v. *Minnesota, supra,* hold any licensing or prior restraint of the press unconstitutional, and I heartily agree. But precedents from that field cannot reasonably be transposed to the street-meeting field. The impact of publishing on public order has no similarity with that of a street meeting. Publishing does not make private use of public property. It reaches only those who choose to read, and, in that way, is analogous to a meeting held in a hall where those who come do so by choice. Written words are less apt to incite or provoke to mass action than spoken words, speech being the primitive and direct communication with the emotions. Few are the riots caused by publication alone, few are the mobs that have not had their immediate origin in harangue. The vulnerability of various forms of communication to community control must be proportioned to their impact upon other community interests.

It is suggested that a permit for a street meeting could be required if the ordinance would prescribe precise standards for its grant or denial. . . .

Of course, standards for administrative action are always desirable, and the more exact the better. But I do not see how this Court can condemn municipal ordinances for not setting forth comprehensive First Amendment standards. This Court never has announced what those standards must be, it does not now say what they are, and it is not clear that any majority could agree on them. In no field are there more numerous individual opinions among the Justices. . . . It seems hypercritical to strike down local laws on their faces for want of standards when we have no standards. And I do not find it required by existing authority. I think that where speech is outside of constitutional immunity the local community or the State is left a large measure of discretion as to the means for dealing with it. . . .

Turning then to the permit system as applied by the Court of Appeals, whose construction binds us, we find that issuance the first time is required. Denial is warranted only in such unusual cases as where an applicant has had a permit which has been revoked for cause and he asserts the right to continue the conduct which was the cause for revocation. If anything less than a reasonable certainty of disorder was shown, denial of a permit would be improper. The procedure by which that decision is reached commends itself to the orderly mind—complaints are filed, witnesses are heard, opportunity to cross-examine is given, and decision is reached by what we must assume to be an impartial and reasonable administrative officer, and, if he denies the permit, the applicant may carry his cause to the courts. He may thus have a civil test of his rights without the personal humiliation of being arrested as presenting a menace to public order. It seems to me that this procedure better protects freedom of speech than to let everyone speak without leave, but subject to surveillance and to being ordered to stop in the discretion of the police. . . .

If any two subjects are intrinsically incendiary and divisive, they are race and religion. Racial fears and hatreds have been at the root of the most terrible riots that have disgraced American civilization. They are ugly possibilities that overhang every great American city. The "consecrated hatreds of sect" account for more than a few of the world's bloody disorders. These are the explosives which the Court says Kunz may play with in the public streets, and the community must not only tolerate but aid him. I find no such doctrine in the Constitution.

In this case there is no evidence of a purpose to suppress speech, except to keep it in bounds that will not upset good order. If there are abuses of censorship or discrimination in administering the ordinance, as well there may be, they are not proved in this case. This Court should be particularly sure of its ground before it strikes down, in a time like this, the going practical system by which New York has sought to control its street-meeting problem. . . .

It should be noted that the Court did not flatly proscribe the requirement of a permit in the *Kunz* decision. But where such requirements pertain, they cannot admit of official discretion which would allow arbitrary or capricious distinctions among applicants. Thus the *Kunz* majority was following the line of reasoning used earlier in *Cox* v. *New Hampshire* (1941) with respect to a parade permit requirement. The *Cox* case is important as indicating that the phrase "no prior restraint" is not altogether apt as a description of First Amendment application. To bar speeches or meetings unless a permit has been obtained is certainly to set up a hurdle, albeit nondiscretionary, which is a type of restraint prior to the exercise of the rights of speech or assembly. This does not argue against the propriety of such requirements, but it points up the caution that one should not erect a judicially interpretative phrase to the status of the First Amendment itself.

COX v. STATE OF NEW HAMPSHIRE
312 U.S. 569 (1941)

Mr. Chief Justice Hughes delivered the opinion of the Court.

Appellants are five "Jehovah's Witnesses" who, with sixty-three others of the same persuasion, were convicted in the municipal court of Manchester, New Hampshire, for violation of a state statute prohibiting a "parade or procession" upon a public street without a special license. . . .

The facts, which are conceded by the defendants to be established by the evidence, are these: The sixty-eight defendants and twenty other persons met at a hall in the City of Manchester on the evening of Saturday, July 8, 1939, "for the purpose of engaging in an information march." The company was divided into four or five groups, each with about fifteen to twenty persons. Each group then proceeded to a different part of the business district of the city and there "would line up in single-file formation and then proceed to march along the sidewalk, 'single-file,' that is, following one another." Each of the defendants carried a small staff with a sign reading "Religion is a Snare and a Racket" and on the reverse "Serve God and Christ the King." Some of the marchers carried placards bearing the statement "Fascism or Freedom. Hear Judge Rutherford and Face the Facts." The marchers also handed out printed leaflets announcing a meeting to be held at a later time in the hall from which they had started, where a talk on government would be given to the public free of charge. Defendants did not apply for a permit and none was issued. . . .

Appellants urge that each of the defendants was a minister ordained to preach the gospel in accordance with his belief and that the participation of these ministers in the march was for the purpose of disseminating information in the public interest and was one of their ways of worship. . . .

There appears to be no ground for challenging the ruling of the state court that appellants were in fact engaged in a parade or procession upon the public streets. . . .

Civil liberties, as guaranteed by the Constitution, imply the existence of an organized society maintaining public order without which liberty itself would be lost in the excesses of unrestrained abuses. The authority of a municipality to impose regulations in order to assure the safety and convenience of the people in the use of public highways has never been regarded as inconsistent with civil liberties but rather as one of the means of safeguarding the good order upon which they ultimately depend. The control of travel on the streets of cities is the most familiar illustration of this recognition of social need. Where a restriction of the use of highways in that relation is designed to promote the public convenience in the interest of all, it cannot be disregarded by the attempted exercise of some civil rights which in other circumstances would be entitled to protection. One would not be justified in ignoring the familiar red traffic light because he thought it his religious duty to disobey the municipal command or sought by that means to direct public attention to an announcement of his opinions. As regulation of the use of the streets for parades and processions is a traditional exercise of control by local government, the question in a particular case is whether that control is exerted so as not to deny or unwarrantedly abridge the right of assembly and the opportunities for the communication of thought and the discussion of public questions immemorially associated with resort to public places. . . .

In the instant case, we are aided by the opinion of the Supreme Court of the State which construed the statute and defined the limitations of the authority conferred for the granting of licenses for parades and processions. The court observed . . . that communication "by the distribution of literature or by the display of placards and signs" was in no respect regulated by the statute; that the regulation with respect to parades and processions was applicable only "to organized formations of persons using the highways"; and that "the defendants separately or collectively in groups not constituting a parade or procession," were "under no contemplation of the act." In this light, the court thought that interference with liberty of speech and writing seemed slight; that the distribution of pamphlets and folders by the groups "traveling in unorganized fashion" would have had as large a circulation, and that "signs carried by members of the groups not in marching formation would have been as conspicuous, as published by them while in parade or procession."

It was with this view of the limited objective of the statute that the state court considered and defined the duty of the licensing authority and the rights of the appellants to a license for their parade, with regard only to considerations of time, place and manner so as to conserve the public convenience. The obvious advantage of requiring application for a permit was noted as giving the public authorities notice in advance so as to afford opportunity for proper policing. And the court further observed that, in fixing time and place, the license served "to prevent confusion by overlapping parades or processions, to secure convenient use of the streets by other travelers, and to minimize the risk of disorder." But the court held that the licensing board was not vested with arbitrary power or an unfettered discretion; that its discretion must be exercised with "uniformity of method of treatment upon the facts of each application, free from improper or inappropriate considerations and from unfair discrimination;" that a "systematic, consistent and just order of treatment, with reference to the convenience of public use of the highways, is the statutory mandate." The defendants, said the court, "had a right, under the act, to a license to march when, where and as they did, if after a required investigation it was found that the convenience of the public in the use of the streets would not thereby be unduly disturbed, upon such conditions or changes in time, place and manner as would avoid disturbance."

If a municipality has authority to control the use of its public streets for parades or processions, as it undoubtedly has, it cannot be denied authority to give consideration, without unfair discrimination, to time, place and manner in relation to the other proper uses of the streets. We find it impossible to say that the limited authority conferred by the licensing provisions of the statute in question as thus construed by the state court contravened any constitutional right.

There remains the question of license fees which, as the court said, had a permissible range from $300 to a nominal amount. The court construed the Act as requiring "a reasonable fixing of the amount of the fee." "The charge," said the court, "for a circus parade or a celebration procession of length, each drawing crowds of observers, would take into account the greater public expense of policing the spectacle, compared with the slight expense of a less expansive and attractive parade or procession, to which the charge would be adjusted." The fee was held to be "not a revenue tax, but one to meet the expense incident to the administration of the act and to the maintenance of public order in the matter licensed." There is nothing contrary to the Constitution in the charge of a fee limited to the purpose stated. The suggestion that a flat fee should have been charged fails to take account of the difficulty of framing a fair schedule to meet all circumstances, and we perceive no constitutional ground for denying to local governments that flexibility of adjustment of fees which in the light of varying conditions would tend to conserve rather than impair the liberty sought.

There is no evidence that the statute has been administered otherwise than in the fair and non-discriminatory manner which the state court has construed it to require. . . .

Nor is any question of peaceful picketing here involved, as in *Thornhill* v. *Alabama*, 310 U.S. 88. . . . The statute, as the state court said, is not aimed at any restraint of freedom of speech, and there is no basis for an assumption that it would be applied so as to prevent peaceful picketing as described in the cases cited.

The argument as to freedom of worship is also beside the point. No interference with religious worship or the practice of religion in any proper sense is shown, but only the exercise of local control over the use of streets for parades and processions.

The judgment of the Supreme Court of New Hampshire is 　*Affirmed.*

The issue of the validity of the fee requirement prior to parading was discussed separately in the *Cox* case and the requirement was upheld. The decision cannot be read, however, as supporting all license taxes on the exercise of First Amendment rights. The Court's discussion was confined to the problems of administering the municipal function of policing traffic in the public ways. Other types of religious exercise requiring no such special attention could be treated quite differently by the Court in dealing with license tax requirements. However, in the next year after *Cox,* the Court was faced with a challenge to a municipal ordinance which imposed a license tax on all persons who sold or canvassed for the sale of printed matter. There was no discrimination against sellers of religious literature; the license fee applied to all alike. Jehovah's Witnesses in Opelika, Alabama, raised the issue of abridgment of religious freedom in the application of such a fee requirement to their missionary efforts. In a five-to-four decision in *Jones* v. *Opelika*, 316 U.S. 584 (1942), the Court upheld the ordinance as applied to the Jehovah's Witnesses. The opinion for the majority stated that "The First Amendment does not require a subsidy in the form of fiscal exemption." This judgment was vacated in the following year, however, when in *Murdock* v. *Pennsylvania*, 319 U.S. 105 (1943), the Court reversed its position and held such fees unconstitutional as applied to the sale of religious literature. In this case Jehovah's Witnesses attacked the license requirement of the City of Jeanette, Pennsylvania. Justice Douglas, speaking for a majority of five, stated:

The hand distribution of religious tracts is an age-old form of missionary evangelism—as old as the history of printing presses. It has been a potent force in various religious movements down through the years. This form of evangelism is utilized today on a large scale by various religious sects whose colporteurs carry the Gospel to thousands upon thousands of homes and seek through personal visitations to win adherents to their faith. It is more than preaching; it is more than distribution of religious literature. It is a combination of both. Its purpose is as evangelical as the revival meeting. This form of religious activity occupies the same high estate under the First Amendment as do worship in the churches and preaching from the pulpits. It has the same claim to protection as the more orthodox and conventional exercises of religion. It also has the same claim as the others to the guarantees of freedom of speech and freedom of the press.

It was alleged in justification for the license fee that the religious literature was distributed with a solicitation of funds, and thus utilized ordinary commercial methods. Justice Douglas responded that the mere fact that the religious literature is "sold" by itinerant preachers rather than "donated" does not transform evangelism into a commercial enterprise. "If it did, then the passing of the collection plate in church would make the church service a commercial project. The constitutional rights of those spreading their religious beliefs through the spoken and printed word are not to be gauged by standards governing retailers or wholesalers of books." He stated further that an itinerant evangelist does not become "a mere book agent by selling the Bible or religious tracts to help defray his expenses or to sustain him."

The Justice was careful to say, however, that he did not mean that religious groups and the press are free from all financial burdens of government. Normal income taxes or property taxes levied on one who engages in religious activities are a different matter. But in this case, it was "a flat tax imposed on the exercise of a privilege granted by the Bill of Rights," and therefore a prior restraint on the free exercise of religion.

The *Murdock* decision was followed in *Follett* v. *Town of McCormick*, 321 U.S. 573 (1944), where a similar municipal tax was sought to be imposed on a Jehovah's Witness who maintained his home in the municipality and who earned his living by means of the sale of religious literature. [For discussions of some of the earlier Jehovah's Witnesses cases, see Hollis W. Barber, "Religious Liberty v. Police Power—Jehovah's Witnesses," 41 *Am. Pol. Sci. Rev.* 226 (1947); Edward F. Waite, "The Debt of Constitutional Law to Jehovah's Witnesses," 28 *Minn. L. Rev.* 209 (1944).]

THE "FREE EXERCISE" CLAUSE AND JUDICIAL SETTLEMENT OF CHURCH DISPUTES

Church organizations are no less subject to rifts and dissensions than are other groups, despite their presumably nobler aims. When these differences involve matters of religious beliefs and doctrines, then the warring factions are left to their own devices, if peaceable, to settle the disputes. But when, as is sometimes the case, the differences shift over to issues of property rights, then questions are raised which have traditionally been within the purview of the civil courts. To say this, however, is not to throw the door open to judicial interference in the property relationships of church groups. For it is clear that courts, as well as legislative bodies, have potentialities for interfering with religion through the simple device of awarding title to the properties to the specific faction which the court chooses to promote. This is the danger area in the judicial settlement of church disputes. When arguments arise between factions over who gets the pulpit, how can the courts select one of the groups as the official, legally constituted congregation without being guilty of abridging religious freedom? The courts cannot evade the responsibility of settling property disputes peaceably, but they cannot invade the sphere of religion by interjecting their own views on matters of doctrine. How can they reconcile these requirements? The United States Supreme Court faced this question for the first time in 1872 in the case of *Watson* v. *Jones*.

WATSON v. JONES
13 Wallace 679 (1872)

[A number of Southern churches withdrew from the General Assembly of the Presbyterian Church and formed the Presbyterian Church of The Confederate States, following a division of opinion over the question of slavery. The congregation of the Walnut Street Church of Louisville, Kentucky, split irreconcilably over the question of adherence to the northern or southern branch and came to court to settle the property issues. The Trial Court held for the anti-slavery group, and the appellate court affirmed.]

Mr. Justice Miller delivered the opinion of the Court.

This case belongs to a class, happily rare in our courts, in which one of the parties to a controversy, essentially ecclesiastical, resorts to the judicial tribunals of the State for the maintenance of rights which the Church has refused to acknowledge, or found itself unable to protect. Much as such dissensions among the members of a religious society should be regretted, a regret which is increased when passing from the control of the judicial and legislative bodies of the entire organization to which the society belongs, an appeal is made to the secular authority; the courts when so called on must perform their functions as in other cases. . . .

The questions which have come before the civil courts concerning the rights to property held by ecclesiastical bodies, may, so far as we have been able to examine them, be profitably classified under three general heads, which of course do not include cases governed by considerations applicable to a church established and supported by law as the religion of the State.

1. The first of these is when the property which is the subject of controversy has been, by the deed or will of the donor, or other instrument by which the property is held, by the express terms of the instrument devoted to the teaching, support or spread of some specific form of religious doctrine or belief.

2. The second is when the property is held by a religious congregation which, by the nature of its organization, is strictly independent of other ecclesiastical associations, and so far as church government is concerned, owes no fealty or obligation to any higher authority.

3. The third is where the religious congregation or ecclesiastical body holding the

property is but a subordinate member of some general church organization in which there are superior ecclesiastical tribunals with a general and ultimate power of control more or less complete in some supreme judicatory over the whole membership of that general organization.

In regard to the first of these classes it seems hardly to admit a rational doubt that an individual or an association of individuals may dedicate property by way of trust to the purpose of sustaining, supporting and propagating definite religious doctrines or principles, providing that in doing so they violate no law of morality, and give to the instrument by which their purpose is evidenced, the formalities which the laws require. And it would seem also to be the obvious duty of the court, in a case properly made, to see that the property so dedicated is not diverted from the trust which is thus attached to its use. So long as there are persons qualified within the meaning of the original dedication, and who are willing to teach the doctrines or principles prescribed in the act of dedication, and so long as there is any one so interested in the execution of the trust as to have a standing in court, it must be that they can prevent the diversion of the property or fund to other and different uses. This is the general doctrine of courts of equity as to charities, and it seems equally applicable to ecclesiastical matters.

In such case, if the trust is confided to a religious congregation of the independent or congregational form of church government, it is not in the power of the majority of that congregation, however preponderant, by reason of a change of views on religious subjects, to carry the property so confided to them to the support of new and conflicting doctrine. A pious man building and dedicating a house of worship to the sole and exclusive use of those who believe in the doctrine of the Holy Trinity, and placing it under the control of a congregation which at the time holds the same belief, has a right to expect that the law will prevent that property from being used as a means of support and dissemination of the Unitarian doctrine, and as a place of Unitarian worship. Nor is the principle varied when the organization to which the trust is confided is of the second or associated form of church government. The protection which the law throws around the trust is the same. And though the task may be a delicate one and a difficult one, it will be the duty of the court in such cases, when the doctrine to be taught or the form of worship to be used is definitely and clearly laid down, to inquire whether the party accused of violating the trust is holding or teaching a different doctrine, or using a form of worship which is so far variant as to defeat the declared objects of the trust. . . .

The second class of cases which we have described has reference to the case of a church of a strictly congregational or independent organization, governed solely within itself, either by a majority of its members or by such other local organism as it may have instituted for the purpose of ecclesiastical government; and to property held by such a church, either by way of purchase or donation, with no other specific trust attached to it in the hands of the church than that it is for the use of that congregation as a religious society.

In such cases, where there is a schism which leads to a separation into distinct and conflicting bodies, the rights of such bodies to the use of the property must be determined by the ordinary principles which govern voluntary associations. If the principle of government in such cases is that the majority rules, then the numerical majority of members must control the right to the use of the property. If there be within the congregation officers in whom are vested the powers of such control, then those who adhere to the acknowledged organism by which the body is governed are entitled to the use of the property. The minority in choosing to separate themselves into a distinct body, and refusing to recognize the authority of the governing body, can claim no rights in the property from the fact that they had once been members of the church or congregation. This ruling admits of no inquiry into the existing religious opinions of those who comprise the legal or regular organization; for, if such was permitted, a very small minority, without any officers of the church among them, might be found to be the only faithful supporters of the religious dogmas of the founders of the Church. There being no such trust imposed upon the property when purchased or given, the court will not imply one for the purpose of expelling from its use those who by regular succession and order constitute the Church, because they may have changed in some respect their views of religious truth. . . .

But the third of these classes of cases is the one which is oftenest found in the courts, and which, with reference to the number and difficulty of the questions involved, and to other considerations, is every way the most important.

It is the case of property acquired in any of the usual modes for the general use of a religious congregation which is itself part of a large and general organization of some religious denomination, with which it is more or less intimately connected by religious views and ecclesiastical government.

The case before us is one of this class, growing out of a schism which has divided the congregation and its officers and the presbytery and synod, and which appeals to the courts to determine the right to the use of the property so acquired. Here is no case of property devoted forever by the instrument which conveyed it, or by any specific declaration to its owner, to the support of any special religious dogmas, or any peculiar form of worship, but of property purchased for the use of a religious congregation, and so long as any existing religious congregation can be ascertained to be that congregation, or its regular and legitimate successor, it is entitled to the use of the property. In the case of an independent congregation we have pointed out how this identity, or succession, is to be ascertained, but in cases of this character we are bound to look at the fact that the local congregation is itself but a member of a much larger and more important religious organization, and is under its government and control, and is bound by its orders and judgments. There are in the Presbyterian system of ecclesiastical government, in regular succession, the Presbytery over the session or local church, the Synod over the Presbytery, and the General Assembly over all. These are called in the language of the church organs "judicatories," and they entertain appeals from the decisions of those below, and prescribe corrective measures in other cases.

In this class of cases we think the rule of action which should govern the civil courts, founded in a broad and sound view of the relations of church and state under our system of laws, and supported by a preponderating weight of judicial authority is, that, whenever the questions of discipline or of faith, or ecclesiastical rule, custom or law have been decided by the highest of these church judicatories to which the matter has been carried, the legal tribunals must accept such decisions as final, and as binding on them, in their application to the case before them. . . .

In this country the full and free right to entertain any religious belief, to practice any religious principle, and to teach any religious doctrine which does not violate the laws of morality and property, and which does not infringe personal rights, is conceded to all. The law knows no heresy, and is committed to the support of no dogma, the establishment of no sect. The right to organize voluntary religious associations to assist in the expression and dissemination of any religious doctrine, and to create tribunals for the decision of controverted questions of faith within the association, and for the ecclesiastical government of all the individual members, congregations and officers within the general association, is unquestioned. All who unite themselves to such a body do so with an implied consent to this government, and are bound to submit to it. But it would be a vain consent and would lead to the total subversion of such religious bodies, if any one aggrieved by one of their decisions could appeal to the secular courts and have them reversed. It is of the essence of these religious unions, and of their right to establish tribunals for the decision of questions arising among themselves, that those decisions should be binding in all cases of ecclesiastical cognizance, subject only to such appeals as the organism itself provides for. . . .

[Here Justice Miller reviews other cases decided in state courts on similar questions of disposition of religious disputes.]

We cannot better close this review of the authorities than in the language of the Supreme Court of Pennsylvania, in the case of *The German Ref. Ch.* v. *Seibert*: "The decisions of ecclesiastical courts, like every other judicial tribunal, are final, as they are the best judges of what constitutes an offense against the word of God and the discipline of the Church. Any other than those courts must be incompetent judges of matters of faith, discipline and doctrine; and civil courts, if they should be so unwise as to attempt to supervise their judgments on matters which come within their jurisdiction, would only involve themselves in a sea of uncertainty and doubt which would do anything but improve either religion or good morals.". . .

But we need pursue this subject no further. Whatever may have been the case before the Kentucky court, the appellants in the case presented to us have separated themselves wholly from the church organization to which they belonged when this controversy commenced. They now deny its authority, denounce its action and refuse to abide by its judgments. They have first erected themselves into a new organization, and have since joined themselves to another totally different, if not hostile, to the one to which they belonged when the difficulty first began. Under any of the decisions which we have examined, the appellants, in their present position, have no right to the property, or to the use of it, which is the subject of this suit. . . .

Affirmed.

Justice Miller's clear and careful categorization of property questions in ecclesiastical disputes coming before the civil courts is still followed today. He described three types of cases and stated the governing principle for each. First, if the property has been set up in trust for the propagation of a specific doctrine, then the civil courts will enforce such purpose irrespective of the desires of the governing body of the church or the majority of its members. If no such arrangement is present, however, then the applicable rule for disposition of the property turns on whether the body is a self-governing congregational church or a hierarchical (centrally-organized) church. In the former case, the court applies a majority-rule principle and seeks to determine which faction in the dispute constitutes the majority. In the latter case, however, it is immaterial whether the protesting faction constitutes a majority or not. The court will follow the decision of the proper hierarchical or institutional authority, and its inquiry is limited to determining what that authority's decision is.

Watson v. *Jones* was used in 1952 as authority for holding unconstitutional a New York statute which undertook to determine proprietary use of the St. Nicholas Cathedral in New York. Two separate factions claimed the cathedral, each contending that it was the duly authorized proprietor or agent of the Russian Orthodox Church. By statute the legislature of New York in 1945 attempted to free the Russian Orthodox churches in that state from control of the Moscow church authorities—the Patriarch of Moscow and the Holy Synod—and leave them under the control of the Russian Church in America—a North American organization exclusively. Thus one faction claimed occupancy by virtue of an appointment by the Patriarch of Moscow, while the opposing group claimed under the statute. The New York Court of Appeals, following the statute, held for the latter group. In *Kedroff* v. *St. Nicholas Cathedral*, 344 U.S. 94 (1952), the United States Supreme Court reversed. After examining the complicated factual setting of the case, Justice Reed, speaking for the majority, stated:

> We conclude that [the statute] undertook by its terms to transfer the control of the New York churches of the Russian Orthodox religion from the central governing hierarchy of the Russian Orthodox Church, the Patriarch of Moscow and the Holy Synod, to the governing authorities of the Russian Church in America, a church organization limited to the diocese of North America and the Aleutian Islands. This transfer takes place by virtue of the statute. Such a law violates the Fourteenth Amendment. It prohibits in this country the free exercise of religion. Legislation that regulates church administration, the operation of the churches, the appointment of clergy, by requiring conformity to church statutes "adopted at a general convention (sobor) held in the City of New York..." prohibits the free exercise of religion. Although this statute requires the New York churches to "in all other respects conform to, maintain and follow the faith, doctrine, ritual, communion, discipline, canon law, traditions and usages of the Eastern Confession (Eastern Orthodox or Greek Catholic Church)," their conformity is by legislative fiat and subject to legislative will....

> This legislation...in the view of the Court of Appeals, gave the use of the churches to the Russian Church in America on the theory that this church would most faithfully carry out the purposes of the religious trust. Thus dangers of political use of church pulpits would be minimized. Legislative power to punish subversive action cannot be doubted. If such action should be actually attempted by a cleric, neither his robe nor his pulpit would be a defense.... Here there is a transfer by statute of control over churches. This violates our rule of separation between church and state. That conclusion results from the purpose, meaning and effect of the New York legislation stated above, considered in the light of the history and decisions considered below....

> [Here Justice Reed discusses hierarchical churches and gives a detailed treatment of *Watson* v. *Jones*.]

> ...The opinion radiates...a spirit of freedom for religious organizations, an independence from secular control or manipulation—in short, power to decide for themselves, free from state interference, matters of church government as well as

those of faith and doctrine. Freedom to select the clergy, where no improper methods of choice are proven, we think, must now be said to have a federal constitutional protection as a part of the free exercise of religion against state interference. . . .

The Supreme Court reversed and remanded the *Kedroff* case to the New York Court of Appeals. That court then reached the same decision as it had earlier, but this time on common-law grounds. In *Kreshik* v. *St. Nicholas Cathedral*, 363 U.S. 190 (1960), the Supreme Court reversed again. In a *per curiam* opinion the Court stated:

[T]he decision now under review rests on the same premises which were found to have underlain the enactment of the statute struck down in *Kedroff*. . . . But it is established doctrine that "[i]t is not of moment that the State has here acted solely through its judicial branch, for whether legislative or judicial, it is still the application of state power which we are asked to scrutinize.". . . Accordingly, our ruling in *Kedroff* is controlling here, and requires dismissal of the complaint.

MISCELLANEOUS ESTABLISHMENT AND FREE EXERCISE QUESTIONS

In concluding the discussion of freedom of religion, two additional issues should at least be noted. The first is the question of the validity of tax exemptions granted to church property and income tax deductions for contributions to religious organizations. Logically, one might argue that if direct appropriations of money by governments to religious organizations are an unconstitutional establishment of religion, then a tax exemption which results in a net financial gain for the same religious groups should rest on the same principle. Whether logical or not, however, history has indicated a clear differentiation by the courts between appropriations and tax exemptions, and the latter have been uniformly sustained. This but raises another question, however, and that is the question of defining a religious institution entitled to the exemption, since the mere claim cannot be permitted to be conclusive of the question of entitlement under the law. Such an examination inescapably leads the courts into the determination of whether a particular group claiming the exemption is a religious group, and thus, like it or not, in such issues the civil courts are in one sense passing judgment on religious belief. [For a detailed treatment of the cases and issues raised, see David Fellman, *op. cit.*, pp. 43–51; Arvo Van Alstyne, "Tax Exemption of Church Property," 20 *Ohio St. L. J.* 461 (1959); Note, "Constitutionality of Tax Exemptions Accorded American Church Property," 30 *Albany L. Rev.* 58 (1966).]

In *Walz* v. *Tax Commission of the City of New York*, 397 U.S. 664 (1970), the Court held, with only one dissent, that the granting of tax exemptions to religious organizations did not violate the religion clauses of the First Amendment since (1) the inclusion within the exemption provisions of a broad class of nonprofit organizations such as libraries, playgrounds, and hospitals indicated that the legislation was not aimed at establishing or supporting religion, and (2) the exemptions created only a minimal and remote involvement between church and state. (See Chapter 9 for the opinion.)

A second issue is the degree to which considerations of religion may enter into the disposition by the courts of various questions of family relationships, such as adoption, appointment of guardians, divorce, and premarital agreements concerning religious training of children. In an adoption case in Massachusetts, for example, the Massachusetts Supreme Court upheld its state statute which virtually bars adoption by couples of a different faith than that of the child's mother, even though the mother consented to the arrangement in the specific instance. [Petition of *Goldman*, 331 Mass. 647, 121 N.W. 2d 843 (1954), *cert. denied*, 348 U.S. 942 (1955).] On matters of awarding to one parent custody of children, following separation, the courts usually hold that if the parent is otherwise qualified, differences in religious views are not an impediment. [For a detailed consideration of these and related questions, see David Fellman, *op. cit.*, pp. 55–59; Thomas Emerson and David Haber, *Political and Civil Rights in the United States*, 2d. ed., 2 vols. (Buffalo: Dennis & Co., 1958), pp. 1155–1157, 1185, 1191; Elvin E. Overton, "Religion and Adoption," 23 *Tenn. L. Rev.* 951 (1955); Leo Pfeffer, "Religion in the Upbringing of Children," 35 *B. U. L. Rev.* 333 (1955).]

In addition to the *Walz* case, above, the Court in recent years has handed down other noteworthy decisions in the area of religious freedom. In *Flast* v. *Cohen*, 392 U.S. 83 (1968), the Court departed from the 1923 rule of *Frothingham* v. *Mellon* (which had held that mere taxpayer status is insufficient to accord standing to challenge a Congressional appropriation) to the extent that taxpayer suits are permitted if the challenge is based on a claim that the federal appropriation violates the religion clauses of the First Amendment. In *Board of Education* v. *Allen*, 392 U.S. 236 (1968), the Court followed the *Everson* rationale in holding constitutional the State's policy of lending secular textbooks to children attending parochial schools. But in *Lemon* v. *Kurtzman*, 403 U.S. 602 (1971), the Court held that statutes of Rhode Island and Pennsylvania, which provided for salary supplements and other assistance for instructional purposes for nonpublic schools, including sectarian schools, represented an unconstitutional establishment of religion.

Epperson v. *Arkansas*, 393 U.S. 97 (1968), invalidated a 1928 Arkansas law which forbade the teaching of "the theory or doctrine that mankind ascended or descended from a lower order of animals." The Court held that the anti-evolution law represented a preference for a particular religious doctrine and thus conflicted with the First Amendment's establishment and free exercise of religion clauses. (See Chapter 9 for the opinions in the *Walz*, *Allen*, *Lemon*, and *Epperson* cases.)

CHAPTER 6

Freedom of Speech, Press, and Assembly

THE freedoms of speech, press, and assembly occupy a peculiar position relative to the democratic process, and one shared only by the various aspects of the right to participate in elections. Trial by jury, freedom from self-incrimination, and the right to counsel are assuredly important procedural guarantees against arbitrary deprivation of life and liberty. But the democratic process could be maintained even if these guarantees were changed. The First Amendment guarantees freedom from establishment of religion, and there is apparently widespread approval of this policy in the United States. But a change to some specific established church in this nation would have no necessary impact on the characterization of the United States as a democratic nation. England has an established church and yet is clearly democratic by the usual procedural standards. To restrict substantially the rights of speech, press, assembly, and voting, however, is to cut the arteries that feed the heart of the democratic model. However one may choose to define democracy, the list of characteristics must include at least certain minimal procedural features: widespread adult suffrage, reasonably frequent elections, reasonable access to the ballot on the part of candidates, popular selection of major policy-making officials, and decision by majority rule. Those rights which are necessary to ensure free interchange of ideas and to guarantee that a continuing and shifting majority may be arrived at freely would certainly seem to be in a special category in terms of constitutional immunity. The most important institutions for the preservation of the democratic process are those which safeguard the opportunity for the reversal of public policy if a sufficient majority demands it. The important rights in this category would be access to the ballot, both as a voter and as a candidate, and the freedoms of speech, press, and assembly. Serious inroads on the exercise of any of these rights may result in a corresponding curtailment of the ease with which public policy can be changed, even though a majority may desire the change. Thus while encroachments on other types of personal rights might be inconvenient or even obnoxious, the dangers to democratic form must be considerably less as long as the channels for formulating public opinion and focusing majority demands remain open. It is this general proposition which accounts for the apparently paradoxical position in which many champions of personal liberties find themselves with respect to treatment of Communists in the United States. Free speech and association are vital in a democracy, but some restraints even on these must be permitted if there is a real danger that the group using them to gain political power will close off the channels and institutions by which reversal of policy can be accomplished by majority demand.

The conclusion that certain rights guaranteed in the Constitution are in a special position in a democracy is not drawn from any specific phraseology of the Constitution. It is derived logically from the assumption that the democratic system is the appropriate organizational scheme for a reasonably educated society but one in which knowledge will always be incomplete. The channels of communication, of receiving new information and of persuasion, and the institutions for legally influencing the determination of public policy deserve special care if the democratic model is to function according to blueprint. Such a view is somewhat akin to the "preferred position" doctrine which for a time enjoyed considerable publicity in the opinions of the Court. That doctrine, however, was squarely tied to the First Amendment in its entirety and was never extended to cover voting rights as well, as does the statement here.

THE SCOPE OF THE RIGHTS

The words "speech, press, and assembly" have certain obvious connotations which have required no special analysis to fit them under the First Amendment coverage of these words. A candidate's speech requesting votes, the publication of books and newspapers, and a meeting to discuss public questions are clearly within the scope of application of the First Amendment. Certain other aspects of these words have, however, been less clearly subsumed under the proper interpretation of the bare phraseology of the First Amendment, and their addition has been slower and somewhat more controversial. Probably the best illustration of this slow expansion of the scope of the rights is in the position of motion pictures under the First Amendment. The question of whether commercial movies were entitled to constitutional protection as speech and press first reached the Supreme Court in 1915, in *Mutual Film Corporation* v. *Industrial Commission*, 236 U.S. 230. The Court in that case held that the exhibition of motion pictures was a "business pure and simple, originated and conducted for profit like other spectacles, not to be regarded, nor intended to be regarded by the Ohio Constitution . . . as part of the press of the country or as organs of public opinion." This view held until 1952, when the Court overruled that portion of the *Mutual Film Corporation* decision in *Burstyn* v. *Wilson*, 343 U.S. 495. The Court stated squarely in the latter case that the "liberty of expression by means of motion pictures is guaranteed by the First and Fourteenth Amendments."

In 1940 the Court held that picketing of a plant in the course of a labor dispute came within the meaning of "speech" in the First Amendment. The case was *Thornhill* v. *Alabama,* 310 U.S. 88, and the opinion for a nearly unanimous Court stated:

In the circumstances of our times the dissemination of information concerning the facts of a labor dispute must be regarded as within that area of free discussion that is guaranteed by the Constitution. . . . The range of activities proscribed by Section 3448, whether characterized as picketing or loitering or otherwise, embraces nearly every practicable, effective means whereby those interested—including the employees directly affected—may enlighten the public on the nature and causes of a labor dispute. The safeguarding of these means is essential to the securing of an informed and educated public opinion with respect to a matter which is of public concern.

In *Cox* v. *State of New Hampshire,* 312 U.S. 569 (1941), the Court made the logical extension from *Thornhill* and accepted the view that parades could be properly brought under the rubric of speech and assembly protected by the Constitution.

The "press" protected by the First Amendment extends to handbills and circulars, as well as the standard forms of books and magazines and newspapers. As the Court stated in *Lovell* v. *Griffin,* 303 U.S. 444 (1938):

The liberty of the press is not confined to newspapers and periodicals. It necessarily embraces pamphlets and leaflets. These indeed have been historic weapons in the defense of liberty, as the pamphlets of Thomas Paine and others in our own history abundantly attest. The press in its historic connotation comprehends every sort of publication which affords a vehicle of information and opinion.

Nor has the Court ignored the impact of technological developments on the traditional forms of speech and press. As indicated earlier, in 1952 it held that movies were a form of expression guaranteed by the First and Fourteenth Amendments. And in 1948, in *Saia* v. *New York,* 334 U.S. 558, the Court held that the use of amplifying systems in delivering speeches did not take them out of the area of protection of the First Amendment. Justice Douglas stated for the Court, "Loud-speakers are today indispensable instruments of effective public speech. The sound truck has became an accepted method of political campaigning. It is the way people are reached."

Finally, the right of assembly has been expanded beyond the simple concept of a physical assemblage to include the even more significant right of association. In *NAACP* v. *Alabama,* 357 U.S. 449 (1958), Justice Harlan, speaking for a unanimous Court, stated:

Effective advocacy of both public and private points of view, particularly controversial ones, is undeniably enhanced by group association, as this Court has more than once recognized by remarking upon the close nexus between the freedoms of speech and assembly.... It is beyond debate that freedom to engage in association for the advancement of beliefs and ideas is an inseparable aspect of the "liberty" assured by the Due Process Clause of the Fourteenth Amendment, which embraces freedom of speech.

Even these few cases illustrate the breadth which the Court is willing to accord to the words of the First Amendment. The words "speech," "press," and "assembly" are not applied in coldly formalistic fashion. Instead, it is the substance of the rights which is examined and their importance in a free democratic system. Thus, as Justice Harlan put it in the NAACP case, what the First Amendment protects is "effective advocacy of both public and private points of view." To introduce novel vehicles of expression, then, is merely to change the angle from which resulting problems of reconciliation might be viewed; it is not to step outside the First Amendment's scope of application.

As has already been discussed, the rights guaranteed by the First Amendment are explicitly guaranteed against abridgment by Congress. It has also been noted that over the past several decades the Court has, through a succession of decisions, gradually "incorporated" these same rights into the liberties which the "due process" clause of the Fourteenth Amendment protects against invasion by the state. In the area of First Amendment rights, then, it is usually safe to use First Amendment cases and Fourteenth Amendment cases interchangeably in discussing the validity of restrictions placed by government—whether state or federal—on the exercise of those rights. The process of "incorporation" began with *Gitlow* v. *New York*, 268 U.S. 652 (1925). Benjamin Gitlow was indicted in the supreme court of New York for the crime of criminal anarchy, as defined by statute. His conviction was affirmed by the New York appellate courts. The case was taken on writ of error to the United States Supreme Court under the contention that the statute was repugnant to the "due process" clause of the Fourteenth Amendment. The Court affirmed the judgment of the New York Court of Appeals, but on the issue of whether a state law unduly restrictive of freedom of speech and press could be held to violate the Fourteenth Amendment the Court gave, almost casually, one of its most momentous decisions. Justice Sanford, for the Court, said, "For present purposes we may and do assume that freedom of speech and of the press—which are protected by the First Amendment from abridgment by Congress—are among the fundamental personal rights and liberties protected by the due process clause of the Fourteenth Amendment from impairment by the States." With such a modest statement did the Court begin the vastly important process of "incorporation" of the First Amendment rights into the Fourteenth Amendment's "liberty" safeguarded by the concept of due process of law.

Freedom of assembly, the third of the rights covered in this chapter, was brought under the protection of the Fourteenth Amendment's "due process" clause in 1937 in *De Jonge* v. *Oregon, 299* U.S. 353. The appellant in that case was indicted for violation of the Criminal Syndicalism Law of Oregon, was found guilty as charged, and was sentenced to imprisonment for seven years. The law defined "criminal syndicalism" as "the doctrine which advocates crime, physical violence, sabotage or any unlawful acts or methods as a means of accomplishing or effecting industrial or political change or revolution." The charge was that De Jonge assisted in the conduct of a meeting called under the auspices of the Communist Party. The defense contended that the meeting was lawful, orderly, and public, and that no unlawful conduct was taught or advocated at the meeting. In holding the Fourteenth Amendment applicable to assemblies, as well as to speech and press, the Court, through Chief Justice Hughes, first cited *Gitlow* v. *New York*. The opinion then stated:

> Freedom of speech and of the press are fundamental rights which are safeguarded by the due process clause of the Fourteenth Amendment of the Federal Constitution. ... The right of peaceable assembly is a right cognate to those of free speech and free press and is equally fundamental. ... The First Amendment of the Federal Constitution expressly guarantees that right against abridgment by Congress. But explicit mention there does not argue exclusion elsewhere. For the right is one that cannot be denied without violating those fundamental principles of liberty and justice which lie at the base of all civil and political institutions,—principles which the Fourteenth Amendment embodies in the general terms of its due process clause.

Two important points should be noted, then, concerning the Constitution's protection of speech, press, and assembly. First, the rights have been broadly construed to include picketing, parading, carrying placards, distributing handbills or circulars, using amplifying equipment, movies, and organizational associations as well as mere congregations of people. Second, the rights guaranteed in the First Amendment against abridgment by the national government have been incorporated totally into the "liberty" guaranteed in the Fourteenth Amendment against state encroachment.

PREVIOUS RESTRAINTS

It should be obvious that the First Amendment was not intended and has not been construed to protect every utterance, publication, or assembly. The traditional approach is to consider that certain well-recognized exceptions to the exercise of First Amendment rights were tacitly included in defining the scope of the Amendment's protections. As Justice Thomas M. Cooley stated, with respect to the Bill of Rights, "They are conservatory instruments rather than reformatory." [*Weimer* v. *Bunbury,* 30 Mich. 201, 214 (1874).] Despite the broad language, then, existing limitations on the exercise of those rights were not necessarily abolished.

Since the First Amendment rights are not absolute, the essential problem to be faced is the delineation of the kinds of restraints on speech, press, and assembly which are constitutionally permissible from those which are not. There are widely differing views on the appropriate answer to this problem, and the present chapter depicts the application of some of these views to the central areas of controversy surrounding First Amendment rights. There is one area, however, on which there seems to be fairly general agreement. This is in the theory that the First Amendment forbids the imposition of most *prior* restraints on the exercise of First Amendment rights. The standard citation is Blackstone's *Commentaries* (IV, 151), in which he states that "the liberty of the press . . . consists in laying no *previous* restraints upon publications and not in freedom from censure for criminal matter when published." Broadening the statement to include other rights, it would indicate that government cannot hinder speech or press or assembly *before* the speaking or printing or assembling takes place, but can punish or obstruct as it may choose *afterward*. As Thomas Jefferson often urged, Blackstone was no model for those interested in human liberty to follow. Probably the most trenchant statements on this aspect of Blackstone are those of Professor Zechariah Chafee, Jr., in his book *Free Speech in the United States:* [1]

This Blackstonian theory dies hard, but it ought to be knocked on the head once for all. In the first place, Blackstone was not interpreting a constitution, but trying to state the English law of his time, which had no censorship and did have extensive libel prosecutions. Whether or not he stated that law correctly, an entirely different view of the liberty of the press was soon afterwards enacted in Fox's Libel Act, . . . so that Blackstone's view does not even correspond to the English law of the last hundred and twenty-five years. Furthermore, Blackstone is notoriously unfitted to be an authority on the liberties of American colonists, since he upheld the right of Parliament to tax them, and was pronounced by one of his own colleagues to have been "we all know, an anti-republican lawyer."

Not only is the Blackstonian interpretation of our free speech clauses inconsistent with eighteenth-century history, . . . but it is contrary to modern decisions, thoroughly artificial, and wholly out of accord with a common-sense view of the relations of state and citizen. In some respects this theory goes altogether too far in restricting state action. The total prohibition of previous restraint would not allow the government to prevent a newspaper from publishing the sailing dates of transports or the number of troops in a sector. It would forbid the removal of an indecent poster from a billboard. . . .

On the other hand, it is hardly necessary to argue that the Blackstonian definition gives very inadequate protection to the freedom of expression. A death penalty for writing about socialism would be as effective suppression as a censorship. The government which holds twenty years in prison before a speaker and calls him free to talk resembles the peasant described by Galsworthy:

"The other day in Russia an Englishman came on a street-meeting shortly after the first revolution had begun. An extremist was addressing the gathering and

[1] Zechariah Chafee, Jr. *Free Speech in the United States* (Cambridge: Harvard University Press, 1948), pp. 9–11. Reprinted by permission of the publishers.

telling them that they were fools to go on fighting, that they ought to refuse and go home, and so forth. The crowd grew angry, and some soldiers were for making a rush at him; but the chairman, a big burly peasant, stopped them with these words: 'Brothers, you know that our country is now a country of free speech. We must listen to this man, we must let him say anything he will. But, brothers, when he's finished, we'll bash his head in!' "

Professor Chafee has thus pointed out that the Blackstonian statement is at the same time too extreme a restriction on governmental powers of censorship and too liberal in its grant of governmental power to punish after the fact. The Court has not treated the former issue definitively, but it has clearly refused to apply the First Amendment so as to permit the kinds of punishment which would have the same stifling effect as prior restraints. It is the impact of the restriction on the exercise of First Amendment rights which is the important consideration, rather than the mere formal determination of whether the restraining hand of government is laid on before or after the exercise of the right. Nevertheless, the Court has taken a near absolutist position on the invalidity of prior restraints. It is apt to use a balancing test on the issue of liability for punishment after the speech, publication, or assembly, but the rule generally is a firm one relative to prior restraints. A case illustrative of the Court's approach is *Near* v. *Minnesota,* dealing with limitations on the press.

NEAR *v.* MINNESOTA
283 U.S. 697 (1931)

Mr. Chief Justice Hughes delivered the opinion of the Court.

Chapter 285 of the Session Laws of Minnesota for the year 1925 . . . provides for the abatement, as a public nuisance, of a "malicious, scandalous and defamatory newspaper, magazine or other periodical." Section 1 of the act is as follows:

"Section 1: Any person who, as an individual, or as a member or employee of a firm, or association or organization, or as an officer, director, member or employee of a corporation, shall be engaged in the business of regularly or customarily producing, publishing or circulating, having in possession, selling or giving away,

(a) an obscene, lewd and lascivious newspaper, magazine, or other periodical, or

(b) a malicious, scandalous and defamatory newspaper, magazine or other periodical,

is guilty of a nuisance, and all persons guilty of such nuisance may be enjoined, as hereinafter provided. . . .

"In actions brought under (b) above, there shall be available the defense that the truth was published with good motives and for justifiable ends and in such actions the plaintiff shall not have the right to report [sic] to issues or editions of periodicals taking place more than three months before the commencement of the action.". . .

Under this statute, [section one, clause (b)], the county attorney of Hennepin county brought this action to enjoin the publication of what was described as a "malicious, scandalous and defamatory newspaper, magazine and periodical," known as "The Saturday Press," published by the defendants in the city of Minneapolis. . . .

Without attempting to summarize the contents of the voluminous exhibits attached to the complaint, we deem it sufficient to say that the articles charged in substance that a Jewish gangster was in control of gambling, bootlegging and racketeering in Minneapolis, and that law enforcing officers and agencies were not energetically performing their duties. Most of the charges were directed against the chief of police; he was charged with gross neglect of duty, illicit relations with gangsters, and with participation in graft. The county attorney was charged with knowing the existing conditions and with failure to take adequate measures to remedy them. The mayor was accused of inefficiency and dereliction. One member of the grand jury was stated to be in sympathy with the gangsters. A special grand jury and a special prosecutor were demanded to deal with the situation in general, and, in particular, to investigate an attempt to assassinate one Guilford, one of the original defendants, who, it appears from the articles, was shot by gangsters after the first issue of the periodical had been published. There is no question but that the articles made serious accusations against the public officers named and others in connection with the prevalence of crimes and the failure to expose and punish them.

[Initially an order was made by the district court of the State directing the defendants to show cause why a temporary injunction should not issue and meanwhile forbidding the defendants to circulate certain editions of the periodical and from publishing or circulating future editions "containing malicious, scandalous and defamatory matter of the kind alleged in plaintiff's complaint herein or otherwise."

The defendants demurred to the complaint, challenging the constitutionality of the statute. The district court overruled the demurrer, certified the question of constitutionality to the state supreme court, and the supreme court held the statute to be valid. Thereupon, Near answered the complaint and denied that the articles were malicious, scandalous or defamatory as alleged. He expressly invoked the protection of the "due process" clause of the Fourteenth Amendment.]

The district court made findings of fact, which followed the allegations of the complaint and found in general terms that the editions in question were "chiefly devoted to malicious, scandalous and defamatory articles," concerning the individuals named. The court further found that the defendants through these publications "did engage in the business of regularly and customarily producing, publishing and circulating a malicious, scandalous and defamatory newspaper," and that "the said publication under said name of The Saturday Press, or any other name, constitutes a public nuisance under the laws of the state." Judgment was thereupon entered adjudging that "the newspaper, magazine and periodical known as The Saturday Press," as a public nuisance, "be and is hereby abated." The judgment perpetually enjoined the defendants "from producing, editing, publishing, circulating, having in their possession, selling or giving away any publication whatsoever which is a malicious, scandalous or defamatory newspaper, as defined by law," and also "from further conducting said nuisance under the name and title of said The Saturday Press or any other name or title."

The defendant Near appealed from this judgment to the supreme court of the state, again asserting his right under the Federal Constitution, and the judgment was affirmed upon the authority of the former decision. 179 Minn. 40. With respect to the contention that the judgment went too far, and prevented the defendants from publishing any kind of a newspaper, the court observed that the assignments of error did not go to the form of the judgment and that the lower court had not been asked to modify it. The court added that it saw no reason "for defendants to construe the judgment as restraining them from operating a newspaper in harmony with the public welfare, to which all must yield," that the allegations of the complaint had been found to be true, and though this was an equitable action defendants had not indicated a desire "to conduct their business in the usual and legitimate manner."

From the judgment as thus affirmed, the defendant Near appeals to this court.

This statute, for the suppression as a public nuisance of a newspaper or periodical, is unusual, if not unique, and raises questions of grave importance transcending the local interests involved in the particular action. It is no longer open to doubt that the liberty of the press and of speech is within the liberty safeguarded by the due process clause of the Fourteenth Amendment from invasion by state action. It was found impossible to conclude that this essential personal liberty of the citizen was left unprotected by the general guaranty of fundamental rights of person and property. . . .

The appellee insists that the questions of the application of the statute to appellant's periodical, and of the construction of the judgment of the trial court, are not presented for review; that appellant's sole attack was upon the constitutionality of the statute, however it might be applied. The appellee contends that no question either of motive in the publication, or whether the decree goes beyond the direction of the statute, is before us. . . .

With respect to these contentions it is enough to say that in passing upon constitutional questions the court has regard to substance and not to mere matters of form, and that, in accordance with familiar principles, the statute must be tested by its operation and effect. . . . That operation and effect we think are clearly shown by the record in this case. We are not concerned with mere errors of the trial court, if there be such, in going beyond the direction of the statute as construed by the supreme court of the state. It is thus important to note precisely the purpose and effect of the statute as the state court has construed it.

First. The statute is not aimed at the redress of individual or private wrongs. Remedies for libel remain available and unaffected. The statute, said the state court, "is not directed at threatened libel but at an existing business which, generally speaking, involves more than libel." It is aimed at the distribution of scandalous matter as "detrimental to public morals and to the general welfare," tending "to disturb the peace of the community" and "to provoke assaults and the commission of crime." In order to obtain an injunction to suppress the future publication of the newspaper or periodical, it is not necessary to prove the falsity of the charges that have been made in the publication condemned. In the present action there was no allegation that the matter published was not true. It is alleged, and the statute requires the allegation, that the publication was "malicious." But, as in prosecutions for libel, there is no requirement of proof by the state of malice in fact as distinguished from malice inferred from the mere publication of the defamatory matter. The judgment in this case proceeded upon the mere proof of publication. The statute permits the defense, not of the truth alone, but only that the truth was published with good motives and for justifiable ends. It is apparent that under the statute the publication is to be regarded as defamatory if it injures reputation, and that it is scandalous if it circulates charges of reprehensible conduct, whether criminal or otherwise, and the publication is thus deemed to invite public reprobation and to constitute a public scandal. . . .

Second. The statute is directed not simply at the circulation of scandalous and defamatory statements with regard to private citizens, but at the continued publication by newspapers and periodicals of charges against public officers of corruption, malfeasance in office, or serious neglect of duty. Such charges by their very nature create a public scandal. They are scandalous and defamatory within the meaning of the statute, which has its normal operation in relation to publications dealing prominently and chiefly with the alleged derelictions of public officers.

Third. The object of the statute is not punishment, in the ordinary sense, but suppression of the offending newspaper or periodical. The reason for the enactment, as the state court has said, is that prosecutions to enforce penal statutes for libel do not result in "efficient repression or suppression of the evils of scandal.". . . Under this statute, a publisher of a newspaper or periodical, undertaking to conduct a campaign to expose and to censure official derelictions, and devoting his publication principally to that purpose, must face not simply the possibility of a verdict against him in a suit or prosecution for libel, but a determination that his newspaper or periodical is a public nuisance to be abated, and that this abatement and suppression will follow unless he is prepared with legal evidence to prove the truth of the charges and also to satisfy the court that, in addition to being true, the matter was published with good motives and for justifiable ends.

This suppression is accomplished by enjoining publication and that restraint is the object and effect of the statute.

Fourth. The statute not only operates to suppress the offending newspaper or periodical but to put the publisher under an effective censorship. . . .

If we cut through mere details of procedure, the operation and effect of the statute in substance is that public authorities may bring the owner or publisher of a newspaper or periodical before a judge upon a charge of conducting a business of publishing scandalous and defamatory matter—in particular that the matter consists of charges against public officers of official dereliction—and unless the owner or publisher is able and disposed to bring competent evidence to satisfy the judge that the charges are true and are published with good motives and for justifiable ends, his newspaper or periodical is suppressed and further publication is made punishable as a contempt. This is the essence of censorship.

The question is whether a statute authorizing such proceedings in restraint of publication is consistent with the conception of the liberty of the press as historically conceived and guaranteed. In determining the extent of the constitutional protection, it has been generally, if not universally, considered that it is the chief purpose of the guaranty to prevent previous restraints upon publication. The struggle in England, directed against the legislative power of the licenser, resulted in renunuciation of the censorship of the press. . . . Here, as Madison said, "The great and essential rights of the people are secured against legislative as well as against executive ambition. They are secured, not by laws paramount to prerogative, but by constitutions paramount to laws. This security of the freedom of the press requires that it should be exempt not only from previous restraint by the executive, as in Great Britain, but from legislative restraint also." Report on the Virginia Resolutions, Madison's Works, vol. 4, p. 543. This court said, in *Patterson* v. *Colorado*, 205 U.S. 454, 462: "In the first place, the main purpose of such constitutional provisions is 'to prevent all such *previous restraints* upon publications as had been practised by other governments,' and they do not prevent the subsequent punishment of such as may be deemed contrary to the public welfare.". . .

. . . In the present case, we have no occasion to inquire as to the permissible scope of subsequent punishment. For whatever wrong the appellant has committed or may commit, by his publications, the state appropriately affords both public and private redress by its libel laws. As has been noted, the statute in question does not deal with punishments; it provides for no punishment, except in case of contempt for violation of the court's order, but for suppression and injunction, that is, for restraint upon publication.

The objection has also been made that the principle as to immunity from previous restraint is not absolutely unlimited. But the limitation has been recognized only in exceptional cases. "When a nation is at war many things that might be said in time of peace are such a hindrance to its effort that their utterance will not be endured so long as men fight and that no court could regard them as protected by any constitutional right." *Schenck* v. *United States*, 249 U.S. 47, 52. No one would question but that a government might prevent actual obstruction to its recruiting service or the publication of the sailing dates of transports or the number and location of troops. On similar grounds, the primary requirements of decency may be enforced against obscene publications. The security of the community life may be protected against incitements to acts of violence and the overthrow by force of orderly government. The constitutional guaranty of free speech does not "protect a man from an injunction against uttering words that may have all the effect of force. *Gompers* v. *Bucks Stove & Range Co.*, 221 U.S. 418, 439." *Schenck* v. *United States, supra.* These limitations are not applicable here. Nor are we now concerned with questions as to the extent of authority to prevent publications in order to protect private rights according to the principles governing the exercise of the jurisdiction of courts of equity. (See 29 *Harvard Law Rev.* 640.)

The exceptional nature of its limitations places in a strong light the general conception that liberty of the press, historically considered and taken up by the Federal Constitution, has meant, principally, although not exclusively, immunity from previous restraints or censorship. . . .

The importance of this immunity has not lessened. While reckless assaults upon public men, and efforts to bring obloquy upon those who are endeavoring faithfully to discharge official duties, exert a baleful influence and deserve the severest condemnation in public opinion, it cannot be said that this abuse is greater, and it is believed to be less, than that which characterized the period in which our institutions took shape. Meanwhile, the administration of government has become more complex, the opportunities for malfeasance and corruption have multiplied, crime has grown to most serious proportions, and the danger of its protection by unfaithful officials and of the impairment of the fundamental security of life and property by criminal alliances and official neglect, emphasizes the primary need of a vigilant and courageous press, especially in great cities. The fact that the liberty of the press may be abused by miscreant purveyors of scandal does not make any the less necessary the immunity of the press from previous restraint in dealing with official misconduct. Subsequent punishment for such abuses as may exist is the appropriate remedy, consistent with constitutional privilege. . . .

Equally unavailing is the insistence that the statute is designed to prevent the circulation of scandal which tends to disturb the public peace and to provoke assaults and the commission of crime. Charges of reprehensible conduct, and in particular of official malfeasance, unquestionably create a public scandal, but the theory of the constitutional guaranty is that even a more serious public evil would be caused by authority to prevent publication.. . . .

Judgment reversed.

[Mr. Justice Butler wrote a dissenting opinion, concurred in by Justices Van Devanter, McReynolds, and Sutherland.]

The majority opinion in the case did not reach the issue of whether the publisher was constitutionally free of any liability for the specific charges made in his newspaper. The point stressed was that in view of the post-publication remedy of a libel action, the injunction against future publication of similar charges was in the nature of a previous restraint. While the decision might be construed as a bar to the use of the injunctive remedy as a limitation on the press, a later case shows that the injunction is constitutionally permissible in special circumstances if the procedural safeguards are adequate. The case is *Kingsley Books, Inc.* v. *Brown,* decided in 1957. [But see Chap. 9 for the "Pentagon Papers" decision in *New York Times* v. *U.S.,* 403 U.S. 713 (1971).]

KINGSLEY BOOKS, INC. *v.* BROWN

354 U.S. 436 (1957)

Mr. Justice Frankfurter delivered the opinion of the Court.

This is a proceeding under Sec. 22-a of the New York Code of Criminal Procedure.. . . This section supplements the existing conventional criminal provision dealing with pornography by authorizing the chief executive, or legal officer, of a municipality to invoke a "limited injunctive remedy," under closely defined procedural safeguards, against the sale and distribution of written and printed matter found after due trial to be obscene, and to obtain an order for the seizure, in default of surrender, of the condemned publications.

A complaint dated September 10, 1954, charged appellants with displaying for sale paper-covered obscene booklets, fourteen of which were annexed, under the general title of "Nights of Horror." The complaint prayed that appellants be enjoined from further distribution of the booklets, that they be required to surrender to the sheriff for destruction all copies in their possession, and, upon failure to do so, that the sheriff be commanded to seize and destroy those copies. The same day the appellants were ordered to show cause within four days why they should not be enjoined *pendente lite* from distributing the booklets. Appellants consented to the granting of an injunction *pendente lite* and did not bring the matter to issue promptly, as was their right under subdivision 2 of the challenged section, which provides that the persons sought to be enjoined "shall be entitled to a trial of the issues within two days of the conclusion of the trial." After the case came to trial, the judge, sitting in equity, found that the booklets annexed to the complaint and introduced in evidence were clearly obscene—were "dirt for dirt's sake"; he enjoined their further distribution and ordered their destruction. He refused to enjoin "the sale and distribution of later issues" on the ground that "to rule against a volume not offered in evidence would . . . impose an unreasonable prior restraint upon freedom of the press.". . .

Neither in the New York Court of Appeals, nor here, did appellants assail the legislation insofar as it outlaws obscenity. The claim they make lies within a very narrow compass. Their attack is upon the power of New York to employ the remedial scheme of Section 22-a. . . . Resort to this injunctive remedy, it is claimed, is beyond the constitutional power of New York in that it amounts to a prior censorship of literary product and as such is violative of that "freedom of thought, and speech" which has been "withdrawn by the Fourteenth Amendment from encroachment by the states.". . . Reliance is particularly placed upon *Near* v. *Minnesota*. . . .

We need not linger over the suggestion that something can be drawn out of the Due Process Clause of the Fourteenth Amendment that restricts New York to the criminal process in seeking to protect its people against the dissemination of pornography. It is not for this Court thus to limit the State in resorting to various weapons in the armory of the law. Whether proscribed conduct is to be visited by a criminal prosecution or by a *qui tam* action or by an injunction or by some or all of these remedies in combination, is a matter within the legislature's range of choice. . . . If New York chooses to subject persons who disseminate obscene "literature" to criminal prosecution and also to deal with such books as deodands of old, or both, with due regard, of course, to appropriate opportunities for the trial of the underlying issue, it is not for us to gainsay its selection of remedies. . . .

. . . The phrase "prior restraint" is not a self-wielding sword. Nor can it serve as a talismanic test. The duty of closer analysis and critical judgment in applying the thought behind the phrase has thus been authoritatively put by one who brings weighty learning to his support of constitutionally protected liberties: "What is needed," writes Professor Paul A. Freund, "is a pragmatic assessment of its operation in the particular circumstances. The generalization that prior restraint is particularly obnoxious in civil liberties cases must yield to more particularistic analysis." The Supreme Court and Civil Liberties, 4 *Vand. L. Rev.* 533, 539.

Wherein does Section 22-a differ in its effective operation from the type of statute upheld in *Alberts?* Section 311 of California's Penal Code provides that "Every person who willfully and lewdly . . . keeps for sale . . . any obscene . . . book . . . is guilty of a misdemeanor. . . ." Section 1141 of New York's Penal Law is similar. One would be bold to assert that the *in terrorem* effect of such statutes less restrains booksellers in the period before the law strikes than does Section 22-a. Instead of requiring the bookseller to dread that the offer for sale of a book may, without prior warning, subject him to a criminal prosecution with the hazard of imprisonment, the civil procedure assures him that such consequences cannot follow unless he ignores a court order specifically directed to him for a prompt and carefully circumscribed determination of the issue of obscenity. Until then, he may keep the book for sale and sell it on his own judgment rather than steer "nervously among the treacherous shoals.". . .

Criminal enforcement and the proceeding under Section 22-a interfere with a book's solicitation of the public precisely at the same stage. In each situation the law moves after publication; the book need not in either case have yet passed into the hands of the public. . . .

Nor are the consequences of a judicial condemnation for obscenity under Section 22-a more restrictive of freedom of expression than the result of conviction for a misdemeanor. In *Alberts*, the defendant was fined $500, sentenced to sixty days in prison, and put on probation for two years on condition that he not violate the obscenity statute. Not only was he completely separated from society for two months but he was also seriously restrained from trafficking in all obscene publications for a considerable time. Appellants, on the other hand, were enjoined from displaying for sale or distributing only the particular booklets theretofore published and adjudged to be obscene. Thus, the restraint upon appellants as merchants in obscenity was narrower than that imposed on Alberts.

Section 22-a's provision for the seizure and destruction of the instruments of ascertained wrongdoing expresses resort to a legal remedy sanctioned by the long history of Anglo-American law. See Holmes, The Common Law, 24–26. . . .

It only remains to say that the difference between *Near* v. *Minnesota, supra,* and this case is glaring in fact. The two cases are no less glaringly different when judged by the appropriate criteria of constitutional law. Minnesota empowered its courts to enjoin the dissemination of future issues of a publication because its past issues had been found offensive. In the language of Mr. Chief Justice Hughes, "This is of the essence of censorship.". . . As such, it was found unconstitutional. This was enough to condemn the statute wholly apart from the fact that the proceeding in *Near* involved not obscenity but matters deemed to be derogatory to a public officer. Unlike *Near,* Section 22-a is concerned solely with obscenity and, as authoritatively construed, it studiously withholds restraint upon matters not already published and not yet found to be offensive.

The judgment is

Affirmed.

Mr. Chief Justice Warren, dissenting. . . .

Mr. Justice Douglas, joined by Mr. Justice Black, dissenting. . . .

Mr Justice Brennan, dissenting. . . .

The jury represents a cross-section of the community and has a special aptitude for reflecting the view of the average person. Jury trial of obscenity therefore provides a peculiarly competent application of the standard for judging obscenity which, by its definition, calls for an appraisal of material according to the average person's application of contemporary community standards. A statute which does not afford the defendant, of right, a jury determination of obscenity falls short, in my view, of giving proper effect to the standard fashioned as the necessary safeguard demanded by the freedoms of speech and press for material which is not obscene. Of course, as with jury questions generally, the trial judge must initially determine that there is a jury question, *i.e.,* that reasonable men may differ whether the material is obscene. . . .

[On prior restraint generally, see Zechariah Chafee, Jr., *Free Speech in the United States* (Cambridge: Harvard University Press, 1948), pp. 9–30, 400–435; Paul A. Freund, "The Supreme Court and Civil Liberties," 4 *Vand. L. Rev.* 533, 537–545 (1951); Thomas I. Emerson, "The Doctrine of Prior Restraint," 20 *Law and Contemp. Prob.* 648 (1955).]

Although the New York Court of Appeals was unanimous in upholding the constitutionality of the law, the statute passed muster before the United States Supreme Court by the slender margin of five-to-four. Thus "only a little encroachment," to quote Justice Douglas, is strongly resisted when it smacks of previous restraint and the heavy hand of a censor; and this even in a case where the finding of obscenity was not under attack. Concern over previous restraints is, of course, both understandable and supportable. Censorship denies the proscribed book the light of day altogether, with no chance for an impact on the reading public. If the book is in fact one which it is illegal to sell or display for sale, then one might raise the question of whether it is not indeed more desirable to keep it off the shelf altogether. This is to overlook the crucial stage of the problem, however, which is the actual determination of whether the book falls within the statutory ban. Three aspects of this fact-finding stage deserve careful scrutiny before a decision can be reached on the issue of denial of First Amendment rights. These are (1) the test to be employed to determine whether or not the publication is proscribed by law (whether under obscenity, national security provisions, or others), (2) the procedures to be followed in arriving at a decision, and (3) the special competence required of the person or persons who actually make the finding. To the majority in *Kingsley Books* it appeared that examination of such factors as these was a more appropriate approach (the "pragmatic assessment" suggested by Professor Freund) than the use of the phrase "prior restraint" as a talismanic test.

The real difficulty in attempting to apply a "prior restraint" test to limitations on the press (and its included forms, such as movies) lies in the fact that a multistage process is involved. A manuscript is prepared, then it is published, then it is distributed in volume to various distributors and retailers, and finally it is actually placed in the hands of the reading public. To complicate the process further, advance copies of some books are specially printed and sent out for review or other purposes prior to the general publication date. Must the government wait to proceed under its criminal laws until members of the public have actually purchased copies at retail outlets to avoid the claim of "prior restraint"? If only one copy need be sold at retail to avoid such a charge, then it might be argued, as did Justice Frankfurter in *Kingsley Books,* that the practical distinction is nonexistent. At what stage do restraints clearly become "prior" restraints?

In applying the doctrine to freedom of speech, without the several stages involved in press cases, there are fewer difficulties. Either the speech is permitted to be given or it is not. If not, there may be an issue of prior restraint. But if penalities are imposed afterward, no such issue is presented. Thus in *Thomas* v. *Collins,* 323 U.S. 516 (1945), the question presented was the constitutionality of an injunction issued under a Texas statute which forbade solicitation of members for labor unions without an organizer's card having first been obtained from the Secretary of State. Five members of the United States Supreme Court held the requirement to be unconstitutional. Justice Rutledge, for the majority, stated:

> If the exercise of the rights of free speech and free assembly cannot be made a crime, we do not think this can be accomplished by the device of requiring previous registration as a condition for exercising them and making such a condition the foundation for restraining in advance their exercise and for imposing a penalty for violating such a restraining order.

In *Staub* v. *City of Baxley*, 355 U.S. 313 (1958), a direct permit ordinance was tested. Rather than mere registration of solicitors, the requirement was that persons soliciting membership in any organization which required fees or dues of members must apply to the mayor and council for a permit, and such applications could be granted or denied following consideration of the character of the applicant, the nature of the organization and its effects upon the general welfare of the citizens. The Court reversed a conviction for solicitation of membership in a labor union without the required permit. Justice Whittaker, for the majority of seven, stated:

It is undeniable that the ordinance authorized the Mayor and Council of the City of Baxley to grant "or refuse to grant" the required permit in their uncontrolled discretion. It thus makes enjoyment of speech contingent upon the will of the Mayor and Council of the City, although that fundamental right is made free from congressional abridgment by the First Amendment and is protected by the Fourteenth from invasion by state action. For these reasons, the ordinance, on its face, imposes an unconstitutional prior restraint upon the enjoyment of First Amendment freedoms and lays "a forbidden burden upon the exercise of liberty protected by the Constitution." *Cantwell* v. *Connecticut*. . . .

Of course, if a registration requirement, imposed as a condition to be met before exercising the right of speech, is unconstitutional, then, *a fortiori*, the requirement of a permit with discretionary power to grant or deny would also be invalid. A similar holding obtained in the case of *Cantwell* v. *Connecticut*, discussed in the previous chapter, involving a permit requirement for the solicitation of funds for religious organizations.

Hague v. *CIO*, 307 U.S. 496 (1939), concerned the validity of a Jersey City ordinance which barred the leasing of a hall for a public speech or the holding of public meetings without a permit from the chief of police. Members of a labor union sought permission to hold public meetings in the city for the "organization of unorganized workers into labor unions." Permission was refused on the ground that there was reason to believe that such meetings would lead to riot and disorder. They then sought and obtained an injunction prohibiting the city from interfering with their rights of free speech and peaceable assembly. The Court affirmed the lower court's decision and held the ordinance void on its face.

While the Court has fairly consistently struck down attempts to license the exercise of free speech, especially where issuance of permits is discretionary, there are at least two areas where a permit requirement is not *per se* invalid. One is the case of the speech given on public property where there is apt to be competition for the location. In *Kunz* v. *New York*, 340 U.S. 290 (1951), involving the application of a permit requirement for the use of the streets and sidewalks for speeches in New York City, and in *Niemotko* v. *Maryland*, 340 U.S. 268 (1951), involving the operation of an "amorphous practice" (as the Chief Justice called it) of requiring a permit from the city council before holding a meeting in a public park, there is an indication that a permit requirement which is completely nondiscretionary and is used merely for the purpose of notification and for scheduling use in orderly fashion would not be considered an unconstitutional restraint. Chief Justice Vinson, speaking for the majority in *Niemotko*, stated:

This Court has many times examined the licensing systems by which local bodies regulate the use of their parks and public places. . . . In those cases this Court condemned statutes and ordinances which required that permits be obtained from local officials as a prerequisite to the use of public places, on the grounds that a license requirement constituted a prior restraint on freedom of speech, press and religion, and, *in the absence of narrowly drawn, reasonable and definite standards for the officials to follow*, must be invalid. [Emphasis added.]

It would seem that a little prior restraint may be tolerated if there is some substantial community interest to be served in imposing the limitation. Thus, again, Justice Frankfurter's conclusion may be recalled, to the effect that the phrase "prior restraint" is not a self-wielding sword.

In another area of speech and press the Court has shown even more flexibility in its applications of the rule of no previous restraint. This is the matter of licensing of motion pictures. A very few states and less than a score of cities have provisions requiring that an exhibitor obtain a permit prior to the showing of any motion picture publicly. These laws or ordinances generally allow the licensing agency to refuse a permit if the film is obscene or would tend to corrupt morals or incite to crime. In *Burstyn, Inc.* v. *Wilson*, 343 U.S. 495 (1952), the Court first held that "expression by means of motion pictures is included within the free speech and free press guaranty of the First and Fourteenth Amendments." The controversy arose over the decision of the New York Board of Regents to rescind a license granted earlier for the showing of the film *The Miracle* on the ground that it fell under the statutory ban against exhibiting "sacrilegious" movies. The Court refused to rule squarely on the issue of the constitutionality of licensing movies. Instead the decision to reverse was based on the narrower ground of adequacy of standards in the use of the word "sacrilegious." Justice Clark, for the Court, stated:

New York's highest court says there is "nothing mysterious" about the statutory provision applied in this case: "It is simply this: that no religion, as that word is understood by the ordinary, reasonable person, shall be treated with contempt, mockery, scorn and ridicule. . . ." This is far from the kind of narrow exception to freedom of expression which a state may carve out to satisfy the adverse demands of other interests of society. In seeking to apply the broad and all-inclusive definition of "sacrilegious" given by the New York courts, the censor is set adrift upon a boundless sea amid a myriad of conflicting currents of religious views, with no charts but those provided by the most vocal and powerful orthodoxies. New York cannot vest such unlimited restraining control over motion pictures in a censor.

The Court followed a similar approach in reversing several subsequent state court decisions on the apparent ground of inadequacy of standards. Without explanation and citing only the *Burstyn* case in *per curiam* decisions, the Court reversed: New York's denial of a license for the showing of *La Ronde* (under the statutory standard of "immoral" and "tending to corrupt morals") in *Commercial Pictures* v. *Regents*, 346 U.S. 587 (1954); Ohio's ban on the film *M* (which had been found to "undermine confidence in the enforcement of law and government" and which could lead "unstable persons to increased immorality and crime") in *Superior Films* v. *Department of Education of Ohio*, 346 U.S. 587 (1954); and a Kansas ban on *The Moon is Blue* (under a statutory standard barring films that were "obscene, indecent, or immoral, or such as tend to debase or corrupt morals") in *Holmby Productions* v. *Vaughn*, 350 U.S. 870 (1955).

Not until 1961 did the Court squarely come to grips with the issue of whether the licensing requirement for the exhibiting of motion pictures was *per se* an unconstitutional prior restraint. The case was *Times Film Corporation* v. *City of Chicago*.

TIMES FILM CORPORATION *v.* CITY OF CHICAGO
365 U.S. 43 (1961)

Mr. Justice Clark delivered the opinion of the Court.

Petitioner challenges on constitutional grounds the validity on its face of that portion of Section 155-4 of the Municipal Code of the City of Chicago which requires submission of all motion pictures for examination prior to their public exhibition. Petitioner is a New York corporation owning the exclusive right to publicly exhibit in Chicago the film known as "Don Juan." It applied for a permit as Chicago's ordinance required, and tendered the license fee but refused to submit the film for examination. The appropriate city official refused to issue the permit and his order was made final on appeal to the Mayor. The sole ground for denial was petitioner's refusal to submit the film for examination as required. Petitioner then brought this suit seeking injunctive relief ordering the issuance of the permit without submission of the film and restraining the city officials from interfering with the exhibition of the picture. Its sole ground is that the provision of the ordinance requiring submission of the film constitutes, on its face, a prior restraint within the prohibition of the First and Fourteenth Amendments. The District Court dismissed the complaint on the grounds, *inter alia,* that neither a substantial federal question nor even a justiciable controversy was presented. . . . The Court of Appeals affirmed. . . . The precise question at issue here never having been specifically decided by this Court, we granted certiorari. . . .

We are satisfied that a justiciable controversy exists. The section of Chicago's ordinance in controversy specifically provides that a permit for the public exhibition of a motion picture must be obtained; that such "permit shall be granted only after the motion picture film for which said permit is requested has been produced at the office of the commissioner of police for examination;" that the Commissioner shall refuse the permit if the picture does not meet certain standards; and that in the event of such refusal the applicant may appeal to the Mayor for a *de novo* hearing and his action shall be final. Violation of the ordinance carries certain punishments. The petitioner complied with the requirements of the ordinance, save for the production of the film for examination. The claim is that this concrete and specific statutory requirement, the production of the film at the office of the Commissioner for examination, is invalid as a previous restraint on freedom of speech. . . . Admittedly, the challenged section of the ordinance imposes a previous restraint, and the broad justiciable issue is therefore present as to whether the ambit of constitutional protection includes complete and absolute freedom to exhibit, at least once, any and every kind of motion picture. It is that question alone which we decide. We have concluded that Section 155-4 of Chicago's ordinance requiring the submission of films prior to their public exhibition is not, on the grounds set forth, void on its face. . . .

. . . [T]here is not a word in the record as to the nature and content of "Don Juan." We are left entirely in the dark in this regard, as were the city officials and the other reviewing courts. Petitioner claims that the nature of the film is irrelevant, and that even if this film contains the basest type of pornography, or incitement to riot, or forceful overthrow of orderly government, it may nonetheless be shown without prior submission for examination. The challenge here is to the censor's basic authority; it does not go to any statutory standards employed by the censor or procedural requirements as to the submission of the film. . . .

Petitioner would have us hold that the public exhibition of motion pictures must be allowed under any circumstances. The State's sole remedy, it says, is the invocation of criminal process under the Illinois pornography statute, . . . and then only after a transgression. But this position, as we have seen, is founded upon the claim of absolute privilege against prior restraint under the First Amendment—a claim without sanction in our cases. To illustrate its fallacy we need only point to one of the "exceptional cases" which Chief Justice Hughes enumerated in *Near* v. *State of Minnesota* . . . namely, "the primary requirements of decency [that] may be enforced against obscene publications.". . . Chicago emphasizes here its duty to protect its people against the dangers of obscenity in the public exhibition of motion pictures. To this argument petitioner's only answer is that regardless of the capacity for, or extent of such an evil, previous restraint cannot be justified. With this we cannot agree. We recognized in *Burstyn, supra,* that "capacity for evil . . . may be relevant in determining the permissible scope of control,". . . and that motion pictures were not "necessarily subject to the precise rules governing any other particular method of expression. Each method," we said, "tends to present its own peculiar problems.". . . Certainly petitioner's broadside attack does not warrant, nor could it justify on the record here, our saying that—aside from any consideration of the other "exceptional cases" mentioned in our decisions—the State is stripped of all constitutional power to prevent, in the most effective fashion, the utterance of this class of speech. It is not for this Court to limit the State in its selection of the remedy it deems most effective to cope with such a problem, absent, of course, a showing of unreasonable strictures on individual liberty resulting from its application in particular circumstances. *Kingsley Books, Inc.,* v. *Brown, supra.* . . . We, of course, are not holding that city officials may be granted the power to prevent the showing of any motion picture they deem unworthy of a license. . . .

As to what may be decided when a concrete case involving a specific standard provided by this ordinance is presented, we intimate no opinion. The petitioner has not challenged all—or for that matter any—of the ordinance's standards. Naturally we could not say that every one of the standards, including those which Illinois' highest court has found sufficient, is so vague on its face that the entire ordinance is void. At this time we say no more than this—that we are dealing only with motion pictures and, even as to them, only in the context of the broadside attack presented on this record.

Affirmed.

Mr. Chief Justice Warren, with whom Mr. Justice Black, Mr. Justice Douglas and Mr. Justice Brennan join, dissenting.

I cannot agree with either the conclusion reached by the Court or with the reasons advanced for its support. To me, this case clearly presents the question of our approval of unlimited censorship of motion pictures before exhibition through a system of administrative licensing. Moreover, the decision presents a real danger of eventual censorship for every form of communication be it newspapers, journals, books, magazines, television, radio or public speeches. The Court purports to leave these questions for another day, but I am aware of no constitutional principle which permits us to hold that the communication of ideas through one medium may be censored while other media are immune. Of course each medium presents its own peculiar problems, but they are not of the kind which would authorize the censorship of one form of communication and not the others. I submit that in arriving at its decision the Court has interpreted our cases contrary to the intention at the time of their rendition and, in exalting the censor of motion pictures, has endangered the First and Fourteenth Amendment rights of all others engaged in the dissemination of ideas. . . .

I hesitate to disagree with the Court's formulation of the issue before us, but, with all deference, I must insist that the question presented in this case is *not* whether a motion picture exhibitor has a constitutionally protected, "complete and absolute freedom to exhibit, at least once, any and every kind of motion picture." . . . Surely, the Court is not bound by the petitioner's conception of the issue or by the more extreme positions that petitioner may have argued at one time in the case. The question here presented is whether the City of Chicago—or, for that matter, any city, any State or the Federal Government—may require all motion picture exhibitors to submit all films to a police chief, mayor or other administrative official, for licensing and censorship prior to public exhibition within the jurisdiction. . . .

Let it be completely clear what the Court's decision does. It gives official license to the censor, approving a grant of power to city officials to prevent the showing of any moving picture these officials deem unworthy of a license. It thus gives formal sanction to censorship in its purest and most far-reaching form, to a classical plan of licensing that, in our country, most closely approaches the English licensing laws of the seventeenth century which were commonly used to suppress dissent in the mother country and in the colonies. . . . The Court treats motion pictures, food for the mind, held to be within the shield of the First Amendment, . . . little differently than it would treat edibles. . . . By its decision, the Court gives its assent to unlimited censorship of moving pictures through a licensing system, despite the fact that Chicago has chosen this most objectionable course to attain its goals without any apparent attempt to devise other means so as not to intrude on the constitutionally protected liberties of speech and press. . . .

The statute in *Kingsley* specified that the person sought to be enjoined was to be entitled to a trial of the issues within one day after joinder and a decision was to be rendered by the court within two days of the conclusion of the trial. The Chicago plan makes no provision for prompt judicial determination. In *Kingsley,* the person enjoined had available the defense that the written or printed matter was not obscene if an attempt was made to punish him for disobedience of the injunction. The Chicago ordinance admits no defense in a prosecution for failure to procure a license other than that the motion picture was submitted to the censor and a license was obtained. . . .

The censor performs free from all of the procedural safeguards afforded litigants in a court of law. . . . The likelihood of a fair and impartial trial disappears when the censor is both prosecutor and judge. There is a complete absence of rules of evidence; the fact is that there is usually no evidence at all as the system at bar vividly illustrates. How different from a judicial proceeding where a full case is presented by the litigants. The inexistence of a jury to determine contemporary community standards is a vital flaw. . . .

A revelation of the extent to which censorship has recently been used in this country is indeed astonishing. The Chicago licensors have banned newsreel films of Chicago policemen shooting at labor pickets and have ordered the deletion of a scene depicting the birth of a buffalo in Walt Disney's *Vanishing Prairie.* [Journal and Reporter citations for this and following censor actions omitted.] Before World War II, the Chicago censor denied licenses to a number of films portraying and criticizing life in Nazi Germany including the March of Time's *Inside Nazi Germany.* . . . Recently, Chicago refused to issue a permit for the exhibition of the motion picture *Anatomy of a Murder* based upon the bestselling novel of the same title, because it found the use of words "rape" and "contraceptive" to be objectionable. . . . The Memphis censors banned *The Southerner* which dealt with poverty among tenant farmers because "it reflects on the south.". . . Maryland censors restricted a Polish documentary film on the basis that it failed to present a true picture of modern Poland. . . . Memphis banned *Curley* because it contained scenes of white and Negro children in school together. . . . *Witchcraft,* a study of superstition through the ages, was suppressed for years because it depicted the devil as a genial rake with amorous leanings, and because it was feared that certain historical scenes, portraying the excesses of religious fanatics, might offend religion. *Scarface,* thought by some as the best of the gangster films, was held up for months; then it was so badly mutilated that retakes costing a hundred thousand dollars were required to preserve continuity. The New York censors banned *Damaged Lives,* a film dealing with venereal disease, although it treated a difficult theme with dignity and had the sponsorship of the American Social Hygiene Society. . . . And this is but a smattering produced from limited research. Perhaps the most powerful indictment of Chicago's licensing device is found in the fact that between the Court's decision in 1952 in *Joseph Burstyn, Inc.* v. *Wilson, supra,* and the filing of the petition for certiorari in 1960 in the present case, not once have the state courts upheld the censor when the exhibitor elected to appeal. Brief for American Civil Liberties Union as *amicus curiae,* pp. 13–14. . . .

The contention may be advanced that the impact of motion pictures is such that a licensing system of prior censorship is permissible. There are several answers to this, the first of which I think is the Constitution itself. Although it is an open question whether the impact of motion pictures is greater or less that that of other media, there is not much doubt that the exposure of television far exceeds that of the motion picture. See S. Rep. No. 1466, 84th Cong., 2d Sess. 5. But, even if the impact of the motion picture is greater than that of some other media, that fact constitutes no basis for the argument that motion pictures should be subject to greater suppression. This is the traditional argument made in the censor's behalf; this is the argument advanced against newspapers at the time of the invention of the printing press. The argument was ultimately rejected in England, and has consistently been held to be contrary to our Constitution. No compelling reason has been predicated for accepting the contention now. . . .

. . . I would reverse the decision below.

[Mr. Justice Douglas also wrote a dissenting opinion in which the Chief Justice and Mr. Justice Black concurred.]

The validity of motion picture licensing was again challenged in *Freedman* v. *Maryland*, 380 U.S. 51 (1965). The statute required submission of all films to a state board, which would approve all such films which "are moral and proper" and disapprove those considered by the board to be obscene or tending to corrupt morals or incite to crime. In *Freedman*, unlike *Times Film*, the challenge was specifically directed to the inhibiting effect of the delays in making final determinations permitted by the statutory and administrative procedures, and also to the fact that the burden of carrying litigation was thrown on the exhibitor. The Court, with two dissents, affirmed the *Times Film* holding that a licensing requirement for movies was not *per se* unconstitutional, but it held the Maryland statute procedurally defective and thus violative of the constitutional guaranty of freedom of expression. The Court did not specify just how Maryland should change its procedures to meet the test of constitutionality, but Justice Brennan's opinion for the Court stated that "a model is not lacking: In *Kingsley Books, Inc.* v. *Brown* . . . we upheld a New York injunctive procedure designed to prevent the sale of obscene books. That procedure postpones any restraint against sale until a judicial determination of obscenity following notice and an adversary hearing." Justices Douglas and Black reiterated their views expressed in *Times Film* that movies "are entitled to the same degree and kind of protection under the First Amendment as other forms of expression." [See John R. Verani, "Motion Picture Censorship and the Doctrine of Prior Restraint," 3 *Houston L. Rev.* 11 (1965); Ernest Giglio, "Prior Restraint of Motion Pictures," 69 *Dick. L. Rev.* 379 (1965).]

It may be seen from the various opinions expressed in the cases presented thus far that discussion of the specific doctrine of previous restraint tends to slide over into the more generalized concept of censorship. The latter word is quite commonly employed in the literature to denote any form of restraint, before or after publication, aside from criminal prosecutions, which effectively impairs consumption of the various forms of speech or press. Thus a decision of the Postmaster General to classify a magazine as not entitled to the second-class mailing privilege is certainly not a previous restraint, in the traditional usage, but it will clearly reduce (or possibly rule out altogether) the circulation of the magazine. Since the terms are sometimes used interchangeably in discussions of previous restraint, it is appropriate to consider here some of the postpublication administrative practices which limit freedom of speech and press.

Periodicals which are granted the second-class mail privilege have by this fact gained a valuable asset. Without such a privilege the standard postage rates would be so high for many such publications that costs would be prohibitive. Even if this were not the result, the periodical would suffer a serious competitive disadvantage. The Court has held that Congress need not open the privilege to publications of all types, and Congress has set conditions which must be met in order to qualify. The relevant requirement (one of four) is:

Except as otherwise provided by law, the conditions upon which a publication shall be admitted to the second class are as follows . . . *Fourth.* It must be originated and published for the dissemination of information of a public character, or devoted to literature, the sciences, arts, or some special industry, and having a legitimate list of subscribers. Nothing herein contained shall be so construed as to admit to the second-class rate regular publications designed primarily for advertising purposes, or for free circulation, or for circulation at nominal rates.

Esquire Magazine was granted a second-cass permit in 1933. In 1943, pursuant to 39 USCA Sec. 232, the Postmaster General held a hearing and revoked the permit. The publisher then brought suit to enjoin the Postmaster General from revoking the permit. The Supreme Court considered the issue in *Hannegan* v. *Esquire, Inc.,* 327 U.S. 146 (1946). Justice Douglas, for a unanimous Court, stated that the Postmaster General acted improperly. The opinion cites the Postmaster General's statements in support of the conclusion to revoke. It should be noted that the decision to revoke was not based on a finding of obscenity, for in that case the magazine would be altogether nonmailable. It rested, instead, on a conclusion that the fourth condition set down by Congress was not met:

The plain language of this statute does not assume that a publication must in fact be "obscene" within the intendment of the postal obscenity statutes before it can be found not to be "originated and published for the dissemination of information of a public character, or devoted to literature, the sciences, arts, or some special industry."

Writings and pictures may be indecent, vulgar, and risque and still not be obscene in a technical sense. Such writings and pictures may be in that obscure and treacherous borderland zone where the average person hesitates to find them technically obscene, but still may see ample proof that they are morally improper and not for the public welfare and the public good. When such writings or pictures occur in isolated instances their dangerous tendencies and malignant qualities may be considered of lesser importance.

When, however, they become a dominant and systematic feature they most certainly cannot be said to be for the public good, and a publication which uses them in that manner is not making the "special contribution to the public welfare" which Congress intended by the Fourth condition.

A publication to enjoy these unique mail privileges and special preferences is bound to do more than refrain from disseminating material which is obscene or bordering on the obscene. It is under a positive duty to contribute to the public good and the public welfare. . . .

Justice Douglas pointed out that most of the magazine issues offered in evidence and under attack were predominantly made up of material which was not challenged. He continued:

But petitioner's predecessor found that the objectionable items, though a small percentage of the total bulk, were regular recurrent features which gave the magazine its dominant tone or characteristic. These include jokes, cartoons, pictures, articles, and poems. They were said to reflect the smoking-room type of humor, featuring, in the main, sex. Some witnesses found the challenged items highly objectionable, calling them salacious and indecent. Others thought they were only racy and risque. Some condemned them as being merely in poor taste. Other witnesses could find no objection to them.

An examination of the items makes plain, we think, that the controversy is not whether the magazine publishes "information of a public character" or is devoted to "literature" or to the "arts." It is whether the contents are "good" or "bad." To uphold the order of revocation would, therefore, grant the Postmaster-General a power of censorship. Such a power is so abhorrent to our traditions that a purpose to grant it should not be easily inferred. . . .

We may assume that Congress has a broad power of classification and need not open second-class mail to publications of all types. The categories or publications entitled to that classification have indeed varied through the years. And the Court held in *Ex parte Jackson*, 96 U.S. 727, that Congress could constitutionally make it a crime to send fraudulent or obscene material through the mails. But grave constitutional questions are immediately raised once it is said that the use of mails is a privilege which may be extended or withheld on any grounds whatsoever. . . . Under that view the second-class rate could be granted on condition that certain economic or political ideas not be disseminated. The provisions of the Fourth condition would have to be far more explicit for us to assume that Congress made such a radical departure from our traditions and undertook to clothe the Postmaster General with the power to supervise the tastes of the reading public of the country.

It is plain, as we have said, that the favorable second class rates were granted periodicals meeting the requirements of the Fourth condition, so that the public good might be served through a dissemination of the class of periodicals described. But that is a far cry from assuming that Congress had any idea that each applicant for the second class rate must convince the Postmaster-General that his publication positively contributes to the public good or public welfare. . . .

It should be noted that the Court's decision in the *Esquire* case came off as an issue of statutory intent rather than First Amendment application. It thus left undetermined the constitutional area of restrictions which Congress might impose as limitations on the second-class mail privilege. In *Donaldson* v. *Read Magazine*, 333 U.S. 178 (1948), however, the Court sustained a Court order forbidding the delivery of mail and money orders to a magazine conducting a puzzle contest which the Postmaster General had found to be fraudulent. The Court stated that freedom of the press does not include the right to raise money by deception of the public. The mail-block sanction (prohibiting the delivery of *all* mail to offending sources of "obscene" publications and other articles) is a formidable weapon in the hands of the Post Office Department. Under a 1960 act of Congress, the mail-block sanction may not be used without an order from a federal court. At one time the Department declared nondeliverable such works as James Jones's *From Here to Eternity*, as well as some of the works of John O'Hara, John Steinbeck, and Ernest Hemingway. [See Edward De Grazia, "Obscenity and the Mail: A Study of Administrative Restraint," 20 *Law and Contemporary Problems* 608–620 (Autumn, 1955).] Under its interpretation of the Foreign Agents Registration Act of 1938, the Post Office Department has held that it can seize and destroy foreign propaganda coming into this country via the mails. Under this interpretation it delayed a shipment of seventy-five copies of Lenin's *State and Revolution* to be used in a history course at Brown University until the university authorities satisfied the Department as to the usefulness of the book to the University and the restrictions placed on its accessibility. [See generally, Jay A. Sigler, "Freedom of the Mails: A Developing Right," 54 *Geo. L. J.* 30 (1965).]

Another form of administrative proceeding involving censorship from time to time has been the enforcement of custom controls on the importation of books or paintings. Until the law was changed by Congress in 1930, customs officials prevented the entry of such classics as Voltaire's *Candide, The Arabian Nights,* and Boccaccio's *Decameron,* as well as a number of modern works. The fact that many of the books were published in the United States did not seem to affect the application of the section barring "obscene" works. In 1930 the Congress amended the Tariff Act to authorize importation of classics and books of recognized scientific and literary merit when imported for noncommercial purposes. The act also provided that upon seizure of a book, the collector was required to notify the federal district attorney, who was to institute proceedings in the federal district court for the forfeiture of the book. Any party in interest could demand a trial by jury. In 1933 a copy of *Ulysses* was seized by the customs officials, but in an important decision by Judge Woolsey, the book was held not to come within the statutory ban on "obscene" works and therefore was not subject to seizure and confiscation. The case was *United States v. One Book Called "Ulysses,"* 5 F. Supp. 182 (1933). The decision was affirmed by the Court of Appeals, 72 F. 2d 705 (1934), and resulted in relative freedom from customs censorship. Nonetheless, the Tariff Act provision, Title 19 United States Code, Section 1305, remains and may be applied in appropriate cases if supported by judicial order. [See Jay A. Sigler, "Customs Censorship," 15 *Clev.-Mar. L. Rev.* 58 (1966).]

It can be said that the Court has taken a strong stand against previous restraints on First Amendment rights, although the opinions do indicate a few exceptional situations where such restraints might be allowable. Censorship devices which operate after publication but still effectively bar public consumption of a film, book, or painting, have been treated less stringently, but the Court examines the standards employed by the censors with great care. Thus it is not unconstitutional to require that movie films be licensed for showing, but the statutory guidelines for denial of license must be carefully drawn. Book publishers may print their books, but they may not send obscene books through the mail. Further, the Post Office Department might request and receive a court order setting up a mail-block sanction against offending publishers. The publishers might get the books as far as the retailers, only to face an injunction barring the sale of their books at that juncture. And, finally, the customs bureau is directed to stop the importation of obscene books into the United States.

What is the Court's attitude on restraints imposed after the speech is made or after the book has been made available to the public? As Chafee pointed out so clearly, the Blackstone approach would leave the speaker or the writer at the mercy of the law once he had exercised his right to put his ideas before the public. Such an attitude would make a mockery of the constitutional guarantees. Recognizing this, the Court and thoughtful writers on the subject have explored several approaches in their attempts to set out workable doctrines as decisional rules for determining the permissible areas of restraint on First Amendment rights. The development of these approaches is taken up in the following section.

DOCTRINES ADVANCED AS TESTS OF CONSTITUTIONALITY OF FIRST AMENDMENT RESTRAINTS

Probably the best known judicial test in the First Amendment area is the "clear and present danger" test formulated by Justice Holmes in *Schenck* v. *United States* in 1919. The case presented the delicate issue of the area of criticism and dissent allowable during time of war. The decision holds that the rights of speech and press are not and were not intended to be absolute rights, but must be subject to certain reasonable restraints. At the same time, Justice Holmes, for a unanimous Court, set out his controversial proposition regarding the requirements necessary to support such restraints.

SCHENCK v. UNITED STATES
249 U.S. 47 (1919)

Mr. Justice Holmes delivered the opinion of the Court.

This is an indictment in three counts. The first charges a conspiracy to violate the Espionage Act of June 15, 1917, . . . by causing and attempting to cause insubordination, etc., in the military and naval forces of the United States, and to obstruct the recruiting and enlistment service of the United States, when the United States was at war with the German Empire, to-wit, that the defendants willfully conspired to have printed and circulated to men who had been called and accepted for military service under the Act of May 18, 1917, a document set forth and alleged to be calculated to cause such insubordination and obstruction. . . . The second count alleges a conspiracy to commit an offense against the United States, to-wit, to use the mails for the transmission of matter declared to be nonmailable by . . . the Act of June 15, 1917, to-wit, the above mentioned document, . . . The third count charges an unlawful use of the mails for the transmission of the same matter and otherwise as above. The defendants were found guilty on all the counts. They set up the First Amendment to the Constitution forbidding Congress to make any law abridging the freedom of speech, or of the press, and bringing the case here on that ground have argued some other points also of which we must dispose. . . .

The document in question upon its first printed side recited the first section of the Thirteenth Amendment, said that the idea embodied in it was violated by the Conscription Act and that a conscript is little better than a convict. In impassioned language it intimated that conscription was despotism in its worst form and a monstrous wrong against humanity in the interest of Wall Street's chosen few. It said, "Do not submit to intimidation," but in form at least confined itself to peaceful measures such as a petition for the repeal of the act. The other and later printed side of the sheet was headed "Assert Your Rights." It stated reasons for alleging that any one violated the Constitution when he refused to recognize "your right to assert your opposition to the draft," and went on, "If you do not assert and support your rights, you are helping to deny or disparage rights which it is the solemn duty of all citizens and residents of the United States to retain." It described the arguments on the other side as coming from cunning politicians and a mercenary capitalist press, and even silent consent to the conscription law as helping to support an infamous conspiracy. It denied the power to send our citizens away to foreign shores to shoot up the people of other lands, and added that words could not express the condemnation such cold-blooded ruthlessness deserves, &c., &c., winding up, "You must do your share to maintain, support and uphold the rights of the people of this country." Of course the document would not have been sent unless it had been intended to have some effect, and we do not see what effect it could be expected to have upon persons subject to the draft except to influence them to obstruct the carrying of it out. The defendants do not deny that the jury might find against them on this point.

But it is said, suppose that that was the tendency of the circular, it is protected by the First Amendment to the Constitution. Two of the strongest expressions are said to be quoted respectively from well-known public men. It well may be that the prohibition of laws abridging the freedom of speech is not confined to previous restraints, although to prevent them may have been the main purpose, as intimated in *Patterson* v. *Colorado*, 205 U.S. 454, 462. We admit that in many places and in ordinary times the defendants in saying all that was said in the circular would have been within their constitutional rights. But the character of every act depends upon the circumstances in which it is done. *Aikens* v. *Wisconsin*, 195 U.S. 194, 205, 206. The most stringent protection of free speech would not protect a man in falsely shouting fire in a theatre and causing a panic. It does not even protect a man from an injunction against uttering words that may have all the effect of force. *Gompers* v. *Bucks Stove & Range Co.*, 221 U.S. 418, 439. The question in every case is whether the words used are used in such circumstances and are of such a nature as to create a clear and present danger that they will bring about the substantive evils that Congress has a right to prevent. It is a question of proximity and degree. When a nation is at war many things that might be said in time of peace are such a hindrance to its effort that their utterance will not be endured so long as men fight and that no Court could regard them as protected by any constitutional right. It seems to be admitted that if an actual obstruction of the recruiting service were proved, liability for words that produced that effect might be enforced. The Statute of 1917, in Section 4, punishes conspiracies to obstruct as well as actual obstruction. If the act (speaking, or circulating a paper), its tendency and the intent with which it is done, are the same, we perceive no ground for saying that success alone warrants making the act a crime. . . .

Judgments affirmed.

Nine months after the *Schenck* case the Court decided *Abrams* v. *United States,* 250 U.S. 616 (1919). (For an excellent treatment of this case see Chafee, *Free Speech in the United States,* pp. 108–140.) In August 1918, while the United States was still at war with Germany, American troops were ordered to Vladivostok as a move to hinder the success of the Russian Revolution. Abrams and others began meeting in their "third-floor back" in New York's East Side and decided to protest against the attack on the Russian Revolution, with which they strongly sympathized. They printed several thousand leaflets and distributed them. There were general exhortations to munitions workers to strike in order to prevent American interference in the Revolution. There was no evidence that any of the leaflets reached any munitions workers or that anyone was led to stop war work. The five defendants were convicted and sentenced to twenty years imprisonment. The United States Supreme Court affirmed the convictions. The majority found that the defendants had intended to "urge, incite, and advocate" curtailment of production necessary to the war with Germany and were thus guilty of violation of the Sedition Act of 1918. Justice Holmes, with Justice Brandeis concurring, dissented. His opinion stated in part:

I never have seen any reason to doubt that the questions of law that alone were before this Court in the cases of *Schenck, Frohwerk* and *Debs,* . . . were rightly decided. I do not doubt for a moment that by the same reasoning that would justify punishing persuasion to murder, the United States constitutionally may punish speech that produces or is intended to produce a clear and imminent danger that it will bring about forthwith certain substantive evils that the United States constitutionally may seek to prevent. The power undoubtedly is greater in time of war than in time of peace because war opens dangers that do not exist at other times.

But as against dangers peculiar to war, as against others, the principle of the right to free speech is always the same. It is only the present danger of immediate evil or an intent to bring it about that warrants Congress in setting a limit to the expression of opinion where private rights are not concerned. Congress certainly cannot forbid all effort to change the mind of the country. Now nobody can suppose that the surreptitious publishing of a silly leaflet by an unknown man, without more, would present any immediate danger that its opinions would hinder the success of the government arms or have any appreciable tendency to do so.

Publishing those opinions for the very purpose of obstructing, however, might indicate a greater danger and at any rate would have the quality of an attempt. So I assume that the second leaflet if published for the purposes alleged in the fourth count might be punishable. But it seems pretty clear to me that nothing less than that would bring these papers within the scope of this law. . . .

I do not see how anyone can find the intent required by the statute in any of the defendants' words. The second leaflet is the only one that affords even a foundation for the charge, and there, without invoking the hatred of German militarism expressed in the former one, it is evident from the beginning to the end that the only object of the paper is to help Russia and stop American intervention there against the popular government—not to impede the United States in the war that it was carrying on. To say that two phrases taken literally might import a suggestion of conduct that would have interference with the war as an indirect and probably undesired effect seems to me by no means enough to show an attempt to produce that effect. . . .

Persecution for the expression of opinions seems to me perfectly logical. If you have no doubt of your premises or your power and want a certain result with all your heart you naturally express your wishes in law and sweep away all opposition. To allow opposition by speech seems to indicate that you think the speech impotent, as when a man says that he has squared the circle, or that you do not care whole-heartedly for the result, or that you doubt either your power or your premises. But when men have realized that time has upset many fighting faiths, they may come to believe even more than they believe the very foundations of their own conduct that the ultimate good desired is better reached by free trade in ideas—that the best test of truth is the power of the thought to get itself accepted in the competition of the market, and that truth is the only ground upon which their wishes safely can be carried out. That at any rate is the theory of our Constitution. It is an experiment, as all life is an experiment. Every year if not every day we have to wager our salvation upon some prophecy based upon imperfect knowledge. While that experiment is part of our system I think that we should be eternally vigilant against attempts to check the expression of opinions that we loathe and believe to be fraught with death, unless they so imminently threaten immediate interference with the lawful and pressing purposes of the law that an immediate check is required to save the country. I wholly disagree with the argument of the Government that the First Amendment left the common law as to seditious libel in force. I had conceived that the United States through many years had shown its repentance for the Sedition Act of 1798, by repaying fines that it imposed. Only the emergency that makes it immediately dangerous to leave the correction of evil counsels to time warrants making any exception to the sweeping command, "Congress shall make no law . . . abridging the freedom of speech." Of course I am speaking only of expressions of opinion and exhortations, which were all that were uttered here, but I regret that I cannot put into more impressive words my belief that in their conviction upon this indictment the defendants were deprived of their rights under the Constitution of the United States.

It seems to be a reasonable inference from Justice Holmes' pronouncements in the two preceding cases that the Court itself would have the final word on whether a given speech or publication presented the requisite "clear and present danger"—at least where the issue was appropriately raised. In *Gitlow* v. *New York*, 268 U.S. 652 (1925), however, the majority gave the doctrine a different cast. Benjamin Gitlow was convicted in the supreme court of New York of the statutory crime of criminal anarchy in that he and others published and distributed various papers advocating the revolutionary overthrow of the government. He was a member of the Left Wing section of the Socialist party and participated in the publication and circulation of a Left Wing Manifesto in the official organ entitled "The Revolutionary Age." Several thousand copies of the paper were distributed by mail and by direct sale. The manifesto called for a "Communist revolution" and mobilizing the "power of the proletariat in action," through mass industrial revolts developing into mass political strikes and "revolutionary mass action" for the purpose of conquering and destroying the parliamentary state and establishing in its place the "system of Communist Socialism." In his opinion for the Court, affirming the conviction, Justice Sanford said in part:

By enacting the present statute the state has determined, through its legislative body, that utterances advocating the overthrow of organized government by force, violence, and unlawful means, are so inimical to the general welfare, and involve such danger of substantive evil, that they may be penalized in the exercise of its police power. That determination must be given great weight. . . . That utterances inciting to the overthrow of organized government by unlawful means present a sufficient danger of substantive evil to bring their punishment within the range of legislative discretion is clear. Such utterances, by their very nature, involve danger to the public peace and to the security of the state. They threaten breaches of the peace and ultimate revolution. And the immediate danger is none the less real and substantial because the effect of a given utterance cannot be accurately foreseen. . . .

We cannot hold that the present statute is an arbitrary or unreasonable exercise of the police power of the state, unwarrantably infringing the freedom of speech or press; and we must and do sustain its constitutionality.

This being so it may be applied to every utterance—not too trivial to be beneath the notice of the law—which is of such a character and used with such intent and purpose as to bring it within the prohibition of the statute. . . . In other words, when the legislative body has determined generally, in the constitutional exercise of its discretion, that utterances of a certain kind involve such danger of substantive evil that they may be punished, the question whether any specific utterance coming within the prohibited class is likely, in and of itself, to bring about the substantive evil, is not open to consideration. It is sufficient that the statute itself be constitutional, and that the use of the language comes within its prohibition.

It is clear that the question in such cases is entirely different from that involved in those cases where the statute merely prohibits certain acts involving the danger of substantive evil, without any reference to language itself, and it is sought to apply its provisions to language used by the defendant for the purpose of bringing about the prohibited results. . . . And the general statement in the *Schenck* case that the "question in every case is whether the words are used in such circumstances and are of such a nature as to create a clear and present danger that they will bring about the substantive evils,"—upon which great reliance is placed in the defendant's argument,—was manifestly intended, as shown by the context, to apply only in cases of this class, and has no application to those like the present, where the legislative body itself has previously determined the danger of substantive evil arising from utterances of a specified character. . . .

Justice Holmes, joined by Justice Brandeis, dissented from this construction of the "clear and present danger" statement. Since Justice Holmes formulated the statement and wrote the opinion for a unanimous Court when it first appeared in the official reports, and since Justice Sanford was not even on the Court when the *Schenck* case was decided, his attempt to explain the appropriate application of the doctrine might seem to indicate considerable temerity, if not outright effrontery. The majority in *Abrams* had disagreed with Justice Holmes, but no mention was made by them of the clear and present danger test. In his dissent in *Gitlow* Justice Holmes stated in part:

If I am right, then I think that the criterion sanctioned by the full court in *Schenck* v. *United States* . . . applies: "The question in every case is whether the words used·are used in such circumstances and are of such a nature as to create a clear and present danger that they will bring about the substantive evils that [the state] has a right to prevent." It is true that in my opinion this criterion was departed from in *Abrams* v. *United States*, . . . but the convictions that I expressed in that case are too deep for it to be possible for me as yet to believe that it and *Schaefer* v. *United States* . . . have settled the law. If what I think the correct test is applied, it is manifest that there was no present danger of an attempt to overthrow the government by force on the part of the admittedly small minority who shared the defendant's views. It is said that this Manifesto was more than a theory, that it was an incitement. Every idea is an incitement. It offers itself for belief, and, if believed, it is acted on unless some other belief outweighs it, or some failure of energy stifles the movement at its birth. The only difference between the expression of an opinion and an incitement in the narrower sense is the speaker's enthusiasm for the result. Eloquence may set fire to reason. But whatever may be thought of the redundant discourse before us, it had no chance of starting a present conflagration. If, in the long run, the beliefs expressed in proletarian dictatorship are destined to be accepted by the dominant forces of the community, the only meaning of free speech is that they should be given their chance and have their way.

If the publication of this document had been laid as an attempt to induce an uprising against government at once, and not at some indefinite time in the future, it would have presented a different question. The object would have been one with which the law might deal, subject to the doubt whether there was any danger that the publication could produce any result; or, in other words, whether it was not futile and too remote from possible consequences. But the indictment alleges the publication and nothing more.

It appears that the majority in *Gitlow* employed the normal test of reasonableness coupled with the presumption of validity accorded legislative determinations. Speech was to be accorded no different treatment than any other area subject to legislative restraint, and the statutory finding of clear and present danger was to be conclusive upon the courts. It seems equally clear that the Holmes test was either purposely designed or, at the very least, used as a judicial tool for according special protection to the rights of expression against overzealous application of restraints. It did not purport to set up an absolute freedom to speak and publish, but as Justice Holmes applied the phrase it was a useful mechanism for broadening the permissible area of speech and press and for allowing the courts to examine more critically than before the restraints on those rights. Justice Black's gloss on the doctrine affords the maximum scope. In his opinion for the Court in *Bridges* v. *California*, 314 U.S. 252 (1941), he stated, "What finally emerges from the 'clear and present danger' cases is a working principle that the substantive evil must be extremely serious and the degree of imminence extremely high before utterances can be punished." On the other hand, Justice Frankfurter minimized the utility of the phrase. In his concurring opinion in *Pennekamp* v. *Florida*, 328 U.S. 331 (1946), he stated, " 'Clear and present danger' was never used by Mr. Justice Holmes to express a technical legal doctrine or to convey a formula for adjudicating cases. It was a literary phrase not to be distorted by being taken from its context. In its setting it served to indicate the importance of freedom of speech to a free society but also to emphasize that its exercise must be compatible with the preservation of other freedoms essential to a democracy and guaranteed by our Constitution. When those other attributes of a democracy are threatened by speech, the Constitution does not deny power to the states to curb it."

The years since *Schenck* and *Gitlow* have seen a variety of different, even tortured, applications of the clear and present danger doctrine. [See, e.g., the opinions in *Dennis* v. *United States*, 341 U.S. 494 (1951).] It has been subjected to criticism as well as praise, and to avoid this collateral controversy the Court today seems to feel that it can handle First Amendment cases more easily by simply omitting reference to the doctrine altogether. The one exception in recent years is *Wood* v. *Georgia*, 370 U.S. 375 (1962), in which the test was applied to invalidate a conviction for contempt of court based upon a sheriff's criticism of certain judges which allegedly interfered with a grand jury proceeding. Two justices dissented, but all justices accepted the application of the test in the case.

While the customary view has been that the clear and present danger doctrine had as its primary function the *broadening* of the permissible area of First Amendment freedoms, there have been some who have argued that to use such a test is to *restrict* First Amendment rights and therefore to violate the Constitution. The foremost exponent of this view has been Alexander Meiklejohn. The following selection gives his approach, normally referred to as the "absolutist's" approach to defining First Amendment rights of expression.

FREE SPEECH AND ITS RELATION TO SELF-GOVERNMENT [2]

... [N]o one who reads with care the text of the First Amendment can fail to be startled by its absoluteness. The phrase, "Congress shall make no law ... abridging the freedom of speech," is unqualified. It admits of no exceptions. To say that no laws of a given type shall be made means that no laws of that type shall, under any circumstances, be made. That prohibition holds good in war as in peace, in danger as in security. The men who adopted the Bill of Rights were not ignorant of the necessities of war or of national danger. It would, in fact, be nearer to the truth to say that it was exactly those necessities which they had in mind as they planned to defend freedom of discussion against them. Out of their own bitter experience they knew how terror and hatred, how war and strife, can drive men into acts of unreasoning suppression. They planned, therefore, both for the peace which they desired and for the wars which they feared. And in both cases they established an absolute, unqualified prohibition of the abridgment of the freedom of speech. That same requirement, for the same reasons, under the same Constitution, holds good today.

Against what has just been said it will be answered that twentieth-century America does not accept "absolutes" so readily as did the eighteenth century. But to this we must reply that the issue here involved cannot be dealt with by such twentieth-century a priori reasoning. It requires careful examination of the structure and functioning of our political system as a whole to see what part the principle of the freedom of speech plays, here and now, in that system. And when that examination is made, it seems to me clear that for our day and generation, the words of the First Amendment mean literally what they say. And what they say is that under no circumstances shall the freedom of speech be abridged. Whether or not that opinion can be justified is the primary issue with which this argument tries to deal.

But ... this dictum which we rightly take to express the most vital wisdom which men have won in their striving for political freedom is yet—it must be admitted—strangely paradoxical. No one can doubt that, in any well-governed society, the legislature has both the right and the duty to prohibit certain forms of speech. Libellous assertions may be, and must be, forbidden and punished. So too must slander. Words which incite men to crime are themselves criminal and must be dealt with as such. Sedition and treason may be expressed by speech or writing. And, in those cases, decisive repressive action by the government is imperative for the sake of the general welfare. All these necessities that speech be limited are recognized and provided for under the Constitution. They were not unknown to the writers of the First Amendment. That amendment, then, we may take it for granted, *does not forbid the abridging of speech*. But, at the same time, *it does forbid the abridging of the freedom of speech*. It is to the solving of that paradox, that apparent self-contradiction, that we are summoned if, as free men, we wish to know what the right of freedom of speech is. ...

First, we must remember that, in the Constitution as it stood before it was amended by the Bill of Rights, the principle of the freedom of public discussion had been already clearly recognized and adopted. Article I, section 6, of the Constitution,

[2] Abridged from pp. 17–19, 35–40, Alexander Meiklejohn, *Free Speech and Its Relation to Self-Government* (New York: Harper and Brothers, 1948). Copyright 1948 by Harper & Row, Publishers, Incorporated. Reprinted by permission of the publishers.

as it defines the duties and privileges of the members of Congress, says, ". . . and for any speech or debate in either House, they shall not be questioned in any other place." Here is a prohibition against abridgment of the freedom of speech which is equally uncompromising, equally absolute, with that of the First Amendment. Un-qualifiedly, the freedom of debate of our representatives upon the floor of either house is protected from abridging interference. May that protection, under the Constitution, be limited or withdrawn in time of clear and present danger? And if not, why not?

. . . If congressional immunity were not absolute and unconditional, the whole program of representative self-government would be broken down. And likewise, by common consent, the same kind of immunity is guaranteed to the judges in our courts. Everyone knows that the dissenting opinions of members of the Supreme Court are a clear and present threat to the effectiveness of majority decisions. And yet the freedom of the minorities on the bench to challenge and to dissent has not been legally abridged. Nor will it be.

And that fact throws strong and direct light upon the provision of the First Amendment that the public discussions of "citizens" shall have the same immunity. In the last resort, it is not our representatives who govern us. We govern ourselves, using them. And we do so in such ways as our own free judgment may decide. And, that being true, it is essential that when we speak in the open forum, we "shall not be questioned in any other place." It is not enough for us, as self-governing men, that we be governed wisely and justly, by someone else. We insist on doing our own governing. The freedom which we grant to our representatives is merely a derivative of the prior freedom which belongs to us as voters. In spite of all the dangers which it involves, Article I, section 6, suggests that the First Amendment means what it says: In the field of common action, of public discussion, the freedom of speech shall not be abridged.

And, second, the Fifth Amendment—by contrast of meaning, rather than by similarity—throws light upon the First. By the relevant clause of the Fifth Amendment we are told that no person within the jurisdiction of the laws of the United States may be "deprived of life, liberty, or property, without due process of law." And, whatever may have been the original reference of the term "liberty," as used in that sentence when it was written, it has been, in recent times, construed by the Supreme Court to include "the liberty of speech." The Fifth Amendment is, then, saying that the people of the United States have a civil liberty of speech which, by due legal process, the government may limit or suppress. But this means that, under the Bill of Rights, there are two freedoms, or liberties, of speech, rather than only one. There is a "freedom of speech" which the First Amendment declares to be non-abridgable. But there is also a "liberty of speech" which the Fifth Amendment declares to be abridgable. And for the inquiry in which we are engaged, the distinction between these two, the fact that there are two, is of fundamental importance. The Fifth Amendment, it appears, has to do with a class of utterances concerning which the legislature may, legitimately, raise the question, "Shall they be endured?" The First Amendment, on the other hand, has to do with a class of utterances concerning which that question may never legitimately be raised. And if that be true, then the problem which Mr. Holmes has suggested—that of separating two classes of utterances—becomes the problem of defining the difference between, and the relation between, the First and Fifth Amendments, so far as they deal with matters of speech.

The nature of this difference comes to light if we note that the "liberty" of speech which is subject to abridgment is correlated, in the Fifth Amendment, with our rights to "life" and "property." These are private rights. They are individual possessions. And there can be no doubt that among the many forms of individual action and possession which are protected by the Constitution—not from regulation, but from undue regulation—the right to speak one's mind as one chooses is esteemed by us as one of our most highly cherished private possessions. Individuals have, then, a private right of speech which may on occasion be denied or limited, though such limitations may not be imposed unnecessarily or unequally. So says the Fifth Amendment. But this limited guarantee of the freedom of a man's wish to speak is radically different in intent from the unlimited guarantee of the freedom of public discussion, which is given by the First Amendment. The latter, correlating the freedom of speech in which it is interested with the freedom of religion, of press, of assembly, of petition for redress of grievances, places all these alike beyond the reach of legislative limitation, beyond even the due process of law. With regard to them, Congress has no negative powers whatever. There are, then, in the theory of the Constitution, two radically different kinds of utterances. The constitutional status of a merchant advertising his wares, of a paid lobbyist fighting for the advantage of his client, is utterly different from that of a citizen who is planning for the general welfare. And from this it follows that the Constitution provides differently for two different kinds of "freedom of speech."

Now, the basic error which we shall find in the "clear and present danger" principle, as it seeks to separate speech which will be endured from speech which will not be endured, is that it ignores or denies this difference of reference between the First and Fifth amendments. Mr. Holmes and the Supreme Court have ventured to annul the First Amendment because they have believed that the due process clause of the Fifth Amendment could take its place. But if that substitution can be shown to be invalid; if, under the Constitution, we have two essentially different freedoms of speech rather than only one, the position taken by the court becomes untenable. . . .

It can be seen from the foregoing selection that Professor Meiklejohn feels that the "clear and present danger" test, while better than the *Gitlow* approach, is still an improper restraint on freedom of speech if employed in a case involving *public* discussion rather than speech concerning *private* matters. In 1962, in a public interview by Professor Edmond Cahn, Justice Black indicated an even stronger position in favor of freedom of speech than did Professor Meiklejohn. ["Justice Black and First Amendment 'Absolutes'; A Public Interview," 37 *N.Y.U. L. Rev.* 549 (1962).] Some questions and Justice Black's answers follow: [3]

Suppose we start with one of the key sentences in your James Madison Lecture where you said, "It is my belief that there *are* 'absolutes' in our Bill of Rights, and that they were put there on purpose by men who knew what words meant and meant their prohibitions to be 'absolutes.' " Will you please explain your reasons for this.

[3] Reprinted by permission of the *New York University Law Review* and Justice Black.

JUSTICE BLACK: My first reason is that I believe the words do mean what they say. I have no reason to challenge the intelligence, integrity or honesty of the men who wrote the First Amendment. . . .

I learned a long time ago that there are affirmative and negative words. The beginning of the First Amendment is that "Congress shall make no law." I understand that it is rather old-fashioned and shows a slight naivete to say that "no law" means no law. It is one of the most amazing things about the ingeniousness of the times that strong arguments are made, which *almost* convince me, that it is very foolish of me to think "no law" means no law. But what it *says* is "Congress shall make no law respecting an establishment of religion," and so on.

I have to be honest about it. I confess not only that I think the Amendment means what it says but also that I may be slightly influenced by the fact that I do not think Congress *should* make any law with respect to these subjects. . . .

CAHN: Some of your colleagues would say that it is better to interpret the Bill of Rights so as to permit Congress to take what it considers reasonable steps to preserve the security of the nation even at some sacrifice of freedom of speech and association. Otherwise what will happen to the nation and the Bill of Rights as well? What is your view of this?

JUSTICE BLACK: . . . Of course, I want this country to do what will preserve it. I want it to be preserved as the kind of Government it was intended to be. I would not desire to live at any place where my thoughts were under the suspicion of government and where my words could be censored by government, and where worship, whatever it was or wasn't, had to be determined by an officer of the government. That is not the kind of government I want preserved.

I agree with those who wrote our Constitution, that too much power in the hands of officials is a dangerous thing. What was government created for except to serve the people? Why was a Constitution written for the first time in this country except to limit the power of government and those who were selected to exercise it at the moment?

My answer to the statement that this Government should preserve itself is yes. The method I would adopt is different, however, from that of some other people. I think it can be preserved only by leaving people with the utmost freedom to think and to hope and to talk and to dream if they want to dream. I do not think this Government must look to force, stifling the minds and aspirations of the people. Yes, I believe in self-preservation, but I would preserve it as the founders said, by leaving people free. I think here, as in another time, it cannot live half slave and half free. . . .

CAHN: Do you make an exception in freedom of speech and press for the law of defamation? That is, are you willing to allow people to sue for damages when they are subjected to libel or slander?

JUSTICE BLACK: My view of the First Amendment, as originally ratified, is that it said Congress should pass none of these kinds of laws. As written at that time, the Amendment applied only to Congress. I have no doubt myself that the provision, as written and adopted, intended that there should be no libel or defamation law in the United States under the United States Government, just absolutely none so far as I am concerned. . . .

My belief is that the First Amendment was made applicable to the states by the Fourteenth. I do not hesitate, so far as my own view is concerned, as to what should be and what I hope will sometime be the constitutional doctrine that just as it was not intended to authorize damage suits for mere words as distinguished from conduct as far as the Federal Government is concerned, the same rule should apply to the states. . . .

I believe with Jefferson that it is time enough for government to step in to regulate people when they *do* something, not when they *say* something, and I do not believe myself that there is *any* halfway ground if they enforce the protections of the First Amendment. . . .

CAHN: Is there any kind of obscene material, whether defined as hardcore pornography or otherwise, the distribution and sale of which can be constitutionally restricted in any manner whatever, in your opinion?

JUSTICE BLACK: I will say it can in this country, because the courts have held that it can.

CAHN: Yes, but you won't get off so easily. I want to know what you think.

JUSTICE BLACK: My view is, without deviation, without exception, without any ifs, buts, or whereases, that freedom of speech means that you shall not do something to people either for the views they have or the views they express or the words they speak or write.

There is strong argument for the position taken by a man whom I admire very greatly, Dr. Meiklejohn, that the First Amendment really was intended to protect *political* speech, and I do think that was the basic purpose; that plus the fact that they wanted to protect *religious* speech. Those were the two main things they had in mind.

It is the law that there can be an arrest made for obscenity. It was the law in Rome that they could arrest people for obscenity after Augustus became Caesar. Tacitus says that then it became obscene to criticize the Emperor. It is not any trouble to establish a classification so that whatever it is that you do not want said is within that classification. So far as I am concerned, I do not believe there is any halfway ground for protecting freedom of speech and press. If you say it is half free, you can rest assured that it will not remain as much as half free. Madison explained that in his great Remonstrance when he said in effect, "If you make laws to force people to speak the words of Christianity, it won't be long until the same power will narrow the sole religion to the most powerful sect in it." I realize that there are dangers in freedom of speech, but I do not believe there are any halfway marks.

CAHN: Do you subscribe to the idea involved in the clear and present danger rule?

JUSTICE BLACK: I do not.

The "absolutist" position on First Amendment rights has never gained the acceptance of a majority on the Court, but it is a recurring theme in many of the dissenting opinions of Justice Black, who is frequently joined by Chief Justice Warren and Justice Douglas.

Another approach to the judicial handling of restrictions on freedom of expression is the so-called "preferred position" doctrine. In *Thomas* v. *Collins,* 323 U.S. 516 (1945), the doctrine finds its first official expression supported by a majority of the Court. The case dealt with the validity of a labor organizer's conviction for contempt of court for violating an order that he refrain from addressing a meeting until he first registered and obtained an organizer's card as required by Texas law. In holding the requirement invalid, and thus the conviction as well, Justice Rutledge, speaking for the majority, stated:

The case confronts us again with the duty our system places on this Court to say where the individual's freedom ends and the State's power begins. Choice on that border, now as always delicate, is perhaps more so where the usual presumption supporting legislation is balanced by the preferred place given in our scheme to the great, the indispensable democratic freedoms secured by the First Amendment. That priority gives these liberties a sanctity and a sanction not permitting dubious intrusions. And it is the character of the right, not of the limitation, which determines what standard governs the choice.

The "preferred position" doctrine was by no means first stated in *Thomas* v. *Collins*, since variations on this theme were presented at least as early as 1788 in letters of Thomas Paine and Thomas Jefferson. [Edmond Cahn gives an interesting historical analysis in "The Firstness of the First Amendment," 65 *Yale L. J.* 464 (1956).] But this case is the first in which a majority of the Court acquiesced in its use. It seems to have made its first appearance in the judicial opinions in Justice Stone's now famous "footnote 4" in his opinion for the Court in *United States* v. *Carolene Products Company*, 304 U.S. 144, 152, n. 4 (1938). In it he stated:

There may be narrower scope for operation of the presumption of constitutionality when legislation appears on its face to be within a specific prohibition of the Constitution, such as those of the first ten Amendments, which are deemed equally specific when held to be embraced within the Fourteenth. . . .

It is unnecessary to consider now whether legislation which restricts those political processes which can ordinarily be expected to bring about repeal of undesirable legislation, is to be subjected to more exacting judicial scrutiny under the general prohibitions of the Fourteenth Amendment than are most other types of legislation.

In effect, the theory of this doctrine is that the presumption of validity of legislation under attack is reversed when the questioned legislation affects adversely First Amendment freedom of expression. Thus, while formerly the Court took the view that state or federal laws were constitutional until proved otherwise, the "preferred position" concept would shift the burden of proof to the government to show that the attempted restriction was not unconstitutional. By the late 1940's, however, the Court was wavering on the use of this concept, and in 1949 Justice Frankfurter frankly expressed his distrust of its use. The occasion was the Court's consideration of a Trenton, New Jersey, sound truck ordinance in *Kovacs* v. *Cooper*, 336 U.S. 77 (1949). In the course of his opinion concurring with the majority in holding the ordinance constitutional, Justice Frankfurter took issue with Justice Reed's acceptance of the "preferred position" concept. He stated:

My brother Reed speaks of "The preferred position of freedom of speech," though, to be sure, he finds that the Trenton ordinance does not disregard it. This is a phrase that has uncritically crept into some recent opinions of this Court. I deem it a mischievous phrase, if it carries the thought, which it may subtly imply, that any law touching communication is infected with presumptive invalidity. It is not the first time in the history of constitutional adjudication that such a doctrinaire attitude has disregarded the admonition most to be observed in exercising the Court's reviewing power over legislation, "that it is a *constitution* we are expounding," *McCulloch* v. *Maryland*. . . . I say the phrase is mischievous because it radiates a constitutional doctrine without avowing it. . . .

Behind the notion sought to be expressed by the formula as to "the preferred position of freedom of speech" lies a relevant consideration in determining whether an enactment relating to the liberties protected by the Due Process Clause of the Fourteenth Amendment is violative of it. In law also, doctrine is illuminated by history. The ideas now governing the constitutional protection of freedom of speech derive essentially from the opinions of Mr. Justice Holmes.

The philosophy of his opinions on that subject arose from a deep awareness of the extent to which sociological conclusions are conditioned by time and circumstance. Because of this awareness Mr. Justice Holmes seldom felt justified in opposing his own opinion to economic views which the legislature embodied in law. But since he also realized that the progress of civilization is to a considerable extent the displacement of error which once held sway as official truth by beliefs which in turn have yielded to other beliefs, for him the right to search for truth was of a different order than some transient economic dogma. And without freedom of expression, thought becomes checked and atrophied. Therefore, in considering what interests are so fundamental as to be enshrined in the Due Process Clause, those liberties of the individual which history has attested as the indispensable conditions of an open as against a closed society come to this Court with a momentum for respect lacking when appeal is made to liberties which derive merely from shifting economic arrangements. Accordingly, Mr. Justice Holmes was far more ready to find legislative invasion where free inquiry was involved than in the debatable area of economics. See my Mr. Justice Holmes and the Supreme Court, 58 et seq.

The objection of summarizing this line of thought by the phrase "the preferred position of freedom of speech" is that it expresses a complicated process of constitutional adjudication by a deceptive formula. And it was Mr. Justice Holmes who admonished us that "To rest upon a formula is a slumber that, prolonged, means death." Collected Legal Papers, 306. Such a formula makes for mechanical jurisprudence . . .

A careful reading of Justice Frankfurter's opinion might lead to the conclusion that he accepts the idea of a gradation of rights, with freedom of expression on public matters as foremost, but he disapproves of a shorthand "doctrine" to express the differentiation. [For further reading of the "preferred position" concept, as well as a detailed analysis of Justice Frankfurter's position, see Robert B. McKay, "The Preference for Freedom," 34 *N.Y.U. L. Rev.* 1182 (1959).]

More recently the Court has tended to stress a "balancing" test, although some members strongly object to its use, preferring instead something closer to the absolute position. It seems that the first use of the "balancing" test by the Court is to be found in Chief Justice Vinson's opinion for the majority in *American Communications Ass'n, CIO* v. *Douds,* 339 U.S. 382 (1950), in which the Court upheld the non-Communist affidavit provision of the Labor Management Relations Act of 1947. In the course of his opinion he stated:

So far as the *Schenck* case itself is concerned, imminent danger of any substantive evil that Congress may prevent justifies the restriction of speech. . . . But in suggesting that the substantive evil must be serious and substantial, it was never the intention of this Court to lay down an absolutist test measured in terms of danger to the Nation. When the effect of a statute or ordinance upon the exercise of First Amendment freedoms is relatively small and the public interest to be protected is substantial, it is obvious that a rigid test requiring a showing of imminent danger to the security of the Nation is an absurdity. . . .

When particular conduct is regulated in the interest of public order, and the regulation results in an indirect, conditional, partial abridgment of speech, the duty of the courts is to determine which of these two conflicting interests demands the greater protection under the particular circumstances presented. The high place in which the right to speak, think, and assemble as you will was held by the Framers of the Bill of Rights and is held today by those who value liberty both as a means and an end indicates the solicitude with which we must view any assertion of personal freedoms. . . .

On the other hand, legitimate attempts to protect the public, not from the remote possible effects of noxious ideologies, but from present excesses of direct, active conduct are not presumptively bad because they interfere with and, in some of its manifestations, restrain the exercise of First Amendment rights. . . . In essence, the problem is one of weighing the probable effects of the statute upon the free exercise of the right of speech and assembly against the congressional determination that political strikes are evils of conduct which cause substantial harm to interstate commerce and that Communists and others identified by Section 9(h) pose continuing threats to that public interest when in positions of union leadership. We must, therefore, undertake the "delicate and difficult task . . . to weigh the circumstances and to appraise the substantiality of the reasons advanced in support of the regulation of the free enjoyment of the rights." *Schneider* v. *Irvington,* 308 U.S. 147, 161.

Justices Frankfurter, Harlan, and Clark have been leading supporters of the "balancing" test in the period since 1950. In *Dennis* v. *United States,* 341 U.S. 494 (1951), upholding sections of the Smith Act of 1940, Justice Frankfurter made the following statements in his concurring opinion:

The demands of free speech in a democratic society as well as the interest in national security are better served by candid and informed weighing of the competing interests, within the confines of the judicial process, than by announcing dogmas too inflexible for the non-Euclidian problems to be solved.

But how are competing interests to be assessed? Since they are not subject to quantitative ascertainment, the issue necessarily resolves itself into asking, who is to make the adjustment?—who is to balance the relevant factors and ascertain which interest is in the circumstances to prevail? Full responsibility for the choice cannot be given to the courts. Courts are not representative bodies. They are not designed to be a good reflex of a democratic society. Their judgment is best informed, and therefore most dependable, within narrow limits. Their essential quality is detachment, founded on independence. History teaches that the independence of the judiciary is jeopardized when courts become embroiled in the passions of the day and assume primary responsibility in choosing between competing political, economic and social pressures.

Primary responsibility for adjusting the interests which compete in the situation before us of necessity belongs to the Congress. The nature of the power to be exercised by this Court has been delineated in decisions not charged with the emotional appeal of situations such as that now before us. We are to set aside the judgment of those whose duty it is to legislate only if there is no reasonable basis for it. . . .

. . . Free-speech cases are not an exception to the principle that we are not legislators, that direct policy-making is not our province. How best to reconcile competing interests is the business of legislatures, and the balance they strike is a judgment not to be displaced by ours, but to be respected unless outside the pale of fair judgment. . . .

. . . A survey of the relevant decisions indicates that the results which we have reached are on the whole those that would ensue from careful weighing of conflicting interests. The complex issues presented by regulation of speech in public places by picketing, and by legislation prohibiting advocacy of crime have been resolved by scrutiny of many factors besides the imminence and gravity of the evil threatened. The matter has been well summarized by a reflective student of the Court's work. "The truth is that the clear-and-present-danger test is an oversimplified judgment unless it takes account also of a number of other factors: the relative seriousness of the danger in comparison with the value of the occasion for speech or political activity; the availability of more moderate controls than those which the state has imposed; and perhaps the specific intent with which the speech or activity is launched. No matter how rapidly we utter the phrase 'clear and present danger,' or how closely we hyphenate the words, they are not a substitute for the weighing of values. They tend to convey a delusion of certitude when what is most certain is the complexity of the strands in the web of freedoms which the judge must disentangle." Freund, On Understanding the Supreme Court 27–28.

Justice Harlan makes use of the "balancing" test in his opinion for a unanimous Court in NAACP v. Alabama, 357 U.S. 449 (1958), in which the Court held invalid the order of an Alabama court requiring the disclosure of membership rolls of the Alabama affiliates of the National Association for the Advancement of Colored People. Justice Harlan's opinion pointed out that "the production order, in the respects here drawn in question, must be regarded as entailing the likelihood of a substantial restraint upon the exercise by petitioner's members of their right to freedom of association." He then stated: "We turn to the final question whether Alabama has demonstrated an interest in obtaining the disclosures it seeks from petitioner which is sufficient to justify the deterrent effect which we have concluded these disclosures may well have on the free exercise by petitioner's members of their constitutionally protected right of association." The phraseology is thus clearly indicative of the employment of a "balancing" test of constitutionality. And Justice Clark, in his dissenting opinion in *Talley* v. *California*, 362 U.S. 60 (1960), dealing with the constitutionality of a Los Angeles ordinance requiring the name and address of sponsors on any handbills distributed, said: "(B)efore passing upon the validity of the ordinance, I would weigh the interests of the public in its enforcement against the claimed right of Talley."

Justices Black and Douglas have been vigorous opponents of the use of the "balancing" test in the First Amendment area. In *Barenblatt* v. *United States*, 360 U.S. 109 (1959), in which the Court upheld the conviction for contempt of Congress for refusal to answer committee questions concerning Communist Party membership, and in which Barenblatt grounded his refusal on First Amendment protection to belief and associational activity, Justice Black dissented, saying:

The First Amendment says in no equivocal language that Congress shall pass no law abridging freedom of speech, press, assembly or petition. The activities of this Committee, authorized by Congress, do precisely that, through exposure, obloquy and public scorn. . . .

(A) I do not agree that laws directly abridging First Amendment freedoms can be justified by a congressional or judicial balancing process. There are, of course, cases suggesting that a law which primarily regulates conduct but which might also indirectly affect speech can be upheld if the effect on speech is minor in relation to the need for control of the conduct. With these cases I agree. Typical of them are *Cantwell* v. *State of Connecticut*, 310 U.S. 296, and *Schneider* v. *Irvington*, 308 U.S. 147. Both of these involved the right of a city to control its streets. . . . In so holding, we, of course, found it necessary to "weigh the circumstances." But we did not in *Schneider*, any more than in *Cantwell*, even remotely suggest that a law directly aimed at curtailing speech and political persuasion could be saved through a balancing process. . . .

To apply the Court's balancing test under such circumstances is to read the First Amendment to say "Congress shall pass no law abridging freedom of speech, press, assembly and petition, unless Congress and the Supreme Court reach the joint conclusion that on balance the interests of the Government in stifling these freedoms is greater than the interest of the people in having them exercised." This is closely akin to the notion that neither the First Amendment nor any other provision of the Bill of Rights should be enforced unless the Court believes it is *reasonable* to do so. Not only does this violate the genius of our *written* Constitution, but it runs expressly counter to the injunction to Court and Congress made by Madison when he introduced the Bill of Rights.

It can be seen that there are a variety of "doctrines," "principles," or "tests" which have been employed or suggested for determining the validity of restraints on First Amendment freedom of expression. But there is substantial disagreement among the members of the Court and among leading scholars as to the appropriate test to employ. The problem is further complicated by the fact that some of the members of the Court have stated that First Amendment cases must be categorized and different tests employed for the different categories. Justice Black indicated as much in the portion of his dissent in *Barenblatt* quoted above. Thus a street regulation which indirectly affects speech may be handled under a "balancing" test, but a straight restriction on First Amendment freedom of expression may not be. Justice Jackson, in his concurring opinion in the *Dennis* case, suggested a different division. Discussing the "clear and present danger" test he stated:

I would save it, unmodified, for application as a "rule of reason" in the kind of case for which it was devised. When the issue is criminality of a hot-headed speech on a street corner, or circulation of a few incendiary pamphlets, or parading by some zealots behind a red flag, or refusal of a handful of school children to salute our flag, it is not beyond the capacity of the judicial process to gather, comprehend, and weigh the necessary materials for decision whether it is a clear and present danger of substantive evil or a harmless letting off of steam. It is not a prophecy, for the danger in such cases has matured by the time of trial or it was never present. The test applies and has meaning where a conviction is sought to be based on a speech or writing which does not directly or explicitly advocate a crime but to which such tendency is sought to be attributed by construction or by implication from external circumstances. The formula in such cases favors freedoms that are vital to our society, and, even if sometimes applied too generously, the consequences cannot be grave. But its recent expansion has extended, in particular to Communists, unprecedented immunities. Unless we are to hold our Government captive in a judge-made trap, we must approach the problem of a well-organized, nationwide conspiracy, such as I have described, as realistically as our predecessors faced the trivialities that were being prosecuted until they were checked with a rule of reason. . . .

The authors of the clear and present danger test never applied it to a case like this, nor would I. If applied as it is proposed here, it means that the Communist plotting is protected during its period of incubation; its preliminary stages of organization and preparation are immune from the law; the Government can move only after imminent action is manifest, when it would, of course, be too late.

[For further treatment of the various doctrines applied to freedom of expression, see Zechariah Chafee, Jr., *Free Speech in the United States*, *passim;* Thomas I. Emerson, "Toward a General Theory of the First Amendment," 72 *Yale L. J.* 877 (1963); Charles B. Nutting, "Is the First Amendment Obsolete?," 30 *Geo. Wash. L. Rev.* 167 (1961). On the "clear and present danger" test see Chester J. Antieau, "The Rule of Clear and Present Danger—Its Origin and Application," 13 *U. Det. L. J.* 198 (1950); Chester J. Antieau, "The Rule of Clear and Present Danger: Scope of Its Applicability," 48 *Mich. L. Rev.* 811 (1950); Robert B. McKay, "The Preference for Freedom," 34 *N.Y.U.L. Rev.* 1182 (1959). On the "absolutist" approach, see Alexander Meiklejohn, "The Balancing of Self-Preservation Against Political Freedom," 49 *Calif. L. Rev.* 4 (1961), and "The First Amendment is an Absolute," 1961 *Sup. Ct. Rev.* 245. On the "balancing" test see Wallace Mendelson, "On the Meaning of the First

Amendment: Absolutes in the Balance," 50 *Calif. L. Rev.* 821 (1962); Laurent B. Frantz, "The First Amendment in the Balance," 71 *Yale L. J.* 1424 (1962).]

The contrapuntal application of these doctrines in the major areas of First Amendment controversy can be most easily seen in the categorized examination of the cases. The remaining portion of the chapter will be devoted to delineating the scope of protection offered in the more important areas of governmental restraint on freedom of expression.

INTERNAL SECURITY

One of the most notorious instances of governmental repression of freedom of expression in American history was the enactment of the Sedition Act of 1798. There were a number of interesting aspects of the operation of the law. Although the verdict of history has been that it was unconstitutional, the act was never challenged in the United States Supreme Court. The act expired by its own terms in 1801, after two years of operation. And despite the furor the act aroused, only ten persons were convicted under it, although many more were indicted but never tried. One Jared Peck was indicted under the act for circulating a petition to Congress asking that the act be repealed. [For the best account of the Alien and Sedition Acts, see James Morton Smith, *Freedom's Fetters* (Ithaca: Cornell University Press, 1956).] The important portions of the act prohibited the writing, printing, or uttering "any false, scandalous and malicious writings against the government of the United States, or either house of the Congress of the United States, or the President" with intent to defame them, or to bring them into contempt or disrepute, or "to excite any unlawful combinations therein, for opposing or resisting any law of the United States . . . ." The punishment was a fine not exceeding two thousand dollars and imprisonment not exceeding two years.

The next important pieces of federal legislation restricting speech and press did not come until World War I, with the enactment of the Espionage Act of 1917 and the Sedition Act of 1918. As indicated earlier, these acts were upheld in *Schenck* v. *United States* and *Abrams* v. *United States*, along with four other cases decided in the period 1919–1920. The Espionage Act penalized the circulation of false statements made with intent to interfere with military success, or attempts to cause insubordination in the military and naval forces of the United States or to obstruct the recruiting and enlistment service of the United States. The Sedition Act further prohibited speeches or acts obstructing the sale of government bonds, or speaking or writing anything intended to cause contempt for the American form of government, the Constitution, the flag, or the military uniforms, or urging any curtailment of production of things necessary to the prosecution of the war with intent to hinder its prosecution, or supporting the cause of any country at war with us, or opposing the cause of the United States therein.

The penalty was $10,000 fine or twenty years imprisonment or both. Nearly a thousand persons were convicted under these two acts, out of about two thousand cases prosecuted. In his *Free Speech in the United States* Professor Chafee devoted a chapter to these prosecutions. He stated:

> ...Almost all the convictions were for expressions of opinion about the merits and conduct of the war.
>
> It became criminal to advocate heavier taxation instead of bond issues, to state the conscription was unconstitutional though the Supreme Court had not yet held it valid, to say that the sinking of merchant vessels was legal, to urge that a referendum should have preceded our declaration of war, to say that war was contrary to the teachings of Christ. Men have been punished for criticising the Red Cross and the Y.M.C.A., while under the Minnesota Espionage Act it has been held a crime to discourage women from knitting by the remark, "No soldier ever sees these socks." [p. 51.]

More recently the Congress enacted the Alien Registration Act of 1940, better known simply as the Smith Act. The Act contains provisions similar to those of New York's Criminal Anarchy Act of 1902, which was upheld in *Gitlow* v. *New York*. It was not until 1951, however, that the United States Supreme Court decided the issue of the constitutionality of the Smith Act. Prior to that case, *Dennis* v. *United States*, the Act had been invoked only twice. In 1941, eighteen Trotskyites were convicted under the Act, and their convictions were affirmed by the Court of Appeals. [*Dunne* v. *United States*, 138 F. 2d 137 (C.A. 8th, 1943).] The Supreme Court denied certiorari. A second trial, involving alleged pro-Nazis, was dropped before completion in 1944. [*United States* v. *McWilliams*, 163 F. 2d 695 (C.A. D.C., 1947).]

In 1948, eleven top members of the American Communist Party were indicted for conspiracies prohibited by Section 3 of the Smith Act. The trial in the District Court in New York was a marathon proceeding, running for nine months and resulting in conviction. The convictions were affirmed by the court of appeals with an opinion by Judge Learned Hand. [*United States* v. *Dennis*, 183 F. 2d 201 (C.A. 2d, 1950).] The Supreme Court granted certiorari, limiting review to the constitutional issues raised without examining such issues as the sufficiency of the evidence.

DENNIS *v.* UNITED STATES

341 U.S. 494 (1951)

Mr. Chief Justice Vinson announced the judgment of the Court and an opinion in which Mr. Justice Reed, Mr. Justice Burton and Mr. Justice Minton join.

Petitioners were indicted in July, 1948, for violation of the conspiracy provisions of the Smith Act, 54 Stat. 671, 18 U.S.C. (1946 ed.) Section 11.... A verdict of guilty as to all the petitioners was returned by the jury.... The Court of Appeals affirmed the convictions. 183 F. 2d 201. We granted certiorari ... limited to the following two questions: (1) Whether either Section 2 or Section 3 of the Smith Act, inherently or as construed and applied in the instant case, violates the First

Amendment and other provisions of the Bill of Rights; (2) whether either Section 2 or Section 3 of the Act, inherently or as construed and applied in the instant case, violates the First and Fifth Amendments because of indefiniteness.

Sections 2 and 3 of the Smith Act . . . provide as follows:

"Sec. 2.

"(a) It shall be unlawful for any person—

"(1) to knowingly or wilfully advocate, abet, advise, or teach the duty, necessity, desirability, or propriety of overthrowing or destroying any government in the United States by force or violence, or by the assassination of any officer of such government;

"(2) with intent to cause the overthrow or destruction of any government in the United States, to print, publish, edit, issue, circulate, sell, distribute, or publicly display any written or printed matter advocating, advising, or teaching the duty, necessity, desirability, or propriety of overthrowing or destroying any government in the United States by force or violence;

"(3) to organize or help to organize any society, group, or assembly of persons who teach, advocate, or encourage the overthrow or destruction of any government in the United States by force or violence; or to be or become a member of, or affiliate with, any such society, group, or assembly of persons, knowing the purpose thereof. . . .

"Sec. 3. It shall be unlawful for any person to attempt to commit, or to conspire to commit, any of the acts prohibited by the provisions of . . . this title."

The indictment charged the petitioners with wilfully and knowingly conspiring (1) to organize as the Communist Party of the United States of America a society, group and assembly of persons who teach and advocate the overthrow and destruction of the Government of the United States by force and violence, and (2) knowingly and wilfully to advocate and teach the duty and necessity of overthrowing and destroying the Government of the United States by force and violence. The indictment further alleged that Section 2 of the Smith Act proscribes these acts and that any conspiracy to take such action is a violation of Section 3 of the Act. . . .

I

It will be helpful in clarifying the issues to treat next the contention that the trial judge improperly interpreted the statute by charging that the statute required an unlawful intent before the jury could convict. More specifically, he charged that the jury could not find the petitioners guilty under the indictment unless they found that petitioners had the intent "to overthrow . . . the Government of the United States by force and violence as speedily as circumstances would permit.". . .

. . . We hold that the statute requires as an essential element of the crime proof of the intent of those who are charged with its violation to overthrow the Government by force and violence. . . .

II

The obvious purpose of the statute is to protect existing Government, not from change by peaceable, lawful and constitutional means, but from change by violence, revolution and terrorism. That it is within the *power* of the Congress to protect the Government of the United States from armed rebellion is a proposition which requires little discussion. Whatever theoretical merit there may be to the argument that there is a "right" to rebellion against dictatorial governments is without force where the existing structure of the government provides for peaceful and orderly change. We reject any principle of governmental helplessness in the face of preparation for revolution, which principle, carried to its logical conclusion, must lead to anarchy. No one could conceive that it is not within the power of Congress to prohibit acts intended to overthrow the Government by force and violence. The question with which we are concerned here is not whether Congress has such *power*, but whether the *means* which it has employed conflict with the First and Fifth Amendments to the Constitution.

One of the bases for the contention that the means which Congress has employed are invalid takes the form of an attack on the face of the statute on the grounds that by its terms it prohibits academic discussion of the merits of Marxism-Leninism, that it stifles ideas and is contrary to all concepts of a free speech and a free press. Although we do not agree that the language itself has that significance, we must bear in mind that it is the duty of the federal courts to interpret federal legislation in a manner not inconsistent with the demands of the Constitution. . . .

The very language of the Smith Act negates the interpretation which petitioners would have us impose on that Act. It is directed at advocacy, not discussion. Thus, the trial judge properly charged the jury that they could not convict if they found that petitioners did "no more than pursue peaceful studies and discussions or teachings and advocacy in the realm of ideas." He further charged that it was not unlawful "to conduct in an American college and university a course explaining the philosophical theories set forth in the books which have been placed in evidence." Such a charge is in strict accord with the statutory language, and illustrates the meaning to be placed on those words. Congress did not intend to eradicate the free discussion of political theories, to destroy the traditional rights of Americans to discuss and evaluate ideas without fear of governmental sanction. Rather Congress was concerned with the very kind of activity in which the evidence showed these petitioners engaged.

III

. . . No important case involving free speech was decided by this Court prior to *Schenck* v. *United States*, 249 U.S. 47 (1919). . . . Writing for a unanimous Court, Justice Holmes stated that the "question in every case is whether the words used are used in such circumstances and are of such a nature as to create a clear and present danger that they will bring about the substantive evils that Congress has a right to prevent.". . .

. . . But . . . neither Justice Holmes nor Justice Brandeis ever envisioned that a shorthand phrase should be crystallized into a rigid rule to be applied inflexibly without regard to the circumstances of each case. Speech is not absolute, above and beyond control by the legislature when its judgment, subject to review here, is that certain kinds of speech are so undesirable as to warrant criminal sanction. Nothing is more certain in modern society than the principle that there are no absolutes, that a name, a phrase, a standard has meaning only when associated with the considerations which gave birth to the nomenclature. . . . To those who would paralyze our Government in the face of impending threat by encasing it in a semantic straitjacket we must reply that all concepts are relative.

In this case we are squarely presented with the application of the "clear and present danger" test, and must decide what that phrase imports. We first note that many of the cases in which this Court has reversed convictions by use of this or similar tests have been based on the fact that the interest which the State was attempting to protect was itself too insubstantial to warrant restriction of speech. . . . Overthrow of the Government by force and violence is certainly a substantial enough interest for the Government to limit speech. Indeed, this is the ultimate value of any society, for if a society cannot protect its very structure from armed internal attack, it must follow that no subordinate value can be protected. If, then, this interest may be protected, the literal problem which is presented is what has been meant by the use of the phrase "clear and present danger" of the utterances bringing about the evil within the power of Congress to punish.

Obviously, the words cannot mean that before the Government may act, it must wait until the *putsch* is about to be executed, the plans have been laid and the signal is awaited. If Government is aware that a group aiming at its overthrow is attempting to indoctrinate its members and to commit them to a course whereby they will strike when the leaders feel the circumstances permit, action by the Government is required. The argument that there is no need for Government to concern itself, for Government is strong, it possesses ample powers to put down a rebellion, it may defeat the revolution with ease needs no answer. For that is not the question. Certainly an attempt to overthrow the Government by force, even though doomed from the outset because of inadequate numbers or power of the revolutionists, is a sufficient evil for Congress to prevent. The damage which such attempts create both physically and politically to a nation makes it impossible to measure the validity in terms of the probability of success, or the immediacy of a successful attempt. In the instant case the trial judge charged the jury that they could not convict unless they found that petitioners intended to overthrow the Government "as speedily as circumstances would permit." This does not mean, and could not properly mean, that they would not strike until there was certainty of success. What was meant was that the revolutionists would strike when they thought the time was ripe. We must therefore reject the contention that success or probability of success is the criterion.

The situation with which Justices Holmes and Brandeis were concerned in *Gitlow* was a comparatively isolated event bearing little relation in their minds to any substantial threat to the safety of the community. . . . They were not confronted with any situation comparable to the instant one—the development of an apparatus designed and dedicated to the overthrow of the Government, in the context of world crisis after crisis.

Chief Judge Learned Hand, writing for the majority below, interpreted the phrase as follows: "In each case [courts] must ask whether the gravity of the 'evil,' discounted by its improbability, justifies such invasion of free speech as is necessary to avoid the danger." We adopt this statement of the rule. As articulated by Chief Judge Hand, it is as succinct and inclusive as any other we might devise at this time. It takes into consideration those factors which we deem relevant, and relates their significances. More we cannot expect from words.

Likewise, we are in accord with the court below, which affirmed the trial court's finding that the requisite danger existed. The mere fact that from the period 1945 to 1948 petitioner's activities did not result in an attempt to overthrow the Government by force and violence is of course no answer to the fact that there was a group that was ready to make the attempt. The formation by petitioners of such a highly organized conspiracy, with rigidly disciplined members subject to call when the leaders, these petitioners, felt that the time had come for action, coupled with the inflammable nature of world conditions, similar uprisings in other countries, and the touch-and-go nature of our relations with countries with whom petitioners were in the very least ideologically attuned, convince us that their convictions were justified on this score. And this analysis disposes of the contention that a conspiracy to advocate, as distinguished from the advocacy itself, cannot be constitutionally restrained, because it comprises only the preparation. It is the existence of the conspiracy which creates the danger. . . .

IV

[The Chief Justice then considers the contention that the trial judge should have submitted for jury determination the question of whether sufficient danger existed to apply the law rather than making this decision himself as a matter of law.]

When facts are found that establish the violation of a statute the protection against conviction afforded by the First Amendment is a matter of law. The doctrine that there must be a clear and present danger of a substantive evil that Congress has a right to prevent is a judicial rule to be applied as a matter of law by the courts. The guilt is established by proof of facts. Whether the First Amendment protects the activity which constitutes the violation of the statute must depend upon a judicial determination of the scope of the First Amendment applied to the circumstances of the case. . . .

V

There remains to be discussed the question of vagueness—whether the statute as we have interpreted it is too vague, not sufficiently advising those who would speak of the limitations upon their activity. . . .

We hold that Sections 2(a)(1), 2(a)(3) and 3 of the Smith Act, do not inherently, or as construed or applied in the instant case, violate the First Amendment and other provisions of the Bill of Rights, or the First and Fifth Amendments because of indefiniteness. Petitioners intended to overthrow the Government of the United States as speedily as the circumstances would permit. Their conspiracy to organize the Communist Party and to teach and advocate the overthrow of the Government of the United States by force and violence created a "clear and present danger" of an attempt to overthrow the Government by force and violence. They were properly and constitutionally convicted for violation of the Smith Act. The judgments of conviction are

Affirmed.

Mr. Justice Clark took no part in the consideration or decision of this case.

Mr. Justice Frankfurter, concurring in affirmance of the judgment. . . .

The language of the First Amendment is to be read not as barren words found in a dictionary but as symbols of historic experience illumined by the presuppositions of those who employed them. Not what words did Madison and Hamilton use, but what was it in their minds which they conveyed? Free speech is subject to prohibition of those abuses of expression which a civilized society may forbid. . . . Absolute rules would inevitably lead to absolute exceptions, and such exceptions would eventually corrode the rules. The demands of free speech in a democratic society as well as the interest in national security are better served by candid and informed weighing of the competing interests, within the confines of the judicial process, than by announcing dogmas too inflexible for the non-Euclidian problems to be solved. . . .

Primary responsibility for adjusting the interests which compete in the situation before us of necessity belongs to the Congress. . . .

II

We have recognized and resolved conflicts between speech and competing interests in six different types of cases. . . .

I must leave to others the ungrateful task of trying to reconcile all these decisions. In some instances we have too readily permitted juries to infer deception from error, or intention from argumentative or critical statements. . . . In other instances we weighted the interest in free speech so heavily that we permitted essential conflicting values to be destroyed. . . . Viewed as a whole, however, the decisions express an attitude toward the judicial function and a standard of values which for me are decisive of the case before us.

First.—Free-speech cases are not an exception to the principle that we are not legislators, that direct policy-making is not our province. How best to reconcile competing interests is the business of legislatures, and the balance they strike is a judgment not to be displaced by ours, but to be respected unless outside the pale of fair judgment. . . .

Second.—A survey of the relevant decisions indicates that the results which we have reached are on the whole those that would ensue from careful weighing of conflicting interests. The complex issues presented by regulation of speech . . . have been resolved by scrutiny of many factors besides the imminence and gravity of the evil threatened. . . .

Third.—Not every type of speech occupies the same position on the scale of values. There is no substantial public interest in permitting certain kinds of utterances: "the lewd and obscene, the profane, the libelous, and the insulting or 'fighting' words—those which by their very utterance inflict injury or tend to incite an immediate breach of the peace." *Chaplinsky* v. *New Hampshire*, 315 U.S. 568, 572. We have frequently indicated that the interest in protecting speech depends on the circumstances of the occasion. . . .

The defendants have been convicted of conspiring to organize a party of persons who advocate the overthrow of the Government by force and violence. . . .

On any scale of values which we have hitherto recognized, speech of this sort ranks low. . . .

III

These general considerations underlie decision of the case before us.

On the one hand is the interest in security. The Communist Party was not designed by these defendants as an ordinary political party. . . . The jury found that the Party rejects the basic premise of our political system—that change is to be brought about by nonviolent constitutional process. The jury found that the Party advocates the theory that there is a duty and necessity to overthrow the Government by force and violence. . . .

. . . We may take judicial notice that the Communist doctrines which these defendants have conspired to advocate are in the ascendancy in powerful nations who cannot be acquitted of unfriendliness to the institutions of this country. We may take account of evidence brought forward at this trial and elsewhere, much of which has long been common knowledge. In sum, it would amply justify a legislature in concluding that recruitment of additional members for the Party would create a substantial danger to national security. . . .

On the other hand is the interest in free speech. The right to exert all governmental powers in aid of maintaining our institutions and resisting their physical overthrow does not include intolerance of opinions and speech that cannot do harm although opposed and perhaps alien to dominant, traditional opinion. . . .

. . . A public interest is not wanting in granting freedom to speak their minds even to those who advocate the overthrow of the Government by force. For, as the evidence in this case abundantly illustrates, coupled with such advocacy is criticism of defects in our society. Criticism is the spur to reform. . . . Suppressing advocates of overthrow inevitably will also silence critics who do not advocate overthrow but fear that their criticism may be so construed. No matter how clear we may be that the defendants now before us are preparing to overthrow our Government at the propitious moment, it is self-delusion to think that we can punish them for their advocacy without adding to the risks run by loyal citizens who honestly believe in some of the reforms these defendants advance. It is a sobering fact that in sustaining the conviction before us we can hardly escape restriction on the interchange of ideas. . . .

It is not for us to decide how we would adjust the clash of interests which this case presents were the primary responsibility for reconciling it ours. Congress has determined that the danger created by advocacy of overthrow justifies the ensuing restriction on freedom of speech. . . .

. . . [I]t is relevant to remind that in sustaining the power of Congress in a case like this nothing irrevocable is done. The democratic process at all events is not impaired or restricted. Power and responsibility remain with the people and immediately with their representation. All the Court says is that Congress was not forbidden by the Constitution to pass this enactment and a prosecution under it may be brought against a conspiracy such as the one before us. . . .

Mr. Justice Jackson, concurring.

This prosecution is the latest of never-ending, because never successful, quests for some legal formula that will secure an existing order against revolutionary radicalism. It requires us to reappraise, in the light of our own times and conditions, constitutional doctrines devised under other circumstances to strike a balance between authority and liberty. . . .

If we must decide that this Act and its application are constitutional only if we are convinced that petitioner's conduct creates a "clear and present danger" of violent overthrow, we must appraise imponderables, including international and national phenomena which baffle the best informed foreign offices and our most experienced politicians. We would have to foresee and predict the effectiveness of Communist propaganda, opportunities for infiltration, whether, and when, a time will come that they consider propitious for action, and whether and how fast our existing government will deteriorate. And we would have to speculate as to whether an approaching Communist *coup* would not be anticipated by a nationalistic fascist movement. No doctrine can be sound whose application requires us to make a prophecy of that sort in the guise of a legal decision. The judicial process simply is not adequate to a trial of such far-flung issues. The answers given would reflect our own political predilections and nothing more.

The authors of the clear and present danger test never applied it to a case like this, nor would I. If applied as it is proposed here, it means that the Communist plotting is protected during its period of incubation; its preliminary stages of organization and preparation are immune from the law; the Government can move only after imminent action is manifest, when it would, of course, be too late. . . .

There is lamentation in the dissents about the injustice of conviction in the absence of some overt act. Of course, there has been no general uprising against the Government, but the record is replete with acts to carry out the conspiracy alleged, acts such as always are held sufficient to consummate the crime where the statute requires an overt act. . . .

I do not suggest that Congress could punish conspiracy to advocate something, the doing of which it may not punish. Advocacy or exposition of the doctrine of communal property ownership, or any political philosophy unassociated with advocacy of its imposition by force or seizure of government by unlawful means could not be reached through conspiracy prosecution. But it is not forbidden to put down force or violence, it is not forbidden to punish its teaching or advocacy, and the end being punishable, there is no doubt of the power to punish conspiracy for the purpose. . . .

The law of conspiracy has been the chief means at the Government's disposal to deal with the growing problems created by such organizations. I happen to think it is an awkward and inept remedy, but I find no constitutional authority for taking this weapon from the Government. There is no constitutional right to "gang up" on the Government.

While I think there was power in Congress to enact this statute and that, as applied in this case, it cannot be be held unconstitutional, I add that I have little faith in the long-range effectiveness of this conviction to stop the rise of the Communist movement. . . . No decision by this Court can forestall revolution whenever the existing government fails to command the respect and loyalty of the people and sufficient distress and discontent is allowed to grow up among the masses. . . .

Mr. Justice Black, dissenting. . . .

At the outset I want to emphasize what the crime involved in this case is, and what it is not. These petitioners were not charged with an attempt to overthrow the Government. They were not charged with overt acts of any kind designed to overthrow the Government. They were not even charged with saying anything or writing anything designed to overthrow the Government. The charge was that they agreed to assemble and to talk and publish certain ideas at a later date: The indictment is that they conspired to organize the Communist Party and to use speech or newspapers and other publications in the future to teach and advocate the forcible overthrow of the Government. No matter how it is worded, this is a virulent form of prior censorship of speech and press, which I believe the First Amendment forbids. I would hold Section 3 of the Smith Act authorizing this prior restraint unconstitutional on its face and as applied.

. . . The opinions for affirmance indicate that the chief reason for jettisoning the [clear and present danger] rule is the expressed fear that advocacy of Communist doctrine endangers the safety of the Republic. Undoubtedly, a governmental policy of unfettered communication of ideas does entail dangers. To the Founders of this Nation, however, the benefits derived from free expression were worth the risk. . . . I have always believed that the First Amendment is the keystone of our Government, that the freedoms it guarantees provide the best insurance against destruction of all freedom. At least as to speech in the realm of public matters, I believe that the "clear and present danger" test does not "mark the furthermost constitutional boundaries of protected expression" but does "no more than recognize a minimum compulsion of the Bill of Rights." *Bridges* v. *California,* 314 U.S. 252, 263.

So long as this Court exercises the power of judicial review of legislation, I cannot agree that the First Amendment permits us to sustain laws suppressing freedom of speech and press on the basis of Congress' or our own notions of mere "reasonableness." Such a doctrine waters down the First Amendment so that it amounts to little more than an admonition to Congress. The Amendment as so construed is not likely to protect any but those "safe" or orthodox views which rarely need its protection. . . .

Public opinion being what it now is, few will protest the conviction of these Communist petitioners. There is hope, however, that in calmer times, when present pressures, passions and fears subside, this or some later Court will restore the First Amendment liberties to the high preferred place where they belong in a free society.

Mr. Justice Douglas, dissenting. . . .

The next important case to come before the Court involving the Smith Act was *Yates* v. *United States,* 354 U.S. 298 (1957). Other prosecutions of lesser Communists had taken place in the interval since *Dennis,* but the Court had not reviewed any of the convictions. In *Yates* the Court imposed no limitations upon its grant of certiorari to review the convictions of fourteen Communists under the same Smith Act sections involved in the *Dennis* case. Thus it was free to examine the whole record and consider the sufficiency of the evidence supporting the convictions. Three primary issues were presented in the case. First, the petitioners contended that the conviction for "organizing" the Communist Party was barred by the three-year statute of limitations, since the Party was "organized," within the meaning of the statute, by 1945 at the latest, and the indictment was returned in 1951. Justice Harlan, for the majority, agreed with this contention. He pointed out that the statute did not define what was meant by "organize," and that "In these circumstances we should follow the familiar rule that criminal statutes are to be strictly construed and give to 'organize' its narrow meaning, that is, that the word refers only to acts entering into the creation of a new organization, and not to acts thereafter performed in carrying on its activities, even though such acts may loosely be termed 'organizational.' "

A second issue presented by petitioners was that the instructions to the jury were fatally defective in that the trial court refused to charge that, in order to convict, the jury must find that the advocacy which the defendants conspired to promote was directed at promoting unlawful action and not mere persuasion to accept forcible overthrow as abstract doctrine. The majority agreed with this second contention also. Justice Harlan stated:

In failing to distinguish between advocacy of forcible overthrow as an abstract doctrine and advocacy of action to that end, the District Court appears to have been led astray by the holding in *Dennis* that advocacy of violent action to be taken at some future time was enough. . . . [W]e are unable to regard the District

Court's charge upon this aspect of the case as adequate. The jury was never told that the Smith Act does not denounce advocacy in the sense of preaching abstractly the forcible overthrow of the Government. We think that the trial court's statement that the proscribed advocacy must include the "urging," "necessity," and "duty" of forcible overthrow, and not merely its "desirability" and "propriety," may not be regarded as a sufficient substitute for charging that the Smith Act reaches only advocacy of action for the overthrow of government by force and violence. The essential distinction is that those to whom the advocacy is addressed must be urged to *do* something, now or in the future, rather than merely to *believe* in something.

Although the holding on the first two issues already required reversal of the convictions, the Court went one step further to consider the sufficiency of the evidence against the fourteen petitioners, "to see whether there are individuals as to whom acquittal is unequivocally demanded." After putting aside all evidence relating to the "organizing" charge alone as well as that not directly connected to a charge of advocacy in the sense of a call to forcible action, Justice Harlan found the record "strikingly deficient." As to five of the defendants he found no overt acts to support the conviction other than mere membership in the Party or as officers or functionaries, and their acquittal was ordered. As to the other nine defendants, the majority found evidence indicating "action" in their holding of classes teaching illegal action as well as other participation in "underground apparatus"—which might support a finding of guilty under a proper charge to the jury. The cases of these nine, then, were remanded for new trials.

The *Yates* decision represents somewhat of a withdrawal from the broad language of Chief Justice Vinson in the *Dennis* case, and, in fact, draws in question the very validity of the convictions in the earlier case. Since the decision came off on statutory construction rather than constitutional issues, the Congress might have revised the Smith Act to reach *any* advocacy of overthrow of the government by violence, thus presenting the constitutional issue squarely, but such revision has not been made. Congress did disagree with the Court's construction of the "organizing" section, however, and in 1962 amended the Act to include within the meaning of that section the continued recruitment or expansion of organizational activity.

Neither *Dennis* nor *Yates*, however, reached the question of the validity of the "membership" section of the Smith Act. The section appeared to raise even more serious questions of constitutionality than the two preceding sections, and the Government was somewhat slow to proceed under the "membership" charge alone. In *Scales* v. *United States*, 367 U.S. 203 (1961), the Court ruled on the issue for the first time.

SCALES *v.* UNITED STATES

367 U.S. 203 (1961)

Mr. Justice Harlan delivered the opinion of the Court.

Our writ issued in this case ... to review ... petitioner's conviction under the so-called membership clause of the Smith Act. 18 USC Section 2385. The Act, among other things, makes a felony the acquisition or holding of knowing membership in any organization which advocates the overthrow of the Government of the United States by force or violence.

The validity of this conviction is challenged on statutory, constitutional, and evidentiary grounds, and further on the basis of certain alleged trial and procedural errors. . . . For reasons given in this opinion we affirm the Court of Appeals.

I

Statutory Challenge

Petitioner contends that the indictment fails to state an offense against the United States. The claim is that Section 4(f) of the Internal Security Act of 1950, 64 Stat 987, . . . constitutes a *pro tanto* repeal of the membership clause of the Smith Act by excluding from the reach of that clause membership in any Communist organization. . . .

We turn first to the provision itself, and find that, as to petitioner's construction of it, the language is at best ambiguous if not suggestive of a contrary conclusion. Section 4(f) provides that membership or office-holding in a Communist organization shall not constitute "*per se* a violation of subsection (a) or subsection (c) of this section or of any other criminal statute." Petitioner would most plainly be correct if the statute under which he was indicted purported to proscribe membership in Communist organizations, as such, and to punish membership *per se* in an organization engaging in proscribed advocacy. . . .

. . . The natural tendency of the first sentence of subsection (f) as to the criminal provisions specifically mentioned is to provide clarification of the meaning of those provisions, that is, that an offense is not made out on proof of *mere* membership in a Communist organization. . . .

. . . Although we think that the membership clause on its face goes beyond making mere Party membership a violation, in that it requires a showing both of illegal Party purposes and of a member's knowledge of such purposes, we regard the first sentence of Section 4(f) as a clear warrant for construing the clause as requiring not only knowing membership, but active and purposive membership, purposive that is as to the organization's criminal ends. . . . By its terms, then, subsection (f) does not effect a *pro tanto* repeal of the membership clause; at most it modifies it. . . .

[The opinion then takes up an examination of the legislative history of the Internal Security Act of 1950, and Justice Harlan concludes that it does not bar this prosecution.]

II

Constitutional Challenge to the Membership Clause on its Face

Petitioner's constitutional attack goes both to the statute on its face and as applied . . .

It will bring the constitutional issues into clearer focus to notice first the premises on which the case was submitted to the jury. The jury was instructed that in order to convict it must find that within the three-year limitations period (1) the Communist Party advocated the violent overthrow of the Government, in the sense of present "advocacy of action" to accomplish that end as soon as circumstances were propitious; and (2) petitioner was an "active" member of the Party, and not merely "a nominal, passive, inactive or purely technical" member, with knowledge of the Party's illegal advocacy and a specific intent to bring about violent overthrow "as speedily as circumstances would permit."

The constitutional attack upon the membership clause, as thus construed, is that the statute offends (1) the Fifth Amendment, in that it impermissibly imputes guilt to an individual merely on the basis of his associations and sympathies, rather than because of some concrete personal involvement in criminal conduct; and (2) the First Amendment, in that it infringes free political expression and association. . . .

Fifth Amendment

Any thought that due process puts beyond the reach of the criminal law all individual associational relationships, unless accompanied by the commission of specific acts of criminality, is dispelled by familiar concepts of the law of conspiracy and complicity. . . .

What must be met, then, is the argument that membership, even when accompanied by the elements of knowledge and specific intent, affords an insufficient quantum of participation in the organization's alleged criminal activity, that is, an insufficiently significant form of aid and encouragement to permit the imposition of criminal sanctions on that basis. . . .

In an area of the criminal law which this Court has indicated more than once demands its watchful scrutiny . . . , these factors have weight and must be found to be overborne in a total constitutional assessment of the statute. We think, however, they are duly met when the statute is found to reach only "active" members having also a guilty knowledge and intent, and which therefore prevents a conviction on what otherwise might be regarded as merely an expression of sympathy with the alleged criminal enterprise, unaccompanied by any significant action in its support or any commitment to undertake such action. . . .

First Amendment

Little remains to be said concerning the claim that the statute infringes First Amendment freedoms. It was settled in *Dennis* that the advocacy with which we are here concerned is not constitutionally protected speech, and it was further established that a combination to promote such advocacy, albeit under the aegis of what purports to be a political party, is not such association as is protected by the First Amendment. We can discern no reason why membership, when it constitutes a purposeful form of complicity in a group engaging in this same forbidden advocacy, should receive any greater degree of protection from the guarantees of that Amendment.

If it is said that the mere existence of such an enactment tends to inhibit the exercise of constitutionally protected rights, in that it engenders an unhealthy fear that one may find himself unwittingly embroiled in criminal liability, the answer surely is that the statute provides that a defendant must be proven to have knowledge of the proscribed advocacy before he may be convicted. . . . The clause does not make criminal all association with an organization, which has been shown to engage in illegal advocacy. There must be clear proof that a defendant "specifically intend[s] to accomplish [the aims of the organization] by resort to violence." *Noto v. United States*. . . . Thus the member for whom the organization is a vehicle for the advancement of legitimate aims and policies does not fall within the ban of the statute: he lacks the requisite specific intent "to bring about the overthrow of the government as speedily as circumstances would permit." Such a person may be foolish, deluded, or perhaps merely optimistic, but he is not by this statute made a criminal.

We conclude that petitioner's constitutional challenge must be overruled.

III

Evidentiary Challenge

Only in rare instances will this Court review the general sufficiency of the evidence to support a criminal conviction, for ordinarily that is a function which properly belongs to and ends with the Court of Appeals. We do so in this case and in ... *Noto* v. *United States* ..., our first review of convictions under the membership clause of the Smith Act—not only to make sure that substantive constitutional standards have not been thwarted, but also to provide guidance for the future to the lower courts in an area which borders so closely upon constitutionally protected rights. . . .

[Justice Harlan here examines the testimony introduced to prove the illegal purposes and general "character of the organization of which he is charged with being a member." As to the specific acts of the defendant, Justice Harlan cited testimony and evidence showing that Scales had recruited members, sent out Communist literature, instructed and guided new members, arranged for scholarships to study at official Communist Party schools, and advised one member to "infiltrate the Civilian Defense setup" in New York.]

We conclude that this evidence sufficed to make a case for the jury on the issue of illegal Party advocacy. *Dennis* and *Yates* have definitely laid at rest any doubt but that present advocacy of *future* action for violent overthrow satisfies statutory and constitutional requirements equally with advocacy of *immediate* action to that end. . . . Hence this record cannot be considered deficient because it contains no evidence of advocacy for immediate overthrow. . . .

The sufficiency of the evidence as to other elements of the crime requires no exposition. Scales' "active" membership in the Party is indisputable, and that issue was properly submitted to the jury under instructions that were entirely adequate. The elements of petitioner's "knowledge" and "specific intent". . . require no further discussion of the evidence beyond that already given as to Scales' utterances and activities. Compare *Noto* v. *United States*. . . . They bear little resemblance to the fragmentary and equivocal utterances and conduct which were found insufficient in *Nowak* v. *United States*, 356 U.S. 660. . . .

We hold that this prosecution does not fail for insufficiency of the proof. . . .

The judgment of the Court of Appeals must be

Affirmed.

Mr. Justice Black, dissenting.

. . . My reasons for dissenting from this decision are primarily those set out by Mr. Justice Brennan—that Section 4(f) of the Subversive Activities Control Act bars prosecutions under the membership clause of the Smith Act—and Mr. Justice Douglas—that the Amendment absolutely forbids Congress to outlaw membership in a political party or similar association merely because one of the philosophical tenets of that group is that the existing government should be overthrown by force at some distant time in the future when circumstances may permit. . . .

. . . I think it is important to point out the manner in which this case re-emphasizes the freedom-destroying nature of the "balancing test" presently in use by the Court to justify its refusal to apply specific constitutional protections of the Bill of Rights. In some of the recent cases in which it has "balanced" away the protections of the First Amendment, the Court has suggested that it was justified in the application of this "test" because no direct abridgment of First Amendment freedoms was involved, the abridgment in each of these cases being, in the Court's opinion, nothing more than "an incident of the informed exercise of a valid governmental function." A possible implication of that suggestion was that if the Court were confronted with what it would call a direct abridgment of speech, it would not apply the "balancing test" but would enforce the protections of the First Amendment according to its own terms. This case causes me to doubt that such an implication is justified. Petitioner is being sent to jail for the express reason that he has associated with people who have entertained unlawful ideas and said unlawful things, and that of course is a *direct* abridgment of his freedoms of speech and assembly—under any definition that has ever been used for that term. Nevertheless, even as to this admittedly direct abridgment, the Court relies upon its prior decisions to the effect that the Government has power to abridge speech and assembly if its interest in doing so is sufficient to outweigh the interest in protecting these First Amendment freedoms.

This, I think, demonstrates the unlimited breadth and danger of the "balancing test" as it is currently being applied by a majority of this Court. Under that "test," the question in every case in which a First Amendment right is asserted is not whether there has been an abridgment of that right, not whether the abridgment of that right was intentional on the part of the Government, and not whether there is any other way in which the Government could accomplish a lawful aim without an invasion of the constitutionally guaranteed rights of the people. It is, rather, simply whether the Government has an interest in abridging the right involved and, if so, whether that interest is of sufficient importance, in the opinion of a majority of this Court, to justify the Government's action in doing so. This doctrine, to say the very least, is capable of being used to justify almost any action Government may wish to take to suppress First Amendment freedoms.

Mr. Justice Douglas, dissenting.

When we allow petitioner to be sentenced to prison for six years for being a "member" of the Communist Party, we make a sharp break with traditional concepts of First Amendment rights and make serious Mark Twain's lighthearted comment that "It is by the goodness of God that in our country we have those three unspeakably precious things: freedom of speech, freedom of conscience, and the prudence never to practice either of them.". . .

We legalize today guilt by association, sending a man to prison when he committed no unlawful act. Today's break with tradition is a serious one. It borrows from the totalitarian philosophy. . . .

The case is not saved by showing that petitioner was an active member. None of the activity constitutes a crime. . . .

Belief in the principle of revolution is deep in our traditions. The Declaration of Independence proclaims it. . . .

This right of revolution has been and is a part of the fabric of our institutions. . . .
Mr. Justice Brennan with whom the Chief Justice and Mr. Justice Douglas join, dissenting. . . .

States, of course, have long had various kinds of sedition statutes of their own. No particular problems were presented by such laws, other than those taken up in the cases above, until the enactment of the Smith Act. The issue then presented was one of national supremacy: did the federal law supersede the state laws on sedition and thereby render them unenforceable? In *Pennsylvania* v. *Nelson,* 350 U.S. 497 (1956), the Court held that in passing the Smith Act Congress intended to occupy the field, and affirmed the Pennsylvania Supreme Court's reversal of a conviction under the state statute. The Court pointed out as additional support for its decision the strong possibility of interference by the state enforcement authorities with the overall program of the federal government.

Although the cases thus far discussed point up some rather sharp differences of opinion among the justices regarding the validity of some of the major antisubversion sections of the Smith Act, the Court is unanimous in its view that *overt acts* in aid of revolution may appropriately be punished. Justices Black and Douglas stressed, however, that restrictions imposed prior to engagement in overt action unconstitutionally inhibit freedom of thought and association. At the core of the differences of opinion on these questions appears to be the divergence of attitude on whether making speeches, organizing groups, and associating for common purposes can appropriately be considered as "overt action." A minority of the Court do not think such stages can be so held, and this conclusion has led them to dissent in a number of cases involving a variety of restrictions primarily directed at subversive organizations. The important right of association is the central issue in many of these cases, particularly those involving the various kinds of non-Communist oaths. [On the validity of state criminal syndicalism laws, see *Brandenburg* v. *Ohio,* 395 U.S. 444 (1969), in Chap. 9.]

In the Taft-Hartley Act of 1947 Congress provided that the services of the NLRB and the protections of the Act would be denied to labor organizations whose officers failed to file affidavits with the Board that they were not Communist Party members and did not believe in overthrow of the government by force. This requirement was upheld in *American Communications Ass'n., CIO* v. *Douds,* 339 U.S. 382 (1950). Chief Justice Vinson in his opinion for the Court stated:

Government's interest here is not in preventing the dissemination of Communist doctrine or the holding of particular beliefs because it is feared that unlawful action will result therefrom if free speech is practiced. Its interest is in protecting the free flow of commerce from what Congress considers to be substantial evils of conduct that are not the products of speech at all. Section 9(h), in other words, . . . regulates harmful conduct which Congress has determined is carried on by persons who may be identified by their political affiliations and beliefs.

Justices Jackson and Frankfurter concurred in the result as to the non-membership portion but dissented as to the "belief" portion of the affidavit. Justice Black dissented on the ground that both provisions were unconstitutional. He stated that "Never before has this Court held that the Government could for any reason attaint persons for their political beliefs or affiliations. It does so today."

Many states and cities have adopted policies demanding non-Communist oaths from governmental employees. In 1948 Los Angeles adopted an ordinance requiring all employees to file an oath stating that they had neither advocated overthrow of the government by violence nor been a member of an organization which advocated such action and also to file an affidavit stating whether they were or ever had been a member of the Communist Party. The validity of the ordinance was tested in *Garner* v. *Board of Public Works*, 341 U.S. 716 (1951). Five members of the Court held that both the oath and the affidavit were valid, although Justice Clark, for the majority, said "We assume that *scienter* is implicit in each clause of the oath." Thus innocent membership was not to be punished. Two members of the Court felt that the affidavit was valid but not the oath, since the ordinance did not by its terms clearly specify "knowing" membership as the basis for denial of employment. Justices Douglas and Black considered both requirements to be bills of attainder and ex post facto.

The following year, in *Wieman* v. *Updegraff*, 344 U.S. 183 (1952), the Court unanimously invalidated an oath requirement of Oklahoma which barred from governmental employment persons who were or had been members of proscribed organizations, irrespective of their knowledge of the purposes of such organizations. Justice Clark, for the Court, stated:

> Under the Oklahoma Act, the fact of association alone determines disloyalty and disqualification; it matters not whether association existed innocently or knowingly. To thus inhibit individual freedom of movement is to stifle the flow of democratic expression and controversy at one of its chief sources. We hold that the distinction observed between the case at bar and *Garner* . . . is decisive. Indiscriminate classification of innocent with knowing activity must fall as an assertion of arbitrary power. The oath offends due process.

Employees have also been removed from public positions when found to belong to subversive organizations. New York's Feinberg Law, passed in 1949, provided that after an inquiry and notice and hearing the Board of Regents should prepare a list of subversive organizations. Thereafter membership in any of these organizations should constitute prima facie evidence of disqualification for employment in the public schools. The law was upheld by the Supreme Court in *Adler* v. *Board of Education of the City of New York*, 342 U.S. 485 (1952). Justice Minton, speaking for the majority, stated that persons have no right to work for the state in the school system on their own terms. If they do not choose to work for the school system upon the reasonable terms laid down by the proper authorities of New York, "they are at liberty to retain their beliefs and associations and go elsewhere."

Public employees have also been dismissed for refusal to answer questions about membership in subversive organizations, even when the alleged association took place many years earlier. A Brooklyn College professor was discharged on the ground that claiming the Fifth Amendment privilege before a Senate committee, which had questioned him concerning his political affiliations prior to 1941, was "equivalent to a resignation" under the Charter of the City of New York. In *Slochower* v. *Board of Higher Education*, 350 U.S. 551 (1956), the Court reversed the judgment, but at the same time it suggested that the city could use whatever facts it chose to make an inquiry to see whether Slochower's continued employment was "inconsistent with a real interest of the State."

New York City accepted the suggestion, and two employees who refused to answer questions concerning Communist membership were discharged. Lerner, a subway conductor, was removed as a person of "doubtful trust and reliability" for his "lack of candor," and Beilan, a public school teacher, was dismissed for "incompetency." The judgments were affirmed by the Court in *Lerner* v. *Casey*, 357 U.S. 468 (1958) and *Beilan* v. *Board of Public Education*, 357 U.S. 399 (1958), respectively. A similar result obtained in a Los Angeles County employee's dismissal for refusal to testify concerning his subversive activity before a subcommittee of the House Un-American Activities Committee in the face of a state statute requiring all public employees to give such testimony "on pain of discharge." *Nelson* v. *County of Los Angeles*, 362 U.S. 1 (1960).

The application of associational or belief tests to examinations for admission to the bar presents a specialized aspect of the same problem. In 1945, in the case of *In Re Summers*, 325 U.S. 561, the Court sustained Illinois' denial of admission to the bar of an applicant on the sole ground that as a conscientious objector to military service, he could not in good faith take the required oath to support the constitution of the state. Justice Reed, speaking for the majority of five, stressed that "the responsibility for choice as to the personnel of its bar rests with Illinois." He stated further, however, that men could not be excluded from the practice of law "or indeed from following any other calling, simply because they belong to any of our religious groups." But he did not find any such discrimination in the action of the Illinois Supreme Court. Justice Black, for the four dissenting members, objected that by its requirement Illinois had set up a test oath "designed to impose civil disabilities upon men for their beliefs rather than for unlawful conduct."

In 1957 the Court had occasion to examine, at least partially, the issue of whether Communist membership could constitutionally be made a basis for denial of admission to the bar. The case was *Schware* v. *Board of Bar Examiners*, 353 U.S. 232 (1957). Three aspects of Schware's past conduct led the New Mexico Board to conclude that "he failed to satisfy the Board of the requisite moral character." (1) From 1934 to 1937 he had used several aliases, apparently to avoid anti-Semitism; (2) he had been arrested several times, including twice for "suspicion of criminal syndicalism," although not convicted; and (3) from 1932 to 1940 he had been a member of the Communist Party, having joined at the age of 18 in his last year of high school. At the hearing he made a strong case for exemplary conduct since 1940, with three years of honorable service as a paratrooper, the operation of a business to support his family and his law school study, and the testimony of teachers and associates in support of his character. The State Supreme Court affirmed the denial of admission and stressed the previous Communist membership. The United States Supreme Court unanimously reversed, although the members split six-to-three on their reasons. Justice Black, for the majority, said: "We conclude that his past membership in the Communist Party does not justify an inference that he presently has bad moral character." Justice Frankfurter, in the concurring opinion, took a somewhat narrow view in saying: "to hold, as the [state] court did, that Communist affiliation for six to seven years up to 1940, fifteen years prior to the court's assessment of it, in and of itself made the petitioner 'a person of questionable character' is so dogmatic an inference as to be wholly unwarranted."

It does not appear that the holding in *Schware* bars the state from taking past Communist membership into account in making decisions regarding admissions to the bar, but it clearly cannot be considered as conclusively establishing bad moral character or as alone a ground for denial of admission.

As in the public employment cases, the problem of refusal to answer questions concerning Communist membership as affecting acceptability has been presented. In the first Konigsberg case, *Konigsberg* v. *State Bar of California*, 353 U.S. 252 (1957), the relevant requirement used as a basis for denial of admission to the bar was that applicants must be of good moral character and not advocate the overthrow of the government. The Court held that the denial of a license, based largely upon the applicant's refusal to answer questions concerning Communist Party membership, violated due process, since the record did not warrant finding that he failed to prove that he was of good moral character and did not advocate overthrow. At subsequent hearings before the bar committee Konigsberg again refused to answer questions relating to membership in the Communist Party, and again the committee declined to certify him. In the second Konigsberg case, *Konigsberg* v. *State Bar of California*, 366 U.S. 36 (1961), the Court held, in a five-to-four decision, that the state could properly deny the application on the ground that by refusing to answer the questions, the applicant had obstructed the committee in the performance of its required investigation into his qualifications. According to the majority, this was permissible despite the fact that the applicant's evidence of good moral character was unrebutted and he unequivocally asserted his disbelief in violent overthrow and stated that he had never knowingly been a member of an organization advocating such action. The applicant had refused, however, to answer questions dealing with Communist Party membership on the ground that they unconstitutionally impinged upon rights of free speech and association. Justice Harlan, for the Court, cited *Beilan* v. *Board of Public Education* in stating: "As regards the questioning of public employees relative to Communist Party membership it has already been held that the interest in not subjecting speech and association to the deterrence of subsequent disclosure is outweighed by the State's interest in ascertaining the fitness of the employee for the post he holds, and hence that such questioning does not infringe constitutional protections." He went on to conclude that the "State's interest in having lawyers who are devoted to the law in its broadest sense, including not only its substantive provisions, but also its procedures for orderly change, is clearly sufficient to outweigh the minimal effect upon free association occasioned by compulsory disclosure in the circumstances here presented."

A vigorous dissenting opinion was filed by Justice Black, with two justices concurring, and another by Justice Brennan. They argued that both on constitutional grounds and as a matter of a finding based on the record, the denial of license should have been reversed.

A similar result was reached in *In Re Anastaplo*, 366 U.S. 82 (1961), dealing with an Illinois decision to deny admission to the bar to an applicant who refused to answer questions about membership in the Communist Party.

The cases above indicate a somewhat ambivalent attitude on the part of the Court toward the extent to which membership in the Communist Party may be considered relevant in denying or terminating various kinds of public or quasi-public employment. One explanation for the ambivalence during the period spanned by the cases (1952–1961) is that not until 1958, in the decision in *NAACP* v. *Alabama* (discussed below), did the Court squarely recognize a constitutional right of association. Once having accorded this right First Amendment status, however, subsequent decisions demonstrate greater reluctance to uphold governmental restrictions which directly impinge on the right of association. *Scales* v. *United States*, decided in 1961, pointed to a new rule: mere membership in the Communist Party, without active furtherance of unlawful purposes, could not constitutionally be punished. The *Scales* decision came off on statutory rather than constitutional grounds, but the constitutional implications were clear, nonetheless.

In *Elfbrandt* v. *Russell*, 384 U.S. 11 (1966), the Court held unconstitutional an Arizona loyalty oath for state employees which subjected to discharge and prosecution for perjury any person who took the oath and "knowingly and willfully becomes or remains a member of the communist party" or any other organization having as one of its purposes the overthrow of the government of Arizona. A majority of five held the statute invalid since it did not require a showing that an employee was an active member with the specific intent of assisting in achieving the unlawful ends of a proscribed organization. Justice Douglas, for the majority, said "This Act threatens the cherished freedom of association protected by the First Amendment." He said further:

Those who join an organization but do not share its unlawful purposes and who do not participate in its unlawful activities surely pose no threat, either as citizens or as public employees. Laws such as this which are not restricted in scope to those who join with the "specific intent" to further illegal action impose, in effect, a conclusive presumption that the member shares the unlawful aims of the organization.

The decision in *Elfbrandt* invited a new attack on New York's Feinberg Law. Several faculty members of the State University of New York brought suit in a federal district court for declaratory and injunctive relief against the New York plan, formulated partly in statutes and partly in administrative regulations. A three-judge court upheld the plan, but on direct appeal, in *Keyishian* v. *Board of Regents of New York,* 385 U.S. 589 (1967), the Supreme Court reversed, overruling *Adler* and holding the Feinberg Law to be unconstitutional.

Three sections of the New York law were challenged as being unconstitutionally vague: (1) a section requiring removal for "treasonable or seditious" utterances or acts; (2) a section barring employment of any person who "by word of mouth or writing willfully and deliberately advocates, advises or teaches the doctrine" of forceful overthrow of government; and (3) a section requiring the disqualification of an employee involved with the distribution of written material "containing or advocating, advising or teaching the doctrine" of forceful overthrow, and who himself "advocates, advises, teaches, or embraces the duty, necessity or propriety of adopting the doctrine contained therein."

A majority of five held these sections to be unconstitutionally vague, on the ground that they were "plainly susceptible to sweeping and improper application," and might "reasonably be construed to cover mere expression of belief." As to the provisions of the Feinberg Law making Communist Party membership, as such, prima facie evidence of disqualification, the majority followed *Elfbrandt* in holding that "legislation which sanctions membership unaccompanied by specific intent to further the unlawful goals of the organization or which is not active membership violates constitutional limitations."

In the course of his opinion for the majority, Justice Brennan gave an impressive statement in support of academic freedom:

Our Nation is deeply committed to safeguarding academic freedom, which is of transcendent value to all of us and not merely to the teachers concerned. That freedom is therefore a special concern of the First Amendment, which does not tolerate laws that cast a pall of orthodoxy over the classroom. "The vigilant protection of constitutional freedoms is nowhere more vital than in the community of American schools.". . . . The classroom is peculiarly the "marketplace of ideas." The Nation's future depends upon leaders trained through wide exposure to that robust exchange of ideas which discovers the truth "out of a multitude of tongues, [rather] than through any kind of authoritative selection."

A special problem involving the right of association concerns governmental power, by statute or order, to compel individuals to disclose their membership in various organizations or to compel organizations to disclose their membership lists. The major recent cases on these questions have held that the Constitution protects against such compulsory disclosure.

NAACP v. *Alabama,* 357 U.S. 449 (1958) involved the validity of an Alabama court order directing the disclosure of membership lists in the Alabama affiliate of the NAACP. The organization offered to produce all requested papers and information except those showing names and addresses of officers and members. The Alabama court held the NAACP in contempt and a fine of $100,000 was adjudged. The United States Supreme Court unanimously held the registration requirement invalid. Speaking for the Court, Justice Harlan stated:

Effective advocacy of both public and private points of view, particularly controversial ones, is undeniably enhanced by group association, as this Court has more than once recognized by remarking upon the close nexus between the freedoms of speech and assembly. . . . It is beyond debate that freedom to engage in association for the advancement of beliefs and ideas is an inseparable aspect of the "liberty" assured by the Due Process Clause of the Fourteenth Amendment, which embraces freedom of speech. . . . Of course, it is immaterial whether the beliefs sought to be advanced by association pertain to political, economic, religious or cultural matters, and state action which may have the effect of curtailing the freedom to associate is subject to the closest scrutiny.

The main problem presented in the case was to distinguish the Alabama requirement from the Klan registration law of New York which the Court had held constitutional in *New York ex rel. Bryant* v. *Zimmerman,* 278 U.S. 63 (1928). On this point Justice Harlan stated:

That case involved markedly different considerations in terms of the interest of the State in obtaining disclosure. . . . In its opinion, the Court took care to emphasize the nature of the organization which New York sought to regulate. The decision was based on the particular character of the Klan's activities, involving acts of unlawful intimidation and violence, which the Court assumed was before the state legislature when it enacted the statute, and of which the Court itself took judicial notice. . . . And we conclude that Alabama has fallen short of showing a controlling justification for the deterrent effect on the free enjoyment of the right to associate which disclosure of membership lists is likely to have.

[See Joseph B. Robison, "Protection of Associations From Compulsory Disclosure of Membership," 58 *Col. L. Rev.* 614 (1958).]

Despite the distinction which the opinion indicated between the Klan registration law and the NAACP registration, the holding in the NAACP case raises doubts as to the continued vitality of the *Zimmerman* decision.

In *Shelton* v. *Tucker*, 364 U.S. 479 (1960), the Court dealt with an Arkansas statute which compelled every teacher in a state-supported school to file annually an affidavit listing every organization to which he had belonged or regularly contributed within the preceding five years. Plaintiffs challenged the validity of the statute under the Fourteenth Amendment "due process" clause. By the narrow margin of five-to-four the Court held the requirement unconstitutional. All members of the Court agreed that the state has a right to investigate the competence and fitness of those whom it hires to teach in its schools. They further appeared to agree that some check into the associational ties would be relevant to the matter of competence. But the majority felt that to inquire into *every* such organizational relationship—church affiliation, political party, social club and others—was to permit unlimited scope to such an inquiry and therefore to violate the freedom of association. As Justice Stewart stated for the majority, "Many such relationships could have no possible bearing upon the teacher's occupational competence or fitness."

Justice Frankfurter, dissenting, felt that the state was entitled to know whether a teacher might "have so many divers associations, so many divers commitments, that they consume his time and energy and interest at the expense of his work or even of his professional dedication." He also stated that, on the record, he could not attribute to the state a purpose to inhibit constitutional rights. But he added, "Of course, if the information gathered by the required affidavits is used to further a scheme of terminating the employment of teachers solely because of their membership in unpopular organizations, that use will run afoul of the Fourteenth Amendment."

The more recent issue of compulsory disclosure of membership involves the application of the Subversive Activities Control Act of 1950 (which is Title I of the Internal Security Act of 1950), which requires the registration with the Attorney General of all Communist-action organizations, as well as all Communist-front organizations. In the case of an organization which is ordered to register by the Subversive Activities Control Board, registration must take place within thirty days of the date upon which the Board's order becomes final. Registration is to be accompanied by a statement containing, among other information, the names and addresses of each person who has been an officer and each person who has been a member during the past twelve months. Once an organization has registered, it must file an annual report containing the same information required in the registration statement. The procedures and requirements of registration for Communist fronts are identical with those for Communist-action organizations, except that fronts need not list their nonofficer members.

Under Section 7(h) of the Act, if the officers of a Communist-action organization fail to register as ordered by the Board, then the individual members are required to register themselves within sixty days after the registration order becomes final. Section 8 provides criminal penalties to be imposed upon organizations, officers and individuals who fail to register or to file statements as required: a fine of not more than $10,000 for each offense by an organization; a fine of not more than $10,000 or imprisonment for not more than five years or both for each offense by an officer or individual; and each day of failure to register constituting a separate offense.

After more than a year of hearings, the Subversive Activities Control Board in 1953 issued an order requiring that the Communist Party of the United States register in the manner prescribed by the Act. After protracted litigation, the Court of Appeals for the District of Columbia Circuit affirmed the registration order. The Party petitioned the Supreme Court for review, basing its objections to the order on three broad grounds: alleged procedural errors in the Board's taking of testimony, improper construction of the Act, and the unconstitutionality of the Act as constituting a bill of attainder, as violative of freedom of expression and association, and as violative of the privilege against self-incrimination. By a five-to-four vote the Court upheld the judgment of the court of appeals in *Communist Party of the United States* v. *Subversive Activities Control Board*, 367 U.S. 1 (1961).

The majority, through Justice Frankfurter, held that many of the alleged consequences of the Act were prematurely presented and the prejudicial effects only speculative, without support in the record. They refused, therefore, to reach several of the claims of appellants. The majority specifically held, however, that the Act was not a bill of attainder, since the Act applies to a class of activity, not to the Communist Party as such. On the claim of violation of freedom of expression and association, Justice Frankfurter stated, "The present case differs from *Thomas* v. *Collins* and from *National Association for Advancement of Colored People*, *Bates*, and *Shelton* in the magnitude of the public interests which the registration and disclosure provisions are designed to protect and in the pertinence which registration and disclosure bear to the protection of those interests." He reviewed the legislative findings of the threat to national security from the Communist-action organizations and the purpose of the Act as preventing "the world-wide Communist conspiracy from accomplishing its purpose in this country." He stated further:

Congress, when it enacted the Subversive Activities Control Act, did attempt to cope with precisely such a danger. In light of its legislative findings, based on voluminous evidence collected during years of investigation, we cannot say that that danger is chimerical, or that the registration requirement of Section 7 is an ill-adjusted means of dealing with it. In saying this, we are not insensitive to the fact that the public opprobrium and obloquy which may attach to an individual listed with the Attorney General as a member of a Communist-action organization is no less considerable than that with which members of the National Association for the Advancement of Colored People were threatened in *National Association for Ad-*

vancement of Colored People and *Bates*. But while an angry public opinion, and the evils which it may spawn, are relevant considerations in adjudging . . . the validity of legislation that, in effecting disclosure, may thereby entail some restraints on speech and association, the existence of an ugly public temper does not, as such and without more, incapacitate government to require publicity demanded by rational interests high in the scale of national concern. Where the mask of anonymity which an organization's members wear serves the double purpose of protecting them from popular prejudice and of enabling them to cover over a foreign-directed conspiracy, infiltrate into other groups, and enlist the support of persons who would not, if the truth were revealed, lend their support, . . . it would be a distortion of the First Amendment to hold that it prohibits Congress from removing the mask.

An additional claim of the Party was that the registration requirements of the Act could not be imposed and exacted consistently with the Fifth Amendment's self-incrimination clause. It was argued that the officers of the Party are compelled, in the very act of filing a signed registration statement, to admit that they *are* Party officers—an admission which the Court has held incriminating. Justice Frankfurter's response was that the claim was premature:

Manifestly, insofar as this contention is directed against the provisions . . . requiring that designated officers file registration statements in default of registration by an organization, it is prematurely raised in the present proceeding. The duties imposed by those provisions will not arise until and unless the Party fails to register. At this time their application is wholly contingent and conjectural. . . .

The sequel to the case came in 1965 in the case of *Albertson* v. *Subversive Activities Control Board*, 382 U.S. 70 (1965). After the Communist Party had failed to comply with an order requiring it to furnish the Attorney General a list of the Party's members, the Attorney General, acting pursuant to provisions of the Subversive Activities Control Act, requested that the Subversive Activities Control Board grant orders requiring petitioners to register as individual members of the Party. The Board granted the orders, and the Court of Appeals for the District of Columbia affirmed, expressing the view that the constitutional issues raised by the petitioners were not ripe for adjudication and would be ripe only in a prosecution for failure to register if the petitioners did not register. The United States Supreme Court voted unanimously to reverse, holding that the orders violated the Fifth Amendment privilege against self-incrimination. Justice Brennan, for the Court, stated that admission of membership may be used to prosecute the registrant under the membership clause of the Smith Act. He stated further:

Section 4(f) of the Act, the purported immunity provision, does not save the registration orders from petitioners' Fifth Amendment challenge. . . . [T]he immunity granted by §4(f) is not complete. . . . With regard to the act of registering . . . §4(f) provides only that the admission of Party membership thus required shall not per se constitute a violation of §§4(a) and (c) or any other criminal statute, or "be received in evidence" against a registrant in any criminal prosecution; it does not preclude the use of the admission as an investigatory lead, a use which is barred by the privilege.

It is not an easy matter to sum up the Court's delineation of the constitutional rights to free expression when applied to matters touching on internal security, especially as related to restrictions on Communists. But a few signposts have been erected, indicating at least general directions. At the outset, it is apparent that in the hard cases involving the issue of freedom of expression versus internal security the Court takes a long, close look at the procedures used in applying the given restrictions. While procedural matters have generally been dealt with in a previous chapter, the point here is that where freedom of expression is being abridged, the statutory and constitutional procedural requirements are apt to be applied somewhat more rigorously than in some other areas. Once these requirements are met, however, the Court has permitted both the national and the state governments to impose a variety of restrictions on Communists. [For a compilation of such restrictions and court decisions relative to them, see the Fund for the Republic publication, *Digest of the Public Record of Communism in the United States* (New York: Fund for the Republic, 1955).] Both governments may bar active Communists from employment. In addition, a refusal to answer official inquiries concerning such participation can be taken into account in determining "competence" or "good moral character" in connection with retention of governmental employment or admission to the bar. But where associational tests range too widely and reach ordinarily lawful organizational ties, then the Court tends to hold that First Amendment rights of belief and association have been abridged. Thus it may be true that there is no "right" to government employment, but this is not to say that governments can set requirements which are unrelated to the proper performance of the employment position or which classify applicants in an unreasonable fashion.

The Court has upheld a congressional requirement that before becoming eligible for the services of the National Labor Relations Board, and thus the statutory benefits of the Wagner Act, a labor organization must file with the Board an affidavit executed by each officer of such organization that he is not a member of the Communist Party or affiliated with it. In 1959, however, this requirement of the Taft-Hartley Act was replaced by a provision making it a crime for a member of the Communist Party to serve as an officer or employee of a labor union (except in clerical or custodial positions). In *United States* v. *Brown,* 381 U.S. 437 (1965), the Court by a five-to-four vote held this section unconstitutional as a bill of attainder. The Chief Justice, for the majority, stated that the statute did not "set forth a generally applicable rule decreeing that any person who commits certain acts or possesses certain characteristics .... shall not hold union office, and leave to courts and juries the job of deciding what persons have committed the specified acts or possessed the specified characteristics." Instead it simply designated the persons—members of the Communist Party —and such designation "is not the substitution of a semantically equivalent phrase" and is therefore a bill of attainder.

In *Schneiderman* v. *United States*, 320 U.S. 118 (1943), the Court indicated that Congress might exclude all Communist aliens from entering the United States. And in *Harisiades* v. *Shaughnessy*, 342 U.S. 580 (1952), it was held that Congress could constitutionally deport all aliens who had been members of the Communist Party, including even those whose membership had ceased prior to the passage of the statute requiring such deportation. Thus aliens and immigrants are in a particularly vulnerable position. [See Milton R. Konvitz, *Civil Rights in Immigration* (Ithaca: Cornell University Press, 1953); Lena L. Orlow, "The Immigration and Nationality Act in Operation," 29 *Temple L. Q.* 153 (1956); Blanch L. Freedman, "The Loyalty-Security Program—Its Effect in Immigration and Deportation," 15 *Law. Guild Rev.* 135 (1955); Comment, "The Alien and the Constitution," 20 *U. of Chi. L. Rev.* 547 (1953).]

The advocacy of revolution can constitutionally be punished unless it is limited to the advocacy of *belief in the doctrine* of overthrow of the government by violence. And organizing a group or becoming an active member of a group dedicated to teaching the overthrow of the government by violence may constitutionally be punished. Restrictions on Communists unsupported by a showing of potential danger to the nation or to maintenance of order appear to be subjected to close scrutiny, however. Thus in *Aptheker* v. *Secretary of State*, 378 U.S. 500 (1964), the Court held that Section 6 of the Subversive Activities Control Act, which bars the application for or use of a passport by a member of an organization ordered to register by the Board as a Communist-action organization, was an undue restriction on the right to travel abroad and therefore an unconstitutional abridgment of the liberty guaranteed by the Fifth Amendment. [See Leonard B. Boudin, "The Constitutional Right to Travel," 56 *Colum. L. Rev.* 47 (1956).] More recently, in *Lamont* v. *Postmaster General*, 381 U.S. 301 (1965), the Court held unconstitutional a federal statute requiring a request in writing as a prerequisite to the delivery of nonsealed mail from abroad which was classified as containing Communist propaganda material. This case is particularly noteworthy in that for the first time in our history the United States Supreme Court held a *federal* statute unconstitutional as an abridgment of First Amendment rights. [See Jay A. Sigler, "Freedom of the Mails: a Developing Right," 54 *Geo. L. J.* 30 (1965).]

At least in the treatment of citizens, it appears that the Court is more willing to take up cases dealing with anti-Communist restrictions than it was in the decade following World War II and is requiring a relatively close relationship between the restriction and the protection of the nation's security before upholding the peripheral attacks on Communists.

[The literature on loyalty-security problems is enormous. See Thomas I. Emerson, David Haber, and Norman Dorsen, *Political and Civil Rights in the United States,* 3rd ed., 2 Vols. (Boston: Little, Brown, 1967), Chap. III, especially the bibliographic references. See also, John L. O'Brian, *National Security and Individual Freedom* (Cambridge: Harvard University Press, 1955); Harold W. Chase, *Security and Liberty: The Problem of Native Communists, 1947–1955* (Garden City: Doubleday & Co., 1955); Walter Gellhorn, ed., *The States and Subversion* (Ithaca: Cornell University Press, 1952).]

REGULATION OF TRAFFIC AND MAINTENANCE OF PUBLIC PEACE AND ORDER

The state may place the exercise of speech and assembly under reasonable police regulations for a variety of purposes, and some of the most oft-cited illustrations of this power are in the areas of traffic control and the preservation of public order. Of course the previously treated decisions dealing with prior restraints are applicable in this area, just as in other types of expression, but if the state avoids this error, it is permitted a reasonable range of control.

A good illustration of the Court's view of an improper and a proper statutory handling of a permissible area of regulation is to be seen in two cases dealing with the regulation of sound amplification equipment in urban streets and parks. In *Saia* v. *New York,* 334 U.S. 558 (1948), the Court found a prior restraint in a city ordinance forbidding the use of sound amplification devices except for "public dissemination ... of items of news and matters of public concern ... provided that the same be done under permission obtained from the Chief of Police." Refused a second permit on the ground that complaints had been reported concerning his prior speeches and sermons using a loud-speaker, appellant, a minister of the Jehovah's Witnesses, delivered a speech, without a permit and again using a loud-speaker, in a park normally used for recreation purposes. By a five-to-four majority the Court held the ordinance unconstitutional on its face as a prior restraint on the right of free speech. It should be noted, however, that the opinion for the Court pointed out that reasonable regulation of the use of loud-speaker was within the range of state power. Justice Douglas, for the majority, stated:

Noise can be regulated by regulating decibels. The hours and place of public discussion can be controlled. But to allow the police to bar the use of loud-speakers because their use can be abused is like barring radio receivers because they too make a noise. The police need not be given the power to deny a man the use of his radio in order to protect a neighbor against sleepless nights. The same is true here.

Any abuses which loud-speakers create can be controlled by narrowly drawn statutes. When a city allows an official to ban them in his uncontrolled discretion, it sanctions a device for suppression of free communication of ideas. In this case a permit is denied because some persons were said to have found the sound annoying. In the next one a permit may be denied because some people find the ideas annoying. Annoyance at ideas can be cloaked in annoyance at sound. The power of censorship inherent in this type of ordinance reveals its vice.

Justice Frankfurter, joined in dissent by Justices Reed and Burton, pointed out that there is an important difference in ordinary human speech and the use of modern amplifying devices which "afford easy, too easy, opportunities for aural aggression." Considering this and the fact that people had complained, it did not seem to him unreasonable or unconstitutional to refuse a license to the appellant for the time and place requested. Justice Jackson dissented separately, stating that this was not even a free speech issue.

[C]an it be that society has no control of apparatus which, when put to unregulated proselyting, propaganda and commercial uses, can render life unbearable? It is intimated that the city can control the decibels; if so, why may it not prescribe zero decibels as appropriate to some places? It seems to me that society has the right to control, as to place, time and volume, the use of loud-speaking devices for any purpose, provided its regulations are not unduly arbitrary, capricious or discriminatory.

The second loud-speaker case also came off on a five-to-four vote, but this time upholding a regulation. The case was *Kovacs* v. *Cooper*, 336 U.S. 77 (1949), involving the validity of a Trenton, New Jersey, ordinance which provided: "That it shall be unlawful for any person, firm or corporation . . . to play, use or operate for advertising purposes, or for any other purpose whatsoever, on or upon the public streets, alleys or thoroughfares in the City of Trenton, any device known as a sound truck, loud speaker or sound-amplifier, or radio or phonograph with a loud speaker or sound amplifier, or any other instrument known as a calliope or any instrument of any kind or character which emits therefrom loud and raucous noises and is attached to and upon any vehicle operated or standing upon said streets or public places aforementioned."

Although five justices held the regulation valid, there was no opinion for the Court. Justice Reed, speaking for three members, seemingly accepted the construction placed on the ordinance by the New Jersey Supreme Court, namely that the ordinance applied only to vehicles with sound amplifiers "emitting loud and raucous noises" and did not prohibit sound trucks altogether. On this basis he stated "We think that the need for reasonable protection in the homes or business houses from the distracting noises of vehicles equipped with such sound amplifying devices justifies the ordinance."

Justice Frankfurter concurred, repeating the views expressed in his *Saia* dissent. Justice Jackson also concurred separately saying:

I join the judgment sustaining the Trenton ordinance because I believe that operation of mechanical sound-amplifying devices conflicts with quiet enjoyment of home and park and with safe and legitimate use of street and market place, and that it is constitutionally subject to regulation or prohibition by the state or municipal authority. . . .

But I agree with Mr. Justice Black that this decision is a repudiation of that in *Saia* v. *New York*. . . . Like him, I am unable to find anything in this record to warrant a distinction because of "loud and raucous" tones of this machine . . . Trenton, as the ordinance reads to me, unconditionally bans all sound trucks from the city streets. Lockport relaxed its prohibition with a proviso to allow their use, even in areas set aside for public recreation, when and where the Chief of Police saw no objection. Comparison of this our 1949 decision with our 1948 decision, I think, will pretty hopelessly confuse municipal authorities as to what they may or may not do.

Justice Black, joined by Justices Douglas and Rutledge, dissented on the ground that the "ordinance is on its face, and as construed and applied in this case by that state's courts, an absolute and unqualified prohibition of amplifying devices on any of Trenton's streets at any time, at any place, for any purpose, and without regard to how noisy they may be." He indicated clearly, however, that reasonable regulation would meet the test of constitutionality. The opinion stated:

I would agree without reservation to the sentiment that "unrestrained use through-out a municipality of all sound amplifying devices would be intolerable." And of course cities may restrict or absolutely ban the use of amplifiers on busy streets in the business area. A city ordinance that reasonably restricts the volume of sound, or the hours during which an amplifier may be used, does not in my mind infringe the constitutionally protected area of free speech. It is because this ordinance does none of these things, but is instead an absolute prohibition of all uses of an amplifier on any of the streets of Trenton at any time that I must dissent.

Justice Murphy dissented separately.

While reconciliation of the two cases may not be easy, a head-count of the voting in the cases shows that Chief Justice Vinson was the only member to change his vote from *Saia* to *Kovacs* relative to the power to enforce the respective ordinances. Since he did not write an opinion in either case, it is not possible to state precisely the basis for his shift. Once again, however, it is clear from a reading of the opinions that an ordinance limiting the volume, time, and place of the use of sound trucks or public sound amplification equipment in some reasonable manner would pass constitutional muster.

The problem of regulating street processions while at the same time avoiding the pitfall of prior restraint and affording broad protection to First Amendment rights was well illustrated in the case of *Cox* v. *New Hampshire*, 312 U.S. 569 (1941), discussed earlier. The Court upheld a reasonable and nondiscriminatory permit requirement for the holding of parades as a proper municipal regulation of the use of the streets.

Feiner v. *New York*, 340 U.S. 315 (1951) illustrates the application of a municipal ordinance prohibiting disorderly conduct to the attempted exercise of free speech. Feiner addressed a group of listeners on a street corner in Syracuse, New York. A racially mixed crowd of some seventy-five or eighty people gathered on the sidewalks and spilled into the street. He urged the audience to attend a speech later that night on the subject of racial discrimination, and during the appeal referred to President Truman as a "bum," to the American Legion as "a Nazi Gestapo," and to the Mayor of Syracuse as a "champagne-sipping bum." He also said that "colored people don't have equal rights and they should rise up in arms and fight for them."

Two officers were sent to the meeting and stated that the crowd was restless and there was some pushing, shoving, and milling around. One man said to the police officers, "If you don't get that S.O.B. off, I will go over and get him off there myself." The police officers told Feiner to stop speaking, and when he refused, arrested him for disorderly conduct. In finding Feiner guilty the trial judge concluded that the police officers were justified in taking action to prevent a breach of the peace, and the New York Court of Appeals affirmed.

A majority of six in the United States Supreme Court considered that the facts clearly indicated sufficient evidence of a possible breach of the peace to warrant Feiner's arrest for disorderly conduct. The Chief Justice, speaking for the majority, stated that "Petitioner was neither arrested nor convicted for the making or the content of his speech. Rather it was the reaction which it actually engendered." He stated further:

We are well aware that the ordinary murmurings and objections of a hostile audience cannot be allowed to silence a speaker, and are also mindful of the possible danger of giving overzealous police officials complete discretion to break up otherwise lawful public meetings. . . . But we are not faced here with such a situation. It is one thing to say that the police cannot be used as an instrument for the oppression of unpopular views, and another to say that, when as here the speaker passes the bounds of argument or persuasion and undertakes incitement to riot, they are powerless to prevent a breach of the peace.

Justices Black and Douglas gave vigorous dissenting opinions, Justice Minton concurring with the latter. Justice Black stated:

As to the existence of a dangerous situation on the street corner, it seems farfetched to suggest that the "facts" show any imminent threat of riot or uncontrollable disorder. It is neither unusual nor unexpected that some people at public street meetings mutter, mill about, push, shove, or disagree, even violently, with the speaker. Indeed, it is rare where controversial topics are discussed that an outdoor crowd does not do some or all of these things. Nor does one isolated threat to assault the speaker forbode disorder. . . .

Moreover, assuming that the "facts" did indicate a critical situation, I reject the implication of the Court's opinion that the police had no obligation to protect petitioner's constitutional right to talk. But if, in the name of preserving order, they ever can interfere with a lawful public speaker, they first must make all reasonable efforts to protect him. Here the policemen did not even pretend to try to protect petitioner.... Their duty was to protect petitioner's right to talk, even to the extent of arresting the man who threatened to interfere. Instead, they shirked that duty and acted only to suppress the right to speak.

The decision in the *Feiner* case indicates the importance of the fact-finding aspect of the cases. The members of the Court sometimes disagree on the law and sometimes on the way that the facts should be read. While the appellate courts do not as a rule upset lower court findings of fact, the United States Supreme Court has often pointed out that in First Amendment cases it will feel free to make its own determination of the facts. The majority in *Feiner* found the facts to support a conviction for disorderly conduct, while the minority read them differently and concluded that the problem was one of a hostile audience interfering with a lawful speech. As to the law, however, it is clear that a reasonably administered municipal prohibition against disorderly conduct may be upheld even though it regulates speech or assembly.

Chaplinsky v. *New Hampshire*, 315 U.S. 568 (1942), involved a state law providing that:

No person shall address any offensive, derisive or annoying word to any other person who is lawfully in any street or other public place, nor call him by any offensive or derisive name, nor make any noise or exclamation in his presence and hearing with intent to deride, offend or annoy him or to prevent him from pursuing his lawful business or occupation.

The state court construed the statute as prohibiting "words likely to cause an average addressee to fight," or "face-to-face words plainly likely to cause a breach of the peace by the addressee." Appellant was a Jehovah's Witness who, after getting into an argument on a public sidewalk, called a city marshal a "damned Fascist" and a "Goddamned racketeer." His conviction under the statute was unanimously upheld by the United States Supreme Court against a claim of invasion of First Amendment freedom of expression. Justice Murphy, for the Court, stated:

There are certain well-defined and narrowly limited classes of speech, the prevention and punishment of which have never been thought to raise any Constitutional problem. These include the lewd and obscene, the profane, the libelous, and the insulting or "fighting" words—those which by their very utterance inflict injury or tend to incite an immediate breach of the peace. It has been well observed that such utterances are no essential part of any exposition of ideas and are of such slight social value as a step to truth that any benefit that may be derived from them is clearly outweighed by the social interest in order and morality.

A case frequently cited in the context of "fighting words" is *Terminiello* v. *Chicago*, 337 U.S. 1 (1949), although the decision in the United States Supreme Court did not come off on that issue. Terminiello spoke in an auditorium in Chicago to a crowd of about 800 persons. He criticized Democrats, Jews, and Communists in a speech full of racial and political hatred. A crowd of over a thousand gathered outside in protest, yelling "Fascists, Hitlers!" A cordon of police assigned to the meeting was unable to stop the smashing of doors, the breaking of windows, and other acts of violence. Terminiello was arrested and convicted of violating a breach of the peace ordinance. In charging the jury, however, the judge defined breach of the peace to include speech which "stirs the public to anger, invites dispute, brings about a condition of unrest or creates a disturbance." By a five-to-four vote the Court reversed the conviction on the ground that the charge to the jury interpreting the statute permitted the punishment of speech that was protected by the Constitution. Justice Douglas, for the majority, stated:

A function of free speech under our system of government is to invite dispute. It may indeed best serve its high purpose when it induces a condition of unrest, creates dissatisfaction with conditions as they are, or even stirs people to anger. Speech is often provocative and challenging. It may strike at prejudices and preconceptions and have profound unsettling effects as it presses for acceptance of an idea. . . . The ordinance as construed by the trial court seriously invaded this province. It permitted conviction of petitioner if his speech stirred people to anger, invited public dispute, or brought about a condition of unrest. A conviction resting on any of those grounds may not stand.

There were dissents on the ground that no one had raised any issue regarding the charge to the jury at any stage of the proceedings, and thus the question was not open to them. Justices Jackson and Burton further dissented on the ground that the jury was justified in finding a breach of the peace in the facts of the case, and the conviction should have been affirmed.

In view of the basis for the majority decision, the *Terminiello* case must be confined to the issue of whether speech which invites dispute and stirs the public to anger can for those reasons only be restricted. Thus it stands as no authority for what a municipality can or cannot do to punish a man who says the things which Terminiello did under the circumstances of his speech. The Court simply did not reach that question in deciding the case.

A different problem is presented, however, when the speech is not of "such slight social value" and where there is neither a presumption that the behavior and speech are likely to provoke the average person to retaliation (as in *Chaplinsky*) nor a clearly supported finding that a breach of the peace is imminent. This was the situation in *Edwards* v. *South Carolina*, 372 U.S. 229 (1963).

EDWARDS *v.* SOUTH CAROLINA
372 U.S. 229 (1963)

Mr. Justice Stewart delivered the opinion of the Court.

The petitioners, 187 in number, were convicted in a magistrate's court in Columbia, South Carolina, of the common-law crime of breach of the peace. Their convictions were ultimately affirmed by the South Carolina Supreme Court.... We granted certiorari ... to consider the claim that these convictions cannot be squared with the Fourteenth Amendment of the United States Constitution.

There was no substantial conflict in the trial evidence. Late in the morning of March 2, 1961, the petitioners, high school and college students of the Negro race, met at the Zion Baptist Church in Columbia. From there, at about noon, they walked in separate groups of about 15 to the South Carolina State House grounds, an area of two city blocks open to the general public. Their purpose was "to submit a protest to the citizens of South Carolina, along with the Legislative Bodies of South Carolina, our feelings and our dissatisfaction with the present condition of discriminatory actions against Negroes, in general, and to let them know that we were dissatisfied and that we would like for the laws which prohibited Negro privileges in this State to be removed."

Already on the State House grounds when the petitioners arrived were 30 or more law enforcement officers, who had advance knowledge that the petitioners were coming. Each group of petitioners entered the grounds through a driveway and parking area known in the record as the "horseshoe." As they entered, they were told by the law enforcement officials that "they had a right, as a citizen, to go through the State House grounds, as any other citizen has, as long as they were peaceful." During the next half hour or 45 minutes, the petitioners, in the same small groups, walked single file or two abreast in an orderly way through the grounds, each group carrying placards bearing such messages as "I am proud to be a Negro," and "Down with segregation."

During this time a crowd of some 200 to 300 onlookers had collected in the horseshoe area and on the adjacent sidewalks. There was no evidence to suggest that these onlookers were anything but curious, and no evidence at all of any threatening remarks, hostile gestures, or offensive language on the part of any member of the crowd. The City Manager testified that he recognized some of the onlookers, whom he did not identify, as "possible trouble makers," but his subsequent testimony made clear that nobody among the crowd actually caused or threatened any trouble. There was no obstruction of pedestrian or vehicular traffic within the State House grounds. ... Although vehicular traffic at a nearby street intersection was slowed down somewhat, an officer was dispatched to keep traffic moving. There were a number of bystanders on the public sidewalks adjacent to the State House grounds, but they all moved on when asked to do so, and there was no impediment of pedestrian traffic. Police protection at the scene was at all times sufficient to meet any foreseeable possibility of disorder.

In the situation and under the circumstances thus described, the police authorities [actually the order issued from the City Manager, as the footnote excerpts from the trial record show] advised the petitioners that they would be arrested if they did not disperse within 15 minutes. Instead of dispersing, the petitioners engaged in what the City Manager described as "boisterous," "loud," and "flamboyant" conduct, which, as his later testimony made clear, consisted of listening to a "religious harangue" by one of their leaders, and loudly singing "The Star Spangled Banner" and other patriotic and religious songs, while stamping their feet and clapping their hands. After 15 minutes had passed, the police arrested the petitioners and marched them off to jail.

Upon this evidence the state trial court convicted the petitioners of breach of the peace, and imposed sentences ranging from a $10 fine or five days in jail, to a $100 fine or 30 days in jail. In affirming the judgments, the Supreme Court of South Carolina said that under the law of that State the offense of breach of the peace "is not susceptible of exact definition," but that the "general definition of the offense" is as follows:

"In general terms, a breach of the peace is a violation of public order, a disturbance of the public tranquility, by any act or conduct inciting to violence..., it includes any violation of any law enacted to preserve peace and good order. It may consist of an act of violence or an act likely to produce violence. It is not necessary that the peace be actually broken to lay the foundation for a prosecution for this offense. If what is done is unjustifiable and unlawful, tending with sufficient directness to break the peace, no more is required. Nor is actual personal violence an essential element in the offense...."

The petitioners contend that there was a complete absence of any evidence of the commission of this offense, and that they were thus denied one of the most basic elements of due process of law.... Whatever the merits of this contention, we need not pass upon it in the present case. The state courts have held that the petitioners' conduct constituted breach of the peace under state law, and we may accept their decision as binding upon us to that extent. *But it nevertheless remains our duty in a case such as this to make an independent examination of the whole record.* [Emphasis supplied.] ... And it is clear to us that in arresting, convicting, and punishing the petitioners under the circumstances disclosed by this record, South Carolina infringed the petitioners' constitutionally protected rights of free speech, free assembly, and freedom to petition for redress of their grievances.

... The circumstances in this case reflect an exercise of these basic constitutional rights in their most pristine and classic form. The petitioners felt aggrieved by laws of South Carolina which allegedly "prohibited Negro privileges in this State." They peaceably assembled at the site of the State Government and there peaceably expressed their grievances "to the citizens of South Carolina, along with the Legislative Bodies of South Carolina." Not until they were told by police officials that they must disperse on pain of arrest did they do more. Even then, they but sang patriotic and religious songs after one of their leaders had delivered a "religious harangue." There was no violence or threat of violence on their part, or on the part of any member of the crowd watching them. Police protection was "ample."

This, therefore, was a far cry from the situation in *Feiner* v. *New York*, ... where two policemen were faced with a crowd which was "pushing, shoving, and milling around,". . . here at least one member of the crowd "threatened violence if the police did not act,". . . where "the crowd was pressing closer around petitioner and the officer,". . . and where "the speaker passes the bounds of argument or persuasion and undertakes incitement to riot.". . . And the record is barren of any evidence of "fighting words." See *Chaplinsky* v. *New Hampshire.* . . .

We do not review in this case criminal convictions resulting from the even-handed application of a precise and narrowly drawn regulatory statute evincing a legislative judgment that certain specific conduct be limited or proscribed. If, for example, the petitioners had been convicted upon evidence that they had violated a law regulating traffic, or had disobeyed a law reasonably limiting the periods during which the State House grounds were open to the public, this would be a different case. . . . These petitioners . . . were convicted upon evidence which showed no more than that the opinions which they were peaceably expressing were sufficiently opposed to the views of the majority of the community to attract a crowd and necessitate police protection. . . .

For these reasons we conclude that these criminal convictions cannot stand.

Reversed.

Mr. Justice Clark, dissenting. . . .

. . . Petitioners, of course, had a right to peaceable assembly, to espouse their cause and to petition, but in my view the manner in which they exercised those rights was by no means the passive demonstration which this Court relates; rather, as the City Manager of Columbia testified, "a dangerous situation was building up" which South Carolina's courts expressly found had created "an actual interference with traffic and an imminently threatened disturbance of the peace of the community." Since the Court does not attack the state courts' findings and accepts the convictions as "binding" to the extent that the petitioners' conduct constituted a breach of the peace, it is difficult for me to understand its understatement of the facts and reversal of the convictions. . . .

. . . Here the petitioners were permitted without hindrance to exercise their rights of free speech and assembly. Their arrests occurred only after a situation arose in which the law-enforcement officials on the scene considered that a dangerous disturbance was imminent. The County Court found that "the evidence is clear that the officers were motivated solely by a proper concern for the preservation of order and the protection of the general welfare in the face of an actual interference with traffic and an imminently threatened disturbance of the peace of the community." In affirming, the South Carolina Supreme Court said the action of the police was "reasonable and motivated solely by a proper concern for the preservation of order and prevention of further interference with traffic upon the public streets and sidewalks.". . .

. . . [I]n *Feiner* v. *New York* . . . we upheld a conviction for breach of the peace in a situation no more dangerous than that found here. There the demonstration was conducted by only one person and the crowd was limited to approximately 80. . . . Here 200 youthful Negro demonstrators were being aroused to a "fever pitch" before a crowd of some 300 people who undoubtedly were hostile. . . . It is my belief that anyone conversant with the almost spontaneous combustion in some Southern communities in such a situation will agree that the City Manager's action may well have averted a major catastrophe.

The gravity of the danger here surely needs no further explication. The imminence of that danger has been emphasized at every stage of this proceeding, from the complaints charging that the demonstrations "tended directly to immediate violence" to the State Supreme Court's affirmance on the authority of Feiner (US) *supra*. This record, then, shows no steps backward from a standard of "clear and present danger." But to say that the police may not intervene until the riot has occurred is like keeping out the doctor until the patient dies. I cannot subscribe to such a doctrine. . . .

I would affirm the convictions.

The "demonstration" has developed into a widely used weapon in the arsenal of peaceful protest. In many of its forms it is simply a variation of the old tool of the picket line. Since it has normally been used to protest a practice or custom much more widespread than the boundaries of a single company, however, and involves an attempt to change entire communities' practices, it carries with it more of the traditional aspects and justifications for considering it as an exercise of freedom of speech than do some of the more narrowly drawn picketing issues. Certainly the majority opinion in *Edwards* illustrates this interpretation. Justice Stewart said, "The circumstances in this case reflect an exercise of these basic constitutional rights in their most pristine and classic form." This is not to say that there is an absolute right to "demonstrate" in large crowds in any and every circumstance, but it is a clear warning that so long as the participants are not engaged in clearly unlawful conduct, the state must show a strong justification for any interference and the justification must be supported by the facts, subject to independent examination by the United States Supreme Court. The position was reiterated in *Henry* v. *Rock Hill*, 376 U.S. 776 (1964), reversing convictions for breach of the peace where there had been a peaceful assemblage at a city hall, with the participants carrying signs and singing songs to protest segregation and where no violence had occurred.

A touchier question was presented in the review of a conviction for picketing in front of a courthouse in Baton Rouge, Louisiana. The appellant Cox was convicted on three charges: (1) breach of the peace, (2) obstructing public passages, and (3) picketing before a courthouse. The charges were based on his conduct during a demonstration of some 2,000 Negro college students protesting racial discrimination. The convictions were separated into two appeals, the first, No. 24, dealing with the first two charges and the second, No. 49, dealing with the charge of picketing before the courthouse. The Court voted unanimously to reverse the convictions on the first charge of breach of the peace. While there was disagreement on the bases for reversal, most of the justices used reasoning similar to that in the *Edwards* case. Justice Black concurred on the ground that the breach of the peace statute on its face and as construed by the state courts was so broad as to be unconstitutionally vague. On the second charge the Court voted seven-to-two for reversal. *Cox* v. *Louisiana*, 379 U.S. 536 (1965). Justice Goldberg, for five members of the Court, held that the conviction for unlawfully obstructing public passages was an unwarranted abridgment of the leader's freedom of speech and assembly because the city authorities permitted or prohibited parades or street meetings in their completely uncontrolled discretion. He stated that, "Although the statute here involved on its face precludes all street assemblies and parades, it has not been so applied and enforced by the Baton Rouge authorities. City officials who testified for the state clearly indicated that certain meetings and parades are permitted in Baton Rouge, even though they have the effect of obstructing traffic, provided prior approval is obtained." Justices Black and Clark concurred on the separate ground that since the statute expressly permitted picketing for the publication of labor union views, to deny picketing for other free speech uses was forbidden by the "equal protection" clause of the Fourteenth Amendment. Justices White and Harlan dissented from the reversal of the conviction of obstructing public passages, stating that the statute had not been applied as an "open-ended licensing statute."

The appeal on the third charge of picketing before a courthouse is reported separately as *Cox v. Louisiana,* 379 U.S. 559 (1965), and the Court reversed by a vote of five-to-four. The conviction was for violations of a Louisiana statute which prohibited picketing or parading in or near a state court "with the intent of interfering with, obstructing or impeding the administration of justice, or with the intent of influencing any judge, juror, witness, or court officer, in the discharge of his duty." Justice Goldberg, speaking for the majority, denied appellant's contention that the statute was invalid on its face. He pointed out that the statute was modeled after an identical statute pertaining to the federal judiciary, passed by Congress in 1949 (64 Stat. 1018) and "unlike the two previously considered, is a precise, narrowly drawn regulatory statute which proscribes certain specific behavior." He stated further:

There can be no question that a State has a legitimate interest in protecting its judicial system from the pressures which picketing near a courthouse might create. Since we are committed to a government of laws and not of men, it is of the utmost importance that the administration of justice be absolutely fair and orderly. This Court has recognized that the unhindered and untrammeled functioning of our courts is part of the very foundation of our constitutional democracy. . . . The constitutional safeguards relating to the integrity of the criminal process attend every stage of a criminal proceeding, starting with arrest and culminating with a trial "in a courtroom presided over by a judge.". . . . There can be no doubt that they embrace the fundamental conception of a fair trial, and that they exclude influence or domination by either a hostile or friendly mob. There is no room at any stage of judicial proceedings for such intervention; mob law is the very antithesis of due process.

On the issue of abridgment of First Amendment rights the opinion stated:

Nor does such a statute infringe upon the constitutionally protected rights of free speech and free assembly. The conduct which is the subject of this statute—picketing and parading—is subject to regulation even though intertwined with expression and association.

The majority went on to find, further, that in applying the statute the state could properly arrest and convict for the kind of demonstration held in this instance—a protest gathering objecting to the arrest of a number of the students and held in the vicinity of the courthouse where the students' trials would take place and where the judges were located who would be trying the students' cases. Justice Goldberg made a distinction between regulations of "speech in its pristine form," such as newspaper comment or a telegram by a citizen to a public official, and "expression mixed with particular conduct." Noting that the case involved the latter form of expression, he concluded that appellant's argument that no clear and present danger was presented should be rejected on the ground that the legislature could properly have made a determination "based on experience that such conduct inherently threatens the judicial process."

Despite these statements in support of a general power to forbid what was done by the demonstrators in this case, however, the majority voted to reverse the convictions on the ground that prior permission was granted by the police and that the meeting did not acquire any illegal aspects afterward which would make refusal to obey a dispersal order a legitimate basis for arrest and conviction on the charge of picketing before a courthouse. The opinion pointed out that the demonstration took place on the far side of the street from the courthouse steps, and that the record showed that the officials present gave permission for Cox to conduct the demonstration at this point. This testimony "was corroborated by the State's witnesses themselves." Justice Goldberg said that "under all the circumstances of this case, after the public officials acted as they did, to sustain appellant's later conviction for demonstrating where they told him he could 'would be to sanction an indefensible sort of entrapment by the State— convicting a citizen for exercising a privilege which the State had clearly told him was available to him.' [*Raley* v. *Ohio*, 360 U.S. 423 (1959).] The 'due process' clause does not permit convictions to be obtained under such circumstances." He stated further:

This is not to say that had the appellant, entirely on his own, held the demonstration across the street from the courthouse within the sight and hearing of those inside, or *a fortiori*, had he defied an order of the police requiring him to hold this demonstration at some point further away out of the sight and hearing of those inside the courthouse, would we reverse the conviction as in this case. . . .

There remains just one final point: the effect of the Sheriff's order to disperse. The State in effect argues that this order somehow removed the prior grant of permission and reliance on the officials' construction that the demonstration on the far side of the street was not illegal as being "near" the courthouse. Appellant was led to believe that his demonstration on the far side of the street violated no statute. He was expressly ordered to leave, not because he was peacefully demonstrating too near the courthouse, nor because a time limit originally set had expired, but because officials erroneously concluded that what he said threatened a breach of the peace. . . . Appellant correctly conceived, as we have held in No. 24, 379 U.S. 536, that this was not a valid reason for the dispersal order. He therefore was still justified in his continued belief that because of the original official grant of permission he had a right to stay where he was for the few additional minutes required to conclude the meeting. In addition, even if we were to accept the State's version that the sole reason for terminating the demonstration was that appellant exceeded the narrow time limits set by the police, his conviction could not be sustained. Assuming the place of the meeting was appropriate—as appellant justifiably concluded from the official grant of permission—nothing in this courthouse statute, nor in the breach of the peace or obstruction of public passages statutes with their broad sweep and application that we have condemned in No. 24 authorizes the police to draw the narrow time line, unrelated to any policy of these statutes, that would be approved if we were to sustain appellant's conviction on this ground. Indeed, the allowance of such unfettered discretion in the police would itself constitute a procedure such as that condemned in No. 24. . . .

Of course this does not mean that the police cannot call a halt to a meeting which though originally peaceful, becomes violent. Nor does it mean that, under properly drafted and administered statutes and ordinances, the authorities cannot set reasonable time limits for assemblies related to the policies of such laws and then order them dispersed when these time limits are exceeded. . . . We merely hold that, under circumstances such as those present in this case, appellant's conviction cannot be sustained on the basis of the dispersal order.

Nothing we have said here or in No. 24 . . . is to be interpreted as sanctioning riotous conduct in any form or demonstrations, however peaceful their conduct or commendable their motives, which conflict with properly drawn statutes and ordinances designed to promote law and order, protect the community against disorder, regulate traffic, safeguard legitimate interests in private and public property, or protect the administration of justice and other essential governmental functions.

Four of the justices dissented in the second *Cox* case. Justice Black said, "I fail to understand how the Court can justify the reversal of these convictions because of a permission which testimony in the record denies was given, which could not have been authoritatively given anyway, and which even if given was soon afterwards revoked." He stated further:

Justice cannot be rightly administered, nor are the lives and safety of prisoners secure, where throngs of people clamor against the processes of justice right outside the courthouse or jailhouse doors. The streets are not now and never have been the proper place to administer justice. Use of the streets for such purposes has always proved disastrous to individual liberty in the long run, whatever fleeting benefits may have appeared to have been achieved. And minority groups, I venture to suggest, are the ones who always have suffered and always will suffer most when street multitudes are allowed to substitute their pressures for the less glamorous but more dependable and temperate processes of the law. Experience demonstrates that it is not a far step from what to many seems the earnest, honest, patriotic, kind-spirited multitude of today, to the fanatical, threatening, lawless mob of tomorrow. And the crowds that press in the streets for noble goals today can be supplanted tomorrow by street mobs pressuring the courts for precisely opposite ends.

Justice Clark, also dissenting, made a finding of facts different from that of the majority. He stated:

But the Court excuses Cox's brazen defiance of the statute—the validity of which the Court upholds—on a much more subtle ground. It seizes upon the acquiescence of the Chief of Police arising from the laudable motive to avoid violence and possible bloodshed to find that he made an on-the-spot administrative determination that a demonstration confined to the west side of St. Louis Street—101 feet from the courthouse steps—would not be "near" enough to the court building to violate the statute. It then holds that the arrest and conviction of appellant for demonstrating there constitutes an "indefensible sort of entrapment," citing *Raley* v. *Ohio*. . . .

With due deference, the record will not support this novel theory. . . .

... [T]he Chief testified that when Cox and the 2,000 Negroes approached him on the way to the courthouse that he was faced with a "situation that was accomplished." From the beginning they had been told not to proceed with their march; twice officers had requested them to turn back to the school; on each occasion they had refused. Finding that he could not stop them without the use of force the Chief told Cox that he must confine the demonstration to the west side of St. Louis Street across from the courthouse.

All the witnesses, including the appellant, state that the time for the demonstration was expressly limited.... [I]t is a novel construction of the facts to say that the grant of permission to demonstrate for a limited period of time was an administrative determination that the west side of the street was not "near" the courthouse ... The only way the Court can support its finding is to ignore the time limitation and hold—as it does *sub silentio*—that once Cox and the 2,000 demonstrators were permitted to occupy the sidewalk they could remain indefinitely.... This, I submit, is a complete frustration of the power of the State....

Nor can I follow the Court's logic when it holds that the case is controlled by *Raley* v. *Ohio, supra.* In *Raley* the petitioners whose convictions were reversed were told that they had a right to exercise their privilege and refuse to answer questions propounded to them in an orderly way during the conduct of a hearing.... Here the demonstrators were determined to go to the courthouse regardless of what the officials told them regarding the legality of their acts.... The demonstration, as I have previously noted, was a *fait accompli.* In view of these distinctions, I can see no enticement or encouragement by agents of the state sufficient to establish a *Raley*-type entrapment....

Reading the facts in a way most favorable to the appellant would, in my opinion, establish only that the Chief of Police consented to the demonstration at that location. However, if the Chief's action be consent, I never knew until today that a law enforcement official—city, state or national—could forgive a breach of the criminal laws. I missed that in my law school, in my practice and for two years while I was head of the Criminal Division of the Department of Justice.

[Justice White, joined by Justice Harlan, also dissented from the reversal of conviction on the picketing charge.]

The second *Cox* case is excerpted at some length to stress two points. First, the members of the Court indicated unanimity of opinion that the state may, under properly drawn statutes, regulate the time, place, duration, and manner of use of the streets for public assemblies, and may promote law and order, regulate traffic, safeguard legitimate interests in private and public property, and protect the administration of justice and other essential governmental functions. Such interests are sufficiently substantial to permit limitations on the exercise of even First Amendment rights, so long as the statutes are narrowly drawn to give fair notice of what is prohibited and to avoid grants of undue discretionary authority to officials administering the laws. Second, the Court will closely scrutinize the record in First Amendment cases and will make its own finding of the "facts" in the cases. And though there may be agreement on the law controlling the case, a particular set of circumstances described in the record below may lead to sharp disagreements among the members of the Court as to how the circumstances should be interpreted. [See *Gregory* v. *Chicago*, 394 U.S. 111 (1969), the "Note on War Protestors," and *Tinker* v. *Des Moines School District*, 393 U.S. 503 (1969) in Chap. 9.]

Picketing has been recognized as containing the elements of expression and communication since *Thornhill* v. *Alabama*, 310 U.S. 88 (1940). As the second *Cox* case indicated, however, this fact does not prevent appropriate restrictions on the place, purpose, and character of such picketing. The relevant cases on state regulations of picketing are reviewed by Justice Frankfurter in his opinion for the Court in *International Brotherhood of Teamsters* v. *Vogt*, decided in 1957.

INTERNATIONAL BROTHERHOOD OF TEAMSTERS *v.* VOGT
354 U.S. 284 (1957)

Mr. Justice Frankfurter delivered the opinion of the Court.

This is one more in the long series of cases in which this Court has been required to consider the limits imposed by the Fourteenth Amendment on the power of a State to enjoin picketing.... Respondent owns and operates a gravel pit in Oconomowoc, Wisconsin, where it employs 15 to 20 men. Petitioner unions sought unsuccessfully to induce some of respondent's employees to join the unions and commenced to picket the entrance to respondent's place of business with signs reading, "The men on this job are not 100 percent affiliated with the A.F.L." In consequence, drivers of several trucking companies refused to deliver and haul goods to and from respondent's plant, causing substantial damage to respondent. Respondent thereupon sought an injunction to restrain the picketing....

[The Wisconsin Supreme Court] held that "One would be credulous, indeed, to believe under the circumstances that the union had no thought of coercing the employer to interfere with its employees in their rights to join or refuse to join the defendant union." Such picketing, the court held, was for "an unlawful purpose," since Wis. Stat. Section 111.06 (2) (b) made it an unfair labor practice for an employee individually or in concert with others to "coerce, intimidate or induce any employer to interfere with any of his employees in the enjoyment of their legal rights ... or to engage in any practice with regard to his employees which would constitute an unfair labor practice if undertaken by him on his own initiative." Relying on *Building Service Employees International Union* v. *Gazzam*, 339 U.S. 532, and *Pappas* v. *Stacey*, 151 Me. 36, 116 A. 2d 497, the Wisconsin Supreme Court therefore affirmed the granting of the injunction....

Apart from remedying the abuses of the injunction in this general type of litigation, legislatures and courts began to find in one of the aims of picketing an aspect of communication. This view came to the fore in *Senn* v. *Tile Layers Protective Union*, 301 U.S. 468, where the Court held that the Fourteenth Amendment did not prohibit Wisconsin from authorizing peaceful stranger picketing by a union that was attempting to unionize a shop and to induce an employer to refrain from working in his business as a laborer.

Although the Court had been closely divided in the *Senn* case, three years later, in passing on a restrictive instead of a permissive state statute, the Court made sweeping pronouncements about the right to picket in holding unconstitutional a statute that had been applied to ban all picketing, with "no exceptions based upon

either the number of persons engaged in the proscribed activity, the peaceful character of their demeanor, the nature of their dispute with an employer, or the
restrained character and the accurateness of the terminology used in notifying the
public of the facts of the dispute." *Thornhill* v. *Alabama,* 310 U.S. 88. As the
statute dealt at large with all picketing, so the Court broadly assimilated peaceful
picketing in general to freedom of speech, and as such protected against abridgment
by the Fourteenth Amendment.

These principles were applied by the Court in *A.F. of L.* v. *Swing,* 312 U.S. 321,
to hold unconstitutional an injunction against peaceful picketing, based on a State's
common-law policy against picketing when there was no immediate dispute between
employer and employee. On the same day, however, the Court upheld a generalized
injunction against picketing where there had been violence because "it could
justifiably be concluded that the momentum of fear generated by past violence
would survive even though future picketing might be wholly peaceful." *Milk
Wagon Drivers Union* v. *Meadowmoor Dairies,* 312 U.S. 287, 294.

Soon, however, the Court came to realize that the broad pronouncements, but not
the specific holding, of *Thornhill* had to yield "to the impact of facts unforeseen,"
or at least not sufficiently appreciated. . . . Cases reached the Court in which a State
had designed a remedy to meet a specific situation or to accomplish a particular
social policy. These cases made manifest that picketing, even though "peaceful,"
involved more than just communication of ideas and could not be immune from all
state regulation. "Picketing by an organized group is more than free speech, since it
involves patrol of a particular locality and since the very presence of a picket line
may induce action of one kind or another, quite irrespective of the nature of the
ideas which are being disseminated." *Bakery and Pastry Drivers & Helpers* v. *Wohl,*
315 U.S. 769, 776 (concurring opinion) ; see *Carpenters & J. Union* v. *Ritter's Cafe,*
315 U.S. 722, 725–728.

These latter two cases required the Court to review a choice made by two States
between the competing interests of unions, employers, their employees, and the
public at large. In the *Ritter's Cafe* case, Texas had enjoined as a violation of its
antitrust law picketing of a restaurant by unions to bring pressure on its owner
with respect to the use of nonunion labor by a contractor of the restaurant owner
in the construction of a building having nothing to do with the restaurant. The
Court held that Texas could, consistent with the Fourteenth Amendment, insulate
from the dispute a neutral establishment that industrially had no connection with
it. This type of picketing certainly involved little, if any, "communication.". . .

The implied reassessments of the broad language of the *Thornhill* case were finally
generalized in a series of cases sustaining injunctions against peaceful picketing, even
when arising in the course of a labor controversy, when such picketing was counter
to valid state policy in a domain open to state regulation. The decisive reconsideration came in *Giboney* v. *Empire Storage & Ice Co.,* 336 U.S. 490. A union, seeking
to organize peddlers, picketed a wholesale dealer to induce it to refrain from selling
to nonunion peddlers. The state courts, finding that such an agreement would constitute a conspiracy in restraint of trade in violation of the state antitrust laws,
enjoined the picketing. This Court affirmed unanimously.

"It is contended that the injunction against picketing adjacent to Empire's place
of business is an unconstitutional abridgment of free speech because the picketers
were attempting peacefully to publicize truthful facts about a labor dispute. . . .
But the record here does not permit this publicizing to be treated in isolation. For

according to the pleadings, the evidence, the findings, and the argument of the appellants, the sole immediate object of the publicizing adjacent to the premises of Empire, as well as the other activities of the appellants and their allies, was to compel Empire to agree to stop selling ice to nonunion pedlers. Thus all of appellants' activities . . . constituted a single and integrated course of conduct, which was in violation of Missouri's valid law. In this situation, the injunction did no more than enjoin an offense against Missouri law, a felony.". . .

The Court therefore concluded that it was "clear that appellants were doing more than exercising a right of free speech or press. . . . They were exercising their economic power together with that of their allies to compel Empire to abide by union rather than by state regulation of trade.". . .

The following Term, the Court decided a group of cases applying and elaborating on the theory of *Giboney*. In *Hughes* v. *Superior Court of California*, 339 U.S. 460, the Court held that the Fourteenth Amendment did not bar use of the injunction to prohibit picketing of a place of business solely to secure compliance with a demand that its employees be hired in percentage to the racial origin of its customers. "We cannot construe the due process clause as prohibiting California from securing respect for its policy against involuntary employment on racial lines by prohibiting systematic picketing that would subvert such policy.". . . The Court also found it immaterial that the state policy had been expressed by the judiciary rather than by the legislature.

On the same day, the Court decided *International Brotherhood of Teamsters Union* v. *Hanke*, 339 U.S. 470, holding that a State was not restrained by the Fourteenth Amendment from enjoining picketing of a business, conducted by the owner himself without employees, in order to secure compliance with a demand to become a union shop. Although there was no one opinion for the Court, its decision was another instance of the affirmance of an injunction against picketing because directed against a valid public policy of the State. . . .

A similar problem was involved in *Local Union No. 10, United Association of Journeymen, Plumbers and Steamfitters* v. *Graham*, 345 U.S. 192, where a state court had enjoined, as a violation of its "Right to Work" law, picketing that advertised that nonunion men were being employed on a building job. This Court found that there was evidence in the record supporting a conclusion that a substantial purpose of the picketing was to put pressure on the general contractor to eliminate nonunion men from the job and, on the reasoning of the cases that we have just discussed, held that the injunction was not in conflict with the Fourteenth Amendment.

This series of cases, then, established a broad field in which a State, in enforcing some public policy, whether of its criminal or its civil law, and whether announced by its legislature or its courts, could constitutionally enjoin peaceful picketing aimed at preventing effectuation of that policy.

In the light of this background, the Maine Supreme Judicial Court in 1955 decided, on an agreed statement of facts, the case of *Pappas* v. *Stacey*, 151 Me. 36, 116 A.2d 497. From the statement, it appeared that three union employees went on strike and picketed a restaurant peacefully "for the sole purpose of seeking to organize other employees of the Plaintiff, ultimately to have the Plaintiff enter into collective bargaining and negotiations with the Union. . . ." Maine had a statute providing that workers should have full liberty of self-organization, free from restraint by employers or other persons. The Maine Supreme Judicial Court drew the inference from the agreed statement of facts that "there is a steady and exacting pressure upon the employer to interfere with the free choice of the employee in the matter of organization. To say that the picketing is not designed to bring about such action is to forget an obvious purpose of the picketing—to cause economic loss to the business during noncompliance by the employees with the request of the union." It therefore enjoined the picketing, and an appeal was taken to this Court. . . .

The *Stacey* case is this case. . . . The cases discussed above all hold that, consistent with the Fourteenth Amendment, a State may enjoin such conduct.

Of course, the mere fact that there is "picketing" does not automatically justify its restraint without an investigation into its conduct and purposes. State courts, no more than state legislatures, can enact blanket prohibitions against picketing. *Thornhill* v. *Alabama* . . . and *A.F. of L.* v. *Swing*. . . . The series of cases following *Thornhill* and *Swing* demonstrate that the policy of Wisconsin enforced by the prohibition of this picketing is a valid one. In this case, the circumstances set forth in the opinion of the Wisconsin Supreme Court afford a rational basis for the inference it drew concerning the purpose of the picketing. No question was raised here concerning the breadth of the injunction, but of course its terms must be read in the light of the opinion of the Wisconsin Supreme Court, which justifies it on the ground that the picketing was for the purpose of coercing the employer to coerce his employees. . . .

Affirmed.

Mr. Justice Whittaker took no part in the consideration or decision of this case.

Mr. Justice Douglas, with whom the Chief Justice and Mr. Justice Black concur, dissenting.

The Court has now come full circle. In *Thornhill* v. *Alabama* . . . we struck down a state ban on picketing on the ground that "the dissemination of information concerning the facts of a labor dispute must be regarded as within that area of free discussion that is guaranteed by the Constitution." Less than one year later, we held that the First Amendment protected organizational picketing on a factual record which cannot be distinguished from the one now before us. *A.F. of L.* v. *Swing*. . . . Of course, we have always recognized that picketing has aspects which make it more than speech. . . . That difference underlies our decision in *Giboney* v. *Empire Storage & Ice Co.* . . . . There picketing was an essential part of "a single and integrated course of conduct, which was in violation of Missouri's valid law.". . . Speech there was enjoined because it was an inseparable part of conduct which the State constitutionally could and did regulate.

But where, as here, there is no rioting, no mass picketing, no violence, no disorder, no fisticuffs, no coercion—indeed nothing but speech—the principles announced in *Thornhill* and *Swing* should give the advocacy of one side of a dispute First Amendment protection. . . .

Today, the Court signs the formal surrender. State courts and state legislatures cannot fashion blanket prohibitions on all picketing. . . . State courts and state legislatures are free to decide whether to permit or suppress any particular picket line for any reason other than a blanket policy against all picketing. I would adhere to the principle announced in *Thornhill*. I would adhere to the result reached in *Swing*. I would return to the test enunciated in *Giboney*—that this form of expression can be regulated or prohibited only to the extent that it forms an essential part of a course of conduct which the State can regulate or prohibit. I would reverse the judgment below.

State interference in labor disputes may, in addition to the Fourteenth Amendment issues of freedom of expression, raise jurisdictional issues under the National Labor Relations Act when the activity involves a business covered by that Act. In such instances the line of decisions holds that the Congress has the power to preempt the field, and, in the absence of violence necessitating action by the state, the NLRB must make the determination of whether it has exclusive competence to take jurisdiction. [See, for example, *San Diego Building Trades Council* v. *Garmon*, 359 U.S. 236 (1959), and *Guss* v. *Utah Labor Relations Board*, 353 U.S. 1 (1957), holding that if a business is one covered by the NLRA, the state is barred from resolving a labor dispute, even though a violation of the Act is alleged, and in the face of a decision by the NLRB to decline to handle the dispute because of the minimal amount of interstate business involved.] The enactment of the Landrum-Griffin amendments to the NLRA in 1959 was designed to clear up some of the jurisdictional problems between the state and the Board. [See Frank I. Michelman, "State Power to Govern Concerted Employee Activities," 74 *Harv. L. Rev.* 641 (1961).] Given the power of Congress to preempt the field, of course, the issues remaining in this area are statutory rather than constitutional.

SPECIAL ASPECTS OF FREEDOM OF PRESS

While the broader aspects of the topics previously discussed apply to all forms of expression—speech, press, and assembly—and thus have not been dealt with in their applications to isolated First Amendment rights, there are certain special problems which have arisen in connection with the press and other news media which require separate treatment. Among the foremost is that of reconciling the demands of a free press with the need for fair administration of justice. Another is the definition and proper treatment of obscene publications within the demands of the First Amendment. In addition there are problems of delineating the appropriate area of regulation of the press in its character as a normal commercial enterprise, and the application of state laws in such areas as libel and the regulation of distribution of handbills. Insofar as regulations may run afoul of the general interdiction against prior restraints, the earlier discussion of that rule in this chapter applies, as in the important free press case *Near* v. *Minnesota*. In general, this section will deal with the constitutional issues presented by some of the postpublication regulations or burdens on the various facets of the press.

FREE PRESS V. FAIR ADMINISTRATION OF JUSTICE

While a democratic society must accord a high place to the freedom of news media to inform the public, the right to a fair trial, both in civil and criminal cases, is entitled to no less regard. A conflict between these two values arises when newspaper or radio or television communications prior to a trial or during a trial are of such a nature as to threaten the impartiality of verdicts or sentences. The issue with respect to criminal cases has been dealt with to some extent in the earlier chapter on the rights of the accused.

Under his common-law powers the judge in Anglo-American courts has long had the power to punish for contempt persons who interfere with or obstruct the administration of justice. The application of this power to a newspaper, of course, raises First Amendment questions. In the companion cases of *Bridges* v. *California* and *Times-Mirror Company* v. *Superior Court of California,* 314 U.S. 252 (1941), the Court for the first time had occasion to review a state's exercise of the contempt power in punishing a publisher for statements appearing during the course of a trial. Justice Black, in his opinion for the Court, recited the facts:

The Los Angeles Times Editorials. The Times-Mirror Company, publisher of the Los Angeles Times, and L. D. Hotchkiss, its managing editor, were cited for contempt for the publication of three editorials. Both found by the trial court to be responsible for one of the editorials, the company and Hotchkiss were each fined $100. The company alone was held responsible for the other two, and was fined $100 more on account of one, and $300 more on account of the other.

The $300 fine presumably marks the most serious offense. The editorial thus distinguished was entitled "Probation for Gorillas?" After vigorously denouncing two members of a labor union who had previously been found guilty of assaulting nonunion truck drivers, it closes with the observation: "Judge A. A. Scott will make a serious mistake if he grants probation to Matthew Shannon and Kennan Holmes. This community needs the example of their assignment to the jute mill." Judge Scott had previously set a day (about a month after the publication) for passing upon the application of Shannon and Holmes for probation and for pronouncing sentence. . . .

The Bridges Telegram. While a motion for a new trial was pending in a case involving a dispute between an A.F. of L. union and a C.I.O. union of which Bridges was an officer, he either caused to be published or acquiesced in the publication of a telegram which he had sent to the Secretary of Labor. The telegram referred to the judge's decision as "outrageous"; said that attempted enforcement of it would tie up the port of Los Angeles and involve the entire Pacific Coast; and concluded with the announcement that the C.I.O. union, representing some twelve thousand members, did "not intend to allow state courts to override the majority vote of members in choosing its officers and representatives and to override the National Labor Relations Board."

Apparently Bridges' conviction is not rested at all upon his use of the word "outrageous." The remainder of the telegram fairly construed appears to be a statement that if the court's decree should be enforced there would be a strike. It is not claimed that such a strike would have been in violation of the terms of the decree, nor that in any other way it would have run afoul of the law of California. On no construction, therefore, can the telegram be taken as a threat either by Bridges or the union to follow an illegal course of action.

[By a five-to-four vote the Court reversed the contempt citations in both cases.

Justice Black, for the majority, examined and refuted the argument that "the power of judges to punish by contempt out-of-court publications tending to obstruct the orderly and fair administration of justice in a pending case was deeply rooted in English common law at the time the Constitution was adopted," and therefore the usual constitutional immunity guaranteed to other types of utterances could not be applied in this case. The opinion stated further:]

... [W]e are convinced that the judgments below result in a curtailment of expression that cannot be dismissed as insignificant. If they can be justified at all, it must be in terms of some serious substantive evil which they are designed to avert. The substantive evil here sought to be averted has been variously described below. It appears to be double: disrespect for the judiciary; and disorderly and unfair administration of justice. The assumption that respect for the judiciary can be won by shielding judges from published criticism wrongly appraises the character of American public opinion. For it is a prized American privilege to speak one's mind, although not always with perfect good taste, on all public institutions. And an enforced silence, however limited, solely in the name of preserving the dignity of the bench, would probably engender resentment, suspicion, and contempt much more than it would enhance respect.

The other evil feared, disorderly and unfair administration of justice, is more plausibly associated with restricting publications which touch upon pending litigation. The very word "trial" connotes decisions on the evidence and arguments properly advanced in open court. Legal trials are not like elections, to be won through the use of the meeting-hall, the radio, and the newspaper. But we cannot start with the assumption that publications of the kind here involved actually do threaten to change the nature of legal trials, and that to preserve judicial impartiality, it is necessary for judges to have a contempt power by which they can close all channels of public expression to all matters which touch upon pending cases. We must therefore turn to the particular utterances here in question and the circumstances of their publication to determine to what extent the substantive evil of unfair administration of justice was a likely consequence, and whether the degree of likelihood was sufficient to justify summary punishment.

[As to the *Times-Mirror* editorials, the opinion pointed out that from the past position of the paper on labor controversies there could have been little doubt of its attitude toward the probation of the two union members. Justice Black stated:]

In view of the paper's long-continued militancy in this field, it is inconceivable that any judge in Los Angeles would expect anything but adverse criticism from it in the event probation were granted. Yet such criticism after final disposition of the proceedings would clearly have been privileged. Hence, this editorial, given the most intimidating construction it will bear, did no more than threaten future adverse criticism which was reasonably to be expected anyway in the event of a lenient disposition of the pending case. To regard it, therefore, as in itself of substantial influence upon the course of justice would be to impute to judges a lack of firmness, wisdom, or honor, which we cannot accept as a major premise.

[The majority felt that there was no more danger of intimidation or interference with justice in the Bridges telegram than in the editorials and reversed the judgment in this case also.

Justice Frankfurter filed a long dissenting opinion, concurred in by Chief Justice Stone and Justices Roberts and Byrnes. He said, "A trial is not a 'free trade in ideas,' nor is the best test of truth in a courtroom 'the power of the thought to get itself accepted in the competition of the market.' " He continued:]

A court is a forum with strictly defined limits for discussion. It is circumscribed in the range of its inquiry and in its methods by the Constitution, by laws, and by age-old traditions. Its judges are restrained in their freedom of expression by historic compulsions resting on no other officials of government. They are so circumscribed precisely because judges have in their keeping the enforcement of rights and the protection of liberties which, according to the wisdom of the ages, can only be enforced and protected by observing such methods and traditions. . . .

It is suggested that threats, by discussion, to untrammeled decisions by courts are the most natural expressions when public feeling runs highest. But it does not follow that states are left powerless to prevent their courts from being subverted by outside pressure when the need for impartiality and fair proceeding is greatest. To say that the framers of the Constitution sanctified veiled violence through coercive speech directed against those charged with adjudications is not merely to make violence an ingredient of justice; it mocks the very ideal of justice by respecting its forms while stultifying its uncontaminated exercise.

The case illustrates the milder strictures employed in the United States against newspaper comment while a case is *sub judice*. In England the rule is much tighter, and the fines are apt to be far more severe. In 1949 the Lord Chief Justice fined the London *Daily Mirror* £10,000 and sentenced the editor to three months in jail for comments published concerning a murder trial then under way. [See Donald M. Gillmor, "Free Press and Fair Trial in English Law," 22 *Wash. & Lee L. Rev.* 17 (1965).] In the United States Supreme Court the cases indicate that the evidence supporting a contempt finding must point to a strong threat of subversion of justice before such a judgment will be upheld. In *Pennekamp* v. *Florida*, 328 U.S. 331 (1946), the publisher of the *Miami Herald* was fined for contempt for having published various editorials and a cartoon criticizing a local judge for interfering with the prosecutor's attempts to combat crime in the Miami area. The Supreme Court reversed. Even though some of the cases were still pending, the Court unanimously held that the criticism did not create a danger to fair judicial administration of the "clearness and immediacy necessary to close the doors of permissible public comment." And in *Craig* v. *Harney*, 331 U.S. 367 (1947), a divided Court held that publication, while a motion for a new trial was pending, of an unfair report of the facts of a civil case, accompanied by criticism of the judge for taking the case from the jury, was protected by the Constitution. The press called the action of the trial judge "arbitrary action" and a "travesty on justice." It deplored the fact that the elected judge was a "layman" and not a "competent attorney." The case dealt with an attempt by a property owner to evict a serviceman from business property for nonpayment of rent, and public opinion seemingly was strongly in favor of the serviceman. The jury had twice returned a verdict in his favor despite an instructed verdict for the

plaintiff. The motion for new trial followed the jury's third verdict in compliance with the judge's instruction. Subsequently the newspaper personnel
involved in the editorials and reports were adjudged guilty of contempt.
Justice Douglas, speaking for the majority voting to reverse, stated:

A judge who is part of such a dramatic episode can hardly help but know that
his decision is apt to be unpopular. But the law of contempt is not made for the
protection of judges who may be sensitive to the winds of public opinion. Judges
are supposed to be men of fortitude, able to thrive in a hardy climate. Conceivably
a campaign could be so managed and so aimed at the sensibilities of a particular
judge and the matter pending before him as to cross the forbidden line. But the
episodes we have here do not fall in that category. Nor can we assume that the trial
judge was not a man of fortitude.

[Justice Frankfurter, joined by Chief Justice Vinson, dissented, pointing out that
the newspapers involved were under common control and were the only papers of
general circulation in the area. He stated:]

It can hardly be a compelling presumption that such papers so controlled had
no influence, at a time when patriotic fervor was running high, in stirring up sentiment of powerful groups in a small community in favor of a veteran to whom, it
was charged, a great wrong had been done. It would seem a natural inference,
as the court below in effect found, that these newspapers whipped up public
opinion against the judge to secure reversal of his action and then professed merely
to report public opinion. We cannot say that the Texas Court could not properly
find that these newspapers asked of the judge, and instigated powerful sections of
the community to ask of the judge, that which no one has any business to ask
of a judge, except the parties and their counsel in open court, namely, that he
should decide one way rather than another.

[Justice Jackson dissented separately, saying:]

From our sheltered position, fortified by life tenure and other defenses to judicial
independence, it is easy to say that this local judge ought to have shown more
fortitude in the face of criticism. But he had no such protection. He was an elective
judge, who held for a short term. I do not take it that an ambition of a judge to
remain a judge is either unusual or dishonorable. Moreover, he was not a lawyer,
and I regard this as a matter of some consequence. A lawyer may gain courage to
render a decision that temporarily is unpopular because he has confidence that his
profession over the years will approve it, despite its unpopular reception, as has been
the case with many great decisions. But this judge had no anchor in professional
opinion. Of course, the blasts of these little papers in this small community do
not jolt us, but I am not so confident that we would be indifferent if a news
monopoly in our entire jurisdiction should perpetrate this kind of an attack on us.

The previous decisions have presented the problem of unusual pressures
on judges by newspapers to have them dispose of cases in particular ways.
A problem is also presented when pretrial publicity in criminal cases is
of such a nature as to threaten impartial decisions by jurors. The usual procedure for developing this issue is to appeal a conviction on the ground
that a fair trial was denied because of the prejudicial effect of the publicity.
In *Shepherd* v. *Florida,* 341 U.S. 50 (1951), this was one of the grounds

suggested in requesting a reversal of the conviction of four Negroes. The majority reversed, although the decision came off on the ground that discrimination had been practiced in the selection of the grand jury. Justices Frankfurter and Jackson, however, argued further that inflammatory newspaper comment made a fair trial in the community impossible.

Contempt proceedings have also been initiated against persons publishing prejudicial comment upon pending criminal cases. A Maryland trial court, in 1949, punished for contempt a broadcasting company which prior to a murder trial had announced that the person arrested had confessed to the crime, that he had a long criminal record, and that he went to the scene of the crime with officers, re-enacted the crime, and dug up the knife which he had used to commit the murder. The Maryland court of appeals reversed the contempt conviction on the basis of *Bridges, Pennekamp,* and *Craig.* The United States Supreme Court denied certiorari, *Maryland* v. *Baltimore Radio Show,* 338 U.S. 912 (1950), but Justice Frankfurter filed an opinion stressing the point that such denial should not be construed as approving the decision below. He set out in an appendix the course of English decisions dealing with situations in which publications were claimed to have injuriously affected the prosecutions for crime awaiting jury determination, and as to freedom of press in England cited the Report of the Royal Commission on the Press, Cmd. No. 7700, and the debate thereon in the House of Commons, July 28, 1949. (467 H.C. Deb., 5th Ser., 2683–2794)

In *Irvin* v. *Dowd,* 366 U.S. 717 (1961), the petitioner was indicted for murder in Indiana and was granted a change of venue to an adjoining county. His request for a second change of venue and a continuance, sought on the ground of local prejudice, was denied. He was convicted and sentenced to death. After lengthy litigation, the issue came to the United States Supreme Court on certiorari to review a denial of habeas corpus. By unanimous vote the Court vacated the judgment, holding that pretrial publicity had prejudiced the chances for a fair trial in the second county. Justice Clark's opinion for the Court states:

> Finally, and with remarkable understatement, the headlines reported that "impartial jurors are hard to find." The panel consisted of 430 persons. The court itself excused 268 of those on challenges for cause as having fixed opinions as to the guilt of petitioner. . . . An examination of the 2,783-page *voir dire* record shows that 370 prospective jurors or almost 90 percent of those examined on the point (10 members of the panel were never asked whether or not they had any opinion) entertained some opinion as to guilt—ranging in intensity from mere suspicion to absolute certainty. . . . With his life at stake, it is not requiring too much that petitioner be tried in an atmosphere undisturbed by so huge a wave of public passion and by a jury other than one in which two-thirds of the members admit, before hearing any testimony, to possessing a belief in his guilt.

A flagrant example of pretrial publicity is presented in *Rideau* v. *Louisiana,* 373 U.S. 73 (1963). Following a confession televised from a jail cell, Rideau moved for a change of venue. The motion was denied, and the defendant was tried, convicted, and sentenced to death for murder. On certiorari, the United States Supreme Court reversed, with the majority holding that due process required a trial before a jury drawn from a community of people who had not seen and heard the televised interview. The facts are recited in Justice Stewart's opinion for the Court:

[A] man robbed a bank in Lake Charles, Louisiana, kidnapped three of the bank's employees, and killed one of them. A few hours later the petitioner . . . was apprehended by the police and lodged in . . . jail in Lake Charles. The next morning a moving picture film with a sound track was made of an "interview" in the jail between Rideau and the Sheriff of Calcasieu Parish. This "interview" lasted approximately 20 minutes. It consisted of interrogation by the sheriff and admissions by Rideau that he had perpetrated the bank robbery, kidnapping, and murder. Later the same day the filmed "interview" was broadcast over a television station in Lake Charles, and some 24,000 people in the community saw and heard it on television. The sound film was again shown on television the next day to an estimated audience of 53,000 people. The following day the film was again broadcast by the same television station, and this time approximately 29,000 people saw and heard the "interview" on their television sets. Calcasieu Parish has a population of approximately 150,000 people. . . .

Three members of the jury which convicted him had stated on *voir dire* that they had seen and heard Rideau's televised "interview" with the sheriff on at least one occasion. . . . Rideau's counsel had requested that these jurors be excused for cause, having exhausted all of their peremptory challenges, but these challenges for cause had been denied by the trial judge.

[In holding the denial of the motion for change of venue and the subsequent trial unconstitutional, Justice Stewart stated:]

For anyone who has ever watched television the conclusion cannot be avoided that this spectacle, to the tens of thousands of people who saw and heard it, in a very real sense *was* Rideau's trial—at which he pleaded guilty to murder. Any subsequent court proceedings in a community so pervasively exposed to such a spectacle could be but a hollow formality.

Justices Clark and Harlan dissented on the ground that the record did not show that the adverse publicity "fatally infected the trial." On this basis they distinguished the case from *Irvin* v. *Dowd*.

The most vivid recent situation involving the clash between the freedom of the news media and the right of an accused to an impartial determination of his guilt took place following the assassination of President Kennedy in November 1963. A crime of such magnitude was bound to lead to enormous pressures on the police and prosecutor for even the most trivial piece of information concerning the assassin which could be transmitted by radio, television, and newspaper to people all over the world. And much that would be considered of an evidentiary nature was released to these media prior to and after the arrest of Lee Harvey Oswald. Had he not been murdered prior to the trial, a serious question would have been presented of whether the three days of saturation coverage precluded an impartial jury determination. The President's Commission on the Assassination took cognizance of this aspect of the events and in the official report, issued in 1964, stated as the last of twelve recommendations:

The commission recommends that the representatives of the bar, law enforcement associations, and the news media work together to establish ethical standards concerning the collection and presentation of information to the public so that there will be no interference with pending criminal investigations, court proceedings, or the right to a fair trial.

In 1965 the Court faced the issue of whether televising and broadcasting a criminal trial of considerable notoriety denied the accused due process of law. The case involved a state prosecution for swindling against Billie Sol Estes in Texas. At a pretrial hearing the defense moved to prevent telecasting, broadcasting by radio and news photography and also moved for a continuance. In a two-day hearing arguments were heard on these motions. These hearings were carried live by both radio and television, and news photography was permitted throughout. At least twelve cameramen were present, "cables and wires were snaked across the courtroom floor, three microphones were on the judge's bench and others were beamed at the jury box and the counsel table," as Justice Clark described the scene. A venire of jurymen had been summoned and was present in the courtroom during the entire hearing. The motion for continuance was granted. At the trial itself, a booth was constructed at the back of the courtroom with an aperture to permit cameramen an unrestricted view of the courtroom. All television cameras and newsreel photographers were restricted to the area of the booth when shooting film or telecasting. Live telecasting was permitted only for the opening and closing arguments of the state, the return of the jury's verdict, and its receipt by the trial judge. Videotapes of the entire proceeding without sound were permitted, however, although the cameras operated only intermittently. Estes was convicted, and the Texas Court of Criminal Appeals affirmed, over the claim of denial of due process under the Fourteenth Amendment because of the televising and broadcasting of proceedings.

By the narrow margin of five-to-four the Court reversed in *Estes* v. *Texas*, 381 U.S. 532 (1965), although the majority was divided on the applicable rule governing the televising and broadcasting of criminal trials. Thus the holding of the case is limited to the use of these media in trials of considerable notoriety. Justice Harlan, in a concurring opinion, indicated that he would not necessarily vote the same way in a trial less highly publicized and involving a "run-of-the-mill case."

The state argued that no prejudice had been shown by petitioner as a result of the televising and that the public has a right to know what goes on in the courts. Justice Clark, for the majority, responded that our system of law must prevent even the probability of unfairness, and even though "one cannot put his finger on its specific mischief and prove with particularity wherein he was prejudiced," it *may* cause prejudice to an accused. Add to this the fact that 48 of the states and the Federal Rules bar the use of television in the courtroom and the conclusion was that "its use would be inconsistent with our concepts of due process in this field."

As to the dangers, Justice Clark enumerated four potential threats to the fair administration of justice: (1) the distraction of jurors because of their self-consciousness and unease when being televised, (2) the impairment of the quality of testimony because of the witnesses' knowledge that they are being viewed by a vast audience, (3) the additional burden and responsibility placed on the trial judge because of the necessity for supervision of the telecasting, leading perhaps to the diversion of attention from the proper conduct of the trial, and (4) the impact of television on the defendant as a form of mental harassment. He stated further, "A defendant on trial for a specific crime is entitled to his day in court, not in a stadium, or a city or nationwide arena. The heightened public clamor resulting from radio and television coverage will inevitably result in prejudice."

Chief Justice Warren, joined by Justices Douglas and Goldberg, stated flatly that he believed "that it violates the Sixth Amendment for federal courts and the Fourteenth Amendment for state courts to allow criminal trials to be televised to the public at large." On the issue of guaranteeing a public trial, he stated that this requirement was met when "a courtroom has facilities for a reasonable number of the public to observe the proceedings, which facilities are not so small as to render the openness negligible and not so large as to distract the trial participants from their proper function, when the public is free to use these facilities, and when all those who attend the trial are free to report what they observed at the proceedings."

The dissenters in the case were unwilling to lay down a flat constitutional bar to televised criminal trials and stressed the point that no actual prejudice was proved in the case. They indicated that a lack of information on the effect of cameras in the courtroom should make the Court wary of a decision which would preclude intelligent assessment of the probable hazards involved in their use.

In an important decision in 1966, *Sheppard* v. *Maxwell*, the Court undertook to suggest some appropriate steps which trial judges should employ to safeguard against prejudicial reporting in criminal trials. The occasion was the review of proceedings at a notorious murder trial.

SHEPPARD *v.* MAXWELL

384 U.S. 333 (1966)

[Petitioner, accused of murdering his wife, was tried before a jury in the Court of Common Pleas of Cuyahoga County, Ohio. Both before and during the trial, which began two weeks before an election in which the trial judge and the chief prosecutor were candidates for judgeships, the petitioner was the subject of extensive newspaper, radio, and television publicity. The publicity included many matters unfavorable to the defendant which were never presented in court. The trial judge denied various requests by defense counsel for a continuance, change of venue, mistrial, and interrogation of the jurors as to their exposure to the publicity. During the trial, which lasted nine weeks, reporters were seated at a press table inside the bar, a few feet from the jury box, and most of the seats in the courtroom were filled with representatives of the news media. Radio broadcasting was done from a room next to the room where the jury recessed and deliberated. Courtroom proceedings which were supposed to be private were overheard and reported by the press, and the noise of newsmen moving in and out of the courtroom made it difficult for counsel and witnesses to be heard. The trial judge made no effort to control the release of leads, information, and gossip to the press by the prosecuting attorneys, the coroner, police officers, or witnesses. Petitioner was convicted of second degree murder. The Ohio Supreme Court affirmed, and the United States Supreme Court denied certiorari. Several years later, petitioner instituted habeas corpus proceedings in a federal district court, which held that he had been denied a fair trial and was entitled to be released. The Court of Appeals reversed. The Supreme Court granted certiorari.]

Mr. Justice Clark delivered the opinion of the Court. . . .

The principle that justice cannot survive behind walls of silence has long been reflected in the "Anglo-American distrust for secret trials.". . . A responsible press has always been regarded as the handmaiden of effective judicial administration, especially in the criminal field. Its function in this regard is documented by an impressive record of service over several centuries. The press does not simply publish information about trials but guards against the miscarriage of justice by subjecting the police, prosecutors, and judicial processes to extensive public scrutiny and criticism. This Court has, therefore, been unwilling to place any direct limitations on the freedom traditionally exercised by the news media for "[w]hat transpires in the court room is public property.". . .

But the Court has also pointed out that "[l]egal trials are not like elections, to be won through the use of the meeting-hall, the radio, and the newspaper.". . .

While we cannot say that Sheppard was denied due process by the judge's refusal to take precautions against the influence of pretrial publicity alone, the court's later rulings must be considered against the setting in which the trial was held. In light of this background, we believe that the arrangements made by the judge with the news media caused Sheppard to be deprived of that "judicial serenity and calm to which [he] was entitled.". . . The fact is that bedlam reigned at the courthouse during the trial and newsmen took over practically the entire courtroom, hounding most of the participants in the trial, especially Sheppard. . . .

The carnival atmosphere at trial could easily have been avoided since the courtroom and courthouse premises are subject to the control of the court. As we stressed in *Estes*, the presence of the press at judicial proceedings must be limited when it is apparent that the accused might otherwise be prejudiced or disadvantaged. Bearing in mind the massive pretrial publicity, the judge should have adopted stricter rules governing the use of the courtroom by newsmen, as Sheppard's counsel requested. The number of reporters in the courtroom itself could have been limited at the first sign that their presence would disrupt the trial. They certainly should not have been placed inside the bar. Furthermore, the judge should have more closely regulated the conduct of newsmen in the courtroom. For instance, the judge belatedly asked them not to handle and photograph trial exhibits lying on the counsel table during recesses.

Secondly, the court should have insulated the witnesses. All of the newspapers and radio stations apparently interviewed prospective witnesses at will, and in many instances disclosed their testimony. . . .

Thirdly, the court should have made some effort to control the release of leads, information, and gossip to the press by police officers, witnesses, and the counsel for both sides. Much of the information thus disclosed was inaccurate, leading to groundless rumors and confusion. . . . Under such circumstances, the judge should have at least warned the newspapers to check the accuracy of their accounts. And it is obvious that the judge should have further sought to alleviate this problem by imposing control over the statements made to the news media by counsel, witnesses, and especially the Coroner and police officers. The prosecution repeatedly made evidence available to the news media which was never offered in the trial. Much of the "evidence" disseminated in this fashion was clearly inadmissible. The exclusion of such evidence in court is rendered meaningless when a news media makes it available to the public. . . .

More specifically, the trial court might well have proscribed extrajudicial statements by any lawyer, party, witness, or court official which divulged prejudicial matters, such as the refusal of Sheppard to submit to interrogation or take any lie detector tests; any statement by Sheppard to officials; the identity of prospective witnesses or their probable testimony; any belief in guilt or innocence; or like statements concerning the merits of the case. . . . In addition, reporters who wrote or broadcasted prejudicial stories, could have been warned as to the impropriety of publishing material not introduced in the proceedings. . . .

From the cases coming here we note that unfair and prejudicial news comment on pending trials has become increasingly prevalent. Due process requires that the accused receive a trial by an impartial jury free from outside influences. Given the pervasiveness of modern communications and the difficulty of effacing prejudicial publicity from the minds of the jurors, the trial courts must take strong measures to ensure that the balance is never weighed against the accused. . . . Neither prosecutors, counsel for defense, the accused, witnesses, court staff nor enforcement officers coming under the jurisdiction of the court should be permitted to frustrate its function. Collaboration between counsel and the press as to information affecting the fairness of a criminal trial is not only subject to regulation, but is highly censurable and worthy of disciplinary measures.

. . . The case is remanded to the District Court with instructions to issue the writ and order that Sheppard be released from custody unless the State puts him to its charges again within a reasonable time.

It is so ordered.

Mr. Justice Black dissents.

[On the subject of fair trial and free press, see George D. Haimbaugh, Jr., "Free Press v. Fair Trial: The Contribution of Mr. Justice Frankfurter," 26 *U. Pitt. L. Rev.* 491 (1965); Carolyn Jaffe, "The Press and the Oppressed—A Study of Prejudicial News Reporting in Criminal Cases," 56 *J. Crim. L.* 1 (1965); Vermont Royster, "Free Press and a Fair Trial,"

43 *N.C.L. Rev.* 364 (1965); Symposium, "Free Press vs. Fair Trial," 41 *N. Dak. L. Rev.* 7, 156 (1964–65); Edward G. Hudon, "Freedom of the Press versus Fair Trial: the Remedy Lies with the Courts," 1 *Valparaiso U. L. Rev.* 8 (1966); A.B.A. Advisory Comm. on Fair Trial and Free Press, *Standards Relating to Fair Trial and Free Press, Tentative Draft* (New York: Institute of Judicial Administration, 1966); Hearings on S.290 before the Subcommittee on Constitutional Rights and the Subcommittee on Improvements in Judicial Machinery of the Senate Committee on the Judiciary, *Free Press and Fair Trial,* 89th Cong., 1st Sess. (1965); Association of the Bar of the City of New York, Special Committee on Radio, Television, and the Administration of Justice, *Freedom of the Press and Fair Trial: Final Report with Recommendations* (New York: Columbia University Press, 1967).]

Libel

In the past it has been commonplace to cite libelous and obscene publications as exceptions to the general rule of constitutional protection afforded the press. In more recent years, however, questions have been raised as to whether even these kinds of publications should necessarily be placed outside the pale of First Amendment protection. Justice Black, in a public interview quoted earlier [37 *N.Y.U.L. Rev.* 549 (1962)], stated that he had no doubt that the First Amendment intended that there should be no libel or defamation law in the United States, and that the Constitution was not intended "to authorize damage suits for mere words as distinguished from conduct."

The Court has not yet adopted the absolute protection argued for by Justice Black, but when the allegedly libelous statements are directed toward official conduct, the Court indicated in *New York Times Co.* v. *Sullivan,* 376 U.S. 254 (1964), that actual malice must be shown to support a judgment against the press. The importance of the case is indicated by the opening sentence in Justice Brennan's opinion for the Court: "We are required in this case to determine for the first time the extent to which the constitutional protections for speech and press limit a State's power to award damages in a libel action brought by a public official against critics of his official conduct."

The action was brought in Montgomery, Alabama, by a city commissioner of public affairs whose duties included the supervision of the police department. The action was brought against the *New York Times* for publication of a paid advertisement describing the mistreatment of Negro students protesting segregation in Montgomery, and also against four individuals whose names, among others, appeared in the advertisement. The advertisement stated in part:

In Montgomery, Alabama, after students sang "My Country, 'Tis of Thee" on the State Capitol steps, their leaders were expelled from school, and truckloads of police armed with shotguns and tear-gas ringed the Alabama State College Campus. When the entire student body protested to state authorities by refusing to re-register, their dining hall was padlocked in an attempt to starve them into sub-mission. . . .

Again and again the Southern violators have answered Dr. King's peaceful protests with intimidation and violence. They have bombed his home almost killing his wife and child. They have assaulted his person. They have arrested him seven times—for "speeding," "loitering" and similar "offenses." And now they have charged him with "perjury"—a *felony* under which they could imprison him for *ten years*. . . .

The respondent contended that both paragraphs accused the Montgomery police, and hence him, as the commissioner who supervised the police, of answering Dr. King's protests with intimidation and violence. Further, as Justice Brennan stated, "It is uncontroverted that some of the statements contained in the two paragraphs were not accurate descriptions of events which occurred in Montgomery." The campus dining hall was not pad-locked, the police did not "ring" the campus, although there were large numbers deployed near it, and Dr. King had been arrested only four times rather than seven, for example.

The jury awarded plaintiff damages of $500,000 against all defendants, and the judgment on the verdict was affirmed by the Supreme Court of Alabama on the grounds that the statements in the advertisement were libelous *per se,* false, and not privileged, and that the evidence showed malice on the part of the newspaper.

Justice Brennan's opinion for six members of the Court stated in part:

[W]e consider this case against the background of a profound national commit-ment to the principle that debate on public issues should be uninhibited, robust, and wide-open, and that it may well include vehement, caustic, and sometimes un-pleasantly sharp attacks on government and public officials. . . . The present adver-tisement, as an expression of grievance and protest on one of the major public issues of our time, would seem clearly to qualify for the constitutional protection. The question is whether it forfeits that protection by the falsity of some of its factual statements and by its alleged defamation of respondent.

Authoritative interpretations of the First Amendment guarantees have con-sistently refused to recognize an exception for any test of truth—whether admin-istered by judges, juries, or administrative officials—and especially one that puts the burden of proving truth on the speaker. . . . The constitutional protection does not turn upon "the truth, popularity, or social utility of the ideas and beliefs which are offered." *NAACP* v. *Button.* . . .

Injury to official reputation affords no more warrant for repressing speech that would otherwise be free than does factual error. Where judicial officers are involved, this Court has held that concern for the dignity and reputation of the courts does not justify the punishment as criminal contempt of criticism of the judge or his decision. . . . If judges are to be treated as "men of fortitude, able to thrive in a hardy climate," . . . surely the same must be true of other government officials, such as elected city commissioners. Criticism of their official conduct does not lose its constitutional protection merely because it is effective criticism and hence diminishes their official reputations.

If neither factual error nor defamatory content suffices to remove the constitutional shield from criticism of official conduct, the combination of the two elements is no less inadequate. . . .

The state rule of law is not saved by its allowance of the defense of truth. A defense for erroneous statements honestly made is no less essential here than was the requirement of proof of guilty knowledge which, in Smith v. California, . . . we held indispensable to a valid conviction of a bookseller for possessing obscene writings for sale. . . .

A rule compelling the critic of official conduct to guarantee the truth of all his factual assertions—and to do so on pain of libel judgments virtually unlimited in amount—leads to a . . . "self-censorship." . . . Under such a rule, would-be critics of official conduct may be deterred from voicing their criticism, even though it is believed to be true and even though it is in fact true, because of doubt whether it can be proved in court or fear of the expense of having to do so. . . . The rule thus dampens the vigor and limits the variety of public debate. It is inconsistent with the First and Fourteenth Amendments.

The constitutional guarantees require, we think, a federal rule that prohibits a public official from recovering damages for a defamatory falsehood relating to his official conduct unless he proves that the statement was made with "actual malice" —that is, with knowledge that it was false or with reckless disregard of whether it was false or not.

The Court then made an independent examination of the record and the opinion states, "[W]e consider that the proof presented to show actual malice lacks the convincing clarity which the constitutional standard demands, and hence that it would not constitutionally sustain the judgment for respondent under the proper rule of law." The case was remanded, however, "for further proceedings not inconsistent with this opinion." Justices Black, Douglas, and Goldberg concurred in the result, but felt that the immunity against libel actions should go further. Justice Goldberg's opinion stated that the constitutional protection "affords to the citizen and to the press an absolute, unconditional privilege to criticize official conduct despite the harm which may flow from excesses and abuses."

The rule of the New York Times case was followed in Garrison v. Louisiana, 379 U.S. 64 (1964), in reversing a conviction for criminal defamation. During a dispute with the judges of a criminal court of New Orleans, the district attorney for the parish held a press conference at which he attributed a large backlog of pending criminal cases to the inefficiency, laziness, and excessive vacations of the judges, and accused them of hampering his enforcement of the vice laws by refusing to authorize the expenses for the necessary investigations. The Court held that the New York Times rule limiting the awarding of civil damages in cases of alleged false criticism of public officials to instances of actual malice was also applicable to criminal sanctions for such criticism. [For more recent developments, see "Note on Libel" in Chap. 9.]

HANDBILL REGULATION AND "GREEN RIVER" ORDINANCES

The earlier cases involving restraints on the distribution of handbills were largely decided on the basis that such limitations constituted prior restraints on free speech and press. Justice Frankfurter gives a brief résumé of the cases in his concurring opinion in *Kunz* v. *New York,* 340 U.S. 290 (1951):

The easiest cases have been those in which the only interest opposing free communication was that of keeping the streets of the community clean. This could scarcely justify prohibiting the dissemination of information by handbills or censoring their contents. In *Lovell* v. *City of Griffin,* 303 U.S. 444 (1937), an ordinance requiring a permit to distribute pamphlets was held invalid where the licensing standard was "not limited to ways which might be regarded as inconsistent with the maintenance of public order or as involving disorderly conduct, the molestation of the inhabitants, or the misuse or littering of the streets.". . . In *Hague* v. *C.I.O.,* 307 U.S. 496 (1939), a portion of the ordinance declared invalid prohibited the distribution of pamphlets. In *Schneider* v. *New Jersey, Town of Irvington,* 308 U.S. 147 (1939), three of the four ordinances declared invalid by the Court prohibited the distribution of pamphlets. In *Jamison* v. *Texas,* 318 U.S. 413 (1943), the Court again declared invalid a municipal ordinance prohibiting the distribution of all handbills.

Other cases have dealt with regulations of commercial handbills and with an ordinance requiring that handbills disclose the name of the distributor. *Valentine* v. *Chrestensen,* 316 U.S. 52 (1942), is an illustration of the former. The respondent had printed a handbill advertising tours of a former navy submarine, which he owned, at a stated admission fee. He was told by the police commissioner that distribution of such a handbill would violate the city sanitary code which prohibited distribution of commercial and advertising matter in the streets. He was told that an exception was made for literature devoted to "information" or public matters. He then printed on the reverse side of his handbills a protest against the city dock department for refusing him wharfage facilities for the exhibition of his submarine. He was advised that this form still violated the ordinance and was restrained from distributing the handbills. The Court unanimously upheld the ordinance as applied to such handbills, clearly differentiating between the state's power to proscribe the dissemination of information and opinion and its power to regulate commercial advertising.

In *Talley* v. *California,* 362 U.S. 60 (1960), the Court reviewed the conviction of appellant who was convicted in a Los Angeles Municipal Court for violating a municipal ordinance making it a criminal offense to distribute "any handbill in any place under any circumstances," unless it had printed on it the names and addresses of the persons who prepared, distributed, or sponsored it. The Court divided six-to-three in reversing the conviction. Justice Black, speaking for the Court, found the ordinance void on its face, citing *Lovell* v. *Griffin.* Counsel for the state urged that the ordinance was aimed at providing a way to identify those responsible for fraud, false advertising, and libel. Justice Black stated, however, that "the ordinance is in no manner so limited, nor have we been referred to any legislative history indicating such a purpose." He stated further:

There can be no doubt that such an identification requirement would tend to restrict freedom to distribute information and thereby freedom of expression. . . .

Anonymous pamphlets, leaflets, brochures and even books have played an important role in the progress of mankind. Persecuted groups and sects from time to time throughout history have been able to criticize oppressive practices and laws either anonymously or not at all. . . .

We have recently had occasion to hold in two cases that there are times and circumstances when States may not compel members of groups engaged in the dissemination of ideas to be publicly identified. *Bates* v. *Little Rock* . . . ; *National Association for Advancement of Colored People* v. *Alabama*, . . . The reason for those holdings was that identification and fear of reprisal might deter perfectly peaceful discussions of public matters of importance. This broad Los Angeles ordinance is subject to the same infirmity. We hold that it, like the Griffin, Georgia, ordinance, is void on its face.

Justice Clark, joined by Justices Frankfurter and Whittaker, dissented. He pointed out that Talley had made no showing that a restraint upon his freedom of speech would result from the enforcement of the ordinance and concluded that "the substantiality of Los Angeles' interest in the enforcement of the ordinance sustains its validity." He also stated that the case was controlled by prior decisions in which "this Court has approved laws requiring no less than Los Angeles' ordinance:" one upholding an Act of Congress requiring newspapers using the second-class mails to publish the names of their editors, publishers, and owners; a second upholding the Federal Regulation of Lobbying Act requiring registration; and, third, the stated policy of a majority of states prohibiting the anonymous distribution of materials relating to candidates and elections.

"Green River" ordinances (so-called because of earlier adoption by the City of Green River, Wyoming) are those which prohibit various kinds of door-to-door solicitation without the prior permission of the householder. In *Martin* v. *Struthers*, 319 U.S. 141 (1943), a divided Court held that a municipality could not constitutionally prohibit a person from going from door to door knocking on doors and ringing doorbells for the purpose of distributing to the householder a handbill announcing a religious meeting. The community's interest in preventing crime and in assuring privacy in an industrial community where many residents worked night shifts and had to sleep during the day was held insufficient to justify the ordinance in the case of persons involved in religious communication by handbill. Justice Frankfurter filed a strong dissent stressing the need to recognize the householder's privacy.

In *Breard* v. *City of Alexandria*, 341 U.S. 622 (1951), however, the Court sustained a similar ordinance applying to various kinds of commercial solicitation. Appellant was a representative of Keystone Readers Service, Inc., and was arrested while going from door to door soliciting subscriptions for nationally known magazines. He argued that the ordinance was an abridgment of his freedom of speech and press. Justice Reed, speaking for the majority, stated:

... We agree that the fact that periodicals are sold does not put them beyond the protection of the First Amendment. The selling, however, brings into the transaction a commercial feature. ...

The case that comes nearest to supporting appellant's contention is *Martin* v. *Struthers*. ... There a municipal ordinance forbidding anyone summoning the occupants of a residence to the door to receive advertisements was held invalid as applied to the free distribution of dodgers "advertising a religious meeting." Attention was directed in note 1 of that case to the fact that the ordinance was not aimed "solely at commercial advertising." It was said: "The ordinance does not control anything but the distribution of literature, and in that respect it substitutes the judgment of the community for the judgment of the individual householder."

The decision to release the distributor was because: "Freedom to distribute information to every citizen wherever he desires to receive it is so clearly vital to the preservation of a free society that, putting aside reasonable police and health regulations of time and manner of distribution, it must be fully preserved."

There was dissent even to this carefully phrased application of the principles of the First Amendment. As no element of the commercial entered into this free solicitation and the opinion was narrowly limited to the precise fact of the free distribution of an invitation to religious services, we feel that it is not necessarily inconsistent with the conclusion reached in this case. ...

This makes the constitutionality of Alexandria's ordinance turn upon a balancing of the conveniences between some householders' desire for privacy and the publisher's right to distribute publications in the precise way that those soliciting for him think brings the best results. The issue brings into collision the rights of the hospitable housewife, peering on Monday morning around her chained door, with those of Mr. Breard's courteous, well-trained but possibly persistent solicitor, offering a bargain on culture and information through a joint subscription to *Satevepost, Pic* and *Today's Woman*. ...

... We think those communities that have found these methods of sale obnoxious may control them by ordinance. ... We see no abridgment of the principles of the First Amendment in this ordinance.

[Justice Black, joined by Justice Douglas, dissented. He stated:]

Today's decision marks a revitalization of the judicial views which prevailed before this Court embraced the philosophy that the First Amendment gives a preferred status to the liberties it protects. I adhere to that preferred position philosophy. It is my belief that the freedom of the people of this Nation cannot survive even a little governmental hobbling of religious or political ideas, whether they be communicated orally or through the press.

The constitutional sanctuary for the press must necessarily include liberty to publish and circulate. In view of our economic system, it must also include freedom to solicit paying subscribers. Of course homeowners can if they wish forbid newsboys, reporters or magazine solicitors to ring their doorbells. But when the homeowner himself has not done this, I believe that the First Amendment ... bars laws like the present ordinance which punish persons who peacefully go from door to door as agents of the press.

MISCELLANEOUS REGULATIONS APPLICABLE TO THE PRESS

While the press is accorded special protection under the First and Fourteenth Amendments, newspapers are not for this reason exempt from all ordinary regulatory measures fairly applied by state or national governments. Newspapers are, after all, commercial enterprises and may be subjected to normal governmental restraints generally applicable to other business operations. The crucial test in any given case is whether the regulation was adopted as a device to limit the freedom of the press.

Newspapers are liable for ordinary taxes, but may a tax be exacted as punishment of newspapers for political opposition? This was the issue in *Grosjean* v. *American Press Co.*, 297 U.S. 233 (1936). In 1934 the Louisiana legislature, dominated by Huey Long, imposed a tax of 2 percent of gross receipts on all newspapers in the state with a circulation of more than 20,000 copies a week. Thirteen newspapers, all hostile to Long, were affected by the tax, while there were four other daily papers and some 120 weekly newspapers, favorable to Long, which were not subject to the tax. Justice Sutherland, speaking for a unanimous Court, examined the pattern of British taxation of newspapers in the eighteenth and nineteenth centuries, remarking that "These duties were quite commonly characterized as 'taxes on knowledge,' a phrase used for the purpose of describing the effect of the exactions and at the same time condemning them." He concluded that the First and Fourteenth Amendments were meant to bar taxes imposed to restrict the free flow of information.

It is not intended by anything we have said to suggest that the owners of newspapers are immune from any of the ordinary forms of taxation for support of the government. But this is not an ordinary form of tax, but one single in kind, with a long history of hostile misuse against the freedom of the press.

The predominant purpose of the grant of immunity here invoked was to preserve an untrammeled press as a vital source of public information. . . . The tax here involved is bad not because it takes money from the pockets of the appellees. If that were all, a wholly different question would be presented. It is bad because, in the light of its history and of its present setting, it is seen to be a deliberate and calculated device in the guise of a tax to limit the circulation of information to which the public is entitled in virtue of the constitutional guaranties. A free press stands as one of the great interpreters between the government and the people. To allow it to be fettered is to fetter ourselves.

In view of the persistent search for new subjects of taxation, it is not without significance that, with the single exception of the Louisiana statute, so far as we can discover, no state during the one hundred fifty years of our national existence has undertaken to impose a tax like that now in question.

The form in which the tax is imposed is in itself suspicious. It is not measured or limited by the volume of advertisements. It is measured alone by the extent of the circulation of the publication in which the advertisements are carried, with the plain purpose of penalizing the publishers and curtailing the circulation of a selected group of newspapers.

Having reached the conclusion that the act imposing the tax in question is unconstitutional under the due process of law clause because it abridges the freedom of the press, we deem it unnecessary to consider the further ground assigned that it also constitutes a denial of the equal protection of the laws.

Several national regulations adopted under the commerce power have been successfully applied to the press against claims of First Amendment violation. In *The Associated Press* v. *National Labor Relations Board*, 301 U.S. 103 (1937), the Court held that the National Labor Relations Act could be applied to the newspaper business just as it could to other business enterprises in interstate commerce. The case arose after the Board had ordered the reinstatement of a copy editor for the Associated Press who had been fired for attempting to organize a union. The Court said, "The publisher of a newspaper has no special immunity from the application of general laws. . . . The regulation here in question has no relation whatever to the impartial distribution of news."

A similar holding obtained in *Oklahoma Press Publishing Co.* v. *Walling*, 327 U.S. 186 (1946), in which a newspaper publisher was held subject to the provisions of the Fair Labor Standards Act. And in *Associated Press* v. *United States*, 326 U.S. 1 (1945), it was held that the Sherman Antitrust Act could constitutionally be applied to newspapers, and for the Associated Press to enforce its bylaws severely restricting competition was an unreasonable restraint of trade in violation of the Act. Justice Black, for the majority, said, "The First Amendment affords not the slightest support for the contention that a combination to restrain trade in news and views has any constitutional immunity."

OBSCENITY AND PORNOGRAPHY

Earlier forms of censorship were primarily concerned with stamping out heresy or sedition. More recently, while considerations of security are important, the principal impetus for control of publications and movies is a concern for morality and the prohibition of obscenity. The common-law crime of "obscene libel" developed in England in the early part of the eighteenth century. The established rule of the old common law received its formulation in the opinion of Chief Justice Cockburn in the case of *Regina* v. *Hicklin* (1868), L.R. 3 Q. B. 360. The case dealt with a pamphlet purporting to describe the morals—or lack of morals—of Catholic priests in connection with the confessional. The long title was *The Confessional Unmasked: showing the depravity of the Roman Priesthood, the iniquity of the Confessional and the questions put to females in confession*. It was printed and circulated at cost by an anti-Catholic group which had as its main purpose the election of Protestants to Parliament. The case involved a request for a destruction order, rather than a prosecution, and in allowing the order the Chief Justice laid down the test for obscenity:

> I think the test of obscenity is this, whether the tendency of the matter charged as obscenity is to deprave and corrupt those whose minds are open to such immoral influences, and into whose hands a publication of this sort may fall.

This rule has apparently been followed by the English courts down to the enactment of the Obscene Publications Act of 1959, which changed "tendency" to "effect" and omitted the application to "those whose minds are open to such immoral influences." [On the English law generally, see Norman St. John-Stevas, *Obscenity and the Law* (New York: Macmillan, 1956) and John Chandos, editor, *To Deprave and Corrupt* (New York: Association Press, 1962).]

The objection to the Hicklin test, of course, is that it fixes a standard for the community's reading matter geared to the feeblest mentality or most suggestible individual in the community. While the test may have been followed to some extent by American judges, it was explicitly rejected in 1933 by federal judge John Woolsey in *United States* v. *One Book Called Ulysses,* 5 F. Supp. 182 (1933), a case involving a customs official's denial of entry of James Joyce's *Ulysses.* [*Aff'd.* 72 F. 2d 705 (1934) by Judges Augustus N. and Learned Hand.] Since then American judges have preferred to use as a standard of judgment the effect of the book upon normal, average, healthy persons.

The United States Supreme Court made a historic decision in 1957 when it ruled squarely for the first time on the subject of the censorship of books. The case was *Butler* v. *Michigan,* 352 U.S. 380 (1957). The state statute made it a misdemeanor to sell to the *general reading public* any obscene book, "tending to incite minors to violent or depraved or immoral acts," or "tending to the corruption of the morals of youth." The appellant was convicted of violating the statute by selling a copy of a paper-bound reprint of John Griffin's *The Devil Rides Outside.*

The Court unanimously voted to set aside the conviction. Justice Frankfurter, for the Court, stated:

> The State insists that, by thus quarantining the general reading public against books not too rugged for grown men and women in order to shield juvenile innocence, it is exercising its power to promote the general welfare. Surely, this is to burn the house to roast the pig. . . . We have before us legislation not reasonably restricted to the evil with which it is said to deal. The incidence of this enactment is to reduce the adult population of Michigan to reading only what is fit for children.

At the same term of Court, and also for the first time, the problem of legislative control of publications alleged to be obscene was considered. The opinion was written jointly for the companion cases of *Roth* v. *United*

States and *Alberts* v. *California,* 354 U.S. 476 (1957). Roth was convicted in a federal court of violating the federal statute which forbids the mailing of obscene literature, by sending a publication called *American Aphrodite.* Alberts was convicted for advertising such books as *Sword of Desire, She Made It Pay,* and *The Business Side of the Oldest Business,* in violation of a California law which forbids the writing, publishing, or selling of obscene books.

ROTH *v.* UNITED STATES

ALBERTS *v.* CALIFORNIA

354 U.S. 476 (1957)

Mr. Justice Brennan delivered the opinion of the Court....

The dispositive question is whether obscenity is utterance within the area of protected speech and press.* Although this is the first time the question has been squarely presented to this Court, either under the First Amendment or under the Fourteenth Amendment, expressions found in numerous opinions indicate that this Court has always assumed that obscenity is not protected by the freedoms of speech and press....

The guaranties of freedom of expression in effect in 10 of the 14 States which by 1792 had ratified the Constitution, gave no absolute protection for every utterance. Thirteen of the 14 States provided for the prosecution of libel, and all of those States made either blasphemy or profanity, or both, statutory crimes. As early as 1712, Massachusetts made it criminal to publish "any filthy, obscene, or profane song, pamphlet, libel or mock sermon" in imitation or mimicking of religious services.... Thus, profanity and obscenity were related offenses.

In light of this history, it is apparent that the unconditional phrasing of the First Amendment was not intended to protect every utterance.... At the time of the adoption of the First Amendment, obscenity law was not as fully developed as libel law, but there is sufficiently contemporaneous evidence to show that obscenity, too, was outside the protection intended for speech and press....

All ideas having even the slightest redeeming social importance—unorthodox ideas, controversial ideas, even ideas hateful to the prevailing climate of opinion—have the full protection of the guaranties, unless excludable because they encroach upon the limited area of more important interests. But implicit in the history of the First Amendment is the rejection of obscenity as utterly without redeeming social importance. This rejection for that reason is mirrored in the universal judgment that obscenity should be restrained, reflected in the international agreement of over 50 nations,** in the obscenity laws of all of the 48 States, and in the 20 obscenity laws enacted by the Congress from 1842 to 1956.... We hold that obscenity is not within the area of constitutionally protected speech or press.

It is strenuously urged that these obscenity statutes offend the constitutional guaranties because they punish incitation to impure sexual *thoughts,* not shown to be related to any overt antisocial conduct which is or may be incited in the persons stimulated to such *thoughts....*

However, sex and obscenity are not synonymous. Obscene material is material

---

* No issue is presented in either case concerning the obscenity of the material involved.

** Agreement for the Suppression of the Circulation of Obscene Publications, 37 stat. 1511; Treaties in Force 209 (U.S. Department State, October 31, 1956).

which deals with sex in a manner appealing to prurient interest.* * * The portrayal of sex, *e.g.*, in art, literature and scientific works, is not itself sufficient reason to deny material the constitutional protection of freedom of speech and press. Sex, a great and mysterious motive force in human life, has indisputably been a subject of absorbing interest to mankind through the ages; it is one of the vital problems of human interest and public concern. . . .

The early leading standard of obscenity allowed material to be judged merely by the effect of an isolated excerpt upon particularly susceptible persons. *Regina* v. *Hicklin* [1868] L.R. 3 Q.B. 360. Some American courts adopted this standard but later decisions have rejected it and substituted this test: whether to the average person, applying contemporary community standards, the dominant theme of the material taken as a whole appeals to prurient interest. The *Hicklin* test, judging obscenity by the effect of isolated passages upon the most susceptible persons, might well encompass material legitimately treating with sex, and so it must be rejected as unconstitutionally restrictive of the freedoms of speech and press. On the other hand, the substituted standard provides safeguards adequate to withstand the charge of constitutional infirmity. . . .

It is argued that the statutes do not provide reasonably ascertainable standards of guilt and therefore violate the constitutional requirements of due process. . . .

Many decisions have recognized that these terms of obscenity statutes are not precise. This Court, however, has consistently held that lack of precision is not itself offensive to the requirements of due process. . . . These words [obscene, lewd, lascivious, or filthy or indecent], applied according to the proper standard for judging obscenity, already discussed, give adequate warning of the conduct proscribed and mark ". . . boundaries sufficiently distinct for judges and juries fairly to administer the law.". . .

[Chief Justice Warren concurred in the result.]

[Justice Harlan concurred in *Alberts* and dissented in *Roth*. He stated that "Congress has no substantive power over sexual morality," and such powers as the federal government has in this field are insufficient to support a statute so broadly phrased as to reach the transmission of books which, under the judge's charge "tend to stir sexual impulses and lead to sexually impure thoughts." He stated further that he did not think the federal statute could be constitutionally construed to reach other than "what the Government has termed as 'hard-core' pornography."]

Mr. Justice Douglas, with whom Mr. Justice Black concurs, dissenting.

When we sustain these convictions, we make the legality of a publication turn on the purity of thought which a book or tract instills in the mind of the reader. I do not think we can approve that standard and be faithful to the command of the First Amendment, which by its terms is a restraint on Congress and which by the Fourteenth is a restraint on the States. . . .

By these standards punishment is inflicted for thoughts provoked, not for overt

* * * *I.e.*, material having a tendency to excite lustful thoughts. . . .

We perceive no significant difference between the meaning of obscenity developed in the case law and the definition of the A.L.I., Model Penal Code, Section 207.10 (2) (Tent. Draft No. 6, 1957), *viz.*:

". . . A thing is obscene if, considered as a whole, its predominant appeal is to prurient interest, i.e., a shameful or morbid interest in nudity, sex, or excretion, and if it goes substantially beyond customary limits of candor in description or representation of such matters. . . ." . . .

acts nor antisocial conduct. This test cannot be squared with our decisions under the First Amendment. . . . This issue cannot be avoided by saying that obscenity is not protected by the First Amendment. The question remains what is the constitutional test of obscenity?

The tests by which these convictions were obtained require only the arousing of sexual thoughts. Yet the arousing of sexual thoughts and desires happens every day in normal life in dozens of ways. Nearly 30 years ago a questionnaire sent to college and normal school women graduates asked what things were most stimulating sexually. Of 409 replies, 9 said "music"; 18 said "pictures"; 29 said "dancing"; 40 said "drama"; 95 said "books"; and 218 said "man." Alpert, Judicial Censorship of Obscene Literature, 52 Harv. L. Rev. 40, 73 . . . .

If we were certain that impurity of sexual thoughts impelled to action, we would be on less dangerous ground in punishing the distributors of this sex literature. But it is by no means clear that obscene literature, as so defined, is a significant factor in influencing substantial deviations from the community standards. . . .

The absence of dependable information on the effect of obscene literature on human conduct should make us wary. It should put us on the side of protecting society's interest in literature, except and unless it can be said that the particular publication has an impact on action that the government can control.

As noted, the trial judge in the *Roth* case charged the jury in the alternative that the federal obscenity statute outlaws literature dealing with sex which offends "the common conscience of the community." That standard is, in my view, more inimical still to freedom of expression.

. . . Certainly that standard would not be an acceptable one if religion, economics, politics or philosophy were involved. How does it become a constitutional standard when literature treating with sex is concerned?

Any test that turns on what is offensive to the community's standards is too loose, too capricious, too destructive of freedom of expression to be squared with the First Amendment. Under that test, juries can censor, suppress what they don't like, provided the matter relates to "sexual impurity" or has a tendency "to excite lustful thoughts." This is community censorship in one of its worst forms. It creates a regime where in the battle between the literati and the Philistines, the Philistines are certain to win. If experience in this field teaches anything, it is that "censorship of obscenity has almost always been both irrational and indiscriminate.". . .

I would give the broad sweep of the First Amendment full support. I have the same confidence in the ability of our people to reject noxious literature as I have in their capacity to sort out the true from the false in theology, economics, politics, or any other field.

It seems clear that the majority in *Roth* was trying to set out a rule which would afford substantial protection to speech and press against attempts at censorship. It seems equally clear that the rule is not particularly helpful except in its requirements that the work be considered as a whole and that its effect be judged by the standard of the average person rather than the abnormal reader. There are still problems of determining what contemporary community standards are and what is meant by "appeals to prurient interest." [On the problems of definition, see two articles by William Lockhart and Robert McClure, "Censorship of Obscenity: The Developing Constitutional Standards," 45 *Minn. L. Rev.* 5 (1960), and "Obscenity Censorship: The Core Constitutional Issue—What Is Obscene?", 7 *Utah L. Rev.* 289 (1961).]

The difficulties in applying the *Roth* rule are well illustrated in the variety of opinions filed in *Jacobellis* v. *Ohio,* 378 U.S. 184 (1964). The manager of a motion picture theater in Ohio was convicted of violating an Ohio obscenity statute by possessing and exhibiting a French film entitled *The Lovers.* As Justice Brennan described it, the film "involves a woman bored with her life and marriage who abandons her husband and family for a young archaeologist with whom she has suddenly fallen in love. There is an explicit love scene in the last reel of the film, and the state's objections are based almost entirely upon that scene." The Court divided six-to-three in reversing the conviction, but the majority were unable to agree on an opinion. There were three separate opinions for the members voting to reverse and two for the dissenters.

Justice Brennan, joined by Justice Goldberg, first stated that a jury's verdict on the issue of obscenity could not be conclusive on the Court since the question "necessarily implicates an issue of constitutional law." He stated:

The suggestion is appealing, since it would lift from our shoulders a difficult, recurring, and unpleasant task. But we cannot accept it. Such an abnegation of judicial supervision in this field would be inconsistent with our duty to uphold the constitutional guarantees....

In other areas involving constitutional rights under the Due Process Clause, the Court has consistently recognized its duty to apply the applicable rules of law upon the basis of an independent review of the facts of each case....

He reiterated the *Roth* statement that the reason that obscenity can be proscribed is that it is utterly without redeeming social importance. The corollary of this, he said, was that material dealing with sex in a manner that advocates ideas or that has literary or scientific or artistic value or any other form of social importance may not be branded as obscenity and denied the constitutional protection.

As to the aspect of the *Roth* rule calling for testing obscenity by "contemporary community standards," Justices Brennan and Goldberg argued that "the constitutional status of an allegedly obscene work must be determined on the basis of a national standard." They could see no justification for allowing the constitutional limits for defining obscenity "to vary with town or county lines."

Justice Black, joined by Justice Douglas, concurred in the reversal, but took an absolutist stand against censorship. He stated:

My reason for reversing is that I think the conviction of appellant or anyone else for exhibiting a motion picture abridges freedom of the press as safeguarded by the First Amendment, which is made obligatory on the States by the Fourteenth.

[Justice Stewart concurred, but gave yet another view of the area of constitutional exclusion. He stated:]

I have reached the conclusion, which I think is confirmed at least by negative implication in the Court's decisions since *Roth* and *Alberts*, that under the First and Fourteenth Amendments criminal laws in this area are constitutionally limited to hard-core pornography. I shall not today attempt further to define the kinds of material I understand to be embraced within that shorthand description; and perhaps I could never succeed in intelligibly doing so. But I know it when I see it, and the motion picture involved in this case is not that.

[Justice White concurred without opinion.]

[Chief Justice Warren, joined by Justice Clark, dissented. He stated:]

For all the sound and fury that the *Roth* test has generated, it has not been proved unsound, and I believe that we should try to live with it—at least until a more satisfactory definition is evolved. . . .

It is my belief that when the Court said in *Roth* that obscenity is to be defined by reference to "community standards," it meant community standards—not a national standard, as is sometimes argued. I believe that there is no provable "national standard," and perhaps there should be none. At all events, this Court has not been able to enunciate one, and it would be unreasonable to expect local courts to divine one. It is said that such a "community" approach may well result in material being proscribed as obscene in one community but not in another, and, in all probability, that is true. But communities throughout the Nation are in fact diverse, and it must be remembered that, in cases such as this one, the Court is confronted with the task of reconciling rights of the diverse communities within our society and of individuals.

We are told that only "hard core pornography" should be denied the protection of the First Amendment. But who can define "hard core pornography" with any greater clarity than "obscenity"? . . .

In my opinion, the use to which the various materials are put—not just the words and pictures themselves—must be considered in determining whether or not the materials are obscene. A technical or legal treatise on pornography may well be inoffensive under most circumstances but, at the same time, "obscene" in the extreme when sold or displayed to children. . . .

In light of the foregoing, I would reiterate my acceptance of the rule of the *Roth* case. . . . However, protection of society's right to maintain its moral fiber and the effective administration of justice require that this Court not establish itself as an ultimate censor, in each case reading the entire record, viewing the accused material, and making an independent *de novo* judgment on the question of obscenity. Therefore, once a finding of obscenity has been made below under a proper application of the *Roth* test, I would apply a "sufficient evidence" standard of review—requiring something more than merely any evidence but something less than "substantial evidence on the record [including the allegedly obscene material] as a whole." . . .

Justice Harlan, dissenting, repeated the view, stated in dissent in *Roth*, that two different tests should be employed in determining "what is bannable on the score of obscenity" by the federal and state governments. He suggested that the *Roth* test should be used "in holding the Federal Government with a tight rein," while the states should be permitted greater latitude.

The diversity of views expressed by the members of the Court on the proper definition and delineation of the Court's function in reviewing obscenity cases underlines the need for caution in attempting a generalized rule in such cases. In the light of the procedure employed by the Court in such review—reading the books or viewing the films under attack—the present attitude of the majority may after all be not too far from that expressed by Justice Stewart with reference to pornography: perhaps he couldn't define it, "but I know it when I see it."

Whatever may be the definition, "hard-core pornography" appears to be the type of literature and films which the majority of the Court will agree to have banned. In two *per curiam* decisions, for example, the Court reversed without opinion the decisions of two separate United States Courts of Appeals which had upheld trial court findings that certain magazines were obscene and therefore nonmailable. *One, Inc.* v. *Olesen, Postmaster of Los Angeles*, 355 U.S. 371 (1958), held to be mailable (and thus presumably not obscene) the magazine *One—The Homosexual Magazine*, which appeared to the trial court to have been written to appeal to the tastes and interests of homosexuals. A similar holding obtained in *Sunshine Book Company* v. *Summerfield*, 355 U.S. 372 (1958), concerning the mailability of *Sunshine and Health*, a nudist magazine which the trial court had found obscene because of its photographs showing male and female nudes in excessive detail. In each case the Court merely cited *Roth* v. *United States* in reversing.

A recent gloss was added to the law of obscenity in two decisions in 1966. In *Ginzburg* v. *United States*, 383 U.S. 463 (1966), defendants challenged their convictions for having violated the federal obscenity statute by using the mail for distributing allegedly obscene literature—namely, the magazine *Eros*, containing articles and photo essays on love and sex; a biweekly newsletter, dedicated to "keeping sex an art and preventing it from becoming a science"; and "The Housewife's Handbook on Promiscuity." On certiorari, the Supreme Court by a five-to-four vote affirmed the convictions. In so holding, the majority stated that even though the publications, standing alone, might not be obscene, the question of obscenity "may include consideration of the setting in which the publications were presented as an aid to determining the question of obscenity, and assume without deciding that the prosecution could not have succeeded otherwise." "We view the publications against a background of commercial exploitation of erotica solely for the sake of their prurient appeal." The Court found ample evidence to support a finding that the publisher pointedly directed his advertising and distribution campaign to prurient appeal. Justice Brennan stated:

Besides testimony as to the merit of the material, there was abundant evidence to show that each of the accused publications was originated or sold as stock in trade of the sordid business of pandering—"the business of purveying textual or graphic matter openly advertised to appeal to the erotic interest of their customers."

With respect to the "Handbook," the government drew a distinction between the author's solicitation and that of petitioners. The author had printed the work privately and circulated persons whose names appeared on membership lists of medical and psychiatric associations, asserting its value as an adjunct in therapy. According to the United States Attorney, the author "never had widespread indiscriminate distribution of the Handbook and, consequently, the Post Office Department did not interfere." The majority of the Court accepted this distinction in applying the definition of obscenity, stating:

Petitioners, however, did not sell the book to such a limited audience, or focus their claims for it on its supposed therapeutic or educational value; rather, they deliberately emphasized the sexually provocative aspects of the work, in order to catch the salaciously disposed.

Thus the majority added to the *Roth* test of obscenity another consideration, whether in the context of the production, sale, and publicity for the publication there is substantial evidence of "exploitation by those who would make a business of pandering to 'the widespread weakness for titillation by pornography.' " And the finding of the latter fact "in close cases . . . may be probative with respect to the nature of the material in question and thus satisfy the *Roth* test."

There were four separate dissenting opinions. Justice Stewart expressed the views that (1) the defendants were denied due process because they were never charged with "commercial exploitation," or "pandering," or "titillation"; (2) no federal statute made conduct of this kind a criminal offense; (3) any such criminal statute would be unconstitutionally vague; and (4) the Court had no power to deny a defendant the First Amendment protections because it disapproves of his sordid business.

A second obscenity case, decided on the same day, was *Mishkin* v. *New York*, 383 U.S. 502 (1966). Mishkin was convicted of violating New York law by preparing obscene books, publishing obscene books, and possessing obscene books with intent to sell them. Fifty books were involved in the case. As stated by Justice Brennan, "They portray sexuality in many guises. Some depict relatively normal heterosexual relations, but more depict such deviations as sado-masochism, fetishism, and homosexuality." By a six-to-three vote the Court affirmed the conviction. Appellant attacked his conviction on three grounds: (1) the statutory proscriptions against "sadistic" or "masochistic" or "obscene" materials are impermissibly vague and thus the statute is invalid on its face; (2) the books were not in fact obscene; and (3) the proof of *scienter* was inadequate.

The Court stated that the New York courts have interpreted "obscenity" to cover only so-called "hard-core pornography," and since this is a more rigorous test than the *Roth* definition, the constitutional criteria are satisfied. The second challenge rested in part on the *Roth* requirement that the material be judged on the basis of its appeal to the "average" or "normal" person. It was argued that material concerning deviant sexual practices, such as flagellation, fetishisms, and lesbianism, do not satisfy the prurient-appeal requirement because the "average" person would be disgusted rather than erotically stimulated. In response Justice Brennan, for the majority, stated:

> We adjust the prurient-appeal requirement to social realities by permitting the appeal of this type of material to be assessed in terms of the sexual interests of its intended and probable recipient group; and since our holding requires that the recipient group be defined with more specificity than in terms of sexually immature persons, it also avoids the inadequacy of the most-susceptible-person facet of the *Hicklin* test.

On the issue of *scienter*, the Court quoted the New York Court of Appeals statement that "It is not innocent but *calculated purveyance* of filth which is exorcised," and stated that there was adequate proof that appellant was aware of the character of the material which he purposely had prepared and sold.

In a third case decided on the same day, *A Book Named "John Cleland's Memoirs of a Woman of Pleasure"* v. *Attorney General of Massachusetts*, 383 U.S. 413 (1966), the Court reviewed the judgment of a Massachusetts court of equity that the book *Memoirs of a Woman of Pleasure* (commonly known as *Fanny Hill*), written by John Cleland in about 1750, was obscene. By a six-to-three vote the Court reversed, but the majority was so badly split that there was no "opinion for the Court." Three justices, through Justice Brennan, held that the *Roth* test required a finding that the book be *"utterly* without redeeming social value" to be classified as obscene; that each of the three facets of the *Roth* test is to be applied independently; and that "the social value of the book can neither be weighed against nor canceled by its prurient appeal or patent offensiveness." Thus the Massachusetts court erred in holding that a book need not be "unqualifiedly worthless before it can be deemed obscene." The opinion brought this holding in line with *Ginzburg* by stating that there was no evidence presented that the book was "commercially exploited for the sake of prurient appeal, to the exclusion of all other values," but that such a finding might justify the conclusion that the book was utterly without redeeming social importance.

Justice Black concurred on the ground that the First Amendment denies to governments the power to censor speech or press regardless of the particular subject discussed. Justice Douglas concurred on the ground that government has no power to censor the expression of ideas. Justice Stewart concurred on the ground that only "hard-core pornography" could be proscribed under the First Amendment, and that *Fanny Hill* was not in that category.

The clear import of these decisions is to allow communities greater leverage in their attempts to repress the burgeoning business of the smut-mills. [See the "bibliography" appended to Justice Brennan's opinion in *Ginzburg.*] At the same time it represents a retreat from the trend toward greater freedom of the press since World War II. It remains to be seen what peripheral impact these decisions will have on the freedom of the press in general.

The Court in several instances has reversed lower court judgments because of defective procedural guarantees without squarely reaching the issue of obscenity. Chief Justice Warren referred to this problem in his dissent in *Jacobellis:*

> There has been some tendency in dealing with this area of the law for enforcement agencies to do only that which is easy to do—for instance, to seize and destroy books with only a minimum of protection. As a result, courts are often presented with procedurally bad cases and, in dealing with them, appear to be acquiescing in the dissemination of obscenity. But if cases were well prepared and were conducted with the appropriate concern for constitutional safeguards, courts would not hesitate to enforce the laws against obscenity. Thus, enforcement agencies must realize that there is no royal road to enforcement; hard and conscientious work is required.

Illustrative of the close scrutiny of procedures by the Court is the decision in *A Quantity of Copies of Books* v. *Kansas,* 378 U.S. 205 (1964), decided on the same day as *Jacobellis.* Under a Kansas statute authorizing the seizure of allegedly obscene books before an adversary determination of their obscenity, and, after that determination, their destruction by burning or otherwise, the Attorney General of Kansas obtained an order from a state court directing that certain paperback novels in the possession of the P-K News Service be seized and impounded, pending a hearing. Although not required by the statute, the Attorney General identified the novels by title, and the district judge conducted a 45-minute *ex parte* inquiry in which he examined seven of the books. Concluding that the books appeared to be obscene, the judge issued a warrant authorizing the seizure of all books identified by title in the information. Thirty-one of the titles, 1,715 books in all, were seized and impounded. At a hearing ten days later, P-K moved to quash the information and the warrant on the ground that since P-K was not afforded an opportunity first to argue the issue of obscenity the procedure was unconstitutional because it operated as a prior restraint on the circulation and dissemination of books. The motion was denied, and following a final hearing the court held all 31 novels to be obscene and ordered the sheriff to stand ready to destroy the copies on further order. The Supreme Court of Kansas affirmed.

On appeal, the United States Supreme Court reversed, but the seven justices voting for reversal were unable to agree upon an opinion in support of the decision. Justice Brennan, speaking also for Chief Justice Warren, Justice White and Justice Goldberg, stated:

The steps taken beyond the express requirements of the statute were thought by the Attorney General to be necessary under our decision in *Marcus* v. *Search Warrant of Property*, 367 U.S. 717 (1961), decided a few weeks before the Information was filed. *Marcus* involved a proceeding under a strikingly similar Missouri search and seizure statute and implementing rule of court. . . . In *Marcus* the warrant gave the police virtually unlimited authority to seize any publications which they considered to be obscene, and was issued on a verified complaint lacking any specific description of the publications to be seized, and without prior submission of any publications whatever to the judge issuing the warrant. We reversed a judgment directing the destruction of the copies of 100 publications held to be obscene, holding that, even assuming that they were obscene, the procedures leading to their condemnation were constitutionally deficient for lack of safeguards to prevent suppression of non-obscene publications protected by the Constitution.

It is our view that since the warrant here authorized the sheriff to seize all copies of the specified titles, and since P-K was not afforded a hearing on the question of the obscenity even of the seven novels before the warrant issued, the procedure was likewise constitutionally deficient. This is the teaching of *Kingsley Books, Inc.* v. *Brown*, 354 U.S. 436 (1957). . . . The New York injunctive procedure there sustained does not afford *ex parte* relief but postpones all injunctive relief until "both sides have had an opportunity to be heard.". . . In *Marcus* we explicitly said that *Kingsley Books* "does not support the proposition that the State may impose the extensive restraints imposed here on the distribution of these publications prior to an adversary proceeding on the issue of obscenity, irrespective of whether or not the material is legally obscene.". . . A seizure of all copies of the named titles is indeed more repressive than an injunction preventing further sale of the books. . . . We therefore conclude that in not first affording P-K an adversary hearing, the procedure leading to the seizure was constitutionally deficient. . . .

Nor is the order under review saved because, after all 1,719 copies were seized and removed from circulation, P-K News Service was afforded a full hearing on the question of the obscenity of the novels. For if seizure of books precedes an adversary determination of their obscenity, there is danger of abridgment of the right of the public in a free society to unobstructed circulation of nonobscene books.

The Justice was careful to point out in his opinion, however, that the decision intimated no view on whether the books in question were in fact obscene.

Justices Black and Douglas reiterated their views expressed in Justice Douglas' dissent in *Roth*, that book-burning statutes were in plain violation of the First Amendment, irrespective of the procedures employed.

Justice Stewart concurred separately, stating that if the books had been hard-core pornography, which he did not so find, the procedures followed would be valid, but since they were not the state could not "by any pro-

cedure constitutionally suppress them, any more than Kansas could constitutionally make their sale or distribution a criminal act."

Justice Harlan, joined by Justice Clark, dissented. The main thrust of
his argument was directed toward the opinion by Justice Brennan. He contended that the Kansas procedure was unlike that in *Marcus*, and thus the
case did not control. He argued that the procedure was sufficiently similar
to that in *Kingsley Books* to justify affirmance, rather than reversal, under
the rule of that case. Looking beyond the statute to the procedures followed by the Attorney General in Kansas, he stated:

> While the New York statute allows an almost immediate hearing on the obscenity
> issue, it would be unrealistic to suppose that most persons who allegedly have or sell
> obscene materials will be able to prepare for such a hearing in four days, the time
> between the issuance of the complaint and the *pendente lite* injunction in *Kingsley
> Books*. In practical terms, therefore, the New York scheme, as approved by this
> Court, does contemplate restraint before a hearing on the merits.

Justice Harlan also attacked the implication that the statute constituted
a prior restraint: "Since there may be lurking in my Brother Brennan's opinion the unarticulated premise that this Kansas procedure is impermissible
because it operates as a 'prior restraint,' I deem it appropriate to make a few
observations on that score." He argued that the doctrine of prior restraint
was one requiring a case-to-case approach and was not a "talismanic test."
Thus a slight prior restraint in the case of obscene books might not be as
serious as in the case of newspapers. He stated:

> If controversial political writings attack those in power, government officials may
> benefit from suppression although society may suffer. In the area of obscenity, there
> is less chance that decision-makers will have interests which may affect their estimate
> of what is constitutionally protected and what is not. It is vital to the operation of
> democratic government that the citizens have facts and ideas on important issues
> before them. A delay of even a day or two may be of crucial importance in some
> instances. On the other hand, the subject of sex is of constant but rarely particularly
> topic interest.

Another aspect of the enforcement of obscenity laws was the basis for
reversal in *Smith* v. *California*, 361 U.S. 147 (1959). Smith was the proprietor of a bookstore and was convicted of violating a Los Angeles ordinance which made it unlawful to possess any obscene or indecent book in
any place where books were sold or kept for sale. The ordinance was construed as imposing a strict criminal liability, without requiring any element
of *scienter,* i.e., knowledge by the defendant of the contents of the book
upon which the criminal charge was based. The Court unanimously reversed the conviction, although there were five separate opinions. Justice
Brennan, speaking for five members, held that the requirement of strict
liability on the bookseller unconstitutionally hindered freedom of speech
and press. He stated:

[I]f the bookseller is criminally liable without knowledge of the contents, and the ordinance fulfills its purpose, he will tend to restrict the books he sells to those he has inspected; and thus the State will have imposed a restriction upon the distribution of constitutionally protected as well as obscene literature. . . . If the contents of bookshops and periodical stands were restricted to material of which their proprietors had made an inspection, they might be depleted indeed. . . . The bookseller's self-censorship, compelled by the State, would be a censorship affecting the whole public, hardly less virulent for being privately administered.

In *Bantam Books, Inc.* v. *Sullivan*, 372 U.S. 58 (1963), the Court dealt with the constitutionality of certain forms of informal suppression of distribution of books by a state commission. The Rhode Island legislature created the "Rhode Island Commission to Encourage Morality in Youth" which, among other duties, was charged with educating the public concerning any obscene publications and with investigating and recommending the prosecution of all violations of relevant statutes. The Commission evolved the practice of sending notices to distributors that certain designated books or magazines had been found to be objectionable for sale, distribution or display to persons under 18 years of age, asking for their cooperation, and reminding them of the Commission's duty to recommend prosecution of sellers of obscenity. Copies of the lists of objectionable publications were also circulated to local police departments, and the distributors were so advised. The normal result of such notification was for the distributor to halt further circulation of the listed publications, to withdraw from retailers all unsold copies, and to return all unsold copies to the publishers.

Appellants, four New York publishers of paperback books, brought the action in the Superior Court of Rhode Island (1) to declare the law creating the Commission unconstitutional and (2) to declare unconstitutional and enjoin the acts and practices of the Commission under the law. With only one dissent, the Court held that the law creating the Commission was valid, but the practice of informal suppression constituted a system of prior administrative restraints. The opinion for the majority noted that "although the Commission's supposed concern is limited to youthful readers, the 'cooperation' it seeks from distributors invariably entails the complete suppression of the listed publications; adult readers are equally deprived of the opportunity to purchase the publications in the State." The fact that such a result could be accomplished without any judicial determination of the issue of obscenity was a fatal defect in its failure to furnish the procedural safeguards required for restricting the freedom of the press.

As indicated in the earlier discussion of the doctrine of prior restraint, the Court has not held that they are unconstitutional *per se*. And despite the Court's traditional attitude of disfavor toward prior restraints, it held in *Times Film Corp.* v. *City of Chicago*, 365 U.S. 43 (1961), that a municipality's requirement of a license prior to the exhibition of a motion picture film was not unconstitutional. The Court's concern with procedural safeguards adequate to ensure that freedom of expression will not be unduly inhibited, however, led it to circumscribe very closely the municipality's powers under such a licensing requirement in *Freedman* v. *Maryland*, 380 U.S. 51 (1965).

Appellant challenged the constitutionality of the Maryland motion picture censorship statute by exhibiting the film *Revenge at Daybreak* without first submitting it to the state board of censors. He was convicted of violating the statute, although the state conceded that the picture would have received a license if properly submitted. The Court unanimously reversed, holding the Maryland procedures deficient under the First and Fourteenth Amendments. The *Times Film* holding was not overruled, but the Court held the statute invalid as a prior restraint because (1) upon the censor's disapproval of a film, the exhibitor must assume the burden of instituting judicial proceedings and of persuading the courts that the film is protected expression, (2) once the censor has acted against a film, exhibition is barred pending judicial review, however protracted, and (3) there was no assurance of prompt judicial determination of the issues. Justice Brennan stated:

> Risk of delay is built into the Maryland procedure, as is borne out by experience; in the only reported case indicating the length of time required to complete an appeal, the initial judicial determination has taken four months and final vindication of the film on appellate review, six months.

Citing *Bantam Books, Inc.* v. *Sullivan* and *A Quantity of Books* v. *Kansas*, he stated that "because only a judicial determination in an adversary proceeding ensures the necessary sensitivity to freedom of expression, only a procedure requiring a judicial determination suffices to impose a valid final restraint." He pointed out that it was up to the state to decide how to incorporate the necessary procedural safeguards, but suggested that the New York procedure relative to books, which the Court upheld in *Kingsley Books, Inc.* v. *Brown*, might usefully serve as a model.

Although the *Freedman* case did not raise any issue of obscenity, it is clearly relevant to such a discussion because the primary thrust of movie censorship is in that direction. The holding does not bar licensing requirements, but it softens the impact of such practices to some extent.

A final aspect of censorship for obscenity should be noted. This is in the informal official action and the private pressures which may be brought to limit distribution of various publications. *Bantam Books* illustrated one kind of informal official action and one on which a court test was successfully brought. Others are not so readily apparent and may not be amenable to litigation at all. David Fellman in *The Censorship of Books* states: [4]

> The most important form of official censorship of books in this country arises from the fact that our governments—national, state, and local—are the biggest purchasers of books in the country. In fact, they buy about one-half of all hardcover books. Books are purchased by government for schools, public libraries, the

---

[4] David Fellman, *The Censorship of Books* (Madison: University of Wisconsin Press, 1957), p. 14.

armed forces, overseas information libraries, hospitals, etc. And of course the right to buy includes the right to refuse to buy, if for no other reason than that not all books can be bought. The buyer must make selections, and the making of selections necessarily involves some form of censorship. Thus the Army has banned the second Kinsey book on the sexual life of American females.

[On the subject of informal official censorship generally, see Comment, "Censorship of Obscene Literature by Informal Governmental Action," 22 *Univ. of Chi. L. Rev.* 216 (1954).]

Substantial extralegal controls may flow from the pressures exerted by various private groups. In some instances these are matters of self-regulation, as in the Motion Picture Production Code, adopted by the Motion Picture Association of America. [See also the Code of the Comics Magazine Association of America, reprinted in 1 *Cath. Law.* 60 (1955).] The pressure groups operating outside the industry, however, pose a different problem. These groups may have substantial impact on the availability of motion pictures or books or, at the least, on the volume of consumption. Two influential groups of this type are the Legion of Decency, which reviews and classifies movies, and the National Office for Decent Literature, which reviews paperback books primarily. Lists are prepared by each of these groups and are available to interested persons. According to one writer [see Note, "Entertainment: Public Pressures and the Law," 71 *Harv. L. Rev.* 326 (1957).], the NODL does not attempt to implement its decisions on a local level, but recommends procedures to be followed. It suggests that local committees call on stores selling paperbacks and frequented by younger people. Using the NODL list as a guide, the committee requests the store owner to remove the objectionable books. If he acquiesces, it is suggested that such cooperation be mentioned from the pulpit or in parish publications. The same writer states that some parish groups provide a special seal to be placed in cooperating merchants' windows and parish members are requested to patronize only the stores displaying the seal of approval. Obviously the extralegal private pressures can have a substantial impact on the publications available for sale even to adult readers if the local groups are militant, well-organized, and representative of a sizable number of consumers. To oppose such action, in the minds of many, is to draw the battle lines between purity and pruriency, and thus the opposition is apt to be less well-organized and in the more vulnerable position of having to defend the right to sell and purchase publications of very poor quality, although not obscene. The compromise solution attempted in some states is to adopt statutes forbidding the sale to persons under eighteen years of age of publications which fail to meet the *Roth* test. The assumption appears to be that the Court will allow more latitude in banning sales to such persons than to adults because of the special interest of the state relative to juveniles. At the same time, adults will not have their reading choices abridged by a standard which will limit them to only "what is fit for children." Some legislators apparently have supported this type of control in the hope that it will forestall the more severe private censorship, even though they may not be convinced that reading habits are necessarily a causal factor in juvenile misbehavior. [For indications that nonreading rather than reading "bad" books is the more serious problem in juvenile delinquency, see Sheldon Glueck and Eleanor Glueck, *Unraveling Juvenile Delinquency* (New York: Commonwealth Fund, 1950), and Walter Gellhorn, *Individual Freedom and Governmental Restraints* (Baton Rouge: Louisiana State University Press, 1956), Chap. 2.]

See Chapter 9 for the opinions in *Stanley* v. *Georgia,* 394 U.S. 557 (1969), holding invalid a state law barring *possession* of obscene matter, and *United States* v. *Reidel,* 402 U.S. 351 (1971), upholding the federal law prohibiting the use of the mails for the delivery of obscene matter.

CHAPTER 7

Equal Protection of the Law

MUCH of the developing law in the area of civil rights can in essence be characterized as a drive for equality under the law. The concept of equality has played an important part in American legal and political development since its overt statement by Thomas Jefferson in the Declaration's famous words, "We hold these truths to be self-evident, that all men are created equal. . . ." The movement has been sporadic and has taken differing directions and emphases, sometimes stressing the economic, at other times the legal or the social. In the Revolutionary and post-Revolutionary period substantial gains were made in the area of religious equality, with the gradual elimination of taxes for religious support, disestablishment, and the removal of restrictions on public worship for some of the minority sects. During the Jacksonian period religious tests for office-holding began to disappear and political equality was further extended by the removal of property qualifications for both voters and candidates for public office. In economic thought it was one of the firm tenets of Jacksonian democracy that progress could be assured for all if the legislative policy of granting exclusive grants of privilege could be stopped and everyone afforded equal opportunity to engage in business enterprise. The Civil War era saw the adoption of a minimal program of racial equality in the abolition of slavery. Even in the period of Manchester Liberalism in the latter third of the nineteenth century when the doctrines of Herbert Spencer held sway, it was a somewhat twisted concept of equality which was interwoven into the fabric of social Darwinism. All men had an equal opportunity to compete for economic survival and leadership. By fencing off government from entering the struggle to lay down ground rules for the economic "game," equality was supposedly secured and the victors were entitled to the spoils because they were the fittest. The theory, of course, took no account of the fact that the competition could never be equal between persons who entered the struggle with substantially unequal financial assets. A great deal of legislation since the adoption of the Sherman Antitrust Act in 1890 has been prompted by the desire to equalize the competitive battle in the economic arena, including labor's bargaining position as against management.

In the earlier part of the twentieth century, and still in evidence today, a major aspect of the movement for equality was the drive for equal rights for women. The acquisition of the right to vote, to serve on juries, to compete for jobs and careers on somewhat more nearly equal terms with men, and the achievement of more substantial property and personal rights within the marriage relationship have been important facets of the overall trend. The Civil Rights Act of 1964 is expected to have a substantial impact in the area of equal employment opportunities for women and equal pay for equal work, although experience under the Act to date is too brief for accurate assessment of these provisions.

Today, a major effort is being undertaken by the national government to ensure the minimal requirements of food, housing, education, and economic opportunity under the theory that true equality of opportunity can only be achieved by removing restraints based on race or religion or sex and by guaranteeing to all participants at least the basic tools and ingredients for attempting to develop to their full potential.

The general advances sketched out above represent programs achieved by the political branches, however, rather than through judicial applications of a constitutional doctrine of equal protection of the laws. In the judicial arena the issues raised under the Fourteenth Amendment's "equal protection" clause (and a similar requirement as sometimes read into the Fifth Amendment "due process" clause) can usually be resolved into one of two questions: (1) Was the specific law involved administered impartially? or (2) Did the legislature, in adopting a specific law providing for differential treatment of different segments of the public, set up a reasonable classification of the objects or persons treated, in view of the overall purposes of the law?

An early case on the first issue was *Yick Wo v. Hopkins,* 118 U.S. 356 (1886). The board of supervisors of San Francisco enacted an ordinance providing that no one should carry on a laundry within the county "without having first obtained the consent of the board of supervisors, except the same be located in a building constructed either of brick or stone." Yick Wo, a Chinese subject resident in San Francisco, petitioned for a license to carry on a laundry in the same building in which he had been doing so for twenty-two years. His application was refused, and he was arrested and fined $10 for continuing in business without the license. After failure to pay the fine he was committed to jail, where he petitioned for a writ of habeas corpus. He had received certificates from the fire wardens and the health officer showing that his premises were safe and in sanitary condition. At the time the ordinance was passed, there were about 320 laundries in San Francisco of which about 240 were owned and operated by Chinese. It was admitted that all applications for a license made by Chinese persons were refused, while the petitions of all others, with one exception, were granted. About 150 Chinese were arrested for noncompliance, while, as stated in Yick Wo's petition, "those who are not subjects of China and who are conducting eighty-odd laundries under similar conditions, are left unmolested." The Supreme Court of California discharged the writ, but the

United States Supreme Court reversed, holding the application of the law violative of the "equal protection" clause.

Justice Matthews, for the Court, stated:

In the present cases we are not obliged to reason from the probable to the actual, and pass upon the validity of the ordinances complained of, as tried merely by the opportunities which their terms afford, of unequal and unjust discrimination in their administration. For the cases present the ordinances in actual operation, and the facts shown establish an administration directed so exclusively against a particular class of persons as to warrant and require the conclusion that ... they are applied by the public authorities charged with their administration ... with a mind so unequal and oppressive as to amount to a practical denial by the State of that equal protection of the laws which is secured ... by the broad and benign provisions of the Fourteenth Amendment.... Though the law itself be fair on its face and impartial in appearance, yet, if it is applied and administered by public authority with an evil eye and an unequal hand, so as practically to make unjust and illegal discriminations between persons in similar circumstances, material to their rights, the denial of equal justice is still within the prohibition of the Constitution....

A similar issue, although in quite another context, was presented in *Niemotko* v. *Maryland*, 340 U.S. 268 (1951). Niemotko and others who were Jehovah's Witnesses, scheduled Bible talks in the public park of Havre de Grace, Maryland. Although there was no ordinance prohibiting or regulating the use of this park, it had been the custom for organizations and individuals desiring to use it for meetings and celebrations of various kinds to obtain a permit from the park commissioner. In conformity with this practice, the group requested permission to use the park on four consecutive Sundays. The park commissioner refused.

The group appealed this refusal to the city council, and a hearing was held by the council. The evidence indicated that the only questions asked of the Witnesses at the hearing pertained to their alleged refusal to salute the flag, their views on the Bible, and other issues irrelevant to unencumbered use of the public parks. After the hearing, the council denied the request, although permits had been customarily granted for similar purposes, including meetings of religious and fraternal organizations. Niemotko was later arrested for attempting to hold the meeting without a permit and convicted of disorderly conduct. The Maryland appellate court denied certiorari, and on appeal the United States Supreme Court unanimously held the convictions violative of equal protection of the laws. Chief Justice Vinson, for the Court, stated:

The conclusion is inescapable that the use of the park was denied because of the City Council's dislike for or disagreement with the Witnesses on their views. The right to equal protection of the laws, in the exercise of those freedoms of speech and religion protected by the First and Fourteenth Amendments, has a firmer foundation than the whims or personal opinions of a local governing body.

Because of limited resources, enforcement agencies often follow policies of selective enforcement of various laws. Presumably if such selectivity is based on race or religion, it would run afoul of the "equal protection" clause, as in the two cases discussed above. But suppose the only basis for the policy is the judicious allocation of scarce policing resources. This situation presents a more difficult question, and one which the Court has not fully explored. In one case, however, the Court expressly recognized the dilemma of the enforcing agency and approved a selective enforcement order of the FTC. The Commission obtained a cease and desist order against one firm engaged in illegal price arrangements. The firm complained that several other business competitors were following the same practices, and that it was unfair to subject one to serious financial loss without at the same time punishing the others. In *Moog Industries* v. *FTC*, 355 U.S. 411 (1958), the Court rejected the argument, and, after stressing the "specialized experienced judgment" of the Commission, concluded that "the Commission alone is empowered to develop that enforcement policy best calculated to achieve the ends contemplated by Congress and to allocate its available funds and personnel in such a way as to execute its policy efficiently and economically." [See: Glenn Abernathy, "Police Discretion and Equal Protection," 14 *S.C.L.Q.* 472 (1962); Wayne R. LaFave, "The Police and Nonenforcement of the Law" (Two Pts.), 1962 *Wis. L. Rev.* 104, 179.]

The second aspect of the problem of equal protection concerns actual classification by the legislature in the application of a statute. It is almost impossible to conceive of a law which does not in some way employ classification. And it would place an intolerable burden on the legislature to have to deal with all evils in the community at once, or even to deal with all aspects of a single evil, in order to meet the test of equal protection. Thus the legislature can, if it chooses, attack community ills more or less piecemeal. It can try to solve problems one at a time, and it can even deal with some aspects of a given problem while ignoring others. In short, the "equal protection" clause does not fasten upon the legislature an iron rule of uniform treatment.

The legislature is thus free to "classify" the objects of its attention, treating some in one fashion and others differently. It is free to discriminate, then. But if it *does* discriminate, the equal protection requirement demands that the legislative classification not be arbitrary and unreasonable and that the distinctions employed bear some rational relationship to the lawful purposes to be accomplished. Even here, however, there is a strong presumption in the courts that discriminations in legislation are based on adequate grounds. As indicated in *Crescent Oil Company* v. *Mississippi*, 257 U.S. 129, 137 (1921), every state of facts sufficient to sustain a classification which can reasonably be conceived of as having existed when the law was adopted will be assumed. Further, since the legislature is free to try to correct one evil without reaching others, it is no defense to show that a challenged law could easily have been broadened to correct other very similar evils. As Justice Holmes stated in *Keokee Consolidated Coke Company* v. *Taylor* 234 U.S. 224 (1914), "it is established by repeated decisions that a statute aimed at what is deemed an evil, and hitting it presumably where experience shows it to be most felt, is not to be upset by thinking up and enumerating other instances to which it might have been applied equally well, so far as the Court can see."

A famous case which involved in part the equal protection issue was *Buck* v. *Bell*, 274 U.S. 200 (1927), in which a state law providing for the sterilization of mental defectives was challenged. A Virginia law of 1924 provided that after complying with very careful procedural requirements to protect patients from possible abuse, *institutionalized* mental defectives could be ordered sterilized. No provision was made for sterilization of such persons who were not living in various institutions specified in the law. The main thrust of argument in the case was that it deprived the affected persons of their liberty without due process of law, and in upholding the provisions the opinion was primarily directed to that issue. The law was also challenged, however, on the ground that the differential treatment accorded institutional inmates and those outside institutions violated the "equal protection" clause. In upholding the statute against this claim, Justice Holmes, for the Court, stated:

But, it is said, however it might be if this reasoning were applied generally, it fails when it is confined to the small number who are in the institutions named and is not applied to the multitudes outside. It is the usual last resort of constitutional arguments to point out shortcomings of this sort. But the answer is that the law does all that is needed when it does all that it can, indicates a policy, applies it to all within the lines, and seeks to bring within the lines all similarly situated so far and so fast as its means allow. Of course so far as the operations enable those who otherwise must be kept confined to be returned to the world, and thus open the asylum to others, the equality aimed at will be more nearly reached.

In 1942 the Court held that an Oklahoma law providing for the sterilization of certain kinds of criminals and not others went beyond the bounds of reasonable classification. The case was *Skinner* v. *Oklahoma*.

SKINNER *v.* OKLAHOMA
316 U.S. 535 (1942)

Mr. Justice Douglas delivered the opinion of the Court....

The statute involved is Oklahoma's Habitual Criminal Sterilization Act.... That Act defines an "habitual criminal" as a person who, having been convicted two or more times for crimes "amounting to felonies involving moral turpitude,"... is thereafter convicted of such a felony in Oklahoma and is sentenced to a term of imprisonment in an Oklahoma penal institution. Machinery is provided for the institution by the Attorney General of a proceeding against such a person in the Oklahoma courts for a judgment that such person shall be rendered sexually sterile. ... Only one other provision of the Act is material here, and that is Section 195, which provided that "offenses arising out of the violation of the prohibitory laws, revenue acts, embezzlement, or political offenses, shall not come or be considered within the terms of this Act."

Petitioner was convicted in 1926 of the crime of stealing chickens, and was sentenced to the Oklahoma State Reformatory. In 1929 he was convicted of the crime of robbery with firearms, and was sentenced to the reformatory. In 1934 he was convicted again of robbery with firearms, and was sentenced to the penitentiary. He was confined there in 1935 when the Act was passed. In 1936 the Attorney General instituted proceedings against him. . . . A judgment directing that the operation of vasectomy be performed on petitioner was affirmed by the Supreme Court of Oklahoma by a five to four decision. . . .

Several objections to the constitutionality of the Act have been pressed upon us. . . . We pass those points without intimating an opinion on them, for there is a feature of the Act which clearly condemns it. That is, its failure to meet the requirements of the equal protection clause of the Fourteenth Amendment.

We do not stop to point out all of the inequalities in this Act. A few examples will suffice. In Oklahoma, grand larceny is a felony. . . . Larceny is grand larceny when the property taken exceeds $20 in value. . . . Embezzlement is punishable "in the manner prescribed for feloniously stealing property of the value of that embezzled.". . . A clerk who appropriates over $20 from his employer's till and a stranger who steals the same amount are thus both guilty of felonies. If the latter repeats his act and is convicted three times, he may be sterilized. But the clerk is not subject to the pains and penalties of the Act not matter how large his embezzlements nor how frequent his convictions. A person who enters a chicken coop and steals chickens commits a felony; and he may be sterilized if he is thrice convicted. If, however, he is a bailee of the property and fraudulently appropriates it, he is an embezzler. . . . Hence, no matter how habitual his proclivities for embezzlement are and no matter how often his conviction, he may not be sterilized. Thus, the nature of the two crimes is intrinsically the same and they are punishable in the same manner. . . .

It was stated in *Buck* v. *Bell, supra,* that the claim that state legislation violates the equal protection clause of the Fourteenth Amendment is "the usual last resort of constitutional arguments.". . . Under our constitutional system the States in determining the reach and scope of particular legislation need not provide "abstract symmetry.". . . They may mark and set apart the classes and types of problems according to the needs and as dictated or suggested by experience. . . . Only recently we reaffirmed the view that the equal protection clause does not prevent the legislature from recognizing "degrees of evil" . . . by our ruling . . . that "the Constitution does not require things which are different in fact or opinion to be treated in law as though they were the same.". . . Thus, if we had here only a question as to a State's classification of crimes, such as embezzlement or larceny, no substantial federal question would be raised. . . . For a State is not constrained in the exercise of its police power to ignore experience which marks a class of offenders or a family of offenses for special treatment. Nor is it prevented by the equal protection clause from confining "its restrictions to those classes of cases where the need is deemed to be clearest.". . .

But the instant legislation runs afoul of the equal protection clause, though we give Oklahoma that large deference which the rule of the foregoing cases requires.

We are dealing here with legislation which involves one of the basic civil rights of man. Marriage and procreation are fundamental to the very existence and survival of the race. . . . There is no redemption for the individual whom the law touches. Any experiment which the State conducts is to his irreparable injury. He is forever deprived of a basic liberty. We mention these matters not to reexamine the scope of the police power of the States. We advert to them merely in emphasis of our view that strict scrutiny of the classification which a State makes in a sterilization law is essential, lest unwittingly, or otherwise, invidious discriminations are made against groups or types of individuals in violation of the constitutional guaranty of just and equal laws. . . . When the law lays an unequal hand on those who have committed intrinsically the same quality of offense and sterilizes one and not the other, it has made as invidious a discrimination as if it had selected a particular race or nationality for oppressive treatment. . . . Sterilization of those who have thrice committed grand larceny, with immunity for those who are embezzlers, is a clear, pointed, unmistakable discrimination. Oklahoma makes no attempt to say that he who commits larceny by trespass or trick or fraud has biologically inheritable traits which he who commits embezzlement lacks. . . . We have not the slightest basis for inferring that that line has any significance in eugenics, nor that the inheritability of criminal traits follows the neat legal distinctions which the law has marked between those two offenses. . . . The equal protection clause would indeed be a formula of empty words if such conspicuously artificial lines could be drawn. . . .

Reversed.

[Chief Justice Stone and Mr. Justice Jackson wrote separate concurring opinions.]

The opinion for the Court explicitly denied any attempt to re-examine the due process issue with respect to sterilization. Yet much of the flavor of the opinion is in due process language. Justice Douglas provides an interesting and novel coupling of the "due process" and "equal protection" clauses. In effect, he states that the more fundamental the right involved and the more serious the restraint or interference with that right, the higher the Court will raise the standard of "reasonableness" which the "equal protection" clause requires of legislative classifications. By the same token, if the restraints involved raise no serious due process issues, the state has far broader latitude in making strange and unusual classifications. Although the Court has not explicitly adhered to such a construction in other cases, it is possible that it might be an unexpressed guideline for individual justices in dealing with equal protection cases. Certainly in matters of economic regulation, an area in which the Court has almost gone out of the business of invalidating legislation on due process grounds, the state has exceedingly large powers of classification. In *Williamson* v. *Lee Optical Company*, 348 U.S. 483 (1955), for example, the Court examined an Oklahoma law which made it unlawful for any person not a licensed optometrist or ophthalmologist to fit lenses to a face or to duplicate or replace lenses except upon written prescriptive authority of a licensed opthalmologist or optometrist. Sellers of ready-to-wear glasses were exempt, however, from the regulations, and the claim was made that the exemption rendered the law invalid under the "equal protection" clause. On the due process issue Justice Douglas, for a unanimous Court, stated:

The day is gone when this Court uses the Due Process Clause of the Fourteenth Amendment to strike down state laws, regulatory of business and industrial conditions, because they may be unwise, improvident, or out of harmony with a particular school of thought.... We emphasize again what Chief Justice Waite said in *Munn* v. *State of Illinois*, ..."For protection against abuses by legislatures the people must resort to the polls, not to the courts."

As to the equal protection issue, Justice Douglas was equally unsympathetic:

The problem of legislative classification is a perennial one, admitting of no doctrinaire definition. Evils in the same field may be of different dimensions and proportions, requiring different remedies. Or so the legislature may think.... Or the reform may take one step at a time, addressing itself to the phase of the problem which seems most acute to the legislative mind.... The legislature may select one phase of one field and apply a remedy there, neglecting the others.... The prohibition of the Equal Protection Clause goes no further than the invidious discrimination. We cannot say that that point has been reached here. For all this record shows, the ready-to-wear branch of this business may not loom large in Oklahoma or may present problems of regulation distinct from the other branch.

A variety of earlier cases hold that the state does not violate the "equal protection" clause by singling out women for special treatment in the exercise of the state's protective power. Classification has been upheld based on differences either in their physical characteristics or in the social conditions surrounding their employment. One of the earliest pieces of social legislation to be held valid by the Court was a law limiting hours of work for women in laundries to a ten-hour workday. [*Muller* v. *Oregon*, 208 U.S. 412 (1908).] In *Radice* v. *New York*, 264 U.S. 292 (1924), a law prohibiting women from working in restaurants at night was upheld. More recently, in *Goesaert* v. *Cleary*, 335 U.S. 464 (1948), the Court sustained a state statute forbidding women to act as bartenders, but making an exception in favor of wives and daughters of the male owners of liquor establishments, although three justices dissented. Justice Frankfurter, for the majority, stated:

We are, to be sure, dealing with a historic calling. We meet the alewife, sprightly and ribald, in Shakespeare, but centuries before him she played a role in the social life of England.... The Fourteenth Amendment did not tear history up by the roots, and the regulation of the liquor traffic is one of the oldest and most untrammeled of legislative powers. Michigan could, beyond question, forbid all women from working behind a bar. This is so despite the vast changes in the social and legal position of women. The fact that women may now have achieved the virtues that men have long claimed as their prerogatives and now indulge in vices that men have long practiced, does not preclude the States from drawing a sharp line between the sexes, certainly in such matters as the regulation of the liquor traffic.... The Constitution does not require legislatures to reflect sociological insight, or shifting social standards, any more than it requires them to keep abreast of the latest scientific standards.

The experiences of World War II, however, had shown to many people clear proof that women could perform just as competently and safeguard their morals at least as well as men in occupations which formerly had been denied them. Women drove taxis, welded, riveted, flew airplanes, and even did heavy construction work. And they did these jobs at all hours of the day and night. Understandably, many such women chafed under the resumption after the war of the so-called "protective" laws limiting the types of employment for women or the hours in which they could work. Their criticisms began to reach legislative bodies and political party platform committees, and they charged that the only thing "protective" about such restrictions was the protection of men from female competition for their jobs. The dissenting opinion of Justice Rutledge, joined by Justices Douglas and Murphy, in the *Goesaert* case indicated a willingness to look more closely into the reasonableness of classifications based on sex. He stated, in part:

The statute arbitrarily discriminates between male and female owners of liquor establishments. A male owner, although he himself is always absent from his bar, may employ his wife and daughter as barmaids. A female owner may neither work as a barmaid herself nor employ her daughter in that position, even if a man is always present in the establishment to keep order. This inevitable result of the classification belies the assumption that the statute was motivated by a legislative solicitude for the moral and physical well-being of women who, but for the law, would be employed as barmaids. Since there could be no other conceivable justification for such discrimination against women owners of liquor establishments, the statute should be held invalid as a denial of equal protection.

In 1967 the United States Supreme Court denied a petition for certiorari to review a Tennessee rule of tort liability involving an unusual aspect of discrimination on the basis of sex. The case was *Krohn* v. *Richardson-Merrell, Inc.,* 406 SW 2d 166 (Tennessee, 1966), a tort action against a drug company following the rendering of a man impotent as a consequence of using the company's drug. As one assignment of injury, the wife claimed damages for loss of consortium. Following the common-law rule, the Tennessee Supreme Court held that the wife could not maintain such an action and rejected her contention that permitting a husband but not a wife to recover for loss of consortium is an impermissible discrimination under the "equal protection" clause.

The Civil Rights Act of 1964, while primarily designed to prevent racial discriminations, includes in the Title VII provisions on Equal Employment Opportunity a provision that it shall be an unlawful employment practice for an employer, as defined by the Act, "to fail or refuse to hire or to discharge any individual, or otherwise to discriminate against any individual with respect to his compensation, terms, conditions, or privileges of employment, because of such individual's . . . sex. . . ." Employment agencies and labor unions are also barred from making classifications or otherwise discriminating on the basis of sex. The Title permits an exception, however, "in those certain instances where . . . sex . . . is a bona fide occupational qualification reasonably necessary to the normal operation of that particular business or enterprise." In order to implement these and other provisions of Title VII, the Equal Opportunity Commission is created by the Act and is given authority "to issue, amend, or rescind suitable procedural regulations to carry out the provisions of this title."

On November 22, 1965, Franklin D. Roosevelt, Jr., Chairman of the Commission, published the first guidelines (30 Federal Register 14926) on how the Commission construed its statutory duties under the provisions barring discriminations based on sex. The statement is made that "The commission does not believe that Congress intended to disturb such laws and regulations which are intended to, and have the effect of, protecting women against exploitation and hazard." It goes on to point out, however, that many laws originally enacted to protect women have ceased to be relevant to the nation's technology or to the expanding role of the woman worker in the economy. And in cases where the clear effect of a law in current circumstances is not to protect women but to subject them to discrimination, the law will not be considered a justification for discrimination. As an example, the Commission said it would honor state restrictions on lifting weights except where the limit is set at an unreasonably low level that could not endanger women.

In yet another area of equal protection questions, the past two or three decades have seen a sharp change in the rights of indigent defendants in criminal cases. The "due process" clauses of the Constitution have long been used to hold government to minimum standards of procedure. More recently, the Court has employed the "equal protection" clause to require still higher standards in order that the impoverished defendant will not be placed at a substantial disadvantage by comparison with the wealthier person in defending against a criminal prosecution. As shown in the earlier chapter on the rights of accused persons, the state must now furnish counsel for any indigent defendant charged with a serious crime, and furnish it at an earlier stage than before. In addition, the right to counsel carries through the appellate stage, as well as the right to a free transcript of record, as further guarantees of equality of treatment.

Despite the importance of these developments, the single most dramatic change in the broad movement toward equal rights since the abolition of slavery has been the reversal in constitutional interpretation which now bars governmental discrimination based on race. For most of the period since 1865 the law looked in two directions with regard to racial discrimination. It was held unconstitutional for the state explicitly to deny to persons because of their race a right enjoyed by members of other races, but, under the decision in *Plessy* v. *Ferguson* in 1896, it was not unconstitutional for the state to dispense governmental benefits and employ its police powers along lines separated on the basis of race. The Louisiana statute upheld in that case required "equal but separate accommodations for the white and colored races" in railway coaches. The phrase has been reversed and since that time has been referred to as the "separate but equal" doctrine. The landmark decision in the area of race discrimination, *Brown* v. *Board of Education of Topeka*, 347 U.S. 483 (1954), although technically confined to education, has been subsequently broadened to a holding that separate facilities are *inherently unequal*, and therefore governmental discrimination on the basis of race cannot meet the test of equal protection of the laws. [The literature on the subject of racial discrimination is enormous, but for an excellent treatment of the development of the law through the *Brown* case, see A. P. Blaustein and C. C. Ferguson, Jr., *Desegregation and the Law* (New Brunswick: Rutgers University Press, 1957). See, also, Jack Greenberg, *Race Relations and American Law* (New York: Columbia University Press, 1959). An invaluable reference source is the *Race Relations Law Reporter* (Nashville: Vanderbilt University School of Law, published quarterly since 1956.)]

Following the bitterly criticized decision in *Dred Scott* v. *Sandford*, 19 Howard 393 (1857), holding that the Constitution did not contemplate acquisition of United States citizenship by Negroes, the Thirteenth, Fourteenth, and Fifteenth Amendments were adopted. As a package, these amendments were clearly intended to elevate the Negro to at least equal *legal* status with other United States citizens. The extent to which they limit private and quasi-public discrimination based on race is actually still a matter of argument, although the question is largely moot since the adoption of the Civil Rights Act of 1964. (The issue of what is considered "state action" under the Fourteenth and Fifteenth Amendments has been discussed earlier in Chapter 3.) But it required nearly a century of litigation to reach a clear holding that all governmental distinctions based on race were unconstitutional. One of the earliest post-Civil War cases on the application of the Fourteenth Amendment to racial discrimination was decided in 1880 and dealt with the constitutionality of a statutory bar to jury service for Negroes. The case was *Strauder* v. *West Virginia* and was decided by a Court whose members had lived through the Civil War and observed the activity of the subsequent Congresses in adopting constitutional amendments and legislation designed to protect the Negro.

STRAUDER *v.* WEST VIRGINIA
100 U.S. 303 (1880)

Mr. Justice Strong delivered the opinion of the Court.

[Strauder, a Negro, was convicted of murder in a West Virginia court by an all-white jury. Under state law only white male citizens were liable for jury service.

A petition for removal of the cause to the federal circuit court on the ground of racial discrimination in the selection of jurors was denied, and the trial proceeded in state court. The state supreme court affirmed the conviction and the United States Supreme Court reviewed the conviction on writ of error.]

[The Fourteenth Amendment] is one of a series of constitutional provisions having a common purpose; namely, securing to a race recently emancipated, a race that through many generations had been held in slavery, all the civil rights that the superior race enjoy. . . . At the time when they were incorporated into the Constitution, it required little knowledge of human nature to anticipate that those who had long been regarded as an inferior and subject race would, when suddenly raised to the rank of citizenship, be looked upon with jealousy and positive dislike, and that state laws might be enacted or enforced to perpetuate the distinctions that had before existed. Discriminations against them had been habitual. . . . They especially needed protection against unfriendly action in the States where they were resident. It was in view of these considerations the Fourteenth Amendment was framed and adopted.

It was designed to assure to the colored race the enjoyment of all the civil rights that under the law are enjoyed by white persons, and to give to that race the protection of the general government, in that enjoyment, whenever, it should be denied by the States. . . .

If this is the spirit and meaning of the amendment, whether it means more or not, it is to be construed liberally, to carry out the purposes of its framers. . . . It ordains that no State shall deprive any person of life, liberty, or property, without due process of law, or deny to any person within its jurisdiction the equal protection of the laws. What is this but declaring that the law in the States shall be the same for the black as for the white; that all persons, whether colored or white, shall stand equal before the laws of the States, and, in regard to the colored race, for whose protection the amendment was primarily designed, that no discrimination shall be made against them by law because of their color? The words of the amendment, it is true, are prohibitory, but they contain a necessary implication of a positive immunity, or right, most valuable to the colored race,—the right to exemption from unfriendly legislation against them distinctively as colored,—exemption from legal discriminations, implying inferiority in civil society, lessening the security of their enjoyment of the rights which others enjoy, and discriminations which are steps towards reducing them to the condition of a subject race. . . .

In view of these considerations, it is hard to see why the statute of West Virginia should not be regarded as discriminating against a colored man when he is put upon trial for an alleged criminal offense against the State. It is not easy to comprehend how it can be said that while every white man is entitled to a trial by a jury selected from persons of his own race or color, or rather, selected without discrimination against his color, and a negro is not, the latter is equally protected by the law with the former. Is not protection of life, and liberty against race or color prejudice a right, a legal right, under the constitutional amendment? And how can it be maintained that compelling a colored man to submit to a trial for his life by a jury drawn from a panel from which the State has expressly excluded every man of his race, because of color alone, however well qualified in other respects, is not a denial to him of equal legal protection? . . .

The Fourteenth Amendment makes no attempt to enumerate the rights it is designed to protect. It speaks in general terms, and those are as comprehensive as possible. Its language is prohibitory; but every prohibition implies the existence of rights and immunities, prominent among which is an immunity from inequality of legal protection, either for life, liberty, or property. Any state action that denies this immunity to a colored man is in conflict with the Constitution. . . .

Reversed.

[Justice Field, joined by Justice Clifford, dissented.]

The bar against state discrimination on race in jury service has been applied uniformly by the Court since *Strauder,* although it extends only to a requirement that racial discrimination not be employed in the selection process and does not command that a given racial distribution be found on a particular jury. (See the discussion of jury trial in Chapter 4.) Thus in *Hernandez* v. *Texas,* 347 U.S. 475 (1954), the Court reversed the conviction of a Mexican-American where the record showed a systematic exclusion of Mexican-Americans from juries.

Despite the sweeping statements in Justice Strong's opinion concerning the scope of protection offered by the Fourteenth Amendment against racial discrimination, the Court, less than twenty years later, in 1896, was prepared to uphold, with only one dissent, the power of the state to require racial segregation. The case was *Plessy* v. *Ferguson,* and the dissenter, Justice Harlan, was the only remaining member who had voted with the majority in the *Strauder* case. (Justice Field also remained, but he had dissented in the earlier case.)

PLESSY v. FERGUSON
163 U.S. 537 (1896)

Mr. Justice Brown . . . delivered the opinion of the court.

[A Louisiana statute, passed in 1890, required all railway companies carrying passengers in the State to provide "equal but separate accommodations for the white and colored races," and also that no person should be permitted to occupy seats in coaches other than the ones assigned to his race. Plessy alleged that he was seven-eighths Caucasian and one-eighth African blood, that he took a seat in a white coach, and upon his refusal to leave the coach was forcibly ejected, imprisoned, and charged with violation of the act. He petitioned for a writ of prohibition directed against the trial court on the ground that the statute was unconstitutional under the Thirteenth and Fourteenth Amendments. The Louisiana Supreme Court held the statute constitutional and denied the relief sought.]

That it does not conflict with the Thirteenth Amendment, which abolished slavery and involuntary servitude, . . . is too clear for argument. Slavery implies involuntary servitude,—a state of bondage; the ownership of mankind as a chattel, or, at least, the control of the labor and services of one man for the benefit of another. . . .

By the Fourteenth Amendment . . . the states are forbidden from making or enforcing any law which shall . . . deny to any person within their jurisdiction the equal protection of the laws. . . .

The object of the amendment was undoubtedly to enforce the absolute equality of the two races before the law, but in the nature of things it could not have been intended to abolish distinctions based upon color, or to enforce social, as distinguished from political, equality, or a commingling of the two races upon terms unsatisfactory to either. Laws permitting, and even requiring, their separation in places where they are liable to be brought into contact do not necessarily imply the inferiority of either race to the other, and have been generally, if not universally, recognized as within the competency of the state legislatures in the exercise of their police power. The most common instance of this is connected with the establishment of separate schools for white and colored children, which has been held to be a valid exercise of the legislative power even by courts of states where the political rights of the colored race have been longest and most earnestly enforced.

One of the earliest of these cases is that of *Roberts* v. *City of Boston*, 5 Cush. 198 (1849), in which the Supreme Judicial Court of Massachusetts held that the general school committee of Boston had power to make provision for the instruction of colored children in separate schools established exclusively for them, and to prohibit their attendance upon the other schools. . . . Similar laws have been enacted by Congress under its general power of legislation over the District of Columbia . . . as well as by the legislatures of many of the states, and have been generally, if not uniformly, sustained by the courts. . . .

The distinction between laws interfering with the political equality of the Negro and those requiring the separation of the two races in schools, theatres, and railway carriages has been frequently drawn by this court. . . .

We consider the underlying fallacy of the plaintiff's argument to consist in the assumption that the enforced separation of the two races stamps the colored race with a badge of inferiority. If this be so, it is not by reason of anything found in the act, but solely because the colored race chooses to put that construction upon it. The argument necessarily assumes that if . . . the colored race should become the dominant power in the state legislature, and should enact a law in precisely similar terms, it would thereby relegate the white race to an inferior position. We imagine that the white race, at least, would not acquiesce in this assumption. The argument also assumes that social prejudices may be overcome by legislation and that equal rights cannot be secured to the Negro except by an enforced commingling of the two races. We cannot accept this proposition. If the two races are to meet upon terms of social equality, it must be the result of natural affinities, a mutual appreciation of each other's merits, and a voluntary consent of individuals. . . .

Legislation is powerless to eradicate racial instincts or to abolish distinctions based upon physical differences, and the attempt to do so can only result in accentuating the difficulties of the present situation. If the civil and political rights of both races be equal, one cannot be inferior to the other civilly or politically. If one race be inferior to the other socially, the Constitution of the United States cannot put them upon the same plane. . . .

The judgment of the court below is, therefore,

Affirmed.

Mr. Justice Brewer did not hear the argument or participate in the decision of this case.

Mr. Justice Harlan, dissenting: . . .

In respect of civil rights, common to all citizens, the Constitution of the United States does not, I think, permit any public authority to know the race of those entitled to be protected in the enjoyment of such rights. . . .

It was said in argument that the statute of Louisiana does not discriminate against either race but prescribes a rule applicable alike to white and colored citizens. But this argument does not meet the difficulty. Everyone knows that the statute in question had its origin in the purpose, not so much to exclude white persons from railroad cars occupied by blacks, as to exclude colored people from coaches occupied or assigned to white persons.... The thing to accomplish was, under the guise of giving equal accommodations for whites and blacks, to compel the latter to keep to themselves while travelling in railroad passenger coaches. No one would be so wanting in candor as to assert the contrary. The fundamental objection, therefore, to the statute is that it interferes with the personal freedom of citizens....

The white race deems itself to be the dominant race in this country. And so it is, in prestige, in achievements, in education, in wealth, and in power. So, I doubt not, it will continue to be for all time, if it remains true to its great heritage and holds fast to the principles of constitutional liberty. But in the view of the Constitution, in the eye of the law, there is in this country no superior, dominant, ruling class of citizens. There is no caste here. Our Constitution is color-blind and neither knows nor tolerates classes among citizens. In respect of civil rights, all citizens are equal before the law. The humblest is the peer of the most powerful. The law regards man as man and takes no account of his surroundings or of his color when his civil rights as guaranteed by the supreme law of the land are involved....

The arbitrary separation of citizens, on the basis of race, while they are on a public highway, is a badge of servitude wholly inconsistent with the civil freedom and the equality before the law established by the Constitution. It cannot be justified upon any legal grounds.

If evils will result from the commingling of the two races upon public highways established for the benefit of all, they be infinitely less than those that will surely come from state legislation regulating the enjoyment of civil rights upon the basis of race. We boast of the freedom enjoyed by our people above all other peoples. But it is difficult to reconcile that boast with a state of the law which, practically, puts the brand of servitude and degradation upon a large class of our fellow citizens, our equals before the law. The thin disguise of "equal" accommodations for passengers in railroad coaches will not mislead anyone, nor atone for the wrong this day done....

It is difficult to reconcile the holding in *Plessy* with the language of Justice Strong in *Strauder* v. *West Virginia*. As Justice Harlan pointed out in his dissent in *Plessy*, it was clear to everyone that the equal but separate provisions in transportation and other laws were designed to perpetuate a caste system, even though the facilities for the two races might be equal. As a matter of fact, segregated facilities were rarely equal, but it was not until almost fifty years later that the Court came to grips with this issue.

If it was not unconstitutional for the state to segregate by race in transportation, then it was felt that it would be equally permissible to segregate in other areas, such as education, or parks, or swimming pools. The so-called "Jim Crow" laws became a pattern in the South and racial segregation in "social" activities was maintained, while under the *Strauder* rule and the Fifteenth Amendment at least most of the "political" arena was presumed to be constitutionally bound to a policy of freedom from racial differentiation. [See C. Vann Woodward, *The Strange Career of Jim Crow*, (New York: Oxford, 1955).]

Even this kind of rough distinction between "social" and "political" did not always obtain, however, as became evident when the issue of racial zoning in residential property came to the Court in 1917. In 1914, the City of Louisville, Kentucky, in order "to prevent conflict and ill-feeling between the white and colored races in the City of Louisville," enacted an ordinance which prohibited any Negro from moving into and occupying a residence in a block in which more than half the houses were occupied by whites and, conversely, prohibited whites from moving into a block in which the houses were predominantly Negro-occupied. Warley, a Negro, contracted with Buchanan for the purchase of a home in a block largely occupied by white residents. Buchanan then refused to complete the sale on the ground that the ordinance forbade it. Warley brought an action for specific performance on the contention that the ordinance violated the Fourteenth Amendment and thus was no defense to an action for specific performance. The Kentucky courts upheld the ordinance, and the case was carried to the United States Supreme Court for review on a writ of error. In *Buchanan* v. *Warley*, 245 U.S. 60 (1917), the Court held the ordinance violative of the Fourteenth Amendment.

Justice Day, speaking for a unanimous Court, stated, in part:

That there exists a serious and difficult problem arising from a feeling of race hostility which the law is powerless to control, and to which it must give a measure of consideration, may be freely admitted. But its solution cannot be promoted by depriving citizens of their constitutional rights and privileges.

As we have seen, this court has held laws valid which separated the races on the basis of equal accommodations in public conveyances, and courts of high authority have held enactments lawful which provide for separation in the public schools of white and colored pupils where equal privileges are given. But in view of the rights secured by the Fourteenth Amendment to the federal Constitution such legislation must have its limitations, and cannot be sustained where the exercise of authority exceeds the restraints of the Constitution. We think these limitations are exceeded in laws and ordinances of the character now before us.

It is the purpose of such enactments, and, it is frankly avowed it will be their ultimate effect, to require by law, at least in residential districts, the compulsory separation of the races on account of color. Such action is said to be essential to the maintenance of the purity of the races, although it is to be noted in the ordinance under consideration that the employment of colored servants in white families is permitted, and near-by residences of colored persons not coming within the blocks, as defined in the ordinance, are not prohibited.

The case presented does not deal with an attempt to prohibit the amalgamation of the races. The right which the ordinance annulled was the civil rights of a white man to dispose of his property if he saw fit to do so to a person of color and of a colored person to make such disposition to a white person.

It is urged that this proposed segregation will promote the public peace by preventing race conflicts. Desirable as this is, and important as is the preservation of the public peace, this aim cannot be accomplished by laws or ordinances which deny rights created or protected by the federal Constitution.

It is said that such acquisitions by colored persons depreciate property owned in the neighborhood by white persons. But property may be acquired by undesirable white neighbors or put to disagreeable though lawful uses with like results.

We think this attempt to prevent the alienation of the property in question to a person of color was not a legitimate exercise of the police power of the State, and is in direct violation of the fundamental law enacted in the Fourteenth Amendment of the Constitution preventing state interference with property rights except by due process of law. That being the case, the ordinance cannot stand.

It should be noted that the decision came off on the ground that for the state so to restrict the property owner was a deprivation of property without due process of law. Technically, then, the holding did not interfere with the earlier interpretation of the "equal protection" clause that racial segregation imposed by law in nonpolitical areas was not barred. It did, however, point up the anomaly in such an interpretation, and the Court was sharply criticized for giving greater protection to the property rights of Negroes than to their personal rights. In rebuttal, it was contended that the Congress following the Civil War had enacted legislation specifically to protect the right of all citizens "to inherit, purchase, lease, sell, hold, and convey real and personal property" (14 Stat. 27, 1866), while it also established schools for the District of Columbia on a racially segregated basis. Thus it was argued that the Congress intended to protect property rights through the Fourteenth Amendment but did not intend for that Amendment to restrict racial segregation imposed by law. As a consequence of the decision in *Buchanan* v. *Warley,* the practice developed of incorporating racially restrictive covenants in deeds conveying property. (The cases involving the validity of the enforcement of such covenants by the state are taken up below.)

Taking the decisions in *Strauder, Plessy,* and *Buchanan* together, it would appear that by the end of World War I a rough rule had been developed that the state could not make racial distinctions in the area of political or property rights, but racial segregation in "social" areas could be imposed by law on a "separate but equal" basis. Added to this is the holding in the *Civil Rights Cases,* 109 U.S. 3 (1883), (discussed in Chapter 3) that the Fourteenth Amendment barred only *state* action of certain types and not racial barriers set up by *private* action. This decision was double-edged in that it not only limited judicial remedies in actions brought under the Fourteenth Amendment, but it also, and to the same extent, limited the scope of legislation adopted by Congress to enforce the provisions of the Fourteenth Amendment. The rule of *Strauder-Plessy-Buchanan,* and the rule of the *Civil Rights Cases,* however, suggested three broad avenues of attack on racial discrimination. Within the framework of these decisions it was still possible to enter the judicial arena and argue (1) that a given right was political in nature and that the state should be barred from making any kind of racial distinctions in its exercise, or (2) that a given facility, required by state law to be segregated, was operated in such fashion that Negroes were not in fact being treated equally with whites, or (3) that a particular form of racial discrimination, though nominally imposed by private action, was in some manner being furthered by the active assistance or participation of the state in such fashion as to bring the imposition within the category of "state action" prohibited by the Fourteenth or Fifteenth Amendments.

The first approach has been used repeatedly in such areas as racial discrimination in jury selection and in voting rights. Despite the clear holding in *Strauder*, the Court has repeatedly found it necessary to review, and reverse, convictions of Negroes where a long-continued pattern of discrimination in the selection of jurors was followed. And in *Pierre* v. *Louisiana*, 306 U.S. 354 (1939), the Court held unanimously that even in the grand jury the Negro defendant was constitutionally entitled to a panel free from selection methods which discriminated against Negroes because of their race. (The discussion of racial discrimination in voting will be reserved for the chapter following.)

The second approach is the one which was ultimately successful in barring racial segregation in public schools in the landmark case of *Brown* v. *Board of Education* in 1954. It is not suggested that the earlier cases brought on this ground were part of an organized, frontal assault on the whole concept of segregation by race. They were, in fact, sporadic, isolated cases, and not until after the end of World War II was there a conscious strategy employed to press the case for exact equality of facilities to the point that separate facilities were by this very fact unequal.

The earlier cases arguing inequality of facilities were brought in situations where the Negro was offered no facilities whatever in an area where they were available to whites. The Court had little difficulty finding a violation of the Fourteenth Amendment in such instances where there was no pretense of affording separate but equal treatment. In *McCabe* v. *Atchison, T. & S.F. Ry.*, 235 U.S. 151 (1914), the Court held void a separate coach law of Oklahoma which permitted carriers to provide sleeping and dining cars only for white persons, notwithstanding the state's contention that there was little demand for them by colored persons. Nearly twenty-five years later a similar issue was presented, this time in the field of education, and again the Court held the state provision to be a violation of the equal protection of the laws. The state of Missouri maintained a law school at its university for white students but had none at the state university for Negroes. It provided by statute for the payment of tuition fees for any of its Negro citizens to study law "at the university of any adjacent state," but refused to admit them to the white law school. In *Missouri ex rel. Gaines* v. *Canada*, 305 U.S. 337 (1938), the Court unanimously held that petitioner had been denied equal protection of the laws. Chief Justice Hughes, speaking for the Court, stated:

The admissibility of laws separating the races in the enjoyment of privileges afforded by the State rests wholly upon the equality of the privileges which the laws give to the separated groups within the State. The question here is not of a duty of the State to supply legal training, or of the quality of the training which it does supply, but of its duty when it provides such training to furnish it to the residents of the State upon the basis of an equality of right. By the operation of the laws of Missouri a privilege has been created for white law students which is denied to negroes by reason of their race. The white resident is afforded legal education within the State; the negro resident having the same qualifications is refused it there and must go outside the State to obtain it. That is a denial of the equality of legal right to the enjoyment of the privilege which the State has set up, and the provision for the payment of tuition fees in another State does not remove the discrimination. . . . That resort may mitigate the inconvenience of the discrimination but cannot serve to validate it.

Nor can we regard the fact that there is but a limited demand in Missouri for the legal education of negroes as excusing the discrimination in favor of whites. We had occasion to consider a cognate question in the case of *McCabe* v. *Atchison, T. & S.F. Ry. Co.* . . . We found that argument to be without merit. It made, we said, the constitutional right "depend upon the number of persons who may be discriminated against, whereas the essence of the constitutional right is that it is a personal one. Whether or not particular facilities shall be provided may doubtless be conditioned upon there being a reasonable demand therefor; but, if facilities are provided, substantial equality of treatment of persons traveling under like conditions cannot be refused. It is the individual who is entitled to the equal protection of the laws, and if he is denied by a common carrier, acting in the matter under the authority of a state law, a facility or convenience in the course of his journey which, under substantially the same circumstances, is furnished to another traveler, he may properly complain that his constitutional privilege has been invaded." *Id.*, 235 U.S. 161, 162. . . .

The *McCabe* and *Gaines* cases can, of course, be confined to the narrow holding that privileges created by law for white persons cannot be denied to Negroes, although they can be constitutionally provided on a segregated basis. There are phrases in the two opinions, however, which suggest that the segregated facilities should in fact be equal. The opinion in *McCabe* states that "substantial equality of treatment . . . cannot be refused." And in *Gaines* the Court refers to "the equality of legal right to the enjoyment of the privilege which the State has set up." Not yet, however, did the Court squarely hold that separate facilities had to be truly equal to meet the requirements of equal protection.

Meanwhile a sort of collateral attack on segregation by race was undertaken in the field of interstate transportation. In *Mitchell* v. *United States*, 313 U.S. 80 (1941), the Court held that for a railroad to deny Pullman car accommodations to a Negro solely because of his race was in violation of the provision of the Interstate Commerce Act forbidding "any undue or unreasonable prejudice or disadvantage in any respect whatsoever." The decision stands with *McCabe* and *Gaines*, however, as a case involving absolute denial of a facility rather than the equality of separately provided facilities. The next approach was to argue that separate facilities required by state law on interstate carriers was an undue burden on interstate commerce. This argument was successful in *Morgan* v. *Virginia*, 328 U.S. 373 (1946), in which the Court held that the mandatory reseating of passengers when a state line was crossed was a burden on interstate commerce not supportable under the police power of the state. In the absence of state laws, however, private regulations of carriers requiring segregation of passengers remained unaffected by this ruling. This gap was closed by the ruling in *Henderson* v. *United States*, 339 U.S. 816 (1950), in which the Court held that the nondiscrimination requirement of the Interstate Commerce Act barred a railroad from enforcing its rule providing for segregated dining facilities on its cars. And *Boynton* v. *Virginia*, 364 U.S. 454 (1960), extended the holding to the terminal and restaurant facilities of interstate bus carriers.

In the same year that the *Henderson* case was decided, the Court decided two other cases in the field of higher education which squarely opened the way for an attack on segregated facilities on the ground that accommodations for Negroes were not in actuality equal to those for white persons. *McLaurin* v. *Oklahoma State Regents*, 339 U.S. 637 (1950), involved a Negro in the graduate school of the University of Oklahoma. Under the requirements of the *Gaines* holding, the state had provided that qualified Negroes could be admitted to white state schools where the Negro school did not offer the requested course of study. Once McLaurin was admitted, however, rigid segregation practices prevailed within the University. He was assigned a special "colored" seat in each classroom, a special table was provided for him in the library, and he was required to eat in a segregated portion of the cafeteria. The Court declared these conditions unconstitutional on the ground that they would "impair and inhibit his ability to study, to engage in discussions and exchange views with other students."

On the same day the Court rendered its decision in *Sweatt* v. *Painter*, 339 U.S. 629 (1950), involving the petition of a Negro for admission to the University of Texas Law School. A separate law school for Negroes was provided by the state, but the petition alleged that its facilities were not substantially equivalent to those of the white school, and therefore he was constitutionally entitled to be admitted to the white school. The Court held unanimously that the petitioner should be admitted to the University of Texas. Chief Justice Vinson, speaking for the Court, said:

> The University of Texas Law School, from which petitioner was excluded, was staffed by a faculty of sixteen full-time and three part-time professors, some of whom are nationally recognized authorities in their field. Its student body num-

bered 850. The library contained over 65,000 volumes. Among the other facilities available to the students were a law review, moot court facilities, scholarship funds, and Order of the Coif affiliation. The school's alumni occupy the most distinguished positions in the private practice of the law and in the public life of the State. It may properly be considered one of the nation's ranking law schools.

The law school for Negroes which was to have opened in February, 1947, would have had no independent faculty or library. The teaching was to be carried on by four members of the University of Texas Law School faculty, who were to maintain their offices at the University of Texas while teaching at both institutions. Few of the 10,000 volumes ordered for the library had arrived; nor was there any full-time librarian. The school lacked accreditation.

Since the trial of this case, respondents report the opening of a law school at the Texas State University for Negroes. It is apparently on the road to full accreditation. It has a faculty of five full-time professors; a student body of 23; a library of some 16,500 volumes serviced by a full-time staff; a practice court and legal aid association; and one alumnus who has become a member of the Texas Bar.

Whether the University of Texas Law School is compared with the original or the new law school for Negroes, we cannot find substantial equality in the educational opportunities offered white and Negro law students by the State. In terms of number of the faculty, variety of courses and opportunity for specialization, size of the student body, scope of the library, availability of law review and similar activities, the University of Texas Law School is superior. What is more important, the University of Texas Law School possesses to a far greater degree those qualities which are incapable of objective measurement but which make for greatness in a law school. Such qualities, to name but a few, include reputation of the faculty, experience of the administration, position and influence of the alumni, standing in the community, traditions and prestige. It is difficult to believe that one who had a free choice between these law schools would consider the question close.

... The law school to which Texas is willing to admit petitioner excludes from its student body members of the racial groups which number 85 per cent of the population of the State and include most of the lawyers, witnesses, jurors, judges and other officials with whom petitioner will inevitably be dealing when he becomes a member of the Texas Bar. With such a substantial and significant segment of society excluded, we cannot conclude that the education offered petitioner is substantially equal to that which he would receive if admitted to the University of Texas Law School. ...

In holding that the Texas practice violated the "equal protection" clause, the Court refused, however, to re-examine the separate but equal doctrine. Nonetheless, the decision and the general tenor of the Court's opinion suggested strongly that the time might be ripe for such a re-examination. To make a point of the opportunities of students for "intellectual commingling" in the *McLaurin* case and to examine and recognize "those qualities which are incapable of objective measurement" such as reputation of the faculty, the school's standing in the community, and the "position and influence of the alumni," as the Court did in *Sweatt* is certainly to give strong intimations that separate facilities in education are inherently unequal and therefore unconstitutional. Actions were brought in several states and in the District of Columbia with the hope that this issue could ultimately be squarely raised in the United States Supreme Court. In December of 1952 the Court heard argument in its appellate review of four cases involving segregated school laws in the states of Kansas, Virginia, South Carolina, and Delaware, and one case involving the validity of maintaining segregated public schools in the District of Columbia. In December of the following year, 1953, the cases were reargued on certain questions propounded by the Court. Finally, on May 17, 1954, the Court handed down its momentous decision that governmentally enforced racial segregation in public schools was unconstitutional. The state cases, decided together and reported officially under the name of the Kansas case, *Brown* v. *Board of Education of Topeka, Kansas,* were based on the "equal protection" clause of the Fourteenth Amendment. The District of Columbia case, *Bolling* v. *Sharpe,* was based on an equal protection requirement as implied in the "due process" clause of the Fifth Amendment.

BROWN *v.* BOARD OF EDUCATION OF TOPEKA

347 U.S. 483 (1954)

Mr. Chief Justice Warren delivered the opinion of the Court.

These cases come to us from the States of Kansas, South Carolina, Virginia, and Delaware. They are premised on different facts and different local conditions, but a common legal question justifies their consideration together in this consolidated opinion.

In each of the cases, minors of the Negro race, through their legal representatives, seek the aid of the courts in obtaining admission to the public schools of their community on a nonsegregated basis. In each instance, they had been denied admission to schools attended by white children under laws requiring or permitting segregation according to race. This segregation was alleged to deprive the plaintiffs of the equal protection of the laws under the Fourteenth Amendment. In each of the cases other than the Delaware case, a three-judge federal district court denied relief to the plaintiffs on the so-called "separate but equal" doctrine announced by this Court in *Plessy* v. *Ferguson,* 163 U.S. 537. Under that doctrine, equality of treatment is accorded when the races are provided substantially equal facilities, even though these facilities be separate. In the Delaware case, the Supreme Court of Delaware adhered to that doctrine, but ordered that the plaintiffs be admitted to the white schools because of their superiority to the Negro schools.

The plaintiffs contend that segregated public schools are not "equal" and cannot be made "equal," and that hence they are deprived of the equal protection of the laws. Because of the obvious importance of the question presented, the Court took jurisdiction. Argument was heard in the 1952 Term, and reargument was heard this Term on certain questions propounded by the Court.

[The order was issued on June 8, 1953, 345 U.S. 972, and requested counsel "to discuss particularly" five questions. The first three questions are answered in the instant case, but questions 4 and 5 are set out for still further argument in the following Term. The five questions were:

"1. What evidence is there that the Congress which submitted and the State legislatures and conventions which ratified the Fourteenth Amendment contemplated or did not contemplate, understood or did not understand, that it would abolish segregation in public schools?

"2. If neither the Congress in submitting nor the States in ratifying the Fourteenth Amendment understood that compliance with it would require the immediate abolition of segregation in public schools, was it nevertheless the understanding of the framers of the Amendment

(a) that future Congresses might, in the exercise of their power under section 5 of the Amendment, abolish such segregation, or

(b) that it would be within the judicial power, in light of future conditions, to construe the Amendment as abolishing such segregation of its own force?

"3. On the assumption that the answers to questions 2(a) and (b) do not dispose of the issue, is it within the judicial power, in construing the Amendment, to abolish segregation in public schools?

"4. Assuming it is decided that segregation in public schools violated the Fourteenth Amendment

(a) would a decree necessarily follow providing that, within the limits set by normal geographic school districting, Negro children should forthwith be admitted to schools of their choice, or

(b) may this Court, in the exercise of its equity powers, permit an effective gradual adjustment to be brought about from existing segregated systems to a system not based on color distinctions?

"5. On the assumption on which questions 4(a) and (b) are based, and assuming further that this Court will exercise its equity powers to the end described in question 4(b),

(a) should this Court formulate detailed decrees in these cases;

(b) if so, what specific issues should the decrees reach;

(c) should this Court appoint a special master to hear evidence with a view to recommending specific terms for such decrees;

(d) should this Court remand to the courts of first instance with directions to frame decrees in these cases, and if so what general directions should the decrees of this Court include and what procedures should the courts of first instance follow in arriving at the specific terms of more detailed decrees?" 345 U.S., 972.

The Attorney General of the United States participated both Terms as *amicus curiae*.]

Reargument was largely devoted to the circumstances surrounding the adoption of the Fourteenth Amendment in 1868. It covered exhaustively consideration of the Amendment in Congress, ratification by the states, then existing practices in racial segregation, and the views of proponents and opponents of the Amendment. This discussion and our own investigation convince us that, although these sources cast some light, it is not enough to resolve the problem with which we are faced. At best, they are inconclusive. The most avid proponents of the post-War Amendments undoubtedly intended them to remove all legal distinctions among "all persons born or naturalized in the United States." Their opponents, just as certainly, were antagonistic to both the letter and the spirit of the Amendments and wished them to have the most limited effect. What others in Congress and the state legislatures had in mind cannot be determined with any degree of certainty.

An additional reason for the inconclusive nature of the Amendment's history, with respect to segregated schools, is the status of public education at that time.

In the South, the movement toward free common schools, supported by general taxation, had not yet taken hold. Education of white children was largely in the hands of private groups. Education of Negroes was almost nonexistent, and practically all of the race were illiterate. In fact, any education of Negroes was forbidden by law in some states. Today, in contrast, many Negroes have achieved outstanding success in the arts and sciences as well as in the business and professional world. It is true that public school education at the time of the Amendment had advanced further in the North, but the effect of the Amendment on Northern States was generally ignored in the congressional debates. Even in the North, the conditions of public education did not approximate those existing today. The curriculum was usually rudimentary; ungraded schools were common in rural areas; the school term was but three months a year in many states; and compulsory school attendance was virtually unknown. As a consequence, it is not surprising that there should be so little in the history of the Fourteenth Amendment relating to its intended effect on public education.

In the first cases in this Court construing the Fourteenth Amendment, decided shortly after its adoption, the Court interpreted it as proscribing all state-imposed discriminations against the Negro race.* The doctrine of "separate but equal" did not make its appearance in this Court until 1896 in the case of *Plessy* v. *Ferguson, supra,* involving not education but transportation.** American courts have since labored with the doctrine for over half a century. In this Court, there have been six cases involving the "separate but equal" doctrine in the field of public education. In *Cumming* v. *County Board of Education*, 175 U.S. 528, and *Gong Lum* v. *Rice*, 275 U.S. 78, the validity of the doctrine itself was not challenged. In more recent cases, all on the graduate school level, inequality was found in that specific benefits enjoyed by white students were denied to Negro students of the same educational qualifications. *Missouri ex rel. Gaines* v. *Canada*, 305 U.S. 337; *Sipuel* v. *Oklahoma*, 332 U.S. 631; *Sweatt* v. *Painter*, 339 U.S. 629; *McLaurin* v. *Oklahoma State Regents*, 339 U.S. 637. In none of these cases was it necessary to re-examine the doctrine to grant relief to the Negro plaintiff. And in *Sweatt* v. *Painter, supra,* the Court expressly reserved decision on the question whether *Plessy* v. *Ferguson* should be held inapplicable to public education.

In the instant cases, that question is directly presented. Here, unlike *Sweatt* v. *Painter,* there are findings below that the Negro and white schools involved have been equalized, or are being equalized, with respect to buildings, curricula, qualifications and salaries of teachers, and other "tangible" factors. Our decision, therefore, cannot turn on merely a comparison of these tangible factors in the Negro and white schools involved in each of the cases. We must look instead to the effect of segregation itself on public education.

In approaching this problem we cannot turn the clock back to 1868 when the Amendment was adopted, or even to 1896 when *Plessy* v. *Ferguson* was written. We must consider public education in the light of its full development and its present place in American life throughout the Nation. Only in this way can it be

---

* *Slaughter-House Cases,* 16 Wall. 36, 67–72 (1873); *Strauder* v. *West Virginia*, 100 U.S. 303, 307–308 (1880).... See also *Virginia* v. *Rives*, 100 U.S. 313 (1880); *Ex parte Virginia*, 100 U.S. 339, 344–345 (1880).

** The doctrine apparently originated in *Roberts* v. *City of Boston*, 59 Mass. 198, 206 (1850), upholding school segregation against attack as being violative of a state constitutional guarantee of equality....,

determined if segregation in public schools deprives these plaintiffs of the equal protection of the laws.

Today, education is perhaps the most important function of state and local governments. Compulsory school attendance laws and the great expenditures for education both demonstrate our recognition of the importance of education to our democratic society. It is required in the performance of our most basic public responsibilities, even service in the armed forces. It is the very foundation of good citizenship. Today it is a principal instrument in awakening the child to cultural values, in preparing him for later professional training, and in helping him to adjust normally to his environment. In these days, it is doubtful that any child may reasonably be expected to succeed in life if he is denied the opportunity of an education. Such an opportunity, where the state has undertaken to provide it, is a right which must be made available to all on equal terms.

We come then to the question presented: Does segregation of children in public schools solely on the basis of race, even though the physical facilities and other "tangible" factors may be equal, deprive the children of the minority group of equal education opportunities? We believe that it does.

In *Sweatt v. Painter, supra,* in finding that a segregated law school for Negroes could not provide them equal educational opportunities, this Court relied in large part on "those qualities which are incapable of objective measurement but which make for greatness in a law school." In *McLaurin* v. *Oklahoma State Regents, supra,* the Court, in requiring that a Negro admitted to a white graduate school be treated like all other students, again resorted to intangible considerations: ". . . his ability to study, to engage in discussions and exchange views with other students, and, in general, to learn his profession." Such considerations apply with added force to children in grade and high schools. To separate them from others of similar age and qualifications solely because of their race generates a feeling of inferiority as to their status in the community that may affect their hearts and minds in a way unlikely ever to be undone. The effect of this separation on their educational opportunities was well stated by a finding in the Kansas case by a court which nevertheless felt compelled to rule against the Negro plaintiffs:

"Segregation of white and colored children in public schools has a detrimental effect upon the colored children. The impact is greater when it has the sanction of the law; for the policy of separating the races is usually interpreted as denoting the inferiority of the negro group. A sense of inferiority affects the motivation of a child to learn. Segregation with the sanction of law, therefore, has a tendency to [retard] the educational and mental development of negro children and to deprive them of some of the benefits they would receive in a racial[ly] integrated school system."

Whatever may have been the extent of psychological knowledge at the time of *Plessy* v. *Ferguson,* this finding is amply supported by modern authority.*** Any language in *Plessy* v. *Ferguson* contrary to this finding is rejected.

*** K. B. Clark, *Effect of Prejudice and Discrimination on Personality Development* (Midcentury White House Conference on Children and Youth, 1950); Witmer and Kotinsky, *Personality in the Making* (1952), c. VI; Deutscher and Chein, "The Psychological Effects of Enforced Segregation: a Survey of Social Science Opinion," 26 *J. Psychol.* 259 (1948); Chein, "What Are the Psychological Effects of Segregation Under Conditions of Equal Facilities?" 3 *Int. J. Opinion and Attitude Res.* 229 (1949); Brameld, *Educational Costs in Discrimination and National Welfare* (MacIver, ed., 1949), 44–48; Frazier, *The Negro in the United States* (1949), 674–681. And see generally Gunnar Myrdal, *An American Dilemma* (1944).

We conclude that in the field of public education the doctrine of "separate but equal" has no place. Separate educational facilities are inherently unequal. Therefore, we hold that the plaintiffs and others similarly situated for whom the actions have been brought are, by reason of the segregation complained of, deprived of the equal protection of the laws guaranteed by the Fourteenth Amendment. This disposition makes unnecessary any discussion whether such segregation also violates the Due Process Clause of the Fourteenth Amendment.

Because these are class actions, because of the wide applicability of this decision, and because of the great variety of local conditions, the formulation of decrees in these cases presents problems of considerable complexity. On reargument, the consideration of appropriate relief was necessarily subordinated to the primary question —the constitutionality of segregation in public education. We have now announced that such segregation is a denial of the equal protection of the laws. In order that we may have the full assistance of the parties in formulating decrees, the cases will be restored to the docket, and the parties are requested to present further argument on Questions 4 and 5 previously propounded by the Court for the reargument this Term. . . .

It is so ordered.

In *Bolling* v. *Sharpe*, 347 U.S. 497 (1954), decided the same day, the Court held that racial segregation enforced by the federal government in the public schools of the District of Columbia was violative of the Fifth Amendment. The case was treated separately since there is no "equal protection" clause applicable to the federal government. The Court, however, had no difficulty in reading the requirement into the "due process" clause of the Fifth Amendment. It was pointed out that classifications may be so arbitrary and unjust as to be violative of due process, and racial discrimination by the federal government fell into this category. Chief Justice Warren, for the Court, stated:

In view of our decision that the Constitution prohibits the states from maintaining racially segregated public schools, it would be unthinkable that the same Constitution would impose a lesser duty on the Federal Government. We hold that racial segregation in the public schools of the District of Columbia is a denial of the due process of law guaranteed by the Fifth Amendment to the Constitution.

In two landmark decisions, then, coming near the end of the term in 1954, the Court held that governmentally enforced racial segregation in the public schools was forbidden by the Constitution. Two points should be noted. First, the Court did not in these decisions state that the Constitution commanded governmental *integration* of the schools. It stated only that the policy of forcible segregation by the governments of the nation was invalid. Second, although *Plessy* v. *Ferguson* was not squarely overruled, and the decisions were technically limited to segregation in public education, the Court did say that any language in *Plessy* "contrary to this finding is rejected," and the clear import of the decision was a renunciation of *Plessy*. The final step in overruling *Plessy* was taken in *Gayle* v. *Brow-*

der, 352 U.S. 903 (1956), which held invalid, under the "equal protection" clause, a city ordinance requiring segregation on motor buses operated within the city of Montgomery, Alabama.

Having held that racial segregation enforced by government in the public schools was unconstitutional, the Court was then faced with the question of how best to implement the decision. As stated in the *Brown* opinion, the Court decided to hear further argument on this question before issuing any enforcement decree. Argument was heard in April 1955, and the opinion and judgments were announced in May 1955.

BROWN *v.* BOARD OF EDUCATION OF TOPEKA
349 U.S. 294 (1955)

Mr. Chief Justice Warren delivered the opinion of the Court.

These cases were decided on May 17, 1954. The opinions of that date, declaring the fundamental principle that racial discrimination in public education is unconstitutional, are incorporated herein by reference. All provisions of federal, state, or local law requiring or permitting such discrimination must yield to this principle. There remains for consideration the manner in which relief is to be accorded.

Because these cases arose under different local conditions and their disposition will involve a variety of local problems, we requested further argument on the question of relief. In view of the nationwide importance of the decision, we invited the Attorney General of the United States and the Attorneys General of all states requiring or permitting racial discrimination in public education to present their views on that question. . . .

These presentations were informative and helpful to the Court in its consideration of the complexities arising from the transition to a system of public education freed of racial discrimination. . . .

Full implementation of these constitutional principles may require solution of varied local school problems. School authorities have the primary responsibility for elucidating, assessing, and solving these problems; courts will have to consider whether the action of school authorities constitutes good faith implementation of the governing constitutional principles. Because of their proximity to local conditions and the possible need for further hearings, the courts which originally heard these cases can best perform this judicial appraisal. Accordingly, we believe it appropriate to remand the cases to those courts.

In fashioning and effectuating the decrees, the courts will be guided by equitable principles. Traditionally, equity has been characterized by a practical flexibility in shaping its remedies and by a facility for adjusting and reconciling public and private needs. These cases call for the exercise of these traditional attributes of equity power. At stake is the personal interest of the plaintiffs in admission to public schools as soon as practicable on a nondiscriminatory basis. To effectuate this interest may call for elimination of a variety of obstacles in making the transition to school systems operated in accordance with the constitutional principles set forth in our May 17, 1954, decision. Courts of equity may properly take into account the public interest in the elimination of such obstacles in a systematic and effective manner. But it should go without saying that the vitality of these constitutional principles cannot be allowed to yield simply because of disagreement with them.

While giving weight to these public and private considerations, the courts will require that the defendants make a prompt and reasonable start toward full compliance with our May 17, 1954 ruling. Once such a start has been made, the courts may find that additional time is necessary to carry out the ruling in an effective manner. The burden rests upon the defendants to establish that such time is necessary in the public interest and is consistent with good faith compliance at the earliest practicable date. To that end, the courts may consider problems related to administration, arising from the physical condition of the school plant, the school transportation system, personnel, revision of school districts and attendance areas into compact units to achieve a system of determining admission to the public schools on a nonracial basis, and revision of local laws and regulations which may be necessary in solving the foregoing problems. They will also consider the adequacy of any plans the defendants may propose to meet these problems and to effectuate a transition to a racially nondiscriminatory school system. During this period of transition, the courts will retain jurisdiction of these cases.

The judgments below, except that in the Delaware case, are accordingly reversed and the cases are remanded to the District Courts to take such proceedings and enter such orders and decrees consistent with this opinion as are necessary and proper to admit to public schools on a racially nondiscriminatory basis with all deliberate speed the parties to these cases. . . .

[For more recent decisions requiring a unitary school system and upholding busing orders, see *Green* v. *School Board of New Kent County,* 391 U.S. 430 (1968), and *Swann* v. *Charlotte-Mecklenburg Board of Education,* 402 U.S. 1 (1971) in Chap. 9.]

Following hard on the heels of the second *Brown* decision, the Court in 1956, in *Gayle* v. *Browder,* extended the *Brown* rule to the field of transportation, and thus to all areas under governmental regulation. By 1956, then, the Court had officially ruled that any governmentally imposed policy of segregation by race in any area of activity was in violation of the equal protection of the laws. In addition, the transportation cases involving interstate commerce, discussed earlier in this chapter, had laid down a firm rule that racial discrimination in interstate carriers or in restaurant and terminal facilities operated in conjunction with an interstate carrier violated the nondiscrimination clause of the Interstate Commerce Act. Thus the second broad avenue of attack on racial segregation—that separate facilities required by law were not equal—resulted in a firm holding that the separate but equal doctrine was unconstitutional.

Such decisions, however, only affected practices in the public sector or those properly brought by Congress within the application of its commerce power. There still remained an enormous area of private or quasi-public operations in which race discrimination was practiced and which could not readily be fitted into the framework of decisions relating to enforcement of racially discriminatory legislation or governmental regulations. For these areas a third attack was developed in the courts. The basic approach was fairly simple, although the development of the legal doctrines to support it required a great deal of expert legal scholarship and sustained pressure-group style strategy of a kind peculiar to the process of "judicial lobbying." [For an account of this aspect of litigation see Clement Vose, *Caucasians Only: The Supreme Court, the N.A.A.C.P., and the Restrictive Covenant Cases* (Berkeley: University of California Press, 1959).] The approach was simply to bring as much activity as possible within the concept of "state action" rather than private action. The Fourteenth Amendment bars racial discrimination imposed by "state action," so the more agencies and activities which could be classified within that category, the fewer sectors would remain in which discrimination could validly be carried on under the Constitution.

The first area of attack under this approach was racial discrimination in the Democratic primaries in the South, with a long series of cases beginning in the 1920's and culminating in a square holding in 1953 that a Democratic primary was a governmental institution and that no person could be barred from participation because of his race. (The voting cases will be discussed in the following chapter.) Since a political right was involved, and since the Fifteenth Amendment clearly prohibited governmental discrimination based on race in voting, it did not require the abrogation of the "separate but equal" doctrine to support the Negro claimant's argument. Thus in the category of political and property rights the "state action" approach could be, and was, utilized even before the demise of "separate but equal." Once the claimed right was clearly brought into the magic circle of political and property rights, it was then only necessary to make a proper showing that the denial of the right was in some fair manner carried out under the aegis of governmental authority and a decision could be obtained that racially discriminatory enforcement would violate the Fourteenth or Fifteenth Amendments.

It was pointed out earlier that following the decision in *Buchanan* v. *Warley*, holding that racial zoning by ordinance violated the Fourteenth Amendment, the practice developed of incorporating racially restrictive covenants in deeds conveying property. By the terms of the contract, a buyer of such property would agree never to sell the property to persons of African descent, or Oriental descent, or whatever other nationality the covenant excluded. Presumably, if the buyer violated the agreement and attempted to convey the property to a person in the excluded category, the original seller could file an action in a court of equity and have the later conveyance set aside. But this raised an interesting constitutional issue. Does the participation of the state, in a judicial proceeding setting aside a contract as contrary to a racially restrictive covenant, inject sufficient governmental activity into the transaction to bring it within the category of "state action" within the meaning of the Fourteenth Amendment? If so, then the rule of *Buchanan* v. *Warley* should govern and such participation should be unconstitutional. If not, then the Fourteenth Amendment would not apply, and private discrimination is not barred by the Constitution. After a number of abortive attempts to present the issue before the United States Supreme Court, various organizations interested in the problem of discrimination in residential property were successful in bringing two cases to the Court for decision in 1948. The cases were *Shelley* v. *Kraemer* and *McGhee* v. *Sipes*, and they illustrate clearly the attack on discrimination through broadening the scope of coverage of "state action."

SHELLEY v. KRAEMER
334 U.S. 1 (1948)

Mr. Chief Justice Vinson delivered the opinion of the Court.

These cases present for our consideration questions relating to the validity of court enforcement of private agreements, generally described as restrictive covenants, which have as their purpose the exclusion of persons of designated race or color from the ownership or occupancy of real property. Basic constitutional issues of obvious importance have been raised. . . .

I

Whether the equal protection clause of the Fourteenth Amendment inhibits judicial enforcement by state courts of restrictive covenants based on race or color is a question which this Court has not heretofore been called upon to consider. . . .

It cannot be doubted that among the civil rights intended to be protected from discriminatory state action by the Fourteenth Amendment are the rights to acquire, enjoy, own, and dispose of property. Equality in the enjoyment of property rights was regarded by the framers of that Amendment as an essential pre-condition to the realization of other basic civil rights and liberties which the Amendment was intended to guarantee. . . .

This Court has given specific recognition to the same principle. *Buchanan* v. *Warley*, 245 U.S. 60 (1917).

It is likewise clear that restrictions on the right of occupancy of the sort sought to be created by the private agreements in these cases could not be squared with the requirements of the Fourteenth Amendment if imposed by state statute or local ordinance. . . .

But the present cases, unlike those just discussed, do not involve action by state legislatures or city councils. Here the particular patterns of discrimination and the areas in which the restrictions are to operate, are determined, in the first instance, by the terms of agreements among private individuals. Participation of the State consists in the enforcement of the restrictions so defined. The crucial issue with which we are here confronted is whether this distinction removes these cases from the operation of the prohibitory provisions of the Fourteenth Amendment.

Since the decision of this Court in the *Civil Rights Cases*, 109 U.S. 3 (1883), the principle has become firmly embedded in our constitutional law that the action inhibited by the first section of the Fourteenth Amendment is only such action as may fairly be said to be that of the States. That Amendment erects no shield against merely private conduct, however discriminatory or wrongful. We conclude, therefore, that the restrictive agreements standing alone cannot be regarded as violative of any rights guaranteed to petitioners by the Fourteenth Amendment. So long as the purposes of those agreements are effectuated by voluntary adherence to their terms, it would appear clear that there has been no action by the State and the provisions of the Amendment have not been violated. . . .

But here there was more. These are cases in which the purposes of the agreements were secured only by judicial enforcement by the state courts of the restrictive terms of the agreements. The respondents urge that judicial enforcement of private agreements does not amount to state action; or, in any event, the participation of the State is so attenuated in character as not to amount to state action within the meaning of the Fourteenth Amendment. Finally, it is suggested, even if the States in these cases may be deemed to have acted in the constitutional sense, their action did not deprive petitioners of rights guaranteed by the Fourteenth Amendment. We move to a consideration of these matters.

II

That the action of state courts and judicial officers in their official capacities is to be regarded as action of the State within the meaning of the Fourteenth Amendment, is a proposition which has long been established by decisions of this Court. That principle was given expression in the earliest cases involving the construction of the terms of the Fourteenth Amendment. . . .

III

Against this background of judicial construction, extending over a period of some three-quarters of a century, we are called upon to consider whether enforcement by state courts of the restrictive agreements in these cases may be deemed to be the acts of those States; and, if so, whether that action has denied these petitioners the equal protection of the laws which the Amendment was intended to secure.

We have no doubt that there has been state action in these cases in the full and complete sense of the phrase. The undisputed facts disclose that petitioners were willing purchasers of properties upon which they desired to establish homes. The owners of the properties were willing sellers; and contracts of sale were accordingly consummated. It is clear that but for the active intervention of the state courts, supported by the full panoply of state power, petitioners would have been free to occupy the properties in question without restraint.

These are not cases, as has been suggested, in which the States have merely abstained from action, leaving private individuals free to impose such discriminations as they see fit. Rather, these are cases in which the States have made available to such individuals the full coercive power of government to deny to petitioners, on the grounds of race or color, the enjoyment of property rights in premises which petitioners are willing and financially able to acquire and which the grantors are willing to sell. . . .

The enforcement of the restrictive agreements by the state courts in these cases was directed pursuant to the common-law policy of the States as formulated by those courts in earlier decisions. . . . We have noted that previous decisions of this Court have established the proposition that judicial action is not immunized from the operation of the Fourteenth Amendment simply because it is taken pursuant to the state's common-law policy. Nor is the Amendment ineffective simply because the particular pattern of discrimination, which the State has enforced, was defined initially by the terms of a private agreement. State action, as that phrase is understood for the purposes of the Fourteenth Amendment, refers to exertions of state power in all forms. And when the effect of that action is to deny rights subject to the protection of the Fourteenth Amendment, it is the obligation of this Court to enforce the constitutional commands.

We hold that in granting judicial enforcement of the restrictive agreements in these cases, the States have denied petitioners the equal protection of the laws and that, therefore, the action of the state courts cannot stand. . . .

Reversed.

Mr. Justice Reed, Mr. Justice Jackson, and Mr. Justice Rutledge took no part in the consideration or decision of these cases.

Since the Court stated that the covenants were not violative of the Constitution but that state enforcement of such clauses was, the *Shelley* decision resulted in a revised method of attempting to maintain racially restrictive covenants. *Barrows* v. *Jackson,* 346 U.S. 249 (1953), raised the question of whether the state violated the Fourteenth Amendment by permitting an action for damages for breach of contract to be maintained in its courts against a property owner who conveyed the property in violation of a racial covenant. A California property owner sold a home to a Negro, contrary to the deed restrictions. She was sued by three neighbors on the ground that the value of their property had dropped sharply since Negroes moved in. The Court held that since California could not incorporate in a statute or enforce in equity such discriminatory policies, it could not furnish its coercive power to force payment of damages and thereby accomplish the same result.

The *Shelley* decision also had its impact on Federal policies which affected housing. The national government has provided both for supervision of mortgage lenders and for assistance in financing homes. The Fourteenth Amendment does not reach private discrimination, but national power to support and regulate lending practices extends to the individual pieces of property covered by such loans or financial support. A year and a half after *Shelley,* the FHA ruled that it would not provide mortgage insurance for property on which racially restrictive covenants were recorded after February 15, 1950 [FHA *Underwriting Manual,* sec. 303 (December, 1949)]. This represented a substantial change in policy, since the earlier *Manual* even contained a model restrictive covenant. The VA has followed similar policies designed to promote open occupancy without respect to race. These kinds of pressures are relatively slight to date, but they illustrate the fact that the executive branch can pick up where the courts leave off and can employ additional tools to further a policy of equal opportunity irrespective of race. [For additional material on government and housing see the 1961 United States Commission on Civil Rights Report No. 4, *Housing* (Washington: United States Government Printing Office, 1961).]

The decisions in *Shelley* and *Barrows* stimulated further litigation in the program to attack racial discrimination via the "state action" route. *Burton* v. *Wilmington Parking Authority,* 365 U.S. 715 (1961), raised the question of whether the policy of racial discrimination followed by a private leaseholder of state property in operating a restaurant was "state action" barred by the Fourteenth Amendment. Eagle Coffee Shoppe, Inc., was a restaurant located in a state-owned automobile parking building in Wilmington, Delaware. The Wilmington Parking Authority, a state agency, leased a portion of the building to Eagle for twenty years, renewable for another ten. The lease contained no requirement that the restaurant services be made available to the general public on a nondiscriminatory basis, and Eagle refused to serve Negroes. In an action for injunctive relief, petitioner claimed that in the circumstances of the lease of state property to serve the public, the action of Eagle was state action violative of the "equal protection" clause of the Fourteenth Amendment. The Delaware Supreme Court held that Eagle was acting in "a purely private capacity" under its lease, that its action was not that of the Authority, and therefore the discriminatory policies were not furthered by state action within the contemplation of the Fourteenth Amendment. The United States Supreme Court reversed. Pointing out some of the interrelationships between the Parking Authority and Eagle, Justice Clark, speaking for the majority, stated that "The State has so far insinuated itself into a position of interdependence with Eagle that it must be recognized as a joint participant in the challenged activity, which, on that account, cannot be considered to have been so 'purely private' as to fall without the scope of the Fourteenth Amendment."

The California experience with the controversial area of open-housing policy presented a novel aspect of the combination of state action and private discrimination. In 1959 California passed the Unruh Act guaranteeing equal accommodations, without regard to race, color, or religion, "in all business establishments of every kind whatsoever," and providing for actions for damages for violation of the law. In 1963 the California legislature adopted the Rumford Fair Housing Act which prohibited racial discriminations in the sale or rental of any private dwelling containing more than four units. In 1964, however, by initiative, the voters of California adopted a constitutional amendment, Art. I, §26, providing in part as follows:

"Neither the State nor any subdivision or agency thereof shall deny, limit or abridge, directly or indirectly, the right of any person, who is willing or desires to sell, lease or rent any part or all of his real property, to decline to sell, lease or rent such property to such person or persons as he, in his absolute discretion, chooses."

The real property covered by the amendment was limited to residential property and contained an exception for state-owned real estate. Petitioners sued under the equal accommodations guaranties of the Unruh Act, alleging that they had been refused apartment accommodations solely on account of their race. An injunction and damages were demanded. Defendants moved for summary judgment on the ground that the equal accommodations sections had been made inapplicable to the renting of apartments by the adoption of §26 of the constitution. The trial court granted the motion, and the California Supreme Court reversed, holding the amendment invalid under the Fourteenth Amendment "equal protection" clause. By a five-to-four vote the United States Supreme Court affirmed, in *Reitman* v. *Mulkey*, 387 U.S. 369 (1967). Justice White, for the majority, stated:

The California court could very reasonably conclude that §26 would and did have wider impact than a mere repeal of existing statutes.... The right to discriminate, including the right to discriminate on racial grounds, was now embodied in the State's basic charter, immune from legislative, executive, or judicial regulation at any level of the state government. Those practicing racial discriminations need no longer rely solely on their personal choice. They could now invoke express constitutional authority, free from censure or interference of any kind from official sources....

...Here the California court, armed as it was with the knowledge of the facts and circumstances concerning the passage and potential impact of §26, and familiar with the milieu in which that provision would operate, has determined that the provision would involve the State in private racial discriminations to an unconstitutional degree. We accept this holding of the California court....

...Here we are dealing with a provision which does not just repeal an existing law forbidding private racial discriminations. Section 26 was intended to authorize, and does authorize, racial discrimination in the housing market. The right to discriminate is now one of the basic policies of the State. The California Supreme Court believes that the section will significantly encourage and involve the State in private discriminations. We have been presented with no persuasive considerations indicating that this judgment should be overturned.

[Justice Harlan wrote an opinion for the four dissenters, saying in part:]

This type of alleged state involvement, simply evincing a refusal to involve itself at all, is of course very different from that illustrated in such cases as *Lombard, Peterson, Evans,* and *Burton, supra,* where the Court found active involvement of state agencies and officials in specific acts of discrimination. It is also quite different from cases in which a state enactment could be said to have the obvious purpose of fostering discrimination.... I believe the state action required to bring the Fourteenth Amendment into operation must be affirmative and purposeful, actively fostering discrimination. Only in such a case is ostensibly "private" action more properly labeled "official." I do not believe that the mere enactment of §26, on the showing made here, falls within this class of cases....

[For more recent developments on open housing, see *Jones* v. *Alfred Mayer Co.*, 392 U.S. 409 (1968) and the Fair Housing law of 1968 in Chap. 9.]

Even prior to the decision in *Shelley*, litigation had occurred raising a question with regard to the status of a nominally private agency which, however, depended heavily on governmental appropriations for its operation. Such a question was presented in 1945 concerning the Enoch Pratt Free Library of Baltimore. Kerr, a Negro, sued for damages and an injunction on complaint that she was refused admission to a library training class conducted by the library to prepare persons for staff positions in the central library and its branches. She charged that the library was performing a governmental function and that she was rejected solely because of race, and that such rejection constituted state action prohibited by the Fourteenth Amendment.

The library was established by Pratt in 1882. He erected a building and established a fund and gave them to the city on condition that the city would create an annuity for the maintenance of the library and the erection of four branches. In giving legal effect to the terms of the gift, the Maryland legislature passed a statute and the city passed three ordinances. The state law named the persons who were to constitute the board of trustees. In 1943 and 1944 the city appropriated more than a half million dollars annually for the library's operation. Salary checks were issued by the city's payroll officer and charged against the library's appropriation. The library budget was included in the regular city budget, and library employees were included within the municipal employees' retirement system.

The Court of Appeals for the Fourth Circuit held that the library's action was state action within the meaning of the Fourteenth Amendment and, in the absence of a similar training program for Negroes, Kerr could not be denied admission. *Kerr* v. *Enoch Pratt Free Library*, 149 F. 2d 212 (4th Cir., 1945). *Cert. denied*, 326 U.S. 721 (1945). The two criteria stressed by the court in holding the library's action to be state action were control by the state over the library's activities and, apparently, the volume and importance of financial assistance afforded by the state.

Since 1960 several cases growing out of convictions for restaurant "sit-in" demonstrations have been carried to the United States Supreme Court. Various arguments were presented by the Negro appellants in these cases, including (1) that the restaurants had, by virtue of state licensing and special state regulation, become state instrumentalities, (2) that for the state police and courts to enforce trespass laws in support of restaurant-keepers' racially discriminatory policies was to inject unconstitutional state action under the *Shelley* rule, and (3) where segregated facilities exist in response to general and widespread community custom, state enforcement of such rules is tantamount to state legislation adopting the rule as law and thus violates the Fourteenth Amendment to the same extent as the segregation ordinance did in *Gayle* v. *Browder*. One such case was *Lombard* v. *Louisiana*, 373 U.S. 267 (1963). In *Peterson* v. *Greenville*, 373 U.S. 244 (1963), decided the same day, the Court reversed trespass convictions in a municipal court, following lunch counter "sit-ins," on the ground that a city ordinance required segregated eating facilities, and the convictions had the effect of enforcing the ordinance in violation of the Fourteenth Amendment. In *Lombard*, however, no such ordinance was involved. After having been refused service at the refreshment counter of a Five-and-Ten Cent store in New Orleans, three Negroes and one white person refused to leave when requested to do so by the restaurant manager. They were convicted in a Louisiana state court of criminal mischief under a statute including within that designation the taking of temporary possession of, or the remaining in, a place of business after being ordered to leave by the person in charge of such business. On appeal the Supreme Court of Louisiana af-firmed. On certiorari, the Supreme Court of the United States reversed. In an opinion by Chief Justice Warren, for eight members of the Court, it was held that despite the absence of an ordinance requiring segregation of restaurant facilities, "we conclude that this case is governed by the princi-ples announced in *Peterson* v. *Greenville.*" This conclusion was reached on the ground that public statements of various city officials in effect reached the level of an official command that segregation be continued and such command "has at least as much coercive effect as an ordinance."

Justice Douglas concurred, but on much more expansive grounds. He stated:

... If this were an intrusion of a man's home or yard or farm or garden, the property owner could seek and obtain the aid of the State against the intruder. For the Bill of Rights, as applied to the States through the Due Process Clause of the Fourteenth Amendment, casts its weight on the side of the privacy of homes. . . .

But a restaurant, like the other departments of this retail store where Negroes were served, though private property within the protection of the Fifth Amend-ment, has no aura of constitutionally protected privacy about it. Access by the public is the very reason for its existence. . . .

State licensing and surveillance of a business serving the public . . . brings its service into the public domain. This restaurant needs a permit from Louisiana to operate; and during the existence of the license the State has broad powers of visitation and control. This restaurant is thus an instrumentality of the State since the State charges it with duties to the public and supervises its performance. The State's interest in and activity with regard to its restaurants extends far beyond any mere income-producing licensing requirement.

There is no constitutional way, as I see it, in which a State can license and supervise a business serving the public and endow it with the authority to manage that business on the basis of *apartheid,* which is foreign to our Constitution.

The majority of the Court has not accepted Justice Douglas' suggestion that a private business becomes a state instrumentality by virtue of state licensing and special state regulation. In *Lombard,* however, the Court did look beyond the requirements of statutes or ordinances and found coercive state action in the public statements of officials sufficient to invalidate tres-pass convictions.

In the 1963 term the Court was faced with more than a dozen cases attacking racial segregation in private establishments along "state action" lines. Five cases were decided on June 22, 1964, in which the issue was at least partially considered, and the Court granted certiorari in two other sit-in trespass cases. The same question was presented, but not decided, in seven other cases which the Court disposed of in various ways on the same day. [For the list of cases see Justice Black's dissenting opinion in *Bell* v. *Maryland,* 378 U.S. 226, 320, 322, n.7 (1964).] In each case decided the Court either reversed convictions for trespass (or variations thereon) or reversed and remanded. In general it can only be said that each decision came off on the peculiar facts of the case, without a clear-cut state action rule emanating. In *Griffin* v. *Maryland* 378 U.S. 130 (1964), the private establishment had hired a deputy sheriff as guard to enforce its policy of racial segregation. The majority found the requisite state action in this arrangement to invoke the Fourteenth Amendment in reversing trespass convictions. In *Robinson* v. *Florida*, 378 U.S. 153 (1964), the Court reversed a sit-in trespass conviction on the ground that the state, through regulations requiring separate facilities for each race in restaurants, had become sufficiently involved to bring the Fourteenth Amendment's prohibitions into operation. In *Barr* v. *City of Columbia*, 378 U.S. 146 (1964), and *Bouie* v. *City of Columbia*, 378 U.S. 347 (1964), criminal trespass convictions were reversed on the ground that not until after the commission of the alleged offenses did the South Carolina Supreme Court construe the statute to apply to the act of remaining on the premises after receiving notice to leave, and to convict appellants of a violation under this construction of the statute was to violate the "due process" clause of the Fourteenth Amendment. [On sit-ins generally, see Earl L. Carl, "Reflections on the Sit-Ins," 46 *Cornell L. Q.* 444 (1961); Marion A. Wright, "The Sit-in Movement: Progress Report and Prognosis," *Wayne L. Rev.* 445 (1963); Thomas P. Lewis, "The Sit-In Cases: Great Expectations," 1963 *Supreme Court Rev.* 101; Monrad G. Paulsen, "Sit-in Cases of 1964: 'But Answer Came There None,'" 1964 *Supreme Court Rev.* 137.]

The case in which the state action argument was most fully discussed, although it was not the ground on which the case was disposed of, was *Bell* v. *Maryland*, 378 U.S. 226 (1964). Twelve Negro students were convicted, in a Maryland court, of criminal trespass as a result of their sit-in demonstration at a restaurant in Baltimore. The convictions were affirmed by the Maryland Court of Appeals. On certiorari, the United States Supreme Court vacated the judgment and remanded the case to the Maryland Court of Appeals. Justice Brennan, speaking for five members of the Court, pointed out that after affirmance by the court of appeals, the State of Maryland and the City of Baltimore had enacted public accommodations laws making it unlawful to deny service on account of race, and that under these circumstances it was appropriate to give the state court an opportunity to decide whether the indictments should be dismissed. The real debate on the state action issue involved six of the justices, with the division being three-to-three on that point.

Justice Goldberg, with whom the Chief Justice joined and Justice Douglas joined in part, stated:

I join in the opinion and the judgment of the Court and would therefore have no occasion under ordinary circumstances to express my views on the underlying constitutional issue. Since, however, the dissent at length discusses this constitutional issue and reaches a conclusion with which I profoundly disagree, I am impelled to state the reasons for my conviction that the Constitution guarantees to all Americans the right to be treated as equal members of the community with respect to public accommodations. . . .

The Thirteenth, Fourteenth and Fifteenth Amendments do not permit Negroes to be considered as second-class citizens in any aspect of our public life. . . . We make no racial distinctions between citizens in exacting from them the discharge of public responsibilities. The heaviest duties of citizenship—military service, taxation, obedience to laws—are imposed evenhandedly upon black and white. . . . Our fundamental law which insures such an equality of public burdens, in my view, similarly insures an equality of public benefits. . . .

[Here follows an analysis of the congressional intent behind the Civil Rights Act of 1866 and the Fourteenth Amendment with the conclusion that the purpose was "to ensure that the constitutional concept of citizenship with all attendant rights and privileges would henceforth embrace Negroes. It follows that Negroes as citizens necessarily became entitled to share the right, customarily possessed by other citizens, of access to public accommodations."]

A State applying its statutory or common law to deny rather than protect the right of access to public accommodations has . . . denied the constitutionally intended equal protection. Indeed, in light of the assumption so explicitly stated in the *Civil Rights Cases,* it is significant that Mr. Justice Bradley, who spoke for the Court, had earlier in correspondence with Circuit Judge Woods . . . concluded that: "Denying includes inaction as well as action. And denying the equal protection of the laws includes the omission to protect, as well as the omission to pass laws for protection." These views are fully consonant with this Court's recognition that state conduct which might be described as "inaction" can nevertheless constitute responsible "state action" within the meaning of the Fourteenth Amendment. See, e.g., *Marsh* v. *Alabama,* . . . *Shelley* v. *Kraemer,* . . . *Terry* v. *Adams,* . . . *Barrows* v. *Jackson.* . . .

In the present case the responsibility of the judiciary in applying the principles of the Fourteenth Amendment is clear. The State of Maryland has failed to protect petitioners' constitutional right to public accommodations and is now prosecuting them for attempting to exercise that right. The decision of Maryland's highest court in sustaining these trespass convictions cannot be described as "neutral," for the decision is as affirmative in effect as if the State had enacted an unconstitutional law explicitly authorizing racial discrimination in places of public accommodation. A State, obligated under the Fourteenth Amendment to maintain a system of law in which Negroes are not denied protection in their claim to be treated as equal members of the community, may not use its criminal trespass laws to frustrate the constitutionally granted right. Nor, it should be added, may a State frustrate this right by legitimating a proprietor's attempt at self-help. . . .

My Brother Douglas convincingly demonstrates that the dissent has constructed a straw man by suggesting that this case involves "a property owner's right to choose his social or business associates.". . . The restaurant involved in this case is concededly open to a large segment of the public. Restaurants such as this daily open their doors to millions of Americans. These establishments provide a public service as necessary today as the inns and carriers of Blackstone's time. It should be recognized that the claim asserted by the Negro petitioners concerns such public establishments and does not infringe upon the rights of property owners or personal associational interests.

Petitioners frankly state that the "extension of constitutional guarantees to the authentically private choices of man is wholly unacceptable, and any constitutional theory leading to that result would have reduced itself to absurdity." Indeed, the constitutional protection extended to privacy and private association assures against the imposition of social equality. As noted before, the Congress that enacted the Fourteenth Amendment was particularly conscious that the "civil" rights of man should be distinguished from his "social" rights. Prejudice and bigotry in any form are regrettable, but it is the constitutional right of every person to close his home or club to any person or to choose his social intimates and business partners solely on the basis of personal prejudices including race. These and other rights pertaining to privacy and private association are themselves constitutionally protected liberties.

We deal here, however, with a claim of equal access to public accommodations. This is not a claim which significantly impinges upon personal associational interests; nor is it a claim infringing upon the control of private property not dedicated to public use. A judicial ruling on this claim inevitably involves the liberties and freedoms both of the restaurant proprietor and of the Negro citizen. The dissent would hold in effect that the restaurant proprietor's interest in choosing customers on the basis of race is to be preferred to the Negro's right to equal treatment by a business serving the public. The history and purposes of the Fourteenth Amendment indicate, however, that the Amendment resolves this apparent conflict of liberties in favor of the Negro's right to equal public accommodations. . . . As the history of the common law and, indeed, of our own times graphically illustrates, the interests of proprietors of places of public accommodation have always been adapted to the citizen's felt need for public accommodations, a need which is basic and deep-rooted. This history and the purposes of the Fourteenth Amendment compel the conclusion that the right to be served in places of public accommodation regardless of color cannot constitutionally be subordinated to the proprietor's interest in discriminatorily refusing service. . . .

Mr. Justice Black, with whom Mr. Justice Harlan and Mr. Justice White join, dissenting.

This case does not involve the constitutionality of any existing or proposed state or federal legislation requiring restaurant owners to serve people without regard to color. The crucial issue which the case does present but which the Court does not decide is whether the Fourteenth Amendment, of itself, forbids a State to enforce its trespass laws to convict a person who comes into a privately owned restaurant, is told that because of his color he will not be served, and over the owner's protest refuses to leave. We dissent from the Court's refusal to decide that question. For reasons stated, we think that the question should be decided and that the Fourteenth Amendment does not forbid this application of a State's trespass laws. . . .

. . . [O]ur affirmance of the state court's holding that the Maryland trespass statute is constitutional as applied would in no way hamper or bar decision of further state questions which the Maryland court might deem relevant to protect the rights of the petitioners in accord with Maryland law. Recognition of this power of state courts after we affirm their holdings on federal questions is a commonplace occurrence. . . .

Petitioners, but not the Solicitor General, contend that their conviction for trespass under the state statute was by itself the kind of discriminatory state action forbidden by the Fourteenth Amendment. This contention, on its face, has plausibility when considered along with general statements to the effect that under the Amendment forbidden "state action" may be that of the Judicial as well as of the Legislative or Executive Branch of Government. But a mechanical application of the Fourteenth Amendment to this case cannot survive analysis. The Amendment does not forbid a State to prosecute for crimes committed against a person or his property, however prejudiced or narrow the victim's views may be. Nor can whatever prejudice and bigotry the victim of a crime may have be automatically attributed to the State that prosecutes. Such a doctrine would not only be based on a fiction; it would also severely handicap a State's efforts to maintain a peaceful and orderly society. Our society has put its trust in a system of criminal laws to punish lawless conduct. To avert personal feuds and violent brawls it has led its people to believe and expect that wrongs against them will be vindicated in the courts. Instead of attempting to take the law into their own hands, people have been taught to call for police protection to protect their rights wherever possible. . . . None of our past cases justifies reading the Fourteenth Amendment in a way that might well penalize citizens who are law-abiding enough to call upon the law and its officers for protection instead of using their own physical strength or dangerous weapons to preserve their rights.

In contending that the State's prosecution of petitioners for trespass is state action forbidden by the Fourteenth Amendment, petitioners rely chiefly on *Shelley* v. *Kraemer, supra*. That reliance is misplaced. . . .

It seems pretty clear that the reason judicial enforcement of the restrictive covenants in *Shelley* was deemed state action was not merely the fact that a state court had acted, but rather that it had acted "to deny to petitioners, on the grounds of race or color, the enjoyment of property rights in premises which petitioners are willing and financially able to acquire and which the grantors are willing to sell.". . . In other words, this Court held that state enforcement of the covenants had the effect of denying to the parties their federally guaranteed right to own, occupy, enjoy, and use their property without regard to race or color. Thus, the line of cases from *Buchanan* through *Shelley* establishes these propositions: (1) When an owner of property is willing to sell and a would-be purchaser is willing to buy, then the Civil Rights Act of 1866 . . . prohibits a State, whether through its legislature, executive, or judiciary, from preventing the sale on the grounds of the race or color of one of the parties. . . . (2) Once a person has become a property owner, then he acquires all the rights that go with ownership. . . . This means that the property owner may, in the absence of a valid statute forbidding it, sell his property to whom he pleases and admit to that property whom he will; so long as both parties are willing parties, then the principles stated in Buchanan and Shelley protect this right. But equally, when one party is unwilling, as when the property owner chooses *not* to sell to a particular person or *not* to admit that person, then, as this Court emphasized in *Buchanan*, he is entitled to rely on the guarantee of due process of law, that is, "law of the land," to protect his free use and enjoyment of property and to know that only by valid legislation, passed pursuant to some constitutional grant of power, can anyone disturb this free use. . . . [P]etitioners would have us say that Hooper's federal right must be cut down and he must be compelled— though no statute said he must—to allow people to force their way into his restaurant and remain there over his protest. We cannot subscribe to such a mutilating, one-sided interpretation of federal guarantees the very heart of which is equal treatment under law to all. We must never forget that the Fourteenth Amendment protects "life, liberty, or property" of all people generally, not just some people's "life," some people's "liberty," and some kinds of "property."....

We, like the Solicitor General, reject the argument that the State's protection of Hooper's desire to choose customers on the basis of race by prosecuting trespassers is enough, standing alone, to deprive Hooper of his right to operate the property in his own way. But we disagree with the contention that there are other circumstances which, added to the State's prosecution for trespass, justify a finding of state action. There is no Maryland law, no municipal ordinance, and no official proclamation or action of any kind that shows the slightest state coercion of, or encouragement to, Hooper to bar Negroes from his restaurant. Neither the State, the city, nor any of their agencies has leased publicly owned property to Hooper. It is true that the State and city regulate the restaurants—but not by compelling restaurants to deny service to customers because of their race. License fees are collected, but this licensing has no relationship to race. Under such circumstances, to hold that a State must be held to have participated in prejudicial conduct of its licensees is too big a jump for us to take. Businesses owned by private persons do not become agencies of the State because they are licensed; to hold that they do would be completely to negate all our private ownership concepts and practices....

Our Brother Goldberg in his opinion argues that the Fourteenth Amendment, of its own force and without the need of congressional legislation, prohibits privately owned restaurants from discriminating on account of color or race....

... [T]here is nothing whatever in the material cited to support the proposition that the Fourteenth Amendment, without congressional legislation, prohibits owners of restaurants and other places to refuse service to Negroes. [Here follows an examination of some of the debates in Congress between 1864 and 1874.]

We have confined ourselves entirely to those debates cited in Brother Goldberg's opinion the better to show how, even on its own evidence, the opinion's argument that the Fourteenth Amendment without more prohibits discrimination by restaurants and other such places rests on a wholly inadequate historical foundation. When read and analyzed, the argument is shown to rest entirely on what speakers are said to have believed bills and statutes of the time were meant to do. Such proof fails entirely when the question is, not what statutes did, but rather what the Constitution does....

... We express no views as to the power of Congress, acting under one or another provision of the Constitution, to prevent racial discrimination in the operation of privately owned businesses, nor upon any particular form of legislation to that end. Our sole conclusion is that Section 1 of the Fourteenth Amendment, standing alone, does not prohibit privately owned restaurants from choosing their own customers....

The issue of the validity of state enforcement of trespass laws in support of a restaurant owner's policy of racial discrimination has largely become moot as a consequence of the enactment of the Civil Rights Act of 1964 (78 Stat. 241). [For an account of the legislative history of the Act, see Congressional Quarterly Service, *Revolution in Civil Rights* (Washington, D.C.: Congressional Quarterly, Inc., 1965), pp. 41–70.] The Act reaches discrimination in places of public accommodation if the operations affect interstate commerce or if supported by state action. The issue of what constitutes state action is still viable, however, in areas not covered by the definition of "public accommodations" in the Act, such as barber shops or local dance halls or private schools. [See Richard A. Lang, Jr., "State Action Under the Equal Protection Clause and the Remaining Scope of Private Choice," 50 *Cornell L.Q.* 473–505 (1965).]

The public accommodations title of the Civil Rights Act of 1964 is similar in coverage to the first two sections of the old Civil Rights Act of 1875 which were held unconstitutional in the *Civil Rights Cases* in 1883. The former is primarily grounded in Congress' power to regulate commerce, however, while the latter was largely based on the Civil War Amendments. The relevant provisions of the new Act are found in Title II.

Title II—Injunctive Relief Against Discrimination in Places of Public Accommodation

Sec. 201. (a) All persons shall be entitled to the full and equal enjoyment of the goods, services, facilities, privileges, advantages, and accommodations of any place of public accommodation, as defined in this section, without discrimination or segregation on the ground of race, color, religion, or national origin.

(b) Each of the following establishments which serves the public is a place of public accommodation within the meaning of this title if its operations affect commerce, or if discrimination or segregation by it is supported by State action:

(1) any inn, hotel, motel, or other establishment which provides lodging to transient guests, other than an establishment located within a building which contains not more than five rooms for rent or hire and which is actually occupied by the proprietor of such establishment as his residence;

(2) any restaurant, cafeteria, lunchroom, lunch counter, soda fountain, or other facility principally engaged in selling food for consumption on the premises including, but not limited to, any such facility located on the premises of any retail establishment; or any gasoline station;

(3) any motion picture house, theater, concert hall, sports arena, stadium or other place of exhibition or entertainment; and

(4) any establishment (A) (i) which is physically located within the premises of any establishment otherwise covered by this subsection, or (ii) within the premises of which is physically located any such covered establishment, and (B) which holds itself out as serving patrons of such covered establishment.

(c) The operations of an establishment affect commerce within the meaning of this title if (1) it is one of the establishments described in paragraph (1) of subsection (b); (2) in the case of an establishment described in paragraph (2) of subsection (b), it serves or offers to serve interstate travelers or a substantial portion of the food which it serves, or gasoline or other products which it sells, has moved in commerce; (3) in the case of an establishment described in paragraph (3) of subsection (b), it customarily presents films, performances, athletic teams, exhibitions, or other sources of entertainment which move in commerce; and (4) in the case of an establishment described in paragraph (4) of subsection (b), it is physically located within the premises of, or there is physically located within its premises, an establishment the operations of which affect commerce within the meaning of this subsection. For purposes of this section, "commerce" means travel, trade, traffic, commerce, transportation, or communication among the several States, or between the District of Columbia and any State, or between any foreign country or any territory or possession and any State or the District of Columbia, or between points in the same State but through any other State or the District of Columbia or a foreign country.

(d) Discrimination or segregation by an establishment is supported by State action within the meaning of this title if such discrimination or segregation (1) is carried on under color of any law, statute, ordinance, or regulation; or (2) is carried on under color of any custom or usage required or enforced by officials of the State or political subdivision thereof; or (3) is required by action of the State or political subdivisions thereof.

(e) The provisions of this title shall not apply to a private club or other establishment not in fact open to the public, except to the extent that the facilities of such establishment are made available to the customers or patrons of an establishment within the scope of subsection (b).

Sec. 202. All persons shall be entitled to be free, at any establishment or place, from discrimination or segregation of any kind on the ground of race, color, religion, or national origin, if such discrimination or segregation is or purports to be required by any law, statute, ordinance, regulation, rule, or order of a State or any agency or political subdivision thereof.

[Sec. 203 prohibits the intimidation or coercion of any person with the purpose of interfering with any right or privilege secured by Sections 201 and 202. Sec. 204 provides for the issuance of restraining orders in the event of such attempted intimidation or coercion, upon application of the aggrieved person, and permits the Attorney General to intervene if he certifies that the case is of general public importance. The court is also permitted, in justifiable cases, to appoint an attorney for the complainant and to authorize the commencement of the civil action without the payment of fees, costs, or security. The court may also allow the prevailing party a reasonable attorney's fee as part of the costs.]

Sec. 206. (a) Whenever the Attorney General has reasonable cause to believe that any person or group of persons is engaged in a pattern or practice of resistance to the full enjoyment of any of the rights secured by this title, and that the pattern or practices is of such a nature and is intended to deny the full exercise of the rights herein described, the Attorney General may bring a civil action in the appropriate district court of the United States by filing with it a complaint ... requesting such preventive relief ... as he deems necessary to insure the full enjoyment of the rights herein described. ...

Sec. 207. (a) The district courts of the United States shall have jurisdiction of proceedings instituted pursuant to this title and shall exercise the same without regard to whether the aggrieved party shall have exhausted any administrative or other remedies that may be provided by law.

(b) The remedies provided in this title shall be the exclusive means of enforcing the rights based on this title, but nothing in this title shall preclude any individual or any State or local agency from asserting any right based on any other Federal or State law not inconsistent with this title, including any statute or ordinance requiring nondiscrimination in public establishments or accommodations, or from pursuing any remedy, civil or criminal, which may be available for the vindication or enforcement of such right.

As expected, cases were initiated very quickly questioning the constitutionality of Title II of the Civil Rights Act of 1964. Two such cases were argued on the opening day of the 1964 term of the Court, only three months after the passage of the Act. *Heart of Atlanta Motel* v. *United States*, 379 U.S. 241 (1964), came on direct appeal from a three-judge district court in Georgia, which had sustained the constitutionality of the Title II provisions and had enjoined the motel owner-operator from discriminating against Negroes on account of race or color. *Katzenbach* v. *McClung*, 379 U.S. 294 (1964), came on direct appeal from a three-judge district court in Alabama, which had held the Act unconstitutional as applied to "Ollie's Barbecue" in Birmingham and enjoined enforcement against the restaurant. Decisions were handed down in these two companion cases in December 1964, only two months after argument and five months after enactment of the law.

The *Heart of Atlanta Motel* case was a broad challenge to virtually the entire Title II portion of the Act. Appellant contended that the Act exceeded congressional power to regulate commerce, deprived it of liberty and property without due process of law, took its property without just compensation, and subjected it to involuntary servitude. The Court unanimously held the Act constitutional, although there was a divided vote on the bases for so holding. In the opinion for the Court, Justice Clark examined the *Civil Rights Cases*, which had held similar provisions of the Civil Rights Act of 1875 unconstitutional. He stated:

We think that decision inapposite, and without precedential value in determining the constitutionality of the present Act. Unlike Title II of the present legislation, the 1875 Act broadly proscribed discrimination in "inns, public conveyances on land or water, theaters, and other public places of amusement," without limiting the categories of affected businesses to those impinging upon interstate commerce. In contrast, the applicability of Title II is carefully limited to enterprises having a direct and substantial relation to the interstate flow of goods and people, except where state action is involved. Further, the fact that certain kinds of businesses may not in 1875 have been sufficiently involved in interstate commerce to warrant bringing them within the ambit of the commerce power is not necessarily dispositive of the same question today.... The sheer increase in volume of interstate traffic alone would give discriminatory practices which inhibit travel a far larger impact upon the nation's commerce than such practices had in the economy of another day. Finally, there is language in the *Civil Rights Cases* which indicates that the Court did not fully consider whether the 1875 Act could be sustained as an exercise of the commerce power....

[The opinion then takes up the evidence and testimony reported in various congressional committee hearings to the effect that racial discrimination had "a qualitative as well as quantitative effect on interstate travel by Negroes." The evidence indicated that the uncertainty of finding facilities for food and lodging, stemming from racial discrimination, "had the effect of discouraging travel on the part of a substantial portion of the Negro community."]

The power of Congress to deal with these obstructions depends on the meaning of the Commerce Clause. Its meaning was first enunciated 140 years ago by the great Chief Justice John Marshall in *Gibbons* v. *Ogden*, 9 Wheat. 1 (1824)....

In short, the determinative test of the exercise of power by the Congress under the Commerce Clause is simply whether the activity sought to be regulated is "commerce which concerns more than one state" and has a real and substantial relation to the national interest.....

It is said that the operation of the motel here is of a purely local character. But, assuming this to be true, "if it is interstate commerce that feels the pinch, it does not matter how local the operation that applies the squeeze." *United States* v. *Women's Sportswear Mfrs. Ass'n.* 336 U.S. 460, 464 (1949).... As Chief Justice Stone put it in *United States* v. *Darby, supra:*

"The power of Congress over interstate commerce is not confined to the regulation of commerce among the states. It extends to those activities intrastate which so affect interstate commerce or the exercise of the power of Congress over it as to make regulation of them appropriate means to the attainment of a legitimate end, the exercise of the granted power of Congress to regulate interstate commerce...."

Thus the power of Congress to promote interstate commerce also includes the power to regulate the local incidents thereof, including local activities in both the States of origin and destination, which might have a substantial and harmful effect upon that commerce. One need only examine the evidence which we have discussed above to see that Congress may—as it has—prohibit racial discrimination by motels serving travelers, however "local" their operations may appear.

Nor does the Act deprive appellant of liberty or property under the Fifth Amendment. The commerce power invoked here by the Congress is a specific and plenary one authorized by the Constitution itself. The only questions are: (1) whether Congress had a rational basis for finding that racial discrimination by motels affected commerce, and (2) if it had such a basis, whether the means it selected to eliminate that evil are reasonable and appropriate. If they are, appellant has no "right" to select its guests as it sees fit, free from governmental regulation.

There is nothing novel about such legislation. Thirty-two States now have it on their books either by statute or executive order and many cities provide such regulation. Some of these Acts go back fourscore years. It has been repeatedly held by this Court that such laws do not violate the Due Process Clause of the Fourteenth Amendment....

...As a result the constitutionality of such state statutes stands unquestioned. "The authority of the Federal Government over interstate commerce does not differ," it was held in *United States* v. *Rock Royal Co-op, Inc.,* 307 U.S. 533 (1939), "in extent or character from that retained by the states over intrastate commerce.."...

...Neither do we find any merit in the claim that the Act is a taking of property without just compensation. The cases are to the contrary....

We find no merit in the remainder of appellant's contentions, including that of "involuntary servitude."... We could not say that the requirements of the Act in this regard are in any way "akin to African slavery." *Butler* v. *Perry*, 240 U.S. 328, 332 (1916).

Katzenbach v. *McClung,* 379 U.S. 294 (1964), raised many of the same questions which were disposed of in the companion motel case. The appellees did raise one additional issue, however, which the Court took care of separately. The restaurant was located some distance from interstate highways and railroad and bus stations, and it catered to local family and white-collar trade. In the preceding year the restaurant had purchased locally approximately $150,000 worth of food, of which about $70,000 was for meat that it bought from a local supplier who had procured it from outside the state. In his opinion for the Court upholding the application of the Act to Ollie's Barbecue, Justice Clark stated the question and gave the response:

. . . There is no claim that interstate travelers frequented the restaurant. The sole question, therefore, narrows down to whether Title II, as applied to a restaurant receiving about $70,000 worth of food which has moved in commerce, is a valid exercise of the power of Congress. The Government has contended that Congress had ample basis upon which to find that racial discrimination at restaurants which receive from out of state a substantial portion of the food served does, in fact, impose commercial burdens of national magnitude upon interstate commerce. The appellees' major argument is directed to this premise. They urge that no such basis existed. It is to that question that we now turn. . . .

[The opinion then refers to testimony at hearings before the Senate Committee on Commerce, including testimony that in areas where discrimination is widely practiced there was less spending per capita by Negroes, after discounting income differences, in restaurants and like establishments. "This diminutive spending springing from a refusal to serve Negroes and their total loss as customers, has, regardless of the absence of direct evidence, a close connection to interstate commerce. The fewer customers a restaurant enjoys the less food it sells and consequently the less it buys."]

We believe that this testimony afforded ample basis for the conclusion that established restaurants in such areas sold less interstate goods because of the discrimination, that interstate travel was obstructed directly by it, that business in general suffered and that many new businesses refrained from establishing there as a result of it. . . .

It goes without saying that, viewed in isolation, the volume of food purchased by Ollie's Barbecue from sources supplied from out of state was insignificant when compared with the total foodstuffs moving in commerce. But, as our late Brother Jackson said for the Court in *Wickard* v. *Filburn*, 317 U.S. 111, 127–128 (1924):

"That appellee's own contribution to the demand for wheat may be trivial by itself is not enough to remove him from the scope of federal regulation where, as here, his contribution, taken together with that of many others similarly situated, is far from trivial.". . .

. . . The activities that are beyond the reach of Congress are "those which are completely within a particular State, which do not affect other States, and with which it is not necessary to interfere, for the purpose of executing some of the general powers of the government." *Gibbons* v. *Ogden*, 9 Wheat 1, 195 (1824). This rule is as good today as it was when Chief Justice Marshall laid it down almost a century and a half ago.

Despite the fact that *Brown* v. *Board of Education* had been decided ten years earlier, little progress toward desegregation in public schools had been made in the deep South by the time of the passage of the Civil Rights

Act of 1964. Title IV of the Act provided for various assistance in the preparation and implementation of plans for the desegregation of public schools and, in addition, provided that the Attorney General could initiate suits to obtain relief for persons denied equal protection in the utilization of public schools or colleges. The primary weapon for ending racial segregation in schools and other federally aided state programs, however, was the Title VI provision for cutting off federal funds as penalty for failure to desegregate. The substantive and main procedural provisions are covered in Sections 601 and 602:

Sec. 601. No person in the United States shall, on the ground of race, color, or national origin, be excluded from participation in, be denied the benefits of, or be subjected to discrimination under any program or activity receiving Federal financial assistance.

Sec. 602. Each Federal department and agency which is empowered to extend Federal financial assistance to any program or activity, by way of grant, loan, or contract other than a contract of insurance or guaranty, is authorized and directed to effectuate the provisions of section 601 with respect to such program or activity by issuing rules, regulations, or orders of general applicability which shall be consistent with achievement of the objectives of the statute authorizing the financial assistance in connection with which the action is taken. No such rule, regulation, or order shall become effective unless and until approved by the President. Compliance with any requirement adopted pursuant to this section may be effected (1) by the termination of or refusal to grant or to continue assistance under such program or activity to any recipient as to whom there has been an express finding on the record, after opportunity for hearing, of a failure to comply with such requirement, but such termination or refusal shall be limited to the particular political entity, or part thereof, or other recipient as to whom such a finding has been made and, shall be limited in its effect to the particular program, or part thereof, in which such noncompliance has been so found, or (2) by any other means authorized by law: *Provided, however,* That no such action shall be taken until the department or agency concerned has advised the appropriate person or persons of the failure to comply with the requirement and has determined that compliance cannot be secured by voluntary means. In the case of any action terminating, or refusing to grant or continue, assistance because of failure to comply with a requirement imposed pursuant to this section, the head of the Federal department or agency shall file with the committees of the House and Senate having legislative jurisdiction over the program or activity involved a full written report of the circumstances and the grounds for such action. No such action shall become effective until thirty days have elapsed after the filing of such report.

On April 29, 1965, the Office of Education of the Department of Health, Education and Welfare issued a statement of policy for the implementation of the Title IV provisions. A key aspect of the policy statement lies in the fact that instead of approaching the problem with a view of *cutting off* funds during the year for school systems which failed to desegregate, the Office of Education demanded that school systems *prove their eligibility* for the funds by filing appropriate plans or court orders for desegregation and assurances of implementation with the Commissioner of Education. The basic requirements of the General Statement of Policies are covered in the following sections:

II. *Methods of Compliance—General.*

Elementary and secondary schools or school systems may qualify for Federal financial assistance by:

A. Executing an Assurance of Compliance (HEW Form 441), if the requirements specified in III below are satisfied; or

B. Submitting a final order of a court of the United States for the desegregation of the school or school system which satisfies the requirements . . . below, together with an Initial Compliance Report . . . ; or

C. Submitting a plan for the desegregation of the school system which the Commissioner of Education determines is adequate to accomplish the purposes of the Civil Rights Act . . . ; together with an Initial Compliance Report . . . ; and

D. Implementing the Assurance, final court order or desegregation plan in good faith so as to effectuate the basic objective set forth in section 601 of Title VI. . . .

III. *Methods of Compliance—Assurance of Compliance (HEW Form 441).* An Assurance of Compliance . . . that will qualify a school system for Federal financial assistance may not be executed by a school system in which:

A. The race, color, or national origin of pupils is a factor in their initial assignment, reassignment, or transfer to a particular school or class within a school; or

B. Teachers or other staff who serve pupils remain segregated on the basis of the race, color, or national origin of the pupils in a school; or

C. Any activity, facility or other service, including transportation, provided or sponsored by a school system is segregated on the basis of race, color, or national origin; or

D. There remain any other practices characteristic of dual or segregated school systems.

IV. *Methods of Compliance—Court Orders.*

A. A school system subject to a final order of a court of the United States will be eligible for Federal financial assistance only if the order directs desegregation of the school system; it does not suffice if the order merely directs school authorities to admit certain named persons or otherwise fails to require the elimination of a dual or segregated system of schools based on race, color, or national origin. . . .

V. *Methods of Compliance—Plans for the Desegregation of School Systems.*

[Eligibility may be obtained by submitting a desegregation plan which provides for assignment of pupils on the basis of appropriate geographic attendance areas or freedom of choice exercised by the pupil and his parents or a combination of geographic attendance areas and freedom of choice and which also provides for desegregation of all facets of the school system described in Part III, above.]

The Office of Education adopted firm policies of reviewing compliance plans. Nonetheless, by the time public school systems were well under way in the fall of 1965, the great bulk of such systems in the deep South had provided adequate evidence of compliance to obtain approval and, thereby, eligibility for federal funds.

A third important provision of the Civil Rights Act of 1964 is the Title VII provision setting up a right of equal employment opportunity irrespective of race, color, religion, sex, or national origin. Though the impact of this Title has not been so immediate or dramatic as that of the equal accommodations sections, the long-term effect of this provision, if implemented, will probably be of more importance in assuring real equality of opportunity for all persons than any of the other provisions of the Act. Equal educational opportunity alone does not instill motivation to learn or to remain in school through advanced grades. And equal access to public accommodations is no great personal triumph for the man whose menial occupation does not pay enough to permit him to stay in motels or eat in restaurants anyhow. Assurance of equal chances to compete and to advance in the economic arena, however, at least offers the potential for encouraging the fuller utilization of educational opportunities and the realization of some of the benefits of the equal accommodations provisions.

The first section of Title VII defines the persons and organizations to which the terms of the Title extend. It covers labor unions, employers engaged in an industry affecting commerce, employment agencies, and others. In general the provisions apply to employers and labor unions with twenty-five or more employees or members, but operating on a sliding scale with exemption the first year for those with less than one hundred, the second year for those with less than seventy-five, the third year for those with less than fifty, and those with less than twenty-five thereafter. Since the effective date for this Title was July 2, 1965, the maximum coverage is reached on July 2, 1968. Section 701 (b) further states that the term "employer" does not include:

(1) the United States, a corporation wholly owned by the Government of the United States, an Indian tribe, or a State or political subdivision thereof, (2) a bona fide private membership club (other than a labor organization) which is exempt from taxation under section 501 (c) of the Internal Revenue Code of 1954: ... *Provided further,* That it shall be the policy of the United States to insure equal employment opportunities for Federal employees without discrimination because of race, color, religion, sex or national origin and the President shall utilize his existing authority to effectuate this policy.

The substantive provisions of the Title are found in the following section:

Sec. 703. (a) It shall be an unlawful employment practice for an employer—
(1) to fail or refuse to hire or to discharge any individual, or otherwise to discriminate against any individual with respect to his compensation, terms,

conditions, or privileges of employment, because of such individual's race, color, religion, sex, or national origin; or

(2) to limit, segregate, or classify his employees in any way which would deprive or tend to deprive any individual of employment opportunities or otherwise adversely affect his status as an employee, because of such individual's race, color, religion, sex, or national origin. . . .

Subsections (b), (c), and (d) impose similar limitations on the referral policies of employment agencies, membership policies of labor unions, and training program policies of either employers or labor organizations.

There are two primary exceptions to the nondiscrimination provisions. First, classification on the basis of religion, sex, or national origin may be made if such classification is "a bona fide occupational qualification reasonably necessary to the normal operation of that particular business or enterprise." (Note that the provision does not permit an exception based on race.) Second, schools may hire employees of a particular religion if they are "in whole or in substantial part, owned, supported, controlled, or managed by a particular religion," or if the curriculum of any such school "is directed toward the propagation of a particular religion."

The final subsection, (j), states that nothing in the title shall be interpreted to require *preferential* treatment based on race, religion, sex, or national origin "on account of an imbalance which may exist" in the number of persons in any category employed by any employer (or admitted to membership in any labor union, etc.) in comparison with the total number of persons in such category in the community. Thus a "quota" system of hiring is not demanded by the title.

Section 705 of Title VII provides for the creation of a five-member Equal Employment Opportunity Commission. It is given the power to furnish various kinds of technical assistance to further compliance with the title, to make such technical studies "as are appropriate to effectuate the purposes and policies of this title," and to perform other advising and consulting functions. It is charged with reporting annually to the Congress and to the President concerning the action it has taken, "and shall make such further reports on the cause of and means of eliminating discrimination and such recommendations for further legislation as may appear desirable." The Commission also has authority to examine witnesses under oath and to require the production of documentary evidence relevant or material to the investigation. The Commission has further authority to issue suitable procedural regulations to carry out the provisions of Title VII.

Combining the Title VII provisions with the nondiscrimination features of government contracts, the present national policy should have a substantial impact on employment and personnel practices in the private sector. Not until educational opportunities have been fully utilized, however, can it be anticipated that there will be numerically proportional advancement for many nonwhites into the more highly skilled or managerial positions.

There is one area of state legislation classifying by race into which the Court did not venture until 1967. This is the statutory bar to marriages between whites and nonwhites, commonly known as antimiscegenation laws. Since miscegenous marriages represent one of the great fears of those who support race discriminations, it is understandable that neither the Court nor the nonwhite racial pressure groups were anxious to press the issue of the validity of such laws, at least until nondiscrimination in the more important areas of social and economic activity had been achieved. The line of decisions respecting classification by race in regulatory legislation, however, clearly presaged a holding that the miscegenation laws were unconstitutional.

At one period in the nineteenth century some thirty-eight states had statutes barring whites from marrying defined categories of nonwhites. During the Civil War period nine states repealed such statutes, and as of 1951, twenty-nine states retained them. [See generally, Harvey M. Applebaum, "Miscegenation Statutes: A Constitutional and Social Problem," 53 Geo. L. J. 49 (1964).] Since that time a number of those states repealed their statutes, and as of 1967, sixteen states remained with statutes outlawing interracial marriage. The statutes differed widely, both in the persons to whom they applied and in the definitions of categories. In general they prohibited whites from marrying nonwhites but did not bar intermarriage among the nonwhite categories, as, for example, between Indians and Negroes. The definition of Negro (or Indian or Oriental) varied, however, and a person of mixed white and Negro ancestry could be a white under the law of one state and a Negro under the law of another.

Shortly after the end of World War II, the California Supreme Court held the California antimiscegenation law unconstitutional, as a denial of equal protection of the law, in Perez v. Lippold [Sharp], 32 Cal, 2d 711, 198 P.2d 17 (1948). The United States Supreme Court had an opportunity to rule on the question in a case involving the Virginia law as applied to an attempted marriage between a white and an Oriental, but avoided a decision on the merits. The case was first remanded to the Virginia court on the ground of deficiencies in the record, and an appeal from the later decision was dismissed. [Naim v. Naim, 350 U.S. 985 (1956).]

More recently the Court took an appeal and rendered a decision in a case which bore closely on the miscegenation question. Defendants were convicted in a Florida state court of having violated a statute which made it a criminal offense for a white person and a Negro of opposite sexes, not married to each other, to habitually live in and occupy in the nighttime the same room. The Florida Supreme Court sustained the statute against a claim of denial of equal protection under the Fourteenth Amendment. On appeal the Court unanimously reversed in McLaughlin v. Florida, 379 U.S. 184 (1964). In his opinion for the Court, Justice White discussed the legislative power to classify and then stated: "Our inquiry, therefore, is whether there clearly appears in the relevant materials some overriding statutory purpose requiring the proscription of the specified conduct when engaged in by the white person and a Negro, but not otherwise. Without such justification the racial classification . . . is reduced to an invidious discrimination forbidden by the Equal Protection Clause." He concluded that promiscuity by the interracial couple presented no particular problems which required separate or different treatment. Florida argued, however, that the interracial co-habitation law was valid because it was ancillary to and served the same purpose as the miscegenation law itself. Justice White responded, "We reject this argument without reaching the question of the validity of the State's prohibition against interracial marriage. . . ."

The Court did reach the question in 1967, however, in an appeal involving the antimiscegenation policy of the state of Virgina. The case testing Virginia's statutes began, ironically, as *Virginia* v. *Loving,* a criminal prosecution for violation of the state's ban on interracial marriages. In *Loving* v. *Virginia,* 388 U.S. 1 (1967), the Court held the prohibition unconstitutional.

LOVING v. VIRGINIA
388 U.S. 1 (1967)

Mr. Chief Justice Warren delivered the opinion of the Court.

This case presents a constitutional question never addressed by this Court: whether a statutory scheme adopted by the State of Virginia to prevent marriages between persons solely on the basis of racial classifications violates the Equal Protection and Due Process Clauses of the Fourteenth Amendment. For reasons which seem to us to reflect the central meaning of those constitutional commands, we conclude that these statutes cannot stand consistently with the Fourteenth Amendment.

In June 1958, two residents of Virginia, Mildred Jeter, a Negro woman, and Richard Loving, a white man, were married in the District of Columbia pursuant to its laws. Shortly after their marriage, the Lovings returned to Virginia and established their marital abode in Caroline County. At the October Term, 1958, of the Circuit Court of Caroline County, a grand jury issued an indictment charging the Lovings with violating Virginia's ban on interracial marriages. On January 6, 1959, the Lovings pleaded guilty to the charge and were sentenced to one year in jail; however, the trial judge suspended the sentence for a period of 25 years on the condition that the Lovings leave the State and not return to Virginia together for 25 years, stating that:

"Almighty God created the races white, black, yellow, malay, and red, and he placed them on separate continents. And but for the interference with his arrangement there would be no cause for such marriages. The fact that he separated the races shows that he did not intend for the races to mix."

[The opinion then describes the various procedural attacks made by the Lovings on the judgment and sentence, culminating in an appeal to the Virginia Supreme Court.]

The Supreme Court of Appeals upheld the constitutionality of the antimiscegenation statutes and, after modifying the sentence, affirmed the convictions. The Lovings appealed this decision. . . .

The two statutes under which appellants were convicted and sentenced are part of a comprehensive statutory scheme aimed at prohibiting and punishing interracial marriages. The Lovings were convicted of violating §20–58 of the Virginia Code:

"*Leaving State to evade law.* If any white person and colored person shall go out of this State, for the purpose of being married, and with the intention of returning, and be married out of it, and afterwards return to and reside in it, cohabiting as man and wife, they shall be punished as provided in §20–59, and the marriage shall be governed by the same law as if it had been solemnized in this State. The fact of their cohabitation here as man and wife shall be evidence of their marriage."

Section 20–59, which defines the penalty for miscegenation, provides:

"*Punishment for marriage.* If any white person intermarry with a colored person, or any colored person intermarry with a white person, he shall be guilty of a felony and shall be punished by confinement in the penitentiary for not less than one nor more than five years."

Other central provisions in the Virginia statutory scheme are §20–57, which automatically voids all marriages between "a white person and a colored person" without any judicial proceeding, and §§20–54 and 1–14 which, respectively, define "white persons" and "colored persons and Indians" for purposes of the statutory prohibitions. The Lovings have never disputed in the course of this litigation that Mrs. Loving is a "colored person" or that Mr. Loving is a "white person" within the meanings given those terms by the Virginia statutes. . . .

I

In upholding the constitutionality of these provisions in the decision below, the Supreme Court of Appeals of Virginia referred to its 1955 decision in *Naim* v. *Naim,* 87 S.E. 2d 749, as stating the reasons supporting the validity of these laws. In *Naim,* the state court concluded that the State's legitimate purposes were "to preserve the racial integrity of its citizens," and to prevent "the corruption of blood," "a mongrel breed of citizens," and "the obliteration of racial pride," obviously an endorsement of the doctrine of White Supremacy. . . . The court also reasoned that marriage has traditionally been subject to state regulation without federal intervention, and, consequently, the regulation of marriage should be left to exclusive state control by the Tenth Amendment.

While the state court is no doubt correct in asserting that marriage is a social relation subject to the State's police power, . . . the State does not contend in its argument before this Court that its powers to regulate marriage are unlimited notwithstanding the commands of the Fourteenth Amendment. . . . [T]he State contends that, because its miscegenation statutes punish equally both the white and the Negro participants in an interracial marriage, these statutes, despite their reliance on racial classifications, do not constitute an invidious discrimination based upon race. . . . In the case at bar . . . we deal with statutes containing racial classifications, and the fact of equal application does not immunize the statute from the very heavy burden of justification which the Fourteenth Amendment has traditionally required of state statutes drawn according to race. . . .

There is patently no legitimate overriding purpose independent of invidious racial discrimination which justifies this classification. The fact that Virginia only prohibits interracial marriages involving white persons demonstrates that the racial classifications must stand on their own justification, as measures designed to maintain White Supremacy. We have consistently denied the constitutionality of measures which restrict the rights of citizens on account of race. There can be no doubt that restricting the freedom to marry solely because of racial classifications violates the central meaning of the Equal Protection Clause.

II

These statutes also deprive the Lovings of liberty without due process of law in violation of the Due Process Clause of the Fourteenth Amendment. The freedom to marry has long been recognized as one of the vital personal rights essential to the orderly pursuit of happiness by free men.

Marriage is one of the "basic civil rights of man," fundamental to our very existence and survival. . . . To deny this fundamental freedom on so unsupportable a basis as the racial classifications embodied in these statutes, classifications so directly subversive of the principle of equality at the heart of the Fourteenth Amendment, is surely to deprive all the State's citizens of liberty without due process of law. The Fourteenth Amendment requires that freedom of choice to marry not be restricted by invidious racial discriminations. Under our Constitution, the freedom to marry, or not marry, a person of another race resides with the individual and cannot be infringed by the State.

These convictions must be reversed.

It is so ordered.

Mr. Justice Stewart, concurring.

I have previously expressed the belief that "it is simply not possible for a state law to be valid under our Constitution which makes the criminality of an act depend upon the race of the actor." *McLaughlin* v. *Florida* . . . (concurring opinion). Because I adhere to that belief, I concur in the judgment of the Court.

Despite the long list of cases denying governments the power to classify by race in regulatory legislation, it should not be assumed that they are barred from taking any cognizance whatever of race or color. There are valid uses for such notations, and as long as data concerning race or color are maintained for legitimate statistical or other valid public purposes, such record-keeping does not violate the constitution. Drivers' licenses presumably may properly require an entry showing race or color as an aid to identification, and certainly birth records and census reports would seem justifiably to contain the same information. In *Tancil* v. *Woolls*, 379 U.S. 19 (1964), the Court, in a *per curiam* opinion, affirmed a three-judge district court's judgment [230 F. Supp. 156 (E.D. Va., 1964)] upholding a Virginia statute which required that the race of the parties be identified in divorce decrees. It is clear, however, that record-keeping by race which may be maintained must not in any way suggest differential treatment, such as occurred in the jury selection cases, for example, or the procedure will not pass muster under the "equal protection" clause.

In 1971 the Court examined the question of whether a city's closing of a public swimming pool, following a court order to integrate the facility, was a violation of the Equal Protection Clause. There was disagreement among the justices as to whether the primary motivation behind the decision to close the pool was to avoid financial loss or to evade the integration order, but the majority held that the action was not unconstitutional. See *Palmer* v. *Thompson*, 403 U.S. 217 (1971), in Chap. 9.

CHAPTER 8

Voting and Apportionment

THE framers of the United States Constitution clearly contemplated that the basic power to regulate elections and fix voter qualifications would rest with the states. Except for the "dead letter" provisions of Section 2 of the Fourteenth Amendment, the only affirmative statements of qualifications of voters are found in Article I, Section 2, and in the Seventeenth Amendment, and these provisions only go so far as to require that persons voting for members of the Congress "shall have the Qualifications requisite for Electors of the most numerous Branch of the State Legislature." Thus the states were left with broad leeway in determining the manner in which elections would be conducted and the persons who could participate in them. The general outlines are similar, but there is still considerable variation from state to state in the requirements for voting and in the situations which will disqualify persons from continuing to exercise the franchise. For example, the age requirement is usually twenty-one years, but Georgia and Kentucky set the age at eighteen, Alaska at nineteen, and Hawaii at twenty. And while the usual residence requirement is one year, some states require only six months and others two years. Approximately one-third of the states employ literacy tests of one kind or another before permitting registration. And while all states now require citizenship, there have been some twenty states which at some time or other have allowed aliens to vote before their naturalization was complete. [See generally, Constance E. Smith, *Voting and Election Laws* (New York: Oceana Publications, 1960).]

If this were the whole of the picture of regulations concerning voting and elections, then any problems would be resolved simply by reference to the respective state laws. Complications are introduced, however, by the fact that the Constitution both gives to Congress certain powers to regulate elections and sets certain limits on the states in the exercise of their regulatory powers over voting and elections. It is in the treatment accorded these two areas by the Congress and the courts in the past hundred years rather than in positive state laws that the major developments have occurred in safeguarding and expanding the basic right to vote.

CONSTITUTIONAL LIMITATIONS ON STATE VOTING REGULATIONS

The provisions of the United States Constitution which serve to limit the states in the area of voting and elections are the Fourteenth Amendment's "equal protection" clause, the Fifteenth Amendment, and the Nineteenth Amendment. In brief, the "equal protection" clause denies the state the power to make unreasonable classifications in the matter of voting, the Fifteenth Amendment prohibits either the states or the United States from abridging the right to vote because of race or color, and the Nineteenth Amendment prohibits either the states or the United States from abridging the right to vote because of sex. It should be noted that in each of the three amendments the prohibitions lie against action carried through by *governments,* and none of the restrictions runs against purely *private* action to interfere with voting. In a case alleging a violation of the "equal protection" clause, the court must make affirmative findings in response to two questions before it can offer a remedy: (1) Was the alleged interference accomplished by means of state action? and (2) Was the interference a result of improper classification either in a statute or in its administration? In a case alleging a violation of the Fifteenth Amendment, the court must also make affirmative findings in response to certain questions, but they are slightly different from those which would be raised in an equal protection claim: (1) Was the alleged interference accomplished by means of either state or federal action? (2) Was the attempted electoral participation of the kind guaranteed in the phrase "right to vote"? and (3) Was the alleged denial of electoral participation based on race or color? Only if the answer to all three questions is in the affirmative can the court offer a remedy. (No particular problems have arisen under the Nineteenth Amendment, and it will be omitted from the discussion following.)

THE WHITE PRIMARY CASES

In the latter part of the nineteenth century the southern states adopted a variety of provisions directed largely toward disfranchisement of the Negro. These included such voter requirements as long residence requirements, payment of a poll tax, literacy tests (often discriminatorily administered), and the production of a receipt proving payment of the previous year's taxes. But as the selection of candidates by primary elections instead of party conventions became general, the main thrust of southern effort was directed toward preventing the Negro from participating in the Democratic primaries. In the "solid South" until fairly recently, winning the Democratic primary was tantamount to election, and thus even if participation in the general elections was permitted, it was largely futile. The first of the white primary cases to reach the Court was *Nixon* v. *Herndon,* 273

U.S. 536 (1927). The Texas election law of 1923 provided that "in no event shall a negro be eligible to participate in a Democratic party primary election held in the State of Texas." This provision might appear at first glance to have been a clear-cut violation of the Fifteenth Amendment. But until 1941 the Court did not take a clear stand that the Fifteenth Amendment "right to vote" included the right to vote in a primary. With this uncertainty the Court in *Nixon* v. *Herndon* chose the safer course of ruling the provision unconstitutional as a denial of equal protection of the laws under the Fourteenth Amendment. A substitute statute was then passed authorizing the state executive committee of every political party to fix qualifications for participating in their respective primaries. The state executive committee of the Democratic party then adopted a rule barring Negroes from participation in its primaries. In *Nixon* v. *Condon*, 286 U.S. 73 (1932), the Court held that this was a delegation of state power to the state executive committee and made its determination conclusive irrespective of any expression of the party's will by its convention, and therefore the committee's action barring Negroes from the party primaries was state action prohibited by the Fourteenth Amendment. Undaunted, the Texas legislature then repealed its statutes regarding party membership and left the matter solely to the parties. In 1932 the state Democratic convention of Texas adopted a resolution limiting membership in the Democratic party, and thereby participation in the primaries, to white persons. When this resolution as well was challenged, in *Grovey* v. *Townsend*, 294 U.S. 699 (1935), the Court's uncertainties regarding the right to participate in a primary election as well as the status of a state party convention's determinations under the "state action" definition combined to produce a decision that the petitioner was not denied "any right guaranteed by the Fourteenth and Fifteenth Amendments." The Court held that arguments directed toward the right to membership in a party and participation in its primaries were confused with the right to vote for one who is to hold a public office. "With the former the state need have no concern, with the latter it is bound to concern itself. . . ." With regard to the status of the Democratic convention, the opinion stated, "We are not prepared to hold that in Texas the state convention of a party has become a mere instrumentality or agency for expressing the voice or will of the state."

In 1941, however, the Court held in *United States* v. *Classic*, 313 U.S. 299 (1941), that a citizen's right to vote in a congressional primary and to have his vote properly counted is a federal right protected by the Constitution. The case arose out of fraud in a Louisiana primary, and the Court held that Article I, Sections 2 and 4, supported congressional authority to regulate federal elections, including the power to deal also with primaries as merely a phase of the electoral process. While this decision did not directly deal with the question of the validity of white primaries, the relevance to the decision in *Grovey* v. *Townsend* was obvious. In short order another case was brought up from Texas for a re-examination of the *Grovey* rule.

And in 1944 in *Smith* v. *Allwright*, 321 U.S. 649, *Grovey* was squarely overruled. Justice Reed, speaking for the majority, stated in part:

... When *Grovey* v. *Townsend* was written, the Court looked upon the denial of a vote in a primary as a mere refusal by a party of party membership. As the Louisiana statutes for holding primaries are similar to those of Texas, our ruling in *Classic* as to the unitary character of the electoral process calls for a reexamination as to whether or not the exclusion of Negroes from a Texas party primary was state action. ...

It may now be taken as a postulate that the right to vote in such a primary for the nomination of candidates without discrimination by the State, like the right to vote in a general election, is a right secured by the Constitution. ...

Primary elections are conducted by the party under state statutory authority. The county executive committee selects precinct election officials and the county, district or state executive committees, respectively, canvass the returns. These party committees or the state convention certify the party's candidates to the appropriate officers for inclusion on the official ballot for the general election. No name which has not been so certified may appear upon the ballot for the general election as a candidate of a political party. No other name may be printed on the ballot which has not been placed in nomination by qualified voters who must take oath that they did not participate in a primary for the selection of a candidate for the office for which the nomination is made.

The state courts are given exclusive original jurisdiction of contested elections and of mandamus proceedings to compel party officers to perform their statutory duties.

We think that this statutory system for the selection of party nominees for inclusion on the general election ballot makes the party which is required to follow these legislative directions an agency of the state in so far as it determines the participants in a primary election. ... If the state requires a certain electoral procedure, prescribes a general election ballot made up of party nominees so chosen and limits the choice of the electorate in general elections for state offices, practically speaking, to those whose names appear on such a ballot, it endorses, adopts and enforces the discrimination against Negroes, practiced by a party entrusted by Texas law with the determination of the qualifications of participants in the primary. This is state action within the meaning of the Fifteenth Amendment. ...

Justice Roberts, in dissenting, stated that "The reason for my concern is that the instant decision, overruling that announced about nine years ago, tends to bring adjudications of this tribunal into the same class as a restricted railroad ticket, good for this day and train only."

Smith v. *Allwright* would seem to have settled the matter of the white primary once and for all, but this was not the case. The South Carolina legislature was called into special session and, taking its cue from the way Justice Reed found state action in the Texas case, repealed all statutes (nearly 150 in all) relating in any way to primaries and proposed amendments to the state constitution to remove any similar provisions in the constitution. The theory was that such action would leave the political party in the same position as any other private club, and its acts would in no way be construed as state action. This done, a Democratic state convention adopted a rule barring Negroes from membership in the Democratic Club and, therefore, from participation in its primaries.

A federal district court issued an injunction against an official of the Democratic Party to prevent his denying Negroes the right to vote in the primaries. [*Elmore* v. *Rice*, 72 F. Supp. 516 (E.D.S.C., 1947).] In *Rice* v. *Elmore*, 165 F. 2d 387 (4th C.C.A., 1947), this ruling was affirmed by the Court of Appeals. [*Cert. denied*, 333 U.S. 875 (1948).] Judge Parker, speaking for the court of appeals, stated:

> The fundamental error in defendant's position consists in the premise that a political party is a mere private aggregation of individuals, like a country club, and that the primary is a mere piece of party machinery. . . . [W]ith the passage of the years, political parties have become in effect state institutions, governmental agencies through which sovereign power is exercised by the people. . . .

The closing chapter in the white primary story saw a return to Texas and a challenge to the racially exclusionary practices of the Jaybird Democratic Association of Fort Bend County, Texas. The Jaybird Association was organized in 1889 and limited its membership to white registered voters. Candidates for county offices submitted their names to the Jaybird Committee and ran in a primary held by the Association prior to the regular Democratic primary. The winners normally ran subsequently in the regular Democratic primary without opposition and won both that and the general election following. In *Terry* v. *Adams*, 345 U.S. 461 (1953), the Court held such a procedure violative of the Fifteenth Amendment. Justice Black, for three of the majority, stated:

> For a state to permit such a duplication of its election processes is to permit a flagrant abuse of those processes to defeat the purposes of the Fifteenth Amendment. The use of the county-operated primary to ratify the result of the prohibited election merely compounds the offense. It violates the Fifteenth Amendment for a state, by such circumvention, to permit within its borders the use of any device that produces an equivalent of the prohibited election. . . .
>
> . . . It is immaterial that the state does not control that part of this elective process which it leaves for the Jaybirds to manage. The Jaybird primary has become an integral, indeed the only effective part, of the elective process that determines who shall rule and govern in the county. The effect of the whole procedure, Jaybird primary plus Democratic primary plus general election, is to do precisely that which the Fifteenth Amendment forbids—strip Negroes of every vestige of influence in selecting the officials who control the local county matters that intimately touch the daily lives of citizens. . . .

Five other members of the Court concurred in the result, but for slightly different reasons. Justice Minton was the lone dissenter, arguing that the actions of the Jaybird Association could not properly be held to be state action. [On the white primary see Douglas Weeks, "The White Primary: 1944–1948," 42 *Am. Pol. Sci. Rev.* 500 (1948); V. O. Key, *Southern Poli-*

tics (New York: Knopf, 1949), pp. 625–643; Thurgood Marshall, "The Rise and Collapse of the 'White Primary,'" 26 *J. of Negro Ed.* 249 (1957).]

THE GRANDFATHER CLAUSES

Among other devices employed to impede voting by Negroes was the "grandfather clause," used by several states beginning in 1895. Without expressly disfranchising the Negro, it facilitated the permanent placement of white residents on the lists of registered voters while continuing to impose serious obstacles upon Negro registration. The typical provision required all prospective electors to be able to read and write any section of the state constitution, but no person who voted prior to January 1st, 1866, or who was a lineal descendant of such person, could be denied the right to register and vote because of his inability to meet this literacy requirement. The clause did not, therefore, bar Negroes from being registered, but because of the operative date, all Negroes had to pass the literacy test while most white persons were exempt. In *Guinn* v. *United States,* 238 U.S. 347 (1915), the Court held that the employment by the state of Oklahoma of a standard based purely upon a period of time before the enactment of the Fifteenth Amendment and which so clearly set up a classification following racial lines was in violation of the protection accorded by that Amendment. Oklahoma promptly adopted a new statute in 1916 which provided that all persons, except those who voted in 1914, who were qualified to vote in 1916 but who failed to register between April 30 and May 11, 1916 (a twelve-day registration period) should be perpetually disfranchised. The Court was not impressed with this obvious subterfuge, and in *Lane* v. *Wilson,* 307 U.S. 268 (1939), held this statute also violative of the Fifteenth Amendment. In a sharply worded opinion, Justice Frankfurter stated that that Amendment "nullifies sophisticated as well as simple-minded modes of discrimination. It hits onerous procedural requirements which effectively handicap exercise of the franchise by the colored race although the abstract right to vote may remain unrestricted as to race."

POLL TAXES AND LITERACY TESTS

There were at one time in the period following Reconstruction some eleven southern states which imposed a poll tax as a prerequisite to voting. The amount of the tax ranged from one to two dollars, and some statutes exempted women and older persons. Whether the tax had greater impact on Negroes than on white persons has been a matter of some dispute. Certainly in the manner of administration and in the fact that it was cumulative in some states it was a factor in discouraging voter registration, whether there was special racial impact or not. Payment was normally voluntary and, since tax bills were not usually sent out, the voter had to keep track of annual deadlines and take the initiative in seeking out the proper officials to whom the poll tax was to be paid. Until a 1953 amendment was adopted, the Alabama tax was cumulative starting with age twenty-one and going through age forty-five. After 1953 the cumulative period was reduced to two years. V. O. Key, in his book *Southern Politics* (New York: Knopf, 1949), pp. 617–618, concluded that the poll tax had little or no bearing on the paucity of Negro voters because of the much greater effect of other methods of disfranchisement. He did feel, however, that removal of the poll tax would increase voting in most southern states by five to ten percent of the potential number of white voters.

The Court in *Breedlove* v. *Suttles*, 302 U.S. 277 (1937), upheld the Georgia poll tax law against the claims of a white male citizen that the law violated the "equal protection" clause, that it abridged the privileges and immunities of United States citizens, and that it violated the Nineteenth Amendment. The law exempted blind persons and women who did not register for voting. Justice Butler, for the Court, answered each claim separately:

1. He asserts that the law offends the rule of equality in that it extends only to persons between the ages of 21 and 60 and to women only if they register for voting and in that it makes payment a prerequisite to registration. . . .

Levy by the poll has long been a familiar form of taxation, much used in some countries and to a considerable extent here, at first in the Colonies and later in the States. . . . Poll taxes are laid upon persons without regard to their occupations or property to raise money for the support of government or some more specific end. The equal protection clause does not require absolute equality. . . .

The tax being upon persons, women may be exempted on the basis of special considerations to which they are naturally entitled. In view of burdens necessarily borne by them for the preservation of the race, the State reasonably may exempt them from poll taxes. . . .

Payment as a prerequisite is not required for the purpose of denying or abridging the privilege of voting. . . . Exaction of payment before registration undoubtedly serves to aid collection from electors desiring to vote, but that use of the State's power is not prevented by the Federal Constitution. . . .

2. To make payment of poll taxes a prerequisite of voting is not to deny any privilege or immunity protected by the Fourteenth Amendment. Privilege of voting is not derived from the United States, but is conferred by the State and, save as restrained by the Fifteenth and Nineteenth Amendments and other provisions of the Federal Constitution, the State may condition suffrage as it seems appropriate. . . .

3. The Nineteenth Amendment . . . applies to men and women alike and by its own force supersedes inconsistent measures, whether federal or state. . . . Its purpose is not to regulate the levy or collection of taxes. The construction for which appellant contends would make the amendment a limitation upon the power to tax. . . . It is fanciful to suggest that the Georgia law is a mere disguise under which to deny or abridge the right of men to vote on account of their sex. . . .

Proposals in Congress for abolishing the poll tax as a prerequisite to voting were advanced for many years, beginning in 1939, but many members expressed reservations concerning the constitutionality of the proposals. Finally, in 1962, a constitutional amendment passed the Congress prohibiting the exacting of any tax as a requirement for voting in federal elections. In was ratified in 1964 as the Twenty-fourth Amendment. At the time, five states still required payment of the poll tax (Alabama, Arkansas, Mississippi, Texas, and Virginia), and they indicated plans to continue the requirement with respect to voting in state and local elections.

In 1963, in anticipation of the promulgation of the Twenty-fourth Amendment, a special session of the Virginia General Assembly was convened. It adopted a requirement that in order to qualify to vote in federal elections one must either pay a poll tax or file a witnessed or notarized certificate of residence. In *Harman* v. *Forssenius*, 380 U.S. 528 (1965), the Court unanimously held the requirement repugnant to the Twenty-fourth Amendment. Chief Justice Warren, for the Court, stated that the requirement of a poll tax clearly violated that Amendment, and "no equivalent or milder substitute may be imposed." He said further, "Any material requirement imposed upon the federal voter solely because of his refusal to waive the constitutional immunity subverts the effectiveness of the Twenty-fourth Amendment and must fall under its ban."

The closing chapter in the long history of the poll tax as a prerequisite to voting was presumably written in 1966. In *Harper* v. *Virginia State Bd. of Elections*, 383 U.S. 663 (1966), the Court by a six-to-three vote held the requirement of payment of a poll tax as a prerequisite to participation in *state* elections unconstitutional under the "equal protection" clause of the Fourteenth Amendment. Justice Douglas, for the majority, stated:

> We conclude that a State violates the Equal Protection Clause of the Fourteenth Amendment whenever it makes the affluence of the voter or payment of any fee an electoral standard. Voter qualifications have no relation to wealth nor to paying or not paying this or any other tax.... The principle that denies the State the right to dilute a citizen's vote on account of his economic status or other such factors by analogy bars a system which excludes those unable to pay a fee to vote or who fail to pay.... To introduce wealth or payment of a fee as a measure of a voter's qualifications is to introduce a capricious or irrelevant factor. The degree of the discrimination is irrelevant. In this context—that is, as a condition of obtaining a ballot—the requirement of fee paying causes an "invidious" discrimination (*Skinner* v. *Oklahoma* ...) that runs afoul of the Equal Protection Clause. Levy "by the poll," as stated in *Breedlove* v. *Suttles*, ... is an old familiar form of taxation; and we say nothing to impair its validity so long as it is not made a condition to the exercise of the franchise. *Breedlove* v. *Suttles* sanctioned its use as "a prerequisite of voting."... To that extent the *Breedlove* case is overruled.

Literacy tests for voting have been used by a number of states for many years. While there is a fairly obvious relationship between literacy and voting (although even here the case may be overstated), the literacy test at the same time lends itself more readily than most other requirements to discriminatory administration. The constitutionality of a Mississippi literacy requirement was attacked in *Williams* v. *Mississippi*, 170 U.S. 213 (1898) on the ground that unfettered discretion was vested in the registrars and that the provisions were administered in a racially discriminatory manner. The Court found the claim of discriminatory administration inadequately pleaded and held that literacy tests which are drafted so as to apply alike to all applicants for the voting franchise would be deemed to be fair on their face, and in the absence of proof of discriminatory enforcement could not be viewed as denying the equal protection of the laws guaranteed by the Fourteenth Amendment.

As recently as 1959, in *Lassiter* v. *Northampton Election Board*, 360 U.S. 45, the Court refused to hold invalid on its face a North Carolina requirement that all voters be able "to read and write any section of the Constitution of North Carolina in the English language." Justice Douglas, speaking for a unanimous Court, stated:

> The states have long been held to have broad powers to determine the conditions under which the right of suffrage may be exercised. . . .
> We do not suggest that any standards which a State desires to adopt may be required of voters. But there is wide scope for exercise of its jurisdiction. Residence requirements, age, previous criminal record . . . are obvious examples indicating factors which a State may take into consideration in determining the qualifications of voters. The ability to read and write likewise has some relation to standards designed to promote intelligent use of the ballot. Literacy and illiteracy are neutral on race, creed, color, and sex, as reports around the world show. Literacy and intelligence are obviously not synonymous. Illiterate people may be intelligent voters. Yet in our society where newspapers, periodicals, books, and other printed matter canvass and debate campaign issues, a State might conclude that only those who are literate should exercise the franchise. . . . It was said last century in Massachusetts that a literacy test was designed to insure an "independent and intelligent" exercise of the right of suffrage. . . . North Carolina agrees. We do not sit in judgment on the wisdom of that policy. We cannot say, however, that it is not an allowable one measured by constitutional standards. . . .

The opinion went on to point out, however, that "a literacy test, fair on its face, may be employed to perpetuate that discrimination which the Fifteenth Amendment was designed to uproot." In such circumstances it would be held to be unconstitutionally applied. The Court found just such a purpose in the enactment of the Boswell Amendment to the Alabama Constitution in 1946 which provided that only persons who could "understand and explain any article of the constitution of the United States" could be registered. A separate provision of the Alabama Code required that applicants for registration establish by evidence to the reasonable satisfaction of the board of registrars that they were qualified to register. In 1949 a complaint was filed in a three-judge federal district court charging that these two provisions, coupled together, vested in the Board of Registrars unlimited discretion to grant to or deny the right to register, and that the provisions had in fact been designed and used to prevent qualified Negro applicants from voting. In *Davis* v. *Schnell*, 81 F. Supp. 872 (D.C., S.D. Ala., 1949), the United States District Court held the requirements unconstitutional and enjoined further enforcement of the provisions. Judge Mullins, speaking for the three-judge court, stated:

We ... find from the evidence that prior to the filing of this suit said Board of Registrars required Negro applicants for registration as electors in Mobile County to attempt to explain at least some article of the United States Constitution, while no such requirement was exacted of white applicants. We also find that the plaintiffs Davis and Cook were refused registration as electors because of their race or color.

[The opinion then cites evidence from the registration records showing that subsequent to the filing of the suit sixty-five colored applicants were registered and fifty-seven were rejected, in each of the latter cases because they could not "understand and explain" an article of the Federal Constitution. The records of eleven white applicants showed that they were denied registration on grounds other than failure to meet the literacy requirement. The evidence showed, further, that the Board generally required Negro applicants to explain or interpret the Constitution and did not generally require white applicants to do so.]

The evidence shows that during the incumbency of the defendant board that more than 2800 white persons have been registered and approximately 104 Negroes. The estimated population of Mobile County is 230,000 of which approximately 64 per cent is white and 36 per cent is colored....

... If an exact meaning of the phrase "understand and explain" were to be discovered by a process of construction in this case, it might be that a suitable and definite standard could be found, which would not give to the board of registrars arbitrary power. However, a careful consideration of the legislative and other history of the adoption of this Amendment to the Constitution of Alabama discloses that the ambiguity inherent in the phrase "understand and explain" cannot be resolved, but, on the contrary, was purposeful and used with a view of meeting the decision of the Supreme Court of the United States in *Smith* v. *Allwright*.... The history of the period immediately preceding the adoption of the Boswell Amendment, of which we take judicial notice, and the evidence in this case prove this....

It, thus, clearly appears that this Amendment was intended to be, and is being used for the purpose of discriminating against applicants for the franchise on the basis of race or color. Therefore, we are necessarily brought to the conclusion that this Amendment to the Constitution of Alabama, both in its object and the manner of its administration, is unconstitutional, because it violates the Fifteenth Amendment. While it is true that there is no mention of race or color in the Boswell Amendment, this does not save it. The Fifteenth Amendment "nullifies sophisticated as well as simple-minded modes of discrimination," and "It hits onerous procedural requirements which effectively handicap exercise of the franchise by the colored race although the abstract right to vote may remain unrestricted as to race."...

The United States Supreme Court affirmed, *per curiam*, in *Schnell* v. *Davis*, 336 U.S. 933 (1949).

On authority of *Schnell* v. *Davis* the Court held invalid a Louisiana requirement that applicants for registration be able to give a "reasonable interpretation" of any section of the Louisiana Constitution or the United States Constitution when read to them by the registrar [*Louisiana* v. *United States*, 380 U.S. 145 (1965)]. In his opinion for the Court Justice Black stated:

. . . The applicant facing a registrar in Louisiana thus has been compelled to leave his voting fate to that official's uncontrolled power to determine whether the applicant's understanding of the Federal or State Constitution is satisfactory. As the evidence showed, colored people, even some with the most advanced education and scholarship, were declared by voting registrars with less education to have an unsatisfactory understanding of the constitution of Louisiana or of the United States. This is not a test but a trap, sufficient to stop even the most brilliant man on his way to the voting booth. The cherished right of people in a country like ours to vote cannot be obliterated by the use of laws like this, which leave the voting fate of a citizen to the passing whim or impulse of an individual registrar. . . .

Other practices designed to hinder Negro registration in Louisiana are described in the chapter entitled "The Louisiana Story" in the 1961 United States Commission on Civil Rights Report, *Voting* (Washington, D.C.: U.S. Government Printing Ofc., 1961). One feature of the registration requirements which appears to be unique is the requirement that the applicant state his exact age in years, months, and days. The report states that a registrar of voters of Plaquemines Parish, who was called on to give a step-by-step demonstration of the proper way to complete the application form, erred in her age computation by almost a month. And there appeared to be some confusion as to whether to include or exclude the day on which the application was filed. Nor was there agreement on whether an error of one day would be fatal to registration.

A group of provisions of the Mississippi Constitution added in 1954 and 1960 resulted in requirements that applicants for registration had to: (1) be able to read and copy in writing any section of the Mississippi Constitution, and (2) give a reasonable interpretation of that section to the county registrar, and (3) demonstrate to the registrar "a reasonable understanding of the duties and obligations of citizenship under a constitutional form of government," and (4) be "of good moral character." Under the *Lassiter* rule the first requirement would seem to be legitimate, if fairly administered. The second and third requirements would appear to fall clearly under the ban of *Louisiana* v. *United States* and would be unconstitutional on their face. The fourth requirement would seem to be similarly deficient without some clear definition in terms of convictions for crime or other clear-cut standards.

FEDERAL LEGISLATION TO PROTECT VOTING RIGHTS

Shortly after the Fifteenth Amendment was ratified in 1870, Congress passed a law to enforce its provisions [Act of May 31, 1870, 42 U.S.C. 1971(a) (1958)]. The relevant section provided:

All citizens of the United States who are otherwise qualified by law to vote at any election by the people in any State, Territory, district, county, city, parish, township, school district, municipality, or other territorial subdivision, shall be entitled and allowed to vote at all such elections, without distinction of race, color, or previous condition of servitude; any constitution, law, custom, usage, or regulation of any State or Territory, or by or under its authority, to the contrary notwithstanding.

[The discussion of this section and other legislation through the Civil Rights Act of 1960 is largely in the words of the 1961 Civil Rights Commission Report, *Voting*, pp. 73–78. See also, Note, "Voting Rights," 3 *Race Rel. L. Rep.* 371 (1958).]

While the Supreme Court has long since struck down much Reconstruction legislation as unconstitutional, this provision, Section 1971(a) of Title 42, survives as a cornerstone of Federal legislation to protect the right to vote.

But this section merely declared a right. It provided no legal remedy. And other relevant Reconstruction legislation has proved difficult to apply, or depends on private initiative. Until the passage of the Civil Rights Act of 1957, therefore, the federal government could do little to combat discriminatory denials of the right to vote. The 1957 act, and its successor act in 1960, opened the way to more direct and effective federal action to protect the fundamental right of electoral participation.

For seventy years the federal government relied almost solely on two sections of the Criminal Code to prevent discrimination in voting. Both were Reconstruction measures, now Sections 241 and 242 of Title 18 of the United States Code. Section 241 penalizes *conspiracies* of two or more persons to "injure, oppress, threaten, or intimidate any citizen in the free exercise or enjoyment of any right . . . secured . . . by the Constitution or laws of the United States. . . ." This provision applies to actions by either state officials or private persons that interfere with voting in federal elections, and also to state officials in state and local elections. (For a detailed analysis of Sections 241 and 242 and for discussion of the general distinction between the federal right to vote and the state right, see Chapter 3.) The other criminal provision, now Section 242, prohibits action "under color of law" which interferes with "rights . . . secured or protected by the Constitution or laws of the United States," including the right not to be discriminated against on grounds of race or color.

Section 241 was involved in the case of *Ex parte Yarbrough*, 110 U.S. 651 (1884), where the Court declared that the right to vote in federal elections arose from the federal Constitution and was, therefore, subject to protection by federal legislation. This was true, said the Court, despite the fact that state laws prescribe the qualifications of electors. Both sections were involved in *United States* v. *Classic*, 313 U.S. 299 (1941), where the Court held for the first time that the guarantees of the Constitution cover primary as well as general elections. (See Chapter 3 for the opinions in these two cases.)

In 1939 Congress enacted, as part of the Hatch Act, another criminal provision to protect the right to vote. It is Section 594 of Title 18 of the

Code and assesses criminal penalties as a misdemeanor for persons who intimidate, threaten, or coerce any other person for the purpose of interfering with his right to vote in federal elections. It does not appear to have been used to date.

Before 1957, in addition to these criminal remedies, three other provisions of the Code laid a basis for *civil* remedies for improper denials of the right to vote. Section 1971(a), quoted above, while it did not provide for specific remedies, did set up the federal right to vote without distinctions as to race or color. And two other sections set up the civil remedies. Section 1983 (the civil counterpart of Section 242) of Title 42 of the Code permits suits to be brought against persons acting "under color of any statute, ordinance, regulation, custom or usage" to deprive citizens of rights secured by the Constitution and laws of the United States. The injured party may bring "an action at law, suit in equity, or other proper proceeding for redress." The suit for injunctive relief or for damages is the usual type of action under this section. It was the basis for action, along with Section 1971(a), in a number of landmark cases, including *Nixon* v. *Herndon, Smith* v. *Allwright,* and *Rice* v. *Elmore.* The other section, Section 1985(3) of Title 42, provides for a suit for damages (but not equitable action) in the case of a conspiracy to deprive persons of the equal protection of the laws or to prevent by force, intimidation, or threat, any qualified voter from voting as he chooses in a federal election. This section has been little used. (See Chapter 3 for the text of these sections and some of their applications.)

In summing up the effect of these provisions, the 1961 Civil Rights Commission *Voting* Report states (p. 75):

> These provisions set the framework for a series of important cases expanding and defining the Federal right to vote—but they were weak. Most of these cases were civil, not criminal. The Federal Government was empowered only to bring criminal cases, and the criminal statutes were unwieldy and difficult to apply. Civil cases, with their flexible remedies and relative ease of proof, could be brought only by private persons, who are not always able to bear the expense and difficulty involved in long and complicated litigation.

Congress made a substantial change in adopting the Civil Rights Act of 1957 (71 Stat. 635). Basically, the Act is an amendment to the old Section 1971. It retains that section as subsection (a) and adds several other subsections. Subsection (b) is also a declaration of rights, adopting substantially the same language as 18 U.S.C. Section 594, the Hatch Act provision to punish for intimidation of voters in federal elections, except that it explicitly mentions primaries as well as general elections and provides for civil suits to be brought by either private parties or the Attorney General. Other provisions of the Act give the federal district courts jurisdiction of such civil proceedings without a requirement that state administrative or other remedies first be exhausted; provide for contempt proceedings in the event of disobedience of court orders under the section; and, by authorizing the appointment of an additional Assistant Attorney General, led to raising the Department of Justice's Civil Rights Section to the status of a full division. The Act also created the Civil Rights Commission.

Experience under the 1957 act indicated that it was still insufficient to stop discriminatory denials of the right to vote. When the Commission issued its first report late in 1959, the Civil Rights Division had instituted only three actions under the section permitting the Attorney General to institute suits, and none had been successful. In one case, because the registrars against whom the suit was brought had previously resigned from office, a federal district court had held that there was no one the federal government could sue. [*U.S.* v. *Alabama,* 171 F. Supp. 720 (M.D. Ala., 1959), *aff'd,* 267 F. 2d 808 (5th Cir., 1960), *vacated,* 362 U.S. 602 (1960).]

As a result of the experience under the 1957 act, the Commission strongly urged the passage of another act to close up several loopholes. The Civil Rights Act of 1960 (74 Stat. 86) reflected the Commission's recommendations. It took care of the problem of resigning registrars by amending the 1957 law to provide that in actions brought under Section 1971(a) and (c), "the act or practice shall also be deemed that of the State and the State may be joined as a party defendant and if, prior to the institution of such proceeding, such official has resigned or has been relieved of his office and no successor assumed such office, the proceeding may be instituted against the State."

Another provision of the 1960 Act—Title III—declared voting records public and required their preservation for a period of twenty-two months following any general or special election. The provision opened the way for inspection and copying by the Attorney General both to help him to decide which cases might warrant prosecution and also to help him in gathering evidence for suits ultimately filed.

Title VI of the 1960 Act made provision for the substitution of federal voting referees for local registration officials when various judicial findings of discriminatory practices were made. The procedural requirements which had to be met preparatory to an actual registration order were quite formidable, however. First, the government had to file suit under Section 1971(a) and (c) and obtain a court finding that "a person has been deprived on account of race or color" of the right to vote. Second, the court was required to find that "such deprivation was or is pursuant to a pattern or practice." Third, any person found to be discriminated against because of race could apply for an order declaring him qualified to vote. To get such an order he had to prove: "(1) he is qualified under State law to vote, and (2) he has since such finding by the court been (a) deprived of or denied under color of law the opportunity to register to vote or otherwise to qualify to vote, or (b) found not qualified to vote by any person acting under color of law." Finally, the court (or an appointed referee) had to hold a hearing on the application and permit the state to appear to challenge the applicant's qualifications. Only then could a specific person be ordered to be registered and allowed to vote. Thus the machinery was provided to combat discrimination against voters, but it was cumbersome machinery indeed.

In the 1963 Report of the United States Commission on Civil Rights the following statement is made (p. 27):

Abridgment of the right to vote on the grounds of race persists in the United States in direct violation of the Constitution. In fulfillment of its statutory obligation, the Commission has previously recommended to the President and the Congress a variety of corrective measures. In 1963 the continuing discriminatory denial of the right to vote has led this Commission to reexamine and reconsider each of its prior voting recommendations. The Commission now believes that the only effective method of guaranteeing the vote for all Americans is the enactment by Congress of some form of uniform voter qualification standards. The Commission further believes that the right to vote must, in many instances, be safeguarded and assured by the Federal Government. Adequate legislation must include both standards and implementation. . . .

In partial response to this and other recommendations, Title I of the Civil Rights Act of 1964 (78 Stat. 241) adds further amendments to Section 1971 of Title 42. It prohibits the employment of differential standards of qualification for applicants for registration, prohibits denial of right to vote in federal elections because of trivial errors or omissions on the part of applicants which are not material to the determination of qualification, and requires that literacy tests be administered wholly in writing and, further, that a certified copy of the tests and his answers be furnished to the applicant upon his request. In addition, the provision set up a rebuttable presumption that completion of the sixth grade in school is sufficient to meet the requirement of literacy which any state might impose.

Political pressures mounted, however, for even stronger federal legislation guaranteeing the right to vote. The answer came with the signing into law of the Voting Rights Act of 1965 (79 Stat. 437) on August 6 of that year. The Act was clearly aimed at the South, where most of the racially discriminatory denials of the franchise occurred, and was designed to sweep away all procedures which in the past had been used to deny the right to vote on racial grounds, whatever rational justification might be presented for the procedures. The key provision of the Act, in this respect, is Section 4, which prohibits the use of "any test or device" in certain defined states or political subdivisions thereof. The section states, in part:

Sec. 4. (a) To assure that the right of citizens of the United States to vote is not denied or abridged on account of race or color, no citizen shall be denied the right to vote in any Federal, State, or local election because of his failure to comply with any test or device in any State with respect to which the determinations have been made under subsection (b) or in any political subdivision with respect to which such determinations have been made as a separate unit, unless the United States District Court for the District of Columbia in an action for a declaratory judgment brought by such State or subdivision against the United States has determined that no such test or device has been used during the five years preceding the filing of the action for the purpose or with the effect of denying or abridging the right to vote on account of race or color. . . .

(b) The provisions of subsection (a) shall apply in any State or in any political subdivision of a state which (1) the Attorney General determines maintained on November 1, 1964, any test or device, and with respect to which (2) the Director of the Census determines that less than 50 per centum of the persons of voting age residing therein were registered on November 1, 1964, or that less than 50 per centum of such persons voted in the presidential election of November 1964. . . .

(c) The phrase "test or device" shall mean any requirement that a person as a prerequisite for voting or registration for voting (1) demonstrate the ability to read, write, understand, or interpret any matter, (2) demonstrate any educational achievement or his knowledge of any particular subject, (3) possess good moral character, or (4) prove his qualifications by the voucher of registered voters or members of any other class.

The Act authorizes the appointment of examiners with authority to examine the qualifications of applicants for registration and, if they are found qualified under state laws not in conflict with the Constitution or federal laws, to place their names on a list of eligible voters. The appointment of such examiners may be authorized by a federal court in appropriate proceedings begun by the Attorney General under Section 3 of the Act, or the Civil Service Commission will appoint such examiners if the Attorney General certifies that in specified areas as defined by Section 4(b) residents are being denied registration on account of race or color and that the appointment of examiners is necessary to enforce the guarantees of the Fifteenth Amendment.

Section 5 of the Act demands that if states or political subdivisions falling within the category defined by Section 4 "enact or seek to administer any voting qualification or prerequisite to voting, or standard, practice, or procedure with respect to voting different from that in force or effect on November 1, 1964," they must either seek a declaratory judgment from the United States District Court for the District of Columbia that such provision will not abridge the right to vote on account of race or color, or submit such provision to the Attorney General, in which case if he does not interpose an objection within sixty days thereafter, the provision may be put into operation. In the latter case, however, the Attorney General's failure to object does not act as a bar to subsequent action to enjoin the enforcement of the new provision.

The Attorney General moved swiftly after the adoption of the Act, and several southern states were brought within the prohibitions of the Act in the late summer of 1965. South Carolina brought an action in the original jurisdiction of the United States Supreme Court challenging the constitutionality of the so-called "triggering" provision, Section 4(b) of the Act (the characterization was by counsel for South Carolina, and referred to the coverage formula and the provisions for findings by the Attorney General and the Director of the Census which would "trigger" application of the coverage formula), as well as the Section 5 provision "freezing" the election procedures as they were on November 1, 1964, and the Section 6 provisions for registration by federal examiners. Five other southern states were permitted to file supporting briefs and participate in oral argument in the case—Alabama, Georgia, Louisiana, Mississippi, and Virginia. Twenty northern and western states filed briefs in support of the government's position that the Act was constitutional, and argument was heard beginning on January 17, 1966.

In less than two months, an exceptionally rapid disposition of the case, the Court handed down its decision upholding the constitutionality of the Act in *South Carolina* v. *Katzenbach*, 383 U.S. 301 (1966). The Act was challenged on the grounds that the coverage formula violated the principle of the equality of states, denied due process by employing an invalid presumption, constituted a forbidden bill of attainder, and impaired the separation of powers by adjudicating guilt through legislation. Chief Justice Warren, for the Court, stated:

Two points emerge vividly from the voluminous legislative history of the Act contained in the committee hearings and floor debates. First: Congress felt itself confronted by an insidious and pervasive evil which had been perpetuated in certain parts of our country through unremitting and ingenious defiance of the Constitution. Second: Congress concluded that the unsuccessful remedies which it had prescribed in the past would have to be replaced by sterner and more elaborate measures in order to satisfy the clear commands of the Fifteenth Amendment. . . .

In recent years, Congress has repeatedly tried to cope with the problem by facilitating case-by-case litigation against voting discrimination. . . .

Despite the earnest efforts of the Justice Department and of many federal judges, these new laws have done little to cure the problem of voting discrimination. . . .

. . . [T]he basic question presented by the case [is]: Has Congress exercised its powers under the Fifteenth Amendment in an appropriate manner with relation to the States?

The ground rules for resolving this question are clear. The language and purpose of the Fifteenth Amendment, the prior decisions construing its several provisions, and the general doctrines of constitutional interpretation, all point to one fundamental principle. As against the reserved powers of the States, Congress may use any rational means to effectuate the constitutional prohibition of racial discrimination in voting. . . .

Congress exercised its authority under the Fifteenth Amendment in an inventive manner when it enacted the Voting Rights Act of 1965. First: The measure prescribes remedies for voting discrimination which go into effect without any need for prior adjudication. This was clearly a legitimate response to the problem, for which there is ample precedent under other constitutional provisions. . . . After enduring nearly a century of systematic resistance to the Fifteenth Amendment, Congress might well decide to shift the advantage of time and inertia from the perpetrators of the evil to its victims. . . .

Second: The Act intentionally confines these remedies to a small number of States and political subdivisions which in most instances were familiar to Congress by name. This, too, was a permissible method of dealing with the problem. Congress has learned that substantial voting discrimination presently occurs in certain sections of the country, and it knew no way of accurately forecasting whether the evil might spread elsewhere in the future. In acceptable legislative fashion, Congress chose to limit its attention to the geographic areas where immediate action seemed necessary. . . . The doctrine of the equality of States, invoked by South Carolina, does not bar this approach, for that doctrine applies only to the terms upon which States are admitted to the Union, and not to the remedies for local evils which have subsequently appeared. . . .

[On the validity of the 1970 Voting Rights Amendments, including the provision for 18-year-old voters, see *Oregon* v. *Mitchell*, 400 U.S. 112 (1970), in Chap. 9. See Chap. 9 also for *Perkins* v. *Matthews*, 400 U.S. 379 (1971), involving the prior approval requirements of the 1965 Voting Rights Act.]

APPORTIONMENT OF LEGISLATIVE SEATS AND THE "EQUAL PROTECTION" CLAUSE

Prior to 1962, attacks on patterns of apportioning seats for legislative bodies based on the claim that such patterns violated the Article IV guarantee of "a republican form of government" or that population inequalities between districts had the effect of producing inequalities in the effective voting power of persons residing in different districts were unsuccessful in the federal courts. *Colegrove* v. *Green*, 328 U.S. 549 (1946), presented a challenge to the arrangement of Illinois' congressional districts, essentially unchanged since 1901. Petitioners asked that the Court restrain the state from holding a general election on the ground that the districts lacked compactness of territory and approximate equality of population, and that the inequality of voting power resulting was in violation of the Fourteenth Amendment and the provisions of Article I respecting the election of members of the House of Representatives. Three justices held that the matter was nonjusticiable. Justice Frankfurter, speaking for these, stated:

We are of opinion that the petitioners ask of this Court what is beyond its competence to grant. This is one of those demands on judicial power which cannot be met by verbal fencing about "jurisdiction." It must be resolved by considerations on the basis of which this Court, from time to time, has refused to intervene in controversies. It has refused to do so because due regard for the effective working of our Government revealed this issue to be of a peculiarly political nature and therefore not meet for judicial determination. . . .

. . . Nothing is clearer than that this controversy concerns matters that bring courts into immediate and active relations with party contests. From the determination of such issues this Court has traditionally held aloof. It is hostile to a democratic system to involve the judiciary in the politics of the people. And it is not less pernicious if such judicial intervention in an essentially political contest be dressed up in the abstract phrases of the law. . . .

The one stark fact that emerges from a study of the history of Congressional apportionment is its embroilment in politics, in the sense of party contests and party interests. . . .

Justice Rutledge concurred in the result, holding that the question *was* justiciable but that the bill should be dismissed because the Court could not provide a proper equitable remedy for the problem.

Justices Black, Douglas and Murphy dissented, asserting that the question was justiciable, that appellants had made out a case for their allegations of injury, and that they were entitled to equitable relief. Justice Black suggested that if the state did not properly redistrict, the courts could order elections at large for members of the House, thereby equalizing voting power within the state.

Only seven members of the Court participated in the *Colegrove* decision. On the question of the Court's power to offer assistance in such a case the vote was four-to-three in the negative. With Justice Rutledge's split vote, however, the Court was divided four-to-three in *favor* of holding that the question presented a justiciable controversy. Thus the bill was dismissed, but the case was hardly a conclusive disposition of the whole question of judicial remedies for malapportionment.

In *South* v. *Peters*, 339 U.S. 276 (1950), an injunction was sought in a federal court to restrain the enforcement of the Georgia county-unit statute. The county-unit system provided that in primary elections the candidate receiving the largest vote in a county received its entire "electoral vote," which ranged from two for the small county to six for the most populous county. The complaint charged that gross inequality of voting power resulted from the system. The Court, citing *Colegrove* v. *Green,* affirmed a dismissal of the petition, with Justices Black and Douglas dissenting.

In *Baker* v. *Carr*, 369 U.S. 186 (1962), the Court for the first time held that allegations that malapportionment of legislative seats denied equal protection presented a justiciable cause of action and one for which the federal courts could fashion appropriate equitable relief upon finding that such apportionment was a denial of equal protection under the Fourteenth Amendment. The case presented a challenge to the apportionment of seats in the Tennessee House of Representatives. It was alleged that Tennessee continued to allocate representation on the basis of a 1901 statute, and that subsequent population changes without reapportionment resulted in a denial to the plaintiffs of the equal protection of the laws by virtue of "the debasement of their votes." The trial court had dismissed the petition on grounds of nonjusticiability. By a six-to-two vote the Court reversed and remanded.

BAKER v. CARR

369 U.S. 186 (1962)

Mr. Justice Brennan delivered the opinion of the Court. . . .

. . . [Petitioners] seek a declaration that the 1901 statute is unconstitutional and an injunction restraining the appellees from acting to conduct any further elections under it. They also pray that unless and until the General Assembly enacts a valid reapportionment, the District Court should either decree a reapportionment by mathematical application of the Tennessee constitutional formulae to the most recent Federal Census figures, or direct the appellees to conduct legislative elections, primary and general, at large. . . .

I

. . . In light of the District Court's treatment of the case, we hold today only (a) that the court possessed jurisdiction of the subject matter; (b) that a justiciable cause of action is stated upon which appellants would be entitled to appropriate relief; and (c) because appellees raise the issue before this Court, that the appellants have standing to challenge the Tennessee apportionment statutes. Beyond noting that we have no cause at this stage to doubt the District Court will be able to fashion relief if violations of constitutional rights are found, it is improper now to consider what remedy would be most appropriate if appellants prevail at the trial.

II

Jurisdiction of the Subject Matter

The District Court was uncertain whether our cases withholding federal judicial relief rested upon a lack of federal jurisdiction or upon the inappropriateness of the subject matter for judicial consideration—what we have designated "nonjusticiability." The distinction between the two grounds is significant. In the instance of nonjusticiability, consideration of the cause is not wholly and immediately foreclosed; rather, the Court's inquiry necessarily proceeds to the point of deciding whether the duty asserted can be judicially identified and its breach judicially determined, and whether protection for the right asserted can be judicially molded. In the instance of lack of jurisdiction the cause either does not "arise under" the Federal Constitution, law or treaties (or fall within one of the other enumerated categories of Art. III, Section 2), or is not a "case or controversy" within the meaning of that section; or the cause is not one described by any jurisdictional statute. . . .

An unbroken line of our precedents sustains the federal courts' jurisdiction of the subject matter of federal constitutional claims of this nature. The first case involved the redistricting of States for the purpose of electing Representatives to the Federal Congress. . . . When the Minnesota Supreme Court affirmed the dismissal of a suit to enjoin the Secretary of State of Minnesota from acting under Minnesota redistricting legislation, we reviewed the constitutional merits of the legislation and reversed the State Supreme Court. *Smiley* v. *Holm,* 285 U.S. 355. . . . When a three-judge District Court . . . permanently enjoined officers of the State of Mississippi from conducting an election of Representatives under a Mississippi redistricting act, we reviewed the federal questions on the merits and reversed the District Court. *Wood* v. *Broom,* 287 U.S. 1. . . .

The appellees refer to *Colegrove* v. *Green,* 328 U.S. 549, as authority that the District Court lacked jurisdiction of the subject matter. Appellees misconceive the holding of that case. The holding was precisely contrary to their reading of it. Seven members of the Court participated in the decision. Unlike many other cases in this field which have assumed without discussion that there was jurisdiction, all three opinions filed in *Colegrove* discussed the question. Two of the opinions expressing the views of four of the Justices, a majority, flatly held that there was jurisdiction of the subject matter. . . .

Several subsequent cases similar to *Colegrove* have been decided by the Court in summary *per curiam* statements. None was dismissed for want of jurisdiction of the subject matter. . . .

. . . In *South* v. *Peters*, 339 U.S. 276, we affirmed the dismissal of an attack on the Georgia "county unit" system but founded our action on a ground that plainly would not have been reached if the lower court lacked jurisdiction of the subject matter. . . .

We hold that the District Court has jurisdiction of the subject matter of the federal constitutional claim asserted in the complaint. . . .

IV

Justiciability

. . . We understand the District Court to have read the cited cases as compelling the conclusion that since the appellants sought to have a legislative apportionment held unconstitutional, their suit presented a "political question" and was therefore nonjusticiable. We hold that this challenge to an apportionment presents no nonjusticiable "political question." The cited cases do not hold the contrary.

Of course the mere fact that the suit seeks protection of a political right does not mean it presents a political question. Such an objection "is little more than a play upon words.". . . Rather, it is argued that apportionment cases, whatever the actual wording of the complaint, can involve no federal constitutional right except one resting on the guaranty of a republican form of government, and that complaints based on that clause have been held to present political questions which are nonjusticiable.

We hold that the claim pleaded here neither rests upon nor implicates the Guaranty Clause and that its justiciability is therefore not foreclosed by our decisions of cases involving that clause. . . .

Our discussion . . . requires review of a number of political question cases, in order to expose the attributes of the doctrine. . . . That review reveals that in the Guaranty Clause cases and in the other "political question" cases, it is the relationship between the judiciary and the coordinate branches of the Federal Government, and not the federal judiciary's relationship to the States, which gives rise to the "political question.". . .

. . . The nonjusticiability of a political question is primarily a function of the separation of powers. . . .

. . . Prominent on the surface of any case held to involve a political question is found a textually demonstrable constitutional commitment of the issue to a coordinate political department; or a lack of judicially discoverable and manageable standards for resolving it; or the impossibility of deciding without an initial policy determination of a kind clearly for nonjudicial discretion; or the impossibility of a court's undertaking independent resolution without expressing lack of the respect due coordinate branches of government; or an unusual need for unquestioning adherence to a political decision already made; or the potentiality of embarrassment from multifarious pronouncements by various departments on one question. . . .

We conclude that the nonjusticiability of claims resting on the Guaranty Clause which arises from their embodiment of questions that were thought "political," can have no bearing upon the justiciability of the equal protection claim presented in this case. . . . Only last Term, in *Gomillion* v. *Lightfoot*, 364 U.S. 339 (1960), we applied the Fifteenth Amendment to strike down a redrafting of municipal boundaries which effected a discriminatory impairment of voting rights, in the face of what a majority of the Court of Appeals thought to be a sweeping commitment to state legislatures of the power to draw and redraw such boundaries. . . .

. . . We conclude that the complaint's allegations of a denial of equal protection present a justiciable constitutional cause of action upon which appellants are entitled to a trial and a decision. The right asserted is within the reach of judicial protection under the Fourteenth Amendment.

The judgment of the District Court is reversed and the cause is remanded for further proceedings consistent with this opinion.

Reversed and remanded.

Mr. Justice Whittaker did not participate in the decision of this case.

Mr. Justice Douglas, concurring. . . .

The traditional test under the Equal Protection Clause has been whether a State has made "an invidious discrimination," as it does when it selects "a particular race or nationality for oppressive treatment.". . .

I agree with my Brother Clark that if the allegations in the complaint can be sustained a case for relief is established. We are told that a single vote in Moore County, Tennessee, is worth 19 votes in Hamilton County, that one vote in Stewart or in Chester County is worth nearly eight times a single vote in Shelby or Knox County. The opportunity to prove that an "invidious discrimination" exists should therefore be given the appellants. . . .

Mr. Justice Clark, concurring. . . .

The controlling facts cannot be disputed. It appears from the record that 37 per cent of the voters of Tennessee elect 20 of the 33 Senators while 40 per cent of the voters elect 63 of the 99 members of the House. But this might not on its face be "invidious discrimination,". . . for a "statutory discrimination will not be set aside if any state of facts reasonably may be conceived to justify it." *McGowan* v. *Maryland*, 366 U.S. 420, 426 (1961).

It is true that the apportionment policy incorporated in Tennessee's Constitution, *i.e.*, state-wide numerical equality of representation with certain minor qualifications, is a rational one. . . . Try as one may, Tennessee's apportionment just cannot be made to fit the pattern cut by its Constitution. . . . We must examine what the Assembly has done. The frequency and magnitude of the inequalities in the present districting admit of no policy whatever. . . . [T]he apportionment picture in Tennessee is a topsy-turvical of gigantic proportions. This is not to say that some of the disparity cannot be explained, but when the entire Table is examined . . . it leaves but one conclusion, namely that Tennessee's apportionment is a crazy quilt without rational basis. . . .

Although I find the Tennessee apportionment statute offends the Equal Protection Clause, I would not consider intervention by this Court into so delicate a field if there were any other relief available to the people of Tennessee. But the majority of the people of Tennessee have no "practical opportunities for exerting their political weight at the polls" to correct the existing "invidious discrimination." Tennessee has no initiative and referendum. I have searched diligently for other "practical opportunities" present under the law. I find none other than through the federal courts. The majority of the voters have been caught up in a legislative strait jacket. Tennessee has an "informed, civically militant electorate" and "an aroused popular conscience," but it does not sear "the conscience of the people's representatives." This is because the legislative policy has riveted the present seats in the Assembly to their respective constituencies, and by the votes of their incumbents a reapportionment of any kind is prevented. The people have been rebuffed at the hands of the Assembly; they have tried the constitutional convention route, but since the call must originate in the Assembly it, too, has been fruitless. They have tried Tennessee courts with the same result, and Governors have fought the tide only to flounder. It is said that there is recourse in Congress and perhaps that may be, but from a practical standpoint this is without substance. To date Congress has never undertaken such a task in any State. We therefore must conclude that the people of Tennessee are stymied and without judicial intervention will be saddled with the present discrimination in the affairs of their state goverment. . . .

. . . If judicial competence were lacking to fashion an effective decree, I would dismiss this appeal. However . . . I see no such difficulty in the position of this case. One plan might be to start with the existing assembly districts, consolidate some of them, and award the seats thus released to those counties suffering the most egregious discrimination. Other possibilities are present and might be more effective. But the plan here suggested would at least release the strangle hold now on the Assembly and permit it to redistrict itself. . . .

Mr. Justice Stewart, concurring. . . .

The complaint in this case asserts that Tennessee's system of apportionment is utterly arbitrary—without any possible justification in rationality. The District Court did not reach the merits of that claim, and this Court quite properly expresses no view on the subject. Contrary to the suggestion of my Brother Harlan, the Court does not say or imply that "state legislatures must be so structured as to reflect with approximate equality the voice of every voter." . . . The Court does not say or imply that there is anything in the Federal Constitution "to prevent a State, acting not irrationally, from choosing any electoral legislative structure it thinks best suited to the interests, temper, and customs of its people." . . .

Mr. Justice Frankfurter, whom Mr. Justice Harlan joins, dissenting.

The Court today reverses a uniform course of decision established by a dozen cases, including one by which the very claim now sustained was unanimously rejected only five years ago. The impressive body of rulings thus cast aside reflected the equally uniform course of our political history regarding the relationship between population and legislative representation—a wholly different matter from denial of the franchise to individuals because of race, color, religion or sex. Such a massive repudiation of the experience of our whole past in asserting destructively novel judicial power demands a detailed analysis of the role of this Court in our constitutional scheme. Disregard of inherent limits in the effective exercise of the Court's "judicial Power" not only presages the futility of judicial intervention in the essentially political conflict of forces by which the relation between population and representation has time out of mind been and now is determined. It may well impair the Court's position as the ultimate organ of "the supreme Law of the Land" in that vast range of legal problems, often strongly entangled in popular feeling, on which this Court must pronounce. The Court's authority—possessed neither of the purse nor the sword—ultimately rests on sustained public confidence in its moral sanction. Such feeling must be nourished by the Court's complete detachment, in fact and in appearance, from political entanglements and by abstention from injecting itself into the clash of political forces in political settlements.

A hypothetical claim resting on abstract assumptions is now for the first time made the basis for affording illusory relief for a particular evil even though it foreshadows deeper and more pervasive difficulties in consequence. The claim is hypothetical and the assumptions are abstract because the Court does not vouchsafe the lower courts—state and federal—guide-lines for formulating specific, definite, wholly unprecedented remedies for the inevitable litigations that today's umbrageous disposition is bound to stimulate in connection with politically motivated reapportionments in so many States. . . . For this Court to direct the District Court to enforce a claim to which the Court has over the years consistently found itself required to deny legal enforcement and at the same time to find it necessary to withhold any guidance to the lower court how to enforce this turnabout, new legal claim, manifests an odd—indeed an esoteric—conception of judicial propriety. One of the Court's supporting opinions, as elucidated by commentary, unwittingly affords a disheartening preview of the mathematical quagmire (apart from divers judicially inappropriate and elusive determinants), into which this Court today catapults the lower courts of the country without so much as adumbrating the basis for a legal calculus as a means of extrication. Even assuming the indispensable intellectual disinterestedness on the part of judges in such matters, they do not have accepted legal standards or criteria or even reliable analogies to draw upon for making judicial judgments. To charge courts with the task of accommodating the incommensurable factors of policy that underlie these mathematical puzzles is to attribute, however flatteringly, omnicompetence to judges. The framers of the Constitution persistently rejected a proposal that embodied this assumption and Thomas Jefferson never entertained it. . . .

In sustaining appellants' claim, based on the Fourteenth Amendment, that the District Court may entertain this suit, this Court's uniform course of decision over the years is overruled or disregarded. Explicitly it begins with *Colegrove* v. *Green, supra,* decided in 1946, but its roots run deep in the Court's historic adjudicatory process. . . .

The *Colegrove* doctrine, in the form in which repeated decisions have settled it, was not an innovation. It represents long judicial thought and experience. From its earliest opinions this Court has consistently recognized a class of controversies which do not lend themselves to judicial standards and judicial remedies. . . .

[The opinion then takes up various categories of cases falling under the "political question" doctrine.]

The influence of these converging considerations—the caution not to undertake decision where standards meet for judicial judgment are lacking, the reluctance to interfere with matters of state government in the absence of an unquestionable and effectively enforceable mandate, the unwillingness to make courts arbiters of the broad issues of political organization historically committed to other institutions and for whose adjustment the judicial process is ill-adapted—has been decisive of the settled line of cases, reaching back more than a century, which holds that Art. IV,

Section 4, of the Constitution, guaranteeing to the States "a Republican Form of Government," is not enforceable through the courts. . . .

The present case involves all of the elements that have made the Guarantee Clause cases non-justiciable. It is, in effect, a Guarantee Clause claim masquerading under a different label. But it cannot make the case more fit for judicial action that appellants invoke the Fourteenth Amendment rather than Art. IV, Section 4, where, in fact, the gist of their complaint is the same. . . .

The notion that representation proportioned to the geographic spread of population is so universally accepted as a necessary element of equality between man and man that it must be taken to be the standard of a political equality preserved by the Fourteenth Amendment—that it is, in appellants' words "the basic principle of representative government"—is, to put it bluntly, not true. However desirable and however desired by some among the great political thinkers and framers of our government, it has never been generally practiced, today or in the past. . . .

Manifestly, the Equal Protection Clause supplies no clearer guide for judicial examination of apportionment methods than would the Guarantee Clause itself. Apportionment, by its character, is a subject of extraordinary complexity, involving —even after the fundamental theoretical issues concerning what is to be represented in a representative legislature have been fought out or compromised—considerations of geography, demography, electoral convenience, economic and social cohesions or divergencies among particular local groups, communications, the practical effects of political institutions like the lobby and the city machine, ancient traditions and ties of settled usage, respect for proven incumbents of long experience and senior status, mathematical mechanics, censuses compiling relevant data, and a host of others. Legislative responses throughout the country to the reapportionment demands of the 1960 Census have glaringly confirmed that these are not factors that lend themselves to evaluations of a nature that are the staple of judicial determinations or for which judges are equipped to adjudicate by legal training or experience or native wit. And this is the more so true because in every strand of this complicated, intricate web of values meet the contending forces of partisan politics. The practical significance of apportionment is that the next election results may differ because of it. Apportionment battles are overwhelmingly party or intra-party contests. It will add a virulent source of friction and tension in federal-state relations to embroil the federal judiciary in them. . . .

Dissenting opinion of Mr. Justice Harlan, whom Mr. Justice Frankfurter joins. . . .

In the last analysis, what lies at the core of this controversy is a difference of opinion as to the function of representative government. It is surely beyond argument that those who have the responsibility for devising a system of representation may permissibly consider that factors other than bare numbers should be taken into account. . . .

In short, there is nothing in the Federal Constitution to prevent a State, acting not irrationally, from choosing any electoral legislative structure it thinks best suited to the interests, temper, and customs of its people. I would have thought this proposition settled by *MacDougall* v. *Green*, . . . in which the Court observed that to "assume that political power is a function exclusively of numbers is to disregard the practicalities of government.". . .

Indeed, I would hardly think it unconstitutional if a state legislature's expressed reason for establishing or maintaining an electoral imbalance between its rural and urban population were to protect the State's agricultural interests from the sheer weight of numbers of those residing in its cities. . . .

In conclusion, it is appropriate to say that one need not agree, as a citizen, with what Tennessee has done or failed to do, in order to deprecate, as a judge, what the majority is doing today. Those observers of the Court who see it primarily as the last refuge for the correction of all inequality or injustice, no matter what its nature or source, will no doubt applaud this decision and its break with the past. Those who consider that continuing national respect for the Court's authority depends in large measure upon its wise exercise of self-restraint and discipline in constitutional adjudication, will view the decision with deep concern. . . .

[Mr. Justice Harlan attached an Appendix entitled "The Inadequacy of Arithmetical Formulas as Measures of the Rationality of Tennessee's Apportionment."]

The potential impact of *Baker* v. *Carr* on state and local government and politics was readily apparent. The decision was rendered on March 26, 1962, and a spate of articles, editorials, studies, and speeches in legislative bodies soon followed. Reaction ranged from anger or dismay at the Court's entry into the "political thicket" to warm expressions of enthusiasm for the cutting of the Gordian knot of malapportionment. Many observers, however, raised questions about the application of the *Baker* decision to such problems as the "country unit" system of Georgia, malapportionment of congressional districts, and the "little federal system" of according equal representation by counties in one house of the state legislature. Answers to these questions were not long in coming. In *Gray* v. *Sanders*, 372 U.S. 368 (1963), the Court held invalid the Georgia county unit system of weighting smaller county votes disproportionately in the Democratic primary where United States Senators and statewide officers were nominated. And while some of the opinions in *Baker* indicated that factors other than population might be relevant in setting up electoral districts, the majority in *Gray* v. *Sanders* held that the only acceptable test in statewide elections was equality of population. Justice Douglas, speaking for eight members of the Court, stated:

. . . If a State in a statewide election weighted the male vote more heavily than the female vote or the white vote more heavily than the Negro vote, none could successfully contend that that discrimination was allowable. . . . How then can one person be given twice or 10 times the voting power of another person in a statewide election merely because he lives in a rural area or because he lives in the smallest rural county? Once the geographical unit for which a representative is to be chosen is designated, all who participate in the election are to have an equal vote—whatever their race, whatever their sex, whatever their occupation, whatever their income, and wherever their home may be in that geographical unit. This is required by the Equal Protection Clause of the Fourteenth Amendment. The concept of "we the people" under the Constitution visualizes no preferred class of voters but equality among those who meet the basic qualifications. The idea that every voter is equal to every other voter in his State, when he casts his ballot in favor of one of several competing candidates, underlies many of our decisions. . . .

The conception of political equality from the Declaration of Independence, to Lincoln's Gettysburg Address, to the Fifteenth, Seventeenth, and Nineteenth Amendments can mean only one thing—one person, one vote. . . .

[Justice Harlan was the only dissenter in the case. In an "I-told-you-so" opinion he pointed to the rash of litigation spawned by the *Baker* decision:]

When *Baker* v. *Carr* . . . was argued at the last Term we were assured that if this Court would only remove the roadblocks of *Colegrove* v. *Green* . . . and its predecessors to judicial review in "electoral" cases, this Court in all likelihood would never have to get deeper into such matters. State legislatures, it was predicted, would be prodded into taking satisfactory action by the mere prospect of legal proceedings.

These predictions have not proved true. As of November 1, 1962, [only eight months after *Baker*] the apportionment of seats in at least 30 state legislatures had been challenged in state and federal courts, and, besides this one, 10 electoral cases of one kind or another are already on this Court's docket. The present case is the first of these to reach plenary consideration. . . .

In the following year, in another Georgia case, *Wesberry* v. *Sanders*, 376 U.S. 1 (1964), the Court applied the "one man, one vote" rule to the matter of equalizing of population among congressional districts within a state. Petitioners lived in Georgia's Fifth Congressional District, in which Atlanta is located, which had a population of 823,680 as contrasted with a population of 394,312 for the average Georgia congressional district. They brought suit in a federal district court to enjoin defendants from conducting an election under the existing congressional districting statute on the ground that it was violative of the Constitution. The district court dismissed for nonjusticiability and want of equity, and on appeal the Supreme Court reversed. In an opinion by Justice Black, for six members of the Court, it was held that the statute was invalid as abridging the requirement of Article I, Section 2, that congressmen be chosen "by the People of the several States." In construing this section, Justice Black stated:

We hold that, construed in its historical context, the command of Art. I, Section 2, that Representatives be chosen "by the People of the several States" means that as nearly as is practicable one man's vote in a congressional election is to be worth as much as another's. This rule is followed automatically, of course, when Representatives are chosen as a group on a statewide basis, as was a widespread practice in the first 50 years of our Nation's history. . . . We do not believe that the Framers of the Constitution intended to permit . . . vote-diluting discrimination to be accomplished through the device of districts containing widely varied numbers of inhabitants. To say that a vote is worth more in one district than in another would not only run counter to our fundamental ideas of democratic government, it would cast aside the principle of a House of Representatives elected "by the People," a principle tenaciously fought for and established at the Constitutional Convention. The history of the Constitution, particularly that part of it relating to the adoption of Art. I, Section 2, reveals that those who framed the Constitution meant that, no matter what the mechanics of an election, whether statewide or by districts, it was population which was to be the basis of the House of Representatives.

[The opinion then treats the debates in the Philadelphia Convention on the structure of the Congress and gives some contemporaneous constructions of the sections dealing with the House of Representatives indicating that equality of voting power was intended.]

While it may not be possible to draw congressional districts with mathematical precision, that is no excuse for ignoring our Constitution's plain objective of making equal representation for equal numbers of people the fundamental goal for the House of Representatives. That is the high standard of justice and common sense which the Founders set for us.

Apparently there was fairly general acceptance of the idea that fairness demanded that one house of the legislature and congressional districts be apportioned on the "one man, one vote" formula. But criticism erupted when in June 1964, in a group of Alabama cases cited as *Reynolds* v. *Sims*, 377 U.S. 533 (1964), the Court held that both houses of a bicameral state legislature were required by the "equal protection" clause to be apportioned strictly on the basis of population. Chief Justice Warren, for a majority of six members of the Court, stated that *Gray* and *Wesberry* were, of course, "not dispositive of or directly controlling on our decision in these cases involving state legislative apportionment controversies." Nevertheless, "*Wesberry* clearly established that the fundamental principle of representative government in this country is one of equal representation for equal numbers of people, without regard to race, sex, economic status, or place of residence within a State." The Chief Justice stated further:

Legislators represent people, not trees or acres. Legislators are elected by voters, not farms or cities or economic interests. As long as ours is a representative form of government, and our legislatures are those instruments of government elected directly by and directly representative of the people, the right to elect legislators in a free and unimpaired fashion is a bedrock of our political system. . . . [I]f a State should provide that the votes of citizens in one part of the State should be given two times, or five times, or 10 times the weight of votes of citizens in another part of the State, it could hardly be contended that the right to vote of those residing in the disfavored areas had not been effectively diluted.

[In response to the claim that a state senate based on one member per county was reasonable because analogous to the Federal Senate, Chief Justice Warren stated:]

Much has been written since our decision in *Baker* v. *Carr* about the applicability of the so-called federal analogy to state legislative apportionment arrangements.* After considering the matter, the court below concluded that no conceivable analogy could be drawn between the federal scheme and the apportionment of seats in the Alabama Legislature under the proposed constitutional amendment. We agree with the District Court, and find the federal analogy inapposite and irrelevant to state

* For a thorough statement of the arguments against holding the so-called federal analogy applicable to state legislative apportionment matters, see, e.g., McKay, Reapportionment and the Federal Analogy (National Municipal League pamphlet 1962); McKay, The Federal Analogy and State Apportionment standards, 38 Notre Dame Law. 487 (1963). See also Merrill, Blazes for a Trail through the Thicket of Reapportionment, 16 Okla. L. Rev. 59, 67-70 (1963).

legislative districting schemes. Attempted reliance on the federal analogy appears often to be little more than an after-the-fact rationalization offered in defense of maladjusted state apportionment arrangements. The original constitutions of 36 of our States provided that representation in both houses of the state legislatures would be based completely, or predominantly, on population. And the Founding Fathers clearly had no intention of establishing a pattern or model for the apportionment of seats in state legislatures when the system of representation in the Federal Congress was adopted. Demonstrative of this is the fact that the Northwest Ordinance, adopted in the same year, 1787, as the Federal Constitution, provided for the apportionment of seats in territorial legislatures solely on the basis of population.

The system of representation in the two Houses of the Federal Congress is one ingrained in our Constitution, as part of the law of the land. It is one conceived out of compromise and concession indispensable to the establishment of our federal republic. Arising from unique historical circumstances, it is based on the consideration that in establishing our type of federalism a group of formerly independent States bound themselves together under one national government. . . .

Political subdivisions of States—counties, cities, or whatever—never were and never have been considered as sovereign entities. Rather, they have been traditionally regarded as subordinate governmental instrumentalities created by the State to assist in the carrying out of state governmental functions. . . . The relationship of the States to the Federal Government could hardly be less analogous. . . .

Since we find the so-called federal analogy inapposite to a consideration of the constitutional validity of state legislative apportionment schemes, we necessarily hold that the Equal Protection Clause requires both houses of a state legislature to be apportioned on a population basis. The right of a citizen to equal representation and to have his vote weighted equally with those of all other citizens in the election of members of one house of a bicameral state legislature would amount to little if States could effectively submerge the equal-population principle in the apportionment of seats in the other house. If such a scheme were permissible, an individual citizen's ability to exercise an effective voice in the only instrument of state government directly representative of the people might be almost as effectively thwarted as if neither house were apportioned on a population basis. Deadlock between the two bodies might result in compromise and concession on some issues. But in all too many cases the more probable result would be frustration of the majority will through minority veto in the house not apportioned on a population basis, . . .

We do not believe that the concept of bicameralism is rendered anachronistic and meaningless when the predominant basis of representation in the two state legislative bodies is required to be the same—population. A prime reason for bicameralism, modernly considered, is to insure mature and deliberate consideration of, and to prevent precipitate action on, proposed legislative measures. Simply because the controlling criterion for apportioning representation is required to be the same in both houses does not mean that there will be no differences in the composition and complexion of the two bodies. Different constituencies can be represented in the two houses. One body could be composed of single-member districts while the other could have at least some multimember districts. The length of terms of the legislators in the separate bodies could differ. The numerical size of the two bodies could be made to differ, even significantly, and the geographical size of districts from which legislators are elected could also be made to differ. And apportionment in one house could be arranged so as to balance off minor inequities in the representation of certain areas in the other house. In summary, these and other factors could be, and are presently in many States, utilized to engender differing complexions and collective attitudes in the two bodies of a state legislature, although both are apportioned substantially on a population basis.

By holding that as a federal constitutional requisite both houses of a state legislature must be apportioned on a population basis, we mean that the Equal Protection Clause requires that a State make an honest and good faith effort to construct districts, in both houses of its legislature, as nearly of equal population as is practicable. We realize that it is a practical impossibility to arrange legislative districts so that each one has an identical number of residents, or citizens, or voters. Mathematical exactness or precision is hardly a workable constitutional requirement. . . .

[Justices Clark and Stewart concurred in the result, but on the ground that the Alabama legislature as constituted and the proposals for reapportionment offered by the state were not rationally based. Justice Clark stated, in part:]

It seems to me that all that the Court need say in this case is that each plan considered by the trial court is "a crazy quilt," clearly revealing invidious discrimination in each house of the Legislature and therefore violative of the Equal Protection Clause. . . .

I, therefore, do not reach the question of the so-called "federal analogy." But in my view, if one house of the State Legislature meets the population standard, representation in the other house might include some departure from it so as to take into account, on a rational basis, other factors in order to afford some representation to the various elements of the State. . . .

Justice Harlan delivered a vigorous dissent in which he examined the history of the Fourteenth Amendment and concluded that "the Equal Protection Clause was never intended to inhibit the States in choosing any democratic method they pleased for the apportionment of their legislatures."

On the same day the Court decided with full opinions five other reapportionment cases in the same vein: *WMCA, Inc.* v. *Lomenzo,* 377 U.S. 633 (New York); *Maryland Committee for Fair Representation* v. *Tawes,* 377 U.S. 656 (Maryland); *Davis* v. *Mann,* 377 U.S. 678 (Virginia); *Roman* v. *Sincock,* 377 U.S. 695 (Delaware); and *Lucas* v. *Forty-Fourth General Assembly of Colorado,* 377 U.S. 713 (Colorado). The following week the Court disposed of cases from nine additional states by memorandum decision. (For a collection of the federal cases on apportionment through June 1964, see the annotation in 12 L. ed. 2d 1282.)

The Colorado case presented a unique facet and deserves separate treatment. In a 1962 election the voters of Colorado adopted a constitutional amendment providing for the apportionment of the House of Representatives on the basis of population, but essentially maintaining the existing apportionment in the Senate, which was based on a combination of population and various other factors. The amendment was adopted by initiative and referendum, by a vote of 305,700 to 172,725. At the same election another apportionment proposal, basing apportionment on population in both houses, was defeated by a vote of 311,749 to 149,822.

The plan adopted, Amendment No. 7, provided for thirty-nine state senators elected from thirty-nine districts varying in population from 19,-983 to 71,871, with a possible 33.2 percent of the state's total population electing a majority of the senate. The maximum population-variance ratio in districts of the state house of representatives was 1.7:1, with a possible 45.1 percent of the state's total population electing a majority of that house.

Suits were brought in a federal district court by taxpayers and voters in the Denver metropolitan area challenging the validity of the apportionment under Amendment No. 7. The three-judge court dismissed the actions on the ground that the apportionment was constitutional. On direct appeal, the Supreme Court reversed by a six-to-three vote.

LUCAS v. COLORADO GENERAL ASSEMBLY
377 U.S. 713 (1964)

Mr. Chief Justice Warren delivered the opinion of the Court....

Several aspects of this case serve to distinguish it from the other cases involving state legislative apportionment also decided this date. Initially, one house of the Colorado Legislature is at least arguably apportioned substantially on a population basis under Amendment No. 7 and the implementing statutory provisions.... Additionally, the Colorado scheme of legislative apportionment here attacked is one adopted by a majority vote of the Colorado electorate almost contemporaneously with the District Court's decision on the merits in this litigation. Thus, the plan at issue did not result from prolonged legislative inaction....

As appellees have correctly pointed out, a majority of the voters in every county of the State voted in favor of the apportionment scheme embodied in Amendment No. 7's provisions, in preference to that contained in proposed Amendment No. 8, which, subject to minor deviations, would have based the apportionment of seats in both houses on a population basis. However, the choice presented to the Colorado electorate, in voting on these two proposed constitutional amendments, was hardly as clear-cut as the court below regarded it. One of the most undesirable features of the existing apportionment scheme was the requirement that, in counties given more than one seat in either or both of the houses of the General Assembly, all legislators must be elected at large from the county as a whole. Thus, under the existing plan, each Denver voter was required to vote for eight senators and 17 representatives. Ballots were long and cumbersome, and an intelligent choice among candidates for seats in the legislature was made quite difficult. No identifiable constituencies *within* the populous counties resulted, and the residents of those areas had no single member of the Senate or House elected specifically to represent them. Rather, each legislator elected from a multi-member county represented the county as a whole. Amendment No. 8, as distinguished from Amendment No. 7, while purportedly basing the apportionment of seats in both houses on a population basis, would have perpetuated, for all practical purposes, this debatable feature of the existing scheme.... Thus, neither of the proposed plans was, in all probability, wholly acceptable to the voters in the populous counties, and the assumption of the court below that the Colorado voters made a definitive choice between two contrasting alternatives and indicated that "minority process in the Senate is what they want" does not appear to be factually justifiable.

Finally, this case differs from the others decided this date in that the initiative

device provides a practicable political remedy to obtain relief against alleged legislative malapportionment in Colorado. . . . Additionally, Colorado courts have traditionally not been hesitant about adjudicating controversies relating to legislative
apportionment. . . .

In *Reynolds* v. *Sims* . . . we held that the Equal Protection Clause requires that
both houses of a bicameral state legislature must be apportioned substantially on a
population basis. Of course, the court below assumed, and the parties apparently
conceded, that the Colorado House of Representatives, . . . pursuant to Amendment
No. 7's dictate . . . , is now apportioned sufficiently on a population basis to comport with federal constitutional requisites. We need not pass on this question, since
the apportionment of Senate seats, under Amendment No. 7, clearly involves departures from population-based representation too extreme to be constitutionally
permissible, and there is no indication that the apportionment of the two houses
of the Colorado General Assembly, pursuant to the 1962 constitutional amendment,
is severable. . . .

. . . Manifestly, the fact that an apportionment plan is adopted in a popular
referendum is insufficient to sustain its constitutionality or to induce a court of
equity to refuse to act. As stated by this Court in *West Virginia State Board of
Education* v. *Barnette,* . . . "One's right to life, liberty, and property . . . and other
fundamental rights may not be submitted to vote; they depend on the outcome
of no elections." A citizen's constitutional rights can hardly be infringed simply
because a majority of the people choose that it be. We hold that the fact that a
challenged legislative apportionment plan was approved by the electorate is without federal constitutional significance, if the scheme adopted fails to satisfy the
basic requirements of the Equal Protection Clause, as delineated in our opinion in
Reynolds v. *Sims.* . . .

. . . [A]ppellees' argument, accepted by the court below, that the apportionment
of the Colorado Senate, under Amendment No. 7, is rational because it takes into
account a variety of geographical, historical, topographic and economic considerations fails to provide an adequate justification for the substantial disparities from
population-based representation in the allocation of Senate seats to the disfavored
populous areas. . . .

[The decision below was reversed and the case remanded to the District Court
for a determination of whether appropriate remedies could be fashioned prior to
the 1964 primaries in Colorado or the Amendment No. 7 provisions should be
temporarily utilized for purposes of those elections.]

[Mr. Justice Harlan's dissent in *Reynolds* v. *Sims* also applied to the decision
in *Lucas.*]

Mr. Justice Stewart, whom Mr. Justice Clark joins, dissenting. [A dissenting
opinion in *WMCA, Inc.* v. *Lomenzo,* 377 U.S. 633, at 744, also applicable to *Lucas.*]

It is important to make clear at the outset what these cases are not about. They
have nothing to do with the denial or impairment of any person's right to vote.
Nobody's right to vote has been denied. Nobody's right to vote has been restricted.
Nobody has been deprived of the right to have his vote counted. The voting right
cases which the Court cites are, therefore, completely wide of the mark. Secondly,
these cases have nothing to do with "weighting" or "diluting" of votes cast within
any electoral unit. The rule of *Gray* v. *Sanders* . . . is, therefore, completely without relevance here. Thirdly, these cases are not concerned with the election of
members of the Congress of the United States, governed by Article I of the Con-

stitution. Consequently, the Court's decision in *Wesberry* v. *Sanders* . . . throws no light at all on the basic issue now before us.

The question involved in these cases is quite a different one. Simply stated, the question is to what degree, if at all, the Equal Protection Clause of the Fourteenth Amendment limits each sovereign State's freedom to establish appropriate electoral constituencies from which representatives to the State's bicameral legislative assembly are to be chosen. The Court's answer is a blunt one, and, I think, woefully wrong. The Equal Protection Clause, says the Court, "requires that the seats in both houses of a bicameral state legislature must be apportioned on a population basis.". . .

What the Court has done is to convert a particular political philosophy into a constitutional rule, binding upon each of the 50 states, from Maine to Hawaii, from Alaska to Texas, without regard and without respect for the many individualized and differentiated characteristics of each State, characteristics stemming from each State's distinct history, distinct geography, distinct distribution of population, and distinct political heritage. My own understanding of the various theories of representative government is that no one theory has ever commanded unanimous assent among political scientists, historians, or others who have considered the problem. But even if it were thought that the rule announced today by the Court is, as a matter of political theory, the most desirable general rule which can be devised as a basis for the make-up of the representative assembly of a typical State, I could not join in the fabrication of a constitutional mandate which imports and forever freezes one theory of political thought into our Constitution, and forever denies to every State any opportunity for enlightened and progressive innovation in the design of its democratic institutions, so as to accommodate within a system of representative government the interests and aspirations of diverse groups of people, without subjecting any group or class to absolute domination by a geographically concentrated or highly organized majority.

Representative government is a process of accommodating group interests through democratic institutional arrangements. Its function is to channel the numerous opinions, interests, and abilities of the people of a State into the making of the State's public policy. Appropriate legislative apportionment, therefore, should ideally be designed to insure effective representation in the State's legislature, in cooperation with other organs of political power, of the various groups and interests making up the electorate. In practice, of course, this ideal is approximated in the particular apportionment system of any State by a realistic accommodation of the diverse and often conflicting political forces operating within the State.

. . . The Court today declines to give any recognition to these considerations and countless others, tangible and intangible, in holding unconstitutional the particular systems of legislative apportionment which these States have chosen. Instead, the Court says that the requirements of the Equal Protection Clause can be met in any State only by the uncritical, simplistic, and heavy-handed application of sixth-grade arithmetic. . . .

The fact is, of course, that population factors must often to some degree be subordinated in devising a legislative apportionment plan which is to achieve the important goal of ensuring a fair, effective, and balanced representation of the regional, social, and economic interests within a State. And the further fact is that throughout our history the apportionments of State Legislatures have reflected the strongly felt American tradition that the public interest is composed of many diverse interests, and that in the long run it can better be expressed by a medley of component voices than by the majority's monolithic command. What constitutes a rational plan reasonably designed to achieve this objective will vary from State to State, since each State is unique, in terms of topography, geography, demography, history, heterogeneity and concentration of population, variety of social and economic interests, and in the operation and interrelation of its political institutions. But so long as a State's apportionment plan reasonably achieves, in the light of the State's own characteristics, effective and balanced representation of all substantial interests, without sacrificing the principle of effective majority rule, that plan cannot be considered irrational. . . .

. . . I think that the Equal Protection Clause demands but two basic attributes of any plan of state legislative apportionment. First, it demands that, in the light of the State's own characteristics and needs, the plan must be a rational one. Secondly, it demands that the plan must be such as not to permit the systematic frustration of the will of a majority of the electorate of the State. . . .

Mr. Justice Clark, dissenting. . . .

. . . I cannot agree to the arbitrary application of the "one man, one vote" principle for both houses of a State Legislature. In my view, if one house is fairly apportioned by population (as is admitted here) then the people should have some latitude in providing, on a rational basis, for representation in the other house. The Court seems to approve the federal arrangement of two Senators from each State on the ground that it was a compromise reached by the framers of our Constitution and is a part of the fabric of our national charter. But what the Court overlooks is that Colorado, by an overwhelming vote, has likewise written the organization of its legislative body into its Constitution, and our dual federalism requires that we give it recognition. After all, the Equal Protection Clause is not an algebraic formula. Equal protection does not rest on whether the practice assailed "results in some inequality" but rather on whether "any state of facts reasonably can be conceived that would sustain it"; and one who attacks it must show "that it does not rest upon any reasonable basis, but is essentially arbitrary.". . . Certainly Colorado's arrangement is not arbitrary. On the contrary, it rests on reasonable grounds which, as I have pointed out, are peculiar to that State. . . .

[For an exceptionally careful and thorough analysis of the cases and the views of the critics, see Carl Auerbach, "The Reapportionment Cases: One Person, One Vote—One Vote, One Value," 1964 *Supreme Court Review* 1 (Chicago: Univ. of Chicago Press, 1964).]

A different aspect of the multi-faceted problems of apportionment was taken up by the Court in a case in 1965 involving Georgia's senatorial districts. The legislature had established fifty-four single-member senatorial districts with substantial population equality. In several multidistrict counties, however, the voters elected all the county's senators by a county-wide vote rather than separately, by district-wide votes. Appellees sought a decree that the requirement of county-wide voting in the seven multidistrict counties violated the "equal protection" clause, since their own choice of a senator might be nullified by what voters in other districts of the county desired, while in all single-district counties the voters selected their own senator. In *Fortson* v. *Dorsey*, 379 U.S. 433 (1965), the Court upheld the apportionment scheme, indicating that absent any contention that there was not substantial equality of population among the districts, or evidence to support the assertion that the scheme was intended to minimize or cancel out the voting strength of racial or political elements of the voting population, the statute was constitutional.

In *Sailors* v. *Board of Supervisors*, 387 U.S. 105 (1967), the Court "reserved the question" whether the apportionment of municipal or county legislative agencies was governed by *Reynolds* v. *Sims*. But on the same day a decision was rendered on the validity of a combination at-large and district system of choosing municipal councilmen for the City of Virginia Beach, Virginia.

DUSCH *v.* DAVIS
387 U.S. 112 (1967)

Mr. Justice Douglas delivered the opinion of the Court.

In 1963 the City of Virginia Beach, Virginia, consolidated with adjoining Princess Anne County, which was both rural and urban; and a borough form of government was adopted. There are seven boroughs, one corresponding to the boundaries of the former city and six corresponding to the boundaries of the six magisterial districts. . . . [Three of the boroughs are urban, three rural, and one is primarily tourist. The two smallest boroughs have populations of 733 and 2,504, and the two largest have 23,731 and 29,048.]

Electors of five boroughs . . . instituted this suit against local and state officials claiming that the consolidation plan in its distribution of voting rights violated the principle of *Reynolds* v. *Sims*. . . .

. . . Under the amended charter, the council is composed of 11 members. Four members are elected at large without regard to residence. Seven are elected by the voters of the entire city, one being required to reside in each of the seven boroughs. . . .

In *Sailors* v. *Board of Supervisors, ante,* . . . we reserved the question whether the apportionment of municipal or county legislative agencies is governed by *Reynolds* v. *Sims*. But though we assume *arguendo* that it is, we reverse the Court of Appeals. It felt that *Reynolds* v. *Sims* required "that each legislator, State or Municipal, represent a reasonably like number in population.". . .

The Seven-Four Plan makes no distinction on the basis of race, creed, or economic status or location. Each of the 11 councilmen is elected by a vote of all the electors in the city. The fact that each of the seven councilmen must be a resident of the borough from which he is elected, is not fatal. In upholding a residence requirement for the election of state senators from a multi-district county we said in *Fortson* v. *Dorsey*, 379 U.S. 433, 438:

"It is not accurate to treat a senator from a multi-district county as the representative of only that district within the county wherein he resides. The statute uses districts in multi-district counties merely as the basis of residence for candidates, not for voting or representation. Each district's senator must be a resident of that district, but since his tenure depends upon the county-wide electorate he must be vigilant to serve the interests of all the people in the county, and not merely those of people in his home district; thus, in fact he is the county's and not merely the district's senator."

By analogy the present consolidation plan uses boroughs in the city "merely as the basis of residence for candidates, not for voting or representation." He is nonetheless the city's, not the borough's councilman. In *Fortson* there was substantial equality of population in the senatorial districts, while here the population of the boroughs varies widely. If a borough's resident on the council represented in fact only the borough, residence being only a front, different conclusions might follow. But on the assumption that *Reynolds* v. *Sims* controls, the constitutional test under the Equal Protection Clause is whether there is an "invidious" discrimination....

The Seven-Four Plan seems to reflect a detente between urban and rural communities that may be important in resolving the complex problems of the modern megapolis in relation to the city, the suburbia, and the rural countryside. Finding no invidious discrimination we conclude that the judgment of the Court of Appeals must be and is

Reversed.

Mr. Justice Harlan and Mr. Justice Stewart concur in the result.

The apportionment decisions are, by any test, landmark cases in the history of the Court's work. And they will inevitably have enormous impact on the organization, structure, and operation of state and local government in the United States. The Court has been both praised for its statesmanlike courage and condemned for its heavy-handed entry into matters deemed within the sole prerogative of the States. Illustrative of the former, in a recent book on apportionment, Dean Robert B. McKay states in his summary: "It has been the theme of this volume that the *Reapportionment Cases* have opened the way for revitalization of representative democracy in the United States at the national, state, and even local levels." [*Reapportionment: The Law and Politics of Equal Representation* (New York: Twentieth Century Fund, 1965), pp. 269–270. The book has an excellent bibliography and a valuable appendix summarizing the apportionment history of each of the states.]

Other writers, while accepting the general line of apportionment decisions, have been concerned about some of the unresolved issues and have expressed doubt that the Court has given adequate thought to some of the ramifications of its statements. The following article discusses a few of these questions.

REAPPORTIONMENT PERSPECTIVES: WHAT IS FAIR REPRESENTATION? [1]
By Robert G. Dixon, Jr.

The continuing flow of legislative reapportionment decisions has been hailed as a shimmering symbol of equality and democratic virtue in the election process. The decisions also have been damned as an unconscionable assertion of judicial overlordship over the basic politics of the Nation. Neither of these common reactions contributes to a reasoned dialog on principles of fair representation—a dialog sorely needed if our constitutional crisis in reapportionment is not to degenerate

---

[1] 51 A.B.A.J. 319 (1965). Reprinted by permission of the *American Bar Association Journal* and the author.

into a perpetual numbers game. That there is an intelligible middle position is the theme of this essay.

A declaration of faith is in order at the outset—and it is sincerely intended even though such declarations are the traditional starting point for many an apostate. The Tennessee legislative reapportionment case in 1962, *Baker* v. *Carr,* 369 U.S. 186, was correctly decided, although for the wrong reasons. By 1962 much legislative reapportionment was long overdue in many States and at least some reapportionment was needed in all States. The reapportionment decisions of June 15, 1964, were correctly decided as a natural extension of the meaning implicit in *Baker* v. *Carr,* with the exception of the Colorado case, *Lucas* v. *Forty-fourth General Assembly,* but again for the wrong reasons.

The Nature of the Representation Problem

This odd combination of generally acceptable Supreme Court decisions and unacceptable rationale stems from a basic mistake in the way the conceded mal-apportionment problem has been approached. The mistake, caused in part by the ineptness of defendants' counsel and in part by the narrow approach of plaintiffs' counsel, including the Solicitor General, lies in mischaracterizing the issue in Baker and in placing Baker and the succeeding cases on too narrow a ground. The missing word, the missing basic concept in all of this reapportionment litigation, is representation.

These are not right-to-vote cases, even though voting is involved. They are representation cases, i.e., they are cases concerning the most interesting, the most complex, the most baffling aspect of any democratic political system: namely, the ascertainment of public feeling on innumerable public policy issues through the medium of periodic, partisan selection of district delegates to a multimembered representative assembly.

The guarantee of "republican form of government" clause of the Federal Constitution is responsive to the difficult issue of indirect democracy and fair representation with which the Western World has been grappling ever since it abandoned the direct, or referendum, democracy of the ancient Greeks. The due process clause would also be responsive to the complexity of the representation issue, because of its focus on overall fairness and reasonableness. Either would be an adequate safeguard for preservation of what Justice Stewart referred to in his Maryland opinion as "ultimate effective majority rule." Either would be responsive also to the issue of adequate representation of minority interests and to the correlative issue of gerrymandering to maximize the voting strength of one group of partisans.

But in Baker the Court chose neither the guaranty clause nor the due process clause as its suit of armor for entry into the political thicket. It donned instead the equal protection clause.

The equal protection clause is not responsive to large questions concerning the structure of government—which is what reapportionment involves, ultimately— or concerning the fairness with which variegated popular feeling and shifting popular groupings on various issues are expressed through a district system. Within any district the winner-take-all rule necessarily prevails. The majority, no matter how narrow, gets 100 percent representation for the term of office being filled; the minority, no matter how large, gets zero representation.

Even the Supreme Court's selection of the equal protection clause as the instrument for political revolution in apportionment and districting practices would not have been so unsettling to the cause of political realism if the Court had taken the same flexible approach to equal protection when applied to reapportionment as it has taken when applying this clause to almost all issues other than racial equality. Examples include the State tax cases, the State regulatory power cases and the Sunday closing case. . . . In these cases equal protection emerges as an empirical rule of reasonableness, a rule of fairness in the methods used to achieve a legitimate end. . . .

Reapportionment Decisions—One Man, One Vote

The logic of the reapportionment decisions of June, 1964, is simple and straight-forward. The Court, pursuing its long and in the main quite proper romance with egalitarianism and trapped in its own semantics, defined all of the difficult problems out of existence. In regard to reapportionment, as in regard to race, equal protection is to be a constitutional absolute, in this instance virtually a mathematical absolute. The Court focused on two things, and two things only: one was bare population, with all political allegiances and group interests eliminated; the other was the individual voter, viewed only as a faceless census statistic, and the voter's supposed right to an abstract mathematically equal vote.

In short, the Court does not view these cases as representation cases, or as representative democracy cases at all. It views them as being simply one more round of civil rights cases—but its supposed "civil right of voters" is really only a "civil right of census statistics." This approach explains two other important elements in the Court's reasoning.

First, with the constitutional spotlight focused solely on the abstract "voter" rather than on the group dynamics of American politics, there is no basis for treating his interest in one house of the legislature differently from his interest in the other house. Thus bicameralism, despite the Court's protestations about the possibility of varying the length of terms and sizes of districts in the two houses, becomes a political vermiform appendix rather than an instrument for tempering major-itarianism with requirements of broad consensus. . . .

The second element of the Court's reasoning which flows from its simplistic approach is the irrelevance of the results of statewide popular referendums, even though these are concededly mass exercises in "one man, one vote," like early Grecian direct democracy. On this basis the Colorado voter-approved reapportionment was nullified by the Supreme Court. The Court asked only the question: Can a popular majority override a constitutional civil right? Phrased thus, the answer obviously is "No." But the answer would not have been so easy had the Court asked the more appropriate question, in terms of representative democracy: Is it constitu-tionally unfair for a State with one large metropolitan center, in which 8 percent of the voters can initiate further change, to place one-third of its lawmaking process on some basis other than straight population? [The author considers the Governor and each house of the legislature as exerting one-third of the lawmaking power.]

Remaining "One-man, One-vote" Issues

In effecting much-needed change, *Baker* v. *Carr* also should have been the begin-ning of a fresh analysis of the theoretical and practical problems in effecting fair representation through a district system and of such related issues as the following: Bicameralism; single-member districts as opposed to multimember districts and the special inequities associated with each; the validity of such devices to hear from the minority as cumulative voting, limited voting, and proportional representation; the role of the Governor as legislative leader; and the institutional, geographic, and population bases of political parties. . . .

To date the Court has chosen to avoid the broader representative Government issues to which a concern for political realism and political philosophy would lead it. However, some stubborn issues remain unresolved even under the supposedly objective, clear, equal-population standard for districts.

1. Single member versus multimember districts

One example of a problem of fairness not responsive to a simple census-tract-equality approach is the question of single-member districts as opposed to multi-member districts. Chief Justice Warren in his reapportionment opinions [*Reynolds* v. *Sims,* 377 U.S. 533, at 579] intimated that the States had discretion in this regard, but he was not ruling on representational fairness. The question is still open, so far as the Supreme Court is concerned, whether there may be a constitutional right, in some situations at least, to have a county or city subdistricted, rather than to have its slate of 2, 10, or 20 State legislators elected at large in the county or city.

A Federal district court in Pennsylvania in *Drew* v. *Scranton* [229 F. Supp. 310 (M.D. Pa., 1964), vacated and remanded, 379 U.S. 40 (1964)], found there was such a constitutional right, in order to heighten the prospect of some representation for minorities, and thereafter the Pennsylvania Supreme Court seemed to agree that there was at least a constitutional preference for single-member districts. There may be further litigation if the legislature persists in using some multimember districts. The U.S. Supreme Court ducked the matter by vacating the Federal district court judgment in November, 1964, after the State supreme court had become active.

But the Court did hear oral argument in a Georgia subdistricting case, *Fortson* v. *Dorsey* [379 U.S. 433 (1965)]. A Federal district court had held unconstitutional a multimember district system in Atlanta (Fulton County) in which the seven-man delegation to the State senate was elected at large in the county on a winner-take-all basis, even though each legislator technically was assigned to a subdistrict in the county. Under this system a subdistrict might be represented by a man the subdistrict voters had repudiated, if he was popular in the county as a whole. More important, the county-at-large system of election might make it more difficult for Republican or Negro minorities, although substantial, to elect legislators in proportion to their strength on a regular basis.

The Supreme Court reversed the district court in *Fortson* v. *Dorsey* for lack of proof of inequity. But in a provocative dictum it seemed to move away from its previous, narrow mathematical approach and to suggest a new constitutional right of racial and political party equity in apportionment and districting arrangements. Justice Brennan, speaking for the Court said: ". . . It might well be that, designedly or otherwise a multimember constituency apportionment scheme, under the circumstances of a particular case, would operate to minimize or cancel out the voting strength of racial or political elements of the voting population. When this is demonstrated it will be time enough to consider whether the system still passes constitutional muster."

Regardless of how the constitutional issue is decided, strong arguments on policy grounds can be made in favor of single-member districts or of keeping multimember districts small and infrequent. Subdistricting requires more effort, but is a small price to pay for achieving better representation. Subdistricting (1) keeps the representative closer to the people; (2) heightens the prospect for some representation of divergent viewpoints and minority views; and (3) strengthens the two-party system by avoiding the winner-take-all result of multimember district election.

2. Weighted votes and fractional votes

Another range of additional issues on the frontier of equal protection concerns the constitutionality of weighted vote or fractional vote plans. The New Jersey Supreme Court in December, 1964, voided that State's attempt to use a weighted vote plan for the State senate under which each senator was to receive a vote proportional to the population of his county, starting with a unit of one in the least populous county. [Unreported decision. See New York *Times*, December 16, 1964, p. 1. column 2.] Under this plan the senator from populous Essex County was entitled to 19.1 votes. The New Jersey court did not reach the constitutional issue, but held that a change of this sort required a constitutional amendment and could not be effected merely by changing the rules of the senate.

If and when the constitutional question is reached, weighted voting may be nullified for several reasons. One of the most important reasons would be the consideration that one man casting 19 votes is not as effective in terms of representation as 19 separate voices (or lobbyists). Another would be that 19 men separately elected would provide more opportunity for expression of divergent views. It is noteworthy that both of these arguments involve going beyond the simple mathematical tenor of the Supreme Court's one-man, one-vote decisions. They involve putting reapportionment in the context of the actual complexities of representation —and the difficulties in determining what is fair and effective representation.

Fractional voting is on a firmer ground, both functionally and constitutionally. If applied to one house, as attempted in New York, it would give each small county a live voice in one house at least, even though his vote is only a fraction. The slight exaggeration of rural influence which may flow from ballooning a fractional vote into a whole lobbyist and from giving the small county legislator a whole vote in committee (where it would be almost impossible to operate on a fractional basis) may be viewed as *de minimis*. The counterargument is that a fractional-vote man who was a committee chairman obviously would not be *"de minimis."* Fractional voting is really a misnomer. The essence of the idea is minority representation through spokesmen, not through exaggerated votes.

3. Gerrymandering

Still another range of unresolved issues is encompassed by the term "gerrymandering," a term of no agreed-upon meaning but which always connotes apportionment and districting arrangements designed to transmute one party's actual voter strength into the maximum of legislative seats and to transmute the other party's actual voter strength into the minimum of legislative seats.

Too few persons realize or are willing to admit that gerrymandering in the sense of transmutation of party voter strength is a virtually unavoidable concomitant of any system of election of a multimembered assembly, either from districts or at large, unless some device of proportional representation is used. The reason for the intrinsic inequity of all systems short of proportional representation is that party affiliation is not, like sex, spread fairly evenly through the population. Because of the wild-card factor of party member location, it is impossible to devise a politically neutral apportionment and districting system. . . .

One guideline could be a limitation on use of large multimember districts, because of their winner-take-all characteristic. Another would be to view a district system as suspect—and perhaps shift the burden of proof as was done for the plaintiffs after *Baker* v. *Carr*—whenever it is shown that the system consistently magnifies the legislative strength of one party far beyond its actual statewide voter strength.

4. Political subdivisions and districting

Related to the gerrymandering problem, but transcending it, is the critical need to follow political subdivision lines, particularly county lines, in arranging legislative districts. The reasons are two.

First, if the reapportioners do not follow existing county and political subdivision lines, an infinite range of districting discretion and gerrymandering freedom arises. . . .

The second and more compelling reason for following political subdivision lines is the consideration of effective representation—a consideration which theoretically at least is central to the entire reapportionment struggle. Counties are the building blocks of American political life, thought, and action. In addition to the obvious virtues of stability and continuity, and indeed as a result of them, counties are the basic units for political party organization, for State administration, for planning, zoning and regional arrangements, for civic federation organization, for social organization and for business and industrial organization in most instances. In their own right counties provide an increasingly broad range of services and controls. In mid-20th century America they no longer are the "dark continent of American government." To disregard our natural political units in pursuit of "one man, one vote" would be to cut the vitals out of the American political process.

5. Hearing from the minority

Still another closely related problem which may come to the fore in the next few years is the creation of devices to hear more effectively from the minority. Proportional representation, which I am not advocating, would enable us to hear from all parties, large and small, in proportion to their actual voter strength. But proportional representation is feared because of its tendency to break down the two-party system and to result in legislative majorities resting only on unstable coalitions of minor parties. However, a mixed proportional representation and single-member district system might be considered. In postwar Western occupied Germany the Anglo-American concept of districts and the continental concept of proportional representation collided. The result was to produce for the Federal Republic of Germany a mixed proportional representation and single-member district system which so far has proved to be a very healthy mongrel. Part of the legislature is elected from single-member districts; this ensures intimacy of representation, minimizes party bossism and counteracts the splintering tendency of proportional representation. The other part is elected under a proportional representation list system, thus avoiding the minority party freeze-out, which is a tendency of the pure district system, and substituting representational equity.

Short of a mixed proportional representation and single-member district system, there are other devices to enable hearing from the minority in closer proportion to their numbers than may occur in a pure district system. One is the cumulative vote system under which legislators are elected from three-man districts, each voter having three votes which he may distribute among the candidates equally, or two-one, or three for one. As practiced in Illinois for the lower house since 1870, this has meant that the stronger party got two legislators from each district and the weaker party one. [See George S. Blair, "Cumulative Voting: An Effective Electoral Device in Illinois Politics," (1960)]. Another device is limited voting, which is now in force for a portion of New York's City Council.

6. How "equal" is "equal"?

A question on which many other questions depend is how "equal" is "equal" in regard to the equal-population districts rule. Logically, this could have been mentioned first, but the ramifications are better perceived if one has in mind such other issues as gerrymandering and preserving political subdivisions. Although the Supreme Court did mention the traditional importance of political subdivisions, Chief Justice Warren made it quite clear that population was to be the essential guide when he said: "But neither history alone, nor economic or other sorts of group interests, are permissible factors in attempting to justify disparities from population-based representation.". . .

Two observations need to be made. First, if a strict population standard is to be the only consideration and other representation issues are to be ignored, there is no rational basis for stopping short of a 1-to-1 ratio for all districts, and a population deviation of less than a minuscule 1 or 2 percent. In many States population concentrations will make it necessary to cut some political subdivision lines in districting even if the maximum allowable deviation is as high as 10 or 15 percent. If some units must be cut, why not cut enough to get down to a 1 percent deviation?

Nothing in the Supreme Court decisions so far provides much guidance on this question. Indeed, the constant stress on population equality (even under a census now 5 years old) encourages reapportioners to ignore pre-existing political subdivisions in order to get new districts of minimal deviation, safe from reversal. An unavoidable by-product is to maximize gerrymandering freedom.

The second observation is that the Court not only has tended to focus too narrowly on arithmetic as a virtually exclusive guide to proper reapportionment, but also has approached its reapportionment arithmetic too narrowly. The Court has placed stress on the population variance ratio between the one largest and the one smallest district and on the minimum population which theoretically could elect a majority of the legislature. The Court will take note occasionally of the maximum percentage deviation from the mean or "ideal" district.

If arithmetic is to be the guide, and concededly it must have a major role, the focus should be on the average deviation. It is not at all clear why some isolated, extreme ratios between the largest and smallest districts should be deemed "unfair" or "unconstitutional," provided the average deviation is slight. An occasional extreme ratio or percentage deviation has no adverse impact on majority rule; it may be the best way, if not the only way, to provide effective minority representation along with majority rule. The Court has yet to address itself to this question on a precise factual record.

Foregoing some additional matters, I close with this thought. "One man, one vote" is the symbol of an aspiration for fairness, for avoidance of complexity, and for intelligibility in our representational processes in our mass democracy. This is why all Gallup polls show general public support for the Supreme Court's decisions—although this may be the classic example of the uninformed interviewer asking the uncomprehending interviewee a question which is unavoidably loaded because so oversimplified. But, Gallup polls aside, these aspirations for fairness and for intelligibility are quite proper. The task of honoring them has only begun and will require much refinement of the "one man, one vote" also if something approaching political equity is to be achieved.

The reapportionment decisions have led to probably the most widespread popular re-examination of representation theory since the famous debates on legislative composition in the state constitutional conventions in Massachusetts, New York and Virginia in the decade 1820–1830. Basic "truths" are being scrutinized and tested, to be reconfirmed by some and discarded by others. Even the ancient belief that rural-dominated legislatures block urban demands has been challenged as not borne out by the voting patterns. [See Noel Perrin, "In Defense of Country Votes," *The Yale Review* (Autumn, 1962), pp. 16–24; reprinted in Howard D. Hamilton, editor, *Legislative Apportionment* (New York: Harper & Row, 1964), which presents the background, litigation, and some divergent views on apportionment and representation.] It is doubtful that the more sophisticated nuances of representational theory will find their way into the judicial opinions or the legislative debates, but assuredly the simple phrase "one man, one vote" is insufficient to resolve the variety of problems presented by the commands to reapportion on a basis of equality.

[On the issue of whether multi-member election districts unconstitutionally diminish minority voting power, see *Whitcomb* v. *Chavis*, 403 U.S. 124 (1971), in Chap. 9. On the question of the constitutionally permissible population variation among districts, see *Abate* v. *Mundt*, 403 U.S. 182 (1971), in Chap. 9.]

CHAPTER 9

Additional Recent Cases

ELECTRONIC SURVEILLANCE

KATZ v. UNITED STATES
389 U.S. 347 (1967)

Mr. Justice Stewart delivered the opinion of the Court.

The petitioner was convicted in the District Court for the Southern District of California under an eight-count indictment charging him with transmitting wagering information by telephone from Los Angeles to Miami and Boston, in violation of a federal statute. At trial the Government was permitted, over the petitioner's objection, to introduce evidence of the petitioner's end of telephone conversations, overheard by FBI agents who had attached an electronic listening and recording device to the outside of the public telephone booth from which he had placed his calls. In affirming his conviction, the Court of Appeals rejected the contention that the recordings had been obtained in violation of the Fourth Amendment, because "[t]here was no physical entrance into the area occupied by [the petitioner]." We granted certiorari in order to consider the constitutional questions thus presented. . . .

. . . [T]he Fourth Amendment cannot be translated into a general constitutional "right to privacy." That Amendment protects individual privacy against certain kinds of governmental intrusion, but its protections go further, and often have nothing to do with privacy at all. Other provisions of the Constitution protect personal privacy from other forms of governmental invasion. But the protection of a person's *general* right to privacy—his right to be let alone by other people—is, like the protection of his property and of his very life, left largely to the law of the individual States.

Because of the misleading way the issues have been formulated, the parties have attached great significance to the characterization of the telephone booth from which the petitioner placed his calls. The petitioner has strenuously argued that the booth was "a constitutionally protected area." The Government has maintained with equal vigor that it was not. But this effort to decide whether or not a given "area," viewed in the abstract, is "constitutionally protected" deflects attention from the problem presented by this case. For the Fourth Amendment protects people, not places. What a person knowingly exposes to the public, even in his own home or office, is not a subject of Fourth Amendment protection. . . . But what he seeks to preserve as private, even in an area accessible to the public, may be constitutionally protected. . . .

The Government stresses the fact that the telephone booth from which the petitioner made his calls was constructed partly of glass, so that he was as visible after he entered it as he would have been if he had remained outside. But what he sought to exclude when he entered the booth was not the intruding eye—it was the uninvited ear. He did not shed his right to do so simply because he made his calls from a place where he might be seen. No less than an individual in a business office, in a friend's apartment, or in a taxicab, a person in a telephone booth may rely upon the protection of the Fourth Amendment. One who occupies it, shuts the door behind him, and pays the toll that permits him to place a call is surely entitled to assume that the words he utters into the mouthpiece will not be broadcast to the world. To read the Constitution more narrowly is to ignore the vital role that the public telephone has come to play in private communication.

The Government contends, however, that the activities of its agents in this case should not be tested by Fourth Amendment requirements, for the surveillance technique they employed involved no physical penetration of the telephone booth from which the petitioner placed his calls. It is true that the absence of such penetration was at one time thought to foreclose further Fourth Amendment inquiry, *Olmstead* v. *United States*, . . . for that Amendment was thought to limit only searches and seizures of tangible property. But "[t]he premise that property interests control the right of the Government to search and seize has been discredited." *Warden* v. *Hayden.* . . .

We conclude that the underpinnings of Olmstead and Goldman have been so eroded by our subsequent decisions that the "trespass" doctrine there enunciated can no longer be regarded as controlling. The Government's activities in electronically listening to and recording the petitioner's words violated the privacy upon which he justifiably relied while using the telephone booth and thus constituted a "search and seizure" within the meaning of the Fourth Amendment. . . .

The question remaining for decision, then, is whether the search and seizure conducted in this case complied with constitutional standards. . . . [T]he surveillance was limited, both in scope and in duration, to the specific purpose of establishing the contents of the petitioner's unlawful telephonic communications. The agents confined their surveillance to the brief periods during which he used the telephone booth, and they took great care to overhear only the conversations of the petitioner himself.

Accepting this account of the Government's actions as accurate, it is clear that this surveillance was so narrowly circumscribed that a duly authorized magistrate, properly notified of the need for such investigation, specifically informed of the basis on which it was to proceed, and clearly apprised of the precise intrusion it would entail, could constitutionally have authorized, with appropriate safeguards, the very limited search and seizure that the Government asserts in fact took place. . . .

The Government . . . argues that surveillance of a telephone booth should be exempted from the usual requirement of advance authorization by a magistrate upon a showing of probable cause. We cannot agree. . . . The government agents here ignored "the procedure of antecedent justification . . . that is central to the Fourth Amendment," a procedure that we hold to be a constitutional precondition of the kind of electronic surveillance involved in this case. Because the surveillance here failed to meet that condition, and because it led to the petitioner's conviction, the judgment must be reversed.

Mr. Justice Marshall took no part in the consideration or decision of this case.

Mr. Justice Douglas, with whom Mr. Justice Brennan joins, concurring. . . .

Mr. Justice Harlan, concurring. . . .

Mr. Justice Black, dissenting.

If I could agree with the Court that eavesdropping carried on by electronic means . . . constitutes a "search" or "seizure," I would be happy to join the Court's opinion. . . .

My basic objection is twofold: (1) I do not believe that the words of the Amendment will bear the meaning given them by today's decision, and (2) I do not believe that it is the proper role of this Court to rewrite the Amendment in order "to bring it into harmony with the times" and thus reach a result that many people believe to be desirable. . . .

UNITED STATES v. WHITE
401 U.S. 745 (1971)

Mr. Justice White announced the judgment of the Court and an opinion in which the Chief Justice, Mr. Justice Stewart, and Mr. Justice Blackmun join.

In 1966, respondent James A. White was tried and convicted under two consolidated indictments charging various illegal transactions in narcotics . . . The issue before us is whether the Fourth Amendment bars from evidence the testimony of governmental agents who related certain conversations which had occurred between defendant White and a government informant, Harvey Jackson, and which the agents overheard by monitoring the frequency of a radio transmitter carried by Jackson and concealed on his person. On four occasions the conversations took place in Jackson's home; each of these conversations was overheard by an agent concealed in a kitchen closet with Jackson's consent and by a second agent outside the house using a radio receiver. . . . The jury returned a guilty verdict and defendant appealed. . . .

The Court of Appeals understood *Katz* to render inadmissible against White the agents' testimony concerning conversations which Jackson broadcast to them. We cannot agree. *Katz* involved no revelation to the Government by a party to conversations with the defendant nor did the Court indicate in any way that a defendant has a justifiable and constitutionally protected expectation that a person with whom he is conversing will not then or later reveal the conversation to the police. . . .

Concededly a police agent who conceals his police connections may write down for official use his conversations with a defendant and testify concerning them, without a warrant authorizing his encounters with the defendant and without otherwise violating the latter's Fourth Amendment rights. . . . For constitutional purposes, no different result is required if the agent instead of immediately reporting and transcribing his conversations with defendant, either (1) simultaneously records them with electronic equipment which he is carrying on his person. . . ; (2) or carries radio equipment which simultaneously transmits the conversations either to recording equipment located elsewhere or to other agents monitoring the transmitting frequency. . . .

Inescapably, one contemplating illegal activities must realize and risk that his companions may be reporting to the police. . . .

Nor should we be too ready to erect constitutional barriers to relevant and probative evidence which is also accurate and reliable. An electronic recording will many times produce a more reliable rendition of what a defendant has said than will the unaided memory of a police agent. . . .

Mr. Justice Black . . . concurs in the judgment of the Court for the reasons set forth in his dissent in *Katz* v. *United States*. . . .

Mr. Justice Brennan, concurring in the result. . . .

Mr. Justice Douglas dissenting. . . .

Today no one perhaps notices because only a small, obscure criminal is the victim. But every person is the victim, for the technology we exalt today is every-man's master. . . .

Monitoring, if prevalent, certainly kills free discourse and spontaneous utter-ances. Free discourse—a First Amendment value—may be frivolous or serious, humble or defiant, reactionary or revolutionary, profane or in good taste; but it is not free if there is surveillance. . . .

Now that the discredited decisions in *On Lee* and *Lopez* are resuscitated and re-vived, must everyone live in fear that every word he speaks may be transmitted or recorded and later repeated to the entire world? I can imagine nothing that has a more chilling effect on people speaking their minds and expressing their views on important matters. The advocates of that regime should spend some time in totalitarian countries and learn first-hand the kind of regime they are creating here. . . .

Mr. Justice Harlan, dissenting. . . .

Mr. Justice Marshall, dissenting. . . .

INTERROGATION

OROZCO v. TEXAS
394 U.S. 324 (1969)

Mr. Justice Black delivered the opinion of the Court.

[The evidence introduced at a trial in the Criminal District Court of Dallas County, Texas, in which the defendant was convicted of murder without malice, showed that the defendant, after leaving the scene of a shooting in a cafe, re-turned to his boardinghouse to sleep; that at about 4 a.m. four police officers arrived at the boardinghouse, were admitted by an unidentified woman, and were told that the defendant was asleep in the bedroom; that all four officers entered the bedroom, and, without giving any of the warnings required by *Miranda* v. *Arizona,* asked the defendant's name, whether he had been to the cafe, whether he owned a pistol, and where it was located; and that the defendant gave incrim-inating answers. Rejecting the contention that a material part of the evidence against the defendant had been obtained in violation of his rights against self-incrimination, the Court of Criminal Appeals of Texas affirmed the conviction.]

The State has argued here that since petitioner was interrogated on his own bed, in familiar surroundings, our *Miranda* holding should not apply. It is true that the Court did say in *Miranda* that "compulsion to speak in the isolated setting of the police station may well be greater than in courts or other official investigations, where there are often impartial observers to guard against intimidation or trick-ery." . . . But the opinion iterated and reiterated the absolute necessity for officers interrogating people "in custody" to give the described warnings. See *Mathis* v.

United States, 391 U.S. 1 (1968). According to the officer's testimony, petitioner was under arrest and not free to leave when he was questioned in his bedroom in the early hours of the morning. The *Miranda* opinion declared that the warnings were required when the person being interrogated was "in custody at the station *or otherwise deprived of his freedom of action significant in any way.*" ... (Emphasis supplied.) The decision of this Court in *Miranda* was reached after careful consideration and in lengthy opinions were announced by both the majority and dissenting Justices. There is no need to canvass those arguments again. We do not, as the dissent implies, expand or extend to the slightest extent our *Miranda* decision. We do adhere to our well-considered holding in that case and therefore reverse the conviction below.

Reversed.

Mr. Justice Fortas took no part in the consideration or decision of this case.

Mr. Justice Harlan, concurring. . . .

Mr. Justice White, with whom Mr. Justice Stewart joins, dissenting. . . .

HARRIS *v.* NEW YORK

401 U.S. 222 (1971)

Mr. Chief Justice Burger delivered the opinion of the Court.

We granted the writ in this case to consider petitioner's claim that a statement made by him to police under circumstances rendering it inadmissible to establish the prosecution's case in chief under *Miranda* v. *Arizona* . . . may not be used to impeach his credibility.

The State of New York charged petitioner in a two-count indictment with twice selling heroin to an undercover police officer. . . .

Petitioner took the stand in his own defense. He admitted knowing the undercover police officer but denied a sale on January 4. He admitted making a sale of contents of a glassine bag to the officer on January 6 but claimed it was baking soda and part of a scheme to defraud the purchaser.

On cross-examination petitioner was asked seriatim whether he had made specified statements to the police immediately following his arrest on January 7—statements that partially contradicted petitioner's direct testimony at trial. In response to the cross-examination, petitioner testified that he could not remember virtually any of the questions or answers recited by the prosecutor. . . .

The trial judge instructed the jury that the statements attributed to petitioner by the prosecution could be considered only in passing on petitioner's credibility and not as evidence of guilt. In closing summations both counsel argued the substance of the impeaching statements. The jury then found petitioner guilty of the second count of the indictment. . . .

At trial the prosecution made no effort in its case in chief to use the statements allegedly made by petitioner, conceding that they were inadmissible under *Miranda* v. *Arizona.* . . .

Some comments in the *Miranda* opinion can indeed be read as indicating a bar to use of an uncounseled statement for any purpose, but discussion of that issue was not at all necessary to the Court's holding and cannot be regarded as controlling. *Miranda* barred the prosecution from making its case with statements of an accused made while in custody prior to having or effectively waiving counsel. It does not follow from *Miranda* that evidence inadmissible against an accused in the prosecution's case in chief is barred for all purposes, provided of course that the trustworthiness of the evidence satisfies legal standards. . . .

. . . The impeachment process here undoubtedly provided valuable aid to the jury in assessing petitioner's credibility, and the benefits of this process should not be lost, in our view, because of the speculative possibility that impermissible police conduct will be encouraged thereby. Assuming that the exclusionary rule has a deterrent effect on proscribed police conduct, sufficient deterrence flows when the evidence in question is made unavailable to the prosecution in its case in chief.

Every criminal defendant is privileged to testify in his own defense, or to refuse to do so. . . . The shield provided by *Miranda* cannot be perverted into a license to use perjury by way of a defense, free from the risk of confrontation with prior inconsistent utterances. We hold, therefore, that petitioner's credibility was appropriately impeached by use of his earlier conflicting statements.

Affirmed.

Mr. Justice Black dissents.

Mr. Justice Brennan, with whom Mr. Justice Douglas and Mr. Justice Marshall join, dissenting. . . .

The objective of deterring improper police conduct is only part of the larger objective of safeguarding the integrity of our adversary system. The "essential mainstay" of that system . . . is the privilege against self-incrimination, which for that reason has occupied a central place in our jurisprudence since before the Nation's birth. . . . These values are plainly jeopardized if an exception against admission of tainted statements is made for those used for impeachment purposes. Moreover, it is monstrous that courts should aid or abet the law-breaking police officer. . . . The Court today tells the police that they may freely interrogate an accused incommunicado and without counsel and know that although any statement they obtain in violation of *Miranda* can't be used on the State's direct case, it may be introduced if the defendant has the temerity to testify in his own defense. This goes far toward undoing much of the progress made in conforming police methods to the Constitution. I dissent.

DISRUPTIVE DEFENDANTS

ILLINOIS *v.* ALLEN
397 U.S. 337 (1970)

Mr. Justice Black delivered the opinion of the Court. . . .

One of the most basic of the rights guaranteed by the Confrontation Clause is the accused's right to be present in the courtroom at every stage of his trial. . . . The question presented in this case is whether an accused can claim the benefit of this constitutional right to remain in the courtroom while at the same time he engages in speech and conduct which is so noisy, disorderly, and disruptive that it is exceedingly difficult or wholly impossible to carry on the trial. . . . [The opinion here describes in detail the obstreperous conduct, the interruptions, and abusive language on the part of the defendant, resulting in the judge's order of removal from the courtroom for substantial portions of the trial.]

. . . Although mindful that courts must indulge every reasonable presumption against the loss of constitutional rights, . . . we explicitly hold today that a defendant can lose his right to be present at trial if, after he has been warned by the judge that he will be removed if he continues his disruptive behavior, he nevertheless insists on conducting himself in a manner so disorderly, disruptive, and disrespectful of the court that his trial cannot be carried on with him in the courtroom. Once lost, the right to be present can, of course, be reclaimed as soon as the defendant is willing to conduct himself consistently with the decorum and respect inherent in the concept of courts and judicial proceedings.

It is essential to the proper administration of criminal justice that dignity, order, and decorum be the hallmarks of all court proceedings in our country. The flagrant disregard in the courtroom of elementary standards of proper conduct should not and cannot be tolerated. We believe trial judges confronted with disruptive, contumacious, stubbornly defiant defendants must be given sufficient discretion to meet the circumstances of each case. No one formula for maintaining the appropriate courtroom atmosphere will be best in all situations. We think there are at least three constitutionally permissible ways for a trial judge to handle an obstreperous defendant like Allen: (1) bind and gag him, thereby keeping him present; (2) cite him for contempt; (3) take him out of the courtroom until he promises to conduct himself properly.

Trying a defendant for a crime while he sits bound and gagged before the judge and jury would to an extent comply with that part of the Sixth Amendment's purposes that accords the defendant an opportunity to confront the witnesses at the trial. But even to contemplate such a technique, much less see it, arouses a feeling that no person should be tried while shackled and gagged except as a last resort. . . .

It is not pleasant to hold that the respondent Allen was properly banished from the court for a part of his own trial. But our courts, palladiums of liberty as they are, cannot be treated disrespectfully with impunity. Nor can the accused be permitted by his disruptive conduct indefinitely to avoid being tried on the charges brought against him. It would degrade our country and our judicial system to permit our courts to be bullied, insulted, and humiliated and their orderly progress thwarted and obstructed by defendants brought before them charged with crimes. . . . Being manned by humans, the courts are not perfect and are bound to make some errors. But, if our courts are to remain what the Founders intended, the citadels of justice, their proceedings cannot and must not be infected with the sort of scurrilous, abusive language and conduct paraded before the Illinois trial judge in this case. The record shows that the Illinois judge at all times conducted himself with that dignity, decorum, and patience that befits a judge. Even in holding that the trial judge had erred, the Court of Appeals praised his "commendable patience under severe provocation."

We do not hold that removing this defendant from his own trial was the only way the Illinois judge could have constitutionally solved the problem he had. We do hold, however, that there is nothing whatever in this record to show that the judge did not act completely within his discretion. . . .

The judgment of the Court of Appeals is

Reversed.

Mr. Justice Brennan, concurring. . . .

Mr. Justice Douglas. . . .

We should not reach the merits but should reverse the case for staleness of the record and affirm the denial of relief by the District Court. After all, behind the issuance of a writ of habeas corpus is the exercise of an informed discretion. The question, how to proceed in a criminal case against a defendant who is a mental case, should be resolved only on a full and adequate record. . . .

TRIAL BY JURY

DUNCAN v. LOUISIANA
391 U.S. 145 (1968)

Mr. Justice White delivered the opinion of the Court.

Appellant, Gary Duncan, was convicted of simple battery in the . . . District Court of Louisiana. Under Louisiana law simple battery is a misdemeanor, punishable by a maximum of two years' imprisonment and a $300 fine. Appellant sought trial by jury, but because the Louisiana Constitution grants jury trials only in cases in which capital punishment or imprisonment at hard labor may be imposed, the trial judge denied the request. Appellant was convicted and sentenced to serve 60 days in the parish prison and pay a fine of $150. Appellant sought review in the Supreme Court of Louisiana, asserting that the denial of jury trial violated rights guaranteed to him by the United States Constitution. The Supreme Court . . . denied appellant a writ of certiorari. . . .

The test for determining whether a right extended by the Fifth and Sixth Amendments with respect to federal criminal proceedings is also protected against state action by the Fourteenth Amendment has been phrased in a variety of ways in the opinions of this Court. The question has been asked whether a right is among those " 'fundamental principles of liberty and justice which lie at the base of all our civil and political institutions,' ". . . ; whether it is "basic in our system of jurisprudence,". . . ; and whether it is "a fundamental right, essential to a fair trial,". . . . Because we believe that trial by jury in criminal cases is fundamental to the American scheme of justice, we hold that the Fourteenth Amendment guarantees a right of jury trial in all criminal cases which—were they to be tried in a federal court—would come within the Sixth Amendment's guarantee. Since we consider the appeal before us to be such a case, we hold that the Constitution was violated when appellant's demand for jury trial was refused. . . .

We are aware of prior cases in this Court in which the prevailing opinion contains statements contrary to our holding today that the right to jury trial in serious criminal cases is a fundamental right and hence must be recognized by the States as part of their obligation to extend due process of law to all persons within their jurisdiction. . . . None of these cases, however, dealt with a State which had purported to dispense entirely with a jury trial in serious criminal cases. . . .

The guarantees of jury trial in the Federal and State Constitutions reflect a profound judgment about the way in which law should be enforced and justice administered. A right to jury trial is granted to criminal defendants in order to prevent oppression by the Government. Those who wrote our constitutions knew from history and experience that it was necessary to protect against unfounded criminal charges brought to eliminate enemies and against judges too responsive to the voice of higher authority. . . . The deep commitment of the Nation to the right of jury trial in serious criminal cases as a defense against arbitrary law enforcement qualifies for protection under the Due Process Clause of the Fourteenth Amendment, and must therefore be respected by the States. . . .

. . . It is doubtless true that there is a category of petty crimes or offenses which is not subject to the Sixth Amendment jury trial provision and should not be subject to the Fourteenth Amendment jury trial requirement here applied to the States. Crimes carrying possible penalties up to six months do not require a jury trial if they otherwise qualify as petty offenses. *Cheff* v. *Schnackenberg*, 384 U.S. 373 (1966). But the penalty authorized for a particular crime is of major relevance in determining whether it is serious or not and may in itself, if severe enough, subject the trial to the mandates of the Sixth Amendment....

We need not, however, settle in this case the exact location of the line between petty offenses and serious crimes. It is sufficient for our purposes to hold that a crime punishable by two years in prison is, based on past and contemporary standards in this country, a serious crime and not a petty offense. Consequently, appellant was entitled to a jury trial and it was error to deny it.

The judgment below is reversed and the case is remanded for proceedings not inconsistent with this opinion.

Mr. Justice Fortas, concurring....

Mr. Justice Black, with whom Mr. Justice Douglas joins, concurring....

Mr. Justice Harlan, whom Mr. Justice Stewart joins, dissenting....

WILLIAMS v. FLORIDA
399 U.S. 78 (1970)

Mr. Justice White delivered the opinion of the Court.

[Prior to his trial for robbery in the State of Florida, petitioner filed a pretrial motion to impanel a 12-man jury instead of the six-man jury provided by Florida law in all but capital cases. That motion was denied, and in the subsequent trial petitioner was convicted as charged and was sentenced to life imprisonment. The District Court of Appeal affirmed, rejecting petitioner's claim that his Sixth Amendment rights had been violated.]

In *Duncan* v. *Louisiana* ... we held that the Fourteenth Amendment guarantees a right to trial by jury in all criminal cases which—were they to be tried in a federal court—would come within the Sixth Amendment's guarantee. Petitioner's trial for robbery ... clearly falls within the scope of that holding.... The question in this case then is whether the constitutional guarantee of a trial by "jury" necessarily requires trial by exactly 12 persons, rather than some lesser number— in this case six. We hold that the 12-man panel is not a necessary ingredient of "trial by jury," and that respondent's refusal to impanel more than the six members provided for by Florida law did not violate petitioner's Sixth Amendment rights as applied to the States through the Fourteenth.

We had occasion in *Duncan* v. *Louisiana*, ... to review briefly the oft-told history of the development of trial by jury in criminal cases. That history revealed a long tradition attaching great importance to the concept of relying on a body of one's peers to determine guilt or innocence as a safeguard against arbitrary law enforcement. That same history, however, affords little insight into the considerations which gradually led the size of that body to be generally fixed at 12. Some have suggested that the number 12 was fixed upon simply because that was the number of the presentment jury from the hundred, from which the petty jury developed. Other, less circular but more fanciful reasons for the number 12 have been given, "but they were all brought forward after the number was fixed," and rest on little more than mystical or superstitious insights into the significance of "12." Lord Coke's explanation that the "number of twelve is much respected in holy writ, as 12 apostles, 12 stones, 12 tribes, etc." is typical. In short, while sometime in the 14th century the size of the jury at common law came to be fixed generally at 12, that particular feature of the jury system appears to have been an historical accident, unrelated to the great purposes which gave rise to the jury in the first place. The question before us is whether this accidental feature of the jury has been immutably codified into our Constitution.

This Court's earlier decisions have assumed an affirmative answer to this question. The leading case so construing the Sixth Amendment is *Thompson* v. *Utah*, 170 U.S. 343 (1898).... In reaching its conclusion, the Court announced that the Sixth Amendment was applicable to the defendant's trial when Utah was a territory, and that the jury referred to in the Amendment was a jury "constituted, as it was at common law, of twelve persons, neither more nor less."....

While "the intent of the Framers" is often an elusive quarry, the relevant constitutional history casts considerable doubt on the easy assumption in our past decisions that if a given feature existed in a jury at common law in 1789, then it was necessarily preserved in the Constitution....

We do not pretend to be able to divine precisely what the word "jury" imported to the Framers, the First Congress, or the States in 1789. It may well be that the usual expectation was that the jury would consist of 12, and that hence, the most likely conclusion to be drawn is simply that little thought was actually given to the specific question we face today. But there is absolutely no indication in "the intent of the Framers" of an explicit decision to equate the constitutional and common law characteristics of the jury.... The relevant inquiry, as we see it, must be the function which the particular feature performs and its relation to the purposes of the jury trial. Measured by this standard, the 12-man requirement cannot be regarded as an indispensable component of the Sixth Amendment.

[The opinion here examines the functions of group deliberation, cross-section representation of the community, and protection against governmental oppression, and concludes that these functions are equally well served with juries of six.]

We conclude, in short, as we began: the fact that the jury at common law was composed of precisely 12 is an historical accident, unnecessary to effect the purposes of the jury system and wholly without significance "except to mystics."....

Affirmed.

Mr. Justice Blackmun took no part in the consideration or decision of this case.
Mr. Chief Justice Burger, concurring....
Mr. Justice Harlan, concurring in part and dissenting in part....
Mr. Justice Stewart, concurring....
Mr. Justice Black, with whom Mr. Justice Douglas joins, concurring....
Mr. Justice Marshall, dissenting in part....

COURT-MARTIAL JURISDICTION

O'CALLAHAN *v.* PARKER
395 U.S. 258 (1969)

Mr. Justice Douglas delivered the opinion of the Court.

[Petitioner, a sergeant in the United States Army stationed in Hawaii, while on an evening pass and dressed in civilian clothes, broke into a girl's hotel room in Honolulu and assaulted and attempted to rape her. He was apprehended by a hotel security officer who delivered him to the Honolulu city police for questioning, and after determining that he was a soldier, the city police delivered him to the military police. He was charged with attempted rape, housebreaking, and assault with intent to rape, in violation of the Uniform Code of Military Justice, and was tried and convicted by court-martial on all counts. While under confinement at a federal prison, he filed a petition for habeas corpus in a federal District Court alleging that the court-martial was without jurisdiction to try him for nonmilitary offenses committed off-post while on an evening pass. The District Court dismissed, and the Court of Appeals affirmed.]

A court-martial is not yet an independent instrument of justice but remains to a significant degree a specialized part of the overall mechanism by which military discipline is preserved.

That a system of specialized military courts, proceeding by practices different from those obtaining in the regular courts and in general less favorable to defendants, is necessary to an effective national defense establishment, few would deny. But the justification for such a system rests on the special needs of the military, and history teaches that expanison of military discipline beyond its proper domain carries with it a threat to liberty. . . .

While the Court of Military Appeals takes cognizance of some constitutional rights of the accused who are court-martialed, courts-martial as an institution are singularly inept in dealing with the nice subtleties of constitutional law. . . .

The mere fact that petitioner was at the time of his offense and of his court-martial on active duty in the Armed Forces does not automatically dispose of this case under our prior decisions.

We have held in a series of decisions that court-martial jurisdiction cannot be extended to reach any person not a member of the Armed Forces at the times of both the offense and the trial. Thus, discharged soldiers cannot be court-martialed for offenses committed while in service. *Toth* v. *Quarles.* . . . Similarly, neither civilian employees of the Armed Forces overseas . . . nor civilian dependents of military personnel accompanying them overseas . . . may be tried by court-martial. . . .

The fact that courts-martial have no jurisdiction over nonsoldiers, whatever their offense, does not necessarily imply that they have unlimited jurisdiction over soldiers, regardless of the nature of the offenses charged. Nor do the cases of this Court suggest any such interpretation. . . .

We have concluded that the crime to be under military jurisdiction must be service connected, lest "cases arising in the land or naval forces, or in the Militia, when in actual service in time of War or public danger," as used in the Fifth Amendment, be expanded to deprive every member of the armed services of the benefits of an indictment by a grand jury and a trial by a jury of his peers. . . .

In the present case petitioner was properly absent from his military base when he committed the crimes with which he is charged. There was no connection—not even the remotest one—between his military duties and the crimes in question. The crimes were not committed on a military post or enclave; nor was the person whom he attacked performing any duties relating to the military. Moreover, Hawaii, the situs of the crime, is not an armed camp under military control, as are some of our far-flung outposts.

Finally, we deal with peacetime offenses, not with authority stemming from the war power. Civil courts were open. . . . The offenses did not involve any question of the flouting of military authority, the security of a military post, or the integrity of military property.

We have accordingly decided that since petitioner's crimes were not service connected, he could not be tried by court-martial but rather was entitled to trial by the civilian courts.

Reversed.

Mr. Justice Harlan, whom Mr. Justice Stewart and Mr. Justice White join, dissenting. . . .

The Court does not explain the scope of the "service-connected" crimes as to which court-martial jurisdiction is appropriate, but it appears that jurisdiction may extend to "nonmilitary" offenses in appropriate circumstances. . . .

Whatever role an *ad hoc* judicial approach may have in some areas of the law, the Congress and the military are at least entitled to know with some certainty the allowable scope of court-martial jurisdiction. Otherwise, the infinite permutations of possibly relevant factors are bound to create confusion and proliferate litigation over the jurisdictional issue in each instance. Absolutely nothing in the language, history, or logic of the Constitution justifies this uneasy state of affairs which the Court has today created.

I would affirm the judgment of the Court of Appeals.

ESTABLISHMENT OF RELIGION: TEXTBOOK LOANS

BOARD OF EDUCATION v. ALLEN
392 U.S. 236 (1968)

Mr. Justice White delivered the opinion of the Court.

A law of the State of New York requires local public school authorities to lend textbooks free of charge to all students in grades seven through 12; students attending private schools are included. This case presents the question whether this statute is a "law respecting an establishment of religion, or prohibiting the free exercise thereof," and so in conflict with the First and Fourteenth Amendments to the Constitution, because it authorizes the loan of textbooks to students attending parochial schools. We hold that the law is not in violation of the Constitution. . . .

Everson v. *Board of Education* . . . is the case decided by this Court that is most nearly in point for today's problem. . . .

Everson and later cases have shown that the line between state neutrality to religion and state support of religion is not easy to locate. . . . Based on *Everson*, *Zorach*, *McGowan*, and other cases, *Abington School District* v. *Schempp* . . . fashioned a test subscribed to by eight Justices for distinguishing between forbidden involvements of the State with religion and those contacts which the Establishment clause permits:

"The test may be stated as follows: what are the purpose and the primary effect of the enactment? If either is the advancement or inhibition of religion then the enactment exceeds the scope of legislative power as circumscribed by the Constitution. That is to say that to withstand the strictures of the Establishment Clause there must be a secular legislative purpose and a primary effect that neither advances nor inhibits religion. *Everson* v. *Board of Education*. . . ."

The test is not easy to apply, but the citation of *Everson* by the *Schempp*

Court to support its general standard made clear how the *Schempp* rule would be applied to the facts of *Everson*. The statute upheld in *Everson* would be considered a law having "a secular legislative purpose and a primary effect that neither advances nor inhibits religion." We reach the same result with respect to the New York law. . . .

Of course books are different from buses. Most bus rides have no inherent religious significance, while religious books are common. However, the language of Sec. 701 does not authorize the loan of religious books, and the State claims no right to distribute religious literature. Although the books loaned are those required by the parochial school for use in specific courses, each book loaned must be approved by the public school authorities; only secular books may receive approval. . . . In judging the validity of the statute on this record we must proceed on the assumption that books loaned to students are books that are not unsuitable for use in the public schools because of religious content. . . .

The judgment is affirmed.

Mr. Justice Harlan, concurring. . . .

Mr. Justice Black, dissenting. . . .

I still subscribe to the belief that tax-raised funds cannot constitutionally be used to support religious schools, buy their school books, erect their buildings, pay their teachers, or pay any other of their maintenance expenses, even to the extent of one penny. . . . And I still believe that the only way to protect minority religious groups from majority groups in this country is to keep the wall of separation between church and state high and impregnable as the First and Fourteenth Amendments provide. The Court's affirmance here bodes nothing but evil to religious peace in this country.

Mr. Justice Douglas, dissenting. . . .

Whatever may be said of *Everson*, there is nothing ideological about a bus. There is nothing ideological about a school lunch, or a public nurse, or a scholarship. . . . The textbook goes to the very heart of education in a parochial school. It is the chief, although not solitary, instrumentality for propagating a particular religious creed or faith. How can we possibly approve such state aid to a religion? . . .

The initiative to select and requisition "the books desired" is with the parochial school. Powerful religious-political pressures will therefore be on the state agencies to provide the books that are desired.

These then are the battlegrounds where control of textbook distribution will be won or lost. Now that "secular" textbooks will pour into religious schools, we can rest assured that a contest will be on to provide those books for religious schools which the dominant religious group concludes best reflect the theocentric or other philosophy of the particular church. . . .

ESTABLISHMENT OF RELIGION: STATE SALARY SUPPLEMENTS

LEMON *v.* KURTZMAN

403 U.S. 602 (1971)

Mr. Chief Justice Burger delivered the opinion of the Court.

These two appeals raise questions as to Pennsylvania and Rhode Island statutes providing state aid to church-related elementary and secondary schools. Both statutes are challenged as violative of the Establishment and Free Exercise Clauses of the First Amendment and the Due Process Clause of the Fourteenth Amendment.

Pennsylvania has adopted a statutory program that provides financial support to nonpublic elementary and secondary schools by way of reimbursement for the cost of teachers' salaries, textbooks, and instructional materials in specified secular subjects. Rhode Island has adopted a statute under which the State pays directly to teachers in nonpublic elementary schools a supplement of 15% of their annual salary. Under each statute state aid has been given to church-related educational institutions as well as other private schools. We hold that both statutes are unconstitutional. . . .

(a) Rhode Island Program

The District Court made extensive findings on the grave potential for excessive entanglement that inheres in the religious character and purpose of the Roman Catholic elementary schools of Rhode Island, to date the sole beneficiaries of the Rhode Island Salary Supplement Act. . . .

In *Allen* the Court refused to make assumptions, on a meager record, about the religious content of the textbooks that the State would be asked to provide. We cannot, however, refuse there to recognize that teachers have a substantially different ideological character than books. In terms of potential for involving some aspect of faith or morals in secular subjects, a textbook's content is ascertainable, but a teacher's handling of a subject is not. We cannot ignore the dangers that a teacher under religious control and discipline poses to the separation of the religious from the purely secular aspects of pre-college education.

In our view the record shows these dangers are present to a substantial degree. . . . The teacher is employed by a religious organization, subject to the direction and discipline of religious authorities, and works in a system dedicated to rearing children in a particular faith. These are not lessened by the fact that most of the lay teachers are of the Catholic faith. Inevitably some of a teacher's responsibilities hover on the border between secular and religious orientation.

We need not and do not assume that teachers in parochial schools will be guilty of bad faith or any conscious design to evade the limitations imposed by the statute and the First Amendment. We simply recognize that a dedicated religious person, teaching in a school affiliated with his or her faith and operated to inculcate its tenets, will inevitably experience great difficulty in remaining religiously neutral. . . .

(b) Pennsylvania Program

The Pennsylvania statute also provides state aid to church-related schools for teachers' salaries. . . .

As we noted earlier, the very restrictions and surveillance necessary to ensure that teachers play a strictly nonideological role give rise to entanglements between church and state. The Pennsylvania statute, like that of Rhode Island, fosters this kind of relationship. Reimbursement is not only limited to courses offered in the public schools and materials approved by state officials, but the statute excludes "any subject matter expressing religious teaching, or the morals or forms of worship of any sect." In addition schools seeking reimbursement must maintain accounting procedures that require the State to establish the cost of the secular as distinguished from the religious instruction.

The Pennsylvania statute, moreover, has the further defect of providing state financial aid directly to the church-related school. This factor distinguishes both *Everson* and *Allen,* for in both those cases the Court was careful to point out that state aid was provided to the student and his parents—not to the church-related school. . . . The history of government grants of a continuing cash subsidy indicates that such programs have almost always been accompanied by varying measures of control and surveillance. . . .

A broader base of entanglement of yet a different character is presented by the divisive political potential of these state programs. In a community where such a large number of pupils are served by church-related schools, it can be assumed that state assistance will entail considerable political activity. . . . Candidates will be forced to declare and voters to choose. It would be unrealistic to ignore the fact that many people confronted with issues of this kind will find their votes aligned with their faith.

Ordinarily political debate and division, however vigorous or even partisan, are normal and healthy manifestations of our democratic system of government, but political division along religious lines was one of the principal evils against which the First Amendment was intended to protect. . . .

Mr. Justice Harlan, concurring. . . .

Mr. Justice Douglas, whom Mr. Justice Black joins, concurring. . . .

In *Tilton* v. *Richardson*, 403 U.S. 672 (1971), the Court upheld that portion of the Higher Education Facilities Act of 1963 which provided federal construction grants for college and university facilities (excluding facilities used for sectarian instruction or as places of worship, or those used as part of a program of a school or department of divinity), but held unconstitutional that portion of the Act providing for a 20-year limitation on the religious use of the facilities constructed with federal funds. The Court pointed out that it "cannot be assumed that a substantial structure has no value after that period and hence the unrestricted use of a valuable property is in effect a contribution of some value to a religious body."

Establishment of Religion: Tax Exemptions

WALZ v. TAX COMMISSION OF THE CITY OF NEW YORK
397 U.S. 664 (1970)

Mr. Chief Justice Burger delivered the opinion of the Court.

[The plaintiff, an owner of real property, brought suit in the New York courts to enjoin the New York City Tax Commission from granting property tax exemptions to religious organizations for religious properties used solely for religious worship. Such exemptions were authorized by state constitutional and statutory provisions, but the plaintiff contended that the exemptions indirectly required the plaintiff to make a contribution to religious bodies, thereby violating the religion clauses of the First Amendment. The court dismissed the complaint, and the New York Court of Appeals affirmed.]

The course of constitutional neutrality in this area cannot be an absolutely straight line; rigidity could well defeat the basic purpose of these provisions, which is to insure that no religion be sponsored or favored, none commanded, and none inhibited. . . .

The legislative purpose of a property tax exemption is neither the advancement nor the inhibition of religion; it is neither sponsorship nor hostility. New York, in common with the other States, has determined that certain entities that exist in a harmonious relationship to the community at large, and that foster its "moral or mental improvement," should not be inhibited in their activities by property taxation or the hazard of loss of those properties for nonpayment of taxes. It has not singled out one particular church or religious group or even churches as such; rather, it has granted exemption to all houses of religious worship within a broad class of property owned by nonprofit, quasi-public corporations which include hospitals, libraries, playgrounds, scientific, professional, historical and patriotic groups. The State has an affirmative policy that considers these groups as beneficial and stabilizing influences in community life and finds this classification useful, desirable, and in the public interest. . . .

Determining that the legislative purpose of tax exemption is not aimed at establishing, sponsoring, or supporting religion does not end the inquiry, however. We must also be sure that the end result—the effect—is not an excessive government entanglement with religion. The test is inescapably one of degree. Either course, taxation of churches or exemption, occasions some degree of involvement with religion. Elimination of exemption would tend to expand the involvement of government by giving rise to tax valuation of church property, tax liens, tax foreclosures, and the direct confrontations and conflicts that follow in the train of those legal processes. . . . The exemption creates only a minimal and remote involvement between church and state and far less than taxation of churches. It restricts the fiscal relationship between church and state, and tends to complement and reinforce the desired separation insulating each from the other. . . .

All of the 50 States provide for tax exemption of places of worship, most of them doing so by constitutional guarantees. For so long as federal income taxes have had any potential impact on churches—over 75 years—religious organizations have been expressly exempt from the tax. . . .

Nothing in this national attitude toward religious tolerance and two centuries of uninterrupted freedom from taxation has given the remotest sign of leading to an established church or religion and on the contrary it has operated affirmatively to help guarantee the free exercise of all forms of religious beliefs. . . . If taxation can be seen as this first step toward "establishment" of religion, as Mr. Justice Douglas fears, the second step has been long in coming. Any move which realistically "establishes" a church or tends to do so can be dealt with "while this Court sits.". . .

Affirmed.

Mr. Justice Brennan, concurring. . . .
Mr. Justice Harlan, concurring. . . .
Mr. Justice Douglas, dissenting.

Establishment of Religion:
The Arkansas Anti-Evolution Law

EPPERSON *v.* ARKANSAS

393 U.S. 97 (1968)

Mr. Justice Fortas delivered the opinion of the Court.

This appeal challenges the constitutionality of the "anti-evolution" statute which the State of Arkansas adopted in 1928 to prohibit the teaching in its public schools and universities of the theory that man evolved from other species of life. The statute was a product of the upsurge of "fundamentalist" religious fervor of the twenties. . . .

The present case concerns the teaching of biology in a high school in Little Rock. According to the testimony, until the events here in litigation, the official textbook furnished for the high school biology course "did not have a section on the Darwinian Theory." Then, for the academic year 1965–1966, the school administration, on recommendation of the teachers of biology in the school system, adopted and prescribed a textbook which contained a chapter setting forth "the theory about the origin . . . of man from a lower form of animal."

Susan Epperson . . . was employed . . . to teach 10th grade biology at Central High School. At the start of the next academic year, 1965, she was confronted by the new textbook (which one surmises from the record was not unwelcome to her). She faced at least a literal dilemma because she was supposed to use the textbook for classroom instruction and presumably to teach the statutorily condemned chapter; but to do so would be a criminal offense and subject her to dismissal.

[Miss Epperson then filed an action in the state Chancery Court seeking a declaration that the statute was void and enjoining the state officials from dismissing her for violation of the statute. The Chancery Court held the statute unconstitutional, but on appeal the Supreme Court of Arkansas reversed.]

. . . Arkansas' statute cannot stand. It is of no moment whether the law is deemed to prohibit mention of Darwin's theory, or to forbid any or all of the infinite varieties of communication embraced within the term "teaching." Under either interpretation, the law must be stricken because of its conflict with the constitutional prohibition of state laws respecting an establishment of religion or prohibiting the free exercise thereof. The overriding fact is that Arkansas' law selects from the body of knowledge a particular segment which it proscribes for the sole reason that it is deemed to conflict with a particular religious doctrine; that is, with a particular interpretation of the Book of Genesis by a particular religious group. . . .

As early as 1872, this Court said: "The law knows no heresy, and is committed to the support of no dogma, the establishment of no sect." *Watson* v. *Jones.* . . .

There is and can be no doubt that the First Amendment does not permit the State to require that teaching and learning must be tailored to the principles or prohibitions of any religious sect or dogma. . . . While study of religions and of the Bible from a literary and historic viewpoint, presented objectively as part of a secular program of education, need not collide with the First Amendment's prohibition, the State may not adopt programs or practices in its public schools or colleges which "aid or oppose" any religion. . . . This prohibition is absolute. It forbids alike the preference of a religious doctrine or the prohibition of theory which is deemed antagonistic to a particular dogma. . . .

Reversed.

Mr. Justice Black, concurring. . . .

Mr. Justice Harlan, concurring. . . .

Mr. Justice Stewart, concurring in the result. . . .

PRIOR RESTRAINTS

NEW YORK TIMES CO. *v.* UNITED STATES
403 U.S. 713 (1971)

[In June, 1971, Professor Daniel Ellsberg released to the press a large portion of a 47-volume Pentagon study entitled *History of the United States Decision-Making Process on Vietnam Policy*—some 7,000 pages of material still classified "Top Secret-Sensitive" by the Defense Department. On June 13 the *New York Times* published the first installment of a scheduled five-part series on how the United States got involved in Vietnam. On June 18 *The Washington Post* published the first in its series of articles based on the "Pentagon Papers." The Department of Justice in two separate District Courts requested temporary restraining orders to halt further publication of the papers by the *Times* and the *Post*. Both District Courts denied the requests. On June 19 the Court of Appeals, District of Columbia, temporarily restrained the *Post* from continuing its series, and the District Judge scheduled a hearing for June 21 on the Justice Department's request for an injunction. The Court of Appeals for the Second Circuit issued a restraining order against the *Times* to allow the Government to appeal the District Court decision in New York. After secret hearings in both District Courts, the Court of Appeals for the Second Circuit continued its restraining order and the *Times* filed an appeal to the Supreme Court, while the Court of Appeals in Washington upheld the District Court decision there that the government had failed to prove that the *Post* articles would endanger the national security, but extended the restraining order to give the government time for an appeal to the Supreme Court. Both cases were handled on writs of certiorari and decided on June 30, 1971.]

PER CURIAM.

We granted certiorari in these cases in which the United States seeks to enjoin the *New York Times* and the *Washington Post* from publishing the contents of a classified study entitled "History of U.S. Decision-Making Process on Viet Nam Policy."

"Any system of prior restraints of expression comes to this Court bearing a heavy presumption against its constitutional validity." *Bantam Books, Inc.* v. *Sullivan. . .* ; see also *Near* v. *Minnesota. . . .* The Government "thus carries a heavy burden of showing justification for the enforcement of such a restraint." *Organization for a Better Austin* v. *Keefe. . . .* The District Court for the Southern District of New York in the *New York Times* case and the District Court for the District of Columbia and the Court of Appeals for the District of Columbia Circuit in the *Washington Post* case held that the Government had not met that burden. We agree.

The judgment of the Court of Appeals for the District of Columbia Circuit is therefore affirmed. The order of the Court of Appeals for the Second Circuit is reversed and the case is remanded with directions to enter a judgment affirming the judgment of the District Court for the Southern District of New York. The stays entered June 25, 1971, by the Court are vacated. The mandates shall issue forthwith.

So ordered.

Mr. Justice Black, with whom Mr. Justice Douglas joins, concurring.

I adhere to the view that the Government's case against the *Washington Post* should have been dismissed and that the injunction against the *New York Times* should have been vacated without oral argument when the cases were first presented to this Court. I believe that every moment's continuance of the injunctions against these newspapers amounts to a flagrant, indefensible, and continuing violation of the First Amendment. . . . In my view it is unfortunate that some of my Brethren are apparently willing to hold that the publication of news may sometimes be enjoined. Such a holding would make a shambles of the First Amendment. . . .

In the First Amendment the Founding Fathers gave the free press the protection it must have to fulfill its essential role in our democracy. The press was to serve the governed, not the governors. . . . Only a free and unrestrained press can effectively expose deception in government. And paramount among the responsibilities of a free press is the duty to prevent any part of the government from deceiving the people and sending them off to distant lands to die of foreign fevers and foreign shot and shell. In my view, far from deserving condemnation for their courageous reporting, the *New York Times*, the *Washington Post*, and other newspapers should be commended for serving the purpose that the Founding Fathers saw so clearly. . . .

Mr. Justice Douglas, with whom Mr. Justice Black joins, concurring. . . .

The dominant purpose of the First Amendment was to prohibit the widespread practice of governmental suppression of embarrassing information. It is common knowledge that the First Amendment was adopted against the widespread use of the common law of seditious libel to punish the dissemination of material that is embarrassing to the powers-that-be. . . . The present cases will, I think, go down in history as the most dramatic illustration of that principle. A debate of large proportions goes on in the Nation over our posture in Vietnam. That debate antedated the disclosure of the contents of the present documents. The latter are highly relevant to the debate in progress.

Secrecy in government is fundamentally anti-democratic, perpetuating bureaucratic errors. Open debate and discussion of public issues are vital to our national health. On public questions there should be "open and robust debate." . . .

Mr. Justice Brennan, concurring.

I write separately in these cases only to emphasize what should be apparent: that our judgment in the present cases may not be taken to indicate the propriety, in the future, of issuing temporary stays and restraining orders to block the publication of material sought to be suppressed by the Government. . . .

The error which has pervaded these cases from the outset was the granting of any injunctive relief whatsoever, interim or otherwise. The entire thrust of the Government's claim throughout these cases has been that publication of the material sought to be enjoined "could," or "might," or "may" prejudice the national interest in various ways. But the First Amendment tolerates absolutely no prior judicial restraints of the press predicated upon surmise or conjecture that untoward consequences may result. . . . Thus, only governmental allegation and proof that publication must inevitably, directly and immediately cause the occurrence of an event kindred to imperiling the safety of a transport already at sea can support even the issuance of an interim restraining order. In no event may mere conclusions be sufficient: for if the Executive Branch seeks judicial aid in preventing publication, it must inevitably submit the basis upon which that aid is sought to scrutiny by the judiciary. And therefore, every restraint issued in this case, whatever its form, has violated the First Amendment—and none the less so because that restraint was justified as necessary to afford the court an opportunity to examine the claim more thoroughly. Unless and until the Government has clearly made out its case, the First Amendment commands that no injunction may issue.

Mr. Justice Stewart, with whom Mr. Justice White joins, concurring. . . .

In the absence of the governmental checks and balances present in other areas of our national life, the only effective restraint upon executive policy and power in the areas of national defense and international affairs may lie in an enlightened citizenry—in an informed and critical public opinion which alone can here protect the values of democratic government. . . .

Yet it is elementary that the successful conduct of international diplomacy and the maintenance of an effective national defense require both confidentiality and secrecy. . . .

I think there can be but one answer to this dilemma, if dilemma it be. The responsibility must be where the power is. If the Constitution gives the Executive a large degree of unshared power in the conduct of foreign affairs and the maintenance of our national defense, then under the Constitution the Executive must have the largely unshared duty to determine and preserve the degree of internal security necessary to exercise that power successfully. . . . [I]t is clear to me that it is the constitutional duty of the Executive—as a matter of sovereign prerogative and not as a matter of law as the courts know law—. . . to protect the confidentiality necessary to carry out its responsibilities in the fields of international relations and national defense. . . .

. . . [I]n the cases before us we are asked neither to construe specific regulations nor to apply specific laws. We are asked, instead, to perform a function that the Constitution gave to the Executive, not the Judiciary. . . . I join the judgments of the Court.

Mr. Justice White, with whom Mr. Justice Stewart joins, concurring.

I concur in today's judgments, but only because of the concededly extraordinary protection against prior restraints enjoyed by the press under our constitutional system. I do not say that in no circumstances would the First Amendment permit an injunction against publishing information about government plans or operations. Nor, after examining the materials the Government characterizes as the most sensitive and destructive, can I deny that revelation of these documents will do substantial damage to public interests. Indeed, I am confident that their disclosure will have that result. But I nevertheless agree that the United States has not satisfied the very heavy burden which it must meet to warrant an injunction against publication in these cases, at least in the absence of express and appropriately limited congressional authorization for prior restraints in circumstances such as these. . . .

Mr. Justice Marshall, concurring. . . .

The problem here is whether in this particular case the Executive Branch has authority to invoke the equity jurisdiction of the courts to protect what it believes to be the national interest. . . .

It would . . . be utterly inconsistent with the concept of separation of power for this Court to use its power of contempt to prevent behavior that Congress has specifically declined to prohibit. . . .

Either the Government has the power under statutory grant to use traditional criminal law to protect the country or, if there is no basis for arguing that Congress has made the activity a crime, it is plain that Congress has specifically refused to grant the authority the Government seeks from this Court. In either case this Court does not have authority to grant the requested relief. It is not for this Court to fling itself into every breach perceived by some Government official nor is it for this Court to take on itself the burden of enacting law, especially law that Congress has refused to pass. . . .

Mr. Chief Justice Burger, dissenting. . . .

Only those who view the First Amendment as an absolute in all circumstances —a view I respect, but reject—can find such a case as this to be simple or easy.

This case is not simple for another and more immediate reason. We do not know the facts of the case. No District Judge knew all the facts. No Court of Appeals judge knew all the facts. No member of this Court knows all the facts. . . .

I suggest we are in this posture because these cases have been conducted in unseemly haste. Mr. Justice Harlan covers the chronology of events demonstrating the hectic pressures under which these cases have been processed and I need not restate them. . . .

The consequence of all this melancholy series of events is that we literally do not know what we are acting on. As I see it we have been forced to deal with litigation concerning rights of great magnitude without an adequate record, and surely without time for adequate treatment either in the prior proceedings or in this Court. . . . I agree with Mr. Justice Harlan and Mr. Justice Blackmun but I am not prepared to reach the merits.

I would affirm the Court of Appeals for the Second Circuit and allow the District Court to complete the trial aborted by our grant of certiorari meanwhile preserving the *status quo* in the *Post* case. I would direct that the District Court on remand give priority to the *Times* case to the exclusion of all other business of that court but I would not set arbitrary deadlines. . . .

Mr. Justice Harlan, with whom the Chief Justice and Mr. Justice Blackmun join, dissenting. . . .

With all respect, I consider that the Court has been almost irresponsibly feverish in dealing with these cases. . . .

Forced as I am to reach the merits of these cases, I dissent from the opinion and judgments of the Court. . . .

It is plain to me that the scope of the judicial function in passing upon the activities of the executive Branch of the Government in the field of foreign affairs is very narrowly restricted. This view is, I think, dictated by the concept of separation of powers upon which our constitutional system rests. . . .

I agree that, in performance of its duty to protect the values of the First Amendment against political pressures, the judiciary must review the initial Executive determination to the point of satisfying itself that the subject matter of the dispute does lie within the proper compass of the President's foreign relations power. . . . Moreover, the judiciary may properly insist that the determination that disclosure of the subject matter would irreparably impair the national security be made by the head of the Executive Department concerned—here the Secretary of State or the Secretary of Defense—after actual personal consideration by that officer. . . .

But in my judgment the judiciary may not properly go beyond these two inquiries and redetermine for itself the probable impact of disclosure on the national security....

I can see no indication in the opinions of either the District Court or the Court of Appeals in the *Post* litigation that the conclusions of the Executive were given even the deference owing to an administrative agency, much less that owing to a co-equal branch of the Government operating within the field of its constitutional prerogative....

Mr. Justice Blackmun, dissenting....

With such respect as may be due to the contrary view, this, in my opinion, is not the way to try a law suit of this magnitude and asserted importance. It is not the way for federal courts to adjudicate, and to be required to adjudicate, issues that allegedly concern the Nation's vital welfare....

The First Amendment, after all, is only part of an entire Constitution. Article II of the great document vests in the Executive Branch primary power over the conduct of foreign affairs and places in that branch the responsibility for the Nation's safety. Each provision of the Constitution is important, and I cannot subscribe to a doctrine of unlimited absolutism for the First Amendment at the cost of downgrading other provisions. First Amendment absolutism has never commanded a majority of this Court.... What is needed here is a weighing, upon properly developed standards, of the broad right of the press to print and of the very narrow right of the Government to prevent. Such standards are not yet developed. The parties here are in disagreement as to what those standards should be. But even the newspapers concede that there are situations where restraint is in order and is constitutional....

I therefore would remand these cases....

MAINTENANCE OF PUBLIC PEACE AND ORDER

GREGORY *v.* CHICAGO

394 U.S. 111 (1969)

Mr. Chief Justice Warren delivered the opinion of the Court.

This is a simple case. Petitioners, accompanied by Chicago police and an assistant city attorney, marched in a peaceful and orderly procession from city hall to the mayor's residence to press their claims for desegregation of the public schools. Having promised to cease singing at 8:30 p.m., the marchers did so. Although petitioners and the other demonstrators continued to march in a completely lawful fashion, the onlookers became unruly as the number of bystanders increased. Chicago police, to prevent what they regarded as an impending civil disorder, demanded that the demonstrators, upon pain of arrest, disperse. When this command was not obeyed, petitioners were arrested for disorderly conduct.

Petitioners' march, if peaceful and orderly, falls well within the sphere of conduct protected by the First Amendment.... There is no evidence in this record that petitioners' conduct was disorderly. Therefore, under the principle first established in *Thompson* v. *City of Louisville*,... convictions so totally devoid of evidentiary support violate due process.

The opinion of the Supreme Court of Illinois suggests that petitioners were convicted not for the manner in which they conducted their march but rather for their refusal to disperse when requested to do so by Chicago police. . . . However reasonable the police request may have been and however laudable the police motives, petitioners were charged and convicted for holding a demonstration not for a refusal to obey a police officer. . . .

The judgments are

Reversed.

Mr. Justice Douglas, while joining the separate opinion of Mr. Justice Black, also joins this opinion.

Mr. Justice Stewart and Mr. Justice White concurring. . . .

Mr. Justice Black, with whom Mr. Justice Douglas joins, concurring.

This we think is a highly important case which requires more detailed consideration than the Court's opinion gives it. . . .

. . . [B]oth police and demonstrators made their best efforts faithfully to discharge their responsibilities as officers and citizens, but they were nevertheless unable to restrain these hostile hecklers within decent and orderly bounds. These facts disclosed by the record point unerringly to one conclusion, namely, that when groups with diametrically opposed, deep-seated views are permitted to air their emotional grievances, side by side, on city streets, tranquility and order cannot be maintained even by the joint efforts of the finest and best officers and of those who desire to be the most law-abiding protestors of their grievances.

It is because of this truth, and a desire both to promote order and to safeguard First Amendment freedoms, that this Court has repeatedly warned States and governmental units that they cannot regulate conduct connected with these freedoms through use of sweeping, dragnet statutes that may, because of vagueness, jeopardize these freedoms. In those cases, however, we have been careful to point out the Constitution does not bar enactment of laws regulating conduct, even though connected with speech, press, assembly, and petition, if such laws specifically bar only the conduct deemed obnoxious and are carefully and narrowly aimed at that forbidden conduct. The dilemma revealed by this record is a crying example of a need for some such narrowly drawn law. . . .

The disorderly conduct ordinance under which these petitioners were charged and convicted is not, however, a narrowly drawn law. . . . To the contrary, it might better be described as a meat ax ordinance, gathering in one comprehensive definition of an offense a number of words which have a multiplicity of meanings, some of which would cover activity specifically protected by the First Amendment. . . .

The so-called "diversion tending to a breach of the peace" here was limited entirely and exclusively to the fact that when the policeman in charge of the special police detail concluded that the hecklers observing the march were dangerously close to rioting and that the demonstrators and others were likely to be engulfed in that riot, he ordered Gregory and his demonstrators to leave, and Gregory—standing on what he deemed to be his constitutional rights—refused to do so. . . . To let a policeman's command become equivalent to a criminal statute comes dangerously near making our government one of men rather than of law. . . . There are ample ways to protect the domestic tranquility without subjecting First Amendment freedoms to such a clumsy and unwieldy weapon.

The city of Chicago, recognizing the serious First Amendment problems raised by the disorderly conduct ordinance as it is written, argues that these convictions should nevertheless be affirmed in light of the narrowing construction placed on the ordinance by the Illinois Supreme Court in this case. . . . Whatever the validity of the Illinois Supreme Court's construction, this was simply not the theory on which these petitioners were convicted. In explaining the elements of the offense to the jury, the trial judge merely read the language of the ordinance. The jury was not asked to find whether, as the Illinois Supreme Court's construction apparently requires, there was "an imminent threat of violence," or whether the police had "made all reasonable efforts to protect the demonstrators." Rather, it was sufficient for the jury to decide that petitioners had made "an improper noise" or a "diversion tending to a breach of the peace," or had "collect[ed] in bodies or crowds for unlawful purposes, or for any purpose, to the annoyance or disturbance of other persons.". . .

In agreeing to the reversal of these convictions, however, we wish once more to say that we think our Federal Constitution does not render the States powerless to regulate the conduct of demonstrators and picketers, conduct which is more than "speech," more than "press," more than "assembly," and more than "petition" as those terms are used in the First Amendment. Narrowly drawn statutes regulating the conduct of demonstrators and picketers are not impossible to draft. . . . Speech and press are, of course, to be free, so that public matters can be discussed with impunity. But picketing and demonstrating can be regulated like other conduct of men. We believe that the homes of men, sometimes the last citadel of the tired, the weary and the sick, can be protected by government from noisy, marching, tramping, threatening picketers and demonstrators bent on filling the minds of men, women, and children with fears of the unknown.

For these reasons we concur in the reversal. . . .

Mr. Justice Harlan, concurring in the result. . . .

BRANDENBURG v. OHIO
395 U.S. 444 (1969)

[The defendant, a leader of a Ku Klux Klan group, spoke at a Klan rally at which a large wooden cross was burned and some of the other persons present were carrying firearms. His remarks included such statements as: "Bury the niggers," "the niggers should be returned to Africa," and "send the Jews back to Israel." He was convicted under the Ohio Criminal Syndicalism statute of "advocat[ing] . . . the duty, necessity, or propriety of crime, sabotage, violence, or unlawful methods of terrorism as a means of accomplishing industrial or political reform" and of "voluntarily assembl[ing] with any society, group or assemblage of persons formed to teach or advocate the doctrines of criminal syndicalism." On appeal, he challenged the constitutionality of the statute under the First and Fourteenth Amendments, but the intermediate appellate court of Ohio affirmed, without opinion, and the Supreme Court of Ohio dismissed his appeal.]

PER CURIAM. . . .

In 1927, this Court sustained the constitutionality of California's Criminal Syndicalism Act, . . . the text of which is quite similar to that of the laws of Ohio. *Whitney* v. *California*. . . . The Court upheld the statute on the ground that, without more, "advocating" violent means to effect political and economic change involves such danger to the security of the State that the State may outlaw it. . . . But *Whitney* has been thoroughly discredited by later decisions. See *Dennis* v. *United States*. . . . These later decisions have fashioned the principle that the constitutional guarantees of free speech and free press do not permit a State to forbid or proscribe advocacy of the use of force or of law violation except where such advocacy is directed to inciting or producing imminent lawless action and is likely to incite or produce such action. As we said in *Noto* v. *United States*, ... "the mere abstract teaching ... of the moral propriety or even moral necessity for a resort to force and violence, is not the same as preparing a group for violent action and steeling it to such action.". ... A statute which fails to draw this distinction impermissibly intrudes upon the freedoms guaranteed by the First and Fourteenth Amendments. ...

... [W]e are here confronted with a statute which, by its own words and as applied, purports to punish mere advocacy and to forbid, on pain of criminal punishment, assembly with others merely to advocate the described type of action. Such a statute falls within the condemnation of the First and Fourteenth Amendments. The contrary teaching of *Whitney* v. *California*, *supra*, cannot be supported, and that decision is therefore overruled.

Reversed.

Mr. Justice Black, concurring. ...

Mr. Justice Douglas, concurring. ...

Note on Libel

Greenbelt Cooperative Publishing Ass'n. v. *Bresler*, 398 U.S. 6 (1970), involved a libel action against a newspaper brought by a private real-estate developer. News articles had reported that at city council meetings certain citizens had characterized as "blackmail" the plaintiff's negotiating position with the city council in seeking to obtain zoning variances for certain property owned by the plaintiff at the same time that the city was attempting to buy other property from the plaintiff for school building purposes. The plaintiff contended that the defendants should be held liable for the knowing use of falsehood, since the word "blackmail" was intended to charge the plaintiff with the crime of blackmail, and since the defendants knew that the plaintiff had committed no such crime. The trial court's charge to the jury stated that the plaintiff could recover if the publications had been made with malice *or* with a reckless disregard of whether they were true or false. Judgment was entered for the plaintiff, the Maryland Court of Appeals affirmed, and on certiorari the United States Supreme Court reversed and remanded. The majority held that the plaintiff's status in the course of the negotiations with school officials and the city council brought him clearly within the "public figure" category as defined in *Curtis Publishing Co.* v. *Butts*. Thus the constitutional standard permitted recovery only if it was established that the defamatory publication was false *and* that it was made with knowledge of its falsity or in reckless disregard of whether it was false or true. Further, the majority thought it "simply impossible to believe" that a reader who reached the word "blackmail" would have considered it to be more than "rhetorical hyperbole."

In 1971 the Court reworked the rule of *New York Times* v. *Sullivan* to extend even further the media's protection against libel action. *Rosen-*

bloom v. *Metromedia*, 403 U.S. 29 (1971), involved a libel action against a radio station as a result of news stories of petitioner's arrest for possession of obscene literature, and stories concerning petitioner's lawsuit against certain officials alleging that the magazines he distributed were not obscene and seeking injunctive relief from police interference with his business. The latter stories did not mention petitioner's name, but used the terms "smut literature racket" and "girlie-book peddlers." Following his acquittal of criminal obscenity charges, petitioner sued in a diversity suit in federal court seeking damages under Pennsylvania's libel law. The jury found for petitioner and awarded $25,000 in general damages and $725,000 in punitive damages, which was reduced by the court on remittitur to $25,000. The Court of Appeals reversed, and the Supreme Court affirmed by a five-to-three vote, with Justice Douglas not participating. There was no majority opinion. Justice Brennan wrote an opinion which was joined by the Chief Justice and Justice Blackmun, however, in which the "public official" or "public figure" test was revised to focus on whether the matter publicized was "an event of public or general concern." It was argued that this would protect the media under the *Sullivan* test if the subject matter was of public concern, whether the person involved was public or private. And it would protect the purely *private* activity of even public officials or public figures against careless defamation. Justice Black concurred, reiterating his position that the First Amendment bars all libel actions against the news media "even when statements are broadcast with knowledge they are false." Justice White concurred in the result.

In *Monitor Patriot Co.* v. *Roy*, 401 U.S. 265 (1971), the Court held that the *Sullivan* test applied to a newspaper's characterization of a candidate for the United States Senate as a "former small-time bootlegger." The trial court had charged the jury that if the libel was in the "public sector" and concerned the plaintiff's fitness for office, then the *Sullivan* rule applied. But that if the libel was in the "private sector," the plaintiff need only show that the article was false and had not been published in good faith for a justifiable purpose with a belief founded on reasonable grounds of the truth of the matter published. The jury found against the newspaper, and the New Hampshire Supreme Court affirmed. The United States Supreme Court reversed and remanded, holding that the *Sullivan* test was the proper rule since, as a matter of constitutional law, a charge of criminal conduct, no matter how remote in time or place, could never be irrelevant to a candidate's fitness for office.

OBSCENITY

STANLEY v. GEORGIA
394 U.S. 557 (1969)

Mr. Justice Marshall delivered the opinion of the Court.

An investigation of appellant's alleged bookmaking activities led to the issuance of a search warrant for appellant's home. Under authority of this warrant, federal and state agents secured entrance. . . [W]hile looking through a desk drawer in an upstairs bedroom, one of the federal agents, accompanied by a state officer, found three reels of eight-millimeter film. Using a projector and screen found in an upstairs living room, they viewed the films. The state officer concluded that they were obscene and seized them. Since a further examination of the bedroom indicated that appellant occupied it, he was charged with possession of obscene matter and placed under arrest. He was later indicted for "knowingly hav[ing] possession of obscene matter" in violation of Georgia law. Appellant was tried before a jury and convicted. The Supreme Court of Georgia affirmed. . . .

It is now well established that the Constitution protects the right to receive information and ideas. . . . This right to receive information and ideas, regardless of their social worth . . . is fundamental to our free society. Moreover, in the context of this case—a prosecution for mere possession of printed or filmed matter in the privacy of a person's own home—that right takes on an added dimension. For also fundamental is the right to be free, except in very limited circumstances, from unwanted governmental intrusions into one's privacy. . . .

These are the rights that appellant is asserting in the case before us. He is asserting the right to read or observe what he pleases—the right to satisfy his intellectual and emotional needs in the privacy of his own home. He is asserting the right to be free from state inquiry into the contents of his library. Georgia contends that appellant does not have these rights, that there are certain types of materials that the individual may not read or even possess. Georgia justifies this assertion by arguing that the films in the present case are obscene. But we think that mere categorization of these films as "obscene" is insufficient justification for such a drastic invasion of personal liberties guaranteed by the First and Fourteenth Amendments. Whatever may be the justifications for other statutes regulating obscenity, we do not think they reach into the privacy of one's own home. If the First Amendment means anything, it means that a State has no business telling a man, sitting alone in his own house, what books he may read or what films he may watch. Our whole constitutional heritage rebels at the thought of giving government the power to control men's minds.

And yet, in the face of these traditional notions of individual liberty, Georgia asserts the right to protect the individual's mind from the effects of obscenity. We are not certain that this argument amounts to anything more than the assertion that the State has the right to control the moral content of a person's thoughts. To some, this may be a noble purpose, but it is wholly inconsistent with the philosophy of the First Amendment. . . . Whatever the power of the state to control public dissemination of ideas inimical to the public morality, it cannot constitutionally premise legislation on the desirability of controlling a person's private thoughts. . . .

[Reversed and remanded.]

Mr. Justice Black, concurring. . . .

Mr. Justice Stewart, with whom Mr. Justice Brennan and Mr. Justice White join, concurring in the result. . . .

Even in the much criticized case of *United States* v. *Rabinowitz* . . . the Court emphasized that "exploratory searches . . . cannot be undertaken by officers, with or without a warrant.". . . This record presents a bald violation of that basic constitutional rule. To condone what happened here is to invite a government official to use a seemingly precise and legal warrant only as a ticket to get into a man's home, and, once inside, to launch forth upon unconfined searches and indiscriminate seizures as if armed with all the unbridled and illegal power of a general warrant. . . .

UNITED STATES *v.* REIDEL

402 U.S. 351 (1971)

Mr. Justice White delivered the opinion of the Court.

Section 1461 of Title 18, USC, prohibits the knowing use of the mails for the delivery of obscene matter. The issue presented by the jurisdictional statement in this case is whether Sec. 1461 is constitutional as applied to the distribution of obscene materials to willing recipients who state that they are adults. The District Court held that it was not. We disagree and reverse the judgment. . . .

In *Roth* v. *United States* . . . Roth was convicted under Sec. 1461 for mailing obscene circulars and advertising. The Court affirmed the conviction. . . . *Roth* has not been overruled. It remains the law on this Court and governs this case. . . .

Stanley v. *Georgia* . . . compels no different result. . . . [I]t neither overruled nor disturbed the holding in *Roth*. . . .The Court made its point expressly: "*Roth* and the cases following that decision are not impaired by today's holding. . . ."

The District Court ignored both *Roth* and the express limitations on the reach of the *Stanley* decision. Relying on the statement in *Stanley* that "the Constitution protects the right to receive information and ideas . . . regardless of their social worth,". . . the trial judge reasoned that "if a person has the right to receive and possess this material, then someone must have the right to deliver it to him." He concluded that Sec. 1461 could not be validly applied "where obscene material is not directed at children, or it is not directed at an unwilling public, where the material such as in this case is solicited by adults. . . ."

The District Court gave *Stanley* too wide a sweep. To extrapolate from Stanley's right to have and peruse obscene material in the privacy of his own home a First Amendment right in Reidel to sell it to him would effectively scuttle *Roth*, the precise result that the Stanley opinion abjured. . . .

Reidel is in a wholly different position. He has no complaints about governmental violations of his private thoughts or fantasies, but stands squarely on a claimed First Amendment right to do business in obscenity and use the mails in the process. But *Roth* has squarely placed obscenity and its distribution outside the reach of the First Amendment and they remain there today. *Stanley* did not overrule *Roth* and we decline to do so now. . . .

The judgment of the District Court is reversed.

Mr. Justice Harlan, concurring. . . .

Mr. Justice Marshall, concurring. . . .

Mr. Justice Black, with whom Mr. Justice Douglas joins, dissenting. . . .

NOTE ON WAR PROTESTORS

In *United States* v. *O'Brien*, 391 U.S. 367 (1968), the defendant was convicted for violating federal law by burning his draft card. The Court of Appeals reversed on the ground that the statute was unconstitutional as a law abridging freedom of speech. The Supreme Court reinstated the judgment and sentence of the District Court. Chief Justice Warren, for the majority, said "We cannot accept the view that an apparently limitless variety of conduct can be labelled 'speech' whenever the person engaging in the conduct intends thereby to express an idea." He stated further that the power to classify and conscript manpower for military service is "beyond question," and that the issuance of draft cards was a legitimate and substantial administrative aid in the functioning of the system.

Street v. *New York*, 394 U.S. 576 (1969), involved a conviction for burning an American flag on a street corner. After learning that civil rights leader James Meredith had been shot by a sniper in Mississippi, the accused set fire to his flag. After a policeman approached and learned that Street had burned the flag, the accused stated: "If they did that to Meredith, we don't need an American flag." Following a nonjury trial in the New York City Criminal Court, the accused was convicted and given a suspended sentence for malicious mischief consisting of a violation of a New York statute making it a misdemeanor publicly to mutilate, defile, or cast contempt upon an American flag either by words or act. The conviction was affirmed by the New York Court of Appeals. On appeal, the United States Supreme Court reversed and remanded. A majority of five held that the accused had a constitutional right to express his opinion about the flag, even if his opinion was defiant or contemptuous, and that since he might have been convicted for the words used rather than merely the deed, the case would have to be remanded. Four judges dissented, arguing that the conviction was based on the deed rather than the words and was therefore constitutional.

Several conscientious objector cases of note were decided in 1970 and 1971. *Welsh* v. *United States*, 398 U.S. 333 (1970) involved a draft registrant's application for exemption based on his conscientious scruples against participating in any war and on his belief that killing was morally wrong, but he stated that his views were not "religious" in the traditional sense. The application was denied, and he was convicted of refusing to submit to induction. The Supreme Court reversed the conviction, with five members agreeing that the proper test was whether the opposition to war stemmed from moral, ethical, or religious beliefs about what was right and wrong, and whether such beliefs were held with the strength of traditional convictions.

In *Gillette* v. *United States*, 401 U.S. 437 (1971), however, the Court held that the statutory conscientious objector status did not have to be accorded one who objects to the Vietnam War, but not to participation in a war of national defense or a war sponsored by the United Nations as a peace-keeping measure.

In *Clay (Ali)* v. *United States*, 403 U.S. 698 (1971), the Court reversed the conviction of Muhammad Ali for willful refusal to submit to induction. The *per curiam* opinion stated: "In order to qualify for classification as a conscientious objector, a registrant must satisfy three basic tests.

He must show that he is conscientiously opposed to war in any form. *Gillette* v. *United States*. . . . He must show that this opposition is based upon religious training and belief, as the term has been construed in our decisions. *United States* v. *Seeger*, . . . *Welsh* v. *United States*. . . . And he must show that this objection is sincere." The Court found that Ali's case satisfied all three tests and that the conviction must be reversed.

In *Mulloy* v. *United States*, 398 U.S. 410 (1970), the Court held unanimously that when a local draft board is presented with a nonfrivolous, prima facie claim for a change in classification based on new factual allegations which were not conclusively refuted by other information in the registrant's file, the board's refusal to reopen the classification, thereby depriving the registrant of his right to an administrative appeal, constituted an abuse of discretion, rendering invalid a subsequent order to report for induction, and requiring reversal of a conviction for refusal to submit to induction.

TINKER *v.* DES MOINES SCHOOL DISTRICT

393 U.S. 503 (1969)

Mr. Justice Fortas delivered the opinion of the Court.

Petitioner John F. Tinker, 15 years old, and petitioner Christopher Eckhardt, 16 years old, attended high schools in Des Moines. Petitioner Mary Beth Tinker, John's sister, was a 13-year-old student in junior high school. [As part of a plan formulated by a group of adults and students in the city, the petitioners wore black armbands to their schools to publicize their objections to the hostilities in Vietnam and their support for a truce, despite the fact that they were aware that the school authorities a few days previously had adopted a policy that any student wearing an armband to school would be asked to remove it, on penalty of suspension until he returned without the armband. After refusal to remove the armbands, the students were suspended. Petitioners filed a suit for injunction in federal court. The District Court dismissed the complaint, holding the order a reasonable measure to prevent disturbance of school discipline. The Court of Appeals affirmed.]

The problem presented by the present case does not relate to regulation of the length of skirts or the type of clothing, to hair style or deportment. . . . It does not concern aggressive, disruptive action or even group demonstrations. Our problem involves direct, primary First Amendment rights akin to "pure speech."

The school officials banned and sought to punish petitioners for a silent, passive, expression of opinion, unaccompanied by any disorder or disturbance on the part of petitioners. There is here no evidence whatever of petitioners' interference, actual or nascent, with the school's work or of collision with the rights of other students to be secure and to be let alone. Accordingly, this case does not concern speech or action that intrudes upon the work of the school or the rights of other students. . . .

In order for the State in the person of school officials to justify prohibition of a particular expression of opinion, it must be able to show that its action was caused by something more than a mere desire to avoid the discomfort and unpleasantness that always accompany an unpopular viewpoint. Certainly where there is no finding and no showing that the exercise of the forbidden right would "materially and substantially interfere with the requirements of appropriate discipline in the operation of the school," the prohibition cannot be sustained. . . .

It is also relevant that the school authorities did not purport to prohibit the wearing of all symbols of political or controversial significance. The record shows that students in some of the schools wore buttons relating to national political campaigns, and some even wore the Iron Cross, traditionally a symbol of nazism. The order prohibiting the wearing of armbands did not extend to these. Instead, a particular symbol—black armbands worn to exhibit opposition to this Nation's involvement in Vietnam—was singled out for prohibition. Clearly, the prohibition of expression of one particular opinion, at least without evidence that it is necessary to avoid material and substantial interference with school work or discipline, is not constitutionally permissible.

In our system, state-operated schools may not be enclaves of totalitarianism. School officials do not possess absolute authority over their students. Students in school as well as out of school are "persons" under our Constitution. They are possessed of fundamental rights which the State must respect, just as they themselves must respect their obligations to the State. In our system, students may not be regarded as closed-circuit recipients of only that which the State chooses to communicate. They may not be confined to the expression of those sentiments that are officially approved. In the absence of a specific showing of constitutionally valid reasons to regulate their speech, students are entitled to freedom of expression of their views. . . .

Reversed and remanded.

Mr. Justice Stewart, concurring. . . .

Mr. Justice White, concurring. . . .

Mr. Justice Black, dissenting.

The Court's holding in this case ushers in what I deem to be an entirely new era in which the power to control pupils by the elected "officials of state supported public schools . . ." in the United States is in ultimate effect transferred to the Supreme Court. . . .

Assuming that the Court is correct in holding that the conduct of wearing armbands for the purpose of conveying political ideas is protected by the First Amendment . . . the crucial remaining questions are whether students and teachers may use the school at their whim as a platform for the exercise of free speech— "symbolic" or "pure"—and whether the Courts will allocate to themselves the function of deciding how the pupils' school day will be spent. While I have always believed that under the First and Fourteenth Amendments neither the State nor Federal Government has any authority to regulate or censor the content of speech, I have never believed that any person has a right to give speeches or engage in demonstrations where he pleases and when he pleases. This Court has already rejected such a notion. . . .

While the record does not show that any of these armband students shouted, used profane language or were violent in any manner, a detailed report by some of them shows their armbands caused comments, warnings by other students, the poking of fun at them, and a warning by an older football player that other, nonprotesting students had better let them alone. There is also evidence that the professor of mathematics had his lesson period practically "wrecked" chiefly by disputes with Beth Tinker, who wore her armband for her "demonstration." Even a casual reading of the record shows that this armband did divert students' minds from their regular lessons, and that talk, comments, etc., made John Tinker "self-conscious" in attending school with his armband. While the absence of obscene or boisterous and loud disorder perhaps justifies the Court's statement that the few armband students did not actually "disrupt" the classwork, I think the record overwhelmingly shows that the armbands did exactly what the elected school officials and principals foresaw it would, that is, took the students' minds off their classwork and diverted them to thoughts about the highly emotional subject of the Vietnam war. And I repeat that if the time has come when pupils of state-supported schools, kindergarten, grammar school or high school, can defy and flaunt orders of school officials to keep their minds on their own school work, it is the beginning of a new revolutionary era of permissiveness in this country fostered by the judiciary. The next logical step, it appears to me, would be to hold unconstitutional laws that bar pupils under 21 or 18 from voting, or from being elected members of the Boards of Education. . . .

. . . The truth is that a teacher of kindergarten, grammar school, or high school pupils no more carries into a school with him a complete right to freedom of speech and expression than an anti-Catholic or anti-Semitic carries with him a complete freedom of speech and religion into a Catholic church or Jewish synagogue. Nor does a person carry with him into the United States Senate or House, or to the Supreme Court, or any other court, a complete constitutional right to go into those places contrary to their rules and speak his mind on any subject he pleases. . . .

In my view, teachers, in state-controlled public schools are hired to teach there. Although Mr. Justice McReynolds may have intimated to the contrary in *Meyers* v. *Nebraska, supra,* certainly a teacher is not paid to go into school and teach subjects the State does not hire him to teach as a part of its selected curriculum. Nor are public school students sent to the schools at public expense to broadcast political or any other views to educate and inform the public. The original idea of schools, which I do not believe is yet abandoned as worthless or out of date, was that children had not yet reached the point of experience and wisdom which enabled them to teach all of their elders. It may be that the Nation has outworn the old-fashioned slogan that "children are to be seen not heard," but one may, I hope, be permitted to harbor the thought that taxpayers send children to school on the premise that at their age they need to learn, not teach. . . .

Change has been said to be truly the law of life but sometimes the old and the tried and true are worth holding. The schools of this Nation have undoubtedly contributed to giving us tranquility and to making us a more law-abiding people. Uncontrolled and uncontrollable liberty is an enemy to domestic peace. We cannot close our eyes to the fact that some of the country's greatest problems are crimes committed by the youth, too many of school age. . . . One does not need to be a prophet to know that after the Court's holding today that some students in Iowa schools and indeed in all schools will be ready, able, and willing to defy their teachers on practically all orders. This is the more unfortunate for the schools since groups of students all over the land are already running loose, conducting break-ins, sit-ins, lie-ins, and smash-ins. . . . Students engaged in such activities are apparently confident that they know far more about how to operate public school systems than do their parents, teachers, and elected school officials. It is no answer to say that the particular students here have not yet reached such high points in their demands to attend classes in order to exercise their political pressures. Turned loose with lawsuits for damages and injunctions against their teachers like they are here, it is nothing but wishful thinking to imagine that young, immature students will not soon believe it is their right to control the schools rather than the right of the States that collect the taxes to hire the teachers for the benefit of the pupils. This case, therefore, wholly without constitutional reasons in my judgment, subjects all the public schools in the country to the whims and caprices of their loudest-mouthed, but maybe not their brightest, students. I, for one, am not fully persuaded that school pupils are wise enough, even with this Court's expert help from Washington, to run the 23,390 public school systems in our 50 States. I wish, therefore, wholly to disclaim any purpose on my part, to hold that the Federal Constitution compels the teachers, parents, and elected school officials to surrender control of the American public school system to public school students. I dissent.

Mr. Justice Harlan, dissenting. . . .

RACE DISCRIMINATION IN THE SALE OF PROPERTY

JONES v. ALFRED MAYER CO.
392 U.S. 409 (1968)

Mr. Justice Stewart delivered the opinion of the Court.

In this case we are called upon to determine the scope and the constitutionality of an Act of Congress, 42 U.S.C. Sec. 1982, which provides that:

"All citizens of the United States shall have the same right, in every State and Territory, as is enjoyed by white citizens thereof to inherit, purchase, lease, sell, hold, and convey real and personal property."

[Petitioners filed a complaint in federal court alleging that the respondents had refused to sell them a home in the Paddock Woods community of St. Louis County for the sole reason that petitioner Jones is a Negro. Petitioners sought injunctive and other relief. The District Court dismissed and the Court of Appeals affirmed, concluding that Sec. 1982 applies only to state action and does not reach private refusals to sell.]

At the outset, it is important to make clear precisely what this case does *not* involve. Whatever else it may be, 42 U.S.C. Sec. 1982 is not a comprehensive open housing law. In sharp contrast to the Fair Housing Title (Title VIII) of the Civil Rights Act of 1968, . . . 82 Stat. 73, the statute in this case deals only with racial discrimination and does not address itself to discrimination on grounds of religion or national origin. It does not deal specifically with discrimination in the provision of services or facilities in connection with the sale or rental of a dwelling. . . . It does not empower a federal administrative agency to assist aggrieved parties. It makes no provision for intervention by the Attorney General. And, although it can be enforced by injunction, it contains no provision expressly authorizing a federal court to order the payment of damages. . . .

On its face . . . Sec. 1982 appears to prohibit *all* discrimination against Negroes in the sale or rental of property—discrimination by private owners as well as discrimination by public authorities. Indeed, even the respondents seem to concede that, if Sec. 1982 "means what it says"—to use the words of the respondents' brief—then it must encompass every racially motivated refusal to sell or rent and cannot be confined to officially sanctioned segregation in housing. Stressing what they consider to be the revolutionary implications of so literal a reading of Sec. 1982, the respondents argue that Congress cannot possibly have intended any such result. Our examination of the relevant history, however, persuades us that Congress meant exactly what it said. [The opinion here treats the history of the 1866 Act and concludes that private discrimination was within the reach of Congress' purpose in enacting the law.]

The remaining question is whether Congress has power under the Constitution to do what Sec. 1982 purports to do: to prohibit all racial discrimination, private and public in the sale and rental of property. Our starting point is the Thirteenth Amendment, for it was pursuant to that constitutional provision that Congress originally enacted what is now Sec. 1982....

As its text reveals, the Thirteenth Amendment "is not a mere prohibition of State laws establishing or upholding slavery, but an absolute declaration that slavery or involuntary servitude shall not exist in any part of the United States." ... It has never been doubted, therefore, "that the power vested in Congress to enforce the article by appropriate legislation," *ibid.*, includes the power to enact laws "direct and primary, operating upon the acts of individuals, whether sanctioned by State legislation or not.". . . .

Thus, the fact that Sec. 1982 operates upon the unofficial acts of private individuals, whether or not sanctioned by state law, presents no constitutional problem. If Congress has power under the Thirteenth Amendment to eradicate conditions that prevent Negroes from buying and renting property because of their race or color, then no federal statute calculated to achieve that objective can be thought to exceed the constitutional power of Congress simply because it reaches beyond state action to regulate the conduct of private individuals. The constitutional question in this case, therefore, comes to this: Does the authority of Congress to enforce the Thirteenth Amendment "by appropriate legislation" include the power to eliminate all racial barriers to the acquisition of real and personal property? We think the answer to that question is plainly yes....

Reversed.

Mr. Justice Douglas, concurring....

Mr. Justice Harlan, whom Mr. Justice White joins, dissenting....

For reasons which follow, I believe that the Court's construction of Sec. 1982 as applying to purely private action is almost surely wrong, and at the least is open to serious doubt....

On April 11, 1968, Congress adopted the Civil Rights Act of 1968, 82 Stat. 73, Title VIII of which is a "Fair Housing" provision. Section 804 is the substantive section of the Title, and it makes unlawful: (a) the refusal to sell or rent a dwelling to any person because of race, color, religion, or national origin; (b) discrimination in terms, conditions, or privileges of sale or rental of a dwelling because of race, color, religion, or national origin; (c) printing or publishing of any notice or advertisement with respect to the sale or rental of a dwelling that indicates any preference or limitation based on race, color, religion, or national origin; (d) representation to any person because of race, color, religion, or national origin that any dwelling is not available for inspection, sale, or rental when such dwelling is in fact so available; and (e) the inducement, for profit, of any person to sell or rent by representation regarding the entry into the neighborhood of a person of a particular race, color, religion, or national origin.

In general, enforcement of Title VIII is by negotiation or, if necessary, by civil suit filed by the Secretary of Housing and Urban Development in United States District Court. Where a pattern or practice of resistance to the provisions of Title VIII appears, the Attorney General may bring a civil action.

PUBLIC SCHOOL DESEGREGATION

GREEN *v.* SCHOOL BOARD OF NEW KENT COUNTY
391 U.S. 430 (1968)

Mr. Justice Brennan delivered the opinion of the Court.

The question for decision is whether, under all the circumstances here, respondent School Board's adoption of a "freedom-of-choice" plan which allows a pupil to choose his own public school constitutes adequate compliance with the Board's responsibility "to achieve a system of determining admission to the public schools on a nonracial basis. . .". . . .

Petitioners brought this action in March, 1965, seeking injunctive relief against respondent's continued maintenance of an alleged racially segregated school system. New Kent County is a rural county in Eastern Virginia. About one-half of its population of some 4,500 are Negroes. There is no residential segregation in the county; persons of both races reside throughout. The school system has only two schools, the New Kent school on the east side of the county and the George W. Watkins school on the west side. . . . The School Board operates one white combined elementary and high school (New Kent), and one Negro combined elementary and high school (George W. Watkins). There are no attendance zones. Each school serves the entire county. . . . Under [the State's Pupil Placement Act] children were each year automatically reassigned to the school previously attended unless upon their application the State Board assigned them to another school. . . . To September, 1964, no Negro pupil had applied for admission to the New Kent school under this statute and no white pupil had applied for admission to the Watkins school. . . .

It was such dual systems that 14 years ago *Brown I* held unconstitutional and a year later *Brown II* held must be abolished; school boards operating such school systems were *required* by *Brown II* "to effectuate a transition to a racially nondiscriminatory school system.". . . It is of course true that for the time immediately after *Brown II* the concern was with making an initial break in a long-established pattern of excluding Negro children from schools attended by white childen. The principal focus was on obtaining for those Negro children courageous enough to break with tradition a place in the "white" schools. . . . Under *Brown II* that immediate goal was only the first step, however. The transition to a unitary, nonracial system of public education was and is the ultimate end to be brought about; it was because of the "complexities arising from the transition to a system of public education freed of racial discrimination" that we provided for "all deliberate speed" in the implementation of the principles of *Brown I.* . . .

The School Board contends that it has fully discharged its obligation by adopting a plan by which every student, regardless of race, may "freely" choose the school he will attend. The Board attempts to cast the issue in its broadest form by arguing that its "freedom-of-choice" plan may be faulted only by reading the Fourteenth Amendment as universally requiring "compulsory integration," a reading it insists the wording of the Amendment will not support. But that argument ignores the thrust of *Brown II*.... *Brown II* was a call for the dismantling of well-entrenched dual systems tempered by an awareness that complex and multi-faceted problems would arise which would require time and flexibility for a successful resolution. School boards such as the respondent then operating state-compelled dual systems were nevertheless clearly charged with the affirmative duty to take whatever steps might be necessary to convert to a unitary system in which racial discrimination would be eliminated root and branch.... The constitutional rights of Negro school children articulated in *Brown I* permit no less than this; and it was to this end that *Brown II* commanded school boards to bend their efforts.... The burden on a school board today is to come forward with a plan that promises realistically to work, and promises realistically to work *now*....

We do not hold that "freedom of choice" can have no place in such a plan. We do not hold that a "freedom-of-choice" plan might of itself be unconstitutional, although that argument has been urged upon us. Rather, all we decide today is that in desegregating a dual system a plan utilizing "freedom of choice" is not an end in itself....

The New Kent School Board's "freedom-of-choice" plan cannot be accepted as a sufficient step to "effectuate a transition" to a unitary system. In three years of operation not a single white child has chosen to attend Watkins school and although 115 Negro children enrolled in New Kent school in 1967 ... 85% of the Negro children in the system still attend the all-Negro Watkins school. In other words, the school system remains a dual system. Rather than further the dismantling of the dual system, the plan has operated simply to burden children and their parents with a responsibility which *Brown II* placed squarely on the School Board. The Board must be required to formulate a new plan and, in light of other courses which appear open to the Board, such as zoning, fashion steps which promise realistically to convert promptly to a system without a "white" school and a "Negro" school, but just schools.... [Reversed and remanded.]

It is so ordered.

SWANN *v.* CHARLOTTE-MECKLENBURG BOARD OF EDUCATION

402 U.S. 1 (1971)

[The Charlotte-Mecklenburg school system, which includes the city of Charlotte, North Carolina, had more than 84,000 students in 107 schools in the 1968–1969 school year. Approximately 29% of the pupils were Negro, about two-thirds of whom (some 14,000 students) attended 21 schools which were at least 99% Negro. This resulted from a desegregation plan approved by the District Court in 1965, at the start of this litigation. In 1968 petitioner Swann moved for further relief based on *Green* v. *County School Board*. The District Court ordered the school board in 1969 to provide a plan for faculty and student desegregation. Finding the board's submission unsatisfactory, the Court appointed an expert (Finger) to submit a desegregation plan. The Court in 1970 adopted the board's plan, as modified, for the junior and senior high schools, and the

Finger plan for the elementary schools. The latter plan desegregated all the elementary schools by the technique of grouping two or three outlying schools with one black inner city school, by transporting black students from grades one through four to the outlying white schools, and by transporting white students from the fifth and sixth grades from the outlying white schools to the inner city black school. The Court of Appeals affirmed portions of the order but vacated the order respecting elementary schools, fearing that the plan would unreasonably burden the pupils and the Board.]

Mr. Chief Justice Burger delivered the opinion of the Court.

We granted certiorari in this case to review important issues as to the duties of school authorities and the scope of powers of federal courts under this Court's mandates to eliminate racially separate public schools established and maintained by state action. . . .

This case and those argued with it arose in states having a long history of maintaining two sets of schools in a single school system deliberately operated to carry out a governmental policy to separate pupils in schools solely on the basis of race. That was what *Brown* v. *Board of Education* was all about. These cases present us with the problem of defining in more precise terms than heretofore the scope of the duty of school authorities and district courts in implementing *Brown I* and the mandate to eliminate dual systems and establish unitary systems at once. . . .

The problems encountered by the district courts and courts of appeal make plain that we should now try to amplify guidelines, however incomplete and imperfect, for the assistance of school authorities and courts. . . .

If school authorities fail in their affirmative obligations under these holdings, judicial authority may be invoked. Once a right and a violation have been shown, the scope of a district court's equitable powers to remedy past wrongs is broad, for breadth and flexibility are inherent in equitable remedies. . . .

The school authorities argue that the equity powers of federal district courts have been limited by Title IV of the Civil Rights Act of 1964, 42 U.S.C. Sec. 2000c. The language and the history of Title IV shows that it was not enacted to limit but to define the role of the Federal Government in the implementation of the *Brown I* decision. . . . [Section 2000c-6 provides that "nothing herein shall empower any official or court of the United States to issue any order seeking to achieve a racial balance in any school by requiring the transportation of pupils or students from one school to another . . . to achieve such racial balance. . . ."]

The proviso in Sec. 2000c-6 is in terms designed to foreclose any interpretation of the Act as expanding the *existing* powers of federal courts to enforce the Equal Protection Clause. There is no suggestion of an intention to restrict those powers or withdraw from courts their historic equitable remedial powers. The legislative history of Title IV indicates that Congress was concerned that the Act might be read as creating a right of action under the Fourteenth Amendment in the situation of so-called "de facto segregation," where racial imbalance exists in the schools but with no showing that this was brought about by discriminatory action of state authorities. In short, there is nothing in the Act which provides us material assistance in answering the question of remedy for state-imposed segregation in violation of *Brown I*. The basis of our decision must be the prohibition of the Fourteenth Amendment that no State shall "deny to any person within its jurisdiction the equal protection of the laws.". . .

In *Green,* we pointed out that existing policy and practice with regard to faculty, staff, transportation, extra-curricular activities, and facilities were among the most important indicia of a segregated system. . . . Independent of student assignment, where it is possible to identify a "white school" or a "Negro school" simply by reference to the racial composition of teachers and staff, the quality of school buildings and equipment, or the organization of sports activities, a *prima facie* case of violation of substantive constitutional rights under the Equal Protection Clause is shown. . . .

The construction of new schools and the closing of old ones is one of the most important functions of local school authorities and also one of the most complex. . . . The result of this will be a decision which, when combined with one technique or another of student assignment, will determine the racial composition of the student body in each school in the system. Over the long run, the consequences of the choices will be far reaching. People gravitate toward school facilities, just as schools are located in response to the needs of people. . . . It may well promote segregated residential patterns which, when combined with "neighborhood zoning," further lock the school system into the mold of separation of the races. Upon a proper showing a district court may consider this in fashioning a remedy. . . .

(1) *Racial Balances or Racial Quotas.* . . .

We do not reach in this case the question whether a showing that school segregation is a consequence of other types of state action, without any discriminatory action by the school authorities, is a constitutional violation requiring remedial action by a school desegregation decree. This case does not present that question and we therefore do not decide it. . . .

In this case it is urged that the District Court has imposed a racial balance requirement of 71%–29% on individual schools. The fact that no such objective was actually achieved—and would appear to be impossible—tends to blunt that claim, yet in the opinion and order of the District Court . . . we find that court directing:

"that efforts should be made to reach 71–29 ratio in the various schools so that there will be no basis for contending that one school is racially different from the others. . . ."

The District Judge went on to acknowledge that variation "from that norm may be unavoidable." This contains intimations that the "norm" is a fixed mathematical racial balance reflecting the pupil constituency of the system. If we were to read the holding of the District Court to require, as a matter of substantive constitutional right, any particular degree of racial balance or mixing, that approach would be disapproved and we would be obliged to reverse. The constitutional command to desegregate schools does not mean that every school in every community must always reflect the racial composition of the school system as a whole. . . .

Awareness of the racial composition of the whole school system is likely to be a useful starting point in shaping a remedy to correct past constitutional violations. In sum, the very limited use made of mathematical ratios was within the equitable remedial discretion of the District Court.

(2) One-Race Schools.

The record in this case reveals the familiar phenomenon that in metropolitan areas minority groups are often found concentrated in one part of the city.... Schools all or predominately of one race in a district of mixed population will require close scrutiny to determine that school assignments are not part of state-enforced segregation.

In light of the above, it should be clear that the existence of some small number of one-race, or virtually one-race, schools within a district is not in and of itself the mark of a system which still practices segregation by law....

The court should scrutinize such schools, and the burden upon the school authorities will be to satisfy the court that their racial composition is not the result of present or past discriminatory action on their part....

(3) Remedial Altering of Attendance Zones.

The maps submitted in these cases graphically demonstrate that one of the principal tools employed by school planners and by courts to break up the dual school system has been a frank—and sometimes drastic—gerrymandering of school districts and attendance zones. An additional step was pairing, "clustering," or "grouping" of schools with attendance assignments made deliberately to accomplish the transfer of Negro students out of formerly segregated Negro schools and transfer of white students to formerly all-Negro schools. More often than not, these zones are neither compact nor contiguous; indeed they may be on opposite ends of the city. As an interim corrective measure, this cannot be said to be beyond the broad remedial powers of a court.

Absent a constitutional violation there would be no basis for judicially ordering assignment of students on a racial basis. All things being equal, with no history of discrimination, it might well be desirable to assign pupils to schools nearest their homes. But all things are not equal in a system that has been deliberately constructed and maintained to enforce racial segregation. The remedy for such segregation may be administratively awkward, inconvenient, and even bizarre in some situations and may impose burdens on some; but all awkwardness and inconvenience cannot be avoided in the interim period when remedial adjustments are being made to eliminate the dual school systems....

We hold that the pairing and grouping of noncontiguous school zones is a permissible tool and such action is to be considered in light of the objectives sought....

(4) Transportation of Students.

The scope of permissible transportation of students as an implement of a remedial decree has never been defined by this Court and by the very nature of the problem it cannot be defined with precision. No rigid guidelines as to student transportation can be given for application to the infinite variety of problems presented in thousands of situations.... The District Court's conclusion that assignment of children to the school nearest their home serving their grade would not produce an effective dismantling of the dual system is supported by the record.

Thus the remedial techniques used in the District Court's order were within that court's power to provide equitable relief; implementation of the decree is well within the capacity of the school authority.

The decree provided that the buses used to implement the plan would operate on direct routes. . . . The trips for elementary school pupils average about seven miles and the District Court found that they would take "not over 35 minutes at the most." This system compares favorably with the transportation plan previously operated in Charlotte under which each day 23,600 students on all grade levels were transported an average of 15 miles one way for an average trip requiring over an hour. In these circumstances, we find no basis for holding that the local school authorities may not be required to employ bus transportation as one tool of school desegregation. Desegregation plans cannot be limited to the walk-in school.

An objection to transportation of students may have validity when the time or distance of travel is so great as to risk either the health of the children or significantly impinge on the educational process. District courts must weigh the soundness of any transportation plan in light of what is said in subdivisions (1), (2), and (3) above. . . .

On the facts of this case, we are unable to conclude that the order of the District Court is not reasonable, feasible and workable. . . .

It does not follow that the communities served by such systems will remain demographically stable, for in a growing, mobile society, few will do so. Neither school authorities nor district courts are constitutionally required to make year-by-year adjustments of the racial composition of student bodies once the affirmative duty to desegregate has been accomplished and racial discrimination through official action is eliminated from the system. This does not mean that federal courts are without power to deal with future problems; but in the absence of a showing that either the school authorities or some other agency of the State has deliberately attempted to fix or alter demographic patterns to affect the racial composition of the schools, further intervention by a district court should not be necessary. . . .

The order of the District Court . . . is . . . affirmed.

It is so ordered.

CLOSING OF PUBLIC FACILITIES TO AVOID RACIAL INTEGRATION

PALMER *v.* THOMPSON

403 U.S. 217 (1971)

Mr. Justice Black delivered the opinion of the Court.

[After federal litigation had resulted in a judgment declaring unconstitutional a Mississippi city's operation of public swimming pools on a racially segregated basis—four for whites only and one for Negroes only—the city council decided not to operate public swimming pools at all, and the pools were closed. Some Negro residents brought suit in federal court seeking to require the city to reopen the pools and to operate them on a desegregated basis. The District Court declined to issue an injunction, and the Court of Appeals affirmed.]

Petitioners rely chiefly on the first section of the Fourteenth Amendment which forbids any State to "deny to any person within its jurisdiction the equal protection of the laws." There can be no doubt that a major purpose of this Amendment was to safeguard Negroes against discriminatory state laws—state laws that fail to give Negroes protection equal to that afforded white people. . . . Here there has unquestionably been "state action" because the official local government legislature, the city council, has closed the public swimming pools of Jackson. The question, however, is whether this closing of the pools is state action that denies "the equal protection of the laws" to Negroes. It should be noted first that neither the Fourteenth Amendment nor any act of Congress purports to impose an affirmative duty on a State to begin to operate or to continue to operate swimming pools. Furthermore, this is not a case where whites are permitted to use public facilities while blacks are denied access. It is not a case where a city is maintaining different sets of facilities for blacks and whites and forcing the races to remain separate in recreational or educational activities. . . .

Unless, therefore, as petitioners urge, certain past cases require us to hold that closing the pools to all denied equal protection to Negroes, we must agree with the courts below and affirm.

Although petitioners cite a number of our previous cases, the only two which even plausibly support their argument are *Griffin* v. *County School Board of Prince Edward County*, 377 U.S. 218 (1964), and *Reitman v. Mulkey*, 387 U.S. 369 (1967). For the reasons that follow, however, neither case leads us to reverse the judgment here.

A. In *Griffin* the public schools of Prince Edward County, Virginia, were closed under authority of state and county law, and so-called "private schools" were set up in their place to avoid a court desegregation order. . . . In Prince Edward County the "private schools" were open to whites only and these schools were in fact run by a practical partnership between state and county, designed to preserve segregated education. We pointed out in *Griffin* the many facets of state involvement in the running of the "private schools.". . . That case can give no comfort to petitioners here. This record supports no intimation that Jackson has not completely and finally ceased running swimming pools for all time. . . .

B. Petitioners also claim that Jackson's closing of the public pools authorizes or encourages private pool owners to discriminate on account of race and that such "encouragement" is prohibited by *Reitman* v. *Mulkey, supra*.

In *Reitman*, California had repealed two laws relating to racial discrimination in the sale of housing by passing a constitutional amendment establishing the right of private persons to discriminate on racial grounds in real estate transactions. This Court [held] that the constitutional amendment was an official authorization of racial discrimination which significantly involved the State in the discriminatory acts of private parties. . . . *Reitman* v. *Mulkey* was based on a theory that the evidence was sufficient to show the State was abetting a refusal to rent an apartment on racial grounds. On this record, *Reitman* offers no more support to petitioners than does *Griffin*.

Petitioners have also argued that respondents' action violates the Equal Protection Clause because the decision to close the pools was motivated by a desire to avoid integration of the races. But no case in this Court has held that a legislative act may violate equal protection solely because of the motivations of the men who voted for it. . . .

It is true there is language in some of our cases interpreting the Fourteenth and Fifteenth Amendments which may suggest that the motive or purpose behind a law is relevant to its constitutionality. *Griffin* v. *Prince Edward County, supra; Gomillion* v. *Lightfoot*, 364 U.S. 339 (1960). But the focus in those cases was on the actual effect of the enactments, not upon the motivation which led the States to behave as they did. . . . Here the record indicates only that Jackson once ran segregated public swimming pools and that no public pools are now maintained by the city. . . . It shows no state action affecting blacks differently from whites. . . . The judgment is

Affirmed.

Mr. Chief Justice Burger, concurring. . . .

Mr. Justice Blackmun, concurring. . . .

Mr. Justice Douglas, dissenting. . . .

I conclude that though a State may discontinue any of its municipal services—such as schools, parks, pools, athletic fields, and the like—it may not do so for the purpose of perpetuating or installing apartheid or because it finds life in a multiracial community difficult or unpleasant. If that is its reason, then abolition of a designated public service becomes a device for perpetuating a segregated way of life. That a State may not do. . . .

Mr. Justice White, with whom Mr. Justice Brennan and Mr. Justice Marshall join, dissenting. . . .

Let us assume a city has been maintaining segregated swimming pools and is ordered to desegregate them. Its express response is an official resolution declaring desegregation to be contrary to the city's policy and ordering the facilities closed rather than continued in service on a desegregated basis. To me it is beyond cavil that on such facts the city is adhering to an unconstitutional policy and is implementing it by abandoning the facilities. It will not do in such circumstances to say that whites and Negroes are being treated alike because both are denied use of public services. The fact is that closing the pools is an expression of official policy that Negroes are unfit to associate with whites. . . . The Equal Protection Clause is a hollow promise if it does not forbid such official denigrations of the race the Fourteenth Amendment was designed to protect. . . .

Mr. Justice Marshall, with whom Mr. Justice Brennan and Mr. Justice White join, dissenting. . . .

. . . [W]hen the officials of Jackson, Mississippi, in the circumstances of this case, detailed by Mr. Justice White, denied a single Negro child the opportunity to go swimming simply because he is a Negro, rights guaranteed to that child by the Fourteenth Amendment were lost. The fact that the color of his skin is used to prevent others from swimming in public pools is irrelevant. . . .

CONGRESSIONAL POWER OVER VOTER QUALIFICATIONS

OREGON *v.* MITCHELL
400 U.S. 112 (1970)

Mr. Justice Black, announcing the judgments of the Court in an opinion expressing his own view of the cases.

In these suits the States resist compliance with the Voting Rights Act Amendments of 1970, . . . 84 Stat. 314, because they believe that the Act takes away from them powers reserved to the States by the Constitution to control their own elections. By its terms the Act does three things. First: It lowers the minimum age of voters in both state and federal elections from 21 to 18. Second: Based upon a finding by Congress that literacy tests have been used to discriminate against voters on account of their color, the Act enforces the Fourteenth and Fifteenth Amendments by barring the use of such tests in all elections, state and national. Third: The Act forbids States from disqualifying voters in national elections for presidential and vice presidential electors because they have not met state residency requirements.

For the reasons set out in Part I of this opinion, I believe Congress can fix the age of voters in national elections . . . but cannot set the voting age in state and local elections. For reasons expressed in separate opinions, my Brothers Douglas, Brennan, White, and Marshall join me in concluding that Congress can enfranchise 18-year-old citizens in national elections, but dissent from the judgment that Congress cannot extend the franchise to 18-year-old citizens in state and local elections. For reasons expressed in separate opinions, my Brothers The Chief Justice, Harlan, Stewart, and Blackmun join me in concluding that Congress cannot interfere with the age for voters set by the States for state and local elections. They, however, dissent from the judgment that Congress can control voter qualifications in federal elections. In summary, it is the judgment of the Court that the 18-year-old vote provisions . . . are constitutional and enforceable insofar as they pertain to federal elections and unconstitutional and unenforceable insofar as they pertain to state and local elections.

For the reasons set out in Part II of this opinion, I believe that Congress, in the exercise of its power to enforce the Fourteenth and Fifteenth Amendments, can prohibit the use of literacy tests or other devices used to discriminate against voters on account of their race in both state and federal elections. For reasons expressed in separate opinions, all of my Brethren join me in the judgment. Therefore the literacy test provisions of the Act are upheld.

. . . I believe Congress can set residency requirements and provide for absentee balloting in elections for presidential and vice presidential electors. [Seven justices concur in this judgment.] My Brother Harlan . . . considers that the residency provisions of the statute are unconstitutional. Therefore the residency and absentee balloting provisions of the Act are upheld. . . .

. . . In the very beginning the responsibility of the States for setting the qualifications of voters in congressional elections was made subject to the power of Congress to make or alter such regulations if it deemed advisable. This was done in Art. I, Sec. 4, of the Constitution which provides:

"The Times, Places and Manner of holding Elections for Senators and Representatives, shall be prescribed in each state by the legislature thereof; *but the Congress may at any time by Law make or alter such Regulations,* except as to the Place of Chusing Senators." (Emphasis supplied.) . . .

Any doubt about the powers of Congress to regulate congressional elections, including the age and other qualifications of the voters should be dispelled by the opinion of this Court in *Smiley* v. *Holm* . . . (1932). There, Chief Justice Hughes writing for a unanimous Court discussed the scope of congressional power under Sec. 4 at some length. He said:

"The subject matter is the 'times, places and manner of holding elections for Senators and Representatives.' It cannot be doubted that these comprehensive words embrace authority to provide a complete code for congressional elections. . . . The phrase 'such regulations' plainly refers to regulations of the same general character that the legislature of the State is authorized to prescribe with respect to congressional elections. In exercising this power, the Congress may supplement these state regulations or may substitute its own. . . . It 'has a general supervisory power over the whole subject.' " . . .

Similarly, it is the prerogative of Congress to oversee the conduct of presidential and vice presidential elections and to set the qualifications for voters for electors for those offices. It cannot be seriously contended that Congress has less power over the conduct of presidential elections than it has over congressional elections.

On the other hand, the Constitution was also intended to preserve to the States the power . . . to establish and maintain their own separate and independent governments. . . . It is obvious that the whole Constitution reserves to the States the power to set voter qualifications in state and local elections, except to the limited extent that the people through constitutional amendments have specifically narrowed the powers of the States. . . .

. . . I would hold that the literacy test ban of the 1970 Amendments is constitutional under the Enforcement Clause of the Fifteenth Amendment. . . . In this legislation Congress has recognized that discrimination on account of color and racial origin is not confined to the South, but exists in various parts of the country. Congress has decided that the way to solve the problems of racial discrimination is to deal with nationwide discrimination with nationwide legislation. Compare *South Carolina* v. *Katzenbach, supra.* . . .

In Title II of the Voting Rights Act Amendments Congress also provided that in presidential and vice presidential elections, no voter could be denied his right to cast a ballot because he had not lived in the jurisdiction long enough to meet its residency requirements. Furthermore, Congress provided uniform national rules for absentee voting in presidential and vice presidential elections. In enacting these regulations for national elections Congress was attempting to insure a fully effective voice to all citizens in national elections. What I said in Part I of this opinion applies with equal force here. Acting under its broad authority to create and maintain a national government, Congress unquestionably has power under the Constitution to regulate federal elections. . . .

Mr. Justice Douglas.

I dissent from the judgment of the Court insofar as it declares Sec. 302 unconstitutional as applied to state elections and concur in the judgment as it affects federal elections but for different reasons. I rely on the Equal Protection Clause and on the Privileges and Immunities Clause of the Fourteenth Amendment. . . .

Congress might well conclude that a reduction in the voting age from 21 to 18 was needed in the interests of equal protection. . . . Equality of voting by all who are deemed mature enough to vote is certainly consistent "with the letter and spirit of the constitution.". . . I would sustain the choice which Congress has made. . . .

Mr. Justice Harlan, concurring in part and dissenting in part. . . .

. . . I am of the opinion that the Fourteenth Amendment was never intended to restrict the authority of the States to allocate their political power as they see fit and therefore that it does not authorize Congress to set voter qualifications, in either state or federal elections. I find no other source of congressional power to lower the voting age as fixed by state laws, or to alter state laws on residency, registration, and absentee voting, with respect to either state or federal elections. The suspension of Arizona's literacy requirement, however, can be deemed an appropriate means of enforcing the Fifteenth Amendment, and I would sustain it on that basis. . . .

Mr. Justice Brennan, Mr. Justice White, and Mr. Justice Marshall dissent from the judgment insofar as it declares Sec. 302 unconstitutional as applied to state and local elections, and concur in the judgment in all other respects....

... [T]here is no question but that Congress could legitimately have concluded that the use of literacy tests anywhere within the United States has the inevitable effect of denying the vote to members of racial minorities whose inability to pass such tests is the direct consequence of previous governmental discrimination in education.... Five years of experience with the 1965 Act persuaded Congress that a nationwide ban on literacy and other potentially discriminatory tests was necessary to prevent racial discrimination in voting throughout the country....

Section 202 of the 1970 Amendments abolishes all durational state residence requirements restricting the right to vote in presidential elections.... For more than a century, this Court has recognized the constitutional right of all citizens to unhindered interstate travel and settlement....

By definition, the imposition of a durational residence requirement operates to penalize those persons, and only those persons, who have exercised their constitutional right of interstate migration.... Congress has explicitly found both that the imposition of durational residence requirements abridges the right of free interstate migration and that such requirements are not reasonably related to any compelling state interests.... Accordingly, we find ample justification for the congressional conclusion that Sec. 202 is a reasonable means for eliminating an unnecessary burden on the right of interstate migration. *United States* v. *Guest, supra.* ...

We believe there is serious question whether a statute granting the franchise to citizens over 21 while denying it to those between the ages of 18 and 21 could, in any event, withstand present scrutiny under the Equal Protection Clause. Regardless of the answer to this question, however, it is clear to us that proper regard for the special function of Congress in making determinations of legislative fact compels this Court to respect those determinations unless they are contradicted by evidence far stronger than anything that has been adduced in these cases. We would uphold Sec. 302 as a valid exercise of congressional power under Sec. 5 of the Fourteenth Amendment....

Mr. Justice Stewart, with whom the Chief Justice and Mr. Justice Blackmun join, concurring in part and dissenting in part....

I agree with the Court in sustaining the congressional ban on state literacy tests, for substantially the same reasons relied upon by Mr. Justice Black. I also agree that the action of Congress in removing the restrictions of state residency requirements in presidential elections is constitutionally valid.... And finally, I disagree with the Court's conclusion that Congress could constitutionally reduce the voting age to 18 for federal elections, since I am convinced that Congress was wholly without constitutional power to alter—for the purpose of *any* elections —the voting age qualifications now determined by the several States....

Congress, in my view, has the power under the Constitution to eradicate political and civil disabilities which arise by operation of state law following a change in residence from one State to another. Freedom to travel from State to State— freedom to enter and abide in any State in the Union—is a privilege of United States citizenship.... In the light of these considerations, Sec. 202 presents no difficulty....

Contrary to the submission of my Brother Black, Article I, Sec. 4, does not create in the federal legislature the power to alter the constitutionally established qualifications to vote in congressional elections. ... The "manner" of holding elections can hardly be read to mean the *qualifications* for voters, when it is remembered that Sec. 2 of the same Article I explicitly speaks of the "qualifications" for voters in elections to choose Representatives. It is plain, in short, that when the Framers meant qualifications they said "qualifications." That word does not appear in Article I, Sec. 4. ...

To be sure, recent decisions have established that state action regulating suffrage is not immune from the impact of the Equal Protection Clause. But we have been careful in those decisions to note the undoubted power of a State to establish a qualification for voting based on age. ... I cannot but conclude that Sec. 302 was beyond the constitutional power of Congress to enact.

The Twenty-sixth Amendment to the Constitution was ratified on June 10, 1971, in the record time of three months, seven days. It reinstates the 18-year-old vote provision held unconstitutional in *Oregon* v. *Mitchell* by providing:

"The right of citizens of the United States, who are 18 years of age or older, to vote shall not be denied or abridged by the United States or by any State on account of age."

Prior Approval Requirements of Voting Rights Act of 1965

PERKINS *v.* MATTHEWS
400 U.S. 379 (1971)

Mr. Justice Brennan delivered the opinion of the Court. ...

[Section 5 of the Voting Rights Act of 1965 requires that changes in voting standards or procedures in those States covered by the Act receive prior approval from the District Court for the District of Columbia or be submitted to the Attorney General and receive no objection from him before becoming operative. The city of Canton, Mississippi, (1) changed the locations of certain polling places, (2) annexed adjacent areas, thereby enlarging the number of eligible voters, and (3) changed from ward to at-large election of aldermen, all without following the prior submission procedures outlined in the Voting Rights Act. Certain voters and candidates for election to city offices filed an action in federal court to enjoin the city elections, on the ground that the Act had been violated by instituting the electoral changes without a judgment that such changes did not have a discriminatory purpose or effect. Pending the convening of a three-judge court, a single judge issued a temporary restraining order. The three-judge court, after hearing, dissolved the injunction and dismissed the complaint. The elections were then held in October, 1969, with the challenged changes in effect. The case was heard on direct appeal by the Supreme Court.]

The three-judge court misconceived the permissible scope of its inquiry into appellants' allegations. ... The inquiry should have been limited to the determination whether "a state requirement is covered by Sec. 5, but has not been subjected to the required federal scrutiny." ... What is foreclosed to such district court is what Congress expressly reserved for consideration by the District Court of the

District of Columbia or the Attorney General—the determination whether a covered change does or does not have the purpose or effect "of denying or abridging the right to vote on account of race or color.". . .

[The opinion then gives an examination of each of the three changes in electoral procedure and concludes that since there is a potential for racial discrimination in the purpose or effect of each change, they should have followed the approval procedures outlined in Sec. 5 of the Voting Rights Act.]

The appellants have urged that, in addition to reversing the District Court judgment, the Court should set aside the elections held in October, 1969, and order new elections held forthwith in which the changes challenged in this case may not be enforced. . . . Since the District Court is more familiar with the nuances of the local situation than are we, and has heard the evidence in this case, we think the question of the appropriate remedy is for that court to determine, in the first instance, after hearing the views of both parties.

The judgment of the District Court is reversed, and the case is remanded to that court with instructions to issue injunctions restraining the further enforcement of the changes until such time as the appellees adequately demonstrate compliance with Sec. 5, and for further proceedings consistent with this opinion.

It is so ordered.

Mr. Justice Blackmun, with whom the Chief Justice joins, concurring. . . .

Mr. Justice Harlan, concurring in part and dissenting in part.

Our role in this case, as the Court correctly recognizes, is limited to determination whether Sec. 5 of the Voting Rights Act of 1965 . . . required the city of Canton to obtain federal approval of the way it proposed to run its 1969 elections. For this reason, I am unable to join the dissenting opinion of Mr. Justice Black, . . . although like him I see little likelihood that the changes here involved had a discriminatory purpose or effect.

I agree with the Court, and for substantially the reasons it gives, that the city should have submitted the relocation of polling places for federal approval. But I cannot agree that it was obliged to follow that course with respect to the other two matters here at issue. . . .

. . . Section 5 requires submission of changes "with respect to voting" only.

The Court seems to interpret this restriction as including any change in state law which has an effect on voting, if changes of that type have "a potential for racial discrimination in voting.". . . At least in the absence of a contrary administrative interpretation, I would not go beyond *Allen* [v. *State Board of Elections*] to hold that annexations are within the scope of Sec. 5. The Court's assertion that the Attorney General does in fact interpret the Act differently seems to me to give too much weight to the passing remark of an Assistant Attorney General. [The opinion here points out that there were over 40 municipal annexations in South Carolina in 1967–1968 and over 100 boundary changes in Georgia cities in 1965–1969, only one of which was submitted to the Attorney General.]

I must confess that I am somewhat mystified by the Court's discussion of the appropriate remedy in this case. . . . I would direct the holding of new elections if and only if the city fails to obtain approval from the appropriate federal officials within a reasonable time. . . . In any event, the District Court is entitled to more guidance on this score than the Court provides.

Mr. Justice Black dissenting.

In *South Carolina* v. *Katzenbach* . . . I dissented vigorously from the majority's conclusion that every part of Sec. 5 of the Voting Rights Act was constitutional. The fears which precipitated my dissent in *Katzenbach* have been fully realized in this case. The majority, relying on *Katzenbach,* now actually holds that the City of Canton, Mississippi, a little town of 10,000 persons, cannot change four polling places for its election of aldermen without first obtaining federal approval. . . .

The city altered four of the local polling places. Two were moved because the old polling places had been located on private property and the owners would no longer consent to the use of their property for voting. I find it incredible to believe that Congress intended that the people of Canton would have to travel to Washington to get the Attorney General's consent to rent new polling places. Another polling place was moved because the old one did not have sufficient space to accommodate voting machines. Finally, the fourth place was moved from a courthouse to a public school to eliminate interference with courtroom proceedings. It is difficult for me to imagine a matter more peculiarly and exclusively fit for local determination than the location of polling places for the election of town aldermen. Nor is there the slightest indication that any of these changes were motivated by or resulted in racial discrimination. . . . Presumably, the majority is ready to hold, if necessary, that the City of Canton could not change from ballots to voting machines without obtaining similar federal approval. I dissent from any such utter degradation of the power of the States to govern their own affairs. . . .

. . . It is beyond my comprehension how the change from wards to an at-large election can discriminate against Negroes on account of their race in a city that has an absolute majority of Negro voters. . . .

This Act attempts to reverse the proper order of things. Now the Congress presumes—a presumption which the Court upholds—that state statutes regulating voting are discriminatory and enjoins their enforcement until the State can convince distant federal judges or politically appointed officials that the statute is not discriminatory. This permits the Federal Government to suspend the effectiveness or enforcement of a state act *before* discrimination is proved. But I think the Federal Government is without power to suspend a state statute before discrimination is proved. The inevitable effect of such a reversal of roles is what has happened in this case—a nondiscriminatory state practice or statute is voided wholly without constitutional authority.

Except as applied to a few southern States in a renewed spirit of Reconstruction, the people of this country would never stand for such a perversion of the separation of authority between state and federal governments. Never would New York or California be required to come begging to the City of Washington before they could enforce the valid enactments of their own legislatures. Never would this law have emerged from congressional committee had it applied to the entire United States. Our people are more jealous of their own local governments than to permit such a bold seizure of their authority.

Finally, I dissent from the remedy adopted by the Court. . . . I am convinced that if the majority were to confront the issue of an appropriate remedy now, the Court would not void the election or compel the city to hold a new election. To the contrary, the 1969 election would be upheld because the alleged violations of the Act are so very minor and so clearly technical. We should not forget that while it is easy for judges to order new elections, it will be neither easy nor inexpensive for the little city of Canton to comply with such an order. . . .

Multi-Member Election Districts and the Equal Protection Clause

WHITCOMB v. CHAVIS

403 U.S. 124 (1971)

[Suit was filed in a three-judge federal court in Indiana attacking Indiana's state legislative apportionment insofar as it created a single district of Marion County for the at-large election of eight state senators and fifteen state assembly-men. The District Court redistricted Marion County into single-member districts on the ground that the multi-member district minimized the voting power of the cognizable racial minority in the county's ghetto and, further, redistricted the entire state on the ground that the state was malapportioned. The Court affirmed the latter judgment to the extent that redistricting would be required, but portions of the opinions dealing with this latter issue are omitted from the extracts following.]

Mr. Justice White delivered the opinion of the Court with respect to the validity of the multi-member election district in Marion County. . . .

The question of the constitutional validity of multi-member districts has been pressed in this Court since the first of the modern reapportionment cases. These questions have focused not on population-based apportionment but on the quality of representation afforded by the multi-member district as compared with single-member districts. . . . That voters in multi-member districts vote for and are represented by more legislators than voters in single-member districts has so far not demonstrated an invidious discrimination against the latter. But we have deemed the validity of multi-member district systems justiciable, recognizing also that they may be subject to challenge where the circumstances of a particular case may "operate to minimize or cancel out the voting strength of racial or political elements of the voting population.". . . We have not yet sustained such an attack. . . .

On the record before us plaintiffs' position comes to this: that although they have equal opportunity to participate in and influence the selection of candidates and legislators, and although the ghetto votes predominantly Democratic and that party slates candidates satisfactory to the ghetto, invidious discrimination nevertheless results when the ghetto, along with all other Democrats, suffers the disaster of losing too many elections. But typical American legislative elections are district-oriented, head-on races between candidates of two or more parties. As our system has it, one candidate wins, the others lose. Arguably the losing candidates' supporters are without representation since the men they voted for have been defeated; arguably they have been denied equal protection of the laws since they have no legislative voice of their own. This is true of both single-member *and* multi-member districts. But we have not yet deemed it a denial of equal protection to deny legislative seats to losing candidates, even in those so-called "safe" districts where the same party wins year after year. . . .

The District Court's holding, although on the facts of this case limited to guaranteeing one racial group representation, is not easily contained. It is expressive of the more general proposition that any group with distinctive interests must be represented in legislative halls if it is numerous enough to command at least one seat and represents a majority living in an area sufficiently compact to constitute a single-member district. This approach would make it difficult to reject claims of Democrats, Republicans, or members of any political organization ... who in one year or another, or year after year, are submerged in a one-sided multi-member district vote. There are also union oriented workers, the university community, religious or ethnic groups occupying identifiable areas of our heterogeneous cities and urban areas. Indeed, it would be difficult for a great many, if not most, multi-member districts to survive analysis under the District Court's view unless combined with some voting arrangement such as proportional representation or cumulative voting aimed at providing representation for minority parties or interests. At the very least, affirmance of the District Court would spawn endless litigation concerning the multi-member district systems now widely employed in this country....

[Reversed and remanded.]

Mr. Justice Harlan. . . .

This case is nothing short of complete vindication of Mr. Justice Frankfurter's warning 10 years ago "of the mathematical quagmire (apart from divers judicially inappropriate and elusive determinants) into which this Court today catapults the lower courts of the country.". . . Hopefully, the day will come when the Court will frankly recognize the error of its ways in ever having undertaken to restructure state electoral processes.

I would reverse the judgment below and remand the case to the District Court with directions to dismiss the complaint.

Mr. Justice Douglas, with whom Mr. Justice Brennan and Mr. Justice Marshall concur, dissenting. . . .

It is said that if we prevent racial gerrymandering today, we must prevent gerrymandering of any special interest group tomorrow, whether it be social, economic, or ideological. I do not agree. Our Constitution has a special thrust when it comes to voting; the Fifteenth Amendment says the right of citizens to vote shall not be "abridged" on account of "race, color, or previous condition of servitude."

Our cases since *Baker* v. *Carr* have never intimated that "one man, one vote" meant "one white man, one vote." Since "race" may not be gerrymandered, I think the Court emphasizes the irrelevant when it says that the effect on "the actual voting power" of the blacks should first be known. They may be all Democratic or all Republican; but once their identity is purposefully washed out of the system, the system, as I see it, has a constitutional defect. It is asking the impossible for us to demand that the blacks first show that the effect of the scheme was to discourage or prevent poor blacks from voting or joining such party as they chose. On this record, the voting rights of the blacks have been "abridged," as I read the Constitution. . . .

I would affirm the judgment.

CONSTITUTIONALLY PERMISSIBLE POPULATION VARIATION AMONG DISTRICTS

ABATE *v.* MUNDT

403 U.S. 182 (1971)

Mr. Justice Marshall delivered the opinion of the Court.

In this case, petitioners challenge the constitutionality of a reapportionment plan proposed in response to both federal and state court findings of malapportionment in Rockland County, New York. The Court of Appeals for the State of New York upheld the plan. We affirm.

[The plan created a county legislature with districts corresponding to the county's five towns, one legislator being assigned to the smallest town and the number of legislators for each other town being the number of times its population exceeded that of the smallest town. Rounding off fractions to the nearest integer caused variations of 11,577 population-per-legislator in one town to 13,020 population-per-legislator in another town. The result was a 4.8% overrepresentation of one town and a 7.1% underrepresentation of another, for a total voting inequality of 11.9%.]

It is well established that electoral apportionment must be based on the general principle of population equality and that this principle applies to state and local elections, *Avery* v. *Midland County,* 390 U.S. 474 (1968). "Mathematical exactness or precision is hardly a workable constitutional requirement,". . . but deviations from population equality must be justified by legitimate state considerations, *Swann* v. *Adams,* 385 U.S. 440 (1966). Because voting rights require highly sensitive safeguards, this Court has carefully scrutinized state interests offered to justify deviations from population equality.

In assessing the constitutionality of various apportionment plans, we have observed that viable local governments may need considerable flexibility in municipal arrangements if they are to meet changing societal needs, . . . and that a desire to preserve the integrity of political subdivisions may justify an apportionment plan which departs from numerical equality. . . . These observations, along with the facts that local legislative bodies frequently have fewer representatives than do their state and national counterparts and that some local legislative districts may have a much smaller population than do congressional and state legislative districts, lend support to the argument that slightly greater percentage deviations may be tolerable for local government apportionment schemes. . . . Of course, this Court has never suggested that certain geographic areas or political interests are entitled to disproportionate representation. Rather our statements have reflected the view that the particular circumstances and needs of a local community as a whole may sometimes justify departures from strict equality. . . .

We emphasize that our decision is based on the long tradition of overlapping function and dual personnel in Rockland County government and on the fact that the plan before us does not contain a built-in bias tending to favor particular political interests or geographic areas. And nothing we say today should be taken to imply that even these factors could justify substantially greater deviations from population equality. But we are not prepared to hold that Rockland County reapportionment plan violates the Constitution, and, therefore, we affirm.

Mr. Justice Harlan concurs in the result. . . .

Mr. Justice Stewart concurs in the judgment.

Mr. Justice Brennan, with whom Mr. Justice Douglas joins, dissenting. . . .

. . . I believe that our recent decisions in *Avery* v. *Midland County,* 390 U.S. 474 (1968), *Kirkpatrick* v. *Preisler,* 394 U.S. 526 (1969), and *Wells* v. *Rockefeller,* 394 U.S. 542 (1969), require reversal and I therefore dissent. . . .

In *Kirkpatrick* . . . we explained that because "[t]oleration of even small deviations detracts from" the constitutional command of "equal representation for equal numbers of people," only those "limited population variances which are unavoidable despite a good faith effort to achieve absolute equality or for which justification is shown" are permissible. . . . "[T]he State must justify each variance, no matter how small.". . . . On the record presented here it is clear that such a good-faith effort has not been made. Nor can it be said that sufficient justification has been demonstrated for an 11.9% deviation from voting equality.

The plan approved here allegedly represents as close to mathematical exactness as is possible without changing existing political boundaries or using weighted or fractional votes. But a plan devised under these constraints is not devised in the good-faith effort that the Constitution requires. In *Wells* v. *Rockefeller, supra,* we struck down a similar plan. We held than an attempt to maintain existing county lines was insufficient justification for a 12.1% variance. . . . That is precisely what we are dealing with here. The attempt to maintain existing town lines has resulted in a variance from equality of 11.9%. I cannot believe that a .2% differential is the determining factor in approving this apportionment scheme.

Today's result cannot be excused by asserting that local governments are somehow less important than national or state governments. We have already fully applied the principle of one-man, one-vote to local polities. . . . *Avery* v. *Midland County.* . . .

. . . Obviously no other local apportionment scheme can possibly present the same combination of factors relied on by the Court today. In that sense this decision can have little or no precedential value. Nevertheless, I cannot help but regret even this small departure from the basic constitutional concept of one-man, one-vote.

SELECTED REFERENCES

CHAPTER 1

GENERAL

Henry J. Abraham, *The Judicial Process* (rev. ed., New York: Oxford University Press, 1972) Chaps. 8, 9.

Berl I. Bernhard and Ronald B. Natalie, "Between Rights and Remedies," *53 Geo. L. J.* 915 (1965).

Harold J. Berman and William R. Greiner, *The Nature and Functions of Law*, 2d ed. (Brooklyn: Foundation Press, 1966) Chaps. 1–4.

Edmond Cahn, *Can the Supreme Court Defend Civil Liberties?* (New York: Sidney Hillman Foundation, 1956).

Thomas E. Barth, "Perception and Acceptance of Supreme Court Decisions at the State and Local Level," *17 J. of Pub. L.* 308 (1968).

Richard C. Cortner, "Strategies and Tactics of Litigants in Constitutional Cases," *17 J. of Pub. L.* 287 (1968).

Paul Freund, "Civil Rights and the Limits of Law," *14 Buffalo L. Rev.* 199 (1964).

Paul Freund, "The Supreme Court and Civil Liberties," *4 Vand. L. Rev.* 533 (1951).

Arthur Garfield Hayes Conference, "The Proper Role of the United States Supreme Court in Civil Liberties Cases," *10 Wayne L. Rev.* 457 (1964).

Robert H. Jackson, *The Supreme Court in the American System of Government* (Cambridge: Harvard University Press, 1955).

Herbert Jacob, *Justice in America* (Boston: Little, Brown, 1965) Chap. 4.

Samuel Krislov, *The Supreme Court in the Political Process* (New York: Macmillan, 1965) Chaps. 2, 6.

Richard J. Richardson and Kenneth N. Vines, *The Politics of Federal Courts* (Boston: Little, Brown, 1970).

John P. Roche, *Courts and Rights*, 2d ed. (New York: Random House, 1966)

Stephen L. Wasby, *The Impact of the United States Supreme Court: Some Perspectives* (Homewood: Dorsey, 1970).

ACTIVISM AND SELF-RESTRAINT

Charles L. Black, Jr., *The People and the Court: Judicial Review in a Democracy* (New York: Macmillan, 1960).

Martin Shapiro, "Judicial Modesty: Down With the Old!—Up With the New?" *10 U.C.L.A. L. Rev.* 533 (1963).

Edward McWhinney, "The Great Debate: Activism and Self-Restraint and Current Dilemmas in Judicial Policy-Making," *33 N.Y.U. L. Rev.* 775 (1958).

Herbert Wechsler, "Toward Neutral Principles of Constitutional Law," *73 Harv. L. Rev.* 1 (1959).

STANDING AND JUSTICIABILITY

Note, "Advisory Opinions on the Constitutionality of Statutes," *69 Harv. L. Rev.*

1302 (1956).

Note, "Non-Justiciable Controversy," 48 *Va. L. Rev.* 922 (1962).

Victor G. Rosenblum, "Justiciability and Justice: Elements of Restraint and Indifference," 15 *Catholic U. L. Rev.* 141 (1966).

T. P. Lewis, "Constitutional Rights and the Misuse of 'Standing'," 14 *Stan. L. Rev.* 433 (1962).

John P. Frank, "Political Questions," in Edmond Cahn (ed.), *Supreme Court and Supreme Law* (Bloomington: Indiana University Press, 1954), p. 36.

Charles G. Post, Jr., *The Supreme Court and Political Questions* (*The Johns Hopkins University Studies in History and Political Science,* Series 54, No. 4; Baltimore: The Johns Hopkins Press, 1936).

Fritz Scharpf, "Judicial Review and the Political Question: A Functional Analysis," 75 *Yale L. J.* 517 (1966).

DELAY

Hans Zeisel, Harry Kalven, Jr., and Bernard Buchholz, *Delay in the Court* (Boston: Little, Brown, 1959).

APPEALS

Jerome Frank, *Courts on Trial: Myth and Reality in American Justice* (Princeton: Princeton University Press, 1950) Chaps. 3–9, 15.

Samuel Krislov, "The Amicus Curiae Brief: From Friendship to Advocacy," 72 *Yale L. J.* 694 (1963).

Karl Llewellyn, *The Common Law Tradition: Deciding Appeals* (Boston: Little, Brown, 1960).

Kenneth Vines, "The Role of Circuit Courts of Appeal in the Federal Judicial Process," 7 *Midwest J. of Pol. Sci.* 305 (1963).

POVERTY AND JUSTICE

Norman Dorsen, ed., "Poverty, Civil Liberties, and Civil Rights: A Symposium," 41 *N.Y.U. L. Rev.* 328 (1966).

Robert Lefcourt, ed., *Law Against the People* (New York: Random House, 1971).

Report of the Attorney General's Committee on Poverty and the Administration of Criminal Justice, *Poverty and the Administration of Federal Criminal Justice* (Submitted to U.S. Attorney General, February 25, 1963).

Arnold S. Trebach, *The Rationing of Justice: Constitutional Rights and the Criminal Process* (New Brunswick: Rutgers University Press, 1964).

Patricia M. Wald, *Law and Poverty: 1965* (Report to the National Conference on Law and Poverty; Washington, D.C., June, 1965).

JUDICIAL REVIEW OF ADMINISTRATIVE ACTION

Raoul Berger, "Administrative Arbitrariness and Judicial Review," 65 *Colum. L. Rev.* 55 (1965).

Louis L. Jaffe, *Judicial Control of Administrative Action* (Boston: Little, Brown, 1965).

Symposium, "Judicial Review of Police Methods in Law Enforcement," 44 *Tex. L. Rev.* 939 (1966).

CHAPTER 2

Henry J. Abraham, *Freedom and the Court* (rev. ed., New York: Oxford University Press, 1972) Chap. 3.

William J. Brennan, Jr., *The Bill of Rights and the States* (Santa Barbara: Center for Study of Democratic Institutions, 1961).

Robert F. Cushman, "Incorporation: Due Process and the Bill of Rights," 51 *Cornell L. Q.* 467 (1966).

Horace Flack, *The Adoption of the Fourteenth Amendment* (Baltimore: The Johns Hopkins Press, 1908).

Charles Fairman, "Does the Fourteenth Amendment Incorporate the Bill of Rights? The Original Understanding," 2 *Stan. L. Rev.* 5 (1949).

Felix Frankfurter, "Memorandum on 'Incorporation' of the Bill of Rights into the Due Process Clause of the Fourteenth Amendment," 78 *Harv. L. Rev.* 746 (1965).

Louis Henkin, "Selective Incorporation in the Fourteenth Amendment," 73 *Yale L. J.* 74 (1963).

Roger Howell, "The Privileges and Immunities of State Citizenship," *The Johns Hopkins University Studies in History and Political Science,* Vol. XXXVI, No. 3 (Baltimore: The Johns Hopkins Press, 1918).

Alex B. Lacy, Jr., "The Bill of Rights and the Fourteenth Amendment: the Evolution of the Absorption Doctrine," 23 *Wash. and Lee L. Rev.* 37 (1966).

CHAPTER 3

GENERAL

Sydney Brodie, "The Federally-Secured Right to be Free from Bondage," 40 *Geo. L. J.* 367 (1952).

Ian Brownlie, ed., *Basic Documents on Human Rights* (London: Oxford, 1971).

A. B. Caldwell and Sydney Brodie, "Enforcement of the Criminal Civil Rights Statute, 18 U.S.C. 242, in Prison Brutality Cases," 52 *Geo. L. J.* 706 (1964).

Robert K. Carr, *Federal Protection of Civil Rights* (Ithaca: Cornell University Press, 1947).

Tom C. Clark, "A Federal Prosecutor Looks at the Civil Rights Statutes," 47 *Colum. L. Rev.* 175 (1947).

Osmond Fraenkel, "The Federal Civil Rights Laws," 31 *Minn. L. Rev.* 301 (1947).

Eugene Gressman, "The Unhappy History of Civil Rights Legislation," 50 *Mich. L. Rev.* 1323 (1952).

Richard P. Longaker, *The Presidency and Individual Liberties* (Ithaca: Cornell University Press, 1961).

Will Maslow and Joseph B. Robison, "Civil Rights Legislation and the Fight for Equality, 1862–1952," 20 *U. Chi. L. Rev.* 363 (1953).

Note, "Civil Action for Interference with Federal Privilege and Immunity," 3 *Stan. L. Rev.* 142 (1950).

———, "Discretion to Prosecute Federal Civil Rights Crimes," 74 *Yale L. J.* 1297 (1965).

———, "Federal Civil Action against Private Individuals for Crimes Involving Civil Rights," 74 *Yale L. J.* 1462 (1965).

Report of the President's Commission on Civil Rights, *To Secure These Rights* (Washington, D.C.: U.S. Government Printing Ofc., 1947).

1961 Report of the U.S. Commission on Civil Rights (5 vols.): *Voting*, vol. 1; *Education*, vol. 2; *Employment*, vol. 3; *Housing*, vol. 4; *Justice*, vol. 5 (Washington, D.C.: U.S. Government Printing Ofc., 1961).

Report of the U.S. Commission on Civil Rights, *Civil Rights '63* (Washington, D.C.: U.S. Government Printing Ofc., 1963).

Harry H. Shapiro, "Limitations in Prosecuting Civil Rights Violations," 46 *Cornell L. Q.* 532 (1961).

Henry Putzel, Jr., "Federal Civil Rights Enforcement: a Current Appraisal," 99 *U. Pa. L. Rev.* 439 (1951).

Joseph P. Witherspoon, "Civil Rights Policy in the Federal System: Proposals for a Better Use of Administrative Process," 74 *Yale L. J.* 1171 (1965).

Allan Wolk, *The Presidency and Black Civil Rights* (Cranbury, N.J.: Fairleigh Dickinson Univ. Press, 1971).

THE "STATE ACTION" PROBLEM

Glenn Abernathy, "Expansion of the State Action Concept Under the Fourteenth Amendment," 43 *Cornell L. Q.* 375 (1958).

Michael J. Horan, "Law and Social Change: The Dynamics of the 'State Action' Doctrine," 17 *J. of Pub. L.* 258 (1968).

Richard A. Lang, Jr., "State Action Under the Equal Protection Clause of the Fourteenth Amendment and the Remaining Scope of Private Choice," 50 *Cornell L. Q.* 473 (1965).

Thomas P. Lewis, "The Meaning of State Action," 60 *Colum. L. Rev.* 1083 (1960).

Jerre S. Williams, "The Twilight of State Action," 41 *Texas L. Rev.* 347 (1963).

CHAPTER 4

GENERAL

David Fellman, *The Defendant's Rights* (New York: Rinehart, 1958).

David Fellman, *The Defendant's Rights Under English Law* (Madison: University of Wisconsin Press, 1966).

J. A. C. Grant, *Our Common Law Constitution* (Boston: Boston University Press, 1956).

Sanford H. Kadish, "Methodology and Criteria in Due Process Adjudication—A Survey and Criticism," 66 *Yale L. J.* 319 (1957).

Yale Kamisar, ed., *Criminal Justice in Our Time* (Charlottesville: University Press of Virginia, 1965).

Monrad G. Paulsen and Sanford H. Kadish, *Criminal Law and its Processes* (Boston: Little, Brown, 1962).

Leon Radzinowicz and Marvin E. Wolfgang, eds., *Crime and Justice*, 3 vols. (New York: Basic Books, 1971).

Jerome H. Skolnick, *Justice Without Trial* (New York: Wiley, 1966).

Claude R. Sowle, ed., *Police Power and Individual Freedom* (Chicago: Aldine, 1962).

NOTICE

Note, "The Void-for-Vagueness Doctrine in the Supreme Court," 109 *U. Pa. L. Rev.* 67 (1960).

Oliver P. Field, "Ex post Facto in the Constitution," 20 *Mich. L. Rev.* 315 (1922).

Note, "Statutory Criminal Presumptions: Judicial Sleight of Hand," 53 *Va. L. Rev.* 702 (1967).

SEARCHES AND SEIZURES—PRIVACY

Wayne R. LaFave, *Arrest* (Boston: Little, Brown, 1965).

Jacob W. Landynski, *Search and Seizure and the Supreme Court* (Baltimore: The Johns Hopkins Press, 1966).

Nelson B. Lasson, *The History and Development of the Fourth Amendment to the United States Constitution* (Baltimore: The Johns Hopkins Press, 1937).

Ernest W. Machen, Jr., *The Law of Arrest* (Chapel Hill: Inst. of Government, University of North Carolina, 1950).

Note, "Police Power to Stop, Frisk, and Question Suspicious Persons," 65 *Colum. L. Rev.* 848 (1965).

Joseph A. Varon, *Searches, Seizures, and Immunities* (New York: Bobbs-Merrill, 1961).

Welsh S. White, "Effective Consent to Search and Seizure," 113 *U. Pa. L. Rev.* 260 (1964).

Samuel Dash, Richard F. Schwartz, and Robert Knowlton, *The Eavesdroppers* (New Brunswick: Rutgers University Press, 1959).

Morris L. Ernst, *Privacy: The Right to be Let Alone* (New York: Macmillan, 1962).

Symposium, "The Griswold Case and the Right of Privacy," 64 *Mich. L. Rev.* 197 1965).

Samuel D. Warren and Louis D. Brandeis, "The Right to Privacy," 4 *Harv. L. Rev.* 193 (1890).

Alan F. Westin, *Privacy and Freedom* (New York: Atheneum, 1967).

SELF-INCRIMINATION

American Civil Liberties Union, Illinois Division, *Secret Detention by the Chicago Police* (Glencoe: The Free Press, 1959).

Erwin N. Griswold, *The Fifth Amendment Today* (Cambridge: Harvard University Press, 1955).

Fred E. Inbau, *Self-Incrimination* (Springfield: Thomas, 1950).

Fred E. Inbau and John E. Reid, *Criminal Interrogation and Confessions* (Baltimore: Williams & Wilkins, 1962).

Leonard W. Levy, *Origins of the Fifth Amendment* (New York: Oxford, 1968).

Lewis Mayers, *Shall We Amend the Fifth Amendment?* (New York: Harper & Row, 1959).

R. C. Pittman, "The Colonial and Constitutional History of the Privilege Against Self-Incrimination in America," 21 *Va. L. Rev.* 763 (1935).

R. H. Seeburger and R. Stanton Wettick, Jr., "*Miranda* in Pittsburgh—A Statistical Study," 29 *U. Pittsburgh L. Rev.* 1 (1967).

Otis H. Stephens, Jr., "Police Interrogation and the Supreme Court: An Inquiry into the Limits of Judicial Policy-Making," 17 *J. of Pub. L.* 241 (1968).

Arthur E. Sutherland, "Crime and Confession," 79 *Harv. L. Rev.* 21 (1965).

RIGHT TO COUNSEL

William M. Beaney, *The Right to Counsel in American Courts* (Ann Arbor: University of Michigan Press, 1955).

Anthony Lewis, *Gideon's Trumpet* (New York: Random House, 1964).

Lee Silverstein, *Defense of the Poor in Criminal Cases in American State Courts* (Chicago: American Bar Foundation, 1965).

DOUBLE JEOPARDY

Walter T. Fisher, "Double Jeopardy, Two Sovereignties and the Intruding Constitution," 28 *U. Chi. L. Rev.* 591 (1961).

J. A. C. Grant, "Successive Prosecutions by State and Nation," 4 *U.C.L.A. L. Rev.* 1 (1956).

Charles M. Kneier, "Prosecution Under State Law and Municipal Ordinance as Double Jeopardy," 16 *Cornell L. Q.* 201 (1931).

H. A. Meriam and J. V. Thornton, "Double Jeopardy and the Court-Martial," 19 *Brook. L. Rev.* 62 (1952).

Note, "The Right of the State to Appeal in Criminal Cases," 42 *N.C. L. Rev.* 887 (1964).

Note, "Double Jeopardy: Its History, Rationale and Future," 70 *Dick. L. Rev.* 377 (1966).

TRIAL BY JURY

Sir Patrick Devlin, *Trial by Jury* (London: Stevens, 1956).

Harry Kalven, Jr., and Hans Zeisel, *The American Jury* (Boston: Little, Brown, 1966).

Lester B. Orfield, "Trial by Jury in Federal Criminal Procedure," 1962 *Duke L. J.* 29 (1962).

HABEAS CORPUS

Paul M. Bator, "Finality in Criminal Law and Federal Habeas Corpus for State Prisoners," 76 *Harv. L. Rev.* 441 (1963).

Zechariah Chafee, Jr., "The Most Important Human Right in the Constitution," 32 *B.U. L. Rev.* 144 (1952).

Daniel J. Meador, *Habeas Corpus and Magna Carta* (Charlottesville: University Press of Virginia, 1966).

Ronald P. Sokol, *A Handbook of Federal Habeas Corpus* (Charlottesville: Michie Co., 1965).

CRUEL AND UNUSUAL PUNISHMENT

James S. Campbell, "Revival of the Eighth Amendment: Development of Cruel Punishment Doctrine by the Supreme Court," 16 *Stan. L. Rev.* 996 (1964).

Allen Sultan, "Recent Judicial Concepts of 'Cruel and Unusual Punishment,'" 10 *Vill. L. Rev.* 271 (1965).

Arthur E. Sutherland, Jr., "Due Process and Cruel Punishment," 64 *Harv. L. Rev.* 271 (1950).

CHAPTER 5

Chester J. Antieau, Arthur T. Downey, and Edward C. Roberts, *Freedom from Federal Establishment* (Milwaukee: Bruce, 1964).

Donald E. Boles, *The Bible, Religion, and the Public Schools*, 3rd. ed. (Ames: Iowa State University Press, 1965).

Thomas I. Emerson, David Haber, and Norman Dorsen, *Political and Civil Rights in the United States,* 3rd ed., 2 Vols. (Boston: Little, Brown, 1967) Chap. VIII. Superb notes and references.

David Fellman, *Religion in American Public Law* (Boston: Boston University Press, 1965).

Mark DeWolfe Howe, *The Garden and the Wilderness* (Chicago: University of Chicago Press, 1965).

Paul G. Kauper, *Religion and the Constitution* (Baton Rouge: Louisiana State University Press, 1964).

Philip B. Kurland, *Religion and the Law* (Chicago: Aldine, 1962).

David R. Manwaring, *Render Unto Caesar: The Flag Salute Controversy* (Chicago: University of Chicago Press, 1962).

Dallin H. Oaks, ed., *The Wall Between Church and State* (Chicago: University of Chicago Press, 1963).

Leo Pfeffer, *Church, State and Freedom* (Boston: Beacon Press, 1962).

Anson P. Stokes, *Church and State in the United States,* 3 Vols. (New York: Harper, 1950). See also the one-volume condensation by Leo Pfeffer, *Church and State in the United States* (New York: Harper & Row, 1964).

Symposium, "Expanding Concepts of Religious Freedom," 1966 *Wis. L. Rev.* 215 (1966).

William W. Van Alstyne, "Constitutional Separation of Church and State: The Quest for a Coherent Position," 57 *Amer. Pol. Sci. Rev.* 865 (1963).

Hearings before the Subcommittee on Constitutional Amendments of the Committee on the Judiciary, United States Senate, 89th Cong., 2nd Sess., Aug., 1966, on Senate Joint Resolution 148 relating to Prayers in Public Schools.

CHAPTER 6

GENERAL

Edmond Cahn, ed., *The Great Rights* (New York: Macmillan, 1963).

Zechariah Chafee, Jr., *Free Speech in the United States* (Cambridge: Harvard University Press, 1948).

Thomas I. Emerson, David Haber, and Norman Dorsen, *Political and Civil Rights in the United States,* 3rd ed. (Boston: Little, Brown, 1967), Vol. I.

David Fellman, *The Limits of Freedom* (New Brunswick: Rutgers University Press, 1959).

Osmond Fraenkel, *The Supreme Court and Civil Liberties,* 2d ed. (New York: Oceana, 1963).

Milton Konvitz, *Fundamental Liberties of a Free People: Religion, Speech, Press, Assembly* (Ithaca: Cornell University Press, 1957).

DOCTRINES OF INTERPRETATION

Zechariah Chafee, Jr., *op. cit.,* Chap. I.

Thomas I. Emerson, "Toward a General Theory of the First Amendment," 72 *Yale L. J.* 877 (1963).

Laurent B. Frantz, "The First Amendment in the Balance," 71 *Yale L. J.* 1424 (1962).

Alexander Meiklejohn, *Free Speech and its Relation to Self-Government* (New York: Harper, 1948).

Wallace Mendelson, "On the Meaning of the First Amendment: Absolutes in the Balance," 50 *Calif. L. Rev.* 821 (1962).

Martin Shapiro, *Freedom of Speech: The Supreme Court and Judicial Review* (Englewood Cliffs: Prentice-Hall, 1966).

INTERNAL SECURITY

Association of the Bar of the City of New York, Report of the Special Committee on *The Federal Loyalty-Security Program* (New York: Dodd, Mead, 1956).

Ralph S. Brown, Jr., *Loyalty and Security* (New Haven: Yale University Press, 1958).

Digest of the Public Record of Communism in the United States (New York: Fund for the Republic, 1955).

Sidney Hook, *Political Power and Personal Freedom: Critical Studies in Democracy, Communism, and Civil Rights* (New York: Criterion, 1959).

Harold D. Laswell, *National Security and Individual Freedom* (New York: McGraw-Hill, 1950).

John O. Rogge, *The First and the Fifth* (New York: Nelson & Sons, 1960).

Telford Taylor, *Grand Inquest* (New York: Simon & Schuster, 1955).

PRESS

Arthur L. Berney, "Libel and the First Amendment—A New Constitutional Privilege," 51 *Va. L. Rev.* 1 (1965).

Zechariah Chafee, Jr., *Government and Mass Communication* (Chicago: University of Chicago Press, 1947).

William L. Chenery, *Freedom of the Press* (New York; Harcourt, Brace, 1955).

William E. Hocking, *Freedom of the Press* (Chicago; University of Chicago Press, 1947).

Edward G. Hudon, *Freedom of Speech and Press in America* (Washington, D.C.: Public Affairs Press, 1963).

Leonard W. Levy, ed., *Freedom of the Press from Zenger to Jefferson* (New York: Bobbs-Merrill, 1966).

Meyer L. Stein, *Freedom of the Press: A Continuing Struggle* (New York: Messner, 1966).

FREE PRESS AND FAIR TRIAL

American Bar Ass'n Committee on Fair Trial and Free Press, *Standards Relating to Fair Trial and Free Press, Tentative Draft* (New York: Institute of Judicial Administration, 1966).

Association of the Bar of the City of New York, Special Committee on Radio, Television, and the Administration of Justice, *Freedom of the Press and Fair Trial: Final Report with Recommendations* (New York: Columbia University Press, 1967).

Hearings on S. 290 before the Subcommittee on Constitutional Rights and the Subcommittee on Improvements in Judicial Machinery, United States Senate Committee on the Judiciary, 89th Cong., 1st Sess. (1965), *Free Press and Fair Trial*.

Edward G. Hudon, "Freedom of the Press Versus Fair Trial: The Remedy Lies with the Courts," 1 *Valparaiso U. L. Rev.* 8 (1966).

ASSEMBLY AND ASSOCIATION

Glenn Abernathy, *The Right of Assembly and Association* (Columbia: University of South Carolina Press, 1961).

Zechariah Chafee, Jr., "The Internal Affairs of Associations Not for Profit," 43 *Harv. L. Rev.* 993 (1930).

David Fellman, *The Constitutional Right of Association* (Chicago: University of Chicago Press, 1963).

Robert A. Horn, *Groups and the Constitution* (Stanford: Stanford University Press, 1956).

Charles E. Rice, *Freedom of Association* (New York: New York University Press, 1962).

CENSORSHIP OF BOOKS

John Chandos, ed., *To Deprave and Corrupt* (New York: Association Press, 1962).

Harry M. Clor, ed., *Censorship and Freedom of Expression* (Chicago: Rand McNally, 1971).

Robert B. Downs, ed., *The First Freedom* (Chicago: American Library Ass'n., 1960).

Morris L. Ernst and Alan U. Schwartz, *Censorship: The Search for the Obscene* (New York: Macmillan, 1964).

David Fellman, *The Censorship of Books* (Madison: University of Wisconsin Press, 1957).

Walter Gellhorn, *Individual Freedom and Governmental Restraints* (Baton Rouge: Louisiana State University Press, 1958) Chap. 2.

Robert W. Haney, *Comstockery in America* (Boston: Beacon Press, 1960).

Richard P. McKeon, Robert K. Merton, and Walter Gellhorn, *The Freedom to Read* (New York: Bowker, 1957).

James C. N. Paul and Murray L. Schwartz, *Federal Censorship: Obscenity in the Mail* (New York: Free Press of Glencoe, 1961).

The Report of the Commission on Obscenity and Pornography (Washington: U.S. Government Printing Off., 1970).

Norman St. John-Stevas, *Obscenity and the Law* (London: Secker & Warburg, 1956).

Martin Shapiro, "Obscenity Law: A Public Policy Analysis," 20 *J. of Pub. L.* 503 (1971).

CHAPTER 7

Albert P. Blaustein and Clarence C. Ferguson, Jr., *Desegregation and the Law* (New Brunswick: Rutgers University Press, 1957).

Alfred W. Blumrosen, *Black Employment and the Law* (Brunswick: Rutgers University Press, 1971).

Congressional Quarterly Service, *Revolution in Civil Rights* (Washington, D.C.: Congressional Qtrly., Inc., 1965).

Thomas I. Emerson, David Haber, and Norman Dorsen, *Political and Civil Rights in the United States*, 3rd ed., Vol. II (Boston: Little, Brown, 1967). Exhaustive treatment of discrimination, with superb notes and references.

John Frank and Robert F. Munro, "The Equal Protection of the Laws," 50 *Colum. L. Rev.* 131 (1950).

Jack Greenberg, *Race Relations and American Law* (New York: Columbia University Press, 1959).

Oscar Handlin, *Fire-Bell in the Night: The Crisis in Civil Rights* (Boston: Little, Brown, 1964).

Robert J. Harris, *The Quest for Equality: The Constitution, Congress, and the Supreme Court* (Baton Rouge: Louisiana State University Press, 1960).

Pauli Murray and Mary O. Eastwood, "Jane Crow and the Law: Sex Discrimination and Title VII," 34 *Geo. Wash. L. Rev.* 232 (1965).

Race Relations Law Reporter (Nashville: Vanderbilt University School of Law, published quarterly since 1956). An invaluable reference source.

Joseph Tussman and Jacobus ten Broek, "The Original Understanding of 'Equal Protection of the Laws,'" 37 *Calif. L. Rev.* 341 (1949).

Clement E. Vose, *Caucasians Only: The Supreme Court, the NAACP, and the Restrictive Covenant Cases* (Berkeley: University of California Press, 1959).

Arthur I. Waskow, *From Race Riot to Sit-In: 1919 and the 1960's* (Garden City: Doubleday, 1966).

C. Vann Woodward, *The Strange Career of Jim Crow*, 2d ed. (New York: Oxford University Press, 1966).

1961 U.S. Commission on Civil Rights Reports: No. 2, *Education;* No. 3, *Employment;* No. 4, *Housing;* No. 5, *Justice* (Washington, D.C.: U.S. Government Printing Ofc., 1961).

U.S. Commission on Civil Rights, *Law Enforcement: A Report on Equal Protection in the South* (Washington, D.C.: U.S. Government Printing Ofc., 1965).

CHAPTER 8

VOTING

Alfred Avins, "Literacy Tests and the Fourteenth Amendment: the Contemporary Understanding," 30 *Albany L. Rev.* 229 (1966).

William Gillette, *The Right to Vote: Politics and the Passage of the Fifteenth Amendment* (Baltimore: Johns Hopkins Press, 1965).

Alan P. Grimes, *The Puritan Ethic and Woman Suffrage* (New York: Oxford University Press, 1967).

Paul Lewinson, *Race, Class, and Party: A History of Negro Suffrage and White Politics in the South* (New York: Russell and Russell, 1963).

Thurgood Marshall, "The Rise and Collapse of the 'White Primary,'" 26 *J. of Negro Ed.* 249 (1957).

Donald R. Matthews and James W. Prothro, *Negroes and the New Southern Politics* (New York: Harcourt, Brace & World, 1966).

Note, "Private Economic Coercion and the Civil Rights Act of 1957," 71 *Yale L. J.* 537 (1962).

Kirk H. Porter, *History of Suffrage in the United States* (Chicago: Univ. of Chicago Press, 1918).

Donald S. Strong, *Registration of Voters in Alabama* (University, Ala.: Bur. of Pub. Admin., Univ. of Ala., 1956).

William W. Van Alstyne, "The Fourteenth Amendment, the 'Right' to Vote, and the Understanding of the Thirty-Ninth Congress," 1965 *Sup. Ct. Rev.* 33.

1961 U.S. Commission on Civil Rights Report No. 1, *Voting* (Washington, D.C.: U.S. Government Printing Ofc., 1961).

APPORTIONMENT

Robert G. Dixon, Jr., *Democratic Representation* (New York: Oxford, 1968).

Alfred de Grazia, *Essay on Apportionment and Representative Government* (Washington, D.C.: Institute for Social Science Research, 1963).

Howard D. Hamilton, ed., *Legislative Apportionment* (New York: Harper & Row, 1964).

Calvin B. T. Lee, *One Man, One Vote: WMCA and the Struggle for Equal Representation* (New York: Scribner's, 1967).

Robert B. McKay, *Reapportionment: The Law and Politics of Equal Representation* (New York: Twentieth Century Fund, 1965).

C. Herman Pritchett, "Equal Protection and the Urban Majority," 58 *Amer. Pol. Sci. Rev.* 869 (1964).

Glendon Schubert, ed., *Reapportionment* (New York: Scribner's Sons, 1964).

AMENDMENTS TO THE CONSTITUTION
OF THE UNITED STATES

AMENDMENT I.

[Ratification of the first ten amendments was completed December 15, 1791]
Congress shall make no law respecting an establishment of religion, or prohibiting the free exercise thereof; or abridging the freedom of speech, or of the press; or the right of the people peaceably to assemble, and to petition the Government for a redress of grievances.

AMENDMENT II.

A well regulated Militia, being necessary to the security of a free State, the right of the people to keep and bear Arms, shall not be infringed.

AMENDMENT III.

No Soldier shall, in time of peace be quartered in any house, without the consent of the Owner, nor in time of war, but in a manner to be prescribed by law.

AMENDMENT IV.

The right of the people to be secure in their persons, houses, papers, and effects, against unreasonable searches and seizures, shall not be violated, and no Warrants shall issue, but upon probable cause, supported by Oath or affirmation, and particularly describing the place to be searched, and the persons or things to be seized.

AMENDMENT V.

No person shall be held to answer for a capital, or otherwise infamous crime, unless on a presentment or indictment of a Grand Jury, except in cases arising in the land or naval forces, or in the Militia, when in actual service in time of War or public danger; nor shall any person be subject for the same offence to be twice put in jeopardy of life or limb; nor shall be compelled in any criminal case to be a witness against himself, nor be deprived of life, liberty, or property, without due process of law; nor shall private property be taken for public use, without just compensation.

AMENDMENT VI.

In all criminal prosecutions, the accused shall enjoy the right to a speedy and public trial, by an impartial jury of the State and district wherein the crime shall have been committed, which district shall have been previously ascertained by law, and to be informed of the nature and cause of the accusation; to be confronted with the witnesses against him; to have compulsory process for obtaining witnesses in his favor, and to have the Assistance of Counsel for his defence.

AMENDMENT VII.

In Suits at common law, where the value in controversy shall exceed twenty dollars, the right of trial by jury shall be preserved, and no fact tried by a jury, shall be otherwise re-examined in any Court of the United States, than according to the rules of the common law.

AMENDMENT VIII.

Excessive bail shall not be required, nor excessive fines imposed, nor cruel and unusual punishments inflicted.

AMENDMENT IX.

The enumeration in the Constitution, of certain rights, shall not be construed to deny or disparage others retained by the people.

AMENDMENT X.

The powers not delegated to the United States by the Constitution, nor prohibited by it to the States, are reserved to the States respectively, or to the people.

AMENDMENT XIII. [December 18, 1865]

Section 1. Neither slavery nor involuntary servitude, except as a punishment for crime whereof the party shall have been duly convicted, shall exist within the United States, or any place subject to their jurisdiction.

Section 2. Congress shall have power to enforce this article by appropriate legislation.

AMENDMENT XIV. [July 28, 1868]

Section 1. All persons born or naturalized in the United States, and subject to the jurisdiction thereof, are citizens of the United States and of the State wherein they reside. No State shall make or enforce any law which shall abridge the privileges or immunities of citizens of the United States; nor shall any State deprive any person of life, liberty, or property, without due process of law; nor deny to any person within its jurisdiction the equal protection of the laws.

Section 2. Representatives shall be apportioned among the several States according to their respective numbers, counting the whole number of persons in each State, excluding Indians not taxed. But when the right to vote at any election for the choice of electors for President and Vice President of the United States, Representatives in Congress, the Executive and Judicial officers of a State, or the members of the Legislature thereof, is denied to any of the male inhabitants of such State, being twenty-one years of age, and citizens of the United States, or in any way abridged, except for participation in rebellion, or other crime, the basis of representation therein shall be reduced in the proportion which the number of such male citizens shall bear to the whole number of male citizens twenty-one years of age in such State. . . .

Section 5. The Congress shall have power to enforce, by appropriate legislation, the provisions of this article.

AMENDMENT XV. [March 30, 1870]

Section 1. The right of citizens of the United States to vote shall not be denied or abridged by the United States or by any State on account of race, color, or previous condition of servitude.

Section 2. The Congress shall have power to enforce this article by appropriate legislation.

AMENDMENT XIX. [August 26, 1920]

The right of citizens of the United States to vote shall not be denied or abridged by the United States or by any State on account of sex.

Congress shall have power to enforce this article by appropriate legislation.

AMENDMENT XXIV. [February 4, 1964]

Section 1. The right of citizens of the United States to vote in any primary or other election for President or Vice President, for electors for President or Vice President, or for Senator or Repesentative in Congress, shall not be denied or abridged by the United States or any State by reason of failure to pay any poll tax or other tax.

Section 2. The Congress shall have the power to enforce this article by appropriate legislation.

AMENDMENT XXVI. [July 5, 1971]

Section 1. The right of citizens of the United States, who are eighteen years of age or older, to vote shall not be denied or abridged by the United States or by any State on account of age.

Section 2. The Congress shall have power to enforce this article by appropriate legislation.

INDEX

"Absolutist" doctrine, 336, 361–366

Admissibility of illegally obtained evidence, 131–139

Alien Registration Act of 1940, 374

Appellate review, 12, 194–197, 234

Apportionment (*see* Reapportionment)

Arrest, 116–124

Assembly, freedom of, 315–321, 330–334, 344–346, 400–418

Association, freedom of, 332, 383–395, 398

"Balancing" test, 336, 368–373

Ballard, Guy, 291

Bar examinations, 390–392

Becker Amendment, 275

Bias, 198–199

Bible in public schools, 263–278

Biddle, Francis, 94

Bill-drafting, 16, 31–32

Bill of attainder, 398, 523

Blackstone, 44, 139, 335–336, 355

Blood tests, 177–181

Blue Laws, 278–284, 298–302

Breach of the peace, 116, 403, 405–413

Brownell, Herbert, 143

Cahn, Edmond, 364–366

Cairns, Huntington, 94

Carr, Robert, 76

Censorship
    customs bureau, 94, 354–355
    informal, 450–452
    mails, 351–354
    motion pictures, 346–351
    obscenity, 436–452
    (*See also* Prior restraints)

Chafee, Zechariah, Jr., 335–336, 355

Child-care laws and religious freedom, 288–290

Christological observances, 277–278

Church disputes and the courts, 322–328

Civil Rights Act of 1875, 58

Civil Rights Act of 1964, 1, 17, 493–502, 521

Civil Rights Commission, 517–521

Classification, 45, 454–461, 503–506

"Clear and present danger" test, 355–364, 366

Coerced confessions, 163–181

Coerced evidence, 174–181

Communist Party, 374–400

Compliance forms, Office of Education, 499–501

Compulsory disclosure, 162–163, 394–398

Compulsory process for obtaining witnesses, 200

Confrontation, right of, 124, 199–200

Congressional investigations, 151, 152–160, 371

Congressional protection of rights, 48–93, 517–524

Conscientious objectors, 94, 307–308, 578

Contempt, 421–423

Contraband, 113, 116, 121

Contraceptives, 130

Cooley, Thomas M., 334

Corwin, E. S., 97, 258

Cotton, John, 249

Counsel, right to, 181–197
    at arraignment, 192
    background, 181–182
    "effective" representation, 193–194
    Fourteenth Amendment, 184–191
    interrogation, 170–174
    juvenile delinquency proceedings, 192, 201–204
    noncapital crimes, 187–191
    on appeal, 194–197
    petty offenses, 191–192
    Sixth Amendment, 182–184
    waiver, 173, 184

County-unit system, 525, 532
Courtroom disruption, 555
Court-martial, 239, 559
Criminal syndicalism laws, 573
Cruel and unusual punishment, 243–246
Customs censorship, 94, 354–355

Defendants, disruptive, 555
Defendants' rights, 99–246
Delay in courts, 2–3
De minimis rule, 267, 304
Demonstrations, 405–414, 487–493, 571
Denationalization, 244–245
Detectaphones, 145
Draft protests, 577
Double jeopardy, 204–219
  and federalism, 216–219
  retrial after appeal by defendant, 209–212
  retrial after appeal by government, 208–209
  retrial after mistrial, 205–207
  trial for multiple offenses, 212–216

Eavesdropping, 145–150
Eisenhower, Dwight, 95
Elections (see Voting rights)
Electronic surveillance, 140–150, 550
Elementary and Secondary School Act of 1965, 254
Equal employment opportunity, 501–502
Equal Opportunity Commission, 462, 502
Equal protection of the law, 452–506
Establishment of religion (see Religion, establishment of)
Evidence, 113–116, 131–139, 174–181, 199
Executive protection of rights, 47, 93–98
Ex post facto, 104–106

Fair hearing, 197–204
Fair Housing Law of 1968, 583
Faith healers, 291–292
Fanny Hill, 445
Federal rights, 56–58, 91–92

Federalist, 19
Feinberg Law, 389–390, 393
Fellman, David, 450
Finality of administrative decisions, 4–5
Flag-salute cases, 292–298
Free exercise of religion (see Religion, free exercise of)
Freund, Paul A., 342, 344

Gideon Bibles, 275–277
"Grandfather" clauses, 512
"Green River" ordinances, 433–434
Griswold, Erwin, 267

Habeas corpus, 13, 234–243
  and federalism, 237–239
  form of petition, 241–242
  form of writ, 243
  "In custody" requirement, 236
  and military detention, 239–241
  scope, 234–235
Handbill regulation, 432–433
Hatch Act, 518–519
Hearing, 40
Homestead Act, 57
Homosexuals, 443

Immigration, 4–5, 399
Immunity Act of 1954, 155–160
Immunity statutes and federalism, 160–162
"Incorporation," 18, 25, 35, 40–44, 137, 200, 333–334
Informers, 123–124
Injunction, 10–11, 336–343, 351
Inspections, 125–130
Interrogation, 167–174, 553

Judicial limitations, 2–9
Judicial policy-making, 1
Judicial remedies, 9–13, 46
Judicial review, 9, 30–31, 34
Jury trial, 220–234
  "blue-ribbon" juries, 229
  impartiality, 223–24, 233
  incorporation, 557
  petty offenses, 222–223
  race discrimination, 227–228, 232
  size of jury, 558
  systematic exclusions, 224–228

waiver, 222
women, 226–229
Juvenile courts, 192, 201–204
Juvenile delinquency, 452

Ku Klux Klan, 50, 394, 573

Labor disputes, 332, 414–418
Libel, 429–431, 574
Literacy tests, 514–517
Little Rock crisis, 96
Loyalty oaths, 388–394

Mails, 351–354, 399
Mandamus, 9–10
Meiklejohn, Alexander, 361–364
"Mere evidence" rule, 113–116
Military force, 96–97
Mistrial, 205–207
Motion pictures, 331–332, 346–351
    licensing, 346–351, 449–450

National Labor Relations Act, 1
National Office for Decent Literature,
    451
Nonreviewability, 4–5
Notice, 100–104, 107–108

Obscenity, 347, 351, 436–452, 575
Ombudsman, 14

Pandering, 443–444
Parades, 318–321
Peonage, 82
Permit requirements, 312–321, 344–351
Picketing, 332, 410, 414–418
Police brutality, 15, 65
Political questions, 8, 524–532
Poll taxes, 512–514
Polygamy, 285–287
Pornography (see Obscenity)
Prayer in public schools, 263–278
"Preferred position" doctrine, 331, 366–
    368
Presidency and civil rights (see Execu-
    tive protection)
Press, freedom of, 330–334, 336–344,
    346–361, 418–452
    "absolutist" doctrine, 336, 361–366

"balancing" test, 336, 368–373
"clear and present danger" test, 355–
    364, 366
and fair trials, 418–429
    libel, 429–431, 574
    obscenity, 436–452
"preferred position" doctrine, 331,
    366–368
    taxation, 435–436
Presumption of validity, 5–6, 367–368
Primary elections, 53–54
Prior restraints, 310–321, 334–355,
    449–450, 566
Privacy, 130 (see also Searches and
    seizures)
Privileges and immunities, 23–32, 36
Probable cause, 122–124, 127–130
Procedural regularity, 99
Public accommodations provisions, 494–
    498
Public trial, 197, 425–426
Puritanism, 247

Racial discrimination
    education, 472–480, 499–501, 583–
        589
    employment, 501–502
    government contracts, 96
    housing, 582
    juries, 463–465
    military, 95
    miscegenation laws, 503–506
    public accommodations, 494–498, 589
    racial notations, 506
    restrictive covenants, 469, 481–484
    "separate but equal" doctrine, 463,
        465–467, 470–479
    transportation, 465–467, 470–472
    voting, 508–524, 591, 595, 597
    zoning, 468–469
Reapportionment, 524–549
    congressional districts, 533
    county-unit system, 525, 532
    fair representation, 542–549
    justiciable question, 524–532
    multi-member districts, 597
    municipal councils, 541–542
    "one man, one vote," 533
    population variation, 599

rural v. urban blocs, 549
state senates, 534–536
Registration laws, 162–163, 344–345, 395–398
"Released time" programs, 7, 254–263
Religion, establishment of, 248–284
  aid to religious schools, 249–254, 561–565
  anti-evolution laws, 565
  Becker Amendment, 275
  Bible in public schools, 263–278
  Christological observances, 277–278
  governmental neutrality, 248, 304
  prayer in public schools, 263–278
  "released time" programs, 254–263
  salary supplements, 562
  Sunday Closing Laws, 278–284
  tax exemptions, 328, 564
  textbook loans, 561
Religion, free exercise of, 284–329
  child-care laws, 288–290
  church disputes and the courts, 322–328
  conscientious objectors, 307–308
  faith-healers, 291–292
  license fees, 321–322
  patriotic exercises, 292–298
  and the police power, 285–292
  polygamy, 285–287
  prior restraints, 310–321
  protection to sectarian schools, 309–310
  religious oaths, 305–306
  Sabbatarians, 298–304
  snake-handlers, 290
  solicitation of funds, 312–315
  street meetings, 315–321
  tax exemptions, 328
Religious freedom, 247–328
  (see also Religion, establishment of and Religion, free exercise of)
Religious oaths, 305–306
Ribicoff, Abraham, 254
Retroactivity, 106, 139
Rogers, William P., 94–95, 143–144, 219
Roosevelt, Franklin, 94, 95, 96
Rumford Fair Housing Act, 485

Sabbatarians, 298–304
Searches and seizures, 109–140
  administrative search, 125–130
  contraband, 113, 116, 121
  extent of search, 118–121
  incident to lawful arrest, 116–124
  "Mere evidence" rule, 113–116
  movable vehicle, 117, 121–124
  with valid warrant, 109–116
  without warrant, 116–130
Section 241, Title 18, 82–89
Section 242, Title 18, 65
Section 332, Title 10, 96
Section 1983, Title 42, 81
Section 1985 (3), Title 42, 89–91
Sedition, 357, 373
Selective enforcement, 15, 456
Self-incrimination, 150–180, 553–555
  coerced confessions, 163–181
  invocation, 151–155
  and right to counsel, 170–174
  scope, 155–163
Separation of church and state (see Religion, establishment of)
"Silver-platter" doctrine, 137–138
"Sit-in" demonstrations, 487–493
Smith Act, 374–388
Snake-handlers and religious freedom, 290
Speech, freedom of, 330–418
  "absolutist" doctrine, 336, 361–366
  "balancing" test, 336, 368–373
  "clear and present danger" test, 355–364, 366
  motion pictures, 331–332
  permit requirements, 312–321, 344–351
  picketing, 332
  "preferred position" doctrine, 331, 366–368
  public order, 315–319, 400–418
  sedition, 357, 373
  traffic regulations, 319–321, 400–402
Spencer, Herbert, 453
"Standing," 3–4
"State action," 62–80, 469, 481–494, 509–511
State inaction, 80

Sterilization, 457–459
Street meetings, 315–321, 402–404
Subversive Activities Control Act of
    1950, 395–399
Sunday closing laws, 278–284, 298–302
Supersession, 388
Sutherland, Arthur E., Jr., 267

Taft-Hartley Act, 388, 398
Televised trials, 423–426
Testimonial compulsion, 113
Textbook loans, 561
Traffic regulations, 319–321, 400–402
Travel, right to, 399
Trespass, 145–146, 487–493
Truman, Harry, 95

Unruh Act, 485

Void *ab initio*, 139

"Void for vagueness" doctrine, 101–104
Voluntariness of confessions, 166–167
Voting rights, 48–56, 507–524
    federal examiners, 522
    federal legislation, 517–524
    "grandfather" clauses, 512
    literacy tests, 514–517
    poll taxes, 512–514
    primaries, 508
    qualifications, 507
Voting Rights Act of 1965, 521–524

White primaries, 508–511
Wickersham Commission, 181–182
Wigmore, John H., 199
Williams, Roger, 249
Wiretapping, 140–150, 550
Women, equal rights, 453–454, 460–
    462
    jury service, 226–229